EXPLORING INDIA'S SACRED ART

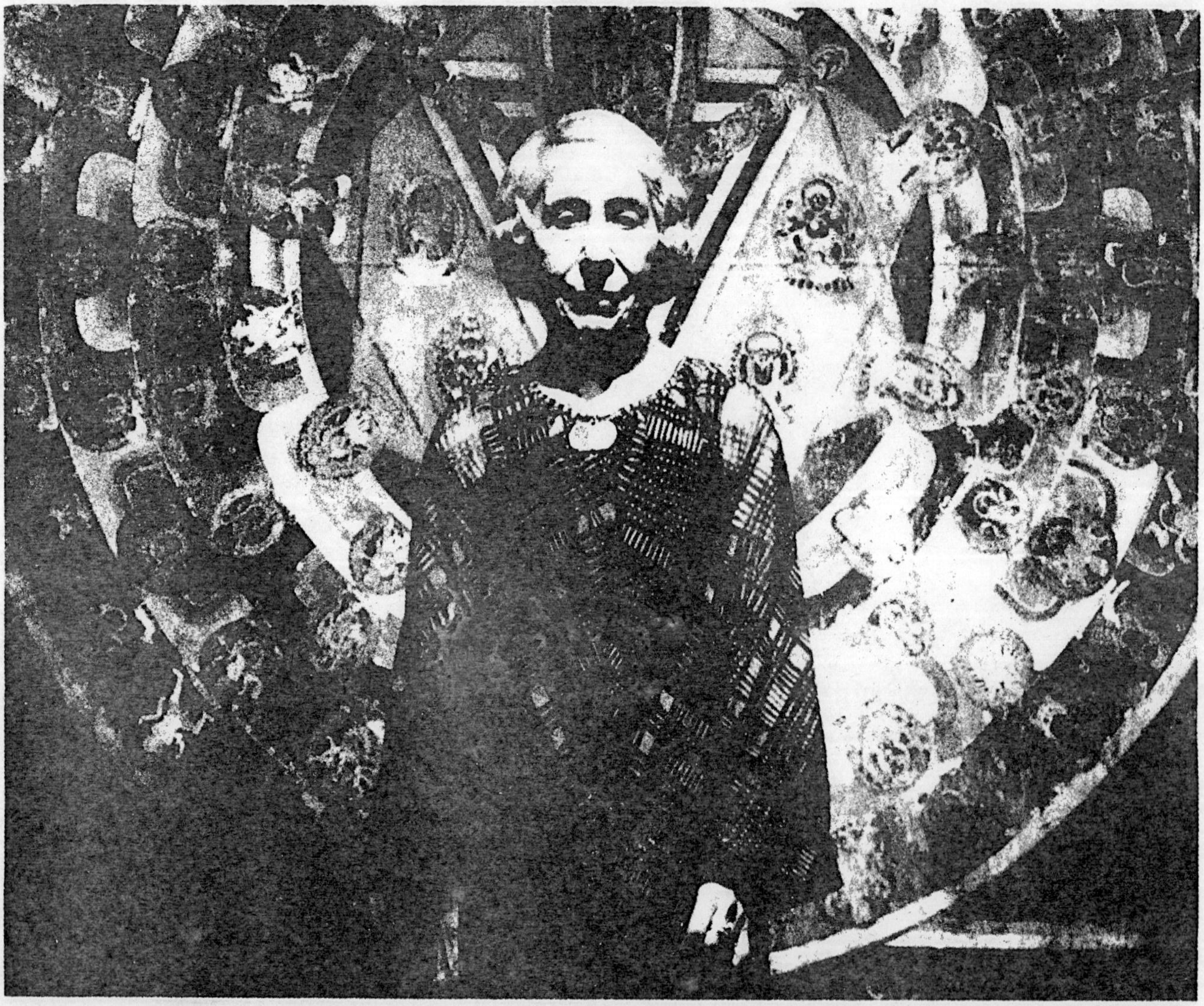

Stella Kramrisch, 1981

EXPLORING INDIA'S SACRED ART

Selected Writings of STELLA KRAMRISCH

edited and with a biographical essay
by Barbara Stoler Miller

INDIRA GANDHI NATIONAL CENTRE FOR THE ARTS
NEW DELHI
AND
MOTILAL BANARSIDASS PUBLISHERS PVT. LTD.
DELHI

First Indian Edition : Delhi, 1994

First Published by University of Pennsylvania Press, Philadelphia, 1983

Published by

INDIRA GANDHI NATIONAL CENTRE FOR THE ARTS
Central Vista, Janpath, New Delhi-110 001
in association with
MOTILAL BANARSIDASS PUBLISHERS PRIVATE LIMITED
Bungalow Road, Jawahar Nagar, Delhi -110 007

ISBN: 978-81-208-1208-6

Printed in India
at Shri Jainendra Press
A-45, Naraina Industrial Area, Phase I
New Delhi-110 028

Contents

PART FOUR: IMAGE AND TEMPLE

PART FIVE: · THEORY AND PRACTICE OF PAINTING

Illustrations

PLATES

5 Representation of Nature in Early Buddhist Sculpture

7 The Image of Mahādeva, Elephanta Island

8 An Image of Aditi-Uttānapad

10 Figural Sculpture of the Gupta Period

11 Pāla and Sena Sculpture

12 Candella Sculpture: Khajuraho

14 Wall and Image in Indian Art

16 Ajanta

FIGURES

Foreword

The foreword to this volume was at the first draft stage when the distinguished and sensitive editor and writer of the biographical essay, Barbara Stoler Miller' passed away. It was difficult to put pen to paper soon after. The final draft ready for the press, was not delivered.

On the night of the 30th August, 1993, I picked up this volume at midnight, opened the pages, read and re-read the remarkable essay on the Image of Mahadeva in the Cave-temple on Elephanta island. I read it, no, experienced it through Stella's being. Her presence was strong. It was the moment of her passing away physically. But she lives in us through her insights, almost revelations on Indian art.

This foreword is dedicated to the memory of the editor and the author, one scholar explorer of the manifaceted Krishna and the *Gita Govinda*, the other revealer of Siva, in all his forms unmanifest and manifest.

Sensitively and discreetly selected essays of a vast body of Stella Kramrisch's works are included in the volume. The five parts represent the manifold contribution of Stella Kramrisch in opening up doors of perception for understanding Indian art.

Ananda Coomaraswamy had eloquently spoken about the anonymous tradition of Indian art. This has been contested by recent scholarship because names have been found and inscriptions discovered. When Coomaraswamy spoke of the anonymous tradition, he was not speaking about signatures and non-signatures. He was speaking about art as subjective and individual expression as distinct from that other Indian stream where the first demand on the artist was to transcend the personal individual almost prior to the act of creation. Impersonalisation was the primary pre-requisite not the end product. Stella Kramrisch gave us another equally or more important insight by dividing Indian art to that which can be understood within the confines of time and date, period and chronology and that which is timeless. The preface to her catalogue on the exhibition *Unknown India* (included here) will remain a watershed in Indian art history studies, if for no other reason, than her classification of the ageless and time variations images.

Within the category of art which is in time and space, the study of Indian art has been, by and large, an exercise in periodisation, and a linear chronological narration. While Stella was conscious of evolution and development of styles and schools in that first little great work "Indian Sculpture", she drew attention specifically to the medieval factor and the transubstantiation of nature into art. She concluded pertinently that to understand Indian art only through the direction of the arrow of linear time was to comprehend one dimension. "Ancient, classical and medieval when taken in the direction of the arrow of time only denote the reactions of people of India the motherland with its creative soil to the people it nourishes", she declared. It is within this framework that she identified 'style' and regional schools. An example of this approach is the essay on Pala and Sena sculpture in this volume.

In the same work *Indian Sculpture*, she courageously and boldly identified the principle of breath *(prana)* in Indian sculpture. In so doing, with a single stroke, she drew attention to the need for understanding Indian sculpture on its own terms from within the tradition rather than the application of criterion of alien traditions. She went further to see how the notions of the gross and the subtle body is concretised through images in stone or other metal. With remarkable facility as also agility, Stella unravelled the structure of Indian art which moves concurrently at the abstract and the figurative planes. Her essay on the *Image of Mahadeva* in the Cave-temple on Elephanta island is and will always remain an essential key to the understanding of Indian art. The twin principles of the unmanifest and manifest of the one and many are articulated in language unsurpassed.

Stella had known and experienced the Himalayan mountains and had investigated the textual traditions of the *Brhat Samhita* and other *Vastu* texts. She had studied the rituals described in the *Satapatha-Brahmana.* It was the interconnection of the Vedic ritual and texts of *Vastu* and the experience of the Himalayas which coalesced into that great work 'The Hindu Temple'. In this work, she brought together textual sources which had so far been comprehended in isolation. For the first time, she established a relationship between not only diverse texts and the fundamental importance of the *Vastu purusa mandala* and the ritual but also to the significance of making temples in the confluence of rivers, of the pure waters of the snows. The temple was both *Purusa* and *Guha*, the co-ordinate of *Meru* and in turn was the vehicle of Man's journey to transcendence. These insights ignited a new line of scholarship on Indian temples architecture post-1960. Coomaraswamy responded not through a review instead through the great essay on *Kandariya Mahadeva.*

Although the volume does not include the last phase of her preoccupation with 'myth' and the Puranas specially *Kurma* and *Siva Purana*, the presence of Siva is the gift of ripened autumnal maturity. She extracted sap and essence from the primordial myths.

The volume is a window to savouring Stella's perceptions and her insights, not the totality of Stella. She travelled far and wide outward and for those who knew her equally and as deeply as is conceivable. For many, she opened new vistas and horizons and may these be explored in full measure by those who follow.

Kapila Vatsyayan

Preface

Stella Kramrisch has been a pioneering interpreter of Indian art and its religious contexts. Her career as a creative scholar, teacher, museum curator, and editor has spanned more than sixty years, during which she has been a dominant force in shaping European, American, and Asian conceptions of Indian culture.

The sources of her scholarly approach are complex, but the style of her work is highly personal. A combination of Western and Indian ideas, as well as dramatic events of her life, have contributed to her conception of art. One important element derives from her early life and education in Vienna before World War I. Another is from almost thirty years in India (1921–1950), where she taught at Calcutta University. A brief biographical essay analyzing her life and work concentrates on these two formative periods. Since 1950, she has lived in the United States, teaching Indian art at the University of Pennsylvania and at the Institute of Fine Arts, New York University, and serving as Curator of Indian art at the Philadelphia Museum. During these years she has focused her energies on a series of major exhibitions and textual studies, culminating in the exhibition "Manifestations of Shiva" and her book *The Presence of Śiva.* In January 1982, Stella was awarded the Indian government's high honor of Padma Bhushan in recognition of her scholarship and devotion to Indian art.

The attempt to place Stella's extraordinary work in the context of her life began as the result of an afternoon Ann Norton and I spent with her in her house near Chester Springs on June 11, 1979. Most of the biographical material originates from Stella herself, but much has been gleaned from conversations and correspondence with her wide circle of colleagues and friends. Among those who have contributed to my understanding of her spirit and her work, special thanks are due to Mildred Archer, Joan and Frederick Baekeland, Maria and Martin Bergmann, Lady Penelope Betjeman (Penelope Chetwode), Schuyler Cammann, Pramod Chandra, Krishna Deva, M. A. Dhaky, Margery and Thomas Dove, Virginia Fields, Theodore Gaster, Pupul Jayakar, Samuel Eilenberg, Arnold Jolles, Barbara Lévi, Roger Lipsey, Porter McCray, Hope and Paul Makler, Pratapaditya Pal, Amy Poster, Irma Rademacher, Joseph Rishel, Meyer Schapiro, Robert Skelton, Craig Smyth, Alexander Soper, Evan Turner, Kapila Vatsyayan, Gordon Wasson, Doris and Ed Wiener, Stuart Cary Welch, and William Wolff.

I am deeply indebted to Alfred Wuerfel for sharing his perspective on life as a non-British foreigner in India during the 1920s and 1930s. Also to Dorothy Norman, for discussing her friendship with Stella and for encouraging me to write the essay.

Ann Norton has contributed her insights as a student of Indian art and as a Jungian analyst. Her participation in the initial selection of papers for this edition was significant, as was her help in securing new photographs. The careful research assistance of Alan Shapiro and Katherine Stern was invaluable.

Archival material and private papers relating to Stella are relatively scarce, but I have found important documents in the manuscript collections of the Library of Congress, The India Office, and the Philadelphia Museum of Art.

The papers for this volume have been chosen with a view to presenting Stella's own most lucid expositions of her basic ideas on Indian religious art. The categories include major descriptive and conceptual studies from different periods of her work, beginning with her first article "The Representation of Nature in Early Buddhist Sculpture (Bharhut-Sanchi)" (1921), which is illustrated here with new photographs from the archive of the Archaeological Survey of India. The most recent essay reprinted here is the introduction to her exhibition catalogue *Unknown India* (1968). After this she concentrated on her book *The Presence of Śiva,* which was published in 1981. She is currently at work on a new study of the Bharhut sculptures.

Although she continued to write in German as well as English during her years in India, much that she wrote was "translated" into her English writings. A notable exception is the article "Die figurale Plastik der Guptazeit," which is noteworthy for the way in which Stella defined characteristics of regional styles of sculpture during the Gupta period. Her visual analyses of individual objects remains unsurpassed. The original article was first translated by Alan Shapiro, and was then revised by me and by Stella, who chose to modify the original text in places to reflect subsequent research. Her first book, *Grundzüge der indischen Kunst* could not be included because of its length, but it has been summarized in the essay.

The selection emphasizes the cultural and symbolic values of Indian art that Stella has concentrated on in her work. The opening section has two articles that discuss the ways art fits into society and communicates religious concepts. The second section has the essay from *Unknown India,* which incorporates her earlier work on folk art, such as kanthās, and various forms of ritual art. The article "Indian Terracottas" is also reprinted. Section three, entitled "The Subtle Body," based on her own term for the form that underlies concrete shapes, includes studies of literary and visual symbolism. In sections four and five, on temple sculpture and painting, formal and technical considerations combine with analyses of symbolic meaning.

The writings selected for this volume are comprehensible in their own terms. They are reprinted here without commentary and with only minor editorial changes. Their diverse styles represent different phases of Stella's scholarly life. Misprints have been corrected, and the transliteration of words from Sanskrit and other Indian languages has been normalized according to currently accepted principles. Since this material was written over a period of about fifty years and was published in many different countries, the forms of bibliographic references and citations vary greatly in the original articles. The notes have therefore been standardized wherever possible to avoid confusion. If read in the context provided by the biographical essay, the writings should not require further explanation. Since Stella's thought is best understood through her own writings, deeper appreciation for her vision of Indian art can be gained by reading her major books: *Grundzüge der indischen Kunst*, *Indian Sculpture*, *The Hindu Temple*, and *The Presence of Śiva*.

Joseph Dye's comprehensive bibliography of her writings, first published in *Marsyas* in 1975 and now brought up to date, is included here. My investigation of Stella's work was based on it.

This volume could not have been published without the editorial skill of Lee Ann Draud of the University of Pennsylvania Press.

Interviews and archival work related to this project took me to India for a month in the winter of 1980–81. This was supported by a grant from the Smithsonian Institution, through the American Institute of Indian Studies. Stella's friends were gracious with their hospitality and their knowledge, yet another measure of the high regard in which she is held throughout the subcontinent.

To Stella herself, teacher and constant resource, I offer the thanks of one who has enjoyed a great adventure.

BARBARA STOLER MILLER
New York
June 1982

Transliteration and Pronunciation Conventions

Indic words are rendered in Roman script, using current international conventions for transliteration. In reading Sanskrit words, the accent is placed on a syllable only when this is long. A syllable is long if it contains a long vowel (*ā*, *ī*, *ū*), a dipthong (*e*, *o*, *ai*, *au*), or a vowel followed by more than one consonant. It should be noted that the aspirated consonants *kh*, *gh*, *ch*, *jh*, *th*, *dh*, *ph*, *bh*, and so on are considered single consonants in the Sanskrit alphabet.

Vowels are given their full value, as in Italian or German:

a as *u* in c*u*t
ā as *a* in f*a*ther
i as *i* in p*i*t
ī as *i* in mach*i*ne
u as *u* in p*u*t
ū as *u* in r*u*le
ṛ a short vowel; as *ri* in *ri*ver
e as *ay* in s*ay*
ai as *ai* in *ai*sle
o as *o* in g*o*
au as *ow* in c*ow*
ṁ nasalizes and lengthens the preceding vowel
ḥ a rough breathing, replacing an original *s* or *r*; lengthens the preceding vowel and occurs only at the end of a syllable or word

Most consonants are analogous to the English, if the distinction between aspirated and nonaspirated consonants is observed; for example, the aspirated consonants *th* and *ph* must never be pronounced as in English *th*in and *ph*ial, but as in ho*th*ouse and she*ph*erd (similarly, *kh*, *gh*, *ch*, *jh*, *dh*, *bh*). The differences between the Sanskrit "cerebral" *ṭ*, *ṭh*, *ḍ*, *ḍh*, *ṇ*, and "dental" *t*, *th*, *d*, *dh*, *n* are another distinctive feature of the language. The dentals are formed with the tongue against the teeth, the cerebrals with the tongue turned back along the palate. Note also:

g as *g* in *g*oat
ṅ as *n* in i*n*k, or si*ng*
c as *ch* in *ch*urch
ñ as *ñ* in Spanish se*ñ*or
ś as *s* is *s*ugar
ṣ as *sh* is *sh*ape

Historical and mythological names are rendered with diacritical marks, but Viṣṇu and Kṛṣṇa are spelled Vishnu and Krishna for the convenience of most readers. The conventional transliteration of Śiva is used.

There has been an attempt to normalize the variety of spellings of Indian place names referred to in Dr. Kramrisch's writings. Ancient sites and places whose modern names have changed significantly are rendered with diacritical marks, e.g., Kauśāmbī (modern Kosam), Pāṭaliputra (modern Patna). Place names in modern use, regardless of their antiquity, do not have diacritical marks, e.g., Bhubaneswar, Mathura.

EXPLORING INDIA'S SACRED ART

Stella Kramrisch: A Biographical Essay

by BARBARA STOLER MILLER

Who, if I cried, would hear me among the angelic
orders? And even if one of them suddenly
pressed me against his heart, I should fade in the strength of his
stronger existence. For beauty's nothing
but beginning of Terror we're still just able to bear,
and why we adore it so is because it serenely
disdains to destroy us. Every angel is terrible.

Stella Kramrisch vividly recalls the angels that have appeared in her experience as sources of consolation and painful beauty since early childhood, when she was drawn to the angels carved inside the ancestral vault on the estate where she lived as a child, and felt their beauty in the fearsome surroundings. For her, the angels were superhuman figures appearing from an invisible realm that was made real by art. Her experience of art is dominated by a sense of wonder as acute as pain in the face of works of creative power. She finds it expressed in the opening lines of Rainer Maria Rilke's conception.[1]

Her rigorous awareness of factual reality and technical details has never kept her from responding to the deeper meaning of a work of art and allowing it to guide her. Among the wealth of images that she has seen, examined, and stored in her eidetic memory, her most profound experiences have focused on the rock-cut Sadāśiva Mahādeva in the cave temple at Elephanta[2] and on the classical Buddha figures of Sarnath. She contrasts the serenity of transfigured nature contained in these forms of Buddha with the deeper, darker cosmic dynamism of the elemental Sadāśiva.

It was through the Sarnath Buddha images that she perceived the process whereby a "subtle body" is translated directly into stone, an insight that underlies her vision of Indian classical art:[3]

4

Exploring India's Sacred Art

Indian art commands a set of visual signs in which the predominating figures are based on the shape of man. These figures, however, do not represent the physical, but rather the subtle body of man. But to visualise this subtle body one must think of it as a combination of fluid, plastic shape and linear rhythms, a transubstantiated form created by the Indian artist, and based on the shape of man. For this shape in life is the place of man's transformation. Art divests it of the accidents of death, stagnation, labour and restlessness, and remakes it as a vessel that holds self-absorption in an unending flux of modelled form and gliding line.

Yoga discipline is as much a prerequisite for the Indian artist as was physical discipline for the Greek. It is as though in Indian art the image is embossed from within by the movement of breath, or circulation, through the vital centres of the living being, unimpeded by the gross matter of the actual physical body. A plastic quality results that is as though carried by the living breath with which the image is filled; conducted by the smooth channels of body and limbs. These smooth channels have a pristine glow and a continuity of outline as though what they hold were an equivalent of the breath of God.

Sadāśiva is the most complete, complex, and esoteric aspect of Śiva, represented as a monumental sculpture at Elephanta. In this image, emitting the convulsed fury of Bhairava on one side and the calm beauty of Umā on the other, Stella discovered the rhythmic tension of opposing forces that express the vitality of Indian religious experience. These are reiterated in other images carved in grottoes inside the cave temple: Naṭarāja, the divine dancer performing the dance of the world's existence, dancing the cosmos into and out of existence, or Ardhanārīśvara, the androgynous god whose body is male on the right and female on the left. Stella has explored every aspect of Śiva's multiple forms through her studies of Indian visual art and religious texts, resulting in her book, *The Presence of Śiva,* and the exhibition "Manifestations of Shiva," to which she devoted a decade of scholarly and curatorial effort.

Stella has always been elusive about facts of her personal life, preferring the complex personality behind her work to remain hidden. Invoking the attitudes of the Indian artist-craftsman with whom she feels deep affinities, she has since her youth consciously tried to think of herself as a "working organism" whose name is significant only as a signature of responsibility to competent works. For her, as for the craftsman, the creative process is a ritual through which the performer transforms himself and his material. The transformative experiences of her own life are what she values most; the spirit that drives her work emerges in her recollections of these experiences. She is a gifted storyteller who takes pleasure in stringing dramatic events into necklaces of tales, enriched by fairytales she heard from childhood servants in Austria, parables of Indian sages, verses by German poets, and visions of her own imagination.

She was born in Moravia at the end of the nineteenth century in a former hunting lodge in the town of Mikulov (Ger. Nikolsburg), Austrian crown land from the mid-nineteenth century until 1918, when Moravia was incorporated into Czechoslovakia following the overthrow of Hapsburg rule. As a child she spoke both Czech and German. An only child, she was carefully nurtured, both intellectually and spiritually.

Her childhood was one of romantic isolation, spent in the Austrian countryside in intimate contact with nature, art, and the supernatural. From the gardeners she learned to believe in the magic of the forest. The gathering and baling of wood to be sent to the city was the source of fantasies about imprisoned nature spirits. Her father taught her to know every flower, fungus, and tree by its German and Latin names. He frequently took her to museums in Vienna. She remembers the ammonites in the Naturhistorisches Museum that fascinated her as a young child, and the two inconspicuous fragments of door jambs from an Indian temple that she discovered there somewhat later. She evokes the happiness of going with her mother or father to hear the Vienna Boys' Choir in the Imperial Chapel on Sundays. A Jew by birth, her father was deeply religious in a nondenominational way.

Her mother imposed severe discipline on her unruly child, including serious study of the violin. She also took her to art exhibitions and encouraged her critical responses to whatever she saw. She supported her daughter's request for ballet lessons; they were taken in secret, against the objections of her father. The lessons continued throughout her school years, and at the age of eighteen she began to give public performances. Her dancing attracted the attention of some avant garde critics and was the basis of her contact with contemporary Austrian and German artists. Her passion for ballet and other forms of dance has endured and colored her conceptions of plastic art.

The Mikulov residence, its castle, and earlier inhabitants are known to have inspired the Austrian poet Franz Grillparzer's brooding, lyrical play *Die Ahnfrau (The Ancestress),* written in 1817. The play, whose heroine is Bertha, the young daughter of Count Zdenko von Borotin, focuses on the curse of the castle that any child who lived there beyond puberty would die. Although Stella does not remember feeling afraid because of the curse, her childhood was filled with rumors of the night-roaming ghost of the ancestress and of treasure buried in the walls of the hunting lodge during the Thirty Years War. Her parents expressed an urgency about leaving and when she was ten years old, the family moved to Vienna.

In Vienna, she attended the city's first humanistic Gymnasium for girls, "Erstes humanistisches Mädchengymnasium in der Rahlgasse," where the rigorous curriculum included Greek as well as Latin. She soon discovered the city's lending libraries and delighted in borrowing quantities of books on any subject. One of these was Leopold von Schroeder's German translation of the *Bhagavadgītā.*[4] Her youthful response to the vision of Krishna revealing himself to the trembling warrior Arjuna on the Kuru battlefield was one of awe and identification with Arjuna's experience:

> You are the infinite power,
> without beginning, middle, or end,
> your arms are infinite
> and your eyes the sun and moon,
> I see you—mouths
> that are blazing fires,
> burning this whole universe
> with your own fiery energy. (*BG* 11:19)

She took as her personal motto Krishna's words to Arjuna:

> Concern yourself only with action,
> never with its fruits.
> The fruits of action should not be your motive,
> nor should you cling to inaction. (*BG* 2:47)

After her discovery of the *Bhagavadgītā,* she sought to learn more about India. When she had exhausted the limited contents of the lending libraries, she went to read in the Theosophical Society and then in the Anthroposophical Society, where she met Rudolf Steiner, its founder. She was impressed by Steiner's interpretations of Indian thought and by his emphasis on the spiritual side of human nature.

The sensibility for India that emerged in her adolescence was developed within an intellectual framework that included serious study of Greek language and culture, German poetry, and philosophy. She avidly read Plato's *Symposium, Phaedo,* and *Critias* and Euripides' *Bacchae.* She responded deeply to Meister Eckhart and also to the mystical lyricism of Heinrich Suso's guide to spiritual life, *Das Büchlein der ewigen Weisheit,* as well as to the writings of Jakob Boehme and Angelus Silesius. When her paternal grandfather was dying, he asked her to read Spinoza to him. Spinoza's intensely mathematical appreciation of the universe and his notion that things make sense when understood in terms of a total structure impressed her. These concepts and his pantheistic interpretation of God as the fullness of Nature, coupled with his emphasis on empirical observation, provided philosophical bases for her readings of Indian religious texts.

Her formal studies were complemented by a keen awareness of contemporary art. When the historic exhibition of Futurist painting came to Vienna in 1912, her experience as a dancer made her sensitive to the rhythms of the paintings and their many-limbed figures. She recalls arguing with her mother about the unconventional forms of Futurist artists. Futurism was only one of several artistic attacks on conventional ideas in Vienna at this time. For Stella, Vienna was less the city of Strauss waltzes than of Gustav Klimt's and Egon Schiele's paintings.[5] Klimt's visual audacity symbolized a new kind of truth for her. He, Schiele, and other contemporary expressionist painters provided counter images to established social relations and challenged the viewer to share in the psychological anguish of the times. Although Freud's *Interpretation of Dreams* sold few copies in the ten years after its publication in 1900, the Viennese expressionist painters read it and drew on its insights in their pictorial revolution. These artists also shared a widespread Germanic interest in Indian spirituality, most concretely articulated by Wassily Kandinsky in his 1912 essay *Über das Geistige in der Kunst.*[6] Stella's thinking about art was shaped by Kandinsky's analysis, though she did not share his admiration for Mme. Blavatsky or theosophy.

When Diaghilev's Ballet Russe was in Vienna in 1912, Stella saw Nijinsky dance "Le Spectre de la Rose." The romantic means that the ballet used to convey the interpenetration of nature and human emotion compelled her eye and mind to focus on details of costume and patterns of movement that revealed a spiritual reality underlying the sensuality of the dance.[7] This synthetic experience of critical analysis and emotional absorption in a work of art proved fundamental to her early encounters with Indian religious art, where human form is expressed in terms of its infinite extensibility in the spiritual universe.

By the time she was sixteen years old Stella had acquired considerable knowledge of Indian culture and gained permission to read in the Oriental Seminar Library of the University of Vienna. Later she became a member of the seminar that Joseph Strzygowski directed in the Institute of Art History. Strzygowski held the first chair of Oriental art to be established in Europe.[8] His main field of interest was Near and Middle Eastern art, archaeology, and architecture. Though he had little formal knowledge of Indian art, he offered to guide her reading and research.

Strzygowski's approach was marked by his theory of continuity between Central Asian and Northern European art in contrast to what he saw as degenerate Mediterranean Hellenism. His aim was to understand European art by searching for its Asiatic roots. His writing was highly speculative rather than systematic. In an article written in 1933 for the first issue of the *Journal of the Indian Society of Oriental Art*, and translated into English by Stella, he applied his views to Indian art. A sense of his style and position can be gleaned from a paragraph of this article:

> Most of the Indian monuments preserved are religious buildings. The more does the profane art of the Mughals appear alien although the Indian share in it is considerable, and this not only in miniature painting, but even in a building like the Taj Mahal which may appear Persian, but its ground plan reveals at a glance the Indian principle, in the way in which the masses are articulated in the interior. We may assume a similar state of things in the more and most ancient art on Indian soil. The scholar whose researches deal with Indian art has always to consult the Vedas while keeping in mind all the while the pre-Aryan art of India.

Although Stella has never followed Strzygowski's strict division of art into the Northern style of nomadic Aryans versus the Southern style of urban Mediterranean civilizations, her early work shows an interest in the influence of race on art.[9] She studied Sanskrit in Vienna with Gomperz and later in Calcutta with D. R. Bhandarkar, thus gaining access to Vedic texts as sources for understanding elusive concepts of Hindu religious art. Her interpretations of Vedic literature have been an essential aspect of her work, though never to the exclusion of later Hindu texts and non-Aryan materials.

Strzygowski's friend Victor Goloubew,[10] the connoisseur and collector, had just returned from India with photographs of Sanchi and Ajanta at the time Stella became a member of Strzygowski's seminar. A set of the photographs was presented to Strzygowski and he made them available to her. They inspired her research on early Buddhist art at Sanchi and Bharhut; this formed the basis of the doctoral dissertation, entitled "Untersuchungen zum Wesen der frühbuddhistischen Bildnerei Indiens," for which she was awarded the doctorate in 1919. Her work was also influenced by the text and illustrations in E. B. Havell's recently published *Indian Sculpture and Painting: Illustrated by Typical Masterpieces with an Explanation of Their Motives and Ideals.*[11] At the time Havell wrote the book he was principal of the Government Art School in Calcutta. He was a passionate advocate of Indian art; he stressed the religious profundity of its anonymous artists at a time when most Europeans refused to recognize the existence of indigenous art in India.

Stella's other teacher at the university was Max Dvořák, who held the chair for European art. His methods differed fundamentally from those of Strzygowski, and they did not like each other. Stella recalls that when they met on the stairs at the university, one looked to the right, the other to the left, and they did not see one another. Dvořák's major contribution to the Vienna School of Art History was his program of integrating art history with the history of ideas. His important essay entitled *Idealismus und Naturalismus in der gotischen Sculptur und Malerei* was written between 1915 and 1917, when she was his student.[12] In it he contrasted the artistic idealism produced by the Christian spirituality of the Middle Ages with the empirical naturalism that dominated Renaissance art. Dvořák's work expressed a nostalgia for the emotional spontaneity that he attributed to the Middle Ages and his passion for spiritual values affected most of his students.

Dvořák had been trained in the formalist method of Alois Riegl, who used the analysis of late Roman textiles to develop a theory of styles that stressed the autonomy of forms. Dvořák stressed that rigorous historical methodology was as crucial to the study of art as was Riegl's formalism, but he encouraged his students to read Riegl's work with care. Stella valued the precision of Riegl's analyses, but not his attempt to construct a comprehensive theory of artistic development.[13]

Another scholar whose work impressed her was Bronislaw Malinowski. She read his early papers on the indigenous people of New Guinea and the Trobriand Islands, with particular interest in his field research techniques and his insistence on the study of different cultures in terms of their internal dynamics.[14]

The events of World War I created economic and cultural chaos in Vienna. At the end of the war, Oxford University invited selected members of the University of Vienna staff to lecture in England. Priority was given to those whose work was "connected with British interests." In order to help his young assistant escape from the misery of postwar Vienna, Strzygowski claimed that Indian art qualified in this category and Stella joined the group going to England in 1919.

She was assigned to give three public lectures on Indian art at Oxford. For her first lecture, she planned to speak on the Hindu temple, although she had never seen one and had seen examples of original temple sculpture for the first time in London. She was introduced by the painter Sir William Rothenstein, then principal of the Royal College of Art in London; he is said to have commented on the "originality" of her eclectic English. As has been her practice ever since, the lecture was delivered without notes. Stella recalls, "After I finished, I went down to the audience. Suddenly I felt the wide-sleeved arms of Rabindranath Tagore around me." Tagore was visiting England in connection with his plans for expanding Santiniketan into an international university called Vishvabharati. The curriculum was designed to nurture artistic creativity, international unity, social reform, and devotion to peace. Tagore invited Stella to join the newly established school of art, Kala Bhavan. She accepted without hesitation. Rather than return to Vienna, she decided to remain in London until she could obtain a visa for travel to India. As an alien ex-enemy, she had to report to the India Office every week and to seek letters of support from various experts, among them Rothenstein. He wrote about her to Tagore in a letter dated April 23, 1921:[15]

> The young Austrian-Slovakian lady came to see me yesterday to ask if I could help her to get a passport for India. But Lord Carmichael tells me that, however willing Mr. Montagu may be, and other people in the India Office, to help you, the Foreign Office, at this particular time, is most unlikely to issue passports to any foreigners save those having clear reasons for going to India and the backing of their embassies so far as their appropriateness is concerned. When things have settled down in India, there will not be the same difficulty; in this particular case I believe you owe me a cock. For I have saved you from the results of an invitation which the recipient, had she been worthy of it, would not have been quite so ready to accept. One wants more than a single meeting, on either side, in such important affairs. Perhaps I am unduly suspicious of the softer sex. But when great things have to be carried through, I doubt whether it is wise to encumber yourself with almond eyed ladies.

Stella persisted despite the obstacles. During the months of waiting, she enrolled as a student in the School of Oriental Studies at London University, where she read Buddhist Abhidharma texts under Louis de La Vallé Poussin. In London she met Moses Gaster, the Rumanian Jewish scholar who was President of the Royal Asiatic Society and Chief Rabbi of the Sephardic communities in England; she frequently visited with him and his family. Gaster dubbed her a "raw egg without a shell" and advised her to harden. He introduced her to Lady Sassoon, whose daughter Lady Ezra, an influential member of Calcutta society, attested to Stella's nonpolitical nature and helped clear the way for her to be issued a visa.[16] After nine months she obtained her visa and immediately set out for Trieste, where she boarded a boat for Bombay.

She stopped in Vienna only long enough to meet her parents at the railway station. It was her last meeting with her father. He died soon after her departure. After 1923, she returned to Vienna for short visits with her mother; these continued until 1940, when the war made travel from India to Europe almost impossible.[17]

Rothenstein, writing again to Tagore in June 1922, described Stella as an "enthusiastic pilgrim."[18] The sea voyage to India allowed her time to meditate on what she would soon see. She spent her first hours there at the cave temple on Elephanta Island.[19]

> I arrived in Bombay very early in the morning and even before going to the hotel, I went to Elephanta in one of those little boats and spent the day there until the sun set. Then something very strange happened: I walked out and saw something glistening in the sand. It was a golden cross, a Jesuit cross. I thought it so extraordinary . . . coming out of the great Siva sanctuary and finding that golden cross there.

She remembers going east across India by train and her first day at Santiniketan:

I arrived there just a little before midnight. It was beautifully calm. It was cold. It was winter and the mimosas were in flower . . . and their scent is lovely. Rabindranath came and he welcomed me. He was followed by a deer. I thought, "It's too good for words; it looks like a dream." He showed me my little room, which was just a cubicle built of mud, with a thatched roof. I did not sleep very much because at five o'clock the bells and gongs started sounding and the students of Santiniketan were chanting one of Tagore's songs. It was the day of the Santiniketan melā, the founding day, so there was a beautiful fair where the villagers came and displayed their handmade goods. I fell in love, first of all, with a toy wooden cart, a ratha, and also with one painting, a sketch of that bare landscape by one of the pupils of Nandalal Bose, who was the principal of Kala Bhavan. That painting, however, was priced at ten rupees and I couldn't afford that because I had seven rupees left, so I spoke to Nandalal Bose and said, "I'm anxious to get it." He said, "Alright, he'll give it to you for seven rupees." These were my last seven rupees. I had nothing else. This was my first day in Santiniketan. It was months before I went to Calcutta.

Writing to Rothenstein shortly after her arrival in India, she apologized for her silence during months "spent in suspense and work." She continued:[20]

I often thought of what you told me, still I feel that having gone through the fire has made me clearer . . . I could not see much of the country up to now, but living in the nearness of Dr. Tagore makes me realise India in full intensity . . . I sincerely hope that the Visva-Bharati will grow and develop. We all try to serve it with our power and it has no other basis than its ideal and our surrender.

Her initial impressions of India were thus dominated by her encounter with Śiva in the cave temple at Elephanta, by the austere natural beauty of the Bengal countryside around Santiniketan, and by the striking figure of Tagore. She admired his skills as a singer, dancer, and social reformer as much as his poetic genius.

She taught Indian art and a survey of Western art at Santiniketan until she joined the faculty of the University of Calcutta in 1923. Even then she remained close to Tagore and his family, often journeying to Santiniketan from Calcutta. She fondly recalls the hours she spent with his oldest brother, Jyotirindranath, a devoted gardener, in his garden of white roses, where he stretched his limbs in a chaise longue toward sunset, and birds came to perch on his arms. She learned about Indian music from one of Tagore's nephews, Dinu Babu, a master of the esrāj, a fretted stringed instrument related to the sarangī.

She also formed friendships with Nandalal Bose and Tagore's nephews Gaganendranath and Abanindranath, who were the founders and leading contemporary artists of the Bengal School. She appreciated their imaginative skills, but found much of the revivalist paintings of Abanindranath to be too romantic and eclectic, despite its Indian subject matter. She noted the strong influence of the styles of Arthur Rackham and Edmond Dulac on Abanindranath's work. She preferred Gaganenranath's daring and at the same time playful experiments with cubist principles, which he employed to create fantastic pictorial architectures of delicate cubes, and his satirical caricature drawings. She found the naive watercolors of Abanindranth's sister, Sunayini Devi, charming for their religious lyricism. When Rabindranath himself suddenly started to paint in 1928, at the age of sixty-seven, Stella was fascinated by the means he found to express impulses that were absent in his writings. In her articles on his drawings and paintings, she compares the mood of his curvilinear forms to art nouveau and to expressionism, particularly that of Edvard Munch.[21]

In Calcutta, Stella had an opportunity to study early Buddhist sculpture on the carved railing of Bharhut stūpa, which had been discovered by General Cunningham in 1873 in a village in the former Nagod State and then transferred to Calcutta for installation in the newly founded Indian Museum. These sculptures encouraged her to publish her view that transcendental states of inner experience are visualized in the forms of Indian plastic art. She delivered a talk on early Buddhist art before the Indian Society of Oriental Art.[22] The lecture appeared in 1921 in *Rūpam*, the journal of the Society, under the title "The Representation of Nature in Early Buddhist Sculpture (Bharhut-Sanchi)."[23] In it, she succinctly presents ideas that resonate throughout her work:

> The oneness of all creation is expressed in early Buddhist sculpture by a gentle harmony and similarity of individual shapes, which characterize every object but are more than a picture of their exterior. Life itself has assumed the shape of artistic form. The Indian understands life as growth. He does not depict the shapes of nature but nature itself, the creative creating power. Earth's life-blood streams through the members of the figures and gives them form according to the celerity of its circulation, which is gently flowing, soft and equipoised at Bharhut. The forms have not yet separated themselves from mother earth, who nourished them and gives them the contemplative life. Each relief is first of all a picture of a spiritual state, and secondary to it, it is the representation of a particular theme.

After hearing her speak, Sir Asutosh Mookerji, Vice-Chancellor of Calcutta University, invited her to become a lecturer in Indian art at the university. Sir Asutosh, a mathematician and judge of the High Court in Calcutta, served as vice-chancellor for two terms (1906–1914, 1921–1923), during which he laid the foundations of a national research university in Calcutta, including colleges of law and medicine and postgraduate departments in sciences, languages, and arts. Sir Asutosh was a Hindu nationalist with a deep respect for India's past, but he was also a social reformer who risked religious ostracism for arranging the remarriage of his eldest daughter, who was a child widow.[24] He invited Stella with full recognition of the social hardships she would face as the only woman and the only European on the faculty of the university, as well as of the unease she would create in British society by her association with Indians. Unfortunately, Sir Asutosh died in 1924. Because she was a Westerner, Stella was discriminated against by his son Syama Prasad, who became vice-chancellor of the university and later a leader of the extremist Hindu Mahasabha. It was only years later, after the publication of her book *The Hindu Temple* in 1946, that she was again received by the family. She recalls Syama Prasad saying to her, "Of the two of us, you are the better Hindu."

University officials, like the British, did not know what to do with Stella. Since her scholarly credentials were impeccable and her devotion to Indian art was apparent, she was made a member of the permanent staff of the University of Calcutta, but was paid a minimal salary because of her non-Indian parentage. However, she was housed on the grounds of the botanical garden of the university, in a building that had been the residence of the wife of one of the university's major benefactors, Sir Taraknath Palit. There she enjoyed the luxury of bathing in Lady Palit's tub of imported Carrara marble. Her closest companion was her pet hyena, Harshi.

People who met her in Calcutta felt her to be absorbed in a private inner life with art and texts, but rarely with people. This was her choice but also a necessity. Aloofness and social isolation in Calcutta were her response to threats, including amorous advances or open hostilities of several Indian men. She knew that a young, unmarried European woman was considered both enticing and dangerously alien. After receiving a number of threatening letters, she applied to the police for a permit to carry a gun. At the very beginning of her career at the University of Calcutta, she had followed the advice of D. R. Bhandarkar, the head of her department, and altered the style of her dresses so that her arms and legs were covered. She was told by him that such modifications of costume were indeed evidence of her "moral improvement."[25]

Her personal difficulties were compounded by political tensions resulting from the partition of Bengal and related British policies. Revolutionary activities during the 1920s included widespread terrorism carried out in the name of the demon-slaying patron goddess of Calcutta, Kālī.[26] Stella was not involved in political events, but the tone of this period would have made a less determined person leave. She stayed to teach and continue her research, sustained by the diversity of art objects she was able to examine in museums, private collections, archaeological sites, and temples all over India.

She devoted her energy and scholarly skills to building Indian art history as an intellectual discipline in which formal history, archaeology, iconography, and religion all had their legitimate roles to play. One of her earliest students, Niharranjan Ray, the late Emeritus Professor of Indian Art at Calcutta University, recalled how she analyzed a piece of plastic art, relating it to its place and time in terms of allied visual and literary materials, always making it "a live object taking its own place in the flowing tide of life." He said, "It was she who taught me how to look at and what to look for in an object of art; she indeed opened my eyes to the aesthetic and spiritual values of Indian art and made me fall in love with it. In those early days of her career in India she used to speak a heavy Germanic English, in somewhat involuted manner, but by the way she threw herself with passionate involvement into whatever she said, in her class lectures as much as in public addresses, she succeeded in communicating her ideas admirably. Her involvement was total and hence contagious."[27]

Another of her early students was Devaprasad Ghose, who became director of the Asutosh Museum of Indian Art when it was established by the university in 1932.[28] In consultation with her, Ghose organized students from villages in the environs of Calcutta to collect examples of folk art. The effort succeeded in preserving a representative collection of Bengali village art, following the plan Sir Asutosh had discussed with Stella before his death.

In Stella's opinion, her most gifted student was Prithwish Neogy, who is now professor of art at the University of Hawaii. She felt that his visual sensitivity was extraordinary. His photographs of Elephanta accompanied her article "The Image of Mahādeva in the Cave-Temple on Elephanta Island." His own published work includes an analysis of the paintings of Binode Behari Mukherjee, one of the most innovative artists of the Bengal School, and an edition of Rabindranath Tagore's writings on art and aesthetics.[29]

Although she was teaching, lecturing, and writing in English, her major work during this period, *Grundzüge der indischen Kunst,* was written in German. It was published in 1924 in Dresden and was widely reviewed in Europe and India; Havell wrote a glowing review in *Rūpam,* as did Heinrich Zimmer in *Orientalistische Literaturzeitung.* [30] When compared with her English writings, the book has a clarity of style and language that her English is still struggling to achieve. Based on materials drawn from two thousand years of Indian art, beginning with early Buddhist sculpture and ending with eighteenth-century Rāgamāla painting, she stresses the religious spirit of Indian art in terms that reflect the theories of the Vienna School. In analogy to Dvořák's distinction between the naturalistic and the idealistic realms of art, she introduces the distinction between dṛṣṭam and adṛṣṭam, manifest and unmanifest. Quoting a poem by the fifteenth-century mystic Kabir, based on an English version by Rabindranath Tagore, she relates this to the Indian conception of conscious and unconscious thought.[31]

> The conscious and unconscious are poles.
> Between them thought has made a swing.
> All beings and all worlds hang there.
> The swing sways ceaselessly.
> Myriad beings exist there.
> The sun and the moon course there.
> Myriad ages pass and the swing goes on.
> Infinite swing: sky, earth, air, and water,
> and God himself taking form.

Her analysis proceeds from the view that a relation between the two poles exists in Indian art through the presence of divine nature in its forms. Objects and concepts are discussed under the themes of myth and form, nature, space, and rhythm. The various sections contain ideas and phrases that became leitmotifs of her later work: the mystery of Śiva's dance is an artistic act sustaining its own law; landscape is a mirror of the soul; time is a gesture of eternity that has its echo suspended in the fullness we call space; rhythm is the natural way in which all life energy develops. Her ideas are presented with reference to large photographs of works from sites such as Bharhut, Amaravati, Sarnath, Ajanta, Mamallapuram, Ellora, and Halebid, as well as several superb sculptures from the Rajshahi Museum in East Bengal.

Within a few years, Stella encountered two remarkable men, each of whom appointed himself her teacher and, in his own way, deepened her view of art. On a visit to the Varendra Research Society in Rajshahi, she met the director, Akshaya Kumar Maitra. When she questioned him about the ancient texts on Indian art, he urged her to study the *Chitrasūtra,* or Rules of Painting, a treatise embedded within the *Viṣṇudharmottara.* He knew that she had been a dancer and would be interested in the relations between dancing and painting expressed in the text. In her foreword to C. Sivaramamurti's recent edition and translation of the *Citrasūtra* she records her initial response to the text:[32]

This unique treatise on painting kept me spellbound when searching the Purāṇas for references to art. A statement in the *Viṣṇudharmottara* (VDhP3.2.4) preceding the *Citrasūtra,* came almost as a revelation: "It is very difficult to understand the rules of painting without a knowledge of dancing."

A trained awareness of movement underlies the *Citrasūtra.* The awareness has for its objects not only voluntary postures and gestures of body and limbs but also the movement of breath within the body. In order to show the former, the rules of foreshortening are taught, in order to show the latter, subtleties of shading had to be mastered by which the body and limbs were given, not only deceptively volumetric fulness, but their planes appeared as if expanding by breathing and throbbing with the pulsations of life. Moreover, the dancer's experience of the flux of movement carried by the body was communicated to the quality of the line, its flowing continuity and modelling sinuosity.

In her eagerness to broadcast the contents of the text, she began translating it with the help of D. R. Bhandarkar. She studied the only available version of the text and quickly published an analysis, along with what she now considers to be an "unscholarly" translation, in *The Calcutta Review* of February 1924. She still finds the rules of the *Citrasūtra* the most relevant compendium on ancient Indian painting and feels that Sivaramamurti's translation clarifies many points she could not document when she read the text in the uncritical Venkatesvara Press edition more than a half century ago.

Akshay Babu, as Stella and his friends called A. K. Maitra, introduced her to other important texts, including the *Hayaśirṣapañcarātra,* a treatise on Hindu temple architecture. She studied the sculptures in the Rajshahi Museum and at local archaeological sites. In 1923 she published "Notes on Bengal Sculpture" and in 1929 "Pāla and Sena Sculpture," which includes many examples from Rajshahi, as well as from the Indian Museum. While analyzing the character and style of these works, she realized the importance of Pāla-Sena sculptures for the study of the dominant Tantric religion of the period, with its emphasis on the creative energy of the female principle. Her understanding was increased by trips with Akshay Babu to the sites of various temples still used for worship, where she shared the religious experience of Hindu rituals of pūjā.

Her youthful love of the German mystics made her susceptible to the songs and sayings of Hindu saints, who seemed to her to convey the spiritual power embodied in Indian art. She felt particular admiration for the living saint Ramana Maharshi, whose teachings provided a background for her own religious experience of Śiva. Śiva revealed himself to Ramana Maharshi on the hill called Arunachala near Tiruvannamalai. His cryptic Tamil devotional poems address God as Arunachala, who is always paradoxical. The poem "Necklace of Nine Gems" is typical:[33]

In the court of Chidambaram,
Śiva, motionless by nature,
dances in rapture for Śakti,
and she stands motionless.
Know that in Arunachala
he stands in solemnity

and she withdraws there
into his unmoving self.

Stella's personal spiritual teacher was a wandering Śaivite Tantric monk who belonged to one of the Aghorī orders.[34] The monk could not stay in any place for long, symbolized by his vow to never let his staff touch the ground. He came to Calcutta periodically and watched her for some time before he announced himself. He spoke no English and communicated with her in Hindi and Sanskrit. He tested her through a drastic Śaiva experience in which she was told to follow him to Kalighat temple, where he had her ascend a funeral pyre and sit on a corpse that was about to be cremated. After the flames began to rise, he let her descend and they waited for the body to be completely burned. Then he told her to gather the ashes, take them home, and rub them on her body. Throughout the entire happening she had implicit faith in its validity as a ritual that confirmed her in her fearlessness and let her understand life with a lightened heart.

Stella's acute sensitivities to nature, to realms of being that transcend the sensible world, and to the tensions of spiritual practice enabled her to engage in this experience of reality's terrible aspect. It expanded her understanding of Śiva. Throughout her life, she has continually opened her imagination and her spirit to difficult means for extending the limits of knowing.

Her personal relationships have always been intense and complex. In 1929 she met and married a Hungarian economist, Laszlo Nemenyi, in Calcutta. He had come to India shortly before in connection with the establishment of the Central Reserve Bank. The work focused his attention on economic problems in the subcontinent, and he stayed to serve as an economic adviser to the government of India. Stella had been reluctant to marry and was determined not to let marriage interfere with her work. She admired her husband's elegance and military discipline, cherishing as his highest praise the words "You are a good soldier!" Though they traveled separately in India and abroad a great deal during their marriage, they enjoyed meeting in a spacious house with beautiful gardens in Calcutta, where they established a household after their marriage, or in Delhi, where Laszlo Nemenyi served in the Ministry of Finance under the viceroy. Stella recalls that during their twenty-one years of marriage, they spent only a fraction of that time together. He was absorbed in work that necessitated his absence from Calcutta and she had little time for social life.

Stella's interest in contemporary Indian art and in tribal and folk arts strengthened her associations with the Tagore brothers, as well as with important Bengali intellectuals like Dinesh Chandra Sen and Gurusaday Dutt. Her work in ancient Indian art brought her into contact with field archaeologists like Sir John Marshall. She met most scholars of art who came to Calcutta, including Ananda K. Coomaraswamy, whom she encountered by chance one day in the Indian Museum. During the years, she spent long hours systematically studying different facets of the museum's collection, with special attention to the Gupta sculptures. These, together with Buddha images from the Sarnath Museum, were the basis for her detailed analysis of Gupta style, "Die figurale Plastik der Guptazeit," which was published in 1931. Her study of classical Buddha images, and related texts, led her to consider the canons for representing divinity in Indian art. She introduced the subject in "Marks of the Great Being: Mahāpuruṣa-lakṣana" (1931) and elaborated on it later in "Emblems of the Universal Being" (1935).

By 1933, she had sufficient scholarly status to be asked to join Abanindranath in editing a new version of the journal of the Indian Society of Oriental Art. The society had grown out of an art club begun in the early years of the twentieth century by a small group of aristocratic Bengalis, like the Tagores, and high-ranking English administrators, such as Lord Kitchener, Military Commander-in-Chief in India, and Sir John Woodroffe, a judge in the Calcutta high court who wrote erudite books on Tantric Hinduism under the name Arthur Avalon. E. B. Havell was also a member. The society sponsored exhibitions and lectures as well as its journal.[35]

The society's journal, formerly known as *Rūpam,* had been suspended because of financial difficulties; Abanindranath and Stella agreed to collaborate in order to save it. They renamed it *Journal of the Indian Society of Oriental Art.* It was difficult to find a printer in Calcutta who was willing to undertake the enterprise, but finally Stella convinced Boothroyd, an Englishman who owned a large press, to do the work. Their association lasted for the fifteen years that she edited the journal. Stella counts Boothroyd and Percy Brown, then Director of the Government School of Art in Calcutta, among the few English people who took a friendly interest in her work.

Abanindranath was at that time Rani Bageswari Professor of Art at the University of Calcutta. Though primarily an artist, he knew Sanskrit and shared Stella's interest in ancient texts. He had published several books on art, and one on folk ritual.[36] His *Sadangā or the Six Limbs of Painting* is a detailed commentary on a Sanskrit verse which lists the essential qualities of painting. Though Sanskrit scholars do not entirely agree with his interpretation of the text, the analysis made his fellow artists aware of the technical and aesthetic sophistication of classical Indian painters. Stella did the real editorial work of the journal, but his support was essential.

For the first issue, she translated two articles from German: "India's Position in the Art of Asia" by Strzygowski and "Some Aspects of Time in Indian Art" by Zimmer. She herself contributed two studies to the issue: "Nepalese Paintings" and "Candella Sculpture: Khajuraho." The latter, using principles she had explored in *Grundzüge,* analyzes the architectural sculpture of a temple complex that was central to her evolving theory about the meaning of the Hindu temple.

In 1933 her *Indian Sculpture* was published in India and England. The book is a scholarly chronological analysis of sculpture from the third millenium B.C. in the Indus Valley to the eighteenth century A.D. in South India, illustrated by 116 photographs of objects representing every known style and period. The book's purpose was not to give an outline of the history of Indian sculpture; instead she defined the conceptual and stylistic trends that characterize each period and then gave densely descriptive analyses of relevant images. She began axiomatically, "There is something so strong, and at the same time unique, in any Indian work of art that its 'Indianness' is felt first of all, and what it is, is seen only on second thought." Her subject was the way in which this essential quality is expressed in the relations of line, surface, volume, and other elements of visualization. Despite recent revisions in the dating of certain objects and sites, the volume remains a unique textbook.[37]

In the same year, her study of Indian painting, "Indische Malerei und Mogulminiatur," appeared in *Asiatische Miniaturmalerei, im Anschluss an Wesen und Werden der Mogulmalerei,* a volume edited by Strzygowski.

During the next decade, she published studies on every aspect of Indian art, mainly in the *Journal of the Indian Society of Oriental Art.* Her discovery of the early Deccani wall paintings at Badami in 1936 brought to light a major tradition of painting. Her analysis of the principles of classical Indian painting, focusing on the frescoes of Ajanta, forms the major part of *A Survey of Painting in the Deccan,* published in 1937. Equally important were her studies of various forms of regional folk art, including "Kanthās," on a textile art of Bengali women, and "Indian Terracottas"; both appeared in 1939.

In the latter article she divided Indian terracotta figurines into "timeless" and "timed" variations. According to her, the "timeless" terracottas are those made by village potters and women within traditions determined by use. The "timed" objects are temporally restricted, often molded variations, whose qualities are influenced by historical factors. This pioneering attempt to categorize terracotta figurines in terms of temporal distribution, forms, techniques, and themes was based on research she did while preparing a catalogue of the collections of the Patna Museum. Stella had been engaged to do the catalogue, but when she presented her work, Professor Banerji Sastri, who was excavating Buxar in the 1930s, demanded that Stella date and name certain objects to support his theory that the site was as old as Mohenjo Daro. She refused and the catalogue was later published without her name, with a note that she did not want her name mentioned.

From 1937–1940, Stella traveled to England to lecture for half of each academic year at the Courtauld Institute, which was founded in 1932 as an institute for the history of European art, affiliated with the University of London. Her courses were designed to introduce Indian art into the curriculum of the institute. For Stella it was also an opportunity to join in discussions with scholars of Western art on issues of philosophy and method.

The major influences on the art historical thought at that time were the works of Ernst Cassirer and Erwin Panofsky. Panofsky was one of the leaders of the Warburg Institute, which had been founded in London in 1905 for the study of classical culture and later merged with the Courtauld Institute. The Warburg scholars saw the art historian as a humanist whose primary concern was not with the style or iconography of a work, but with its symbolic function, which was to be discovered through the study of relevant poetic, religious, philosophical, and political documents. They defended the controversial literary approach to visual art.[38] Stella read Panofsky's recently published *Studies in Iconology* with interest, but she was more impressed by Cassirer's *Philosophie der symbolischen Formen,* which applies principles of Kantian philosophy to investigate the nature of man's symbolic activity. Stella had studied Kant's theories of knowledge and judgment while she was a student in Gymnasium; she thus had a basis for understanding Cassirer's language and mode of analysis. She found his critical approach to the study of culture relevant to her own work on the complex symbolism of the Hindu temple.

In London, she enjoyed the congenial atmosphere of the Courtauld Institute and the chance to know British people outside the restricted social environment of India. She spent time with Penelope Chetwode and her husband John Betjeman at their home in Uffington. They first met in Calcutta in 1929 when Penelope accompanied her parents to spend Christmas with the governor of Bengal, and again in 1933 after her marriage to Betjeman.

She was also delighted to renew her friendship with Betty Heimann, a refugee professor of Sanskrit from Heidelberg who was teaching at the School of Oriental Studies.[39] They had met some years earlier in Calcutta, in the home of German friends Betty was visiting, and based their friendship on mutual interests in Indian philosophy. Betty was a close friend and colleague of Heinrich Zimmer, who had taught at Bonn University. Stella and Betty met him one morning on the train from London to Oxford, where Zimmer was going to deliver one of a series of public lectures. She found it a pleasure to share in their intellectual exuberance. Zimmer was a Sanskrit scholar and cultivated man of letters, married to the daughter of the poet Hugo von Hofmannsthal. He was aware that his image of India was a romantic evocation and he did not want to disturb it by going there. Stella felt that his lack of experience with living Indian culture made him overly subjective.

She greatly admired British courage when she was in London during the blitzkrieg of 1940. She decided to stay in order to accept the invitation of Fritz Saxl, Director of the Warburg Institute, to organize a photographic exhibition entitled "Aspects of Indian Culture," which was held at the Warburg Institute in November and December. Since the Warburg Institute was devoted to the study of Western classical traditions, the invitation was special. In a memorandum prepared for the exhibition, Stella wrote that its intention was "to show how the Indian builder and craftsman have given shape to the religious ideas of the Indian people . . . the monuments convey, by their form and contents, the essential conceptions of the Indian mind."[40]

In his review Herbert Read considered the broader cultural implications of the exhibition:[41]

> The English have been established in India for more than three centuries; for more than eighty years that vast country and its civilisation have been under the direct rule of the British Crown. . . . It is no exaggeration to say that if we as a nation had shown a real sympathy for the culture of this great imperial possession, and a genuine appreciation of its manifestations in architecture, sculpture, painting, music, and dance, we should not now be at such political loggerheads.
>
> This neglect of cultural values which is characteristic of our whole colonial administration has been mitigated by the enterprise of private bodies such as the India Society. It is the India Society which has co-operated with the Warburg Institute in a photographic exhibition of Indian Art now being held in the Imperial Institute buildings, South Kensington. It is an exhibition of the greatest interest, both intrinsically, as a display of the beauty and significance of Indian Art, and incidentally, as a demonstration of what might be called exhibition technique. It has been arranged by Dr. S. Kramrisch, who was lecturer in Indian Art at the Courtauld Institute until it was allowed to become a war casualty (another instance of our philistine contempt for spir-

> itual weapons). The photographs are on a number of screens, in a continuous narrative series. . . . The visitor is first shown the setting of the Indian temple, then the significance of its external form, then the symbolism of the figures which are carved against its walls. . . . A separate section is devoted to the millennium of the "cave" or rock-cut monuments of India . . . and a third section illustrates the contacts and exchanges which Indian art (particularly in the northern border regions of Gandhara and Afghanistan) has had with the classical art of the West. In this section the Warburg Institute is in its special element, and some remarkable parallels are shown. . . .
>
> This exhibition is one of the few cultural activities being carried on in our war-ridden metropolis, and for this reason alone it deserves wide public support; but at any time, and at this time more than ever, it should serve to remind us of our cultural responsibilities, and of our shameful neglect of them in the past.

Stella found the return sea voyage to India in early 1941 a harrowing experience; she did not travel abroad again until after the war. In India, she intensified her effort to understand the symbolic value of the Hindu temple through textual research and field work. Friends say that she would walk ten miles across the jungle or through the alleys of a city to see a temple or a fragment of sculpture. Like a dedicated pilgrim, she journeyed to see remote living temples and abandoned monuments that few foreigners visited.

Among her favorite temples were the Yageśvar temples in the Himalayan foothills north of Almora, on the pilgrimage route to Mānasa Lake. She walked there from Binsar, where she spent every summer for ten years prior to the publication of *The Hindu Temple.* Sir Philip Ramsey, a British officer stationed in Almora in the final years of the eighteenth century, had fallen in love with Binsar and had built a residence there. Subsequently, one or another European intellectual living in India would discover its beauty and stay there in the hot season.

Stella shared a house with Fritz and Barbara Lévi and their daughter. Friedrich Wilhelm Lévi had been professor of mathematics at Berlin University before he was forced to flee in 1936. He accepted an appointment at Calcutta University, thus becoming the second European member of the faculty. He and Stella respected each other's capacities for sustained research on abstruse problems. The peaceful and dramatic surroundings of Binsar were ideal for concentrated work during the university holidays. Lively conversations took place during or after the evening meal, when Stella always dined with the Lévis. They sat at an old oak table in the glow of two kerosene lamps, which the scholars brought from their studies. Discussions ranged from Hindu philosophy and contemporary events to the fundamental plans of the Hindu temple.[42]

Alice Boner and Alain Daniélou were their summer neighbors and Stella valued the chance to exchange ideas with them. She wrote a great deal in Binsar, working on several articles and books in addition to *The Hindu Temple.*[43] She refreshed herself by walking in the hills, gardening, and making jelly from the slightly acid, scarlet flowers of the towering Himalayan rhododendron.

Her extensive readings in Vedic literature and in Varāmihira's *Bṛhatsaṁhitā*, a classical Sanskrit work on astronomy and astrology that relates astronomy to architecture, provided the material for her analysis of the temple.

She studied the texts with pandits and drew plans based on the descriptions. She perceived that a sacred diagram called Vāstupuruṣamaṇḍala was the essential plan of any temple. From this diagram she saw the fantastic vision of a deflated demon, on whom all the gods take their stand, underlying the whole of existence, which is symbolized by the temple. Her Indian colleagues, including the anthropologist Nirmal Kumar Bose, doubted the validity of her interpretation when she presented it to them in outline. Raymond Burnier, the photographer with whom she had worked on an earlier volume, *Surasundari*, thought that she was writing a few introductory remarks to his photographs and was shocked by the sheer volume of her analysis.

Because of the shortage of paper during the war, the two volumes of *The Hindu Temple* were printed in a small edition. The photographs were laboriously reproduced in three colors (black, russet brown, and blue) on cartridge paper. Stella supervised the printing herself; it was done at night on Boothroyd's press, after his pressmen had finished their regular work.

The preface to *The Hindu Temple* summarizes its author's orientation:

> The attempt has here been made to set up the Hindu temple conceptually, from the foundation to its finial. Its structure is rooted in Vedic tradition, and primeval modes of building have contributed their shapes. The principles are given in the sacred books of India and the structural rules in the treatises on architecture. They are carried out in the shrines which still stand throughout the country and which were built in many varieties and styles over a millennium and a half from the fifth century A.D.
>
> The purpose of the Hindu temple is shown by its form. It is the concrete symbol of Reintegration and coheres with the rhythm of the thought imaged in its carvings and laid out in its proportions. Their perfection is a celebration of all the rites enacted during the building of the temple from the ground to its pinnacle. Nothing that is seen on the temple is left unsaid in the verbal tradition nor is any of the detail arbitrary or superfluous. Each has a definite place and is part of the whole.
>
> The Hindu temple is the sum total of architectural rites performed on the basis of its myth. The myth covers the ground and is the plan on which the structure is raised.

The analysis begins with an explanation of Hindu pilgrimage, the sacred site, and the temple plan. The square is shown to be the original sacred space, drawn in the ritual of building a temple in order to enclose the sacred ground and separate it from the profane world. From the start, she insists that everything she is about to describe is ultimately superfluous to the experience of inner realization:

> The place of pilgrimage is the end of the journey to the Centre; but it is not itself the goal and only the means for crossing over to the Centre. . . . For this very reason too no journey need be undertaken at all.

The Hindu Temple established a radical alternative to the narrowly archaeological view expressed in Percy Brown's *Indian Architecture (Buddhist and Hindu),* which Stella reviewed critically soon after its publication in 1944. Her synthetic view of the temple as a symbolic image of the cosmos stresses the integrity of architectural forms, sculptures, myths, rituals, and metaphysical conceptions, as they are visualized in the eye and mind of the worshiper. Seeing the temple as the body of the god who dwells within the sanctum, she analyzes the way in which its walls are structured by abstract designs and sculptures in human and animal form to visualize the power of the divine presence.

The work was praised by scholars of Indian art throughout the world.[44] Although Coomaraswamy did not review it directly, he responded to it by writing "An Indian Temple: The Kandarya Mahadeo." The title refers to an illustration, but he defines his subject as "*the* Hindu temple . . . this subject is one that is made especially appropriate by the recent (1946) publication of Dr. Stella Kramrisch's magnificent work, *The Hindu Temple.*" The article draws on her conception of the temple as the house and body of god, and relates this to his own earlier studies of the symbolism of the door of heaven.[45]

Despite Stella's reputation among international scholars and Indian leaders like Jawaharlal Nehru, who praised her work on many occasions, her relations with Calcutta University colleagues suffered when her husband decided to serve as an economic adviser to the new government of Pakistan after the partition of the subcontinent at the time of Independence. She had planned to spend her life in India, but it became clear that personal and political events made that unrealistic. Her letters of the period express the bitterness she felt. One, written from Colombo on September 7, 1948, to her friend F. Richter, Secretary of the Royal India Society in London, tells of her plans to leave India, and of the influx of students into her courses once rumors of her imminent departure spread.[46] She moved from her apartment into a house in the country, surrounded by fruit trees and orchids; its owner was a nonagenarian who had traveled around the world collecting orchids. She received few visitors and went out only to do library research and to give her lectures.

Two years after moving to Pakistan, Laszlo Nemenyi was found shot to death in his dinner clothes on the beach of Karachi. Some weeks after his death, on May 31, 1950, Stella wrote from Karachi to Sir Frank Brown, Secretary of the East India Association in London:[47]

> Many thanks for your kind words of sympathy. On receiving the terrible message I flew to Karachi and could still see the body of my husband. When, on my return to Calcutta, I remained without news I decided to return to Karachi. Nothing definite is known as yet about the tragedy. . . . It is difficult for me to find the way back to my work.

Stella decided to leave India for a while to gain some distance from recent events. She made anxious provisions for her cats and wrote to W. Norman Brown to accept his standing invitation to come to the University of Pennsylvania as Visiting Professor of Indian Art.[48] She also wrote to Dorothy Norman, the American writer who had visited her earlier that year in Calcutta at the urging of Nehru and Doña Luisa Coomaraswamy.[49] Dorothy met her at the airport and drove her into the city at dawn. Stella was dazzled by her first view of the New York skyline and the practical beauty of its skyscrapers, whose towering structures, she felt, carried their functional inner space together with the human aspirations of those within into the sky and air. Dorothy remembers her delight in the morning light playing on the glass of the Seagram building on Park Avenue.

Through Dorothy and, subsequently, the Far Eastern art historian Alfred Salmony, who invited her to join the editorial board of *Artibus Asiae*, Stella began to meet people who shared her interests in India, art, religion, and ballet. She developed a significant friendship with Natacha Rambova, who was editing the volumes entitled *Egyptian Religious Texts and Representations.*[50] They were both involved with the symbolism of numbers and religious art. Through Stella, Rambova intensified her interest in collecting Himalayan art and eventually donated the collection to the Philadelphia Museum, where Stella was named curator of Indian Art in 1954.

Her visit to Philadelphia had extended to ten years of teaching at the University of Pennsylvania when Stella purchased an eighteenth-century rural schoolhouse near Chester Springs, Pennsylvania. It was set in woods dominated by tall oak, beech, and tulip trees, evoking for her the Vienna woods of her childhood. Underneath the trees surrounding the house she set large recumbent dark stone figures of the bull Nandī, Śiva's vehicle, the god's quintessential animal form of controlled virility.[51] In Śiva temples such bulls are placed in front of the main shrine. Here they effectively controlled a visitor's entry into the magical space of the house, where Stella's diminutive, graceful figure moved like a meticulously carved dancer. She shared the house with pairs of cats, most recently a favored Abyssinian named Sundara and an elusive black cat named Melchior. Stella's affection for her cats is a part of her strong feeling for animals. In India, this feeling was legendary—the Maharaja of Jhalawar had invited her to his tiger hunts until he became convinced that her compassion for the tigers brought the hunters bad luck.

She filled the house with treasures of her passionate and scholarly collecting: extraordinary Indian and Himalayan sculptures and paintings, cases filled with books, polished fossil ammonites, Persian rugs in subtle geometric patterns, Napoleonic china, English and Indian Sheraton as well as American colonial furniture, and a pair of chairs from Sir Philip Ramsey's residence in Binsar. The house, like her own person, was fundamentally austere, despite its wealth of works of art. Within the interior of high ceilings and white walls, objects stood in their own spaces, mutually intensifying one another, blending into a calm ambience. Sunlight filtered through the trees to create changing environments for the contents of the house.

When, after two attempted burglaries, she left the house to move to the city in the fall of 1979, most of her private collection was sent to the Philadelphia Museum. With characteristic determination, she quickly tuned herself to the rhythms of the city. She learned to watch the city streets settle down to sleep from her high terrace, and to enjoy the light of sunrise and sunset altering the interior space of her apartment.

At the University of Pennsylvania, where she taught from 1950 to 1969, Stella's meticulously ordered, highly interpretive lectures stimulated new interest in Indian religious art.[52] In 1964, while she was still teaching there, she was invited to become Professor of Indian Art at the Institute of Fine Arts in New York, a position she actively held until 1982. Students who have worked with her marvel at the intensity of her involvement with the objects and concepts she is analyzing. While teaching, she often seems to be entranced within the sphere of her own energy.

Her dramatic sense of her subject is expressed in *The Art of India through the Ages,* which was published in 1954, dedicated to the memory of Laszlo Nemenyi.[53] The photographs had been prepared in India; they were taken under her direction by the nephew of the man who owned the orchid garden. She recalls how they would wait for days until the sun was in the correct position for photographing a particular image from a special angle. They represent the great monuments of Indian art, as well as many unusual objects. The text is a dense synthesis of her earlier work, beginning with a parable from the *Viṣṇudharmottara:*

> An ancient Indian treatise says that art conduces to fulfilling the aims of life, whose ultimate aim is Release. The compendium opens with a conversation between a king and a sage. The king desires to learn the whole meaning of art, but is told that he must first know the theory of dancing. To this he agrees because the laws of dancing imply the principles that govern painting. But the sage further insists that the king shall begin by studying music and song, for without a knowledge of all the arts, their effect in space and time cannot fully be understood, nor their purpose be achieved.

In reviewing the book, E. M. Forster wrote, "I owe so much to Dr. Kramrisch that I find it difficult to review her book dispassionately. . . . Dr. Kramrisch is concerned with the inner meaning of Indian objects and their relation to the universe."[54]

From 1952 through mid–1960, the Bollingen Foundation supported Stella's research into the religious symbolism underlying Indian thought.[55] The results of her work were published in a series of articles on Vedic mythology, including studies of the numbers one, two, and three in the *Ṛg Veda,*[56] "The Rig Vedic Myth of the Craftsmen,"[57] and "Pūṣan."[58] Concentrating on concrete literary images drawn primarily from the *Ṛg Veda,* she weaves the complex metaphors that attach to each divinity or concept into a theological vision of its significance. Because of their literary basis, these studies seem more abstract than much of her art historical writing, but the approach is analogous, as she makes clear in her article on Pūṣan, the Vedic Lord of the Way:

> "Alles Vergängliche ist nur ein Gleichnis." Whatever is transitory is but a symbol, be it as firm as this earth and high as is the firmament. The shape of the animal, the body of man in all its parts, and man-made objects, all these are drawn into the picture. There they form part of one composition which paints in detail, in as many configurations as inner vision dictates, the nature and myth of the god. The myths are his actions, their stage is the heart and mind *(manas)* of the singer and he draws its lineaments in the frame and order of the cosmos which he sees and knows, in which he lives and is conscious.

In addition to her teaching and research, she worked at the Philadelphia Museum, becoming curator of Indian Art in 1954 and curator emeritus in 1972. Prior to her involvement with the museum, its only important Indian sculpture was the interior of a sixteenth-century temple hall from Madura in South India.[59] The collection was otherwise sparse and haphazard. Her coming attracted objects from private collections to the museum.[60] The position allowed her to expand curatorial skills that she had developed in India, mainly through her work in the Asutosh Museum.

Her book *Indian Sculpture in the Philadelphia Museum*[61] documented and analyzed the collection as it was by 1960. Stone sculptures from the period of the great Indian medieval temples are dominant. In her introduction to the book, she addresses the problem of viewing isolated objects of religious art in a museum:

> The sculptures in the Museum are detached from their original context. They were each part of a larger monument, a special kind of sanctuary or a temple. These monuments had their definite function and meaning. Within its own integrity, each sculpture was part of their total form. The monument with its sculpture was complete in its concreteness when it was seen and used. It was seen with the eye of knowledge and used with ritual competence.
>
> The single sculpture as a work of art in itself and as part of a larger context is the final stage of the inspiration, method, and skill of the Indian artist. As substantiated inspiration the form of each sculpture confronts the onlooker with the power that went into its making. The form is essentially plastic. Viewing and accounting to himself for the particular plasticity of Indian sculpture, the onlooker by way of re-creation may re-invest the sculptures with the concreteness of their intended effect.

During the past two decades, Stella has conceived and organized a series of exhibitions that reflect the breadth and variety of her interests. Each exhibition formed in her mind as she meditated on certain objects and discovered in them concrete representations of Indian religious concepts that were significant for her. She never began with a thesis and searched for images to illustrate it. Instead, she attempted to structure each exhibition by choosing strong visual images whose individual meanings would be amplified by their relations to one another.

In 1960, she added a gallery of Nepalese and Tibetan art to the permanent collections of the Philadelphia Museum.[62] It was opened by the late King of Nepal, Meḥendra Bir Bikram Shah Deva, and his wife. The positive response to this little-known material encouraged her to undertake a more comprehensive exhibition of Nepalese art. She had long been attracted to the stylistic originality and graceful power of native Nepali forms. In 1964 she helped organize an exhibition of the art of Nepal at the Asia Society.[63] She felt uneasy about it, there being insufficient time for considered study. She proceeded with several months of intensive fieldwork in the Kathmandu Valley. She was received by the King of Nepal to discuss the choice of objects with him, and his appreciation for her work led to the loan of several national treasures. The most impressive was a thirty-six inch high, seated, gilt copper statue of the Bodhisattva Avalokiteśvara from the Golden Monastery in Patan. The monks of the monastery had worshiped it with offerings of vermilion powder and pink bougainvillaea flowers to assure the image's safe passage. It was shown with the powder and dried flowers and was returned to Patan wrapped in yellow silk and rose petals.

Her next project, entitled "Unknown India: Ritual Art in Tribe and Village," was shown at the Philadelphia Museum in 1968. She traveled extensively in India for several years to find and borrow striking examples of tribal and folk art, including paintings, textiles, and sculptures in clay, wood, stone, and metal. The exhibit boldly attempted to coordinate aspects of primitive and archaic ritual art from the third millennium B.C. to the twentieth century and from every region of the subcontinent. The catalogue, drawing on her own earlier studies of Indian terracottas and kanthās, is a pioneering attempt to analyze recurrent images and concepts of rural Indian art.[64]

Her most recent exhibition, "Manifestations of Shiva," explored the nature of this paradoxical god, whose mystery has inspired Hindu ritual art for over two thousand years. It included a large selection of paintings, bronzes, and stone sculptures, many of which are monumental stone carvings never before exhibited outside India. While presenting a rich environment of contrasting forms, Stella attempted to communicate a sense of the sacred through the god whose being reveals itself to man as everything and its opposite. Her visual presentation of his complex aspects and relations was intended to create an essential tension between Śiva's inexhaustable manifestations and his ultimate transcendence of all categories.

The organization of the exhibition involved long negotiations with private collectors, museum directors, and government officials in India, Europe, and the United States. Stella made several trips to India. In the spring of 1979, she traveled to India with Arnold Jolles, then acting director of the Philadelphia Museum. He recalls, "In India she saw with young eyes, almost innocent of her knowledge, picking and choosing by the standard of politics, conservation, opportunity, or beauty, and a sense of importance to her. The choices seemed arbitrary at times, but then the words of a poem are too, until they are placed."[65] An official exchange of masterpieces was arranged whereby the Philadelphia Museum would send an exhibition of twentieth-century painting to the National Gallery of Modern Art in New Delhi in return for the loan of important stone sculptures from various museums in India. Notable among these are two recently discovered sandstone reliefs from Pattadakal dating to the eighth century, one showing Śiva as Destroyer of the Three Cities of the Demons, the other as Vanquisher of Death.[66]

The original essay that Stella began as an introduction to the exhibition grew through the years into her scholarly and deeply personal theological statement, *The Presence of Śiva.* The introduction to the catalogue *Manifestations of Shiva* contains a summary of the book. The entire text of *The Presence of Śiva* is woven from her versions of Śiva's myths, drawn from Vedic and Puranic sources. She begins concretely, with an elaborate retelling of the primordial scene of creation, based on a particular hymn of the *Ṛg Veda* (*RV* 10.61.), which speaks of Śiva as Rudra, the Wild God, the hunter with his arrow. The powerful images that emerge from this account are the substructure on which the book is built, culminating in Śiva's cosmic dance of destruction and creation.

> It is when time is about to begin. In the dawn of the world, when the black cow of cosmic night lies with the ruddy cows of morning (*RV* 10.61.4), two figures appear, the Father and the virgin daughter, his own daughter. They are the two actors in the primordial scene. The Father makes love to the daughter. Suddenly he pulls back, his seed falls down to earth, the place of sacrifice. . . . (*RV* 10.61.5–7)
>
> Creation is an act of violence that infringes upon the Uncreate, the undifferentiated wholeness that is before the beginning of things. And yet another act of violence is hinted at, and this is kept secret in these wild and portentous mantras. He is implied, for it is He who is invoked in this hymn. He, the most powerful, who with the arrow in his hand hit the target. . . . (*RV* 10.61.3)

The mystery of creation in this simultaneity of manifestations begins with a fateful shot, the wound it inflicts on the Father, the loss of his seed, its fall to earth, and the birth of the poem and of mankind to be. In the beginning is the word sung by the gods, the celestial intelligence, compassionate witnesses of primal passion and of the deed of the hunter. . . .

Each paragraph of the book sustains the intensity of this opening, adding to the complicated design of images, myths, and metaphysics. The chapters mark nodal points in her conception of Śiva: for example, "The Primordial Scene," "The Archer," "*Liṅga*," "The Androgyne God," "The Family of Śiva." At the end of the book, the sculptures of Elephanta and Ellora are analyzed and presented in detailed photographs. These epic sculptures visually resolve the "lucid frenzy" of Śiva's drama that her text re-creates.

Despite her philosophical training and interest in aesthetics, Stella has consciously avoided formulating a theory of art. Even as a student, she was critical of Heinrich Wölfflin's *Kunstgeschichtliche Grundbegriffe,* in which he attempted to abstract universal patterns of form from his studies of Renaissance and Baroque painting.[67] She felt such theories to be artificial and reductionist. The romantic mysticism of her childhood predisposed her to a more organic approach that would keep her vision open to the complex symbolism of objects and myths. Her own inclinations were confirmed for her from various quarters, such as twentieth-century expressionist painting, Indian religious literature, and the work of Max Dvořák. Later, the images of Elephanta and the Śaiva initiation she underwent deepened her awareness of the relationship between multiple concrete images and cosmic unity. She saw that no single interpretive system, no matter how powerful, could define that relationship without destroying its dynamism.

It is this impulse that governs the style of *The Presence of Śiva,* as well as the exhibition. By lyrically connecting diverse aspects of a myth, or by exhibiting different themes in variant styles and conceptions, she re-creates the dense symbolic atmosphere of Śiva worship.

Her approach is clearly articulated in the critique of Alain Daniélou's manuscript of *Hindu Polytheism* that she prepared for the Bollingen Foundation in 1958.[68] She criticizes Daniélou for "viewing the whole field of contemporary Hindu Polytheism on the basis of the expositions of his Guru, who was Karapātrī, a contemporary Śaiva thinker:

> D's attempt at systematization does not allow him to listen to myth. . . . Symbols are treated as allegories. They have their definite, set meaning. Following Sāṁkhya doctrine . . . D. writes: "All existence is conditioned by the three fundamental qualities of nature, and the three deities which are their personification" . . . and "All worship is intended to keep man within the bonds of manifestation of which the gods are the basic energies." . . . These statements reduce to nothingness the elaborate superstructure of Hindu religio-philosophical thought and D's own effort of laying out the plan of this stupendous superstructure.

She counters his insistence on the primacy of polytheism by criticizing his translations of Vedic texts, including the epigraph to his work, which is taken from the *Śvetāśvatara Upaniṣad* (4.1). His version reads: "The One without color appears by the manifold application of his power with many colors in his hidden power." She criticizes: "The word for *One* is the numeral one *(eka)* and the pronoun *That* represents the limitless transcendental principle. . . . D's substitution of the indefinite pronoun for the numeral one starts his big enterprise on a false key." She translates the verse: "He who is *one (eka)*, without color, assumes by the manifold application of his power, many colours in his hidden purpose."

Verses from the same passage of this Upaniṣad (4.3–4) are used as the epigraph to the catalogue of "Manifestations of Shiva."

> You are woman. You are man.
> You are the youth and the maiden too.
> You, as an old man,
> falter along with a staff. . . .
> You are the dark-blue bird,
> You are the green (parrot) with red eyes.
> You are (the cloud)
> with the lightning in its womb.
> You are the seasons and the seas.
> Having no beginning you are everywhere.
> (You) from whom all worlds are born.

The nature of Stella's work encourages comparison with that of Coomaraswamy and Zimmer. The synthesis of vast Indian textual and visual detail is evident in the way they all relate art to its literary traditions of myth and philosophy. The concepts formulated in their works have exposed the symbolic forms of Indian culture and created a framework within which fruitful research on the history of art continues.

Stella admired Zimmer's cultivated style and his way of integrating myth and art.[69] In her opinion, he never equalled the "intellectual seriousness" of Coomaraswamy, for whom she reserves her highest regard.[70] In a letter to Doña Luisa Coomaraswamy, dated April 20, 1946, she wrote of *Elements of Buddhist Iconography:* "The more energy one has to put into it, the more one becomes aware of a work which like no other has given to Indian studies the direction of the Indian mind."[71]

Stella shares Coomaraswamy's acute sense for the drama of the spiritual process and his passion for understanding the meaning of forms, but her way is not through abstract metaphysics and "Perennial Philosophy."[72] Her own lyrical mysticism keeps her rooted in concrete images, whether visual or literary. For her, a meaningful art object is not merely a metaphysical symbol; it is also vital in its manifest form.

Among Coomaraswamy's central notions is that of "Tradition," which he developed with his friend, the orientalist René Guénon.[73] For him traditional cultures, of which India was the epitome, were essentially spiritual. Scholarly study of ancient cultures, such as Indian and Greek, was a political act, involving severe criticism of the "impoverished reality" of modern society. Stella uses the word "traditional" in her writings in a way that reflects Coomaraswamy's ideas. In her article "Traditions of the Indian Craftsman," for example, she stresses that the artist or craftsman in India acts as a link between the Divine Principle and the worshiper. She shows a consistent sensitivity to what is spiritual, but this does not, for her, imply a rejection of modern life and modern art.

The style in which Stella presents her ideas communicates her vision of Indian art as much as does the content of her analyses. Her skillful integration of visual, textual, and cultural contexts is enhanced by her choice of superb literary and photographic examples. Although she rejects theorizing about art, she has carefully studied Indian treatises on the theory and practice of architecture, sculpture, and painting. Like her friend Alice Boner,[74] she has used these texts in analyzing the symbolic forms of Indian art. Throughout her work, she stresses the interdependence of techniques and spiritual meanings in a creative process whereby something material is transformed into a sacred object.

The writings that are included here have been selected to illustrate essential aspects of Stella's approach to Indian religious art. They are organized according to themes that she herself outlined almost thirty years ago, in an introduction to her review of Benjamin Rowland's *The Art and Architecture of India:*[75]

The continuity of Indian art was carried by an unbroken series of masters. Where the one left off the next tied the threads in a system of forms, a style where images, meaning and function are interknit. This style has its origin in Revelation and its purpose is Release.

Many of the masters are known by their names. They founded schools, whose works over thousands of years mark the spiritual geography of India with temples, sculptures and paintings. These are described in texts, and rules are laid down clearly and flexibly for the benefit of the craftsmen. None of the monuments are inscribed with any of the names of the masters of whom the texts tell. None of the names incised in stone are known to the texts. This would be paradoxical were it not that all the names are but guarantees of the authenticity of the tradition. In the masters who founded local schools and whose names the texts record, the flames of the *genius loci* leaped into the orbit of the original illumination. Those who inscribed their name in stone signed the paradox of anonymity by their obscure lives, which had gone into the competence of their work.

Art in India, as elsewhere, is the form imposed by the artist on life. In India, more than anywhere, form results from performance. The making of the work of art is a ritual. Its magic is active in the form. By performing the rites of art, the craftsman transforms himself and his substance. Form, performance and transformation are simultaneous, inseparable aspects of Indian art. They inhere in its creation and produce their effect in its concrete shape.

With open eyes, the Indian artist sees the world around him. With eyes closed, he sees the world within him. His vision is direct and twofold. Immediate intuition reveals the image and seeing awareness clothes it with lineaments which have the shape of man and his work and evoke the presence of God. The many gods of India, but for their counterfeits in stone and bronze, and their temples, would have no existence on earth.

God is the name, and the work of art is the body and house in which the Formless, the Beyond-Form, the goal of Release and the source of all form reveals itself. The statues and temples are stations on the Road. They are meant to be seen while moving, from image to image, into the sanctuary, in a straight line of procession from the light of day into deepening superluminous darkness, and they are meant to be seen while moving around them in magic circles of recognition and comprehension.

The rites of approach and circumambulation, performed by movement, fix and define the form. Whether enclosed by movement only, or by a wall, the temple, the main work of Indian architecture, is a monument, a gigantic sculpture set up in space; sculpture proliferates on this architectural trunk. Each figure, charged with the impact of the total monument, rests in the balance of its own rounded limbs.

Architecture is given its maximum effect as monumental sculpture enhanced by carvings and paintings. The painted figures are modeled in color as if embossed from within by their breath, which carries their weightless shapes in interlacing waves through the compositions on the walls. All the arts were known to be interconnected by movement, of which dance is the specific form. The figures of Indian sculpture and painting have the bodies and movement of dancers, for nature in her creative mode is known in Indian philosophy under the image of the dancer.

Visual art in India is movement precipitated into measured lines and volumes. Breath was known to be the principle of all living, moving form. It was the criterion of a good painter that he painted his figures as if breathing. The figures of Indian art are modeled on breath. Breath dilates the chest, and is felt to carry the pulsations of life through the body, their vessel, to fingertips and toes. This inner awareness was given permanent shape in art, for it was tested and practiced daily in the discipline of yoga. By concentrated practice of breathing, an inner lightness and warmth were felt to gather into themselves the heaviness of the carnal body and to dissolve it in the weightless "subtle body" built of movement only and emotion, while it retains the semblance of the body of man, which is the place where it is experienced. The "subtle body" is given concrete shape by art, in planes and lines of balanced tensions and unimpeded flux.

This shape inwardly realized in yoga is made concrete in art. Works of art in India are known as existent *(vastu)* and concrete *(mūrti)*. They are approached, comprehended, seen, and touched.

The rite of touching evokes the presence, at the spot touched, of the principle which informs the shape. This refers to the body of man and to that of the image. In his daily rites the orthodox Hindu touches his body all along from hand to foot, repeatedly and particularly where the heart is and the seat of consciousness, also the palms and the fingers. He evokes and assigns to those points of contact the living presence of God. He transforms the body into a residence of the living spirit and confirms his awareness by touch. This realization is his own. It cannot be communicated except by the artist who makes concrete the transformed body and sets it up outside his living continuity.

NOTES

1. Stella quoted these lines from the *Duino Elegies* in German during a discussion of her approach to Indian art, which took place in her house near Chester Springs on June 11, 1979:

> Wer, wenn ich schreie, hörte mich denn aus der Engel
> Ordnungen? und gesetzt selbst, es nähme
> einer mich plötzlich ans Herz: ich verginge von seinem
> stärkeren Dasein. Denn das Schöne ist nichts
> als des Schrecklichen Anfang, den wir noch grade ertragen,
> und wir bewundern es so, weil es gelassen verschmäht,
> uns zu zerstören. Ein jeder Engel ist schrecklich.

The translation is by T. J. B. Leishman and Stephen Spender (London: Hogarth Press, 1968), p. 250. Relevant here is A. K. Coomaraswamy's use of the word "angel" to translate the Sanskrit word deva; his technical discussion of the "angelic" in Sanskrit aesthetics connects with Stella's conception. See *The Transformation of Nature in Art* (Cambridge: Harvard University Press, 1934), p. 121ff.

2. Sadāśiva is how she identifies the colossal main image of the Elephanta Caves in *The Presence of Śiva* (Princeton: Princeton University Press, 1981), p. 445ff. Cf. her earlier analysis "The Image of Mahādeva in the Cave-Temple on Elephanta Island" (1946), reprinted here. Sadyojāta is the name of the frontal face of the image.

3. Quoted in Dorothy Norman, "Conversation with Stella Kramrisch," *Marg*, 6, no. 4 (Deepavali, 1953), p. 3.

4. *Bhagavad-Gita: des Erhabenen Sang* (Jena: Eugen Diederichs Verlag, 1912).

5. For accounts in English of the culture of Hapsburg Vienna before World War I, see William M. Johnson, *The Austrian Mind* (Berkeley: University of California Press, 1972); Allan Janek and Stephen Toulmin, *Wittgenstein's Vienna* (New York: Simon and Schuster, 1973); Nicolas Powell, *Sacred Spring: The Arts in Vienna, 1898–1918* (Greenwich, Conn.: New York Graphics Society, 1974); Alessandra Comini, *The Fantastic Art of Vienna* (New York: Knopf, 1978); Carl E. Schorske, *Fin-de-Siècle Vienna: Politics and Culture* (New York: Knopf, 1980).

6. Translated as *Concerning the Spiritual in Art* in the series Documents of Modern Art (New York: George Wittenborn, 1947).

7. See Richard Buckle, *Diaghilev* (New York: Atheneum, 1979), p. 215. It was during this same season that Alma Mahler invited the young painter Oskar Kokoschka to share her box at the opera to watch the Diaghilev company, marking the start of their notorious love affair; see *Sacred Spring*, p. 171.

8. See Alfred Karasek-Langer, *Verzeichnis der Schriften von Josef Strzygowski* (Klagenfurt: Kommissionsverlag Artur Kollitsch, 1933). Josef Strzygowski (1862–1941) was noted for his studies of early Christian as well as Oriental art. His *Ursprung der christlichen Kirchenkunst* (Leipzig, 1920), translated as *Origin of Christian Church Art* (Oxford, 1920), was to influence W. B. Yeats in writing the Byzantium poems.

9. See Stella Kramrisch, "Influence of Race on Early Indian Art," *Rūpam*, 18 (April 1924): 73–76. This is based on a lecture Sir John Marshall gave at the Society of Oriental Art in Calcutta.

10. In addition to being a skilled photographer, Goloubew was also an avid collector and student of Indian art. *Ars Asiatica* was published in Brussels and Paris under his direction; see his introduction and photographs of two bronze sculptures of Śiva in the Madras museum, as well as his article "La Descente de la Gangā sur la terre à Mavalipuram," in *Sculptures Śaivites, Ars Asiatica*, 3 (1921). Goloubew's collection of Indian miniature paintings is in the Museum of Fine Arts, Boston.

11. London, 1908. For further discussion of this seminal work, see Roger Lipsey, *Coomaraswamy: His Life and Work* (Princeton: Princeton University Press, 1977), pp. 61–70; also, Mary Lago, ed., *Imperfect Encounter: Letters of William Rothenstein and Rabindranath Tagore, 1911–1941* (Cambridge: Harvard University Press, 1972), pp. 2–8ff.

12. Translated by Rudolf J. Klaviter as *Idealism and Naturalism in Gothic Art, by Max Dvořák* (South Bend, Ind.: Notre Dame University Press, 1967).

13. See Meyer Schapiro, "Style," in *Aesthetics Today*, ed. Morris Philipson and Paul J. Gudel (New York: New American Library, 1980), pp. 137–71; Johnson, *The Austrian Mind*, chap. 9, "The Vienna School of Art History"; Henri Zerner, "Alois Riegl: Art, Value, and Historicism," *Daedalus* 105, no. 1 (Winter 1976): 177–88.

14. "The Natives of Mailu: Preliminary Results of the Robert Mond Research Work in British New Guinea," *Transactions of the Royal Society of South Australia* 39 (1915); cf. *Argonauts of the Western Pacific* (New York: Dutton, 1922).

15. *Imperfect Encounter*, p. 281; cf. p. 352, a letter from Rothenstein to Tagore, dated October 27, 1934: "We had a visit from Stella Kramrisch, whom I was most pleased to see again. To my mind she has the profoundest understanding of Indian plastic art of any one I have met. I admire the whole hearted and selfless manner in which she has devoted herself to the art of India. . . ."; also p. 364, dated August 25, 1937: "We heard much of you and your activities from Stella Kramrisch, that able and scholarly woman. . . ."

16. Theodore Gaster graciously shared his reminiscences of Stella's visits to his father's house; she herself recalled the rest.

17. In July 1974, after an absence of several decades, Stella spent a week in Vienna, staying with American friends, Marge and Tom Dove: She visited favorite objects and places: the ammonite collection in the Natural History Museum, Dürer's portrait of Maximilian and the Breu-

gels in the Art Museum, the works of Gustav Klimt and Egon Schiele in the Austrian Gallery of the Nineteenth and Twentieth Centuries, Demel's confectionery, the small mineral shop near the Augustinerkirche where she had purchased her first ammonite almost seventy years earlier. She enjoyed a production of one of the bitterly sarcastic magical farces of Johannes Nestroy, recalling that she had been forbidden to attend the theater as a girl.

In August 1979, the Austrian Cross of Honor for Science and Art was awarded to her in the Indian Gallery of the Philadelphia Museum. She is one of the few American citizens ever to receive it. She had maintained her Austrian citizenship in India even after she married Laszlo Nemenyi, a Hungarian. Later, she took on British citizenship. She was naturalized as an American citizen in 1955, after five years of residence.

18. *Imperfect Encounter,* p. 290.
19. Stella Kramrisch, personal communication.
20. *Imperfect Encounter,* p. 291.
21. The cosmopolitan atmosphere of Santiniketan was further enriched by the residence of European indologists like Sylvain Lévi and Moritz Winternitz. See Krishna Kripilani, *Tagore: A Biography of Rabindranath Tagore* (New York: Grove Press, 1962); also Jaya Appaswamy, *Abanindranath Tagore and the Art of His Times* (New Delhi: Lalit Kala Akademi, 1968). The Kramrisch bibliography lists her writings on the Tagore family and other artists of the Bengal School: 1921, 1923, 1925, 1941, 1942, 1944, 1947, 1951. In 1974 Stella received an honorary Doctor of Literature degree from Visvabharati University for her contribution to Indian art and Tagore's work.
22. The society was comprised of an exclusive group of connoisseurs and scholars; Stella later became an active member. See discussion and note 35 below for details.
23. Reprinted here with recent photographs; the original article was not illustrated, but referred to plates in Cunningham's publications.
24. See *Asutosh Mookerjee: A Biographical Study,* by N. K. Sinha (Calcutta, 1966).
25. Recounted in an interview entitled "Feast, Famine—A Jewel of a Life," by Maryanne Conheim, *Philadelphia Inquirer,* June 4, 1978. An appreciation for the racial and sexual tensions of the period comes from E. M. Forster's *A Passage to India.*
26. Geoffrey Moorhouse, *Calcutta* (New York: Harcourt, Brace, Jovanovich, 1971).
27. Niharranjan Ray, personal communication. Ray later came to disagree with what he saw as his teacher's overreliance on priestly scholastic texts, in the tradition of scholars like Havell and Coomaraswamy, who, he thought, took an overly metaphysical view of traditional Indian life. His own approach is more socioeconomic and political.
28. *Great Art Centres of Calcutta,* ed. Heinz Molle (South Brunswick: A. S. Barnes, 1973).
29. *Binode Behari Mukherjee* (New Delhi: Lalit Kala Akademi, 1965); *Rabinranath Tagore on Art and Aesthetics* (New Delhi: Orient Longmans, 1961).
30. Reviews are listed in the Kramrisch bibliography, 1924, under *Grundzüge.*
31. I have translated the German back into English; Tagore's version, no. 16 in *One Hundred Poems of Kabir* (London: Macmillan, 1915), is based on Kshitimohan Sen's translation into Bengali of the Hindi original, jānh cet acet khambh dōū . . .
32. (New Delhi: Kanak Publications, 1978), p. ix.
33. *The Collected Works of Ramana Maharshi,* ed. Arthur Osborne (Tiruvannamalai: Sri Ramanasram, 1974), p. 99; see Heinrich Zimmer, *Der Weg zum Selbst: Lehre und Leben des indischen Heiligen Shri Raman Maharshi aus Tiruvannamalai,* ed. C. G. Jung (Zürich, 1944); also Lipsey, *Coomaraswamy: His Life and Work,* pp. 219–20.
34. See W. Crooke, "Aghori," *Encyclopedia of Religion and Ethics,* ed. James Hastings (Edinburgh, 1908), vol. 1, pp. 210–13.
35. See "Indian Society of Oriental Art: Its Early Days," a series of notes by Abanindranath Tagore, O. C. Gangoly, James H. Cousins, and the Marquess of Zetland, *Journal of the Indian Society of Oriental Art,* Golden Jubilee Volume (November 1961):96–105.
36. See Appaswamy, *Abanindranath,* p. 27–37.
37. Reprinted in India (Delhi:Motilal Banarsidass, 1981).
38. See Ernst Cassirer, *Philosophie der symbolischen Formen,* 3 vols. (Berlin: Bruno Cassirer, 1923–31); Erwin Panofsky, *Studies in Iconology* (New York: Oxford University Press, 1939); also Katherine E. Gilbert and Helmut Kuhn, *A History of Aesthetics* (London: Thames and Hudson, 1956), pp. 559–63.
39. See Betty Heimann, *Studien zur Eigenart indischen Denkens* (Tübingen, 1930); *Indian and Western Philosophy: A Study in Contrasts* (London, 1937); *The Significance of Prefixes in Sanskrit Philosophical Terminology,* Royal Asiatic Society Monographs, vol. 25 (1951); *Facets of Indian Thought* (London, 1964).
40. Quoted in an undated article from an Indian newspaper, entitled "Indian Culture in

London," India Office Library, Royal Society for India, Pakistan, and Ceylon Collection, India Society papers, MSS. Eur.F.147/78, item 23; this file contains papers about the proposal for the exhibition.

41. *The Listener* 24, no. 619 (Nov. 21, 1940): 729–30; in the issue of Dec. 5, 1940, pp. 801–2, brief notes on the exhibition by E. M. Forster include his personal response: "I came away feeling not only that Hindu art is a remarkable achievement—that I had always realised—but that it was an achievement that I might interpret in view of my own experience and needs."

42. Barbara Lévi, personal communication, May and June 1980.

43. See Kramrisch bibliography, 1936–46; one of her other major projects was *The Arts and Crafts of Travancore,* which she edited with J. H. Cousins and R. Vasudeva Poduval and in which she wrote the chapters on architecture, sculpture, and painting. These were later separately published under the title *Drāviḍa and Kerala in the Art of Travancore* as *Artibus Asiae* Supplement XI. The book was much delayed due to printing problems and was finally published by the Royal India Society and the government of Travancore in 1948. Correspondence relating to it is in the India Office Library, Royal Society for Indian, Pakistan and Ceylon Collection, India Society papers, MSS. Eur.F.147/70. It has recently been reprinted by *Marg.*

44. Reviews are listed in the Kramrisch bibliography, 1946, under *The Hindu Temple;* recent reviews, occasioned by the reprinting of the volumes (New Delhi: Motilal Banarsidass, 1976), include those by Barbara Stoler Miller, *Parabola* 3, no. 1 (1978): 110–12; and by Michael Meister, *The Art Bulletin* 62, no. 1 (March 1980): 180–82.

45. A. K. Coomaraswamy, "An Indian Temple: The Kandarya Mahadeo," *Selected Papers,* vol. 1, ed. Roger Lipsey (Princeton: Princeton University Press, 1977), pp. 3–12; cf. "The Symbolism of the Dome" and "*Svayamātṛṇṇā:* Janua Coeli," 1, pp. 415–520.

46. India Office Library, MSS. Eur.F.147/70, item 38.

47. Ibid., item 90; item 91 is a letter written on the same day to Richter.

48. W. Norman Brown (1892–1975) was professor of Sanskrit and chairman of the Department of South Asia Regional Studies at the University of Pennsylvania; see *Indological Studies in Honor of W. Norman Brown,* ed. Ernest Bender (New Haven, Conn.: American Oriental Society, 1962), for which Stella wrote "Two: Its Significance in the Ṛgveda"; also *Selected Articles by W. Norman Brown,* ed. Rosanne Rocher (Delhi: Motilal Banarsidass, 1979).

On June 15, 1950, the Bollingen Foundation made a grant to the University of Pennsylvania "to bring Dr. Stella Kramrisch to this country to conduct courses at the university . . ."; minutes of the Finance Committee, Bollingen Foundation, by courtesy of William McGuire of Princeton University Press.

49. See note 3 above.

50. Translated with introductions and commentary by Alexandre Piankoff, vols. 1–3, ed. N. Rambova, Bollingen Series, no. 40 (New York: Pantheon Books, 1954–57).

51. When, in 1968, Stella negotiated permissions for the purchase by the Park Commission of Philadelphia of a Nandī sculpture from India for an outdoor sculpture garden at Penn's Landing as part of a bicentennial celebration, she identified Nandī as a symbol of happiness, citing the "pursuit of happiness" in the Declaration of Independence.

52. In May 1981, Stella was awarded an honorary Doctor of Philosophy degree by the University of Pennsylvania in recognition of her contributions as a scholar and teacher.

53. Published in London by Phaidon; subsequently in French, German, and Italian editions (1955, 1957).

54. *The Listener* 52, no. 1344 (December 1954): 977–78.

55. A grant, awarded in March 1952, was for travel to India, photography, and other expenses. In July 1953, she was awarded a fellowship for five years, plus the allocation of part of the budget of the Egyptian Project, "as her work is related to and will be of value to that"; notes of the Finance Committee, Bollingen Foundation, by courtesy of William McGuire. See Library of Congress, Manuscript Division, Bollingen Foundation Records, container 16, file 770.006, entitled "Indian Symbolism"; also *Bollingen Foundation Report: 1945–1965* (New York: Bollingen Foundation, 1967), pp. 83, 107–8. According to Stella, the Bollingen grant was paid to her through the University of Pennsylvania in the form of salary for teaching in the South Asia Regional Studies department.

56. " 'The One' in the Ṛg Veda" (1961); "Two: Its Significance in the Rgveda" (1962); "Triple Structure of Creation in the Ṛg Veda" (1962).

57. Published in 1959, the same year that she published "Natural Science and Technology in Relation to Cultural Institutions and Social Practice in India."

58. Published in 1961, reprinted here; two later articles related in style and use of literary imagery from the *Ṛgveda* and later texts are: "The Indian Great Goddess" (1975) and "The Mahāvīra Vessel and the Plant Pūtika" (1975). The latter relates to R. Gordon Wasson's book,

Soma: Divine Mushroom of Immortality (The Hague: Mouton/New York: Harcourt, Brace and World, 1968). Stella was convinced by the evidence offered in favor of Soma's identification as *Amanita muscaria.* In her article she presents philological and ethnographic material that links the plant Pūtika, a designated surrogate for Soma in Vedic sacrifice, with a mushroom sacred to the Santal tribe of eastern India. This answered one of the main objections against Wasson's mushroom theory: the puzzling absence of other mushrooms in Vedic ritual after Soma was no longer available. See Wasson, "Soma Brought Up-to-Date," *Journal of the American Oriental Society* 99, no. 1: 100–105.

59. W. Norman Brown, *A Pillared Hall from a Temple at Madura* (Philadelphia: University of Pennsylvania Press, 1940).

60. Before 1952 the museum had about seventy small Indian stone pieces, as well as the Madura Mandapa; in 1952 this was supplemented by the acquisition of a private collection of about fifty significant sculptures. After 1954 the Indian Art Department acquired 272 additional objects. The collection was expanded through private donations and two official exchanges with the National Museum in New Delhi. In 1968 two Gothic carvings were exchanged for two eleventh-century Chola granite images, one of Mahāvīra. In 1972 a Flemish Baroque tapestry was exchanged for an eighth-century Pandyan gneiss figure of Aiyanar and a seventh-century Pallava granite figure of a squatting lion, once part of a rock-cut pillar from Mamallapuram. These facts have been supplied by the registrar of the Philadelphia Museum of Art, by permission of the director.

61. University of Pennsylvania Press and Oxford University Press, 1960.

62. "The Art of Nepal and Tibet" (1960).

63. *The Art of Nepal* (1964).

64. *Unknown India* (1968); the introductory essay is reprinted here.

65. Arnold Jolles, personal communication, Nov. 3, 1979.

66. "Manifestations of Shiva" catalogue, pp. 46–49.

67. Published in 1915; 1932 English translation by M. D. Hottinger, *Principles of Art History* (New York: Dover reprint, 1950).

68. Library of Congress, Manuscript Division, Bollingen Foundation Records, container 146, file 670.073, entitled "Hindu Polytheism"; cf. review in the *Journal of the American Oriental Society* 87, no. 3 (1968): 553–60.

69. See her review of Zimmer's *The Art of Indian Asia, Artibus Asiae* 18, no. 3/4 (1955): 328–35.

70. The phrase "intellectual seriousness" is also used of Coomaraswamy by Meyer Schapiro; see Lipsey, *Coomaraswamy,* p. 246. Schapiro has expressed high regard for Stella's work, advising students of medieval art to read *The Hindu Temple.* Stella, in turn, values Schapiro's intellectual "finesse."

71. See Lipsey, *Coomaraswamy,* pp. 216, 220.

72. "Perennial Philosophy," or philosophia perennis, is the term often used by Coomaraswamy to refer to a line of thought passing through the great traditional civilizations; Lipsey, *Coomaraswamy,* p. 274ff.

73. Lipsey, *Coomaraswamy,* p. 265ff. Stella translated two of Guénon's articles for the *Journal of the Indian Society of Oriental Art;* see Kramrisch bibliography, 1937, 1938.

74. See Alice Boner, *Principles of Composition in Hindu Temple Sculpture* (Leiden: Brill, 1962); Ramacandra Kaulacara, *Silpa Prakāśa: Medieval Orissan Sanskrit Text on Temple Architecture,* trans. and annotated A. Boner and S. R. Sarma (Leiden: Brill, 1966), reviewed by Stella in 1968; *New Light on the Sun Temple of Konarak,* trans. and annotated A. Boner and S. R. Sarma with R. P. Das (Benares: Chowkhamba, 1972), reviewed by Stella in 1975.

75. "The Subtle Body of India," *Art News* 52, no. 5 (September 1953):19–20, 60; cf. review of 1955 in the *Journal of the American Oriental Society.*

A Bibliography of the Writings of Stella Kramrisch

COMPILED BY JOSEPH M. DYE III

This bibliography includes Dr. Kramrisch's major published writings, as well as significant reviews of her work. Interviews with Dr. Kramrisch published in periodicals have been listed, while newspaper articles and reviews have not been included.

The bibliographical entries are arranged according to year of publication. Within each year, books are listed first, followed by articles in books, articles in periodicals, notes, book reviews, translations (with one exception), condensations, and interviews. In cases where several books appear within one year, the entries are listed alphabetically by title. In instances where several articles, notes, book reviews, translations, condensations, or interviews appear in one year, the entries are listed within each category alphabetically, by the name of publication; and, in the case of multiple entries within a category (such as several book reviews) published in the same periodical, by series, volume, number, and page number. Reviews of Dr. Kramrisch's works follow the entry to which they apply and are listed alphabetically by the reviewer's last name (when known).

I should like to thank the staff of the Oriental Division of the New York Public Library, and, in particular, Mr. Paar, for most generous assistance. I am also grateful to Mr. Stephen Bendos, Miss Eleanor Pearson, and Mr. L. Qualls for their help.

1919

"Untersuchungen zum Wesen der frühbuddhistischen Bildnerei Indiens." Ph.D. dissertation, University of Vienna, 1919.

1921

"The Representation of Nature in Early Buddhist Sculpture (Bharhut-Sanchi)." *Rūpam,* no. 8 (October 1921), pp. 7–10.

1922

"The Expressiveness of Indian Art." *The Calcutta Review,* 3d ser. 5, nos. 1–2 (October 1922): 1–46; continued and concluded under the same title in *The Calcutta Review,* 3d ser. 5, no. 3 (December 1922):299–342. (Lectures delivered at the Calcutta University on July 27, 1922; July 31, 1922; August 2, 1922; August 5, 1922; August 7, 1922; August 9, 1922.) Reprint. *Journal of the Department of Letters, University of Calcutta* 9 (1923): 55–144.

"The Aesthetics of Young India: A Rejoinder." *Rūpam,* no. 10 (April 1922), pp. 66–67.

"Indian Art and Europe." *Rūpam,* no. 11 (July 1922), pp. 81–86.

"An Indian Cubist." *Rūpam,* no. 11 (July 1922), pp. 107–9.

Review of E. B. Havell, *A Handbook of Indian Art. Journal of the Royal Asiatic Society,* pt. 3 (July 1922), pp. 454–57.

Review of William Cohn, *Alt "budhistische Malerei Japans." Rūpam,* no. 11 (July 1922), p. 103.

Review of Karl With, *Java (Brahmanic, Buddhistic and Indigenous Architecture and Sculpture in Java). Rūpam,* no. 12 (October 1922), pp. 138–42.

1923

Indian Art and Art-Crafts. With R. Srinivasan, T. G. Krishnaswami Pillai, and W. D. S. Brown, foreword by Annie Besant (Adyar Madras: Theosophical Publishing House, 1923). (Lectures delivered in connection with the Arts and Art-Crafts Exhibition held during the Theosophical Society's Annual Convention, December 1922, at Adyar, Madras.) *Review:* N. C. Mehta, *Rūpam,* no. 17 (January 1924), pp. 51–52.

"The Contact of Indian Art with the Art of Other Civilizations." *The Calcutta Review,* 3d ser. 6, no. 3 (March 1923): 514–49. (The Adharchandra Mookerjee Lecture for 1922 delivered on December 16 and 17, 1922.) Reprint. *Journal of the Department of Letters, University of Calcutta,* 10 (1923):76a–110.

"Colossal Copper Statue of Buddha." *The Calcutta Review,* 3d ser. 9, no. 1 (October 1923): 88. (Signed St. K.)

"Some Views from Nasik." *The Calcutta Review,* 3d ser. 9, no. 3 (December 1923): 497–500. (Signed S. K.)

"Notes on Bengal Sculpture." *The Modern Review* 33, no. 1 (January 1923): 57–62.

"The Visarjan Performance of the Visvabharati." *The Modern Review* 34, no. 4 (October 1923): 501–2. (Signed St. K.)

"The Religious and the Grotesque in Indian Art." *The Modern Review* 34, no. 5 (November 1923): 569–79.

"The Present Moment of Art, East and West." *The Visva-Bharati Quarterly* 1, no. 3 (October 1923): 221–25.

"The New Art in Europe." *The Visva-Bharati Quarterly* 1, no. 1 (April 1923): 69–75; wrongly attributed to Stella Kramrisch; corrected and attributed to O. C. Ganguly in *The Visva-Bharati Quarterly* 1, no. 2 (July 1923): inside front cover.

1924

Grundzüge der indischen Kunst (Hellerau bei Dresden: Avalun-Verlag, 1924). *Reviews:* E. B. Havell, *Rūpam,* nos. 27–28 (July–October 1926), pp. 74–77. Serge Oldenburg, *Zapiski Kollegii Vostokovedov pri Azyatskom Musee Akademii Nauk SSR* 2, no. 2 (1927): 390. E. A. Voretzsch, *Asia Major* 3, no. 1 (1926): 140–42. Karl With, *Artibus Asiae* 1, no. 2 (1925): 157–58. H. Zimmer, *Orientalistische Literaturzeitung* 30, no. 3 (March 1927): cols. 191–94.

"The Vishṇudharmottaram: A Treatise on Indian Painting." *The Calcutta Review,* 3d ser. 10, no. 2 (February 1924): 331–86. Reprint. *Journal of the Department of Letters, University of Calcutta* 11 (1924): 1–56. *Review:* H. Zimmer. *Artibus Asiae* 3 (1926): 236–37.

"Windows." *The Calcutta Review,* 3d ser. 10, no. 2 (February 1924): 431–32. (Signed St. K.)

"Indische Malerei der Gegenwart, zur XV. Jahresausstellung der 'India Society of Oriental Art', Calcutta 1924." *Der Cicerone* 16 (1924): 954–62. Reprint. *Jahrbuch der jungen Kunst,* 1924, pp. 234–42.

"Vom Religiösen und Grotesken in der indischen Kunst." *Jahrbuch der asiatischen Kunst* 1 (1924), pp. 102–8.

"Die Wandmalereien zu Kelaṇiya." *Jahrbuch der asiatischen Kunst* 1 (1924): 137–39.

"Influence of Race on Early Indian Art." *Rūpam,* no. 18 (April 1924), pp. 73–76. (Notes on a lecture by Sir John Marshall.)

Review of Ernst Diez, *Einführung in die Kunst des Ostens. Rūpam,* no. 18 (April 1924). p. 91. (Signed S. K.)

1925

"Sunayani Devi." *Der Cicerone* 17 (1925): 87–93.

"Some Wall-Paintings from Kelaṇiya." *The Indian Historical Quarterly* 1, no. 1 (March 1925): 111–16.

1926

Review of H. V. Glasenapp, *Der Jainaismus. The Calcutta Review,* 3d ser. 19, nos. 2–3 (May–June 1926): 388–89.

1927

"Early Indian Sculpture as Found at Barhut; Symbol and Presentation." *Buddhist India, An Illustrated Buddhist Quarterly and Buddhist Gazette* 1, no. 2 (April 1927): 129–35; continued and concluded under the title "Elements of Visualisation in Buddhist Art, as at Barhut . . . continued," in *Buddhist India, An Illustrated Buddhist Quarterly and Buddhist Gazette* 1, no. 3 (July 1927): 201–8 and in 1, no. 4 (October 1927): 285–91.

"Mittelalterliche indische Plastik." *Mitteilungen der Gesellschaft für ostasiatische Kunst* 2, no. 6 (1927): 1–6. (Abstract of a lecture given to the Gesellschaft für ostasiatische Kunst.)

1928

The Vishṇudharmottaram (Pt. III): A Treatise on Indian Painting and Image-Making. Calcutta: University of Calcutta, 1928 (revised and enlarged edition of *The Vishṇudharmottara,* 1924). *Reviews:* Ananda K. Coomaraswamy, *Journal of the American Oriental Society* 52, no. 1 (March 1932): 13–21. A. K. Maitra, *The Calcutta Review,* 3d ser. 28, no. 3 (September 1928): 433–42.

"Buddhist Art in India: Its Development and Extension." *Buddhist India, An Illustrated Buddhist Quarterly and Buddhist Gazette* 2, no. 1 (March 1928): 26–33.

"Three Miniature Metal Images from Comilla." *Rūpam,* nos. 33–34 (January–April 1928), pp. 26–27.

Review of Ramaprasad Chanda, *The Beginnings of Art in Eastern India with Special Reference to Sculptures in the Indian Museum. Ostasiatische Zeitschrift,* n.f. 4 (1927/28): 158–59.

Translation of A. K. Maitra, "Ikonographie der Śiva-Darstellung." *Ostasiatische Zeitschrift,* n.f. 4 (1927/28): 108–19.

"Zur Geschichte indischer Götterbilder mit besonderem Hinweis auf einige neuentdeckte Statuen in Mayurbhañja," by R. Chanda; condensed by Stella Kramrisch from the treatise *Murti ar Mandir. Ostasiatische Zeitschrift,* n. f. 4 (1927/28): 44–47.

1929

Pāla and Sena Sculpture. (?), 1929 (reprinted from *Rūpam,* no. 40). *Reviews:* William Cohn, *Ostasiatische Zeitschrift,* n.f. 8 (1932): 223. R. Heine-Geldern, *Wiener Beiträge zur Kunst- und Kulturgeschichte Asiens* 5 (1931): 77.

"Die indische Kunst." In *Die aussereuropäische Kunst,* edited by Anton Springer. Leipzig: Alfred Kröner Verlag, 1929. *Handbuch der Kunstgeschichte* 6: 231–368.

"Pāla and Sena Sculpture." *Rūpam,* no. 40 (October 1929), pp. 107–26.

Review of P. A. J. Moojen, *Kunst op Bali; inleidende studie tot de bouwkunst. Rūpam,* nos. 38–39 (April–July 1929), pp. 95–97. (Signed S. K.)

Review of N. J. Krom, *Barabudur, Archaeological Description* 2, chap. 11. *Rūpam,* nos. 38–39 (April–July 1929), pp. 97–98. (Signed S. K.)

Translation of Ajit Ghose, "Bemalte Buchdeckel aus alt-Bengalen." *Ostasiatische Zeitschrift,* n.f. 5 (1929): 119–21.

1930

"An Early South Indian 'Bronze'." *Rūpam,* nos. 42–44 (April–October 1930), pp. 16–18.

Review of Jörg Trübner, *Yu und Kuang, zur Typologie der chinesischen Bronzen. Rūpam,* nos. 42–44 (April–October 1930), p. 33. (Signed St. K.)

Review of Gustav Mensching, *Buddhistische Symbolik. Rūpam,* nos. 42–44 (April–October 1930), pp. 33–34. (Signed St. K.)

1931

"Marks of the Great Being: Mahāpuruṣa-lakṣaṇa." In *The Golden Book of Tagore,* edited by Ramananda Chatterjee. Calcutta: The Golden Book Committee, 1931, pp. 286–89.

"A Stone Relief from a Kaliṅga Railing." *The Indian Antiquary* 60, pt. 752 (May 1931): 89–90.

"Die figurale Plastik der Guptazeit." *Wiener Beiträge zur Kunst- und Kulturgeschichte Asiens* 5 (1931): 15–39.

1932

"Landschaft, Tier, und geometrisches Muster in der indischen Kunst." In *Josef Strzygowski-Festschrift.* Klagenfurt: Artur Kollitsch Verlag, 1932, pp. 95–98. (Title printed at the head of the article reads "Tier, Landschaft und Muster in der indischen Kunst.")

1933

Indian Sculpture. The Heritage of India Series. Calcutta: YMCA Publishing House; London, New York: Oxford University Press, 1933. *Reviews:* S. K. Aiyangar, *Journal of Indian History* 12, pt. 3 (December 1933): 445–47. A. C. Banerji, *The Modern Review* 57, no. 1 (January 1935): 74. A. J. Bernet Kempers, *Journal of the Royal Asiatic Society,* pt. 2 (April 1935), p. 399. K. De B. Codrington, *The Burlington Magazine* 64, no. 375 (June 1934): 291–92. G. Coedès, *Bulletin de l'école française d'Extrême-Orient* 33 (1933): 1009–10. Ananda K. Coomaraswamy, *Journal of the American Oriental Society* 54, no. 2 (June 1934): 219–21. Otto Fischer, *Artibus Asiae* 5, nos. 2, 3, 4 (1935): 336–38. W. L. H., *Apollo* 19, no. 109 (January 1934): 45. R. Heine-Geldern, *Wiener Beiträge zur Kunst- und Kulturgeschichte Asiens* 8 (1934): 70. Philip McMahon, *Parnassus* 8, no. 2 (February 1936): 36. O. Strauss, *Orientalistische Literaturzeitung* 38, no. 3 (March 1935): cols. 183–86. K. Takarabe, *Shūkyō Kenkyū,* n.s. 12, no. 1 (1935): 175.

"Indische Malerei und Mogulminiatur." In *Asiatische Miniaturenmalerei, im Anschluss* an *Wesen und Werden der Mogulmalerei,* edited by Josef Strzygowski. Klagenfurt: Verlag Kollitsch, 1933. Arbeiten des I. Kunsthistorischen Instituts der Universität Wien, 50: pp. 112–27. *Reviews:* Laurence Binyon, *The Burlington Magazine* 63, no. 367 (October 1933): 186. Ananda K. Coomaraswamy, *Pantheon* 13, no. 1 (January 1934): viii. G. v. Selle, *Orientalistische Literaturzeitung* 37, no. 6 (June 1934): cols. 379–83. I. Stchoukine, *Gazette des beaux-arts,* 6th ser. 9, no. 842 (March 1933): 188. Melanie Stiassny, *Wiener Beiträge zur Kunst- und Kulturgeschichte Asiens* 7 (1933): 91–92. Shahid Suhrawardy, *Journal of the Indian Society of Oriental Art* 1, no. 2 (December 1933): 149–50.

"The Study of Indian Art." *The Calcutta Review,* 3d ser. 49, no. 1 (October 1933): 60–65.

"Candella Sculpture: Khajuraho." *Journal of the Indian Society of Oriental Art* 1, no. 2 (December 1933): 97–104.

"Nepālese Paintings." *Journal of the Indian Society of Oriental Art* 1, no. 2 (December 1933): 129–47.

Review of G. Yazdani, *Ajanta: The Colour and Monochrome Reproductions of the Ajanta Frescoes Based on Photography,* Part II. *Journal of the Indian Society of Oriental Art* 1, no. 2 (December 1933): 150–51.

Translation of Josef Strzygowski, "India's Position in the Art of Asia." *Journal of the Indian Society of Oriental Art* 1, no. 1 (June 1933): 7–17. (Signed St. K.)

Translation of H. Zimmer, "Some Aspects of Time in Indian Art." *Journal of the Indian Society of Oriental Art* 1, no. 1 (June 1933): 30–51. (Signed St. K.)

1934

"Kaliṅga Temples." *Journal of the Indian Society of Oriental Art* 2, no. 1 (June 1934): 43–60.

"An Illustrated Gīta Govinda Ms." *Journal of the Indian Society of Oriental Art* 2, no. 2 (December 1934): 115–26.

Note appended to K. P. Jayaswal, "Metal Images of Kurkihar Monastery." *Journal of the Indian Society of Oriental Art* 2, no. 2 (December 1934): 77–82.

1935

"A Cedī Head." *Journal of the Indian Society of Oriental Art* 3, no. 1 (June 1935): 79–81.

"Emblems of the Universal Being." *Journal of the Indian Society of Oriental Art* 3, no. 2 (December 1935): 148–65.

Review of R. Heine-Geldern, *The Archaeology and Art of Sumatra. Journal of the Indian Society of Oriental Art* 3, no. 1 (June 1935): 82–83.

1936

Kurkihar, Gaya, and Bodh-Gaya. With S. K. Sarasvati and K. C. Sarkar. Rajshahi: (?), 1936.

"A Celestial Betrothal—In a Sixth Century Indian Wall Painting." *The Illustrated London News* 189, no. 5077 (August 8, 1936): 249.

"Paintings at Bādāmī." *Journal of the Indian Society of Oriental Art* 4, no. 1 (June 1936): 57–61.

"Note on Uṣṇīṣa." *Journal of the Indian Society of Oriental Art* 4, no. 1 (June 1936): 79–83.

Review of F. H. Gravely, *An Outline of Indian Temple Architecture. Journal of the Indian Society of Oriental Art* 4, no. 2 (December 1936): 145–46.

Review of J. M. Somasundaram, *The Great Temple at Tanjore. Journal of the Indian Society of Oriental Art* 4, no. 2 (December 1936): 146.

Review of Hirananda Sastri, *Indian Pictorial Art as Developed in Book-Illustrations. Journal of the Indian Society of Oriental Art* 4, no. 2 (December 1936): 146–47.

1937

A Survey of Painting in the Deccan. London: The India Society in co-operation with the Department of Archaeology, Hyderabad, 1937. *Reviews:* Ludwig Bachhofer, *The Art Bulletin* 21, no. 1 (March 1939): 93–94. Ernst Diez, *Artibus Asiae* 8, no. 1 (1940): 77–79.

"Dakṣiṇa-Citra." *Journal of the Indian Society of Oriental Art* 5 (1937): 218–37.

Translation of René Guénon, "Some Remarks on the Doctrine of Cosmic Cycles." *Journal of the Indian Society of Oriental Art* 5 (1937): 21–28. (Signed St. K.)

Translation of G. Coedès, "Note on the Pillar at Sārnāth." *Journal of the Indian Society of Oriental Art* 5 (1937): 40–41. (Unsigned)

Translation of Josef Strzygowski, "Three Northern Currents in the Art of the Chinese People." *Journal of the Indian Society of Oriental Art* 5 (1937): 42–59. (Unsigned)

Translation of Paul Mus, "Has Brahma Four Faces?" *Journal of the Indian Society of Oriental Art* 5 (1937): 60–73. (Unsigned)

Translation of H. Zimmer, "Tree, Huts, and Temples." *Journal of the Indian Society of Oriental Art* 5 (1937): 111–21. (Unsigned)

1938

"Notes ('Madhupāna' Scenes from Mathurā, etc.; A Śiva Head from Mathurā; Paintings at Bādāmī)." *Journal of the Indian Society of Oriental Art* 6 (1938): 197–203.

Translation of René Guénon, "Initiation and the Crafts." *Journal of the Indian Society of Oriental Art* 6 (1938): 163–68. (Unsigned)

1939

"Indian Terra-cottas." *Journal of the Indian Society of Oriental Art* 7 (1939): 89–110.

"Kanthā." *Journal of the Indian Society of Oriental Art* 7 (1939): 141–67.

"A Painted Ceiling." *Journal of the Indian Society of Oriental Art* 7 (1939): 175–82.

"Medieval Indian Sculpture." *Journal of the Royal Society of Arts* 87, no. 4535 (October 20, 1939): 1180–94.

Translation of René Guénon, "The Arts and Their Traditional Conception." *Journal of the Indian Society of Oriental Art* 7 (1939): 8–12. (Unsigned)

1940

"A Theory of Indian Art." In *Proceedings and Transactions of the Ninth All-India Oriental Conference, Trivandram,* December, 1937. Trivandrum: The Government Press, 1940, pp. 1029–40.

"Einige Typen indischer Deckenmalerei." *Artibus Asiae* 8, no. 1 (1940): 5–15.

"The Hundred Verses of Amaru Illustrated." *Journal of the Indian Society of Oriental Art* 8 (1940): 225–40.

Comments in a discussion of "Arts of Primitive Peoples," by Leonard Adam. *Journal of the Royal Society of Arts* 88, no. 4564 (June 28, 1940): 721.

1941

"Īśānaśivagurudevapaddhati, Kriyāpāda, chaps. 26–27." *Journal of the Indian Society of Oriental Art* 9 (1941): 151–93.

"The Drawings of Rabindranath Tagore." *The Visva-Bharati Quarterly,* n. s. 7, pts. 1 and 2 (May–October 1941): 117–19. Reprint. *Exhibition of Paintings and Drawings by Rabindranath Tagore,* edited by Kamal Mazumdar. Calcutta: Rabindra Parishad, University of Calcutta, 1947. *The Visva-Bharati Quarterly,* n.s. 26, nos. 3 and 4 (1961): 143–46.

1942

"Temple, Door, Throne, Etc." *Journal of the Indian Society of Oriental Art* 10 (1942): 210–52.

"The Genius of Abanindranath Tagore." *The Visva-Bharati Quarterly,* n. s. 8, pts. 1 and 2 (May–October 1942): 65–73. Reprint. *The Visva-Bharati Quarterly,* n.s. 25, nos. 3 and 4 (1960): 123–29; n. s. 37, nos. 3–4 (November 1971–April 1972): 329–38.

1943

"The Orientation of Indian Temples." *Journal of the Indian Society of Oriental Art* 11 (1943): 208–11.

Review of H. G. Quaritch Wales, *Archaeological Researches on Ancient Indian Colonization in Malaya. The Asiatic Review,* n.s. 39, no. 139 (July 1943): 331–32.

1944

Surasundari. Photographs by Raymond Burnier. Calcutta: Indian Society of Oriental Art, 1944. (Signed St. K.)

Foreword to *Jamini Roy,* by Bishnu Dey and John Irwin. Calcutta: Indian Society of Oriental Art, 1944, two unnumbered pages.

"The Superstructure of the Hindu Temple." *Journal of the Indian Society of Oriental Art* 12 (1944): 175–207.

Review of Percy Brown, *Indian Architecture (Buddhist and Hindu). Journal of the Indian Society of Oriental Art* 12 (1944): 211–12.

1945

"Plaster." In *B.C. Law Volume,* Part 1, edited by Dr. D. R. Bhandarkar, Prof. K. A. Nilakanta Sastri, Dr. B. M. Barua, Dr. B. K. Ghosh, Prof. P. K. Gode. Calcutta: Indian Research Institute, 1945, pp. 611–16.

"A Deed of Adoption and Its Reliefs." *Journal of the Indian Society of Oriental Art* 13 (1945): 199–210.

1946

The Hindu Temple. 2 vols. Calcutta: University of Calcutta, 1946. *Reviews:* W. G. Archer, *Man in India* 28, no. 3 (1948): 191–92. Jeannine Auboyer, *La revue de geographie humaine et d'ethnologie* 1, no. 3 (July–September 1948): 125–26. Jeannine Auboyer, *Revue archéologique,* 6th ser. 33 (April–June 1949): 249–50. Hon. Mrs. Betjeman, *Art and Letters,* n.s. 22, no. 2 (1948): 68–70. Nirmal Kumar Bose, *The Modern Review* 82, no. 1 (July 1947): 69. D. Delannoy, *Journal asiatique* 239, no. 2 (1951): 259–60. H. Goetz, *Mārg* 1, no. 4 (1947/48): 61–66. Jean Herbert, *France-Asie* 5, no. 48 (March 1950): 901–5. H. Marchal, *Bulletin de l'école francaise d'Extrême-Orient* 43 (1943–46): 162–66. Haridas Mitra, *The Visva-Bharati Quarterly,* n.s. 15, no. 1 (May 1949–July 1949): 21–29. Alfred Salmony, *Artibus Asiae* 10, no. 3 (1947): 246–48.

"The Image of Mahādeva in the Cave-Temple on Elephanta Island." *Ancient India,* no. 2 (July 1946), pp. 4–8.

1947

"The Banner of Indra." In *Art and Thought,* edited by K. Bharatha Iyer. London: Luzac and Co., 1947, pp. 197–201.

"The Walls of Orissan Temples." *Journal of the Indian Society of Oriental Art* 15 (1947): 178–96.

"Art and the Schools." *The Visva-Bharati Quarterly,* n.s. 13, pts. 1 and 2 (May–October 1947): 169–73.

1948

The Arts and Crafts of Travancore. With J. H. Cousins and R. Vasudeva Poduval. London: The Royal India Society and the Government of Travancore, 1948. Imprint covered by label: Printed 1948 for The Royal India, Pakistan, and Ceylon Society, London and the Government of Travancore. Published 1952 by Bruno Cassirer (Publishers) Ltd., 31 Portland Road, Oxford. *Review:* Odette Viennot, *Arts Asiatiques* 1, fasc. 3 (1954): 235–38.

"Four Images (at the Indian Art Exhibition, Govt. House, New Delhi)." *Roopa-Lekha* 20, no. 2 (1948–49).

1949

"Indian Sculpture." *Introducing India* 2 (1949): 66–82.

Review of W. G. Archer, *The Vertical Man: A Study in Primitive Indian Sculpture. The Visva-Bharati Quarterly* 14, pt. 1 (May–July 1948): 65–66.

Review of Ananda Coomaraswamy, *The Dance of Siva. The Visva-Bharati Quarterly,* n.s. 14, pt. 3 (November 1948–January 1949): 225–26; wrongly attributed to Stella Kramrisch in Index to *The Visva-Bharati Quarterly,* n.s. 14 (1948–49). Review is signed in text by Alain Daniélou.

1950

"Kanthas of Bengal." *Mārg* 3, no. 2 (1949/50): 18–29; continued and concluded: 37.

1951

Introduction to *Abanindranath Tagore: His Early Work,* edited by Ramendranath Chakravarty. Calcutta: Art Section, Indian Museum, 1951, pp. 15–16.

Review of *The Art of India and Pakistan. A Commemorative Catalogue of the Exhibition Held at the Royal Academy of Arts, London* 1947–48, edited by Sir Leigh Ashton. *Artibus Asiae* 14, no. 3 (1951): 256–60.

Review of Chintamoni Kar, *Classical Indian Sculpture (500 B.C. to 500 A.D.). Artibus Asiae* 14, no. 3 (1951): 260.

1952

Review of Jeannine Auboyer, *Arts et styles de l'Inde. Artibus Asiae* 15, no. 3 (1952): 293.

1953

Drāviḍa and Kerala in the Art of Travancore. Ascona: Artibus Asiae, 1953. *Reviews:* Mario Bussagli, *East and West* 5, no. 1 (1954): 46. Charles L. Fabri, *Artibus Asiae* 17, no. 3/4 (1954): 328–30.

"Subtle Body of India." *Art News* 52, no. 5 (September 1953): 19–20; continued and concluded: 60. (Review of *The Art and Architecture of India,* by Benjamin Rowland, Jr.)

Review of *G*[anesh] *D*[atta] *College Bulletin Series,* nos. 2 and 3. *Artibus Asiae* 16, no. 4 (1953): 329.

"Conversation with Stella Kramrisch." *Mārg* 6, no. 4 (Deepavali, 1953): 2–7. (Interview of Stella Kramrisch by Dorothy Norman.)

1954

The Art of India: Traditions of Indian Sculpture, Painting, and Architecture. London: Phaidon, 1954. *Reviews:* W. G. Archer, *The Burlington Magazine* 97, no. 632 (November 1955): 356. Douglas Barrett, *Oriental Art,* n.s. 1, no. 1 (Spring 1955): 34–35. J. LeRoy Davidson, *Art News* 53, no. 9 (January 1955): 32; continued: 60–61. Walter A. Fairservis, Jr., *Archaeology* 20, no. 2 (April 1967): 140–41. E. M. Forster, *The Listener* 52, no. 1344 (Dec. 2, 1954): 977–78. Basil Gray, *Apollo* 61, no. 359 (January 1955): 26. J. I., *The Connoisseur* (Amer. ed.) 36, no. 550 (January 1956): 296. J. E. van Lohuizen-de Leeuw, *Bibliotheca Orientalis* 14, no. 1 (January 1957): 51–53. O., *The Aryan Path* 26, no. 8 (1955): 368–69. *Roopa-Lekha* 25, no. 2 (Winter 1954): 56. Benjamin Rowland, Jr., *College Art Journal* 16, no. 4 (Summer 1955): 389–90. Benjamin Rowland, Jr., *Journal of the American Oriental Society* 75, no. 2 (April–June 1955): 137–39. Walter Spink, *American Anthropologist,* n.s. 59, no. 1 (February 1957): 156–57.

"Rejoinder." *Artibus Asiae* 17, no. 3/4 (1954): 330.

"Dr. S. P. Mookerjee and Indian Art." *The Calcutta Review,* 3d ser. 133, no. 1 (October 1954): 9–10.

1955

Arts de l'Inde: Traditions de la sculpture, de la peinture et de l'architecture. Paris: Phaidon, 1955 (French edition of *The Art of India,* 1954). *Review:* O. Viennot, *Arts asiatiques* 3, no. 2 (1956): 159–60.

Indische Kunst: Traditionen in Skulptur, Malerei und Architektur. Köln-Marienburg: Phaidon, 1955. (German edition of *The Art of India,* 1954.) *Review:* John M. Rosenfield, *Erasmus* 10, nos. 3–4 (February 25, 1957): cols. 96–98.

"The Four-Cornered Citadel of the Gods." *Journal of the American Oriental Society* 75, no. 3 (July–September 1955): 184–87.

"Four Kangra Paintings." *Philadelphia Museum of Art Bulletin* 50, no. 245 (Spring 1955): 40–46.

"India: Unfinished Panorama." *Art News* 54, no. 5 (September 1955): 40; continued and concluded: 57–58. (Review of *The Art of Indian Asia* by H. Zimmer; completed and edited by Joseph Campbell.)

Review of Vilhelm Sloman, *Bizarre Designs in Silks. Artibus Asiae* 18, no. 1 (1955): 107–10.

Review of H. Zimmer, *The Art of Indian Asia,* completed and edited by Joseph Campbell. *Artibus Asiae* 18, no. 3/4 (1955): 328–35.

Review of Benjamin Rowland, *The Art and Architecture of India. Journal of the American Oriental Society* 75, no. 1 (January–March, 1955): 66–68.

1956

"An Image of Aditi-Uttānapad." *Artibus Asiae* 19, no. 3/4 (1956): 259–70.

"Artist, Patron, and Public in India." *The Far Eastern Quarterly* 15, no. 3 (May 1956): 335–42.

"Links Between Early and Later Buddhist Art: 4. Sanchi." *Mārg* 9, no. 2 (March 1956): 29–35.

"Two Indian Embroideries." *Philadelphia Museum of Art Bulletin* 52, no. 251 (Autumn 1956): 14–18.

Review of Hermann Goetz, *The Early Wooden Temples of Chamba. Artibus Asiae* 19, no. 1 (1956): 89–91.

Review of Pierre Rambach and Vitold de Marie-Golish, *The Golden Age of Indian Art, Vth–XIIIth Century. The Far Eastern Quarterly* 15, no. 4 (August 1956): 625–26.

1957

L'Arte dell' India: le tradizioni della scultura, della pittura dell'architettura indiana. Florence: G. C. Sansoni, 1957. (Italian edition of *The Art of India,* 1954.)

"Reflections on the House and Body of God." *Mārg* 10, no. 3 (June 1957): 19–20; continued and concluded: 23.

"Indian Sculpture Newly Acquired." *Philadelphia Museum of Art Bulletin* 52, no. 252 (Winter 1957): 30–38. Corrected in *Philadelphia Museum of Art Bulletin* 52, no. 253 (Spring 1957): 42.

Review of Ananda K. Coomaraswamy, *Mediaeval Sinhalese Art. The Journal of Asian Studies* 16, no. 3 (May 1957): 466–67.

1958

"Traditions of the Indian Craftsman." *Journal of American Folklore* 71, no. 281 (July–September 1958): 224–30. Reprint. In *Traditional India: Structure and Change,* edited by Milton Singer. Philadelphia: American Folklore Society, 1959. Biographical and Special Series 10, pp. 18–24.

"Wall and Image in Indian Art." *Proceedings of the American Philosophical Society* 102, no. 1 (Feb. 17, 1958): 7–13.

Review of Douglas Barrett, *Painting of the Deccan XVI–XVII Century. Artibus Asiae* 21, no. 3/4 (1958): 311–12.

Review of W. G. Archer, *Central Indian Painting. Artibus Asiae* 21, no. 3/4 (1958): 312–13.

Review of Moti Chandra, *Mewar Painting in the Seventeenth Century. Artibus Asiae* 21, no. 3/4 (1958): 313–14.

1959

"The Ṛg Vedic Myth of the Craftsman (The Ṛbhus)." *Artibus Asiae* 22, no. 1/2 (1959): 113–20.

"Early Indian Ivory Carving." *Philadelphia Museum of Art Bulletin* 54, no. 261 (Spring 1959): 55–66.

"Natural Science and Technology in Relation to Cultural Institutions and Social Practice in India." *Philosophy East and West* 9, nos. 1–2 (April–July 1959): 21–23. (Preliminary report of the proceedings of the Third East-West Philosopher's Conference.)

1960

Homage to Khajuraho. With Mulk Raj Anand. Bombay: Mārg Publications, 1960.

Indian Sculpture in the Philadelphia Museum of Art. Philadelphia: University of Pennsylvania Press; London: Oxford University Press, 1960. *Reviews:* F. R. Allchin, *Bulletin of the School of Oriental and African Studies* 26, pt. 1 (1963): 198. A. H. B., *Journal of the Royal Central Asian Society* 49, pts. 3 and 4 (July–October 1962): 351–52. Aschwin Lippe, *The Burlington Magazine* 105, no. 726 (September 1963): 424. Walter Spink, *The Art Bulletin* 45, no. 1 (March 1963): 83–84.

"The Art of Nepal and Tibet." *Philadelphia Museum of Art Bulletin* 55, no. 265 (Spring 1960): 23–38.

Review of Klaus Fischer, *Schöpfungen indischer Kunst. Artibus Asiae* 23, no. 2 (1960): 141–43.

Review of Louis Frédéric, *The Art of India. Artibus Asiae* 23, no. 3/4 (1960): 263–64.

Review of K. Bharatha Iyer, *Indian Art. Artibus Asiae* 23, no. 3/4 (1960): 264.

1961

Indische Kunst: Traditionen in Skulptur, Malerei und Architektur. Zürich: Buchclub Ex Libris, 1961. (Buchclub Ex Libris edition of *The Art of India,* 1954.)

" 'The One' in the Ṛg Veda." In *A Centenary Volume; Rabindranath Tagore, 1861–1961.* New Delhi: Sahitya Akademi, 1961: pp. 410–22.

"Pūṣan." *Journal of the American Oriental Society* 81, no. 2 (April–June 1961): 104–22.

"The Art of Nepal and Tibet." *The Middle Way* 35, no. 4 (February 1961): 135–40; continued and concluded under the same title in *The Middle Way* 36, no. 1 (May 1961): 17–23.

Review of Eric Dickinson and Karl Khandalavala, *Kishangarh Painting. Artibus Asiae* 24, no. 1 (1961): 69–70.

Review of Karl Khandalavala, Moti Chandra, and Pramod Chandra, *Miniature Paintings from the Sri Motichand Khajanchi Collection. Artibus Asiae* 24, no. 1 (1961): 70–71.

Review of Karl Khandalavala, *Pahārī Miniature Painting. Artibus Asiae* 24, no. 1 (1961): 71–72.

Review of Mukul Dey, *Birbhum Terracottas. Artibus Asiae* 24, no. 1 (1961): 72.

Review of Eliky Zannas, *Khajuraho* with historical introduction by Jeannine Auboyer. *Artibus Asiae* 24, no. 1 (1961): 72–73.

Review of Richard Ettinghausen, *Paintings of the Sultans and Emperors of India in American Collections. Artibus Asiae* 24, no. 2 (1961): 146.

Review of Karl Khandalavala, *Pahārī Miniature Painting. Journal of the American Oriental Society* 81, no. 2 (April–June 1961): 136–39.

Review of O. C. Gangoly, *Indian Terracotta Art. The Journal of Asian Studies* 20, no. 4 (August 1961): 559.

Review of D. T. Devendra, *Classical Sinhalese Sculpture. The Journal of Asian Studies* 20, no. 4 (August 1961): 559–60.

1962

"Two: Its Significance in the Ṛgveda." In *Indological Studies in Honor of W. Norman Brown,* edited by Ernest Bender. New Haven, Conn.: American Oriental Society, 1962. American Oriental Series 47, pp. 109–36.

"Natural Science and Technology in Relation to Cultural Patterns and Social Practices in India." In *Philosophy and Culture—East and West,* edited by Charles A. Moore. Honolulu: University of Hawaii Press, 1962, pp. 156–71. (Official report of the proceedings of the Third East-West Philosopher's Conference.)

"The Triple Structure of Creation in the Ṛg Veda." *History of Religions* 2, no. 1 (Summer 1962): 140–75; continued and concluded under the same title in *History of Religions* 2, no. 2 (Winter 1963): 256–85.

Review of Umakant Premanand Shah, *Studies in Jaina Art. Artibus Asiae* 25, no. 1 (1962): 87.

Review of Umakant P. Shah, *Akota Bronzes. Artibus Asiae* 25, no. 1 (1962): 87–88.

Review of Umakant Premanand Shah, *Sculptures from Śāmalājī and Roḍā. Artibus Asiae* 25, no. 1 (1962): 88–89.

Review of Philippe Stern and Mireille Benisti, *Evolution du style indien d'Amaravati. The Journal of Asian Studies* 22, no. 1 (November 1962): 131–32.

1963

"Note on the Bodhisattva Image in the Stanford Museum." *Artibus Asiae* 26, no. 3/4 (1963): 285–89.

"Note with reference to pages 290, 291." *Artibus Asiae* 26, no. 3/4 (1963): 292.

1964

The Art of Nepal. New York: Asia Society, 1964. *Reviews:* E. Conze, *Oriental Art,* n.s. 11, no. 3 (Autumn 1965): 177. Benjamin Rowland, Jr., *The Journal of Asian Studies* 24, no. 3 (May 1965): 548–51.

"Form Elements in the Visual Work of Rabindranath Tagore." *Lalit Kala Contemporary* 2 (December 1964): 37–39.

"The Art of Nepal." *Oriental Art,* n.s. 10, no. 4 (Winter 1964): 225–33.

Review of J. Ph. Vogel, *The Goose in Indian Literature and Art. Journal of the American Oriental Society* 84, no. 4 (October–December 1964): 475–76.

1965

Patna Museum Catalogue of Antiquities. Edited by Parameshwari Lal Gupta. Patna: Patna Museum, 1965.

"The Art of Nepal." *Oriental Art,* n.s. 11, no. 2 (Summer 1965): 123–24.

"Three Nepali Paintings." *Philadelphia Museum of Art Bulletin* 60, no. 285 (Spring 1965): 65–76.

"Department of Oriental Art: Indian Art." *Philadelphia Museum of Art Bulletin* 61, no. 286 (Summer 1965): 118–19.

1966

"Image of Buddha from Gandhara." *Philadelphia Museum of Art Bulletin* 61, no. 289 (Spring 1966): 36–39.

"Indian Art." *Philadelphia Museum of Art Bulletin* 61, no. 290 (Summer 1966): 98–100.

Review of Odette Viennot, *Les divinitiés fluviales Gaṅgā et Yamunā. Artibus Asiae* 28, no. 1 (1966): 98–99.

Review of K. R. Srinivasan, *Cave Temples of the Pallavas. Artibus Asiae* 28, no. 4 (1966): 319–21.

Review of J. E. van Lohuizen-de Leeuw, *Indian Sculptures in the von der Heydt Collection (Rietberg Museum). Artibus Asiae* 28, no. 4 (1966): 321–22.

Review of Stuart Cary Welch and Milo Cleveland Beach, *Gods, Thrones, and Peacocks. The Burlington Magazine* 108, no. 764 (November 1966): 585.

1967

"Indian Art." *Philadelphia Museum of Art Bulletin* 63, no. 295 (October–December, 1967): 52–53.

Review of Balwant Gargi, *Folk Theater of India. The Journal of Asian Studies* 26, no. 3 (May 1967): 504–5.

1968

Unknown India: Ritual Art in Tribe and Village. Philadelphia: The Philadelphia Museum of Art, 1968. *Review:* Mary C. Lanius, *Artibus Asiae* 31, no. 2/3 (1969): 228–29.

Review of Alain Daniélou, *Hindu Polytheism. Journal of the American Oriental Society* 88, no. 3 (July–September 1968): 553–60.

Review of Rāmacandra Kaulācāra, *Śilpa Prakāśa: Medieval Orissan Sanskrit Text on Temple Architecture,* translated and annotated by Alice Boner and Sadāśiva Rath Śarmā. *The Journal of Asian Studies* 27, no. 2 (February 1968): 408–9.

1969

Introduction to *Art of India: Sculpture and Miniature Paintings.* Minneapolis: University of Minnesota, 1969, pp. 4–6.

"Architecture and Sculpture; Painting." In "India" in *Encyclopedia Americana* 14. New York: Americana Corporation, 1969: 803–13.

"Indian Varieties of Art Ritual." In *Myths and Symbols: Studies in Honor of Mircea Eliade,* edited by Joseph M. Kitagawa and Charles H. Long, with the collaboration of Jerald C. Brauer and Marshall G. S. Hodgson. Chicago and London: University of Chicago Press, 1969: 23–45.

Review of V. S. Pathak, *Ancient Historians of India: A Study in Historical Biographies. Artibus Asiae* 31, no. 1 (1969): 93–94.

Review of Sarva Daman Singh, *Ancient Indian Warfare with Special Reference to the Vedic Period. Artibus Asiae* 31, no. 1 (1969): 94–95.

Review of Md. Abdul Waheed Khan, *A Monograph on the Discovery of Mural Paintings of Kalyani Chalukyas at Alladurg. Artibus Asiae* 31, no. 2/3 (1969): 229.

Review of John M. Rosenfield, *The Dynastic Arts of the Kushans. Artibus Asiae* 31, no. 2/3 (1969): 229–32.

Review of Walter Spink, *Ajanta to Ellora. Artibus Asiae* 31, no. 4 (1969): 327–29.

Review of Amalananda Ghosh, *Ajanta Murals. Artibus Asiae* 31, no. 4 (1969): 329.

Review of R. S. Gupta, *The Art and Architecture of Aihole. Artibus Asiae* 31, no. 4 (1969): 329.

Review of Madelaine Hallade, *Gandhāran Art of North India and the Graeco-Buddhist Tradition in India, Persia, and Central Asia. Artibus Asiae* 31, no. 4 (1969): 329–30.

Review of Madanjeet Singh, *Himalayan Art. Artibus Asiae* 31, no. 4 (1969): 330–31.

Review of Heinrich Gerhard Franz, *Buddhistische Kunst Indiens;* Heinrich Gerhard Franz, *Hinduistische und islamische Kunst Indiens. Journal of the American Oriental Society* 89, no. 1 (January–March 1969): 197–98.

1970

The Arts and Crafts of Kerala. With J. H. Cousins and R. Vasudeva Poduval. Cochin: Paico Publishing House, 1970. (*The Arts and Crafts of Travancore,* 1948, enlarged under a new title by R. Vasudeva Poduval.) *Review: Mārg* 24, no. 2 (March 1971): 10–11.

"Indian Art." *Philadelphia Museum of Art Bulletin* 65, no. 304 (July–September 1970): 60.

Review of Curt Maury, *Folk Origins of Indian Art. The Journal of Asian Studies* 30, no. 1 (November 1970): 217–18.

1972

"Śiva, the Archer." In *Indologen Tagung 1971,* edited by H. Härtel. Wiesbaden: Franz Steiner Verlag, 1972, pp. 140–50.

"Śarīravṛkṣa, The Body-Tree," *Journal of the Indian Society of Oriental Art,* n. s. 4 (1971–72): 23–37.

Review of R. Gordon Wasson, *Soma, Divine Mushroom of Immortality. Artibus Asiae* 34, no. 2/3 (1972): 263–67.

1973

Entries in *Treasures of the Philadelphia Museum of Art,* edited by George H. Marcus. Philadelphia: Philadelphia Museum of Art, 1973: 26–30 (Unsigned)

Review of Karl A. Nowotny, *Beiträge zur Geschichte des Weltbildes (Farben und Weltrichtungen). Artibus Asiae* 35, no. 4 (1973): 375–77.

Review of Detlef Ingo Lauf, *Das Erbe Tibets. Artibus Asiae* 35, no. 4 (1973): 377.

1974

"Nepal." In "Arts of Central Asian Peoples: Himalayan Cultures of Nepal and Tibet," in *The New Encyclopaedia Britannica, Macropaedia,* 3. Chicago: Encyclopaedia Britannica, 1974: 1140–41. (Signed S. Kh.)

"South Indian Sculpture." *Apollo,* n.s. 50, no. 149 (July 1974): 12–17.

1975

"Jaina Painting of Western India." In *Aspects of Jaina Art and Architecture,* edited by U. P. Shah and M. A. Dhaky. Ahmedabad: Gujarat State Committee for the Celebration of 2500th Anniversary of Bhagavān Mahāvīra Nirvāṇa, 1975, pp. 385–404.

"The Temple as Puruṣa." In *Studies in Indian Temple Architecture,* edited by Pramod Chandra. New Delhi: American Institute of Indian Studies, 1975: pp. 40–46.

"The Indian Great Goddess." *History of Religions* 14, no. 4 (May 1975): 235–65.

"The Mahāvīra Vessel and the Plant Pūtika." *Journal of the American Oriental Society* 95, no. 2 (April–June 1975): 222–35.

Review of Alice Boner, Sadāśiva Rath Sarmā, and Rajendra Prāsad Dās, *New Light on the Sun Temple of Koṇārka. Artibus Asiae* 37, no. 4 (1975): 306–7.

Review of W. G. Archer, *Indian Paintings from the Punjab Hills: A Survey and History of Pahari Miniature Painting. Artibus Asiae* 37, no. 4 (1975): 307–11.

Review of C. Sivaramamurti, *Nataraja in Art, Thought, and Literature. Artibus Asiae* 37, no. 4 (1975): 311–13.

1976

The Hindu Temple. 2 vols. Delhi: Motilal Banarsidass, 1976. (Reprint of *The Hindu Temple,* 1946) *Reviews:* Michael Meister, *The Art Bulletin* 62, no.1 (March 1980): 180–82. Barbara Stoler Miller, *Parabola* 3, no. 1 (1978): 110–12. Gary Michael Tartakov, *Journal of the Society of Architectural Historians* 38, no. 3 (October 1979): 275–76.

"Eka-Vratya, the Conceptual Monument of Rudra." *Journal of the Indian Society of Oriental Art,* n.s. 8 (Dr. Moti Chandra Commemoration volume, 1976–77, pt. 1): 9–15.

1977

"Liṅga." In *Beiträge zur Indienforschung* (Ernst Waldschmidt zum 80. Geburtstag gewidmet), edited by Herbert Härtel. Berlin: Museum für Indische Kunst, 1977. Veröffentlichungen des Museums für Indische Kunst, 4: pp. 256–66.

1978

Foreword to *Chitrasūtra of the Vishṇudharmottara,* by C. Sivaramamurti. New Delhi: Kanak Publications, 1978: ix–xiv.

1981

Indian Sculpture. Delhi: Motilal Banarsidass (reprint of *Indian Sculpture,* 1933).

Manifestations of Shiva. Philadelphia: Philadelphia Museum of Art, 1981. *Reviews:* Michael W. Meister, *Studies in Visual Communication* 7(Fall 1981): 84–89. Wendy Doniger O'Flaherty, *Connaissance des arts*, no. 16(May 1981), pp. 72–79.

The Presence of Śiva. Princeton: Princeton University Press, 1981. *Reviews:* C. Robert Nixon, *Library Journal,* Feb. 1, 1981. Mira Seth, *Indian Book Chronicle,* Nov. 1, 1981, pp. 352–53. Glenn E. Yocum, *Religious Studies Review* 7(October 1981): 368.

I

PATRON AND PRACTICE

1 Artist, Patron, and Public in India

According to traditional Indian belief and practice every creature has a function (vrata) which he fulfills in the universe. What function did the artist or craftsman fulfill in society, and in that other invisible part of the universe, which he was able to convey by his work to those around him and to posterity?

The distinction often made in the West between artist and craftsman did not affect India. The practitioner of one of the sixty-four recognized branches of art (kalā), which provided channels for every possible kind of creative endowment to be trained and employed, fulfilled his calling in the best way possible to him, and thus carried out his universal task. Vocation and assignment were reciprocal; together they constituted the particular duty (svadharma) whose lifelong discharge satisfied the maker, the person for whom he made the work of art and the standards by which art exists and evokes ever renewed response.

The sixty-four arts[1] are the counterpart to the thirty-two sciences. These two categories, the arts and the sciences, comprise the sum total of knowledge and skill, the one able to convey its contents and the creative experience it reflects through form alone, the other dependent upon words. The distinction is not rigid and certain border disciplines are variously assigned to the one or the other. While the sixty-four arts include the visual arts, music, the dance, drama, and also acrobatics and dressmaking, the perfections of delight which are experienced by the other senses count among their highly specialized branches the culinary art or that of the perfumer, and the more comprehensive art of making love. The degrees of competence in these arts are many and genius is known when met, while there is only a lower limit to payment, fee, or reward. To what extent land, cattle, or silken garments

This essay first appeared in *The Far Eastern Quarterly* (May 1956): 335–42, and is reprinted here by permission.

were added in special cases over and above the customary compensation was regulated by an unwritten code.[2] This discrimination did equal credit to both parties, establishing (as it must have done) degrees of quality and of connoisseurship. A distinction was made, as it must be made, between artist and craftsman with reference to the creative quality of the work of art, but not to the material of which it was made nor to the particular end or delight which it served.

For delight is not mere pleasure. It is not self-indulgence, for delight requires discipline. The keener the perceptiveness the greater the delight. If an artist has to be trained for his task the true connoisseur also requires schooling; both are in need of exercise as well as the opportunity for exercise which they supply the one to the other. Both must start with assets no person can give. They are gifts of God, powers of an intensity greater than those of the discursive mind. But these powers remain incomplete and unfulfilled without the vital contact between artist and patron. Only a disjointed society allows genius to remain unrecognized, wasting away life in solitary communion, its unheard expression crying in a wilderness of numb men.

It is generally assumed that the selectiveness of free competition did not exert its pressures on a calling which, because it was considered "hereditary," was thought to run in smooth channels that endowed the individual with sharpened senses and a high degree of skill. Skill, however, is acquired and not hereditary, nor is heredity a factor to be reckoned with in the transmission of genius. While it was the rule that a son or younger brother learned a craft from his father or elder brother in his workshop, it was not unusual for a young craftsman who had shown promise and was not a relative at all to be educated in the same manner. History has recorded the names and preserved the work of members of one family of architects over more than two-and-a-half centuries; they came from Gujarat to Mewar in Rajasthan in about the year 1389 and were the chief architects of the rulers of Mewar from that time.[3] To this family of architects belonged Maṇḍana who built the Kīrtistambha at Chitor (1440–48), and who was also the author of textbooks on architecture, such as the *Vāsturājavallabha* or the *Rūpamaṇḍana.* An inscription of 1653 in the Jagannātha Rāya temple at Udaipur states that this temple was the work of two architects of the same family. Whether Maṇḍana would have approved of their work we do not know. It does not compare favorably with his own and shows more of the architectural degradation of the later period than of the high standards of the Maṇḍana workshop.

Apprenticeship with a master or with a recognized member of the craftsmen's guilds was a safeguard against low standards, incompetence, or fraud and self-deception. That it did not do away with all of these faults may be read in the threatening words of the *Samarāṅgaṇasūtradhāra* (XLIV, 6–10), a most exhaustive compendium on the visual arts which was compiled in the earlier part or middle of the eleventh century by King Bhoja of Dhārā (Malwa; near modern Indore). From the warning we find that nothing less than death awaits him who would practice architecture without correct knowledge or is mistakenly proud of false knowledge. The king threatens to inflict the death penalty on him as one who ruins the kingdom. This seemingly excessive punishment was justified, for architecture (like the other arts) had a magic effect, not simply an aesthetic one, nor did it fulfill only a utilitarian purpose. It was in the likeness of the architect of the universe, Viśvakarmā, its working principle, that the architect went to his task. Were he to infringe upon any rule or deviate from correct proportion, such neglect or dissonance was felt to be fatal to the structure not only of a particular building, but also to the order of the state. In fact, such injury might even endanger the order in the universe. For this reason "the ghost of such a man, dead before his time, will wander on this wide earth." Having infringed its order, he is doomed to belong nowhere; he who should have been a builder of homes is to remain homeless in a disembodied condition. Another contingency in the practice of the arts is also considered in the same context. It has to do with an artist whose theoretical knowledge is greater than his skill. Such a situation may arise anywhere as soon as the practice of art has reached maturity, has become conscious, and is viewed in retrospect. Of such an artist it is said that he will "faint at the time of action like a timid man on the battlefield." This collapse is equal to nervous failure in which self-deception seems to pass judgment on itself.

King Bhoja, as author or compiler of the great compendium, the *Samarāṅgaṇasūtradhāra,* as patron and head of the state, judges the artist and his shortcomings from a moral point of view, once on the metaphysical level and again on the psychological level. He also takes a third source of failure into account. This is the case of the expert in his craft, the virtuoso who lacks intellectual insight. Of him the king says that "like a blind man he will be misled by anyone" for he is his own dupe, a potential casualty in the field of art.

Surveying this field which covered a considerable part of the king's responsibility, for he was its foremost patron, he proved his knowledge of its nature; not every ruler would have had the same insight or would have recorded it as King Bhoja did. By doing so, however, he followed traditional practice, for an earlier encyclopedia of all the arts, the *Viṣṇudharmottara* (of about the sixth century) is written down as a conversation between a king and a sage. Here the king inquires and the sage instructs in the knowledge of the arts. Such knowledge is not only the domain of one or the other of the sages and seers, but in the sum total of Indian knowledge it forms part of Revelation, the Veda, to which it belongs as applied knowledge, being part of ritual and astrology, and in particular of Tantra, attached to the Atharva Veda.

The artists and craftsmen came from all classes of society. It would seem, however, that the Kshatriyas, the ruler and warrior caste, contributed more patrons than artists, although at least one great artist and sovereign, Mahendravarman, the Pallava king who ruled over a large part of South India, took care to speak of himself in his inscriptions as being a "tiger," which means "preeminent" among painters. It was he who made of the Pallava seaport, Māmallapuram near Madras, a unique work of art.

During the centuries when the great Indian stone temples were built, that is from the sixth century onwards, the Brahman artists performed a double function. As architect-priests (ācārya; sthāpaka) they conceived the building of a particular temple or religious institution, and as the chief architects (sthapati), gave shape to it. With them worked the surveyors (sūtragrahī), the sculptors (takṣaka), modelers, and painters (vardhakī). The Brahman artists and craftsmen, it appears, were heirs to their calling in the Vedic age when they built the altars and fashioned the implements and effigies which formed part of the sacrifice. Vaishya and shudra, too, were artists and craftsmen, the last named, for example, specializing in mat and basketmaking. They also performed the unskilled labor required in large building operations. Although, in general, monetary payment was not made, the artists, craftsmen, and the laborers associated with them were neither poor, nor were they slaves. From a number of the ancient tales (jātakas), which the Buddhists used to illustrate points of doctrine, the high standing and organization of some of the crafts can be gleaned. For example "craft-villages" are described in which practitioners of one craft lived exclusively. However, they were also connected with the land and earned their livelihood both from their craft and from agriculture. In a village of five hundred carpenters, for example, of whom the *Alīnacitta Jātaka* tells, they made prefabricated houses. This village was not far from the city and was also near a forest which furnished timber. The carpenters put together the framework for one and two story houses. They numbered all the pieces from the main posts to the lesser parts. These they sent downstream by river and set up the houses according to the prescribed order. After they received their remuneration, they returned to village to prepare for their next assignment. The head of such a village community of craftsmen was a man of substance, whether he was an architect or, as in the *Sūci Jātaka,* a metal worker, the principal smith in a village of one thousand smiths. He was spoken of as rich and a favorite of the king.

Even in these centuries the guilds maintained standards of work and safeguarded the interests of their members. "To the King's treasurer was given the judgeship of all the guilds. Before that no such office existed, but there was this office ever after" *(Nigrodha Jātaka).* Later on, as recorded in Manu's law books (VIII, 41) of the first or second century, "the King had to establish and to examine the laws of the guilds." These were adjusted to fit life in villages or in towns. If the village was a small one, the craftsman was the endowed servant of the agricultural community; in larger villages a master craftsman controlled his guild; or an entire village practiced one specialized craft. In towns, the guild of craftsmen occupied its own part of the town where—even to this day—certain streets are entirely lined with the workshops of one craft, as in the Tāḍerī Bazaar in Benares. The members of a guild may belong to the same or to different castes, which means that the unifying factor is the craft irrespective of caste. Finally, from within this organized and largely hereditary context, a craftsman or artist could become the temporary or lifelong feudal servant of a king or ruler or of a monastic establishment. Although money payment was unusual, gold was sometimes given to the artists and payment in kind was always made, be it in the form of grants of land, cattle, or a share in the harvest.[4] Whatever the material return, as long as it enabled the artist to live free from anxiety for his daily bread, in the assured knowledge of the purpose of his work and the need which it fulfilled, it met whatever demand a craftsman or artist would legitimately make. That he wanted to be a success, whether in a traditional society or elsewhere, was natural. But success is not necessarily measured in material terms. The pride he took in his work was important. He thought it fitting, as at least one inscription proves, to bestow his name to posterity together with his work. "There has not been and there shall not be in Jambudvīpa any expert (vidvān) in the art of building temples equal to Naraśobha."[5] The temple in Aihole (of the seventh or eighth century) which Naraśobha built is more modest, as a building, than is the tone of the inscription. But one may ask what has happened to the much praised anonymity of the Indian artist? Anonymity in the case of the Indian artist does not imply that he did not want to be known; he did not think of wanting to be known as different from others—as unique; on the contrary, he wanted to be known as conveying surpassingly well what other artists then and in the future would endeavor to convey. His singularity does not stress or seek otherness, but strives for intensity of realization and for power in giving form to content experienced or approached by all those for whom he works.

In some instances it is not the name of any individual artist that the inscription transmits to posterity, but that of the guild as a whole, as for instance on the south gate of the Great Stūpa in Sanchi of the first century, where the ivory carvers of Vidiśā recorded on one of the stone panels that it was their work. If it was their gift, this requires explanation. Buddhist monuments were collective monuments, the work of many artists, guilds, and donors. They were built by contributions from widely distant parts of the country and from all levels of society—merchants, nobles, courtesans, monks, nuns, artisans, and artists. The latter would contribute and donate their own work. The carved panel conspicuously inscribed by the guild of ivory workers as their work, though not outstanding in quality, has a style of its own; the panel next to it, representing the cortege of the gods, is similar in style; it is in fact the very climax of that style and one of the most remarkable carvings in Sanchi. One would like to think of it as the work of the most eminent of the "ivory carvers of Vidiśā," whose name remains unrecorded.

In another instance—they are relatively few in the whole of Indian art—and on the same south gate of the Great Stūpa at Sanchi, the top beam is inscribed so that we know it is "the gift of Ānanda, son of Vāsiṣṭhī, the foreman of the artisans of King Sātakarṇi." It appears from the inscription that Ānanda was the leading court artist of a powerful sovereign, an artist entrusted to carve themes of profoundest meaning and almost programmatic significance. But the quality of the two large reliefs on the inside and the outside of the beam is mediocre, the style popular and archaic. It is closely related to that of the preceding century (first century B.C.) of which the monument of Bharhut is representative. The reliefs completely lack the ingenuity or the buoyant vigor of the work of "the ivory carvers" on the same gate. In a conservative way they are expressive on the one side of a staid acceptance of the calm of life as it flows symmetrically through the lotuses in whose midst the goddess Lakṣmī—the goddess Lotus, the Life-goddess—is stationed, and of the calm of life on the other side as again and again it salutes death, the total extinction, the Parinirvāṇa, of which the thrice repeated stupas are symbolic in this panel.

This competent craftsman, the head of the imperial workshop, had little to say himself. He conveyed a theme, two-faced like the inside and outside of the beam, a theme conveying a meaning as paradoxical as it is perennial in Indian art. The "ivory carvers" of Vidiśā, on the other hand, put their competence and total vitality into at least one of the two panels of which the one is inscribed, and the other is their masterwork. It would be proper to speak of the work of a great artist who was one of the "ivory carvers."

Circumstance, etiquette, and temperament make one craftsman's name prominent and hide another. But whether his name be known or forgotten the artist as creator is beyond earthly reward. As a member of a traditional society, however, he met a social demand. By supplying his work he discharged his duty (dharma) and earned his living. The work of art in India, over and above its completeness as creative act and form, has as its purpose and function the acquisition of merit on a spiritual plane. This merit, however, belongs to the patron or donor. For merit's sake, he has commissioned the work which is to secure for him a lasting place in heaven while still on earth, a blessedness not only for his person, but for his relatives and charges as well. The work of art, as a vehicle to heaven and its bliss, belongs to the patron. He remunerates the artist so that merit should not accrue to the artist, but should remain with the patron. In this way the artist faces each task with a full responsibility ever renewed. While he performs the work for his patron, he gains his artistic stature by giving form to a vision which he alone, then and there, can capture. This immediate intuition and skill, the readiness to convey it with precision, the *Samarāṅgaṇasūtradhāra* says, makes the great masters. Such a master cut out of the rock the stupendous Kailāsanātha temple in Ellora.[6] His name is unknown, but his reaction to his own work is recorded in a copperplate inscription. Seeing his work completed, he exclaimed in wonder: "Oh how did I make it?" doubting his own identity, and bridging by his question the distance between himself, the creator, and the act of creation.

The latter, on having become form, has its lasting function. It remains magically effective. It is this magical potency which the donor or patron believes is working on his behalf.

With this intimate bond of effective magic between patron and art, the role of the artist exceeds that which in the West is assigned to him. For he is not only the creator or maker of objects, that is, works of art, the purveyor of aesthetic delight by which a world beyond the senses becomes visible, tangible, and concrete, so that it can be enjoyed and understood; he also makes them act effectively by means of their aesthetic presence whose magic literally secures for the donor a place in heaven while on earth, and whose virtue acts for the well-being of those who are in the orbit of power or connected with the patron.

In this role as creator-magician and mediator, the artist sheds his anonymity before God. In this capacity he places his likeness next to the image of divinity, standing on a lotus and raised to its level. This is how the two architects Loyaṇa and Kelā of the Vimala Vasahī at Dilwara on Mount Abu had their portraits placed on either side of the goddess Sarasvatī.[7] Their portraits, so far as we know today, begin a series of self-portraits which the architect-sculptors of some of the great religious monuments of Rajasthan inscribed with their names (in Chitor, for example, in Rāṇā Kumbha's "Tower of Glory" where Maṇḍana and his sons shared in the work,[8] and again in the Chaumukh temple in Ranakpur, South Rajasthan [1439] where the architects carved their small likenesses on facets of pillars in the breathtaking halls which they built). All these masters offered their names and persons, as part of their work, to the divinity to whom it was dedicated. As artists and magicians the Indian craftsmen transmuted matter into form, vision into concrete shape, and man beyond his earthly competence. If they composed, as Maṇḍana did, manuals of their art, they did it with the assurance of transmitting traditional knowledge and to assure that they themselves were part of the life wire of a transmundane connection.

Charged with this power their work became concretely real, subtly effective, and transcendentally existent—as predicated in the *Viṣṇusaṁhitā.*[9] The physical presence of the work of art was felt to have power, primarily on the patron and then on all who saw or worshiped it. In this intensity of effect statues were known to weep, to shake, and to address the spectator, as did the royal portrait statues in the drama *Pratimānāṭaka,* or the Būta figure and other images in the Tamil story of *Śilappadikāram.* Furthermore, by technically exploiting the magic nature of things made by art, automata were in use. They are dealt with in the *Samarāṅgaṇasūtradhāra,* whereas the gross abuse of the concrete, material presence of works of art is referred to in earlier Buddhist texts, where sculptured images can be seen as having served the aberrations of some monks,[10] every use having, of necessity, its misuse, but proving nevertheless the power which was felt in the concreteness, the immediate presence of the work of art.

This made the public realize their obligation toward artist and craftsman. If it is laid down in Manu's code (V, 129) that "the hand of a craftsman engaged in his work is always ritually pure," the *Arthaśāstra* decrees capital punishment for any person who caused a craftsman the loss of a hand or an eye.

The value of art and artist being acutely felt, the various ways in which art was harnessed by the ruling power may be illustrated in a few words. In the third century B.C. Emperor Aśoka promulgated his policy of ahiṁsā by means of edicts engraved on free-standing monoliths or on rocks. There the figures of art were used in their traditional symbolic meaning with special application to the contents of the edicts. The forms in which they appeared were either the accepted ones (as in the elephant at Dhauli (Tosali), Orissa, cut out of the living rock) or else they had been transmogrified in a cosmopolitan court art. Not before the time of the Mughals would the latter term again be appropriate. In the slowly unfolding tapestry of Indian history, biography, and art, figures of emperors and kings stand out clearly traced as art patrons who were vitally part of the artistic fabric of their period and instrumental in consolidating its style. Mahendravarman, the Pallava king who ruled in the early seventh century, was a personality of the widest artistic ambiance. He appears to have instilled into the South Indian tradition of sculpture a sophistication which gave rise to the canons of art applied and explored for the next millennium. On a lesser scale, the Rajput ruler, Sansar Chand of Kangra (1775–1823) surrounded himself with a circle of painters who brought classical perfection to the Kangra school of painting with its sensuous delicacy of line, full of lyrical devotion. However, the portraits of the maharaja, himself a devout bhākta, depict none of these sentiments. It is not known what deprived his portraits of just those traits of character which he possessed as a person, and which stimulated the painters who surrounded him so that they distilled in their mythological paintings and epical illustrations the essence of the Kangra tradition and of his patronage. The Kangra school retained the elegance of line and the cool enamel of its colors, though not the same degree of tenderness, into the second half of the nineteenth century. In 1905 an earthquake ended the pictorial idyll that had been the Kangra school, the last phase and style in which traditional Indian art flowered.

In the meanwhile, the dregs of the English Royal Academy conventions had been officially imposed on the teaching of art in India. Even to this day Indian art is blighted by this import, while it is disturbed also because more recently a continental camouflage has entered with a changing impressionist-expressionist, and finally abstract façade, behind which a disoriented generation of artists and "art-lovers" smother their heritage and disguise their obligations. About the same time, at the beginning of this century, a conscious discovery of Indian form began—a groping resuscitation of the ghosts of Mughal, Rajput, Ajanta, and folk painting.

Generations in India follow one another faster than in the West. Today, the young Indian painters of the fourth generation after the rediscovery of indigenous styles are beginning to find themselves and their roots in the traditions of the past and in present-day life. Today, with music and the dance, Indian painting is rising again, while mildew still covers India's once greatest creative field, that of sculpture, next to the wasteland of its modern buildings. The relation of artist, patron, and public today follows the Western pattern, that of a free market without coherent purpose and structure in which the artist fends for fame and livelihood. A politically united India has yet to find in its heart the unity of the spirit that can establish that reciprocity of created and shared values where artist, patron, and public are integrated in the pattern of its traditional civilization.

2 Traditions of the Indian Craftsman

The traditions of the Indian craftsman are the means and ways by which professional activity transforms knowledge of Principle into practice. His particular craft is the sphere in which he is competent to apply this knowledge. The knowledge of Principle is imparted to him through Tradition. Principle is the source and origin of his calling, and is known by the name of Brahma or Viśvarkarmā, the sum total of creative consciousness. The Indian craftsman conceives of his art not as his own, nor as the accumulated skill of ages, but as originating in the divine skill of Viśvakarmā and revealed by him. This is how the sacred texts, the Āgamas, Purāṇas, and Vāstuśāstras trace back the traditions of the craftsman to the fountainhead. As practitioner of Tradition, the craftsman fulfills a double obligation. He is linked in a straight line with the fountainhead, sum total of consciousness, knowledge and inspiration. Its immediate presence in the actual moment of his work is guaranteed by the unbroken line of sages and craftsmen who have transmitted his particular craft to him. He carries it, forms it, and makes it available to the community that shares in Tradition, each according to his particular place and station in life. Tradition embraces the life of the whole community. Thus, the craftsman is involved with his own people more deeply than by common interests or a sphere of cooperative living. Tradition thus is not only an oral transmission of information and beliefs from ancestors to posterity, but also an inherited culture. It is a body of doctrine and discipline, put forth and revealed in the words of the Veda.

The name for any art or craft is śilpa. The meaning of this word is "variegated artistic work," comprising art, skill, craft, labor, ingenuity, rite and ritual, form, and creation. Neither the word "artist," nor "artisan" nor "crafts-

This essay first appeared in *Traditional India: Structure and Change,* ed. Milton Singer (Philadelphia: American Folklore Society, 1959) and is reprinted by permission.

man" are adequate translations of śilpin; for the arts and crafts in Indian partake in the nature of rites whose technical performance had magic power. "Śilpāni, works of art of man," says the *Aitareya Brāhmaṇa* (6. 5.27) "are an imitation of divine forms; by employing their rhythms, a metrical reconstitution is effected of the limited human personality." The range of the crafts extends over the entire culture and comprises the work of the wheelwright and the sculptor, or potter and perfumer, weaver and architect. The number of the arts is unlimited, but they are summed up under sixty-four major headings. These are viewed in twofold respect inasmuch as they belong either to Tantra, and master nature in its magic, or to the arts of love.[1] In addition to these sixty-four techniques (kalā) are the thirty-two sciences (vidyā) whose teaching is mainly verbal.

All these subjects are related to the Veda, which is revelation, the sum total of all knowledge. Architecture, for example, the foremost and comprehensive visual art, is part of the fifth appendix (Vedāṅga) to the Veda, inasmuch as architecture is applied astrology; inasmuch as it is a ritual, it is part of Kalpa, the sixth appendix to the Veda. As an applied knowledge, moreover, it belongs to Tantra (an Upaveda) and, therewith, to the Atharva Veda.[2]

The crafts were hereditary, or the succession was by apprenticeship and adoption, for skill is not inherited. The crafts did not form the prerogative of any caste. The members of a craft share their traditional occupation and the belief in a common origin or mythical ancestor. This is also characteristic of caste, although all members of a caste do not necessarily have the same occupation, and caste remains hereditary even if a man leaves the special occupation which is the traditional work of his caste. According to Parāśara, all the four orders, Brahmans, Kshatriyas, Vaiṣhyas, and Shudras, may practice crafts. Against this liberal pursuit of the arts, however, we have the *Arthaśāstra*, [3] qualifying the Shudras as artisans, and the *Viṣṇusmṛti* (third century),[4] which makes all branches of art the duties of the Shudras.

These conflicting views have India's ethnic past as their background. That Brahmans lived by handicrafts is documented in the jātakas where Brahman carpenters are mentioned. Baudhāyana[5] (fourth century B.C.), describing the preparations for the horse sacrifice, enumerates the artisans who establish themselves near the king, the sacrificer, the carpenters, wheelwrights, brickworkers, potters, and metalworkers. The rathakāra, the chariot-builder, is according to Baudhāyana, a son of a Vaishya father and a Shudra woman. The *Suttavibhaṅga* enumerates wheelwrights and builders among the Untouchables, as they are the issue of a Shudra father and a Brahman mother.

A double set of considerations thus operated in assessing the status of a craft. As far as a craft ministered to the Vedic sacrifice, it had prestige. When the selfsame craft, however, was practiced outside the Vedic pale, it did not carry the same dignity; it was not considered hallowed. Mixed marriages, on the other hand, of the Aryan with the other Indian populations, in anuloma and pratiloma relations, determined the higher or lower status of the practitioner of an occupation.

While the subdivision of the hereditary crafts is on the basis of difference in methods employed, ethnic considerations and social ambitions produced improvement or deterioration in the caste status of the craftsman. The goldsmiths of Maharashtra, for instance, admitted Āhirs who were cattle-herders, to start with, and rated as Shudras. They formed a subcaste of the Sonārs, the Āhir-Sonārs; the word "Āhir" denoting first the subdivision and later on being no more than a surname.[6] Lately the goldsmiths of Maharashtra have started asserting their dignity by refusing to take food at the hands of castes other than Brahman.

The upward trend within a craft, however, has also a deeper cause than social ambition. This was implicitly recognized in the law books. Manu says that the hand of a craftsman engaged in his work is always ritually pure.[7] The *Gautama Dharmaśāstra*[8] postulates that a Brahman may not accept food from an artisan. The law books thus distinguish the craftsman in his social position on the one hand, and in his state of grace on the other—when he is engaged in his work, when he creates and, thereby, gives effect to his being an embodiment of Viśvakarmā.

It is from the latter point of view that the Kammālar, or artisans of South India, dispute the supremacy of the Brahmans. They hold themselves equal in rank with them, claim to be of Aryan descent, and have their own priests. They know themselves descended from Viśvakarmā and his five sons, Manu, Maya, Tvaṣṭar, Śilpaka, and Viśvajña,[9] who are the archetypal ironsmith, worker in wood, brass, and stone, and the goldsmith. The son of anyone of these may follow any of the five crafts.

In Kerala, however, the same classes of craftsmen, the Kammalan, who are Shudras, look to their fellow workers in Tamilnadu, change their tuft of hair from the front to the back of the head, wear the sacred thread and call themselves Brahmans. A variation of this theme is illustrated by a forged deed of adoption from Golkonda, dated in 1294,[10] but actually belonging to the seventeenth century as proved by V. Raghavan. The deed establishes the adoption of a Seth of the Komadi class, a Vaishya, by the Kammālar Deva Brahmās, or Pañca Brahmās, but he remains a Vaishya by caste.

The myth—a form of awareness—of the descent of the craftsmen from Principle, has its counterpart in the myth of the fall of the craftsmen from Principle. This is told in the *Brahmavaivarta Purāṇa.*[11] Viśvakarmā, cursed by an Apsaras descended to earth, was born by a Brahman woman, and became an unparalleled architect. He had nine illegitimate sons, by a Shudra woman, the garlandmaker, blacksmith, potter, metalworker, conch-shell carver, weaver, architect (sūtradhāra), painter (citrakāra), and goldsmith. All were expert in their crafts, but the last three became incompetent to offer sacrifices and unholy because one had stolen gold from a Brahman, the other had failed to carry out the order of a Brahman, and in the painter's case a pictorial composition was defective and not according to the rules.

In this account of the fall, two categories of the lowering of level are taken into consideration. The first accounts for the descent of Principle to the order of the Shudras. This is accepted, for the Shudras were expert in their art. The second category, however, applies to the moral and artistic defection from Principle. This defection is limited to architect, painter-sculptor and goldsmith, the arts which demand the highest intellectual, imaginative, and technical skills. The fall, therefore, is the deeper, for the artistic defection goes hand in hand with a betrayal of Tradition.

The awareness of Tradition is active on all the levels of the craftsman's being. If he infringes on Tradition, if the composition of a painting has no wholeness, the painter shows himself not only as a poor artist but he becomes, thereby, an unholy person. Creative work has the sanctions of a sacrament. In many parts of India to this day, the craftsmen worship their tools at the Daśaharā festival on the day of Viśvakarmā Pūjā. From the time of the sūtras, both the materials and the tools of a craft are known to be sacred, for they are the seat of particular powers. The tree which is to be felled by the carpenter or sculptor is propitiated with offerings; he lays his hand on it with a mantra, asking pardon of the spirits residing in the tree (*Bṛhatsaṁhitā* 57.10–11). The axe which is to fell the tree is anointed with honey and butter so that the tree is not hurt when the transformation through which a shape of nature becomes a work of art is begun by the craftsman.

Before a craftsman takes up his tools for any particular assignment, the axe, the line, the hammer, and all the other instruments are worshiped with incense, flowers, and unhuṣked rice,[12] for they are that extension of the craftsman's hand through which he reaches beyond the ranges of his limited human person. All the work is done in a secluded place, with self-control and concentration. The bricks being invoked as goddesses, the material itself is deified prior to the consecration of the building.

The craftsman was trained from childhood in the workshop of the master, whose son, or younger brother, or apprentice he was. There he learned technique and the dharma, the culture to which he belonged and which he was to become an active part of. From the beginning, he shared in real work and real problems; there was no division of school from life. He learned the trade secrets. With devoted receptiveness, he prepared colors and tools and learned the form and theory of his branch of Tradition. He was initiated into his craft. The initiation was bound up with the particular craft and took it for its basis. His craft will be the field of application of the initiatory knowledge, which is the knowledge of Tradition.

We are acquainted with the rite of initiation of one major and comprehensive art, that of architecture. The initiation of the architect consisted in the drawing and knowledge of a symbolic diagram which is a site plan and ground plan, the Vāstupuruṣamaṇḍala.[13] It is the diagram of existence here on earth. In its symmetry and proportions are stationed all the powers that are active in the cosmos and in man. Their hierarchy is conveyed by their definite allocation on the plan. The plan is a kind of module which has to be applied to any architectural enterprise. Moreover, its meaning is made explicit by its myth, the myth of the Vāstupuruṣa. The myth tells of the condition of man here on earth, of existence itself—of which the plan is a symbol—the cause of his state which is a fall from heaven, and the dangers of this state which are turned into opportunities for the aspirations and ascent of man. The aim of initiation in general, and the architect's initiation in particular, is a waking up of the latent possibilities of the being so that he rises above individual concerns and takes part in the plan of the Great Architect of the Universe.

Each craft has an initiation imparted through the idiom of that craft. For the painter, the free hand drawing of certain abstract curves and curvilineal configurations serves this purpose. These curves are the root form of any design, whether abstract, symbolic, or making use of the shapes of nature. Such curvilineal configurations were the essentials of art teaching in Sinhalese art into the nineteenth century. They are nearly identical with configurations carved in Rajasthan, on a temple of the fifteenth century at Ranakpur.

At all times, and in villages to this day, the craftsman was an organic element of society. He was either a member of a village community or, if he lived in a city, he was a member of a guild of merchant craftsmen living in their own streets and quarters, or else he was a feudal servant of a king, nobleman, or head of a religious order.

In the village, already at the time of the compilation of the jātakas, the craftsman was either the only one of his calling in the community, or else craftsmen of one kind associated in villages of their own; for instance, in a village of 1500 carpenters or 1000 smiths. If he was the only one of his calling in a village, he made his living by an exchange of his service for those of villagers of an equal occupational standing, whereas fixed allotments were made to him from the higher groups, grants of land and other concessions such as free residence, food, and clothing. Perquisites were given on special occasions, but cash payments were rare. Part of the profits of the villager was the share of the king. According to Manu, the king took a five percent tax on objects sold. Security and contentment would, on the whole, have ruled in the village community whereas in the professional villages, competition was keen and rewards uneven. In a twelfth-century inscription from Chingleput,[14] a carpenter refers to himself as owner of the better half of the land of the carpenters in the village. Every craftsman was a cultivator. The state craftsmen, who worked and stayed within the fort at the palace, had land settled on them which was looked after by their family. Other craftsmen came to the palace, or to a religious order, for definite assignments, but worked generally from their own home for local demand. Inscriptions like one of Tanjore, of Rājarāja, the Chola king (985–1018) register the lands assigned to a master carpenter, to other carpenters, goldsmiths, and jewel stitchers.

The craftsmen, other than those of the village community which was self-sufficient, were organized in guilds (śreṇi). These were powerful bodies, particularly in the great cities, some of which were world markets. Although according to *Manu,* 8.41, the king establishes the laws of the guilds, and according to the *Nigrodha Jātaka,* the king's treasurer was the judge of all the guilds, an office established at the time of the redaction of the jātakas—still, according to another jātaka (6.427), the guild of painters laid down its own laws to be respected by the king.

Hereditary officers governed the guilds; membership of a guild was also hereditary. When the son had mastered his father's craft, he took his place in the guild. Each guild comprised all the practitioners of one craft, irrespective of their caste. The income of the guild came from the fees which newcomers had to pay and from fines in case of infringements of rules. The guild laid down the hours and amount of work; they maintained standards of living and of quality, both of material and of design. These, and all contracts were supervised by them, and they negotiated with other guilds. They had standing provisions for helping their members when in need, and sometimes increased their funds by levying contributions on looms or anvils. They collected, also, a certain percentage of sales or profits, or levied a tax on their members' work at a particular temple, for the maintenance of the temple. The guilds, sometimes also contributed the work of their members as a gift to a sacred monument, as did the ivory workers of the town of Vidiśā, in Sanchi of the first century A.D. In that particular case, their work was superlative and by far exceeded the work of the foreman of the artisans of the royal workshop of the Āndhra king, Śatakarṇī, on the same monument. Collective monuments, the work of guilds from various regions, and of individual craftsmen irrespective of caste and creed, and subscribed to by all possible strata of the people, were dedicated to God, whatever his name. This is how the craftsmen were able to give back to Viśvakarmā what he had given them. On the social level, the guilds were represented at public functions when they appeared, for instance, in the amphitheater of Mathura, as described in the *Harivaṁśa,* at the performance of a mythical play. Their pavilions were decorated with flags bearing the implements and emblems of the various crafts.

The king was the foremost patron of the arts. Under Emperor Aśoka (275–231 B.C.), capital punishment was inflicted on any person who impaired the efficiency of a craftsman by causing the loss of a hand or an eye.

There were artists among the kings: Mahendravarman, the Pallava king (seventh century), who called himself a tiger among painters; Akbar, the Great, who was the spiritus rector of his imperial workshops; and other lesser ones, kings who "girt up their loins" carrying out decoration work set as tasks by the sovereign at the marriage of a princess, to which companies of skilled artists had been summoned from every country, as described in the *Harṣacarita*[15] (seventh century). Although royalty was not necessarily confined to the Kshatriya caste, it is enjoined in the *Samarāṅgaṇasūtradhāra* that Meru, the loftiest of all temples, must have a Kshatriya for its patron, while the architect should be a Vaishya or Brahman. A Kshatriya, however, though versed in the science of architecture, must by no means be the architect (SRSu 56:35–43). This injunction is magically motivated. The virtue, or merit, that is in the work of art is communicated to the patron. Without the artist, who works for the patron, that merit would not be there. The magic transfer of merit, the acquisition of a spiritual value, is ritually transmitted to the patron when the work of art becomes his own. The bond of the work with the maker is severed when he receives his remuneration in gold, clothes, and ornaments from the patron. Were they both of the same caste, the transfer would not be complete—a common bond would remain.

The patron who wants to build a village, palace, temple, or bathing pond should select a guru (according to *Śilparatna*) and a śilpin. The name for the patron is yajamāna, the sacrificer, as it has been in Vedic times. The guru who is the architect-priest, the sthāpaka, or ācārya, performs the sacrificial rites for him. It is he who conceives the building to be and who directs the designing architect, the sthapati, or kartṛ, the actual "maker" of the building. With him are associated three other craftsmen: the surveyor, sūtragrahin; the sculptor, takṣaka; and the overseer-plasterer-painter, the vardhakin. The surveyor is the son or disciple of the designing architect, and works under his orders; the sculptor, it is said, should work on his own initiative and in obedience to the designing architect. Here, as throughout all the work, stress is laid on the superlative work, the quality of inspiration which transmutes skill and competence into a formal statement of Principle. This ultimate quality cannot be taught. It is released by the rite of the craftsman's initiation and supported by his entire training. Flawless execution of the rules is one of the conditions, but it does not make the true work of art. The vardhakin, the fourth in the team of craftsmen, consults with the surveyor. All these artists should be honored, for by their creative work and during its execution their status is sacerdotal.

Apart from technical competence, the qualifications of the designing architect are: knowledge of the architectural scripture and of the principles of the other traditional sciences. He should be perfect in body, righteous, kind, free from jealousy, and well born. He should know mathematics and the purāṇas, painting, the various countries, be of a happy disposition, his senses under control, clad in a dhoti and scarf. He should have firm friends. The guru should be a Brahman of high birth, he should know the essence of Vedas and Āgamas, be an initiate, ardent in his work and well versed in Śilpa Śāstra. Their collaboration begins with the ploughing of the ground on which the building is to be. The plough is consecrated by the touch of the guru, the chief architect ploughs the first three rounds. They both perform the rites of ploughing, and Shudras complete the work (*Mānasāra* 5.25). The distinction is made between the craftsmen and the laborers, though unskilled manual labor itself, when it was for a sacred purpose, was performed by members of all castes from the highest downward. Citizens and villagers collected earth from riverbanks and fields (according to *Hayaśīrṣa Pañcarātra*) or they conveyed stone beams for the construction (as for the temple of Sucīndram).

The prestige of the chief architect was high; princes of distant countries came to consult him. They put on splendid garments for their visit and brought presents in their own hands. The anonymity of the Indian craftsman is relative to his task. He has left his ego behind and gives his creative powers to his work. The anonymous builder of the stupendous Kailāsanātha temple of the eighth century in Ellora exclaimed in wonder when he had completed his work: "O, how did I make it?";[16] whereas some craftsmen inscribed their names as a challenge to others to do it better, for they had done their best.

Families of architects are known to us by their work over the centuries. The Bhangora family went from Gujerat to Rajasthan to build for the royal patrons in Mewar, from the fourteenth to the seventeenth century.[17] Maṇḍana was their outstanding member. He built the Kīrtistambha in Chitor (1440–80) and is the author of textbooks (*Rūpamaṇḍana, Vāstu-Rājavallabhā,* etc.) which are still in use by the traditional architects of western India. We also know of patrons and gurus, successive heads of a monastic order, the Saiddhāntikas of Mattamayūra, who, from the ninth to eleventh centuries, built monasteries and temples still in existence all over central India from the west coast to Magadha and laid down their teaching in a detailed textbook of the craft, the *Īśānaśivagurudevapaddhati.*[18] In this book the sustaining power of Tradition and its meaning are expressed by the rites performed when the sthāpaka, the guru, installs the temple. He places in it the seed (bīja) of the temple. While the temple was built, the seed, the causal creative image of the temple, dwelt in the heart-lotus of the guru. On completion of the building, the seed is ritually brought from the heart of the guru and placed in the temple. This seed is consciousness itself (cit). It is then that the sthapati, the architect, gives the entire merit to the patron, for says the same text, "Brahmā himself is the Architect."

II
UNKNOWN INDIA

3 Indian Terracottas

AGELESS TYPES AND TIMED VARIATIONS

The chronology of Indian terracottas has given rise to much speculation and several conclusions have been drawn from the existence of the various types.[1] "Primitive" types have been assigned an early and sometimes a prehistoric date.[2] The "primitive" types, however, are as frequent at Mohenjo-daro in the third millennium B.C. as they are in the Ganges Valley, etc., from the Śuṅga to the Gupta period, (pl. 3-1.1–10) that is, roughly before and during the first half of the first millennium A.D., and their number is not less today, made as they are by the potters and women in the villages of Bengal, Bihar, and so on. Altogether, it is not here a question of any temporal conditions. It is a question not of sequence but of principle. The principle involved is that of ageless types and timed variations. The timeless types persist, essentially changeless; the timed variations result from impresses which the passing moment leaves on them (pls. 3-2, 3-3).

The two types occur side by side on the various levels of the different excavations. Today also the two types continue to be made, the one as "primitive" as ever, the other with all the attributes of style and local adaptations.

If an analogy of these two types of artifacts is sought within the more impressive range of "works" in stone, the changing spectacle of the temples and their images ranges on the one side, the innumerable and changeless liṅgas and Śālagrāma stones (ammonites) on the other. The recorded kinds of liṅgas have not undergone any essential change; today as ever the emblem of Śiva is understood in its implications, and it depends on the extent to which the devotee is qualified to realize some, or all, of them. The same is true about

This essay first appeared in *JISOA* 7 (1939):89–110, and is reprinted here by permission.

the Śālagrāma stone, emblem of Vishnu. The perfection of its form is not due to the work of man. Such as it is, it is shaped by nature.

These observations compel us to view afresh the field of objects of Indian art and cult. There are the ageless types and their timed variations. The latter have hitherto attracted all the attention. The former, if less spectacular and of little interest to an observer of form, are neither less in number nor in importance to the people who make and use them; their unchanging appearance is the work of man or of nature.

The makers then of these objects are: nature and human beings, and among the latter, trained craftsmen who were efficient in work in stone and terracotta. To them are due the many varieties of images and figures fashioned in stone or clay. The village potters make the pots which are in daily use and also those in which dwell the gods; they also make some of their images and the toys. The latter are also made by the women for use in their own household.

The Śālagrāma stone, a black, ovoid or cylindrical shape as emblem and seat of Vishnu, is conclusively perfected in its natural form as are all the other emblems of nature, the Tulsi plant, the holy basil *(Ocimum basilicum)*, or Bodhi trees of any species. In them the stuff they are made of and its shape are accepted as they are, as perfect. No other activity is necessary on the side of man than his entering into a relation with them which makes them effective receptacles of spiritual influences. This is done by rites of consecration. The Śālagrāma stone, in its wholeness round as an egg, becomes a sacred object. The stone, however, needs to be shaped by man, if taken as a fragment of the natural completeness of the hill where it had been quarried, so as to regain wholeness in his hands and by his art. Definite rules are laid down for this purpose so that intrinsic wholeness is established in the artifact by proportionate measurement. Only the craftsman trained in accordance with established tradition can transform the stone. The quality of the work is a conditional expression of the essence which dwells in and altogether fills the form. If the same craftsman also works in clay he transforms it as well, although the technique is another one according to the exigencies of the material. The latter, in the main, demands no tools for its being worked; it is fashioned directly by the hands; it retains its nature in the process. Clay is the essentially plastic and passive, that is, least resisting, material. It is a kind of earth. Earth (Sanskrit: bhū) is substance, the substance of all becoming, the matrix of things to be; it is shapeless itself and undifferentiated.

EARTH

In the process of becoming an "artifact," that is, in the conception by the craftsman, its parts are meted out according to proportionate measurement; differentiation of form[3] sets in, differentiation from the undifferentiated initial stage. Earth or clay is the primeval plastic material, the concrete correspondence of prakṛti, universal substance. That is its nature. In the hands of the person who works it, it becomes commuted into such symbols as are founded on the nature itself of the earth. Images of the "Great Mother" under one name or another are in the majority among the timeless clay symbols found in all the sites, and still made by the women and potters in the villages. Earth, the great mother, is frequently beheld under her aspect as Ṣaṣṭhī[4] and her clay figures are made without cease. Her other names are Aditi,[5] Śrī,[6] Sinīvālī[7]; the Vedas and Brāhmanas express her power; she is the great womb, that which sustains, supports, and contains all.

Mahāmāi, the Great Mother, is known to all; the barest allusion to her feminine appearance suffices and may as well be omitted altogether. Her original shrine is an earthen platform with seven knobs of colored clay at the head.[8] In this instance the knobs carry their meaning in their shape which is that of the sphere, the comprehensive shape of "fullness." It is for their shape also that clods of earth are given as offerings to certain other symbols, to a small mount for instance, erected by the roadside in honor of Dhelhā or Dhelwā Gosāin or Pīr, the "Saint of clods."[9] Every passerby offers such a clod. Every man can shape it. The material easily acquires roundness in the hand of every man and its symbolism is founded on its nature.

A more specialized kind of "everyman" is the village potter; he also makes the timeless symbols in clay. And it is in the nature of the "earth" itself, that women, even if not particularly trained in the craft, should make of it figures which carry an ageless and traditional meaning and which need not change their shape to be properly understood and used by the going and coming generations.

All this applies to toys and images. There is no considerable, if any, difference between the ageless types of figures, human or animal by suggestion, whether they are to be worshipped or played with. The function of the timeless figure is not in itself determined. It becomes so by the relation established with the person who uses it. The meaning of these objects themselves does not change. They are toys to the child and, once they are consecrated, images to the worshiper. By his virtue he then comes up to the total which they symbolize; the child, in its own world, has a similar relation to them. To the Indian child and to the grown-up people in the villages and at all times in Indian tradition, the same things are real, to each according to his power of understanding. There are no "fairy tales for children," and there is no sacred preserve in an otherwise profane world. The ritual of life is binding on everyone from birth to death, and links him with the whole, of which his human presence is an emblem. The earth is another. It is one of the eight forms of Śiva; in the Śāstras it is prescribed to ask forgiveness before planting the foot on the earth after getting up from bed at daybreak.[10] The touch of the hand is not in need of this rite. It performs its own rite in accordance with tradition when following an implicitly understood and, in this respect spontaneous, practice.

The timeless types are made by hand; no mold intervenes between the clay and the maker. They comprise human and animal figures and also chariots; no vegetation forms occur in the ancient sites nor are they made today. The unchanging principle according to which the figures are fashioned reduces the existence of their prototypes to a distribution of simple volumes corresponding to the bulk of body, head, and limbs. By rounding off or flattening, by drawing into points and pinching, by incising lines and affixing pellets (pl.

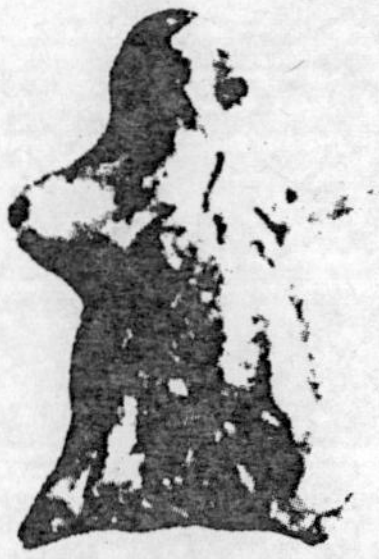

3-1.1

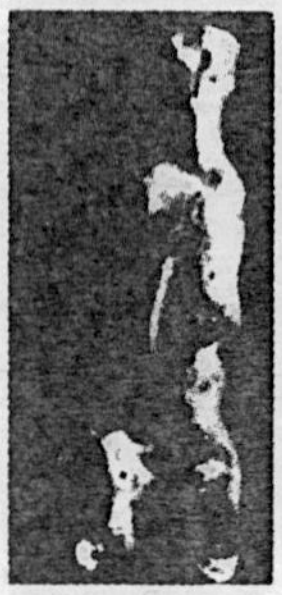

3-1.2

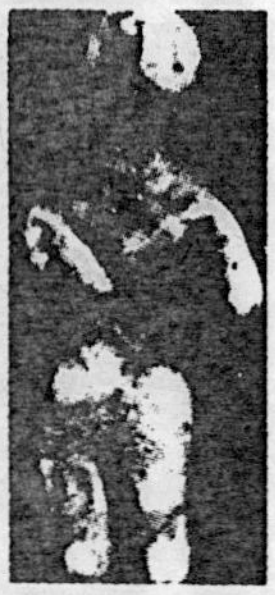

3-1.3

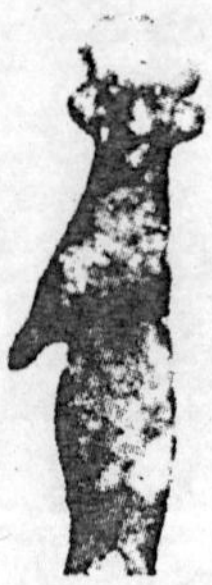

3-1.4

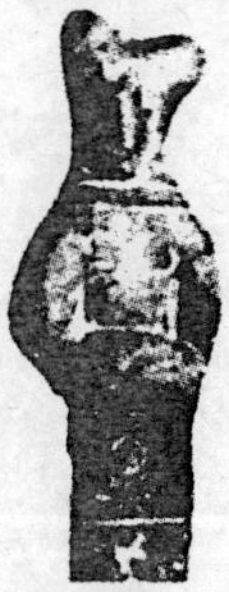

3-1.5

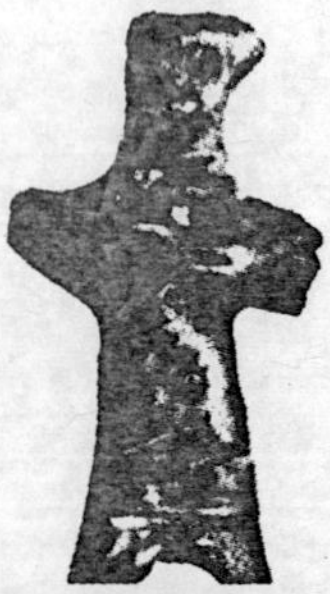

3-1.6

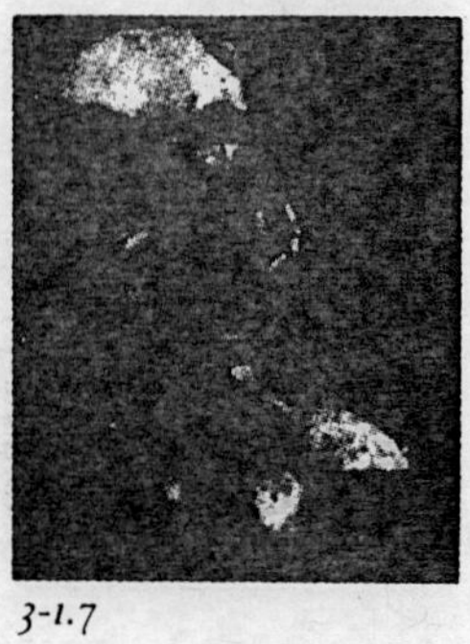

3-1.7

3-1.1–10, 12) the clay is shaped: by the pressure of the hand and such resistance as the substance of the clay offers, its weight yields to the touch. The absence of limbs, arms, or legs, or the fact that they are made as short conical stumps, shows these figurines in the process of acquiring distinct form; they are stages toward rūpa-bheda, differentiation of form.[11]

The figurines (pl. 3-1.1–3) from Buxar, Patna, and Taxila respectively, are some of the possibilities within one type, "star-shaped," with or without arm or leg stumps, more or less drawn out, the entire volume more or less flattened.[12] Plate 3-1.4–6 from Pāṭaliputra are more smooth and flat with lines and ringlets incised; they have animal snouts and horns or spade-like protuberances of the head; these indicate their nonhuman significance; whereas plate 3-1.1–3 may suggest the children, under the protection of Ṣaṣṭhī; they are modeled today clinging to the ample expanses of her fictile images. The spade-shaped head (pl. 3-1.4) does not only belong to these figurines (pl. 3-1.4); it is frequent with female types, from Mohenjo-daro (pl. 3-1.7) and Kauśāmbī (pl. 3-1.9) for example. The importance of the head shape and of the headdress, amplified and detailed in the timebound varieties of female figurines and plaques, will be dealt with further on.

Plate 3-1.8 from Pāṭaliputra, shows the technique of affixed pellets which had been current in the Harappa culture type (pl. 3-1.7), and it has also the slim body without the waist or the hips being especially emphasized. The majority of the female terracotta types outside the Harappa culture combine the notions of potential motherhood and thin-waisted elegance and this is shown by the overstatements in clay, such as plate 3-1.10 and also by a lead plaque (pl. 3-1.11), both from Pāṭaliputra. The latter presents not only the navel which has creative significance and the "mekhalā," but it has also a large, raised crescent which marks with lunar symbolism the place of formation of individual existence.[13]

Flat plaques with serpent heads (pl. 3-1.12)[14] have also the ample hips and thin waist and are distinctly female types. Without arms, and with legs which are barely more than stands for the vase-shaped hip region, they are earthen types in which the "taking shape" is at the same time a technical and a conceptual process. It is equivalent with passages in the Ṛg Veda in which the procession of the sun, or that of dawn (uṣas) is worded. "This footless-maid came earliest forth to footed things." (*RV* 6.59, 6). According to Dr. Coomaraswamy "that is as much as to say that she who had been a 'serpent' now assumes an angelic-human form."[15] In current use, the benign and malevolent aspect of the serpent is recognized, for instance in Bundelkhand, as form of Devī, of the mother goddess.[16]

Such is the emblem of "becoming," of the earth, bhū, of the procession from darkness to light, and also of vāc (voice, word), "which is this earth."[17] Vāc and earth are called Sarparājñī, serpent queen in the *Śatapatha Brāhmaṇa* 4.6.9.16–17. The Sarparājñī hymn (*RV* 10.189.1–3) is also called mānasa stotra, mental laud.[18]

Manasā, the serpent goddess, is worshiped in Bengal anthropomorphically, shaped as a woman wielding serpents, and emblematically as an earthen vessel, often surrounded and surmounted by serpent shapes which issue from it. She is also worshipped as a branch of her sacred tree, Siju *(Euphorbia).*

"Manas," the internal sense,[19] the mental, is not pure intellect; it is not the ultimate consciousness but is the property of man as thinking being, as individuality; it is discursive and reflective. In order to attain the ultimate state of pure consciousness, the functioning of the mental, which is a delimiting, through reason and imagination, has to be stabilized and dissolved and finally becomes extinct.[20]

Manasā is not herself given serpent shape; in both her modes of being fashioned she holds the serpents, in her hands, or as a vessel. She presides over the ambiguity of the serpent, its beneficial and malign potentiality and is herself free from serpent shape. All that the earthen vessel of Manasā has in common with the female serpent emblems in terracotta found in Pāṭaliputra, Buxar, Kauśāmbī, and so on, and belonging to the Śuṅga and Kuṣāṇa phases (i.e., about 100 B.C.–A.D. 100 and later) is the association of the female with the serpent element. The plaque pl. 3-1.12 combines the two in one form. The serpent's head is there on the top, and the transition from serpent to human form begins at the bottom, in the rudimentary feet. On it rests the vessel-outlined body, the receptacle in which life is deposited and from which new life comes forth.

Differentiation as a function of the mind (manas), and the goddess Manasā; differentiation of form (rūpa-bheda) as for instance the evolving of a definite shape such as the hip region or vase shape; the serpent, along with

3-1. "Primitive" or timeless types of Indian terracottas

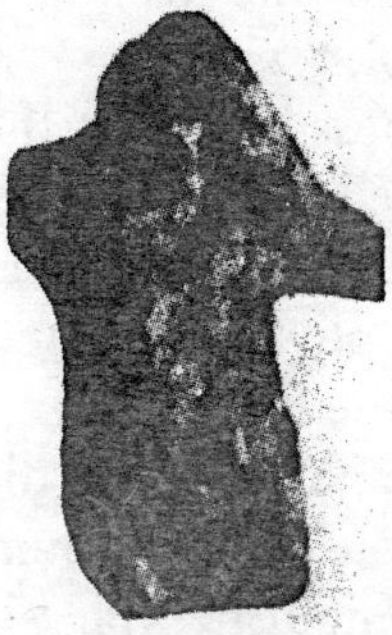

3-1.8

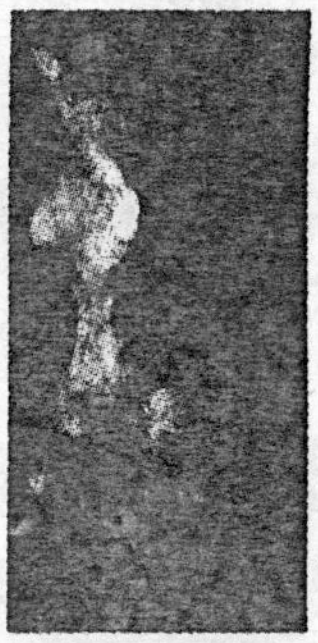

3-1.9

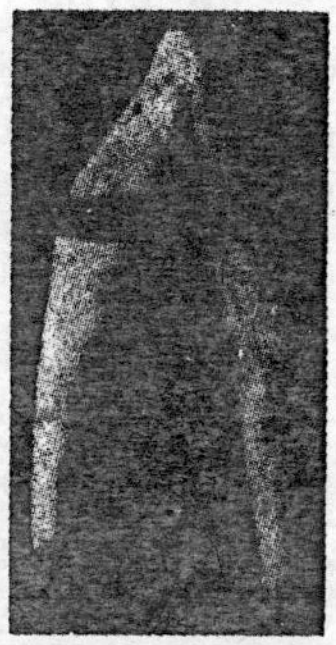

3-1.10

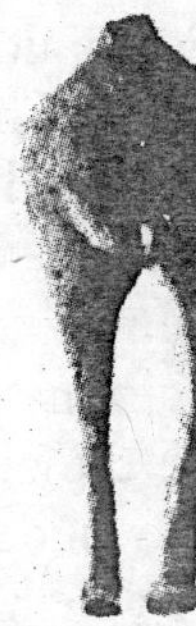

3-1.11

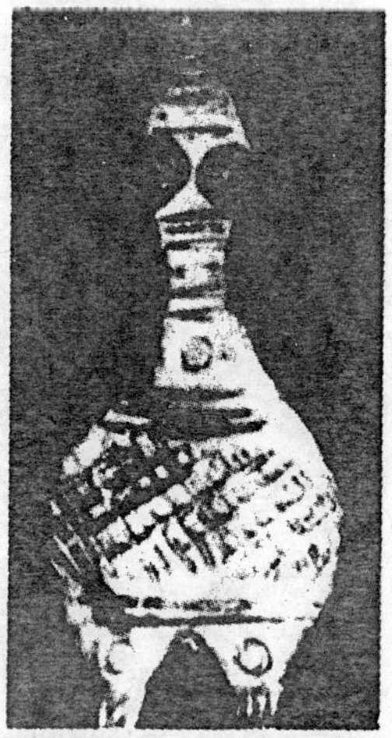

3-1.12

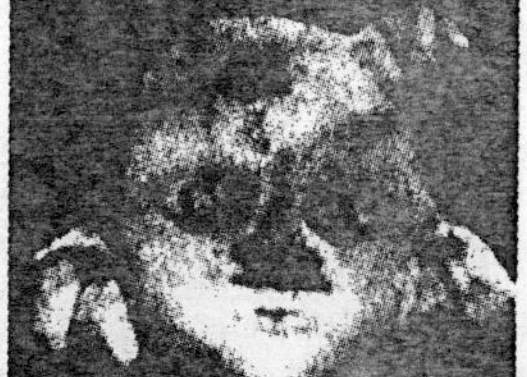

3-1.13

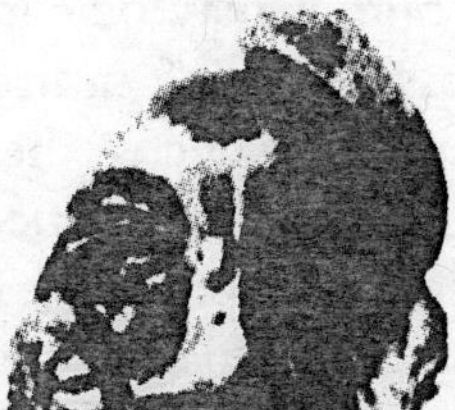

3-1.14

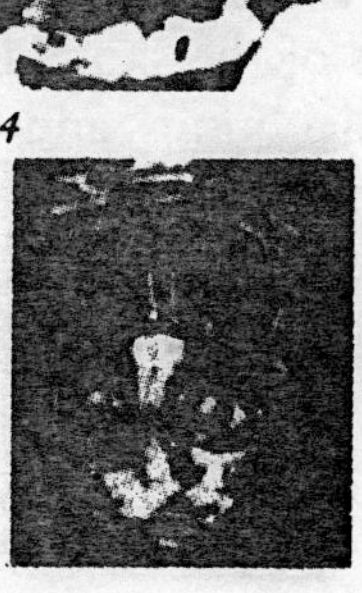

3-1.15

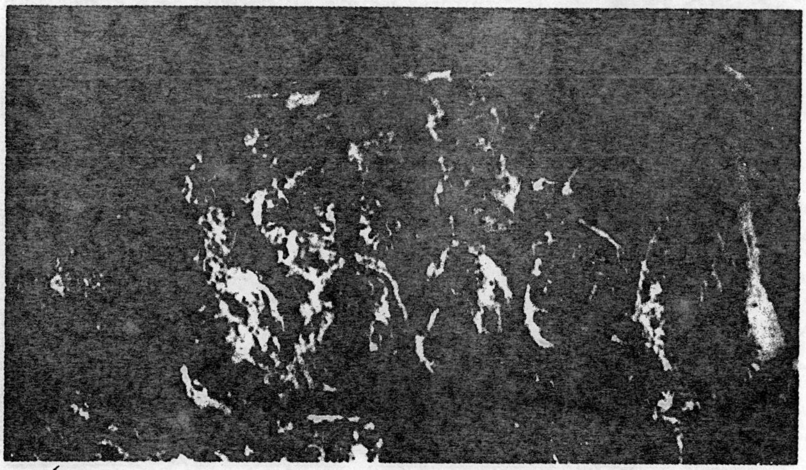

3-1.16

the vessel shape of body or cult object: all these are present in the making of these earthen forms. The material itself, earth, contributes its own fictile nature to the total symbolism.

The serpent as a form of the power of darkness, of the unmanifested, stands for primordial unity; Manasā effects its adjustment to the human level. This is a narrowing down and an application of its power, to the world of man.

PHYSIOGNOMY AND COSTUME

The deity in the darkness, unmanifested, is conceived of in theriomorphic shapes.[21] The figurines (pl. 3-1.4–6) have animal snouts. Physiognomy has to be understood from here in a wider sense than is customary. The "physis," that is, the "becoming," is here seen ontologically with reference to the state—the unmanifested—from where the traits originate in the otherwise "human" appearance. The head or skull is given special importance. It is drawn out into horn shapes. These are disguised in the time-bound varieties of terracottas, as headdress for instance in the Buxar types,[22] and also from Kauśāmbī,[23] and Basarh (pl. 3-2.1, 2) and from Pāṭaliputra (pl. 3-3.5) where bicornate or unicorn arrangements are most elaborate on the female types, whereas turbans or their rudiments are employed in a similar way on the head of male figures, from Pāṭaliputra (pl. 3-1.13, 14) and Mathura[24] (pl. 3-2.12).

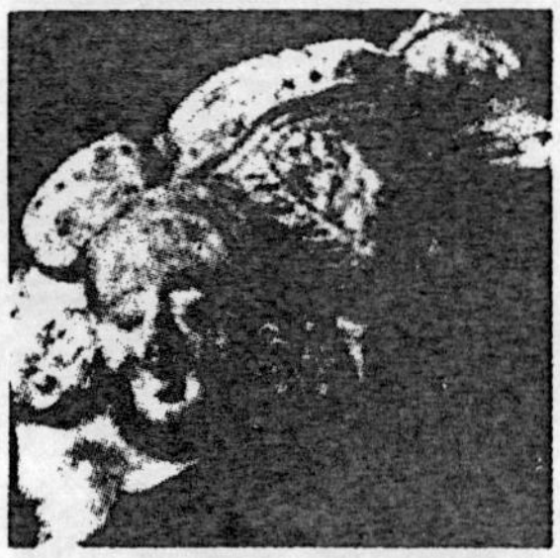

3-2.1

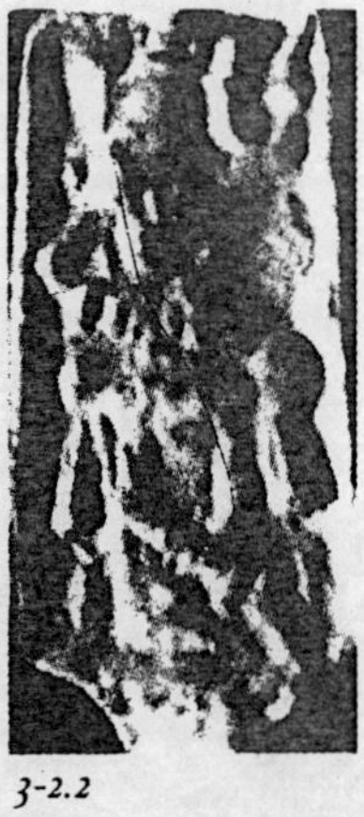

3-2.2

3-2. Timed variations of Indian terracottas

The head is the seat of the higher possibilities of the human being. If endowed with the nonphysical mount of the Uṣṇīṣa,[25] this is situated at a place where according to Indian tradition the human state is left and the more-than-human state is entered, at the moment of physical extinction or of spiritual illumination. It is one of the main signs on the Buddha image and visible when no crown is added. A capacious forehead and skull also distinguish the head of a Buddha, but they are equally conspicuous on the innumerable terracottas, of which a few are illustrated here (female figurines, pl. 3-3). The wide dome of the skull in these figurines and plaques frequently bulges out with lateral bumps, where no "horns" are added. The bumps may be considered a lesser variety of the horns and reduced to the possibilities of anthropomorphic appearance (pl. 3-3.1). In order to achieve a special shape of the head, the skull of the infant is artificially molded in actual practice, for instance in Midnapore, Bengal.[26] The crowns (mukuṭa) carved without exception on all Hindu images encompass such transformed heads. The contents which, while still within the head reach up to the more-than-human levels, shine forth as luminous ray or flame[27] and are visible outside the compass of the skull, also as horns. While still within the head they dilate it into cranial bumps and protuberances. The horns in their theriomorphic implications are the highest residues of the dark "ab intra" aspect which otherwise (pl. 3-1.4–6) also shapes the face of some of these types: at the same time the horns shine forth from the head alike to the rays of sun and moon.

The veil (pl. 3-3.5; from Pāṭaliputra) covers a broad and high conical shape; its central point has the height of the headdress worn to this day by

Banjāra women.[28] The stick put on the apex of the Banjara woman's head is called "singh," i.e., horn.[29] It is given to the woman at marriage. The hair is wound around it and a head cloth is wrapped over it.[30] This "unicorn" variety of the headdress is also favored by the royal ladies of the Ye-tha country and by the women of Hi-mo-ta-lo.[31] The Vedic headdress opaśa might belong to this class.[32] The bicornate headdress is still worn in different ways in Kafiristan and also by other tribes in the Hindu Kush.[33] Terracotta figurines and plaques have it either symmetrical[34] or else with a larger shape or "pouch" on the left. The turbans worn by male types have also the left side more developed, or the "horn" or "turban" is altogether confined to the left side of the skull (pl. 3-1.13, 14, from Pāṭaliputra).

Strands of hair, ribbons, and ornamented plaques make up the enormous pouches or "wings" into which the bicornate headwear bulges in a number of varieties which, each in its own way, belongs to a particular site. Apart from the many specimens of varied type from Pāṭaliputra and Buxar, the most explicit headdress is molded on a plaque, now in the Indian Institute, Oxford, and which must have come from Kauśāmbī.[35] On the right and lesser of the two pouches of her headdress, and along its edge are shown five devices; each of them differs from the others and is placed on top of an amalaka-shaped knob. It appears as if these devices were pinheads, stuck into the beaded and ornamented hair. Five corresponding devices similarly are shown, on the left of the other and lesser fragment from Kauśāmbī. Some of the devices are similar to those current on silver punch marked coins;[36] they are (1) aṅkuśa, (2) a kind of triśūla capped by a horizontal device, (3) an arrowhead; the arrow issues from a vertical pole, (4) a triśūla similar to 2, but capped by a triangular device, (5) a blade-like device. Each of these symbols has a row of beads on top, and such bead chains are profusely laid also on the head,[37] and elsewhere. They are bindu maṇḍalas, garlands of dots. "By knowing the undiminishing bindu maṇḍala the performer attains salvation, the eternal peace.[38] Even if the full significance of the bindu, the dot,[39] was not present to the makers and users of this and other plaques, some of its implied meaning was beheld in connection with that of the other symbols.

The symbols are worn as crests on one pouch-like "horn" of the headdress, of a female figure of lavish beauty and apparel. Such crests are called cūḍa. Śiva, who wears the moon on his Jaṭāmukuṭa, in his braided hair, is called Candracūḍa (moon-crested).[40] The crescent moon is Śiva's share of the products churned from the ocean.[41] The meanings of cūḍa are: protuberance, crest, tuft of hair. The cūḍāmaṇi is a jewel worn on the crest of the head; the cūlāmaṇi-cetiya in the heaven of the thirty-three gods houses the jewel crested turban which the Buddha cast into the air.[42]

Pañcacūḍā, that is, having five crests, is an Apsaras produced at the churning of the ocean.[43] The gods churn the drink of immortality as "quintessence" from the milky sap of the world ocean. They also churn the Pārijāta tree which satisfies all desires, the cup of the moon, the lotus, and others. The Apsaras Rambhā, who is called Pañcacūḍā, is also one of these wish-fulfilling embodiments.[44] On her head she wears five symbols of auspicious meaning.[45] That they are five in number agrees with the general significance of the number five, which is the number of vegetation (flowers have mostly five petals), the symbol of earthly life, the number of Aphrodite; its emblem is the pentagon, pañcakoṇa; it kills all sins. Should the Pañcacūḍā of the two Kauśāmbī plaques enable us to identify the female figure wearing them as the Apsaras Pañcacūḍā, many similar figurines and plaques could be taken to be Apsarases, and especially the alluring, time bound varieties.

CONVEYANCE

Before a survey of the timed variations is made, the ageless types of animal figurines will be considered. They are molded by hand, and reduce the proportions of the respective animal species to those of cylinders, cones, and like geometrical shapes representing their bodies and limbs. The same animals, elephants, horses, and so on, are also molded, subject to the variations of style at the different sites and at different periods (pl. 3-2.4, 5). The supernatural animals, the griffins (pl. 3-2.3; cf. Sanchi, west gate, south pillar) are molded according to the style of the timed varieties. A more explicit description is required to make them recognizable, then lies within the scope of the timeless types. In general, the timed varieties are molded, the ageless types are modeled by hand in large numbers. The single figurines in themselves did matter but little and they could always be replaced. They may not always have been baked, and dissolved into the earth of which they were made.

The main terracotta animals are: horse, elephant, and ram; and other quadrupeds such as the humped bull, the monkey, in Mathura especially, dog, and so forth; furthermore birds, lizards, and frogs, fish and Makara. There are chariots with bulls, and rams used as "tricycles." Horses and elephants, or the spirits of these animals,[46] are the vehicles of the spirits in the villages in India today. In life, the human body is the conveyance. Clay figures of horses and elephants are offered for instance to Ghanaśyāma, one of the chief deities of the Gonds and allied tribes. He was killed by a tiger soon after his wedding. Brahmans who have died a violent death and whose spirits are especially powerful are being presented with clay figurines of the same animals which are placed under a Banyan tree.[47]

The south (dakṣiṇā) is the region of Yama (death). The Dakṣiṇāyana, the southern passage of the sun,[48] is the Pitṛyana. Along it move the ancestors,

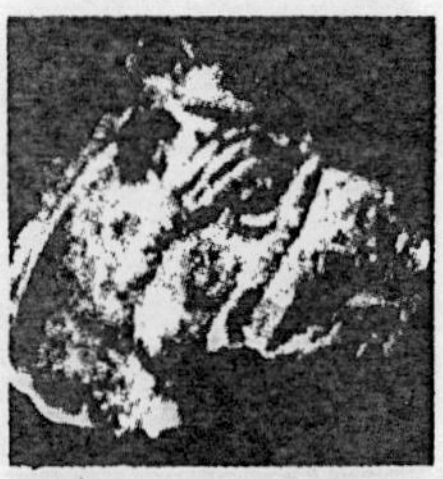

3-2.3

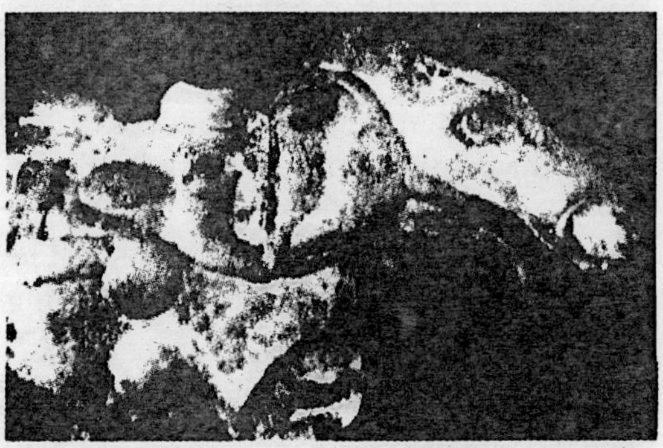

3-2.4

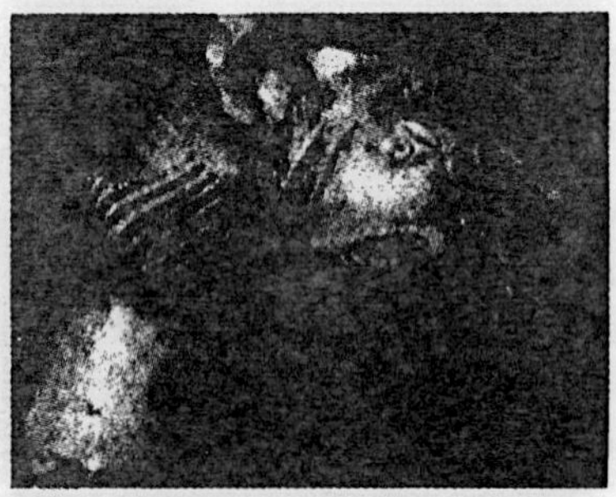

3-2.5

the Pitṛs, on the way of transmigration. Yama, the Pitṛpati (lord of the manes) and Pretarāja (king of the ghosts) is the son of the sun. Horses draw the chariot of the sun. The terracotta horses are the vāhanas of the Pitṛs who are lorded over by Yama, son of the sun; doubly the horses are related to the sun, in its southern course. The sun sinks into the netherworld and rises from the lap of death in the east. The elephant, vāhana of Indra, the recoverer of light, is the guardian of the east.

Elephants, richly caparisoned, and horses are in the nightly procession of the Vetāla (by whom a dead body hanging from a tree is possessed) in the *Vetālapañcaviṁśati*. The terracotta horses and elephants are often caparisoned and especially the elephants are decked out more or less lavishly. On a fragment of an elephant figurine (light grey terracotta with black slip, Śuṅga date) found at Kauśāmbī (Kosam) (pl. 3-1.16), a rug is impressed vertically with alternating rows of circular devices consisting of radial lines around a circle around a dot,[49] and a not quite distinct figure;[50] along its two edges, five ovals hold each a figure with inflated body and a long thin snout. These are figures of Pretas, of the ghosts of the dead. During the year between death and the final judgment of Yama, these feeble creatures suffer from thirst; their body is inflated and they have a pointed snout with a pin prick opening too small to quench its thirst.[51] A Preta cannot touch the ground. They are carried on elephants and horses, offered to them.

The other animals are all vāhanas of the gods, or differently associated with them, as for instance the dove, the messenger of Yama, the god of death. The Makara, vehicle of Varuṇa and Gaṅgā, the elephant as vāhana of Indra, the horses of the sun, all are symbolic conveyances; their multiple meaning is interconnected. Every single animal figurine "conveyed" one or the other aspect. Such a conveyance is not only the animal but also the chariot and cart.[52]

As vehicle in either sense the ram is used and there are two leading types of the so-called "tricycle toys,"[53] one from Kauśāmbī, the other from Basarh. The ram is the vāhana of fire, Agni; its name, aja (agent), means "pushing, drawing, moving." All this it does partly with its horns as far as animal, and partly with its shape and use as "tricycle" which is holed so that wheels are easily attached to it.

On the ageless types, the passing generations have sometimes left their impress, not altogether with the definition of the timed varieties and yet sufficient to date them (pl. 3-1.13–15).[54] The multiple uses to which the ageless types lend themselves offer permanent opportunities for as many applications as there are epochs, localities, and persons trained according to the tradition of their craft.

TIMED VARIATIONS

1) Date and Technique

Some of the small terracotta figurines and plaques have been found in sanctuaries (Maniyar, Matha, Rajgir), others within or near buildings whose foundation walls do not reveal their religious or domestic characters. What matters most is that they were found in large numbers in many buildings of ancient towns, where they must have been in use. That the traditional types and the time-bound varieties occur beside one another is not surprising when it is known that today also the timeless types—female figurines for instance, with a solid cone as the body which affords a relatively large circle to stand on, with pinched faces, pellets affixed for the eyes and no mouth marked—can be found in the same household where Rādhā-Krishna figurines of a banal prettiness have their effect on the same people.

Some of the figurines are modeled on a flat plinth or on a hollow pedestal. Others have no such stand and the majority of plaques were made so as to lean against a wall. They seem to have been placed on shelves or in wall recesses, whereas not a few plaques of Śuṅga date have holes at the top for a cord to be threaded across, and thus to hang them on the wall.

The material of the terracottas is clay, carefully washed with an admixture of mica as the main gritty material to avoid cracking when fired. From the Kuṣāṇa period onward, though only in some varieties, the material is coarse, with a considerable admixture of chopped husks, and the like. The majority of Indian terracottas are baked to various shades of ocher and red; the shade depends on the chemical components in the material and also on the heat and the process of firing. If the air has free access during baking, the iron contained in the clay will be oxidized and this produces the red color; if, however, the combustion is imperfect, the terracotta is grey or black. The latter process is also widely practised; charcoal is kept glowing around an earthen vessel in which the clay object is surrounded and covered with husk. In order to intensify the color of the terracotta, a slip of deeper red color is applied to the red figures as a rule, while the grey-black figures have a rich and shiny black slip or coat of paint.

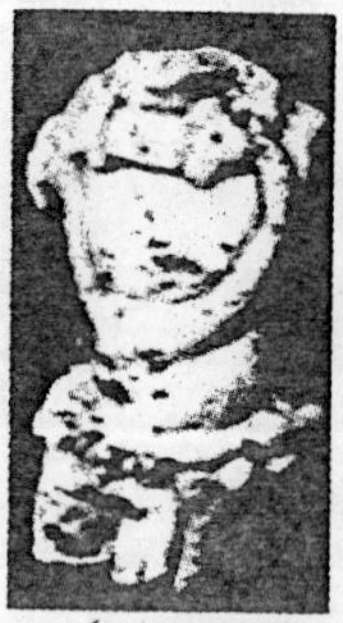

3-2.6

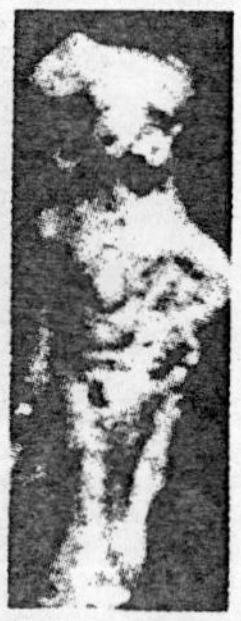

3-2.7

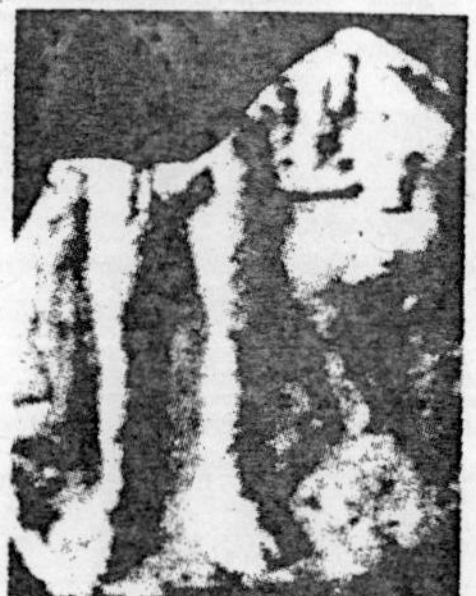

3-2.8

Most of the terracottas of Mathura, prior to the Gupta age, are grey-black, sometimes with a black slip which, however, comes off easily. In all the other sites, the majority of the terracottas show various reds, with red slip. Light grey terracotta objects, however, have also been found at Patna and Kauśāmbī. Objects of the same age, burned to a rich black color, come from Patna and Basarh, and the dark grey terracottas occur sporadically at Buxar, Patna, and other sites. The light grey ware, relatively heavy in weight, shows in most of the specimens traces of a thick black glaze; this moreover was daubed on with light ocher color. This type of decoration (on animal figurines) seems to belong to the late Maurya or Śuṅga age. The thick black glaze occurs also on a few red terracottas. The grey objects must not be taken as a whole to antedate the red ones. The ocher and red colors from Mohenjo-daro onwards are in the majority.

There are traces of polychrome coloring on Mohenjo-daro terracottas.[55] Some of the Pāṭaliputra figurines may have been colored; there is however no distinct trace left. Two fragments from Mathura, of the Śaka and Kuṣāṇa period, and now in the Patna Museum, show remnants of the silver and gold with which they were coated, or else the gold was employed in the polychromy of the plaque.

Neither the method of baking nor the technique of the figurines lend support to speculations about the sequence of the terracottas. From Mohenjo-daro and other Harappan sites on, modeling by hand and the use of molds was common. The former process persists in the timeless types.

In certain well-known series from Mathura and Buxar, the timeless type of body is modeled while the face is molded and dated in all its traits. This may be a technical expedient, for in many other cases only modeled heads are preserved, along with a tenon to be inserted into a body made of one or the other material of which no trace exists. It may, however, also mean that the body retains its timeless significance, whereas the face is "free" to assume any countenance, or none at all; it suffices that its position is marked. This paradox is documented by versions of the Gupta plaque with Pṛthivī from Bhita (*ASIAR* 1911–12, pl. 23, fig. 40), where the squatting feminine body is headed by a lotus flower instead of a face; the body itself is of the timed variety.

Molds, as a rule, are used for the timed variations. Molded faces and affixed headdresses and ornaments are common with all the figurines to which a relatively "early" date may be assigned. The complex and separately affixed devices however, give way later on to completely molded types. Yet even on "Gupta" heads the ear plaques are sometimes separately affixed. Among the later, that is, post-Śuṅga variety of terracottas, plaques remain in vogue, that is, only the front is pressed in the mold; the back, as a rule, is a plain and flat surface. During the Gupta age a type of plaque, very light in weight and of light ocher, is very frequent. From late Suṅga days the practice of molding only the head, along with a tenon, is also maintained. In larger figurines of human and animal shape, the head, as a rule, is massive and the body hollow. It is especially in the Gupta period that such heads are molded in two parts, front and back separately and joined laterally, whereas there are also attempts of molding the two halves separately and joining them along the ridge of the nose. None of the shapes (as observed already) into which the tenoned head was meant to be inserted has been recovered as yet.[56] From the Kuṣāṇa age onward larger heads, usually of a coarse material and provided with tenons, are frequent. They too are pressed in molds; the back frequently makes a curved surface. Also at the same time complete figures in the round, of relatively large size and very frequently representing Pañcika and Hārītī, are common. Grooves, holes in the pupils, and at the corners of the mouth are deepened after molding. A number of findplaces have yielded post-Gupta terracottas. In Belwa, for instance, the reduction of "Gupta" effects to conventional shapes is symptomatic. From our scanty knowledge of later terracottas it must not be thought that their production was diminished. The works of earlier centuries were protected underground and brought to light by excavations, whereas the figurines offered to the gods and worshiped by subsequent generations were exposed to the passing days and their vicissitudes; they were broken, and then forgotten, while fresh ones continued to be made. Large-sized heads from the vicinity of Benares, Belwa, and Gaya, belonging to different ages, have been found recently.

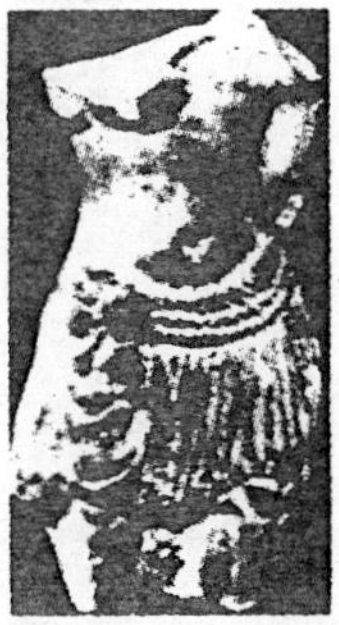
3-2.9

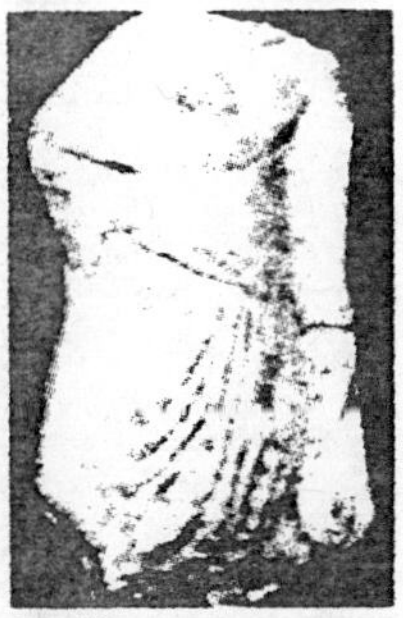
3-2.10

Terracotta figurines and plaques are but part of the output in clay modeling. Different types of clay figures are made for definite pūjās several times every year, and immersed in the rivers immediately afterwards. Temples such as Mirpur Khas, Bhitargaon, Chausa, and Paharpur of the Gupta and subsequent phases, most of which now are dust, had their surfaces covered with

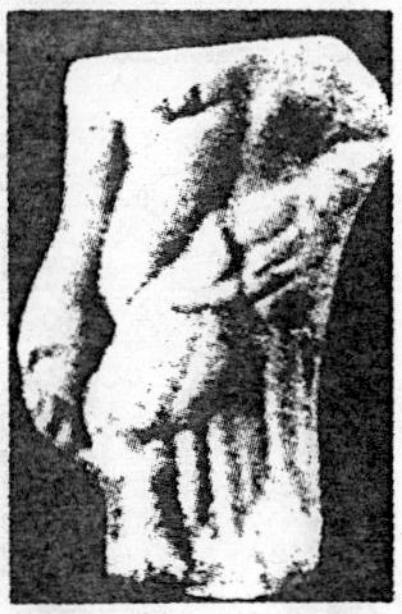
3-2.11

reliefs and figures in terracotta and brick. The tradition was maintained in Bengal till the last century (cf. also the upper stories of South Indian temples). The terracottas hitherto excavated are but a fraction of Indian work in clay; even so they represent an inventory of contemporary Indian form more complete than the stone sculptures give. None of the terracottas is inscribed, and the few inscriptions on stone objects found at some of the sites that have yielded small terracottas are not dated. Paleographically, two refer to the "Mauryan" age, the one on a stone ring excavated in Patna[57] at a level of fourteen feet; the other, on a fragment from a similar stone disc from Kauśāmbī, is in the collection of the Bharata Kalā Pariṣad, Benares. There are, also, inscribed seals from Buxar referable to the same age and others from Patna.[58]

Assuming even that in every instance the depth of the findspot has been accurately recorded, this does not help in any way toward fixing the date of the terracottas. In Basarh, Bulandibagh, and Kumrahar, for example, objects definitely of Kuṣāṇa "style" are found at a much lower depth than work that cannot be later than the late Śuṅga period and in several cases is anterior to it. Gupta terracottas also have been found at the same level as earlier work. There is no such thing as far as terracottas are concerned as a "Maurya level," or the like. The same molds may have been in use for some time. Still, few of the objects as yet found were made in the same mold. This, incidentally, shows that a very small fraction of the whole output is preserved at most of the sites.[59] Numbers of these small, light, and fragile objects, once damaged, may have been thrown away and accumulated in some pit. Earthquakes too are not infrequent, and account for the confusion underground. Some of the most important groups of terracottas, such as those from Mathura, Buxar, and to some extent also the outstanding figurines from Pāṭaliputra, have been assigned various dates.[60]

2) Places

Many recent excavations and finds (cf. *ASIAR* 1935–36, pl. 22, Lauriya Nandangarh; 36) in the northwest [Frontier Provinces, Pakistan—B.S.M.] (Sari-Dheri), from the United Provinces [Uttar Pradesh] to Bengal, in Central India [approximately Madhya Pradesh], and in Hyderabad (Maski) [now in Karnataka] have added a widened range to the possibilities within the timed varieties. Their local features are easily discernible. Each site had its own "manufacture" of the current varieties. These are relatively most distinct in three places, that is, Patna, Buxar, and Mathura. The plentiful recent finds from Kauśāmbī, Bhita, others from Gaya, Bangarh in Bengal, and so on, and also the former finds from Basarh, Set Mahet (Śrāvastī), and Pawaya (Gwalior) appear as local variations and adaptations of the types known from the three sites mentioned.

PĀṬALIPUTRA

The three sites of Bulandibagh, Kumrahar, and the "Patna" excavation are situated within the ancient Pāṭaliputra.[61] An inscribed steatite plaque has been found in the "Patna excavation" with Mauryan characters. This gives the only hitherto available and more or less definite indication toward a dating of some of the terracottas found in "Patna."

Female figures are more numerous than male, and this refers to the ageless types and to the timed and stylistically differentiated alike. The datable varieties are here assembled according to groups; a relative chronology is based on them. A standing figurine from Bulandibagh[62] appears to be the earliest among the standing figurines, the like of which has not been found outside Pāṭaliputra. Made of very fine and hard, grey-buff terracotta, the figurine but for the face was modeled by hand in several separate parts (plinth, costume, jewelry, headwear) which were affixed to the body before firing. There is no considerable affinity between the molded face and that of the carved and colossal shape of the Didarganj Yakṣī, which on grounds of style belongs approximately to the first century B.C. Physiognomically[63] closely related to this figurine is a head of a young girl. A sharpness of slanting surfaces meeting at angles and a somewhat heavy lower part of the face relate more to stone carvings from Bharhut, for instance this bicornate head, than to those of the Maurya phase.

This head is to some extent akin in treatment to carved stone heads from Sarnath.[64] With almost equally "abstract," that is "post" shaped legs as those of the above mentioned figurines, some others show slim and well disciplined bodies with the most delicate touches of modeling on the chest. Skirts of this type of figurines are extravagant with hoops and a flutter that is telling.[65] Greek terracotta figurines—long after the Nike of Paionios—were made in the third century B.C., the skirt forming molds and flutings with less regularity, but more alive with actual movement.[66] The invasion of Pāṭaliputra by Eucratidas, about 175 B.C.[67] may have been instrumental in refreshing the knowledge of Greek art which some of the craftsmen of Pāṭaliputra might have had of types current in Greece some time ago. This knowledge came to stay.

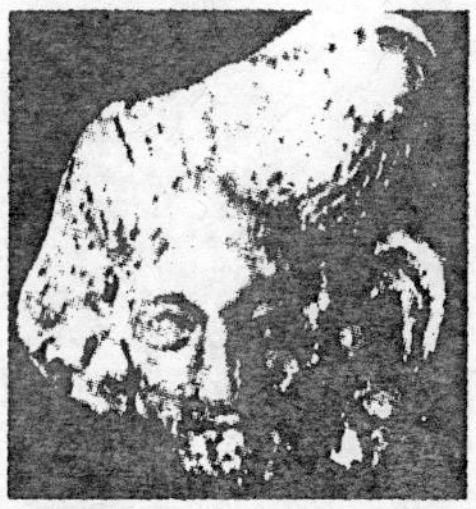

3-2.12

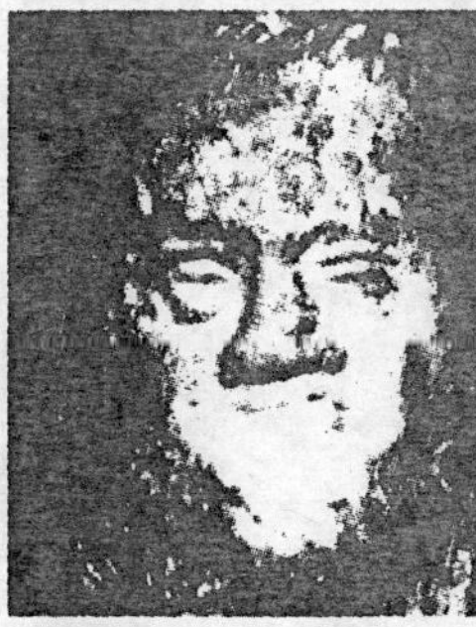

3-2.13

All the figurines have an excessive width and height of the head with lateral bumps, which may be exposed and accentuated even further by the headwear, horns, or turban, or hidden away behind its volume. In the later Śuṅga phase the hair is shown cut in steps with a trapezoidal or zigzag outline against the forehead, not only in Pāṭaliputra, but also in the other findplaces of terracottas. Another mode of emphasizing the very high head is characteristic of very young boyish figures; one of them is carried by a large female figure (from Bulandibagh), another is standing (pl. 3-2.7; top of headdress broken), another young figure (from Patna) is seated in a yogin's "āsana." These boyish figures show the "ūrdhva liṅga," wear some coarsely beaded chains and may be trained in the discipline which leads to yoga; this lends them their youthful looks and radiant countenance. A similar discipline may be read from the upright carriage of the female figurines.

As in the timeless, so also in the timebound feminine figurines, the youthful type, just on the verge of femininity, and the other, emblematic of potential motherhood, occur. A torso[68] belongs to the family of the Yakṣī of Didarganj; in richness of apparel the plaque from Kauśāmbī in the Indian Institute, Oxford, is superior to it.

Figurines modeled by hand and with molded faces, jewelry, and apparel affixed to them continue to be made in the late Śuṅga period (pl. 3-3.2), when plaques become more frequent. With a further increase in the heaviness of the face is now combined a weight of pensiveness sunk into its own depth, glanceless, with eyes closed. The high cheekbones on which the smile was pegged in the earlier figurines have subsided; the face droops with heavy cheeks. The lateral bumps of the head are still there (pl. 3-3.1), although diminished, as if by their contents the weight of the face was fed. There are magnificently modeled busts (pl. 3-3.1); tresses affixed on the back are turgidly rounded and different from the thin stalk shapes affixed on the earlier figurines. With the drooping of the countenance, the entire form physiognomy of the body in other figurines keeps pace.

In the terracottas, nomad fashions on the whole are most conspicuous among male types in Mathura; in Pāṭaliputra the veil worn over the "horn," high on the head on a late Śuṅga or Kānva plaque (pl. 3-3.4), is conspicuous. An almost completely preserved plaque (pl. 3-3.5) shows the entire costume along with a "hooped" kind of dhoti. The heaviness of the Śuṅga countenance remains, in the once more differentiated modeling which also belongs, together with the open-eyed face, to Kuṣāṇa stone sculptures.

Certain types persist from the late Maurya to the Gupta age, and on the type once laid down, successive generations imprint their own physiognomy. One of the series that can thus be traced is that of the female figurine plaque of which the figurine referred to (note 63) is the earliest known example. Not only in Patna (pl. 3-3.2), but also in Kauśāmbī, post-Śuṅga, and Kuṣāṇa, versions (pl. 3-3.3) occur and at the latter site Gupta varieties are fashioned with a high attainment (Municipal Museum, Allahabad). The serial persistence of these types is a parallel—limited in extent—to the traditional types

3-3. Timed variations of Indian terracottas

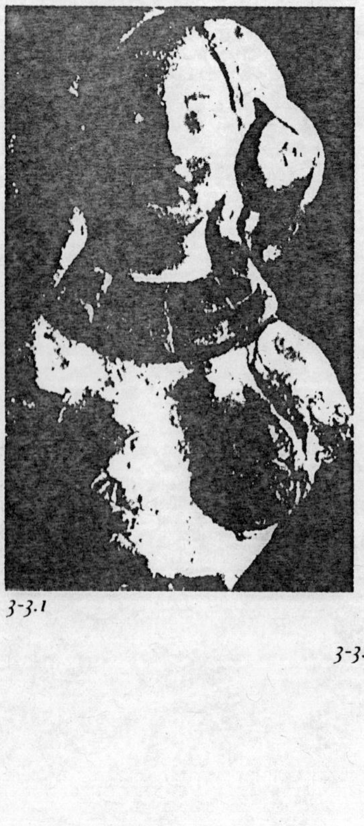

3-3.1

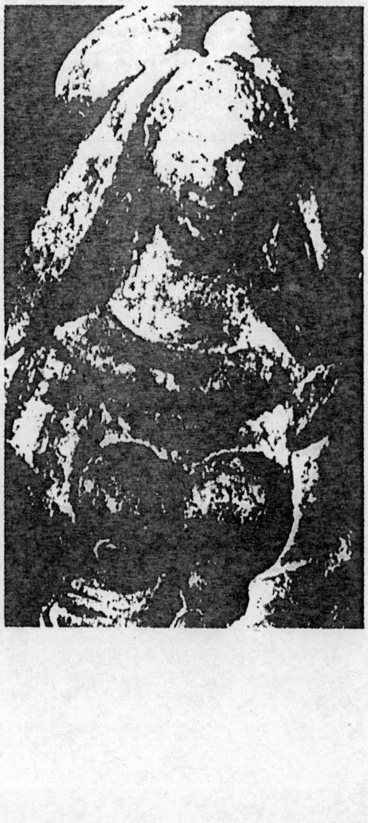

3-3.2

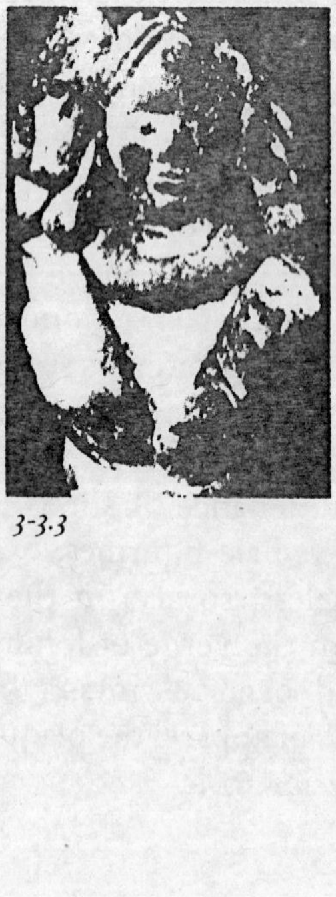

3-3.3

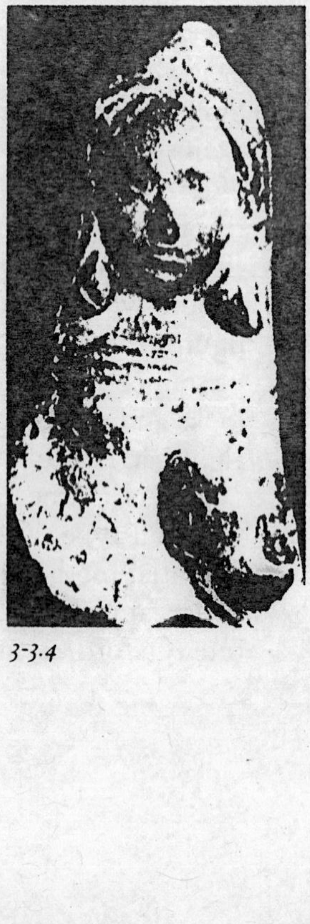

3-3.4

with which the more allusive versions apparently shared the same meaning.

The sequences and transformations to which the female types are subject are equally apparent in the male types; plate 3-2.6 appears in material and form to be a late Maurya or early Śuṅga type of "Yakṣa" proportion while the same type of physique, with a Kuṣāṇa "Hellenistic" modeling and drapery of loin cloth appears in plate 3-2.9.[69] Delicacy due to Hellenistic training is exemplified in plate 3-2.10 and also a recrudescence, in plate 3-2.11, of Scythian origin, also from Bulandibagh. Hellenism is obvious in the fragment (pl. 3-2.8) of the lower part of a plaque with a bare-legged male figure (Hermes?) and a ram on his left. A replica of this plaque is also in the Patna Museum.

BUXAR (SHAHABAD DISTRICT)

The results of Dr. Banerji Sastri's excavation in Buxar, Shahabad District, have been published by him under the title "Remains of a Pre-Historic Civilisation in the Gangetic Valley."[70] Dr. Sastri indicates that the findspot of most of the figurines is fifty-two inches underneath the surface of the riverside, whereas the Brahmī seals with characters "of the third century B.C." were found at a depth of thirty-two inches.

The female types, with faces pressed in the most delicately modeled molds and with varied types of headgear, have bodies of the "ageless" type. Whatever their headgear—which is separately modeled, or molded, and affixed—whether triangular or with lateral "horns," and whatever the ear ornaments (large plaques with floral or wheel-lotus and related motifs or small rings clasping the enormous ear loops), the faces, allowing for slight variations in fullness and quality, belong to one and the same type. It is an entirely modeled type, with the most delicate transitions from forehead to eye and cheek, and a roundness given to the small nose, which makes a stronger accent above the equally small lips. The features seem to hover in the face to the extent of faintness; no lines frame the eye, and the lips, of which no corners are marked, are embedded in oval depressions into which their own smile places them. The smile extends to the cheekbones and, along with the veiled eyes and fullness of face, is a truly Indian equivalent to the "archaic" smile of Greek and Sicilian terracottas of the sixth century A.D. This has no implications regarding their date.

Some heads have a headgear approaching a turban shape similar to turbans worn by male figures in the Bharhut relief. There, however, the central part is much smaller in proportion to the whole broadly bulging mass of the turban. Bead chains (also in Mathura, cf. Bindumaṇḍala, p. 75) frame the high foreheads. Śuṅga faces from Patna in stone and terracotta (Yakṣī, Didarganj, etc.) have this type of modeling. The accents there are stronger. Subsequently, it seems as if the imposing headwear becomes a thing of the past.

The few coarsened "Buxar" types in Patna and Kauśāmbī (pl. 3-2.1), the few Patna types in Buxar, seem to indicate a period of contacts toward the end of the Śuṅga period. A figurine, of Kuṣāṇa type and fully modeled in three dimensions, is one of the noblest contributions in terracotta, from a site which maintained a high level in its work for several centuries.

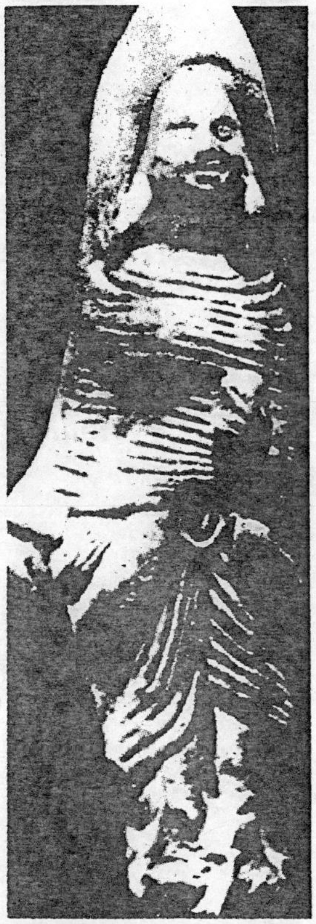

3-3.5

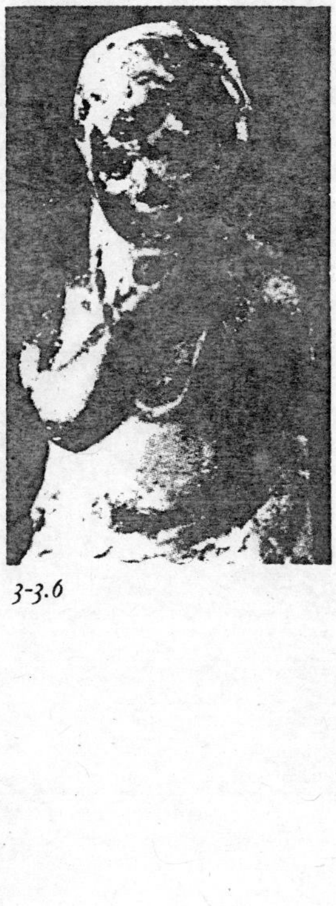

3-3.6

MATHURA

The terracottas from Mathura have already been discussed by several scholars. Differences with regard to the dating of these fictile objects are considerable. The traditional figurines, it has been shown (p. 69), are no more ancient than the time-bound varieties with molded faces. They run parallel. A relative date can be assigned to the molded types. They are not homogeneous and, while retaining the same material (grey or blackish terracotta, shiny black paint or slip) and a certain sameness of type, they are sufficiently varied to show their sequence. The female figurines illustrated in several publications[71] appear to begin the series, if a comparison is made with the Buxar and Pāṭaliputra terracottas. They are seen to align themselves in date with the Buxar figurines. Whether lean or full, there is, if not a smile, yet an animation all over the modeled face. The face is, once more, pegged on the cheekbones even though the wide and open eyes, with their distinctly molded rims, appear to lie flat. This animation is absent from stone carvings prior to 100 B.C.[72]

There are also technical affinities, especially the separately modeled or molded parts affixed before firing, which the figurines from Patna, Buxar, and Mathura share in addition to such motifs as the bicornate headdress. Apart from these points in common, there are at least an equal number of symptoms by which the finds of each site can be distinguished. Not too much stress should be laid on the types of jewelry, tresses of hair, and the like. The rows of beads, for instance, above the parting of the hair or framing the forehead of Mathura figurines of this type (and also of the corresponding Buxar type) are "worn" also by heads of Kuṣāṇa and Gupta date from Mathura.[73] It has been shown already that one type, in its setting of headwear, ornaments, and so forth, can be followed across the centuries (p. 82).[74] Another way of arriving at a relative date is afforded by a comparison with a definitely "Hellenistic" head from Basarh,[75] which belongs to a period after the invasion of Demetrius, that is, to the second quarter of the second century B.C. There, the Hellenistic modeling around the mouth relieves, but does not dissimulate, the hard and taut expanse of the cheeks.

The female types have their male analogies in Mathura and these as well are not of one date; some conform with Śuṅga proportions, others (pl. 3-2.12; pl. 3-3.6) with a "Hellenism" of the Kuṣāṇa school, the "naturalism" of which makes it differ from the "Hellenism" of the Basarh head referred to. These phases correspond, retarded as they are, to the respective phases of Hellenistic sculpture. This may be seen also in plate 3-2.13.[76] The material of the last-mentioned head is red, not grey, terracotta.

Red and ocher terracotta is the prevalent material of the plaques (excepting some of the Śuṅga plaques of Vasudhārā, of black-grey color) from Mathura, as it is elsewhere.

4 Unknown India: Ritual Art in Tribe and Village

THE SETTING

Over the landscape of Indian art tower the great stone temples, the profusion of their sculptures tempered by the elegance of their form. Into the substance itself of the earth, earlier centuries had cut their sanctuaries, had transmuted the living rock into gigantic visions of deity, vibrant in depth. The artists, as a rule, came from the lower strata of the social fabric of India. Many of them were of peasant stock. The organization of their guilds was built upon the close contact between their rural homes and their calling, which took them away from their homes and in which they carried out the visions and speculations of the spiritual elite. This close cooperation having ended, Indian art lost its guidance and patronage. The need was felt no longer to build or excavate a temple that would endure and secure for the patron a place in heaven while still on earth. The villages, however, continued with very little change in their own fabric or in their needs.

The great temples today rise as monuments of the past over a landscape that stayed productive though impoverished in its means, that stayed alive from generation to generation with the course of the years and the seasons, with the waxing and waning of the moon, with sunrise and sunset. All these moments and transitions have their response in innumerable rites and in countless shapes, many of which are not meant to last—molded in clay or made of wood or cotton—for they will be made again and again with the rites of spring or autumn, with the daily rites of evocation. They are part of the sacraments of living, invoking an invisible superhuman presence whose reality is con-

First appeared in *Unknown India: Ritual Art in Tribe and Village* (Philadelphia: The Philadelphia Museum of Art, 1968) and is reprinted by permission.

tacted and communicated by those shapes. But for them it would remain beyond reach and control.

The Indian rural economy of art provides for sculptures to be made as offerings to the deity and to be left untended at the place where they were given, under a tree, near pond or river or in a grove. They accumulate, they decompose, and others take their place. It is not the form which remains and endures, but the performance which makes the form and gives it style, changing with the years as do the leaves on the trees and eventually the trees themselves, yet recognizable in its local varieties as part of the scene where the sculptures stand. Each scene had its "genius loci," called yakṣa. Such genii controlled the sacred geography of India in ancient times when they were called by this name. This was even before the millennium when the stone temples were built as works of monumental sculpture, showing forth on their walls the figure of man transmuted into the likeness of gods (ca. A.D. 500 to 1500). Ancient Indian texts on architecture such as the *Samarāṅgaṇasūtradhāra* of the eleventh century designate the majority of the temples as nagara. This means "belonging to a town." It was there in the towns, preeminently, that a royal patron would endow a temple, greater in its height and splendor and more durable in its material than any palace. It was there that the Brahmans, the priests, laid down the guiding lines and the Kshatriyas, the nobility, set the standards of discriminating taste.

Today, as in former times, there are many large towns in India, but few large temples have been built during the last centuries, under Muslim and British rule. The Great Tradition of architectural sculpture died a slow death. Today, as in former times, the people of India—now about five hundred million—are mainly, that is, 82 percent, rural. Moreover, 80 percent of the rural population worships other gods than Vishnu and Śiva who are worshiped by Brahmans in the large temples.

Only about thirty million are counted today as tribal. Practically half of the tribal population of Middle and South India does not declare itself as Hindu.[1] If outside the pale of Hindu influences, and left to themselves, people neither built temples nor did they make images of their gods. Their religion expresses itself directly in rites in which works of art are the indispensable and focal means of communication with the supernatural, with man's experience of the Real. The Real is sensed in the waking experience. It may be adumbrated in dreams. It is known in trance. Trance, dream, and waking experiences are actual, though they vary in kind and degree and lie in different but interconnected planes. Tribal art gives them form.

Among the tribal people of India, the Gond, Santal, and Bhil are the most numerous groups. They are called aboriginal inasmuch as they were in India before the Aryans arrived in the middle of the second millennium B.C. However, before that time a great urban civilization, with its capital cities in the Punjab and Sind, had extended over a large part of the peninsula (third to second millennium B.C.). The relation of the ancestors of the present tribal people to that great urban civilization of Mohenjo-daro and Harappa is not known.

Tribal art throughout India for the last two thousand years at least must be assumed to have coexisted with traditions commanding greater means and more complex organization. The Buddhist stone railings of the stūpa of Bharhut and the stūpa of the saints, in Sanchi, both collective monuments of sculpture of the second to first century B.C., show the work of many different hands. These stone railings with their carvings are each a symposium of styles, some of which bear affinity to tribal carvings such as those of the Gond who to this day live not far from the sites of these ancient monuments. Buddhism was open to members of any group. The sculptors, however, were not necessarily Buddhists; they came from the lower Hindu strata of ancient Indian or tribal stock. Progressing Hinduization, while dissolving much of the self-supporting and self-sufficient tribal communities, absorbed as much as it destroyed of tribal traditions, while these tribes, where they survived as solid groups, assimilated much from their suppressors, who also were their neighbors. But Hinduism from the start is an alloy of the Brahmanic tradition and the many other and older Indian traditions. Due to this long process of osmosis, tribal art in India, on the whole, lacks the stylistic certitude and perfectedness of the tribal art of Africa, Oceania, and of the American Indian. The art of the Naga, who live on the northeastern frontier of India, although relatively pure, is slighter; the tribal art of Central India cruder; and that of the Bhil more heterogeneous than Congo or Melanesian creations.

Of all the tribal people of India, the small group of the Toda, who live in the Nilgiris, the Blue Hills of South India, have left what may be considered the most ancient relics (about first century A.D.). Terracotta figurines, excavated there, are, it would seem, the work of their ancestors.[2] Some of these figurines have tribal forms, others do not essentially differ in some respects from some of the terracottas found in Mohenjo-daro (pl. 4-1), while in certain respects some of the Mohenjo-daro figurines can be compared with the work by village potters and women made to this day in Bengal.

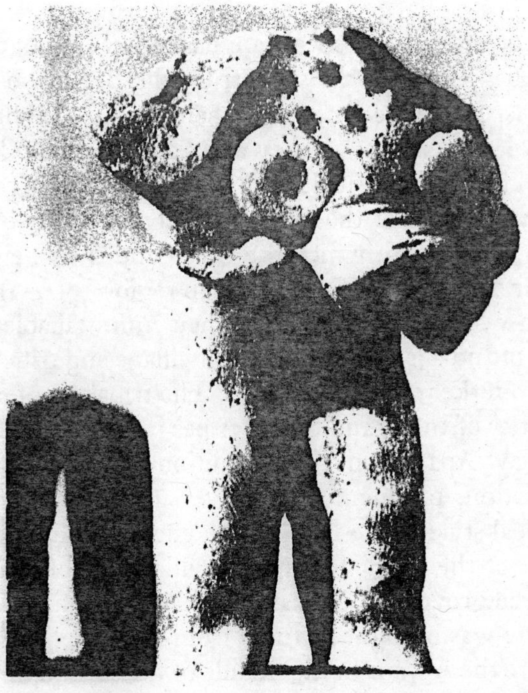

4-1. Humped bull, later part third millennium B.C.; *Mohenjo-daro, Pakistan (National Museum, New Delhi)*

Today the tribal people live in the less accessible parts of the country, not on the open plains, not along the great rivers. Whether they are of the Dravidian or Munda language family, the coherence of each tribe depends upon common rites, on the way the sacraments of life are celebrated and those of death. These make the fundamental identity of tribe and clan. Contacts with the surrounding rural Hindu population act both ways. Traditions are exchanged and prejudices are born. To some of the low-caste Hindus on the fringes of tribal society are delegated, by the tribal people, tasks to which the Hindus themselves do not assign high rank. The age-old profession of the potter is one of them.

In the fourth century B.C., Pāṇini, the great grammarian, distinguished between village craftsmen (grāma-śilpin), and royal craftsmen (raja-śilpin) who worked for a feudal lord. This distinction, however, is not equivalent to one between folk art and court art, though it assigns a different status to the practitioners of certain crafts, the potters being classified among the village craftsmen, their craft being practiced in the village itself. Just as the tribal people, who lived by hunting, foodgathering and shifting cultivation—some only practicing settled agriculture—are looked down upon by their neighbors, the Hindu peasants, with their settled agriculture and full-time specialized occupations, so too the tribal people in psychological revenge consider the lower of the peasant crafts, like that of the potter, below their own dignity. They make the nontribal, low-caste Hindu potters work for them,[3] according to their own instructions. Their snobbery, however, has no effect on the work of the potter. Although he is outside the tribe, bonds of propinquity, and as likely as not of consanguinity, are stronger than prejudice. The object made by the potter, who shapes not only pots but also clay figures, exactly suits his tribal patron and the use for which he requires it. This use again does not essentially differ from the one a villager would have for the potter's work, for instance, for a clay horse.

Similarly, tribal people at present speak languages that are not their own but those of their neighbors. One and the same tribe, the Bhil, whose habitat ranges over a wide area, speak the languages of their nearest neighbor, be it Rajasthani, Gujarati, or Marathi, although they also have their own language, Bhili, an Aryan tongue. The original tribal language however is forgotten, the words which accompany the rites of the Bhil are really not their own. And what about the works of art through which the Bhil—and their neighbors—perform their rites? Their styles differ from region to region (pl. 4-2) as much as the languages through which the Bhil express their unmistakable identity.

The unknown art of India is the art created in village and tribe on social levels below and away from the towering temples. The tribal art of the Naga, on the northeastern frontier of India, and that of tribes in central India remain relatively intact to this day. Apart from these traditions, rural India is a rich ground for cross-fertilization, producing deceptive simplicities of styles in tribe and village. The tribal style of the Bhil, which encompasses a wide area, is shown by the figurine of the Spirit Rider. The village art of South India is represented by the sacred grove with its many and large clay figures, mainly of horses. When the horse was brought to India from its home in Inner Asia is not known. Long before the Aryans in the middle of the second millennium

B.C. had entered India from the north on horseback, the tame horse was represented in Harappan terracotta figurines, unearthed in Lothal and Rangpur.[4] Horse riding later on was a privilege of the aristocracy, the Rajputs, the "sons of kings."

The essentially Indian tribal art form of the wide-ranging figurine of the Bhil Spirit Rider and the essentially Indian village art of the locally circumscribed cult of Aiyanar in which the figure of the horse is exalted show, on the one hand, a tribal identity at the base of a variety of styles and, on the other hand, an autochthonous and localized style brought about by the confluence of many traditions. If these two aspects of a particularly Indian artistic relevance are here singled out in introducing the unknown art of India, a third artistic type, characteristic in its all-Indian application and ramifications, must also be mentioned: the magic diagram, drawn on the floor, a form of art practiced by women only, or by non-Brahman priests on behalf of women.

THE SPIRIT RIDER

The archetype of all the figurines of horsemen which give reality to the Nukto rite of the Bhil has vanished from the scene. Its meaning and function, however, come to life whenever the rite is performed, and the mystery of death-in-life is once more confirmed through the figurine of the rider on his horse. It plays the leading role in this essential tribal rite of the Bhil, although the Bhil neither raise nor use horses. The equestrian figure in art and legend is generally associated with the feudal Hindu Rajputs, the northern neighbors of the Bhil.

The equestrian figure is one of the themes of art by which the tribal world and that of the feudal aristocracy are linked here on earth (pls. 4-2, 4-3). Over and above this, its image is a magic link between heaven and earth. This is its purpose. In this respect, the function of the equestrian figurine is not different from that of the great temples that were erected in the cities. There, the ascent to heaven was built up, stone by stone, each stone carved with an image appropriate to its position in the entire edifice, piled high so that step by step the architectural ritual of the ascent became the monument, the temple. The architectural ritual is put into words in the ancient texts of that science. The oral tradition of the tribal Bhil to this day verifies step by step the journey of the soul that has the Spirit Rider for its acting support.

The liberating function of art is shared by the tribal non-Hindu, the Hindu peasant and the Hindu elite in one tribal-village-urban continuum, where the currents of art from tribe and village to the elite, from the elite to tribe and village, flow both ways.

The tribe of the Bhil, the "sons of the forest" (vanaputra), lives in western India, from the Aravalli Mountains in Rajasthan to the Vindhya range. It is in and near this region that in the course of the last two thousand years the Buddhist cave temples and monasteries of Ajanta were cut out of the rocks, the Jains built the marble temples at Mount Abu, and many Hindu shrines have borne witness to the experience of the numinous. The Bhil were hunters, fishermen, and foodgatherers—they have learned animal husbandry from their neighbors, the Gujar—and they are agriculturists. Although centered in Rajasthan (Mewar), Gujarat, and Khandesh, they also live in loosely connected groups in the mountains and the less readily accessible parts of Sind (in Pakistan), Kutch, and Rajasthan in the northwest and in the state of Andhra Pradesh in the southeast. A small group of them is found as far to the northeast as Bengal.[5] Said to be of pre-Aryan origin, they are classified as proto-Australoid or as Veddid.[6] Their original language is lost; they form a psychological complex without linguistic, physiognomic, economic, or cultural unity.[7] Their spirituality is their own and holds them together.

Formerly they ruled over their own country. This was prior to the arrival of the Rajputs. The Rajputs, the "sons of kings," invaded the country, subsequently Rajasthan, in about the sixth century A.D. They became Kshatriyas, the nobility par excellence of India. Some of these Rajput princes, including the most exalted of them, the Rana of Mewar, at the inception of their rule, had their foreheads marked with the blood of a Bhil. It was drawn from his thumb or big toe.[8] This was an acknowledgment of the precedence of the Bhil as rulers of the country.

The Rajputs are horse owners and riders. The Bhil use the image of the horseman; it is that of a Spirit Rider, the Gothriz Purvez, the Ancestor of the clan. On it is focused the solidarity of the clan; it redeems the dead and liberates the living from the fear of death and the despair of loneliness. Moreover, the Bhil commemorate their fallen heroes, killed in a fight or cattle raid, by setting up stone memorial slabs carved in low relief with an equestrian figure; whereas memorial stones set up for their dead by others, the Rajputs in particular, frequently have a standing figure in front view.[9] The Bhil confer on their ancestors the nobility of the horseman, the chevalier, whereas the Rajputs do not particularly stress the equestrian form of their dead. From the hymns of the Ṛg Veda (second half of the second millennium B.C.) the group of horse and rider is vested with sacredness. Indra, the Creator God, rode the horse for the first time.[10] Later tradition knows the Sun God as rider[11] and the horse itself as fire in all its aspects, on earth and in heaven, the sun on high and the spark of life.[12]

The Bhil ritual for the dead is celebrated in front of the entrance of the house of the deceased.[13] From above its lintel a twelve-runged bamboo ladder is suspended and subsequently also a long string with an arrow—the Bhil were primarily hunters—attached to it. This man-made setting and its paraphernalia contrast with the sacred grove, the central sanctuary of every Bhil settlement. There, an unhewn stone or stones are the symbols of deity. In the cult of the dead, however, man is the symbol. The anthropomorphic image and representation, which are here those of the horseman, are linked with the cult of the dead. Another object required for the great Nukto rite, the rite of the dead, is the figurine of a cow. These figurines are made of the copper anklets of the widow of the deceased. The material itself of the figurines has magical virtue; it takes part in the ritual and undergoes a spiritual alchemy.

The Gothriz Purvez is placed on an altar, the cow on a metal tray. The long string leads to the altar of the Gothriz Purvez and thence to the cow. Now the scene is set. The main actors are the Rawal, the master of ceremonies, the Barwo, the magician, and the Waha, the priest. The Waha, who acts as a Brahman or priest, is a male child from the clan of the dead person.

The preparation for the Nukto rite begins when the Rawal sings to the dying man at the first ghanto, corresponding to the first rung of the ladder: "Alone go, brother, to Bhagavān (the Supreme God) through the seven depths." And at the third ghanto, the Rawal speaks over the dead body: "Come, quite alone." And at the fifth ghanto, it is the spirit (jīva) who speaks: "I am alone, brother, I am alone." The rungs of the bamboo ladder, which the Rawal had hung from the doorframe, represent the twelve stations of the mountain with their obstacles which the jīva, the spirit, has to climb before it is purified and reaches Bhagavan.

The Bhil distinguish between the body, the psychic elements or the ghost (bhūta) and shadow, and the spirit of man. They separate at death. The body is cremated; a heap of stones is piled up under a tree. There the bhūta is appeased in the first three days of the rites, after the death of the body. On the fourth day, the Nukto rites of three days begin. It is then that the Rawal ties the string on the wooden crossbar above the entrance. When the jīva has attained the seventh rung, the stones are scattered; there is now no resting place on earth for any part of the man who died. The spirit rises from one rung of tests and judgment to the next, overcoming the obstacles of each rung. The spirit is purified during the ascent. In the night when the spirit has passed the tenth and eleventh rungs and has been judged in the twelve courts, it goes to Bhagavān. The Rawal has sprinkled the cow with milk to make the spirit pure and white. When the spirit has completed its ascent, during the first Nukto rite, on the fourth day after death, the twelve rungs of the ladder are destroyed, the spirit descends along the string into the arrow, the Rawal having poured water thrice over the cow. By these rites, the spirit is further purified. The spirit now enters the equestrian figurine and the cow and overcomes the Barwo, who, having undergone in the meanwhile the necessary preparations, is in trance. The spirit makes the Barwo select the Waha, a young boy from the clan of the dead, who is now consecrated. The Waha is the Gothriz Purvez; he is possessed by the spirit and is given the same name as the rider figurine on the horse who is the Gothriz Purvez, the Ancestor of the clan, the liberated spirit of the man who had died. The Waha, trembling in his trance, holds the tablet with the figurine of the cow, while the Rawal sings for the khatariz (Kshatriya), the hero, the spirit.

When the figurine of the cow, held by the trembling Waha, has itself ceased to tremble, it is taken in procession to the tree where the stones were collected and then were scattered. The figurine of the cow is buried.

The Rawal tears the string on which the spirit has descended. The Waha is no longer possessed by the spirit. The purified spirit has been accepted in the clan of the ancestors. It dwells with Bhagavān, in the beyond. The Nukto rite has been completed. A meal and mask dance follow.

Without the Nukto rite, the spirit could not have been purified, could not have ascended to Bhagavān and found its place. It would have remained alone, erring between here and there, troubling the heart and mind of the clansmen. The effigy of the spirit, the Gothriz Purvez, the equestrian metal statuette, remains with them. It is not buried as is the figurine of the cow.

The double embodiment of the purified spirit as Ancestor of the clan, in the living body of the entranced youth of the clan, the Waha, and in the equestrian metal statuette proves both to be its temporary abodes. For this, the Waha was made fit by his trance, and the equestrian statuette by its form. The figurine of the cow, too, is temporarily the place where the spirit dwells. But when this figurine ceases to tremble, the spirit has left it, and the little metal cow is buried, having served its purpose. Very few metal figurines of cows exist. The number of equestrian metal figurines is large. They vary considerably in shape, each variation having a formal consistency of its own. They are set up frequently also in household shrines of Rajputs and other Hindus.

Without the figurine of the Gothriz Purvez, the spirit of the dead could not be purified and could not reach Bhagavān, the Supreme God. The figurine, the work of art, is an essential means toward the clan's attainment of a feeling of spiritual worth and earthly security, a feeling of peace and solidarity. The liberated spirit, the khatariz, the hero, comes to dwell in the Nukto rite amidst the clan, in the living, young body of the Waha and in the equestrian statuette.

The Waha discharged the function of a Brahman. For this purpose, he was invested, like a Brahman, with a sacred thread. It is not only in this instance that the Bhil raise a child to the status of a Brahman or recognize in a child a special power.[14] It is the power of the assumed innocence of the child.[15]

The equestrian metal figurines, essential part of rites and trance, were however not made during a trance experience. Invariably cast by the lost wax process, they fall into different stylistic groups. In one particularly spirited variety, a special technique of casting contributed to the tense alertness of its form. But to whatever thought and style-type of figurines horse and rider may belong, they seem to have come from a world of enchantment where innocence and trusting pride went into their conception. Their form lacks not only the tension and determination of similar ancient Iranian metal figurines,[16] but also the cursive, fluid generalization of comparable animal figurines made of clay by Tallensi children of the African Gold Coast.[17] Essentially metallic in character, the pristine, though not primitive, figurines assignable to the Bhil ambience, whether made by Bhil or by Hindu metalsmiths, show rider and horse advancing, as it were, though the legs of the horse are always firmly planted on the ground (pl. 4-2). With one hand the rider holds the reins, as a rule, in the other a staff or weapon. His head is raised, the back is straight. With the four feet of the horse on the ground, the seemingly advancing movement of the group is effected by the position and spacing of the legs of the horse and also by the position and spacing of the neck and head of the horse and the body of the rider, the latter frequently inclining backward. Self-contained and static, the entire group appears as if drawn forward by an invisible pull. Though three dimensional, it is complete in its silhouette. Seen from various angles, rider and horse show themselves in ever new responses of their masses and the connecting voids, left intact by the unobtrusiveness of the rider's legs. Like short, flattened ribbons, the rider's legs adhere to the body of the horse and do not exceed the length of the saddle, as a rule. It is the reins, arms, and weapon which enhance the airiness and onward pull of the group.

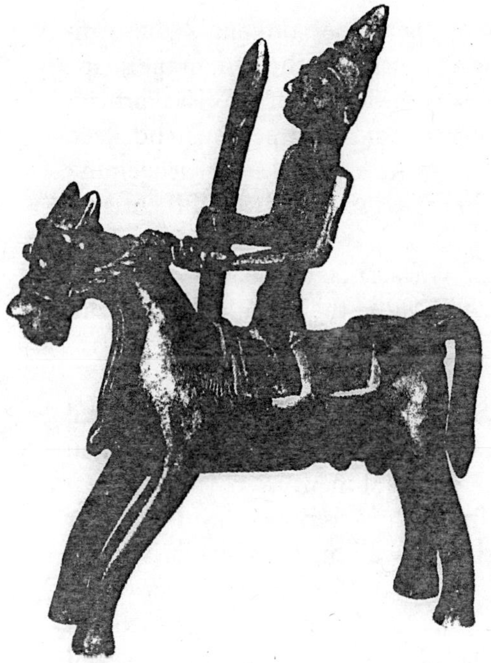

4-2. Equestrian figurine, eighteenth century; Rajasthan

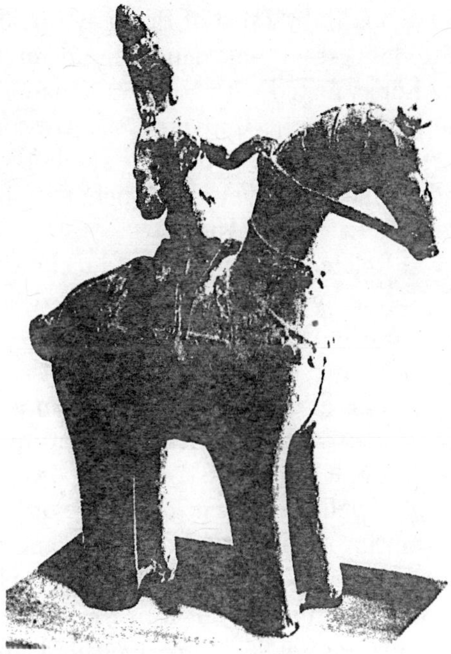

4-3. Equestrian figurine, seventeenth century; South India

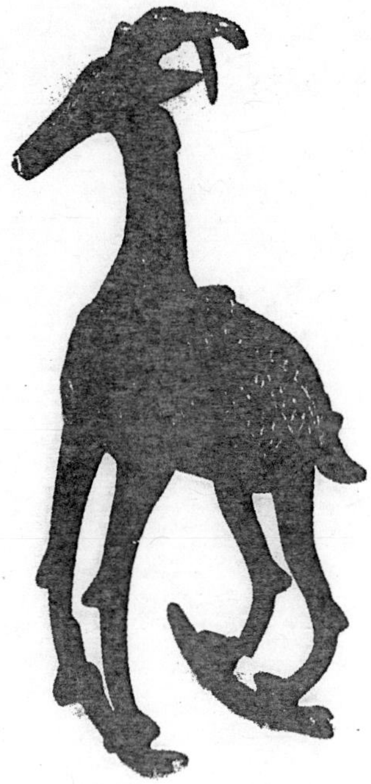

4-4. Antelope, eighteenth century; Bihar

Whether of Don Quixotian elegance as in Rajasthan, or full bodied as also in Rajasthan, Malwa (West Madhya Pradesh), and in Khandesh (Maharashtra), with the rider's face planar and presenting its features as ridges according to the standards of tribal art; or with a three-dimensional face, abstractly modeled and pinched into the peak of the nose; or more naturalistically organized and with the horse's legs flexed and articulated (pl. 4-2)—or simply as sturdy cylinders—each group has a serenely harmonious balance of its own for the liberated spirit, the Ancestor of the clan to dwell in. As this spirit in the Nukto rite takes possession of the Waha, a child, so its image in turn embodies the immortal spirit of childhood as Ancestor of the clan.

Cast by the lost wax process, these figurines are distinct from the nervy zest of the thin-legged horses and frisky riders cast hollow in a special "wire" technique.[18] It is practiced by the quasi-Hinduized metalworkers of the Kainkuya Mal caste, also called Dhokra, a migratory, and partly settled caste of metalsmiths who came from Bihar to Bengal; by the Malar, who are said to have come to Bihar from Madhya Pradesh; and by the Kaser in Bastar, Madhya Pradesh. By their technique of hollow bronze casting, where a ribbed surface results (often it is subsequently smoothed) from placing wax "wires," one-tenth of an inch thick, one against the other, and over them more wax wires, forming an ornamental relief pattern, an eerie elegance is obtained in the figurines from Bihar of which not only the horse, but also the deer or antelope, are chosen embodiments. Like the other small metal images here described, the antelopes too were kept on house altars (pl. 4-4). Warding off evil spirits, they are spirit guardians of manifold meaning. Brahmanic tradition tells of Prajāpati, the Lord of Progeny, the creator "per generationem," who committed incest with his daughter, an antelope.[19] Vivasvānt, the sun, in the shape of a horse, mated with Saṁjñā, a mare. She was the daughter of Viśvakarman, the Maker of the Universe, the creator "per artem."[20] Impetuous and fleet, horse and antelope or deer are symbols of creativeness, full of secret redeeming and protective power.[21] As such, they live in the art of the castes of the metal-workers in eastern India.

Related to their style and technique of work is that of the Kaser, or Ghasia, of Madhya Pradesh. It lacks the gracile fantasy of their work, and its wire texture is more involved and inventive. The figurines are often ponderous,[22] at other times they are fantasmagorias of delicate spikes.

The figurine of the horseman as a Spirit Rider is not always the focal point of a trance experience. As an image of the spirit freed from the human condition, it represents a state of perfection and fulfillment in which immortal heroes dwell. Representing a state of fulfillment, it is credited with the power of granting fulfillment—of wishes and desires. When made of clay it is an offering—to a god or hero like Kasumar Damor, a great magician, helper of the Barwo, and tutelary spirit of the people. At his mountain sanctuary such images, many on wheels, are deposited, and also clay horses, as part of vows and as votive gifts when the need is felt for having a child, regaining health, winning a court case, or for success as a robber.[23] Made of clay, the image is reduced to its minimal form and is part of the vast, timeless world of clay figurines into which history and legend may delve and give specific actuality and meaning to a perennial theme (pl. 4-1).[24] Images of seventy-two horsemen are installed on a platform somewhere in Kutch.[25] They commemorate, legend tells, and keep as potent helpers those white-skinned foreigners said to have come in the thirteenth century from Anatolia and Syria and to have killed the tyrant Punvaro. He had cut off the hands of the architect who had built the city of Patan so that he might not construct anything like it again. The seventy-two horsemen took the fort and killed the chief.[26] Harking back to other, untold memories from Inner Asian horse-herding cultures, these apocalyptic horsemen transmute the fear generated by Muslim invasions into India into a liberating legend in which the evil power does not come from outside but is local, embodied in the tyrant Punvaro. His heinous crime and its punishment are in the Great Indian Tradition. Capital punishment awaits the person who incapacitates a practicing artist[27] and prevents creativeness from functioning. The veneration of the creative act and the annihilation of the obstructor are mythologized in the battle of the Creator God, Indra—who was the first to ride a horse—with the serpent dragon Vṛtra, who had prevented the creative waters from flowing. The heroic horseman—far more than the sacred cow—had taken hold of the imagination of the Indian sculptor in tribe and village.

AUTOCHTHONY

In South India, in almost every Tamil village there is a shrine of Aiyaṇār.[28] Often a large, rough stone without any carving is set up under a tree. It stands for the presence of Aiyaṇār. Such a stone setting belongs to tribal tradition. But Aiyaṇār is a Brahman deity and his worshipers are Dravidian villages. Generally his sanctuary is on the banks of a pond. Its waters fertilize the fields that he protects. In some of his sanctuaries, Aiyaṇār is represented in human shape, a kingly figure riding a horse or an elephant. Horses are offered to him, large terracotta horses, so that he does not lack a mount during the watches of the night when he rides around the village and looks after its safety. He rides with his retinue of heroes—and demons. Two horses at least must be offered to Aiyaṇār each year. The second is for Kaṟuppaṇ, the Dark God, the demon who accompanies him. Over the years, the horses accumulate in the sacred groves. Up to five hundred such large clay horses (up to ten feet or more) may be ready in one sanctuary for the nocturnal rides. New horses are set up, while the old and broken ones are left to decay and return to the earth of which they were made. Under the image of Aiyaṇār a stone liṅga, the phallic symbol of Śiva's creativeness, is buried. The seed of Śiva, from which Aiyaṇār was born, it is said, fell near the banks of the waters.

The numinous lives integrally in Aiyaṇār's sanctuaries, in the waters near by and in the soil, in the trees that enshrine the multitude of clay horses in their upright splendor and in their decay where, fallen to the ground, they are left to return to the earth whose mystery emanates from the total setting and pervades the heterogeneous but utterly consistent legend of Aiyaṇār. These open-air South Indian village sanctuaries are replete with a living art and the living knowledge of the underlying myth whose components and ritual range from Brahmanic to tribal tradition. The salient points of the myth are here put down so that the majesty of form of these clay horses may be comprehended in its proper perspective.

Aiyaṇār, the Lord, is the son of the two great Hindu gods: Śiva, the ascetic Creator-Destroyer; and Vishnu, the Preserver. In order to arouse Śiva, Vishnu assumed the shape of a wonderfully beautiful girl called Mohini or Delusion. She excited Śiva, and he let his seed fall near the waters. From it, Aiyaṇār, the son of Śiva and Vishnu (Hariharaputra), was born. A king, while hunting, found the beautiful babe lying on the ground, crying, but his face radiant with a thousand suns.

The main sanctuary of Aiyaṇār, the Lord, is in the thickly wooded Shabari hills in Kerala near the western coast of South India. There the Lord protects man from evil spirits and endows him with knowledge that leads to salvation. But in the sanctuary of Erumeli in Kerala, Aiyaṇār is worshiped in the form of a hunter.[29] His devotees dance wildly when they worship the Lord of this world of delusion, might, and fear.

Neither the wisdom aspect nor the orgiastic one are overtly part of the divinity of Aiyaṇār in the eastern, Tamil part of South India (he is not known north of the Godavari River), but the mystery of his birth from the two great Hindu gods passed on to the potency of the waters and the earth of any particular locality where Aiyaṇār is worshiped. While he is the same everywhere, each time it is a different Aiyaṇār who is worshiped.[30]

The Lord, Aiyaṇār, the guardian of the land, has his generals and lieutenants. They are heroes (vīra), that is, they are the souls of those who died in battle. They are joined by the host of demons, foremost Kaṟuppaṇ, the Dark

God, who is all that Aiyaṉār is not. He is the adversary to whom blood sacrifices are due. Aiyaṉār is worshiped with flowers and fruits. The dark power within Aiyaṉār, the Hunter, has been hypostatized into Kaṟuppaṉ, his alter ego, the demon as protector. Together they are worshiped by the officiating priest, who also is the maker of their images. He is the village potter, a Kuśavaṉ by caste, son of a Brahman father and a low-cast (Shudra) mother. During worship he becomes possessed by Kaṟuppaṉ, the Dark God, the alter ego of Aiyaṉār. Other names of Aiyaṉār are also Bhūtanātha, Lord of Demons, and Dharma Śāstā, "in front of whom all laws (dharma) of society to which a person belongs must be abandoned" so that his presence is realized.

The terracotta seeds are offered to Aiyaṉār by the village collectively or by individual devotees. Larger than life-size, the horses raise their fiercely noble heads, ready to carry god or demon. The potter-priest gives them basic shapes, which he knows how to modify in keeping with the ardent naturalism of South Indian sculpture. He has seen the rearing stone horses supporting the roofs of the large halls of stone temples of the Vijayanagar style of the sixteenth century.

Himself potter and priest, he molds the clay horses, impressing the clay with tensions experienced in shamanistic possession. The clay itself is taken from a ground of sacred fertility. It holds the liṅga of Śiva and the seed from which Aiyaṉār has sprung. Aiyaṉār, the Lord, scion of the two great Hindu gods, King of Demons, synthesis of deity experienced on the many levels of India's religious structure, depends on the clay horses offered to him for his rides. Their power is vested in the soil from which they are made. It does not extend beyond the Tamil village and its autochthonous art.

Other South Indian open-air sanctuaries are consecrated to the Goddess. In her sevenfold aspect, she is worshiped as the Seven Virgins. The sacred grove may be a square enclosure. The image of the Seven Heavenly Virgins are molded as one mass barely accentuated in its sevenfold undulating identity. The Seven Sisters form a sacred unit and are the tutelary deities of ponds. They go in procession with horses and torches. Whoever sees them, dies.[31] These Seven Virgins, with their will-of-the-wisp, wide-open, painted eyes, hold among themselves the message of death—and the power over birth. They guard against evil. They, too, are offered horses.

The ancient Aryans sacrificed a horse to Varuṇa, the god of the fertilizing waters. In hymnic intoxication, they knew the horse as Varuṇa (*Rg Veda* 1.163.4). They knew it, for the horse had risen from the waters, from the primal fount of life (*RV* 1.163.1). To the South Indian Dravidian peasant of today, this hymnic realization of the fiery animal, the horse, of the fiery spark of life that is in the waters, of the fire that at daybreak seems to arise from the waters as glowing sun and sinks into their darkness and dies, has become uncannily one with the power of Aiyaṉār and also with the eerie, fatal Seven Virgins. They have sprung from the soil, from swamp and pond, these autochthonous goddesses. They are ancient and local and have taken to them the steed that India had known long before the Aryans had come with their horses to India from the north. The Kuśavaṉ, the potter-priest, Aryan-Brahman and aboriginal by his blood, is competent to conceive and make the images of the Seven Sisters in the sanctuary of Muniapaṉ and give it the sacred shape of the square, the symbol of cosmic order. The clear-cut symmetry of this sanctuary combines a mastery over many levels of experience compressed in its extent. In the Seven Virgins and also in many female votive images offered in the sacred groves, primary shapes are suffused with a visionary power. The content of tribal and rural art springs from primary concerns. They are those of life, death, and transcendence in man and of life and death in the cosmos of which he is part.

The form of the work of tribal and rural art of India is, in each of the two hitherto discussed instances, a product of heterogeneous provenance and actuality of purpose. Elsewhere in India, recent tribal art lacks the integrated strength of tribal art in Africa and is generally only an offshoot of what it could have been. Even where its character has not been diluted, its vigor has been sapped. But the loss of character of tribal art is the gain of the rural art of India. By a process of osmosis, the essence of tribal art flowed into rural art. There it has been shown that it is the priest who made the clay horses and other images. While performing the rites, he becomes possessed by Kaṛuppaṉ, the Dark God. Possession and trance of the priest as performer follow upon his work as maker or former of the sculptures that carry or contain the spirit that will possess him.

Among the tribal people of the Bhil, the work of art—an equestrian figurine—was an integral and focal point of a rite. Without it, the rite has no validity. The figurine is a locus of identification with the supernatural. Without it, this identification could not be established. It requires, however, the participation of a priest in trance to become effective. Here, artist and priest, though not combined in one person, are united as form and performer.

The Spirit Riders of the Bhil, Aiyaṉār with his equestrian retinue of heroes and demons, each have their own locale, myths, and rites. The form of the sculptures is their visual equivalent and residue. Less rich in myth and rites are the traditions of the Spirit Riders who guard the villages all over India and whose equestrian images and votive horses are made by the village potters in basic, primary shapes.[32] They all ride without stirrups, on saddled or unsaddled horses.[33] Where no rider is figured plastically, the living human medium in his frenzy may symbolically mount a clay horse by putting his toes on it.[34]

The horse is one of the main themes in the tribal and rural art of India. It rode deep into the interior of the country, carrying the liberated spirit and its own nobility, power, and fertility. It brings wish fulfillment to the poor and the suppressed; it is the hobbyhorse ridden by the followers of Śiva in Bengal at the Gambhīra Festival in the Night of Śiva (Śivarātri), a wooden or bamboo stick with colored paper and string; or it is a dancing horse that takes part in the dance in this festival[35] and also in others, in other seasons of the year, in other parts of the country as in Tanjore, in the south.

The symbol "horse" carries the hopes of everyman in India. It has vivified the creative imagination of village potters and tribal craftsmen and is an outpost of their innumerable styles. Known in India from the remotest past, once more, carrying its Aryan rider, it had entered India from on high, from the north, across the mountains and the social and ethnic strata of the country.

Horses are offered to any village god, male or female.[36] Deposits of clay horses abound not only in the sacred groves of South India or the western hills where Kasumar Dhamor protects his people, but also near the village shrines of Bengal, on the graves of Hindu Tantric and of Muslim saints. By an irony of creative justice, the village potter makes clay horses in their basic timeless shapes, not only for the aboriginal and lowly (the members of the "scheduled castes") but also at the order of the high castes, the Brahmans and Kshatriyas. These spirit horses and riders are massed for worship in a Brahmasthāna.[37] The name means "Place of Brahma" and is the traditional name, in ancient architectural treatises,[38] for the site of the innermost sanctuary of a stone temple of the Great Tradition. The Spirit Rider here represents "the soul of a benevolent, unmarried Brahmin."[39]

The figure of the horse in the art of tribal and rural India retained its basic shape, particularly in the small terracotta images, alongside a form that had become more complex by assimilating to its own simplicity the naturalism that was part of the Great Tradition of Indian sculpture, as in the Tamil village horses, or by raising the little images of the Spirit Rider to expressive, sensitive, stylistically variegated emblems of the Bhil clans and the people of tribal and rural India.

The cow, sacred to the Hindus, and particularly the bull in the shape of Nandī, were given their immortal form in the various schools of sculpture of the Great Tradition. Thence their grandiose, weighty volumes descended, simplified, and carved in stone or wood to the level of folk art. They remain distinct from the primary geometry of the tribal-village art forms.[40]

In ancient times, in the third millennium B.C., the basic form of the bull, impetuously modeled (pl. 4-1), coexisted with its naturalistic shape, in Mohenjo-daro. In a primary shape, the buffalo was found also in the ancient tombs of the Nilgiris of South India.

On the level of village art, animal sculpture retains, though softened at times by descriptive naturalism, its basic, seemingly timeless cast. Ram, boar, and elephant are created as if nourished on the same peaceful pasture. Stylistic varieties among these metal figurines, though slight, are yet sufficient to show the work of a definite region. But it requires a different technique like that of the Dhokra (pl. 4-4) and Kaser figurines or a different material like pith to allow the fantasy of the maker the invention of new skills and forms.

The figure of man in tribal and village art connotes itself; it represents man as he is seen in the waking, dreaming, and trance experience and given form by the artist. It represents preeminently his spirit, the Ancestor. The form of the ancestral spirit-figure, having the shape of man, peoples the tribal world of art. The anthropomorphic image of god was absent from it originally.[41]

An unhewn stone marks the presence of deity. It is daubed with red color, which holds the memory of blood sacrifices. The stone is permanent. It outlasts the perishable, ever renewed offerings made by art. The stone is outside the temporality of man-shaped things.

Unhewn stones, placed under and canopied by the spreading branches of sacred trees are part of the Indian landscape. No conscious attempt is made at a harmonious arrangement. It comes about where the presence of deity is proffered by a visible, though not man-made, sign.

If the tribal and village art of India is seen against the high skyline of the Hindu temples with their countless images of gods, it is seen at the same time within the Indian landscape, which is dotted here and there, wherever you go, by a red-daubed stone, a sign of the presence of deity. While the presence of Aiyaṇār is marked, in principle, by a rough stone, the offerings, the works of art, small or gigantic, made of clay, proclaim his existence.

The tribal-village continuum of rural India extends, even today, into the towns as it must have at any other time. In the Harappan cities of the third millennium B.C., terracotta figurines abounded. They have tubular shapes or conical stumps for limbs, cylindrical or flattened bodies, faces pinched so that pellets for eyes can be affixed on either side of the nose. Similar figurines are made today by the potters or the women of the village. According to the use that will be made of the clay figurines, they will be toys or, if consecrated, ritual objects. While some of the figurines are precise and subtle in proportions and contour, others are sketchy or less competent in execution. But there are, besides these simple, basic types, naturalistically modeled figurines, and others whose faces are molded. Many layers and phases of art, tribal or urban, left their residues in these most ancient towns of the subcontinent, as they did subsequently in other cities.

VARIETIES OF TRIBAL ART

In the tribal Nilgiri tombs, a funerary repertory of clay figurines is accommodated in a variety of types from the basic shapes of naturalistic intent of a buffalo to the seemingly sophisticated distortions of a "primitive" human figurine. In the ancient city of Mathura, which the Greeks called "the city of the gods," a female figurine of primary abstract shape is assignable to the sixth century B.C.; another, with her primary, three-dimensional shape flattened to a superhuman width of the hips, to the third century B.C. Her molded face, however, shows a faint recollection of what could be implications of Greek art just leaving behind its archaic phase. This mother goddess, with her flattened width of hips, looks across space and time to a figurine from Patna of the second or third century A.D. Her basic form is that of a serpent above and woman below.

Primary, basic shapes underlie the complex charm of the ritual metal figurines of the Spirit Rider (pl. 4-2). With less finesse and more immediacy the metal figurines of the tribal Kutiya Kond, on the Andhra Pradesh–Orissa border, capture the movements of an animal, the way it stretches its neck, or those of young people in their insouciance. Cruder technically than the Dhokra figurines discussed, they are related to them. The Kutiya Kond figurines are said to have been meant for the young bridegroom.[42] They were carried in the marriage procession and thus played their part in the sacrament of marriage. They are the most spontaneously animated of the tribal metal figurines. The animation is of two kinds, for the planes of the figurines that are cast in wire-technique show this technique so that the airy texture of the surface, with its raised, crossing or parallel lines, not only directly encloses the core of the body but also suggestively models its volume. Here animal figurines generally are altogether encased in these meshes, whereas the faces and thin limbs of human figures are without them and are modeled freely. The distortions of the latter make them appear agitated and tremulous. In Kond paintings, too—which were done only in dire necessity and were not ever meant to be looked at[43]—the limbs seem to bend and flicker. They are tossed by an excitement that, free from tragic motivation, finds its expressive shape in the metal figurines. Compared with these, the figurines of the Spirit Riders are monumental and impersonal in their presence. They are directed forward toward one goal (pl. 4-2). The Kutiya Kond figurines of animals and man, on the other hand, appear caught in the wilderness of life. Kond figurines are essentially three dimensional; they lack the elegant silhouette of the figurines from western India. The relation of the volumes of a Kond figurine is full of tension. This, together with the crudely spontaneous wire-technique, distinguishes the Kond figurines from those of Bastar with their ornately abstract shapes. Whereas the wire patterns, applied elsewhere in Orissa as well as in Bengal, Bihar, and Bastar, on the smoothed metal ground are meticulous in their regularity and the straight lines of the wires, the Kond figurines wear their sheer wire net texture as if it were a loosely woven, tight-fitting web, its threads pulled this way and that way.

Few attempts have been made to study on the spot the different traditions of tribal art and to define their types of form.[44] The brass figurines differ in every tribe, yet in central India they are always made by the same Hindu caste, the Kaser or Ghasia.[45] Though the caste remains the same, its members were mostly tribal converts. Each tribe would employ Ghasias who lived nearest to them and were their blood relatives. However, even the work of one and the same tribe may vary considerably. This is seen particularly where one and the same subject is represented.[46] Different degrees of Hinduization accrued on the underlying form or left it untouched. It would seem that Hinduization of tribal art increased from the fourteenth century. It was at that time that the Bhil lost the privilege to inaugurate the Rana of Mewar.[47]

A large group of diminutive metal images seems to have its center of production to the south of the Bhil country, in the Deccan, around Nasik (Maharashtra). While the images are sometimes those of Hindu gods, the form is of an archaic, tribal caste; the flat slablike bodies of the figurines carry large heads, the faces projecting with a central peak, that of the nose. Blubber eyes bulge from the cheek slopes on either side of the nose bridge. These uniform, but plastically lively faces form a powerful accent above the puny, planar body. The bulk of the head, as in other tribal form traditions, proportionately exceeds and is here more massively three-dimensional than the rest of the figure. The limbs are tubelike extensions of the body. The figurines are frequently assembled in three-dimensional compositions. They are placed on a disc-shaped base, or the base may be a long, narrow strip. Each type of composition seems to be invented as the occasion demands, and in it the sprightly figures are distributed with zest. They completely exist in space, are freely placed within the spatial area. Truly three-dimensional group compositions are the exception in the Great Tradition of Indian sculpture which carves its images against the walls of the temple or observes a relief treatment even in the freestanding images of the temple sanctuary, as the image is meant to be seen essentially from the front only. The great South Indian bronzes of the Chola Age, apart from the superb modeling of the figures, are timid or constrained in their arrangement when forming a group.[48] In the small figure groups from Nasik, voids and masses interlock, each time in new rhythms and brisk patterns.

According to their ways of life, the tribes use art for specific purposes. The Santal of the Santal Parganas in Bihar occasionally use a carved litter (rāhī) in which the bridal pair is carried. This is not done by any other tribe. The carving of the litter enhances the effect of the procession, which is part of the marriage rite. When a Santal craftsman begins his work on the litter, a pair of pigeons is sacrificed; when the litter is completed and its owner has taken possession, two more pigeons are part of another sacrifice. The activity of carving is part of the marriage rite, as is the procession of the marriage litter. The carvings, in low relief, are narrative: human figures in combined front-profile view, limbs at times overlapped in telling gestures and lively actions of spontaneously formed groups; they are based roughly on one groundline in common, in a cursive notation of figures, human and animal, more voluble and less expert but somehow paralleling Egyptian reliefs. The Santal, too, carve their one-stringed lutes or their fiddles, sometimes in the shape of woman, transfiguring the resonance of the instrument into rotundities known from Hindu sculpture and brought to the tribal level by the simplifications and distortions demanded by the shape of the instrument. The prophetic head with its far-seeing inlaid eyes, traversed at the back by the tuning keys as a kind of ear ornament, carried aloft on a neck of inordinate length, is a noble mask. Through its thin-lipped mouth a god may speak—as he does through the dance mask of another tribe, the Bhuiya (pl. 4-5). Arms and hands closely hug the curved plane of the sounding-box body whose firmness is enhanced visually by the broad collar of the necklace.

Sound and mask, the prophetic voice that speaks through mask and instrument, link auditory and visual experience in one manifestation of the nu-

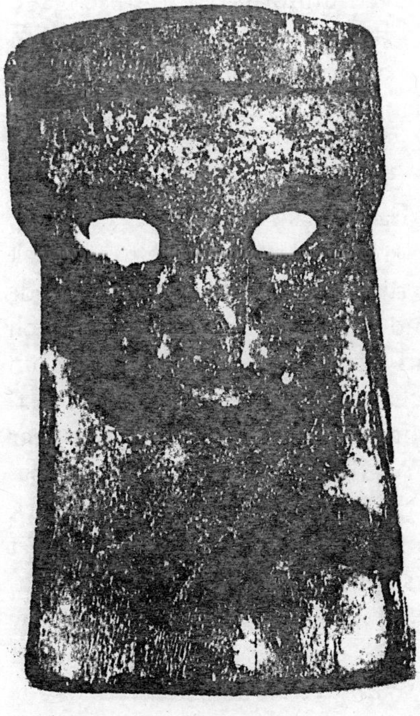

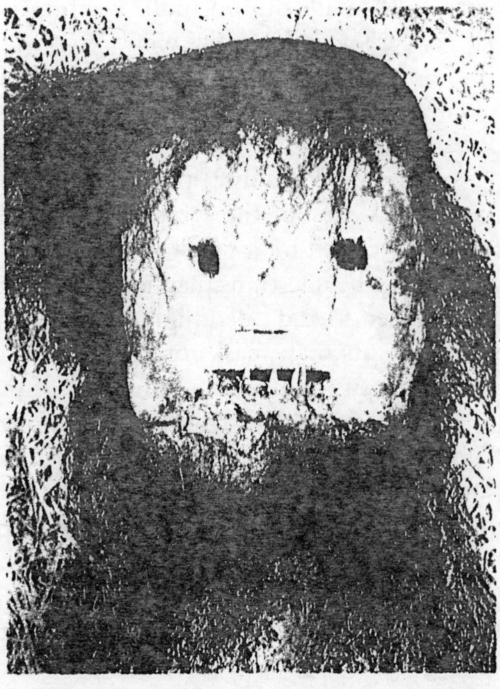

FAR LEFT *4-5. Mask, Bhuiya tribe, twentieth century; Bonai, Orissa-Madhya Pradesh border (National Museum, New Delhi)*

LEFT: *4-6. Mask, Bisonhorn Maria tribe, twentieth century; Bastar, Madhya Pradesh (National Museum, New Delhi)*

minous. The Saora tribe uses musical instruments in divination. The Oraon of Chota Nagpur regard musical instruments with something like religious awe.[49] With the Bhuiya, the gods speak prophetically through the mask while the wearer of the mask dances (pl. 4-5). If the musical instrument, by means of the shape of the human figure, is transformed into an icon, the wearer of the mask loses his identity in the experience of the presence which the mask represents and shields.

Masks are made by the tribal people of central India in assemblages of various materials and colors, in techniques ranging from matting to carving, and in styles from the abstract to grotesque exaggeration (pls. 4-5, 4-6), but with the sole exception of Verrier Elwin, no one has hitherto collected them. The tribal art of India, if collected at the beginning of this century, would have held its own in range and variety in comparison with that of Africa.[50] After that, where it has survived in its purity, it often shows its poverty. Where, smoothed to standards of Hindu art, the tribal proportions are followed, the directness of the underlying tribal form—even in its impoverished state—is lost.

On the nontribal level, and within Hinduism, sannyāsis perform ecstatic mask dances during the Gambhīra Festival of Śiva.[51] Before such an ascetic devotee puts on the wooden mask representing the deity that will take possession of him, he places the mask before the priest who performs the rite that brings life into it (prāṇapratiṣṭhā).

If the mask acts as facade for the temporal presence of the numinous in its wearer, it also protects him from contact with the direct glance of the outsider and makes him immune to the evil eye. In one of its particular usages, the mask (chau) is worn by royal and other dancers of Seraikella in Bihar during the spring rites celebrating Nata Bhairava, the fearful form of Śiva, the Dancer.[52] The chau dance is integrally part of the worship of Śiva. The masks worn today with their blandly wistful, wide-eyed uniform beauty disengage the dancer's face from the emotion expressed by his body. They shield him from a reference of his art to his person. The chau mask in its anonymity is an effective safeguard for the message of the dance conveyed by the movement of the body.

The mask (mohrā) through which the deity speaks is made of brass in the Kulu Valley of the western Himalayas. Each mask is a thanks offering. It is consecrated by a priest (pūjārī), and the shaman talks through the mask answering the questions that have been put to the deity. The masks of the gods are attached to and piled high on a chariot and taken out in procession. Each village has its own masks of the Goddess and her attendant divinities. From their high position on the mountain of the chariot, they inspect the harvest.

These masks of deity, unlike those worn by men, are kept from year to year in the village as property of the deity. A tithe is collected for the preparation of new masks. The money is paid to the craftsmen through the clerk of the village. In this rural setup, the voice of the Goddess is made manifest by its mouthpiece, the mask. The brass masks of the Kulu Valley are plaques showing the crowned head of the Goddess and terminating horizontally below the breast. An ancient mask of the ninth to tenth century[53] is cast in a shape belonging to the Great Tradition of Indian sculpture of that phase. It is the work of a master who must have been chosen for this task by the king who ruled over Kulu. More recent masks are without the opulent, classically formulated naturalism of the great Indian, early medieval tradition. A planar "chest" plaque showing as a rule, a necklace formed of a pair of serpents, symbols of fertility, and a mere suggestion of breasts in very low relief, extends below the mask of the crowned face, molded in high relief and carrying, at times, an aeginetan smile, on its once classical and now schematized features.

Metal and votive plaques accompany the history of the Great Tradition of Indian art.[54] Concurrently and earlier the tribal use of the mask must have been established in India as it was elsewhere since the time of the Cave of the Sorcerer.

The Kulu masks, while looking out on the harvest, look back to a past where metal plaques were given as offerings to the gods, where masks were worn so that the voice of the gods could be heard and where images were made of the gods portraying their ideal beauty. Three different traditions met and helped to create the locally circumscribed Kulu mask. Its isolated survival may indicate an entry of the anthropomorphic image of deity into sculpture by way of the mask as it also shows an appropriation from the Great Tradition of Indian sculpture and its transformation to rural needs and practice.

The Kulu mask and the Nasik group compositions and figurines are each the result of an application to rural practice of the Great Tradition of Indian sculpture. In the Nasik compositions it frequently lent its iconography, though not its manner, to the directional relationship of shapes contained within the volume of one spatial area. In the Kulu Valley, it imbued with its own tradition of form an already complex type of a tribal-rural past.

The tribal art of central India, however, retained its identity in each of the tribal units. If they adopted Hindu symbolism as the Gond did in carving their marriage booths, each post representing a palace of many stories such as that in which Hindu and Buddhist gods are seen to dwell,[55] the figures shown and the stories enacted on the Gond carvings are more closely related to the wall paintings of the Gond, Saora, and other tribes than they are to the representations carved in stone, long ago, on Buddhist and Hindu monuments.[56] At some points, Hindu concepts and symbols such as that of the palace of the gods were adapted by the tribes.[57] At some point, however, craftsmen of tribal extraction contributed their style to monuments of the Great Tradition.

Funerary posts, megalithic or carved in wood, belong not only to the tribal cultures of Central India. They are set up in rural Bengal to this day, and even in the suburbs of Calcutta.[58] These brisakāt (vṛṣakāṣṭha), or "wooden bull posts," show the post transformed into a general likeness of the deceased, man or woman, young or old, whose head is crowned by a "palace" architecture, housing in its first story the figure of a bull, the symbol of righteousness (dharma), and that of a Śiva-liṅga in its top story, the bull being here the means of attaining the highest goal, the domain of Śiva. The ancestral effigy carries as its superstructure an image of Shivaite hopes. Reduced to the bare outlines of form and meaning, such posts are carved today by an old woman sculptor in a crowded street of Calcutta. They are set up near a pond and are left to decay, uncared for, a year after a death has occurred.

From the Spirit Riders of the Bhil and other tribes, such as the Korku, from the horses of Aiyaṇār in South India and those of uncounted village gods throughout the country, to the hobbyhorse ridden by a devotee of Śiva in West Bengal,[59] the work of art was an instrument of communication with the realm of the spirit, the other world. Its form was a creative outcome of the experience of that world. It functioned as a support for wishes and as the only guarantee for their fulfillment. The work of art here fills the void of all that is not within reach and which must be postulated and hoped to be achieved, be it mere wish fulfillment, a feeling of security or the realization in this life of a state beyond it.

Differently located in the creative atmosphere is the art of the Naga tribes. The work of art made by a Naga serves as a repository of magical virtue, of power that leads to achievement and success. The Naga who live on the northeast frontier of India belong to the Tibeto-Burman family. They are a group by themselves, unrelated to the other tribal people of India. They number in all about four hundred thousand, but fall into distinct tribes whose art is linked to their entire social structure. Art with them is a ritual of magic fraught with danger. The artist must prepare himself, restrict his diet, and be chaste before he starts his work.[60] If he breaks one of the rules, he may die.

Some of the Naga are, or were, headhunters. According to them, that part of a man which is his magical virtue adheres to the skull, the other part goes to the land of the dead.[61] The Konyak Naga—some of whom are expert sculptors[62]—carry around their necks tallies of the heads of those they killed in warfare. These are made of wood or brass.[63] In Naga sculpture, the virtue that was in the living, man or animal, seems transferred, as it were, into its created form, where this virtue is enhanced by the ability of the craftsman to do so in creating form.[64] The art of representation is here felt to be a dangerous transmutation, an act of creative magic, for which the artist must brace and discipline his person.

The artist, like the other Naga, here is a warrior. He carves the main pillar of the village dormitory of the men (morung) and its open porch, and the houses of the donors of the Feasts of Merit. He represents animals, real or fantastic ones, warriors, couples, human and animal, dancing couples, tigers or frogs eating the moon. The figures are to be effective: the tigers will make the boys ferocious, the elephants will make them strong, the hornbills will make them fertile. Magically their virtue has gone into their representation and acts on the beholder. This metempsychosis-like transmutation through the medium of art is the Naga contribution to the relation of the artist to his object and to the beholder.

The morung, which is the setting of the Feasts of Merit, and the ritual bamboo mugs (chunga) from which the rice-beer is drunk, are decorated with death-shapes, floating and depleted. Today we see only the end of the Feast of Merit, the end of Naga life as it had been lived. Headhunting now being forbidden, art with the Naga has lost its raison d'etre. Even before that, the carvings of the ritual drinking mugs of the Phom do not differ greatly in quality from the carvings by the great Ang, the sacred chief of his Konyak village,[65] and by his two brothers. They show an almost conscious stylization where slender, weightless figures look like phantoms, suspended in afterthoughts.

The three-dimensional wooden or clay figures, the latter carved like wood, and particularly the wooden grave effigies, however, are free from the decorator's touch. They are set up for the warriors and other important persons for the habitation of their spirit. To the Naga, they are "live" images as long as the spirit dwells in them, but after the proper rites have been performed, the image ceases to be "live" and can be thrown away. Whether severally blocked out in rectilinear planes or more tubular in shape, whether grave effigies or not, the more abstract among the figures are three-dimensional patterns of pathos. It speaks differently from each sculpture, from eyes and mouth that are assimilated to each other. Their three circles, or three slits, intensify an underlying mood. Choice and place of ear-ornaments, colored fibers or cheap buttons, enliven the identity of each figure or group,[66] whatever its style. It may rely on geometric shapes that, though static, cohere by tensions generated by their contrast, or on a relationship of sinuous surface planes and spaces gliding between tenuously defined volumes.

The motivation for decorating the Naga morung and the houses of the donors of the Feasts of Merit, or in the case of the warrior himself, his own person, is the enhancement of life to which the experience of death contributes its share. The work of art, here, is the form given to the meeting of man and the supernatural, of man and the special power, which is not usually or normally his own—and for which the Naga has to kill an enemy or tiger. The artist contributes his work as a part of the total rite of living; it is his function or duty to do so.

He does not always do this willingly. Amongst the Kond, whose young men of one tribal unit, the Kutiya Kond, take pleasure in the small brass figurines made by the Ghasia, "no one paints unless he has to, and nearly every picture has behind it a history of tragedy and sorrow which it was designed to cure."[67] The lively and sometimes tormented line of the small figures in Kond paintings follows a pattern seen in a dream.[68] "Once made, no one ever looks at the painting." Here, apart from the artist himself, even the temporary beholder—who takes part in the funerary rites performed by means of the ancestral image, which then is thrown away—is excluded. The work of art is created and effective between the supernatural and the artist alone. The Kond practice art as self-therapy. They are skeptical about success. "Often the gods change their minds and send dreams demanding that the painting should be rubbed out and a new one prepared."

THE ART RITUAL OF WOMEN

1. Magic Diagrams

The surface for a painting, as a rule, is vertical; if it is horizontal it will be a ceiling or the ground. Classical antiquity had use for pictorial mosaic floors. India knew floor paintings (dhūli-chitra)[69] and to this day they are executed on the ground, mainly with white rice paste but also with colored powders. They are painted in tribal societies as magical diagrams, in different colors.[70]

The magic function of art in India is vested in the diagrams, primarily drawn on the floor.

The art of painting on the floor in rural India is the prerogative of women. Its traditions are handed down from mother to daughter. Her training begins in her fifth or sixth year and she reaches competence in her twelfth year. A non-Brahman priest may be engaged at times. The art of painting on the floor is non-Brahman, though it can be practiced by Brahman women. The women learned it ultimately from traditions more ancient than those of the Aryan Brahmans, and they elaborated them in forms by which the floor is covered with the magic potency in patterns peculiar to each part of India. The material itself of these magic diagrams, the rice powder, is felt to have magical powers. So is the copper, which formed part of the substance of the Bhil Spirit Riders. Rice powder acts magically. It scares away evil spirits.[71] The designs drawn with it on the floor have magical power. They are essentially diagrams. Within the confines, within the more or less intricate geometrical lines of the diagram an invoked presence finds its allotted place. Its power is confined and thereby held in its place and for the purpose for which the diagram was drawn. The magic diagram makes it possible for power to be present, and it brings this presence into the power of the person who has made the diagram. Apart from diagrams drawn by women, yantras, or magical diagrams are, also, part of Tantric Hindu practice.[72] A maṇḍala is such a magic diagram. Maṇḍalas were widely used in Tantric Buddhism. They determine the composition of one of the most characteristic and elaborate types of Buddhist paintings.[73] Tantrics who make a yantra have to avoid food prepared by women and even the sound of a woman's bangles.[74] Is it partly because they have to guard their art from those who had the power to evolve it? The meaning of a yantra goes far beyond that of diagrams drawn by women.

The floor designs drawn mostly freehand by women with rice paste or powder on the earthen ground range from geometrical diagrams by themselves to their association with other symbols such as footprints—which are those of the Great Goddess. These spellbinding configurations are known under many names, such as kōlam, maṇḍana, aripana, according to the style and region in which they evolved.[75] Originally far removed from decoration, all these ritual magic designs are forms of a will directed to an end which is to confine and control a supernatural power and to isolate it from the ground. The effect of these symbolic shapes is at one with their efficacy. They do not form abstract patterns for they are the shape of conceptions. They are intuited and functional diagrams transmitted by women.

Some of these designs are drawn every morning or in the evening; others at each sacrament of life (saṁskāra), at the passage from one state of life to another. They are drawn at the birth of a child, at the boy's investiture with the sacred thread, and at the time of marriage. Others are drawn as acts of devotion when taking a vow (vrata) to achieve a desired result. These are drawn on certain days of the year of special significance in the course of the sun.

The vrata alpona[76] and aripana are richest in design and connotation. The sun, the moon, the stars, the earth are integrated in them and also the things desired by the young girl who draws them, ornaments, a mirror and the like; and the whole cosmos is conjured up to bless and fulfill a young girl's

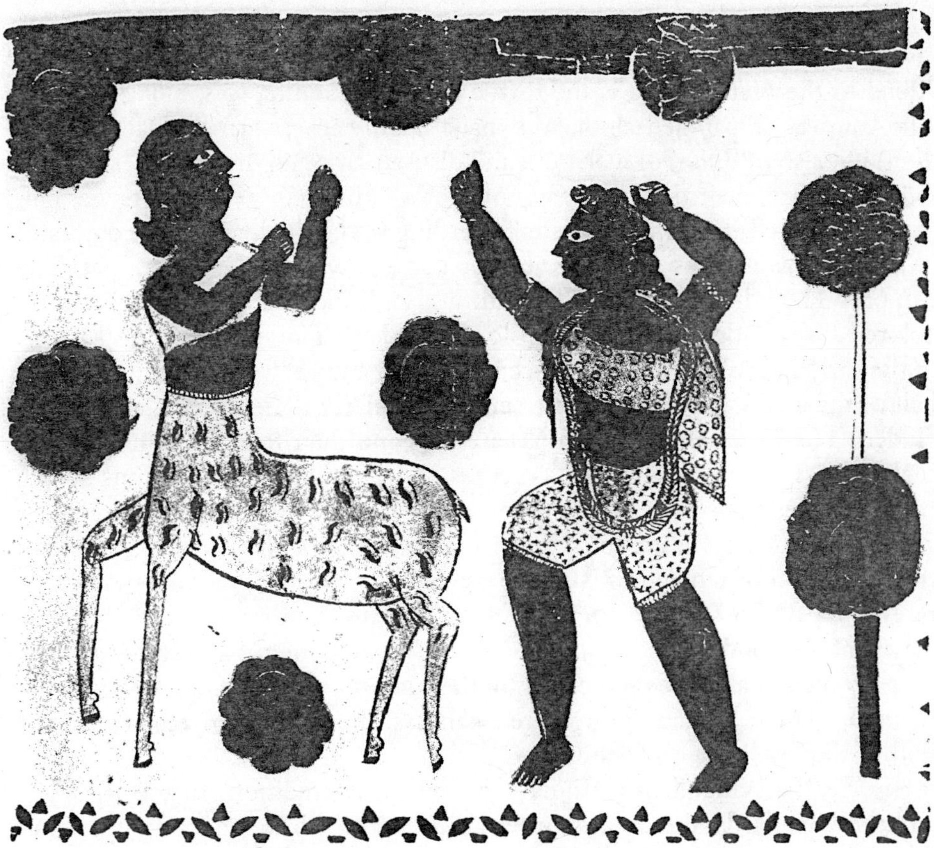

4-7. Ramayana Pat (detail), early nineteenth century; Hooghly, West Bengal

wish—for even a simple wish is not to be fulfilled if no effort is made at the right time to communicate with the powers that work in heaven and on earth. Here it is the magic circle, in other designs—the sacred square, a concatenation of curves or an intersection of polygons—that encloses the magic field. Into it the power of a god is invoked. It is assigned to its enclosure, it is spellbound. It cannot escape; it is controlled. It is held in its confinement, bound in the plane by the outline of the enclosure so that it cannot escape into the ground where, like lightning, it would be rendered impotent.[77]

The most ancient Sanskrit treatise on Indian painting prescribes the worship of the sun god through an eight-petaled lotus flower drawn on the ground.[78] Several other purāṇas[79] speak of the art of drawing the sun on the ground and that the sun was worshiped in a circle in early days.[80] However, this practice was not sanctioned by the Vedas;[81] it belonged to those outside the Vedic pale. The drawing of a magic diagram on the floor, however, became essential in building a Hindu temple.

The power of the supernatural is believed to be controlled magically and made effective at a given spot and time. The art of floor painting is a visual form of magic, a delineation and coercion of the presence of the numinous. Its diagrams avoid becoming stereotyped, they are enriched and evolve where, as in the vrata alpona of eastern India, the hopes and wishes of the artist are precipitated into the design on the floor.

2. *Kanthā Textiles*

Allied to the vrata alpona is the textile art of the kanthā (pls. 4-8, 4-9, 4-10). The kanthā,[82] a patched cloth, was made mainly in eastern Bengal (Bangladesh) but also in Bihar, of worn-out and disused saris and dhotis. After becoming threadbare, their thin, white cotton cloth with its colored borders was cut, patched, quilted, and embroidered. According to the thickness of the quilt and its size, it was used as a cover to be spread, as a wrap to be worn, or folded as a bag. The white ground of the quilt was embroidered and reinforced with colored threads drawn from the colored borders. The colors of the kanthās of the early part of the nineteenth century are mainly red and blue; in the later half of the century, yellows and greens, particularly linden green, are also included. The material of the kanthās are rags and their threads. Joined afresh, these tatters are given a new wholeness. Their embroidered designs spring from this meaning. The kanthā is a work that gives wholeness to things that were of no use any more, to fragments without any significance. This rite of the restitution of wholeness is a domestic one, performed by women, though rarely by Brahman women. The more ornate kanthās are the work of Kāyastha, or middle-class, women from the homes of clerks and scribes. However, women of all castes and classes of the rural population, including Muslim women, owned or had embroidered kanthās. They were given as presents within the family or to friends.

Textile symbolism in India is hallowed by tradition. In the Ṛg Veda and the Upaniṣads, the universe is envisioned as a fabric woven by the gods. The cosmos, the ordered universe, is one continuous fabric with its warp and

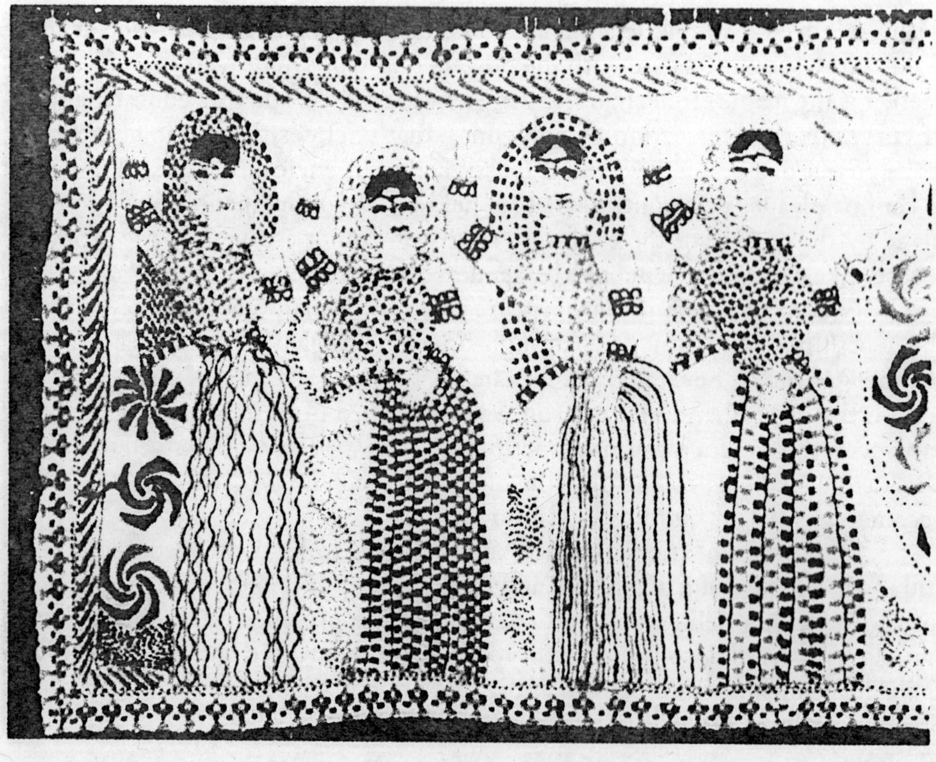

4-8. Kanthā (detail), late nineteenth to early twentieth century; Khulna, East Bengal

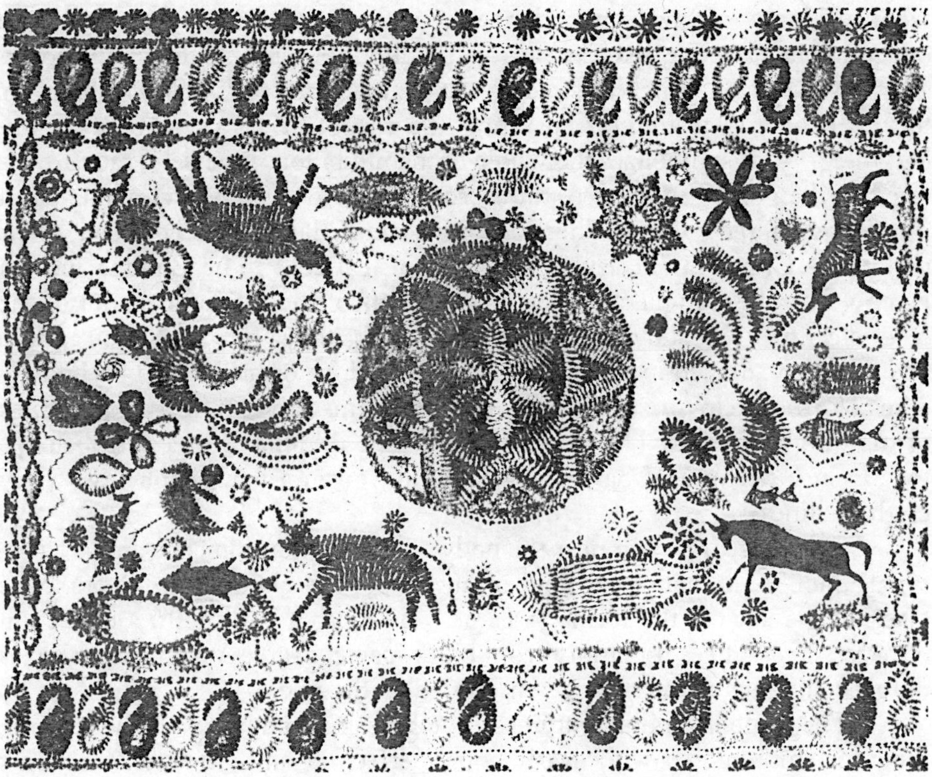

4-9. Kanthā (detail), nineteenth century; Faridpur, East Bengal

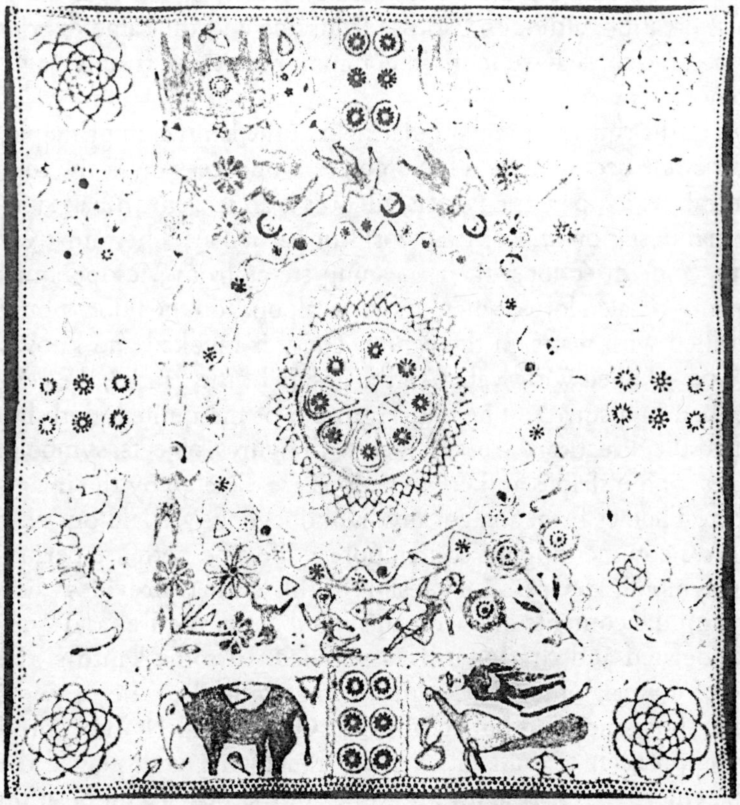

4-10. Kanthā, early nineteenth century; Khulna, East Bengal

woof making a grid pattern.[83] Hence the importance of wholeness, not only of the uncut garment, like the sari or the dhoti, but also of the cloth woven all in one piece, on which a sacred picture is to be painted.[84] Whether as cover for the body or as ground for a painting, the uncut fabric is a symbol of totality and integrity. It symbolizes the whole of manifestation. Inversely, rags are offered to the gods. Cindiyadeo, the Lord of Tatters, gives a new whole cloth if a rag is offered to him. There are rag shrines all over the country. Their goddess is Cithariya Bhavānī, Our Lady of Tatters.[85] The Buddha wore a patchwork robe (sanghati). Some of the reliefs of the Mathura school of the second century A.D. show him thus clad. Lord Caitanya (1485–1533), the apostle and visionary, draped in a kanthā the ecstasies which overwhelmed his body.[86] The colorful patchwork of the robes of saints forms part of miniature paintings of the Mughal period. The patched robe of the Buddha or of a saint belongs to him in his nature of Savior. The rags are given a new wholeness. They clothe holiness.

Clothes being worn near the body are part of its ambience and are personal. Should an enemy get hold of any bit of the cloth, he might practice black magic against the former wearer.[87] The patchwork quilt, a collection of tatters, guarantees immunity from black magic, protection and security, as do even the rags themselves when offered to the gods.

The symbolism inherent in the patchwork of the kanthā is the ground, which is embroidered with nearly equal perfection on both sides.[88] The act of making whole demands perfection throughout. The design is drawn by the embroiderer herself or by another woman. It is neither the work of a professional artist nor is it copied from anywhere. No two kanthās are ever alike; each is an original creation, although kanthās from one and the same district follow certain types and these have more in common than those from villages at a greater distance.

The design of the square or rectangular field of the kanthā, in principle, relies on a central circle occupied by a lotus flower. Four trees mark the four corners. The central, wide-open, many-petaled lotus is an ancient Indian symbol of universal manifestation and of this world in particular. The four trees are symbols of the four directions; their meaning stems from Mesopotamia. The disc of the many-petaled lotus, when drawn as alpona, on the floor, would support a vessel filled with water in the center. Deity is invoked and known to be present in a vessel filled with water. In the design of the kanthā, the central lotus is inscribed in a square. The entire ground of the quilted cloth between the lotus and the directional trees is filled with figures, objects, symbolic devices, and scenes whose shapes and combinations are dictated by the imagination of the artist. Themes from ancient myths and legends are laid out next to scenes and figures commenting on contemporary life, and both are permeated with purely symbolic devices. The design of the kanthās provides wide margins for showing the contents of a woman's mind. Their figures and symbols are freely associated and rhythmically assembled. In some kanthās, the figures are those of animals only. A Muslim kanthā, faithful to the precepts of a noniconic art, shows nothing but scrollwork. On the underlying central and directional composition of the kanthā, as its framework, is displayed the personality of the embroiderer. It shows not only in the planar composition but also in the selection of themes from the common reservoir of the tradition as it is lived by her at the moment of her needlework, but especially in the selection and spacing of the stitches and the resulting texture and form of the embroidery.

The stitches are of the simplest kind, the running stitch being not only the main but also the most ingeniously employed. According to the length and spacing of the single stitches, they circumscribe, and, this is their truly creative function, they organize a surface in a multitude of small squares and triangles so that its speckled texture of ground and embroidery is light or dense with colors. Closely parallel running stitches give a more gliding quality to the ground cover which they produce. Both of these modes and their combinations filling a given surface are bounded by a continuous line, which the backstitch yields. Within its firm contour, be it red or blue, the running stitches, according to their density, not only produce different color values, but together with a particular texture of the surface, they give a tonality of its own to each kanthā. Moreover, they are conducted so as to produce an effect of modeling of its own kind on the textured surface. Modeling by means of running stitches appears to be an invention of the embroiderers of the kanthās. It is a purely textile equivalent of modeling with brush and colors. In this, the "classical" tradition of Indian painting, as in Ajanta, excelled. Visualization in terms of the modeled form, an irrepressible sense of plasticity, are essentially Indian. This age-old and "classical" Indian quality was given form by textile means in the art of the kanthā of East Bengal in the nineteenth century. The effect of modeling is produced by the closely spaced rows of stitches running parallel with the outline of a figure. This brings about an area of uniform texture and tone. Toward the interior of the outlined surface, density and direction of the stitches change, producing other areas set off from their neighbor zones. This, together with the speckled textural effect of the stitches, which leads the eyes in more than one direction, also yields effects akin to op art but having representational intentions. The op art effect is bounded by the outline of the respective figure of elephant or horse.

The figures of the kanthā, "modeled" by these colorful stitches, which allow the white ground to shine through, are also foreshortened, and their limbs may overlap without, however, their giving the effect of any spatial context. The figures are scattered rhythmically over the white ground, and if limbs or figures overlap, their area is part of the embroidered ground, for though the figure may be modeled in terms of stitching, the modeling has no substance to it. It suggests volume by directional movement. Far from creating an illusion of the body, its embroidered form is dematerialized. Often the figures are shown in a contraction of front and profile. At other times, an x-ray view allows one to see across them. As an outcome of this, some kanthās create their own figures, having the shape of a man, with or without a body, the number of limbs also being at the discretion of the artist. This, though, does not refer to their multiplicity which iconography may postulate in the case of the figures of deities but to their reduction, to stumps instead of limbs, contraction of two limbs into one, or omission of one limb or the other according to the needs of identification, rhythm, and compositional clarity.

By the middle of the century, the embroidery stitch is more frequently resorted to than it was earlier. It adds more compact areas and stronger hues to the kanthā. But these stronger accents too sink into the ground of the kanthā. The ground between figures, as often as not, is reinforced all over with stitches running in closely set parallels around each figure. For this, white thread is used and, less frequently, blue or red thread. These colors give a pointilistically muted tonality to the vibrant texture of the ground of kanthās and make them assignable to the turn of the century.

Thematically, the art of the kanthā is an enriched textile version of the art of the aripana or alpona, the painting on the floor, its magic purpose being enhanced by the textile symbolism of its material and the way this is used. Stylistically, its form is entirely its own, adjusting an ancient propensity of India's classical art to its own textile and planar sensibilities.

The art of the kanthā is a rural art. While it is imbued with Hindu myths, it is also perceptive of the life of India in the nineteenth century with some of its manners and fashions derived from those of the West, an imaginative blend of the actuality of living where every day contributes some novelty to be absorbed by the stream of the tradition and integrated into its style. It is an art of leisure. Sophisticatedly primitive, the quilt of the kanthā integrates many layers of the fabric of Indian life, tribal as well as urban, in its conception. The magic that underlies its purpose is that of love—not of coercion, as that of the diagrammatic floor drawings whose purpose is wish fulfillment. A kanthā is given as a present, it is conceived with an outgoing mind and brings the entire personality of the maker to the person for whom it is made. Its composition is a ritual being laid out around the center of the lotus of manifestation. Its symbols have universal validity in the four directions. To their whirls and waves, to the lotus and the life trees are assigned the innumerable figured scenes of the mythic, ever-present past together with episodes of the passing scene.

All of them are firmly stitched into a reconstituted, vibrant wholeness. The kanthā is the form, by textile means, of a creative process of integration within each woman who makes a kanthā.

Succumbing to what were, in India, the belated effects of the Industrial Revolution, the art of the kanthā died after the first quarter of the twentieth century. It is not known when this art began. Its upsurge in a narrowly circumscribed area has not its like elsewhere. Kanthās from Bihar are without the wealth of associated content and textile imagination. Although made by the same technique, their widely spaced design is an adaptation, in terms of embroidery, of the staid, placid lines of a certain type of painting of Bihar. The Bengali kanthās resemble a form of painting in Bengal only insofar as their overall character stems from the magic art of the alpona. As much as the South Indian sanctuaries, teeming with their hundreds of clay horses, clay cattle, and clay human figures offered in sacred groves express in their form the mystery of autochthony, the kanthās of East Bengal are saturated with and express a numinous power, the śakti of this region, working through its women and given form by innumerable disciplined stitches. Both these forms of art, that of the South Indian half-Brahman priest-potter and that of the Bengali Hindu matron—it was the older women, as a rule, who made the kanthās—represent traditional village art in fulfillment of rites of offering.

3. *Painting*

Women in other parts of India have their own inherited traditions of painting. Not only the respective diagrams on the floor are their prerogative. In Mithila, in North Bihar, the women of Brahman families and those of the Kāyastha, or middle class, paint the walls of their homes for the celebration of two of the major sacraments of life.[89] With them, moreover, there is no significant transition within the life of man that is not marked by an aripana on the floor. The paintings act as projections of the meaning of that moment on floor and walls around the person when the rites are performed. Some of the sacraments bound to be observed in each generation are: birth, marriage, the investiture with the sacred thread in the upper castes, and also the first haircut or the piercing of the earlobes. The Maithil wall paintings, done for the sacred thread ceremony and for weddings, have their standard repertory of images, painted according to the stylistic variations peculiar to each social group.[90] Symbols from the aripana or floor diagrams—which are particularly rich in motifs in Mithila—occur also in the wall paintings amidst a generally figural setting. As in the art of the kanthā, freely associated scenes and figures are part of an organized composition whose units, within their precise outlines, seem to float on the white ground of the wall. The women also paint on paper recurrent standard types of figures and compositions of the paintings on the walls. Their distortions commend themselves to eyes familiar with expressive and geometrical form. The paintings on the walls are more permanent than are the floor paintings, whose dried rice paste or colored dust lasts only for the occasion, because the floors are trodden on—dust which has been trodden on has mystical powers[91]—and the image wiped off. The wall paintings decay in less than ten years, and then the time has come for new ones.

The domestic art of the Maithil wall paintings follows the pictorial traditions of the family and caste to which the painter belongs—whereas the textile art of the kanthā precipitates into a given frame of reference the inner world and psychic tensions of its maker. It is the most personal form of a traditional, ritual, and domestic village art.

In the Maithil wall paintings, which may or may not be confined within a frame or border, the figures are evenly distributed over the area to which they adhere with a clear color spread within the circumscribing drawing. Its representational function is simplified, its quality is that of a cognizance not far from toyland. The rhythms, however, of the work of Kāyastha women in spacing the single elements are akin to those of tribal paintings. There they are urgent and stark. Here the single elements are stylized.

All the same, the aspects of tribal and village art hitherto described were imbued with the magic of ritual necessity and fitness. They belonged to a large part to non-Brahmanic and non-Hindu traditions. These visually conceived and executed rites were performed generally by specialized practitioners, like the South Indian Kucavan potter-priests and by women trained to celebrate the visual rites and who, inasmuch as they created form, were artists.

While the women of Mithila celebrate in their paintings the sacraments of the life of man, peasant women in villages of the Punjab, around Delhi, in parts of Uttar Pradesh and Rajasthan celebrate the sacraments of the cosmos;

in seasonal rites the Great Mother, under different names and shapes, is made to inhabit her image, which is the work of the village women during the days when the rites are performed before it. The image of the goddess Hoī, whose body is the square diagram of the cosmos, is assimilated to the shape of man by adding to the square a head and the extremities, or also to that of a house in which man has his dwelling or to both at the same time. The image is painted on a wall of a house in the village. When, however, the Great Goddess as Sānjhī is made to dwell in her image, her shape is a composition of triangles entirely covered with multiform and star-shaped clay discs. They are applied to a coating of mud and cow dung, which is given to an outer wall of a house. The small clay elements painted white and speckled with orange, blue, and yellow cover, a starry array, the dark, triangulated shape of the Goddess. She is accompanied by the small figure of her brother who brings offerings to her on the eighth of the Navarātri rites of nine nights, when his image is added to that of the Great Goddess. On the tenth day the entire painted relief is removed from the wall, which now is painted white and the figure of a peacock is drawn on it, while the remnants of the image are drowned in the village pond.[92] Unique in their technique of relief applique and painting, the Sānjhī representations made by peasant women form part of the visual-tactile creativeness of rural India, which in western India combines not only the effect of mirrors and textiles but of mirrors and mud wall in patterns as free and disciplined as those produced by the stitches of kanthās.

RURAL PRACTICE AND THE GREAT TRADITION

The specialized and professional artist or craftsman belonging to the Hindu tradition worked for a patron in village or town, or for tribal people, or was dependent on an urban public.

Scroll paintings are the work of professional craftsmen (citrakara). They were exhibited in ancient times, for they are mentioned by Pantañjali in the middle of the second century B.C.[93] The long, vertical scroll paintings from West Bengal and Bihar are narrative (pl. 4-7) and thus different from the configurations of the floor and wall paintings of village and tribal art. Their compositions are akin to the complex majority of the carved panels of the corner posts of the Bharhut railing of the second century B.C. that appear to be lithic versions, in relief, of scroll paintings. The practice of painting vertical scrolls has mainly survived in West Bengal and in the Santal Parganas, Bihar, whereas large, horizontal scroll paintings, but also vertical ones, come from Rajasthan. The painters in Bengal belong in the main to the painter caste (citrakara).[94] An ancient text accounts for the low status of the painters. They fell from grace as their paintings transgressed the Brahmanic instructions. They were not painted according to hieratic rules and were therefore defective.[95] This story wants to account for the low status of the citrakaras, to which they had fallen by the thirteenth century. Another community of painters in Bengal are the jādū-paṭuās.[96] They are itinerant aboriginal mendicants, "Hindu" magicians, brassworkers, and painters. They paint for the tribal Santal. Their name, jādū-paṭuā, means "magic-painter." Their styles and also those of the paintings of citrakaras working for the Santal are, on the whole, nearer to tribal brevities than is the opulence of the various Bengali styles of the other citrakaras. Though citrakaras are specialized craftsmen, some of them work in several media. The citrakaras, or painters, often also model in clay. However, they are trained as painters and gain proficiency by painting on the walls of their houses. These exercises are rubbed off daily.[97] Their scrolls were painted in gouache originally, it would seem, on cloth, and subsequently on paper mounted on cloth.

Tribal and village traditions commingle in the painted scrolls. The various schools represented by paintings from different centers carry on each the style created by a local master painter. Some of the early scrolls (ca. 1800) show an awareness of Rajput and Mughal types, though these are recast consistent with a deeper tonality, avoidance of suggestions of the third dimension, and a calmly flowing line. Scrolls painted in Hooghly call to mind qualities of Etruscan painting (pl. 4-7).[98] Later in the nineteenth and in the twentieth century, different "schools" can be localized. The burnt sienna and indigo blue tonality of scrolls from Manbhum, Purulia, West Bengal, holds pent-up emotion packed in dense, contiguous compositions floating in broad, curvilinear rhythms. This "school" is easily distinguished from the archaic, arrested gestures, tensely planar composition, and strong, quiet colors of the Hooghly paintings (pl. 4-7) or from the lyrical, voluble style of many degrees, on white or red ground of the Midnapur paintings where large figures crown the scroll.[99] The subjects painted illustrate Hindu myths. A cycle that kept its popularity over the last thousand years and more are the yama patas, the paintings of the rewards of good and evil to be experienced in the realm of Yama, the Lord of Death.[100]

The scroll paintings (paṭa) were exhibited by the painters who acted as picture showmen and bards at the same time. They recited a passage from scripture and legend while pointing to the respective picture on the scroll, depicting in successive panels the relevant passages. The paṭa or paṭ was hung up on a bamboo frame, the rest of the scroll being rolled up, and the particular incident that a passerby needed for his edification was displayed. The painter-bards on the crossroads are no longer part of the Bengal scene. While their art, in the early twentieth century, borders on religious folk art, the jādū-paṭuās practice magic (jādū) through some of their paintings. These they paint for the tribal Santal. The painter comes with his ready-made schematic portraits of which one or the other is bound to fit the type of the recently dead among the tribal Santal whose house he visits. The dead are believed to wander blindly in the other world until the jādū-paṭuā gives them eyesight by painting the eyes in the "portrait." These "portraits" painted for the Santal are distinguished from the work of the citrakaras by their economy of colors. The scroll paintings intended for Santal audiences, however, lack the relaxedly flowing lines and also the rich warm colors of the Bengali scroll paintings. Their colors are generally light and cool; their crudely vehement economy of line is nearer to tribal wall paintings in Middle India than to the residual opulence of the Bengali village styles.

The paintings done for the Santal represent the tribal tradition among the rural painters, the citrakaras and jādū-paṭuās of eastern India,[101] while the paṭuās, who practiced their calling near the Kālī Temple in Kalighat (now part of Calcutta) produced their pictures for the pilgrims and visitors, many of whom came from Calcutta. Originally, the paṭuās of Kalighat worked in wood. Then they made clay images of Hindu gods to be worshiped at their annual festivals. In between, they painted and made clay and wooden toys.[102]

The paintings particularly associated with them are in watercolor on millmade sheets of paper. They are religious but also satirical in content. They also translate into their own style natural objects, plants, fruits, animals, following the example of the British in India who had been fascinated by the Indian flora and fauna. Kalighat paintings have been called "bazaar paintings,"[103] for they could be bought by anyone and for very little. Made for the man in the street, they supplied him with images he could take home, images which appealed to him on many levels. And they did more than that.

Kalighat paintings translate the narrative style of the village paṭuās into a new monumentality. It owes as much to the classical tradition of Indian painting, as practiced in Ajanta—whose ample fluid curves had glided along an unbroken though weakened chain from master to pupil into the linearized context of the scroll paintings—as it owes to Western classicism brought to Calcutta by the British. Kalighat paintings, at the height of their style in the last quarter of the nineteenth century, condense silhouette and modeling of the figures in sweeping outlines of the continuous brush strokes themselves. The paintings and brush drawings are monumental in their presentation on an otherwise mostly blank page. Preceding the work of Matisse, some of the brush drawings prefigure it. Out of Indian tradition and impressions of Western painting, the "bazaar" painters, descendants of low-caste and hereditary craftsmen created forms as valid as, and akin to, some of the later work by leading artists in the West. In the Kalighat brush drawings of the later nineteenth century, moreover, old slumbering memories of creativeness seem actualized. Sinuosities that had ripened in Indian sculpture in the sixth century and dilated the potent shapes of the Goddess in even a humble offering plaque from the Himalayan foothills or the Punjab in the eighth century sustain the sweep of line of the Kalighat drawings.

Kalighat paintings are an outcome of the residual Great Tradition of Indian painting and of a local, traditional village art and their spontaneous transformation when exposed to currents of Western art active in the nearby city of Calcutta in the nineteenth century. Some of the kanthas show the opposite process, on a different level, by integrating city fashions and foreign types into the rural atmosphere and closely stitched context of their embroidered field.

An altogether different phenomenon however is the form of Jagannatha, carved in wood and painted. The image is set up in its traditional and repeatedly renewed shape in the Temple of Jagannātha, the Lord of the World, in Puri, Orissa.

There, to the south of Bengal, on the east coast, a miraculous thing happened when, according to legend, a log of wood was seen floating in the sea and a mythical king ordered a carpenter to make it into an image of God. The carpenter stipulated that he be left working behind closed doors for twenty-one days. The king opened the door prematurely; the carpenter, who was God himself, vanished. Though the image remained incomplete, it was installed in the temple.[104] The image of Jagannātha, Lord of the World—in his temple of the twelfth century in Puri, an imposing structure built in the Great Tradition and of lavish sophistication—is a log of wood. Just that and nothing else. Large eyes are painted on it and arm stumps branch out. In megalithic cultures, a log of wood is a proxy for a piece of stone, which, in tribe and village, was set up to indicate the presence of deity. The Uriya legend speaks of a miracle that happened when a primeval shape came to be the center of the most meticulously ordained rites of orthodox Hindu worship. The image of Jagannātha stares open-eyed from paintings and wooden images of Orissa. Around it grew an iconographic style of painting entirely its own, a temple-craft based on tribal tradition. Its reverberations were felt in Bengal.

An irruption of a stark shape of tribal art into the Great Tradition is not the rule. It is generally that shapes of the Great Tradition, such as its costumes, are accepted beyond the centers of its activity. Within a feudal society, its many princely and lesser courts and patrons, art had a wide public, the same rural public that listened to its favorite ballads and to the recitation of the sacred myths. The wisdom of India was transmitted orally and visually, written texts were resorted to only when memory had become weakened. Visual transmission was relied upon far more than the written word. The making and beholding of symbols and images were part of living. In Bengal and Bihar, the bard-and-showman exhibited his long scrolls with their neatly divided horizontal panels, each illustrating a phase of the story. In Rajasthan, he showed his wide, horizontal scroll, its composition one overall tessellated field of figures, telling the story of Pābujī, the Rāthor chief, and his coal-black mare.[105] One recognizes the Mewar school of painting but only as far as figures and costumes go. The style of the Pābujī paintings has a planar coherence and epic width unknown to the "miniature" paintings of the Mewar school.

Feudal styles and temple traditions, variously blended, sunk into the fabric of the local practice of art, as it renewed itself celebrating the rites of the seasons in nature and those in the life of man. A series of paintings from Paithan, in Maharashtra, in central India, lays out its epic and mythical themes in a restrainedly heroic manner, another series of paintings from Mysore in the south, more power-inflated, loads its vigorous design and hieratic figures with gold and stylistic ornaments of temple art. The school of Tanjore, in the south, infuses stereotyped Western naturalism into this blend, removing at times its staleness by the naïvité of preoccupations or superstitions which can be satisfied by just this type of art.

In the field of sculpture, the polychrome wood carvings of Kerala on the southwest coast are more than equivalent to the Mysore paintings. Their epic chattiness derives from earlier, near Hoysaḷa idioms; never before have hands been so weighty and fingers so elongated as in this carved and painted exuberance showing the hosts of gods, heroes, and demons on temple beams and cars. Such reliefs are created in, and again help to create, a consistent mood of religious absorption. The spell of autochthony pervades them.[106]

On a corresponding level of autochthonous tradition, metal figurines from the western Himalayas are far from consistent in their form. Daringly or clumsily they present long-lived dregs of classical Western art, reduced simulacra of Himalayan temple art and a pristine aptitude for turning iconography into newly discovered simplicities of form.

Steeped in the rites of their own living traditions of art which went on even when the Great Tradition of the temple builders was given no further scope, the craftsmen throughout India, from about the sixteenth century, supplied the needs of temple worship. Temple cars, in which the image of deity is taken in procession, continued to be built. Indian textbooks on architecture distinguish stationary from mobile architecture. The latter is preeminently that of the temple car. In the two last centuries, it remained a showplace for sacred imagery, fulfilling in its own scale the purpose of the temple: to be seen. To have a look (darśana) of the temple, to see and to ṭake in all that it stands for was the main purpose of a visit to a temple. All the meaning and power inherent in it comes out on its walls as sculpture. The centrifugal impact from the core and center of the temple on to the walls and thence on the beholder generates a dynamism of sculptural form active even in the latest carvings of a wooden temple car, about a century ago. Here, an age-old tradition is still a vital creative urge, manifest in the vehement massing of rhythms which overcome the somewhat stale shapes of the figures. It is by its driving power of rhythmic organization that Indian village art, where it stems from the Great Tradition, is not a folk art. It does not apply to its own scale a great heritage but contributes to it.

The Indian image-maker of the Great Tradition complied with a detailed iconography and iconometry according to his own artistic endowment. The rules let him soar above their firm foundation or they tied him down. If he but followed the rules with sculptural competence, his work became fit for worship. When the Great Tradition no longer prevailed, the village craftsmen shaped images that were iconographically acceptable,[107] though their iconometry was no longer necessarily that of the canons of temple art. Distortions, formerly present but kept in check by these canons, had now a wider scope. In their inflections, the rural, tribal, idiosyncratic tendencies and heritage expressed themselves. God Krishna now plays his games or his flute—which is hardly ever represented in sculpture—in as many distinct modes as the rhythms of modeling and proportions of his body convey in his Rajasthani or Orissan or Bengali image. If Hindu or Jain images are given form by the rural craftsman, they are shaped according to the rhythms of his own way of realizing their presence. On the other hand, and at the same time, he may follow the example of Hindu temple art, and he may visualize the gods and ghosts who protect or threaten his village—instead of marking their presence by an unhewn stone—and invest their images with the substance of Hindu form. He models their figures so that they expand in planes rounded as if by the pulsations of life and breath, which here do not come from their core. Something seems to hold back their luxuriant ease, something that links them to the sterner conceptions of tribal art. At other times, a truly aboriginal conception of a rakṣasa, a man-eating ogre, seems almost to have invented its own technique, a slashed hollow cast whose ribbands streak the cylinders of the legs and furrow the "naturalism" of the head, whereas an image of Navagunjāra is as much a product of local theology as it is an Indian represen-

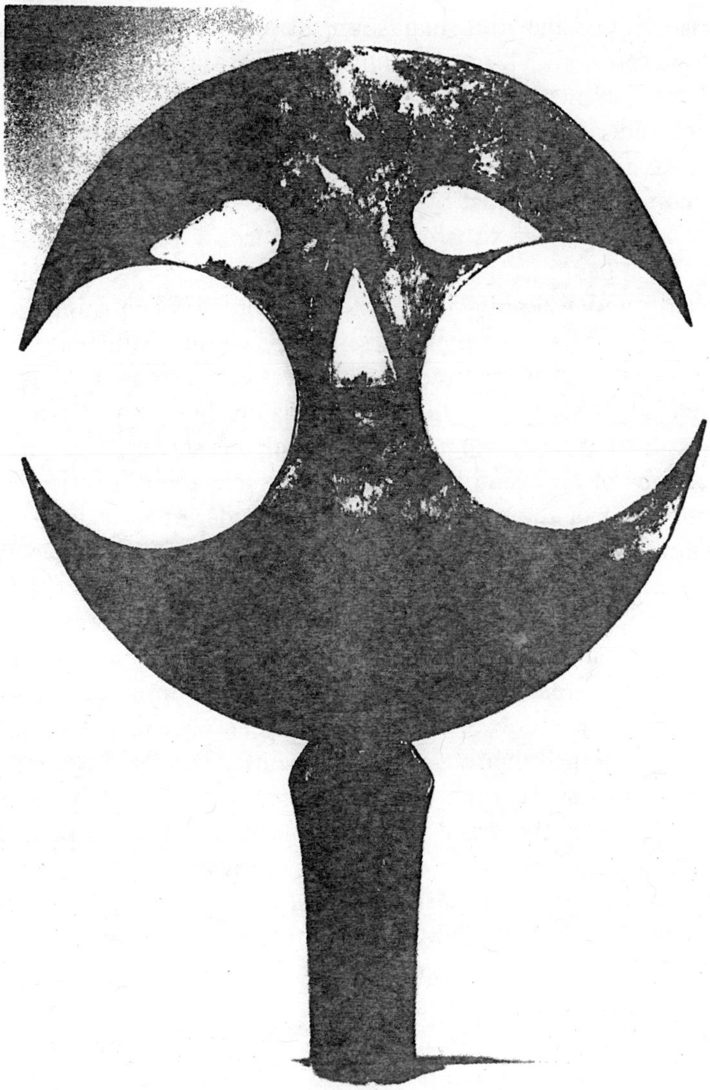

4-11. Asha Danda, twentieth century; Sundarban, West Bengal

tative of the "animal style" and a creation of the village art of Orissa. Ritual implements, such as ritual lamps and vessels and objects of domestic ritual, such as body scrubbers and also magic wands (pl. 4-11), are equally significant works of art. In extraordinary diversity, they emerge from below the cover of the once unifying Great Tradition.

In the domestic art of the kanthā, the embroidered field had taken to its own use the magical disposition of the floor paintings (alpona). The embroidered coverlets of the western Himalayas,[108] though not magically strengthened by the art of stitching, were also made to be gifts. The drawing, however, was often done by professional artists whose work are the Pahārī miniature paintings stemming from several stylistically distinct local centers. The elegance of these embroideries of the higher social classes is set off by others, less ambitious in scale and narrative, where tribal fantasies are at play. Between such extremes of conception, but worked in the same satin stitch with floss silk on gossamer-thin handspun, handwoven cotton, in the colors of Pahari miniatures, are all-over designs of rustic simplicity and visual integrity.

Textiles as covers, wall hangings, and colorful canopies offered their embroidered or appliquéd fields as decorations particularly at marriages but also as a tribute to a dead saint or hero. The symbols and figures of these textiles accompany the ritual of the living and those for the dead in rural India.[109]

Part of the ritual are also the shadow plays with their painted figures. They are ancient means of religious instruction—an involuntary learning by seeing and listening—and entertainment.[110] The puppets, made of painted deer- or goatskin, are either semitransparent, as in the "dance of the leather puppets" of Andhra Pradesh in the eastern Deccan, or, cut out of buffalo skin, they are opaque as are those of Kerala on the southwest coast, their heroic figures belong to the *Rāmāyaṇa.* Seen on the screen, they are but shadows, projections of an exemplary reality. As such, their function is at the other end from that of the masks. The mask shields inner reality, the presence of the numinous, and the person possessed by it from the outer world, while at the same time impressing the outer world with the form of the numinous. Masks are tribal creations. They are essential means of identification with a superhuman reality by one who experiences this reality and, being the form created out of this experience, they are a means of communication between that reality and those who are in need of sensing its presence. The shadow play on the screen, on the other hand, and the painted scrolls, the embroideries, and other kinds of rural art conjure up and trace images inwardly seen. They adumbrate and illustrate the other world so that it may find its place in this world and through its form in art enter the pattern of life.

The gap in intensity in tribal art on the one hand and rural art on the other is closed in India by the penetration of tribal into village art. This blend, by the nineteenth century, took to itself some of the shapes and finally also some of the flavor of Western naturalism such as the British patronized. It was this Western naturalism which took over where Indian "naturalism" of the Great Tradition of temple art had left off. Tribal art, although restricted and impoverished today, had given more to Hindu village art than it received in turn—and what tribal art did receive, it partly received it back. The charm of the equestrian figurines (pls. 4-2, 4-3) seems to have been gathered in this way.

A figurine made by the village potter, or by a woman, if consecrated, plays its part in the rites. If not consecrated, it is a plaything. Toys made of clay, wood, cloth, or pith, simple in the stereometry of their shape, heightened by color, are functional. While they delight sight and touch, they quicken the imagination. Other toys, more detailed in execution because representational in intent, incorporate their once ritual purpose in the ever stimulating qualities of the traditional materials of which they are made. With this added grace, they are easy to look at, being of the same lineage as the figures in the embroideries and scroll paintings made in the village.

III
THE SUBTLE BODY

5 ⚜ The Representation of Nature in Early Buddhist Sculpture (Bharhut-Sanchi)

The oneness of all creation is expressed in early Buddhist sculpture by a gentle harmony and similarity of individual shapes, which characterize every object but are more than a picture of their exterior. Life itself has assumed the shape of artistic form. The Indian understands life as growth. He does not depict the shapes of nature but nature itself, the creative creating power. Earth's life blood streams through the members of figures and gives them form according to the celerity of its circulation, which is gently flowing, soft and equipoised at Bharhut. The forms have not yet separated themselves from Mother Earth, who nourishes them and gives them the contemplative life. Each relief is first of all a picture of this spiritual state, and secondary to it, it is the representation of a particular theme.

In the scene of worship on the Prasenajit Pillar at Bharhut (pl. 5-1), the feet of the figures are not separated from the ground, the tender curved outlines of the figures are accompanied by the folds of hanging drapery. Their swing is similar to that of the branches of the trees which surround the men.

The serenity of the Indian figures is the result of the calmness of mind which invented them. It is the spirit which builds the body. The figures do not seem to have bones and muscles but consist of an entirely uniform plastic mass. Their faces have a sameness of types. All are round and their cheeks seem to be too big because they are not modeled sufficiently (Bharhut, pl. 5-2). The roundness of faces is exaggerated by the headdress, covering the foreheads. This roundness is pronounced by a short nose, small and full lips and almond-shaped eyes which have curved eyebrows. The changes of facial types are always conditioned by a change of quality and style of the relief and are therefore not indicative of different types of races, but show clearly that they are nothing else but a result of artistic formation. The face as an equally measured, well

This essay first appeared in *Rūpam*, no. 8 (October 1921). It was Stella Kramrisch's first published article.

surrounded, symmetrical shape is considered to be a useful element of composition. Some scenes are composed entirely of faces. One head is set next to the other. The aspect of the relief is like that of a number of round buttons, stitched near each other (Bharhut, pl. 5-3). These typical faces without life do not express an inner feeling; they make no attempt toward facial expression, although they have the mystery of smiling peace which blesses the mouth of archaic Greek and early Gothic statues. Their only purpose is to complete the idea of the human figure. It is not that the early Indian artist had no faculty in this direction. He did not consider facial expression as necessary. He was very able to do so if he aimed at it. The representation of Māra's followers (Sanchi, north gate, back view, middle lintel, pl. 5-4) is of a grotesque triviality, obtained by exaggerating the single features of the face which are made to grin sneeringly.

Mostly the figures stand still even if they are supposed to walk (Bharhut, pl. 5-2, upper part). The body is without energy, the movements of actions begin only from the elbow. Hands are made to seize or indicate, and are joined in order to pray (Bharhut, pl. 5-5). The whole energy proceeds from the forearms and hands, the rest of the man takes no part in it and his body swings in a curve that is not influenced by his energy. This produces the effect of all action seemingly to be transposed into the region of dreams. The figures seem to live without any responsibility.

In the representation of the *Yavamajjhakiya Jātaka* (Bharhut, pl. 5-6), the king, sitting on the throne, raises his hand; a woman on his left side raises a chaurī, servants raise their arms holding a stick on which a basket is suspended. No other figure moves. Nevertheless the action is highly dramatic. The relief tells of the fidelity of the queen who stands at the right side of her husband; she is taller than the other people of the court; she withstood the temptations of her lovers, who now are brought before the whole court, imprisoned into the baskets.

BELOW LEFT: 5-1. *Worshiping gods and defeat of Māra; on upright of railing; Bharhut*

BELOW RIGHT: 5-2. *Cakravāka Nagarāja; part view; figure on upright of railing; Bharhut*

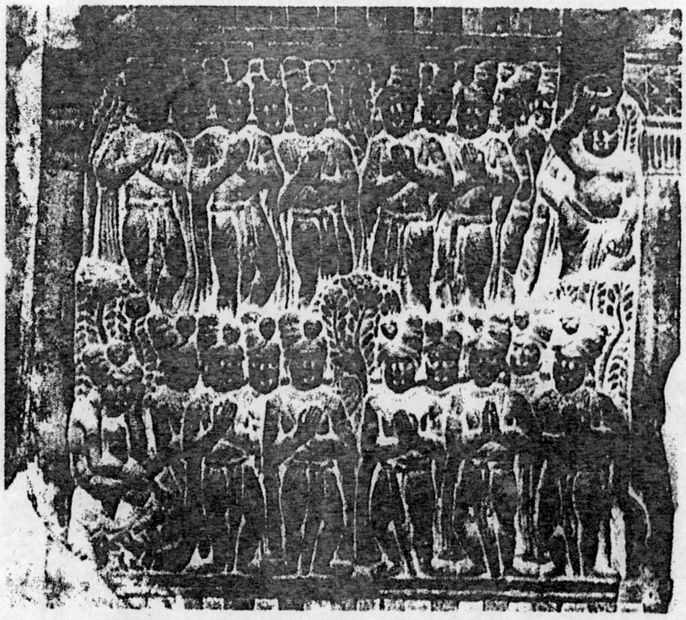

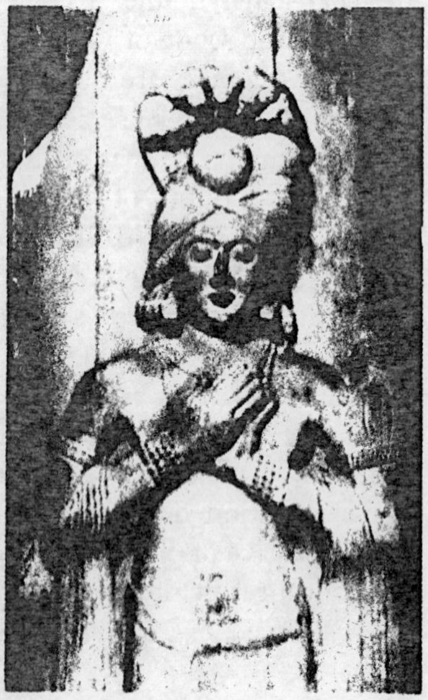

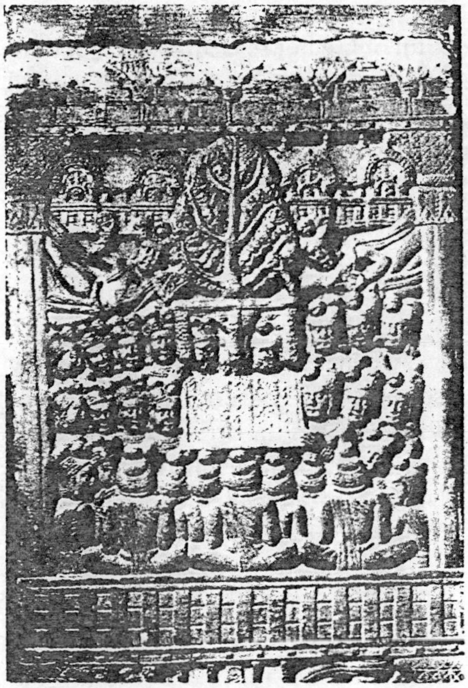

5-3. Buddha teaches Abhidharma in Tushita Heaven; relief on upright of railing; Bharhut

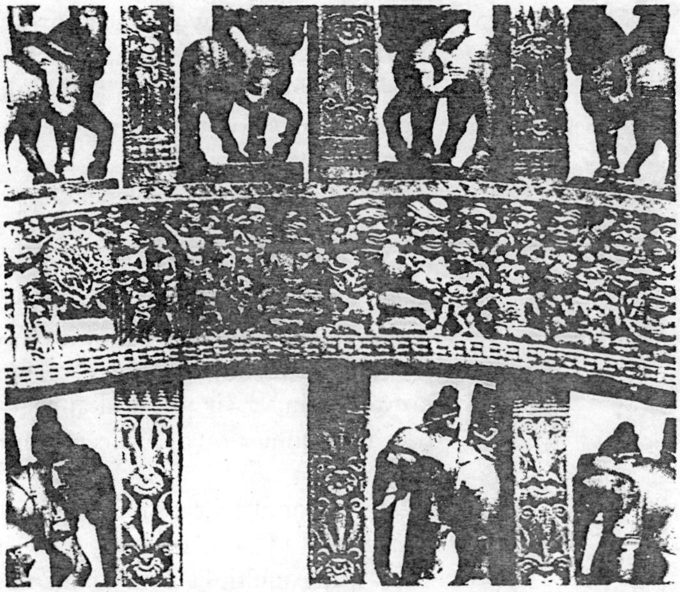

5-4. Māra, the Evil one and his host; part view of middle lintel, back face, north gate, stūpa 1; Sanchi.

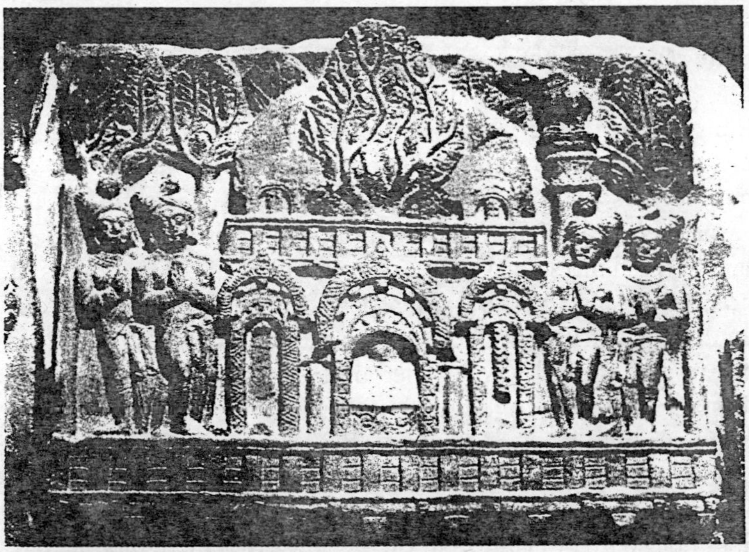

5-5. Bodhighara (Bodhi tree sanctuary) and worshipers; Bharhut

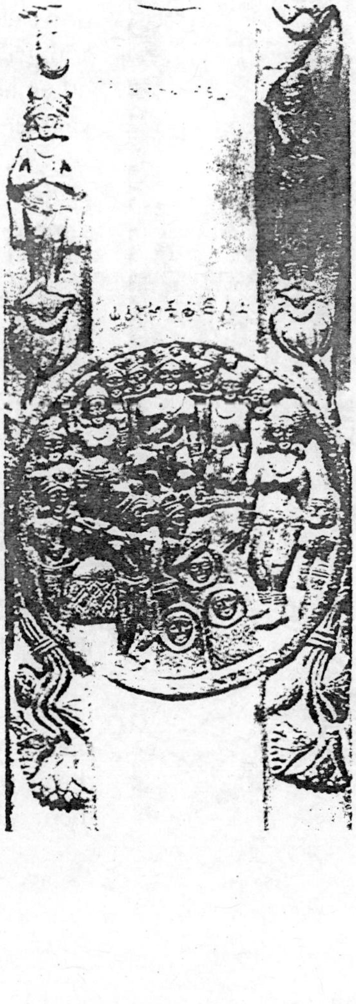

5-6. Yavamajjhakiya Jātaka, *roundel on cross bar of railing; Bharhut*

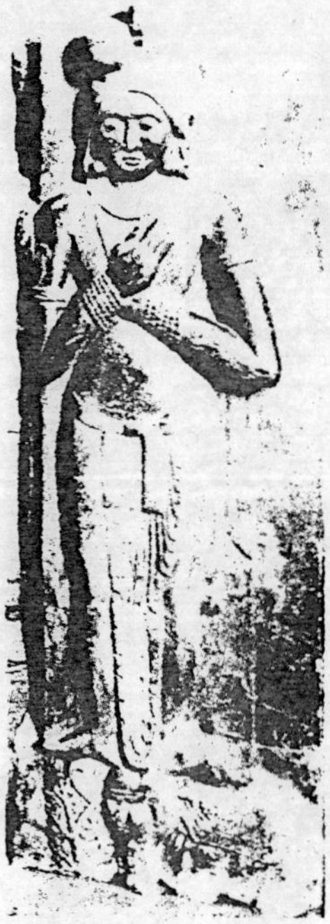

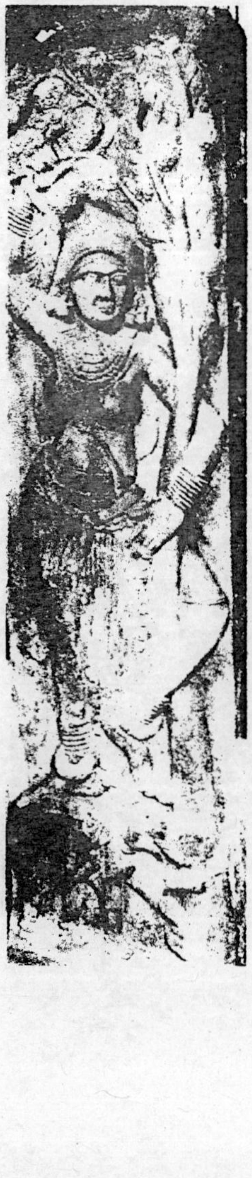

Life as it shows itself in the shapes of nature determines also the artist's forms. The figures are always represented full of life not regarding their action, whether suggesting the peace of religious ceremony or the excitement caused by a miracle. Even when the figures do not move they are full of a latent mobility. It manifests itself in the course of the curved line of the standing yakṣas, yakṣiṇīs, nāgas, and so on (Bharhut, pl. 5-7). The flat and snakelike smooth figures cling along the pillars like tendrils. The flowering tree joins (as a sister to its form), these female figures, which bow the most gracious surrender (Bharhut, pl. 5-8). The legend says that it began to flourish when it was touched by the foot of a woman. So strong is the fullness of life of one of them that she can give it away even to another. Art makes them bloom and grow together. The woman's knee and elbow seem as if they were tender joints of the tree. An inborn feeling of life's community makes the artist from Bharhut and Sanchi form the stems of plants and the arms of man in the same way not regarding their physical appearance or their organic structure. The relation and connection of forms is more intimate than the isolation of the individual.

The multiplication of members, a peculiarity of the later Indian artistic conception of godlikeness can be always recognized here. (In literature, of course, the multiplication of members as an attribute to God's all-filling almightiness has existed long before, for instance the description of Krishna's appearance as given by the *Bhagavadgīta.*) Sometimes the horses have two heads. The reason for this is apparently to let them appear both from outside and inside the gates as complete animals (Sanchi, north gate). Similar inventions with the same purpose occur at Khorsabad and Nineveh, where lions and griffins are represented having five legs. The same principle causes on the other hand a contraction and disappearance of single members. When two yakṣas, leaning on two adjacent sides of one pillar, touch each other on the edge between them, their arms grew together and form a double arm (Bharhut, pl. 5-2) which, seen as a whole, has the harmony of an ornament and is at the same time a perfect two-sided representation of an arm.

In Sanchi the figures awake into a new kind of life. The figures of men as represented by art always show the aspect of mental constitution of their author. Men dreamed at Bharhut both with closed and open eyes, surrendered to the mild waves of life and were carried on them. But here men have awakened. Their actions are no longer only suggested, but take place in their full reality. Every man lives his own life and action means its summit. Men have become active and energetic. But one does not look upon this new sense of life in a different manner from the old one. Because one does not consider it all, one does not judge or criticize it. One is possessed by it and permits oneself to be governed by it. The sense of life has changed but not man's appreciation of life. In both cases life is the urging force whether it bears the man in its rhythm or whether it excites him to spontaneous activity.

The emancipation of the individual consists in his activity. Though the figures stand or bow or join their hands as at Bharhut, has the structure of the body been changed and therewith the character of movements? In Sanchi the artist discovered that the articles are of essential importance for the movement. The bodies lose their bulkiness, become pliable in all their joints, hips, and shoulders. The figures no longer stand clumsy with their whole weight on both feet, but cross their legs graciously over, the head slightly bent aside. One is tempted to suggest that Indian people had learned dancing in the meantime.

The landscape is neither a substantial nor independent part of early Indian art, as for instance in China, where landscape painting is the integration of earth and air, water and mountain, man and universe. Nor does it figure as background of the action. But what may be called landscape takes part in the action and constitutes it. No figure of the "landscape" is superfluous; each has its special importance regarding the representation of the history. The tree for instance, besides its symbolic employment, represents either the dwelling place of one of the chief persons (Bharhut, pl. 5-9) or at times helps to suggest an inundation (Sanchi, water miracle, east gate, left pillar, front face) or the dedication of the Jetavana grove to the Buddha. The landscape character of some of the scenes (for instance in the Vessantara Jātaka, Sanchi north gate, back view, lower lintel, pl. 5-10; or Bharhut, pl. 5-11, as in the adoration of the wisdom tree by the Nāga King Erakapatta) is suggested by the nearness of enormous flowers, of crowded bodies of men, animals, trees, and huts. But

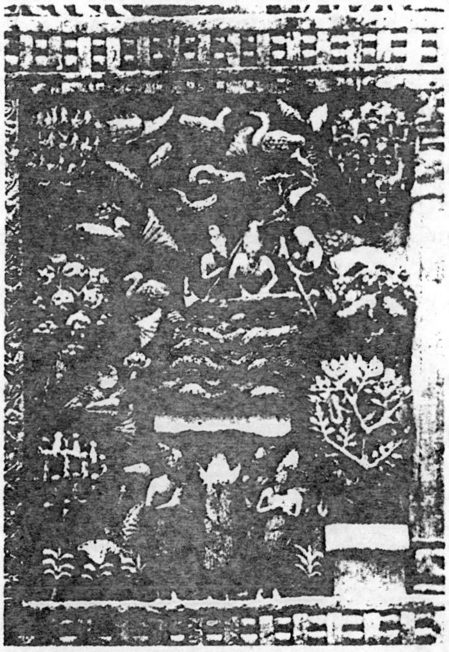

5-9. Water miracle; left pillar, east gate, front face; Sanchi

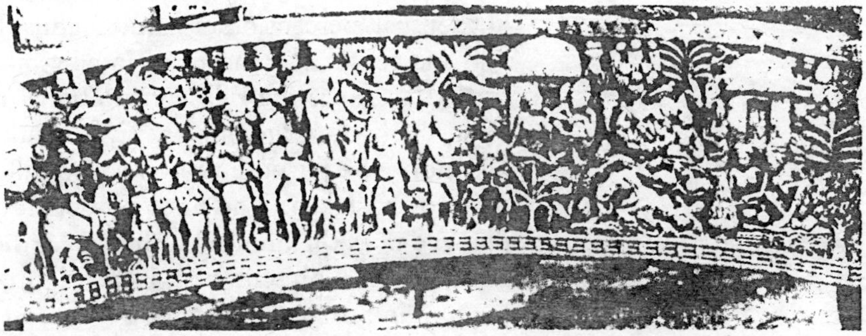

5-10. Vessantara Jātaka; *lower lintel, north gate, back face, stūpa 1; Sanchi*

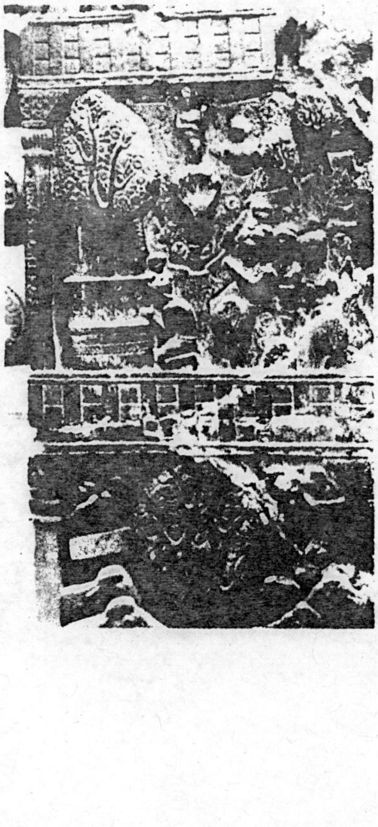

5-11. The Nāga King Erakapatta worships the Buddha; on upright of railing; Bharhut

OPPOSITE PAGE ABOVE:
5-7. Gaṅgīta Yakṣa on upright of railing; Bharhut

OPPOSITE PAGE BELOW:
5-8. Cūlakokā Devatā on upright of railing; Bharhut

this tropical exuberance forms no peculiarity of landscape scenes only, but characterizes all the early Indian artistic inventions and produces in an equal superabundance men, marching to a festival, worshiping animals and flowering trees. One tree, one flower, is sufficient to express and to contain the whole nature. One house or citadel represents similarly a town (Sanchi War of the Relics, west gate, back view, middle lintel, pl. 5-12). Water also is not depicted as an element of landscape. Every so often lakes or rivers may be seen, they have only a narrative meaning (for instance the water miracle or that the crab dwelt in the pool, Sanchi east gate and Bharhut pls. 5-9 and 5-13).

The relation of Indian art to nature is not conditioned by an optic impression of nature's forms but by the artist's inborn and deep love of nature. Not only one sense, the visual, takes an interest in nature, but the artist's whole organism. Thus Indian art is a part of nature itself and is nothing else but man's ratification of his own thankful reality, as a part of nature. But the view of nature as given by art has its roots not only in the vital feelings of the unity of creation, but has to serve the purpose of being intelligible. The early experience, that everything is recognized by its limits, is uttered by art by the means of line, which circumscribes the objects and pronounces the names. Insofar is early Indian art "naturalistic." Outlines have their origin in an intellectual, not sensual, perception of nature. Thus the idea is one constituent of the outline and serves as a means of intelligibility.

These are the two constitutional reasons of early Indian pictorial art. First, the knowledge of a creative nature to which the artist himself belongs. Secondly, the purpose to narrate, to tell exactly so that nothing can be confused or mistaken. The first component may be seen as the plastic capacity, the second as the limiting character of the line. The conscious purpose of the artist is clear representation. Every figure shall give an exact idea of the meaning and importance of the object represented. The tree, for instance, can be recognized by its outline, which is filled in with flowers, leaves, and fruits (Bharhut, pls. 5-9 and 5-10). The size of flowers, leaves, and fruits in relation to the whole tree does not correspond to their real dimensions. Their size is exaggerated and their number reduced. The bigness of each single flower, leaf, or fruit replaces their number; as, for example, the most important part of a throne is its plate. Therefore it must be represented and shown entirely in full size, and that is only possible by a bird's-eye view. So the plate of the throne has a spatial meaning, not effect. Such elements are constant. Their real appearance is neglected, they take no part in the representation as objects but only

5-12. The war of the relics; middle lintel, west gate, back face, stūpa 1; Sanchi

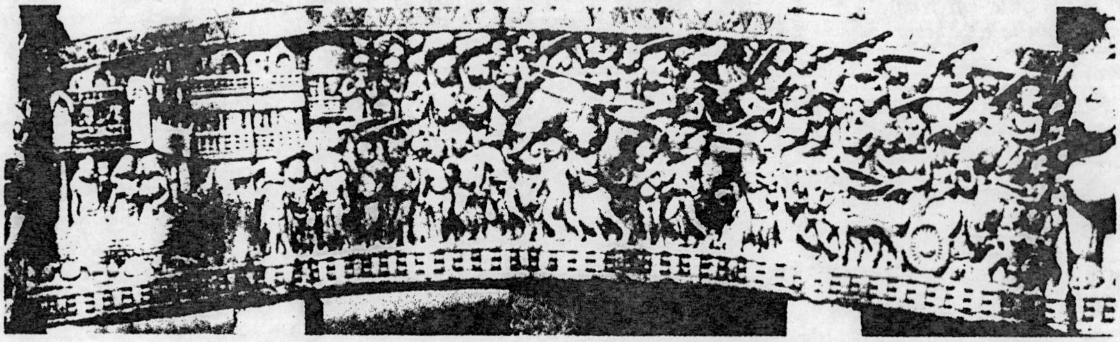

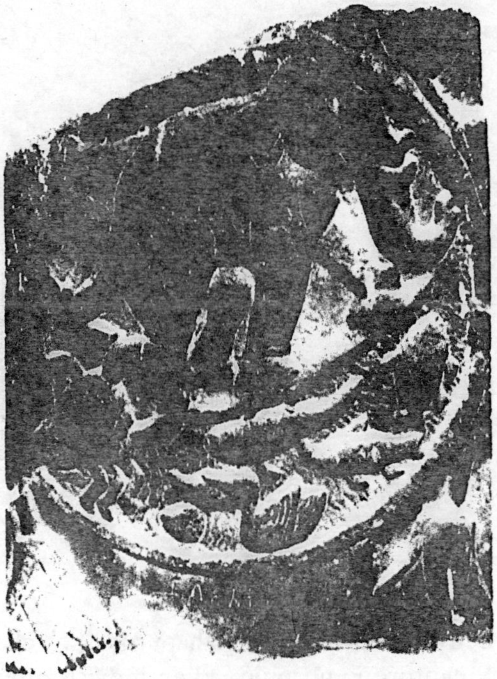

5-13. Kakkaṭa Jātaka;
roundel on upright of railing; Bharhut

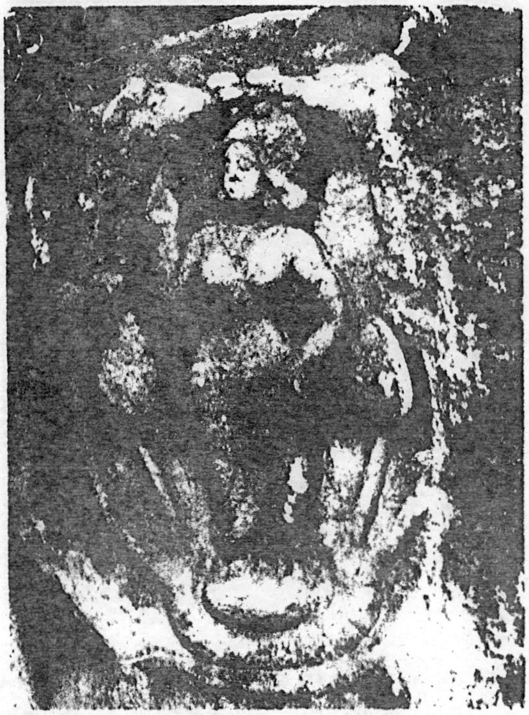

5-14. Gaja-Lakṣmī bathed by elephants; medallion on upper part of upright of railing, Mahābodhi; Bodh-gayā.

as the names of objects and have their own sound whereby they are always recognized by one glance or in the first instance in whatever connection they appear.

The result of this aim, toward clearness and intelligibility, is a disproportion of sizes compared with the real appearance of objects, for instance, the size of waves in proportion to the river, the curls of the lion's mane in relation to the whole size of the animal (Sanchi). These stereotyped signs are the names given to every object by its special peculiarity. They have the economic and mnemotechnic usefulness of abbreviations.

The size of the acting persons themselves changes following the part and importance which the person plays in each representation. As, for instance, in one relief tree and man are of equal size, because the wishing man is not less important than the wish-bestowing tree, while another representation makes elephants and lotus flowers equally small with reference to the mighty human figure of the goddess (pl. 5-14).

Everything is told in the simplest manner and the shortest way, unconstrained and easily, because the man and also the artist were simple. They had not to forget a disturbing manifoldness of the outer world and of their own thought. In a self-consciousness that is as unlimited as it is naïve, men possessed as much of the world as they were interested in. This possession was so safe, so absolute, that men proceeded to build a world which became a symbol of reality.

6 Emblems of the Universal Being

Some of the thirty-two signs[1] of the Universal Being, the Mahāpuruṣa, which mark the image of the Buddha are nonanthropomorphic. They indicate the being of Buddha Lokottara and are "cosmognomical" emblems of his substance, and not physiognomical traits of his body. A meditation on these emblems (pratīkopāsana) consists in beholding each of them as a carrier of the essence which lies in its name and which has an equivalent in its shape. The latter conveys and localizes its activity. Placed on the semblance of an anthropomorphic body the function of these emblems is without regard for its anthropomorphic aspect. There they have but their site.

The image as the site of symbols of activity is the homogeneous soil on which they are made possible. Even apart from distinct marks such as will be dwelt upon, the whole of the image acts as an emblem and while some of its qualities are named severally (among the thirty-two Mahāpuruṣalakṣaṇas and eighty Anuvyañjanas[2]), its entire aspect is analogous by its name and shape to the whole in view of which it is formed.

While a symbol retains its value irrespective of the context in which it appears, an emblem presupposes a cosubstantial level. "Webbed fingers" will be misplaced and meaningless if the fingers belong to a human being or to an image other than that of a Mahāpuruṣa. Each emblem in order to act thus is situated within a field (kṣetra)[3] that supports and is coextensive with the substance (kāya) of the Buddha. Pratīkopāsana dwells on this entire Buddha region while it looks upon its sites and marks as instances, for example, as momentous illustrations of the total meaning. The image itself elicits such a synthetic view. It means what it shows and visibly refers to the principle; "such as it is beheld, such is it said to be."[4]

This essay first appeared in *JISOA* 3 (December 1935): 148–65, and is reprinted here by permission.

The single instances or emblems are localized in different parts of the Buddha image. Its entire body is their field of action, a transubtantiated locality. The Buddha's career on earth is symbolized by the sites of his birth, awakening, first sermon, and death. Each of them is always present; they are beheld simultaneously, symbol next to symbol (Sanchi toraṇas), and what separates them is their situation, their chthonic tie. Analogously the body of the Buddha image is the field simultaneously beheld and distinct in its emblems.

The head of the image of the Buddha is always very high and broad; at the top it may taper into a point,[5] or else, and almost invariably, it is surmounted by a shape, broad and circular at the base and leading hemispherically or conically[6] to a point. The whole of it is always covered with devices that indicate hair.[7] Frequently this heightened shape is surmounted in its turn by a flame device.[8] The apex is specially indicated, and this device is called Uṣṇīṣa.[9] This emblem shows an extension of the body-like appearance of the Buddha beyond its anthropomorphic limits. There and with this elevation it outgrows itself, it is slightly higher than one expects, but by the little that it is higher, it exceeds the limits. "Puruṣa who has a thousand heads, a thousand eyes, a thousand feet, investing the earth in all directions exceeds it by ten (aṅgula) fingers' breadth" (*RV* 10.90.1). Such is the Puruṣa before the sacrifice, and this excess is not distributed in the sacrifice into the manifested world. It remains beyond it, and the Buddha Lokottara comprises it in his substance, which also invests the earth in all directions. Of this exceeding quality of the Buddha substance as Mahāpuruṣa, unqualified (nirguṇa) and not manifested (avyakta), that is, "before the sacrifice," the Uṣṇīṣa is the emblem. The knowledge of it underlies such legends as that of the Brahman who doubted the body of the Buddha to be sixteen feet high and wanted to measure it with a bamboo rod sixteen feet high. But it constantly rose above the end of the rod;[10] or, a stūpa was built around a small stūpa. As the monument progressed in height, the small stūpa always exceeded it by three feet.[11] This outgrowing as an incessant process is marked by a small measure. No measure at all can indicate how far it reaches, for it reaches beyond the manifested world in which measure alone counts. Ten aṅgulas, three feet or four aṅgulas[12] connote exactly the same, that is, a being beyond the limits. It stands for the Mahāpuruṣa as "nirguṇa." Such is the function of the smallness of the emblem. There number does not count; it could be indefinitely large, and it is variably small, "unmeasured in the measured out,"[13] for it does not refer to this world of māyā, to the cosmos which is ordered by number and measure.[14]

The substance of the Buddha image exceeds the semblance of bodily limits and makes it into that of the Lokottara Buddha. This takes place at the apex of the head *(fontanella minor)* where the threshold of Brahman (brahmarandhra) is situated and where the thousand-petaled (sahasrāra) lotus is unfolded downward with its pericarp aloft. This point on high is "the door called Vidhṛtī (tearing asunder) the Nandana, the place of beatitude."[15] Here "where the root of the hair divides, the Puruṣa opens the sides of the head."[16] Further it is said: "The channel (nāḍī) called suṣumṇā (going upwards within the spinal cord to the brahmarandhra) serving as the passage of Prāṇa (breath), through that channel let him proceed upward."[17] "From thence he goes to selflessness and he obtains al(l)-one-ness (kevalatva). Having crossed the limit let him join himself to the limitless in the crown of the head." The Śaivas call it Śivasthānam (abode of Śiva); the Vaiṣṇavas call it Parama Puruṣa.[18]

The "threshold" is the site of the Uṣṇīṣa. At this place the limit is crossed. Here "the Suṣumṇā leads upwards and pierces the solar orb. By it they go the highest path."[19] This is the place of Nirvāṇa and here the breath (prāṇa, i.e., udāna) passes outside. The place of Nirvāṇa is signaled in reliefs in a twofold manner. Flying Vidyādharas hold a stūpa, as if it were a crown, above the Buddha's head,[20] and in Pāla stelae the Parinirvāṇa scene is carved just above the head of the main Buddha image in the middle, the eighth and the highest among the scenes of his career, which are threaded along the edge of the slab.[21]

The site of the Uṣṇīṣa is at the Brahmarandhra. It lies in the place of intersection of the vertical axis, which passes along the body and beyond it, and an imaginary horizontal plane, which rests on top of the skull. Here the Buddha-world comprehensible by the semblance of his body culminates, and this climax of being (bhavāgra) is the point, the moment of transition, from the manifested body of Buddha "to the unborn Dharmakāya by the great perpendicular path."[22] The substance (form) of the image refers to both (p. 165).

Along this great perpendicular path, Prāṇa leads beyond death.[23] It moves along the Suṣumṇā while at the same time "pervading all,"[24] for "breath is the sap of the limbs."[25]

The comprehensive body of the Buddha is pervaded throughout by the agent that leads beyond the body. Within it, breath inflates what it traverses[26] and makes the limbs round.[27] Its pneumatic activity brings about their vegetation aspect, their surging fluid shape. In conformity with this appearance, Hiuen Thsang speaks of the Uṣṇīṣa of the image of Bodh-Gayā as a fleshy cone.[28] The comprehensive substance of the Buddha image remains the same along the vertical axis, below and above the zero point of Nirvāṇa. So it also appears, while in fact the Uṣṇīṣa is an emblem, a thing without qualities, that is, without thingness, real only by the position it occupies and the reference it bears. It is correct to say that the Uṣṇīṣa is not visible to the eyes of ordinary beings.[29] It cannot be, emblem as it is of "nirguṇa" Mahāpuruṣa. In "theory" the Universal Being is invisible to all, and the sages Ekata, Dvita, and Trita had to leave Śvetadvīpa without having been able to see him.[30]

When it is asked "What knowledge is the Tathāgata possessed of so that the protuberance on his head is shining?"[31] The answer is "Who has known this place is never born again."[32] The Uṣṇīṣa that marks the Brahmarandhra, while pointing upward, widens toward the bottom, an inverted shape. It recalls the stūpa in form and meaning.[33] Placed on the zero point, it can be traversed either way along the vertical axis. While it is there that the breath (udāna) goes beyond, it also enters by the same channel. At the site of commutation Vāyu, the wind, enters and Agni, Aditya, and Brahman,[34] and by placing the hand on the Brahmarandhra (of an image of Śiva or Śakti), Prāṇapratiṣṭhā (the establishment of prāṇa within the image) is performed.[35] With the establishment of breath all is established.[36] By breath or by air, as by a thread this world and the other world are strung together and Prāṇa is Brahman (the sūtrātman). In it the Udāna abides.[37] Such is the place of the Uṣṇīṣa, the plummet on the zero point of Sūtrātman and Suṣumṇā.

This does not exhaust the emblematic function of the Uṣṇīṣa, and before approaching its further import the interpretations hitherto made of this symbol have to be considered. The accepted meaning, "protection from the heat," and its interpretation as turban have no reference to the Uṣṇīṣa as carved on the actual images. The early texts *(Mahāpadāna* and *Lakkhaṇa Suttanta, Lalitavistara)* while enumerating the marks of the Mahāpuruṣa do not interpret them. Burnouf already saw that the Buddhists accepted the term Uṣṇīṣa in a particular sense. It is moreover absent from Brahmanical texts. The *Mahābhārata* (Śānti parva 12, 336 and 344) describes the inhabitants of Śvetadvīpa (white island) and Nara and Nārāyaṇa as having heads like umbrellas (chatrākṛtiśīrṣa) and the same character is attributed to the head of the world ruler by the *Bṛhatsaṁhitā.*[38] This attribute refers to the head alone and not to the part which exceeds it. This quality Buddhaghoṣa[39] had before him when he commented on Uṇhīsasīsa as referring to the well-developed forehead and head of the Mahāpuruṣa. It figures separately in the list of Mahāpuruṣa Lakṣaṇas and also among the Anuvyañjanas.[40] It has its prototype in *Atharva Veda* 10.7.32 "the sky his head" and its Tantric elaboration in *Ṣaṭcakra Nirūpaṇa* 40, where Sahasrāra is located in the empyrean (parama vyoma). This lotus has its head turned downwards. In contemporary and traditional Tantric paintings, the petals of the Sahasrāra lotus fall back over the wide expanse of the skull. Śrī Kālīcaraṇa[41] says: The lotus of a thousand petals is like a canopy. It is above all. But in the center where "the subtle Bindu manifests the pure Nirvāṇa Kalā the pericarp of the lotus is directed upwards"[42] and so is also the Uṣṇīṣa.

The position and function of this emblem, its static appearance and dynamic meaning, associated as it is with the flame device and exhaustively commented upon in texts, further enlarge its symbolism and suggest a new translation of the term consonant with its significance.[43] The *Lalitavistara* has it that "after Bhagavān had plunged into deep meditation suddenly from the interstices of the crown of his Uṣṇīṣa there issued the ray of light called the light of knowledge born of itself which brings the remembrance of the former Buddhas. It illuminated all the dwellings of the gods of the pure abodes. The flood of light from the Tathāgata emitted the following Gāthās (verses)."[44] Such knowledge must have been had by Hiuen Thsang speaking about the "fleshy cone" on the Buddha's head; there, he says, appear celestial miracles and the divine puissance shows itself in splendor.[45]

The crown of the Uṣṇīṣa is painted golden yellow in the Māradharṣaṇa scene, Ajanta, cave 1.[46] Its cylindrical shape is cut out in front in a semicircle so as not to hide the dark Uṣṇīṣa. In its upper part the cylinder of the crown is beset with jewels; in its lower part the gold is worked trellis-like. Well could the light issue from the interstices of such a crown. The golden cylinder of the crown may also be taken as a pars pro toto of the golden ray flashed forth from between the eyebrows[47] of the Buddha. "It extended to all the innumerable worlds of the ten quarters. On its return the ray rested on the top of Buddha's head and transformed itself into a golden pillar just like the mount Sumeru wherein the pure and admirable countries of the Buddhas in the ten quarters appeared all at once illuminated."[48] It can be added that the voice (dhvani) of the Buddha is heard sorting from his mouth, the eyebrow hair and the bump.[49] This ray of light is one with the Buddha-word. The Buddha-word in its flood of light comprises all the innumerable worlds in all the Buddha-lands that are and have been. The Buddha-word clothed in light is like another Meru, an "excess" on the higher plane (p. 132) of the comprehensive Buddha-substance encompassed by curves.[50]

The ray is not unsupported. Its radiance is manifested and shines forth once it sorts from the body. Within it the udāna which leads upwards is light.[51] It is the post (skambha) of the inner life,[52] the vital breath.[53] This post of the inner life and the upper ray, the Suṣumṇā in which the Udāna rises into the limitless,[54] lie in one line,[55] below and above the zero point of the Brahmarandhra. This line, following another image, is the Sūtrātman in which the Udāna abides.[56] By it this world, as if by a thread, and the other are strung together.[57] The images are consistent. Thread and channel, post and ray, are the conducts in the central axis of being. It is along them that air and breath, light and fire go the highest path.[58] For Vāyu (air) is Prāṇa (breath), and Prāṇa is Agni (fire).[59] The Maitri Upaniṣad speaks of the "heat" (uṣṇa) produced between the breaths (prāṇa and apāna).[60] "The fiery energy, in the breathing it has its place in the dark heat (uṣṇa) that emanates light proceeding upwards."[61] Parallel with this "cosmognomical" process, the physiological circumstances of Tantric yoga consist in the lower limbs becoming cold while the upper part of the head grows "lustrous," that is, warm. When the yoga is complete, the only trace of warmth to be found in the whole body is at the crown of the head.[62] The passing of warmth and fire in the Udāna which carries them beyond death[63] is the miracle of commutation symbolically situated at the crown of the head.[64] The Uṣṇīṣa is its emblem and its name connotes it, placed as it is on the point on high where the last heat is gleaned[65] to radiate forth as the pure light of which ray or flame are symbols.[66]

It is consistently apparent that the Uṣṇīṣa is neither a turban nor, due to a misunderstanding on the part of the craftsman, a bony protuberance, nor a fleshy growth, although to describe it the two last anthropomorphic secunda comparationis have been used. It is no thing. It is an emblem, and it refers to the super-sensible. It has no prototype in nature. Even on the image: "it is not visible to the eyes of ordinary beings," and though its shape is apprehended, its meaning may not be seen. On some images (Bodhisattva dedicated by Friar Bala)[67] the Uṣṇīṣa was made of precious material[68] or of the pearl Candrakāntā (beloved by the moon). When the moon is about to reflect its light in it, there rises a spring of water.[69] Here the Uṣṇīṣa is not directly emblematic of the breath-fire-sun[70] correspondence but the other luminary, the moon, with its element the water (in which resides the element of fire)[71] is conjured. The symbols in the upper sphere of the human or cosmic appearance are one in essence. Uṣṇīṣa with its flame and ray, the ray emitted from the Ūrṇā between the eyebrows (at the site of the Tantric ājñā cakra with its moon correspondence), the eyes, one taken as the sun and the other as the moon—all these correspondences have to be understood as analogies where the sensible, that is, sun, moon, suture of the skull, eye, and so on, whether cosmic or human, are taken as places of manifestation. That which is beyond manifestation inhabits all these sites to an equal extent and is not comprehended in any. There only its marks (lakṣaṇa) are seen by those who know them.

The Uṣṇīṣa is the foremost lakṣaṇa on the body of the Mahāpuruṣa, the Buddha. His body is the circumambient substance of the breath that moves throughout it and swells its limbs into a steady roundness. This is epitomized and outgrows the limiting anthropomorphic semblance at the top of the head. It is "translated" into the higher level at the instance of Nirvāṇa. Of this the Uṣṇīṣa is the monument.

While the Uṣṇīṣa is the most conspicuous emblem in the Buddha image, the Ūrṇā, the brow-spot, the hairy tuft, plays a large part in the texts (*Saddharmapuṇḍarīka,* etc.). On the images, however, it may or may not be marked. It is situated between the eyebrows, and its place is called Avimukta.[72] According to the *Jābāli Upaniṣad,*[73] the Avimukta lies where the eyebrows are united with the organ of smell. Here is the union of the celestial world and of the higher world.[74] On this point of union Brahman is worshiped. Coomaraswamy[75] speaks of the designation of the spider as Ūrṇavābhi, thread spinner, and of the sun as a spider. The spider image is related to the doctrine of the Sūtrātman. The spider image and its reference to the sun is also related to the webbed fingers and toes (see p. 137). In function the Ūrṇā emblem is allied to the Uṣṇīṣa. It flashes forth light which illuminates the universe. That it is said to be hairy also leads us back to the Uṣṇīṣa, which is covered and surrounded by hair. In the early images a long strand of hair is coiled around it.[76] The accepted formula, however, is that of the curled locks. Coomaraswamy has made it clear[77] that the curly quality means to avoid a "coming to an end." Hiuen Thsang was also in the same tradition describing one hair of the Tathāgatha curled to the right. If pulled it is about one foot long but curled it is no longer than half a thumb.[78] Elsewhere[79] it is stated that a merit equal to that of all the beings of the universe is required in order to give to a single hair the curly appearance of that of the Buddha.

That the hair encloses the power and life of man is a widely current notion. The manifest power of divinity is shown in the growth of hair[80] (cf. parallelism of the meaning of flame, ray, hair). When the future Śākyamuni spreads his hair before Dīpaṅkara Buddha to walk over it, the power of the previous Buddha is transmitted to the Buddha-to-be, in this Bodhisattva-gesture. The whole extent of the Buddha power is rolled into his round locks which curl to the right,[81] as the Pradakṣinā path leads around the stūpa. The locks around and on the Uṣṇīṣa are to be turned to the right, following the course of the sun, the path of life. The craftsmen did not rigorously adhere to this aspect of the symbol. They had more comprehensive means at their disposal to form the substance of the Buddha. Pneumatic dilatation, fluid curves, and the smooth roundness of the body are their modes of visualization for they are aware "that all joints are joint with breath."[82]

The hair emblem, unlike the Uṣṇīṣa, is taken from the physique of man. It is of no importance from where the symbol is taken to be a valid support of the meaning. That the whole power resides in the hair, and that the hair of the Buddha is curled not only on his head in locks, but singly also on his body[83] (although the latter symptom is not shown in images) localizes it on the surface of the Buddha-field (kṣetra) as emitted from its substance. Here a kind of chthonic magic is at play.

For the earth itself is not only ever-active, but it is the constant result of the wind of activity which makes it solid (pārthiva vāyu). All this movement of the entire Buddha-field—its size is measured by chiliocosms—makes the hair on its surface grow in curls, and the words are alive to it which say that the valor of the whole world is required to give to a single hair the curly appearance of that of the Buddha. With all the incessant movement—were it to stop the whole body would collapse[84] which means in terms of form that the image would offer an inert (inane) aspect in mass or color—an inner balance is maintained, the frictionless equipoise of this ceaseless function within the closed world[85] of the Buddha's body and of the corresponding image. This unmoving Prāṇa[86] in current Tantric practice is known in the retention of breath (kumbhaka) which is located in the Suṣumṇā nāḍī, and this channel (see p. 131) is situated in the spinal axis called Merudaṇḍa.

The fifteenth lakṣaṇa enumerated in the *Mahāpadāna* and *Lakkhaṇa Suttantas*[87] speaks of "the frame divinely straight," and this is commented upon by Buddhaghoṣa that the Buddha "will not stoop nor lean backward nor have a crooked spine, but tower up symmetrically." Continuing the description, the eighteenth lakṣaṇa[88] of the *Lakkhaṇa Suttanta,* that "there is no furrow between his shoulders," is commented upon with understanding "from the small of the back upwards the fleshy covering is as a level golden slab." In another connection, furthermore, the *Mahāparinibbāna Suttanta* narrates consistently: "He gazed at Vesālī with an elephant look."[89] Buddhaghoṣa comments that the "Buddhas were accustomed on looking backwards, to turn the whole body round as an elephant does because the bones in their neck were firmly fixed." So they had to be as links of the Merudaṇḍa, through the entire length of which runs the Suṣumṇā, the channel of Prāṇa. The golden slab of the back scrupulously records an appearance which gilded bronze images of the Buddha invariably confirm. But whatever the material of the image, the flat and straight back is the rule and not only of the Buddha image, but of any Indian main deity. Standing or seated their manifestation is as straight as that of a post (skambha) whereas the lesser divinities yield to the flowing movement that goes on in this world (jagat). The Siamese tradition describes the ankles of the Buddha as fixed in such a manner that he can turn his entire body without moving his feet. As support of the world, "the Puruṣa stands like a tree in the sky"[90] and Agni (Vaiśvānara) and Vishnu of both of whom the Buddha can be considered an avatar are over and over again identified with the cosmic column and tree.[91] Within this tradition the Tibetan imagemaker to this day inserts the life-tree, shaped as a truncated pyramid, into the earthen Buddha image.[92]

In touch with the level earth[93] and not supported by lotus flowers (to the end of the Gupta age this is the rule) are the feet of the standing Buddha images. Here as well as in all other images of deities in the rigidly upright stance (kāyotsarga) they are invariably inflated and taut and this often contrasts with the fluid suppleness of the limbs, whatever their volume. As if unwilling to be detached or differentiated from the ground on which they stand or distinct from the mass of the material, the heavy stone or the weighing bronze of which they are fashioned, they convey their affinity to the earth, felt as it is as "pārthiva vāyu."[94] Analogous to the top of the head they too are a place of commutation, for Vāyu here on entering becomes Prāṇa as Prāṇa within the living body is Vāyu.[95] "Brahman (as prāṇa) entered by the tips of the feet,"[96] and this inflation swells them to a great extent before Prāṇa proceeds and equally distributes itself through the limbs while it ascends the high road of the Suṣumṇā. Texts on the making of images agree in describing the feet as full or high like the back of a tortoise,[97] and the *Bṛhatsaṁhitā*[98] distinguishes in the same way the feet of a universal ruler. The Buddha's substance throughout is permeated by movement like the cosmos of which it is the emblem. From the sole of the feet to the point of the Uṣṇīṣa the image is consistently built up. The within encompasses the without, and the Buddha Lokottara of whom all the images are made is thus "fulfilled."[99] Visibly the so-called physical and psychological as well as the cosmic inhere in this emblem of the transcendental. On the whole and in an inverse sense "this also has the shape of man."[100]

The shape of man clings to the image of the Buddha Lokottara. Where it outgrows this semblance is the mark of the Uṣṇīṣa, and where it comprehends its cosmic extent the fingers (and toes) are marked with nets. Jālāṅgulihastapādaḥ (jālābandhahastapādaḥ),[101] etc., are enumerated in the Sanskrit and Pāli lists among the Mahāpuruṣa-lakṣaṇāni. Jāla means net or latticework, and both these meanings are valid in the manner of showing it; whether according to Buddhaghoṣa's comment the "net" refers to the lines of the fingers themselves and toes which intersect like those of a latticed window or whether according to a large number of images a web connects the fingers,[102] the meaning remains the same. The web in between the fingers as shown by many images generally ends not in straight lines but in curves and is frequently reticulated. Whether on, or in between the fingers, the net is not a physical trait. It is an emblem, that is, a meaning visualized. Its prototype is not anthropomorphic and altogether suprasensible. The simile of a net which may further be elaborated into one like that of the Haṁsarāja, the golden mallard,[103] serves as an adequate symbol. As the circumambient mass of the image of the Buddha visualizes his substance and does not portray his appearance, its marks help to show qualities which are implicitly contained in the form of the image. They figure as names and guides. The imaged substance (kāya) of the Buddha, this "kṣetra" of a wide and smooth surface is the emblem (pratīka) of the universe. The universe is frequently pictured in the texts (but also, as will be seen elsewhere, in application) as a net, texture, or fabric. One of its main threads, the Sūtrātman, has been shown already (p. 134).[104] "He verily knows the threads of the warp (tantu) and of the woof (otu) who comprehends all this (universe)."[105] The universe is viewed here as an "haute-lisse" with Agni (Vaiśvānara) or the Sūtrātman as major thread. All contingent existence is shot across it, woven forwards, woven backwards.[106] "That of which they say that it is above the heavens, beneath the earth, embracing heaven and earth, past, present and future, that is woven like warp and woof."[107] Woven, that is, comprehensive is this world fabric, and whatever exists has its place in its network. The universe understood as a woven fabric is tantamount to the cosmos, that is, it is ordered throughout. Microcosmically, referring to the structure of man, it is asked: "Who wove in him breath?"[108] Breath outside the envelope of the body is air and (by air) as by a thread this world and the other world and all creatures are strung together,[109] and "whoso may know the stretched out string in which these progeny are woven in, whoso may know the string of the string, he may know the great Brāhmaṇa."[110] Cut across at any level or else in the vertical direction, the massive world fabric shows its net where everything is fixed in its place. Seen from "outside," that is, when broken through (from a viewpoint in the absolute), the shrine of Brahman is beheld consisting of four nets.[111] What is altogether filled by a thing, that also must be of the same thing up to its limits; its outer surface has the structure of its substance. "Around all beings I went, the web (tantu) of order (ṛta) stretched out for beholding."[112] In a more narrative mode, the *Mahā Sudassana Suttanta* describes the palace of Dhamma hung round with two networks of bells.[113]

The microcosm of man in whom breath is woven is one instance; the building in which man or the deity dwells another instance or microcosm in relation to the world fabric. Not only the palace of Dhamma has networks of bells around. They are also on the railing of Bharhut and surround the entire stūpa.[114] The railing of a Buddhist stūpa or around a sacred tree has the appearance of, and its primary shape actually has been, a trellis. Its cross-bars are termed "sūcī," needle. By its appearance and primary material as well as by the metaphoric name of "sūcī" the railing is a jāla (net, trellis). Besides, a network of bells is laid out on it. Such a pleonasm of allusions is well applied in visual terms. Its concord holds in manifold pictures the same meaning, for it refers to the same vision. The railing pattern, ubiquitous on the facades of early Indian architecture and repeated in stories,[115] appears to have retained its original significance as long as the motif has been applied. Actually and according to the general description given in Buddhist books of an abode "perfectly adorned," such an abode has a surrounding rail and a network ornamental enclosure.[116] Such an abode perfectly adorned is also the throne of the Bodhisattva in Tuṣita heaven. It is spread over with nets of costly texture wherein tinkle innumerable little bells.[117]

The interchangeability of the symbols of body and building, both conceived as indicative of locality to be dwelt in, has been frequently seen.[118] The Buddha in the stūpa is surrounded by the "jāla" of the railing; prenatally as six-tusked elephant he should be covered with golden networks[119] and on being born the Bodhisattva is received by Śakra and Brahman under cover of a beautiful piece of kauśika (silk) cloth.[120] According to the Chinese version[121] the newborn Bodhisattva is caught in a golden net by four angels from the highest heaven.

The net as a whole is not visible on the image of the Buddha. He carries its vestiges, pars pro toto, attached to or on his fingers and toes.[122]

Thus it is beheld as an emblem on his "body." Any section across his substance would be marked correspondingly. Such internal levels or fields cannot be seen exteriorized from the image, but they may be worded. "They will behold here my Buddha field; forming a checkered board of eight compartments with gold threads.[123] Altogether "cosmognomical," the Buddha image comprehends the universe. The Sūtrātman within its vertical axis rises beyond it across the zero point at the Brahmarandhra. Every degree of being can be read on the central rod below that point, every Buddha-field is expanded there. Each degree of being is identical with a mode of knowledge. At the zero point, there can be no identity of any extent. Still, if this is to be conveyed by the image, a symbol, a no-thing may do it: the Uṣṇīṣa.

Jālāṅgulihastapādaḥ and Uṣṇīṣa are concomitant emblems. The fingers and the toes hold up from within the network of the universe the cosmos. The polyvalence of this emblem, which also belongs to Nara and Nārāyaṇa, is shown and worded by its similarity to the web on the extremities of palmipedes, and by the designation of Haṁsarāja (see above). Haṁsa is one of the most ancient names of the sun-bird,[124] and the *Śvetāśvatara Upaniṣad* (3.19 and 25) says of the unique Haṁsa "in the midst of the world he is the fire, he resides in the midst of the waters." If the shrine of Brahman has four nets, the town of Brahman in which dwells the Puruṣa "is all surrounded by Amṛta."[125] The liquid element, water, the sun-bird, the sun with its rays, the spider analogy of the sun, the spider, weaver of its net, the rays that issue from the sun, the very lability of these images as they glide one into the other is caught in the likeness of the membrane of an aquatic sun-bird or else within the lines across the long (and golden) fingers (and toes) of the image of Buddha as Mahāpuruṣa. The network of this Māyā is pierced permanently at the instant of Nirvāṇa. Emblematically the substance of the image rises above its name and form with a form and a name (uṣṇīṣa) that only belong to this symbol.

The balance within this entire and transfigured body (inclusive of the uṣṇīṣa) is indicated by the Lakṣaṇa "nyagrodhaparimaṇḍala,"[126] "the length of his body is equal to the compass of his arms."[127]

Of the pillar and support of the universe the diameter must be wide. For "the Skambha sustains both heaven and earth, the Skambha sustains the six wide directions."[128] Puruṣa pervades all the regions upwards, crosswise,[129] he breathes crosswise.[130] His cosmic cross is the proportion according to which he is extended. The wood of this cross is not dead. It sends forth branches Nyagrodha-like, upward and downward within its circumambient fullness. The sap ascends and descends like breath itself, pervasive, and its channels appear turgid in the round-limbed image of the Buddha as Mahāpuruṣa. The fluid movement of its surface never ends.

Thus balanced within itself the image is a counter-measure (pratimā) of the universe. There are further emblems which also coincide in order to make this apparent.

Although not enumerated in the lists of the thirty-two Mahāpuruṣa Lakṣaṇas and not even among the eighty Anuvyañjanas, the ear is most conspicuous in all the images of the Buddha by its extraordinary size.[131] The great size of the ear emblem shows the corresponding capacity of the organ. "From the ears proceeded hearing, from hearing the quarters of the world (diś).[132] The regions (diś) having become hearing entered the ears."[133] Distance is measured by sound. "A krośa (two miles) is the distance that one can hear the lowing of an ox."[134] The Buddha's ear hears everywhere, it takes in all the sound, all the space of the universe. For sound is a quality of space and within the ear is situated the sense of balance. Immanent within the substance of the Buddha is the universe with all its regions. They have entered the ear qualitatively, that is, as sound. To be accommodated there, the receptacle ever acts in the sense of balance and orientation. Hearing and the heard, balance and space, the containing and the contained coincide. The substance of the Buddha comprehends the extent of the universe. The ear-emblem marks the place of commutation where distance, that is, all the regions find their equivalent in balance.

It is another way of showing the "banyan circumference" (nyagrodha-parimaṇḍala) of the Buddha's body, the equal extent of its fathom and its length, and its cosmic (ordered) structure.[135] The Buddha-pratimā "conforms" with the Mahāpuruṣa, the Buddha Lokottara. It shows its marks interconnected and their meaning coincides. The single emblems are ultimately synonymous. They name what the knowing "see with the heart and distinguish with the intellect."[136] They put it into form, the knowing and competent craftsmen.

7 The Image of Mahādeva in the Cave-Temple on Elephanta Island

The great rock-cut Śiva temple on Elephanta Island is one of the best known monuments of its kind in India, by reason partly of the grandeur of its sculptures and partly of its proximity to Bombay. Nevertheless the colossal carving of triple-headed Śiva which looms out of the rock in the innermost recess of the cave has never been adequately illustrated. The dim, unemphatic light which gives it an added quality of power and mystery does not facilitate the task of the photographer. Recently, however, Mr. Prithwish Neogy, one of Professor Stella Kramrisch's pupils in the University of Calcutta, experimented with sun reflectors and artificial light and supervised the taking of a number of new photographs, some of which are reproduced here.

The triune head which, with its shoulders, rises to a height of seventeen feet ten inches above a molded base, itself nearly three feet high, faces the principal (northern) entrance of the temple at the end of a double row of seven pillars. This vista, in fact, cuts across the major structural axis, which lies east and west, with the liṅga shrine standing free within the western end (fig. 1). Nevertheless the huge Śiva panel is the focus of the whole design. Like the doorways of the shrine itself, it is guarded by dvārapālas or doorkeepers, each some thirteen feet high. Behind, two pilasters flank a recess ten-and-a-half feet deep, within which the heads emerge cliff-like from the native rock. In the highest relief, they have at the same time a proper attachment to their material environment and something of the independence and imminent mobility of sculpture in the round.

This essay first appeared in *Ancient India,* no. 2 (July 1946), pp. 4–8, and is reprinted with the introductory note of Sir Mortimer Wheeler by permission. More recent evidence makes the cave sculptures datable to the mid-sixth century A.D. Dr. Kramrisch in her paper "The Great Cave-Temple of Śiva in Elephanta: Levels of Meaning and Their Form," delivered at the Śiva Symposium at the University of Pennsylvania in May 1981, refers to the central face as Sadyojāta, rather than Tatpuruṣa, and this revision has been made here.

This is not the context in which to discuss the plan of the temple or the features of the other sculptures which adorn it. Suffice it to say that, though not dated by inscription, the type of column used, with āmlā capital and circular fluted shaft springing from a rectangular pier, is of a kind which was in use at Badami in the latter part of the sixth century A.D. *and was still in use at Ellora two centuries later. On this evidence the cave is ascribed to the seventh or eighth century* A.D. *The more subjective evidence of sculptural style may be thought to point to the earlier of the two centuries. Certainly the bold and vital handling of mass is consistent with the age which, alike in the south and the north of India, saw the first complete fulfillment of medieval art.*

The great sculpture of Mahādeva is an image of the fully manifest Supreme Śiva. In the middle is the face of Sadyojāta; the faces of Aghora and Vāmadeva are collateral. The breadth of the shoulders belongs to the central face; the chest, showing but the slightest modeling, is smooth and young. It is as if breathing and holding the breath, as is shown by the ebbing curves of the necklace laid on its raised surface. It is hemmed in on the right and the left by the hands; the right hand is raised—it is damaged; the left rests on the base and holds a ripe fruit with its point up. The shoulders are also those of the lateral faces. These are turned against them, and it is on their backs that their hands come to rest. The one on the spectator's left, belonging to the wrathful face, has a serpent rearing its head from between its fingers, while the one on the right, belonging to the blissful face, holds a lotus flower and is delicately poised on the shoulder. Thus beset with emblems and hands, their fingers pointing upwards in the middle of the bust, closing in where they rest upon the shoulders, the broad body fills the width of the recess like an altar beset with offerings.

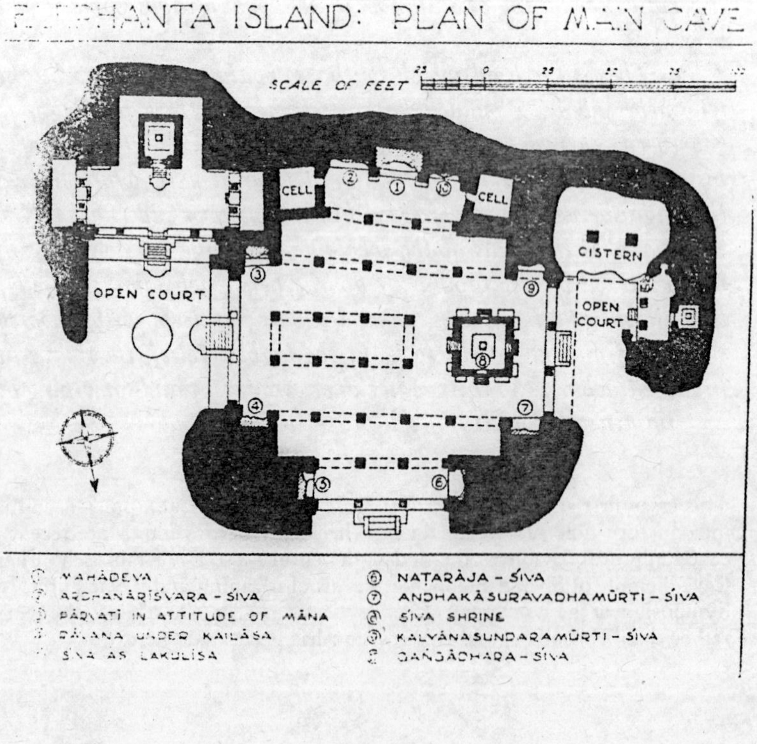

Figure 1. Elephanta Island: Plan of main cave

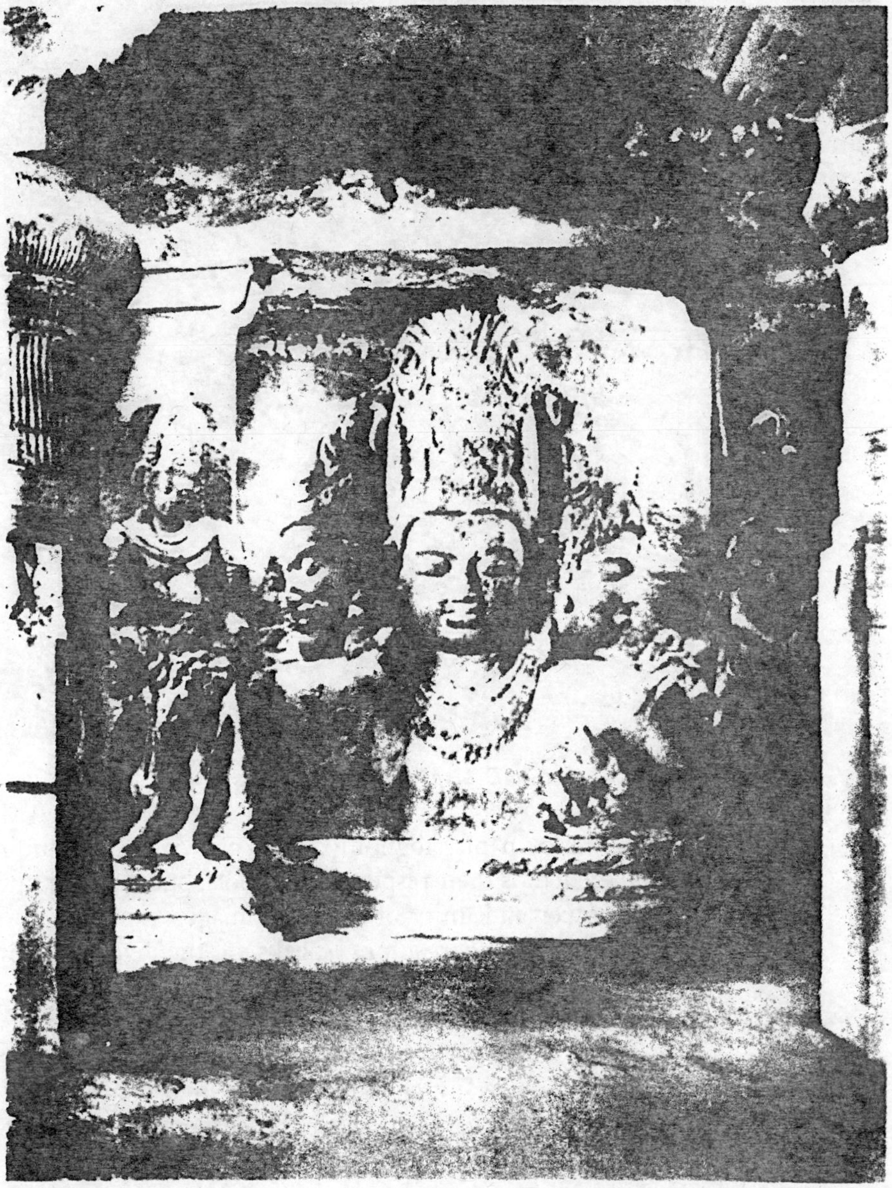

7-1. *Mahādeva*

The middle boldly projecting, the frontal image surges upwards straight and strong as a pillar, with silence on its face and radiance on its crown. The heads on the right and the left repeat the ascent of the central pillar, clinging to it collaterally with their high curving crowns, and forming with it the outline of a strong triple arch which firmly binds together the outline of the triple image.

Each of the three faces is steeped in its own mood, a closed world, each silent, unseeing, each turned away from the other, but each blossoming in generous curves round the stem whence they originate and derive their stability. They are carved in widely sweeping surfaces which bind the crowned triune head in depth just as the triple "arch" binds it vertically. Hands and flowers, serpent, hair, and jewels are laid against the smoothness of face and body. Each

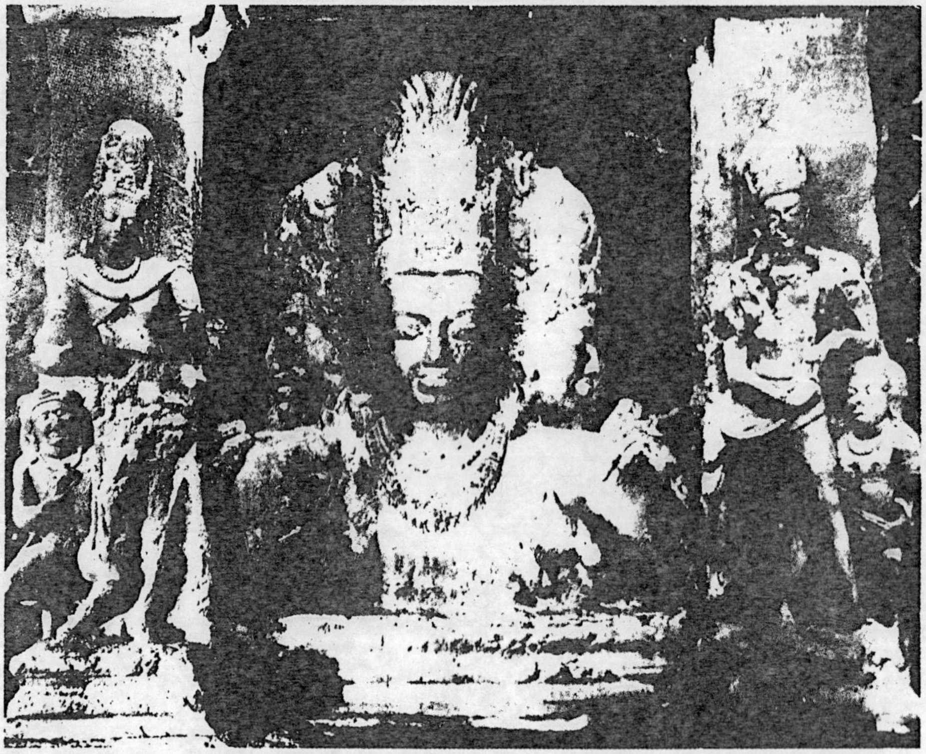

7-2. Mahādeva with Dvārapālas

face has its own physiognomy, each crown correspondingly its own ornaments, the hands their respective symbols; but they are upheld and comprised by the power and unity of the total image.

The *Viṣṇudharmottara* speaks of the five faces of Śiva (Śambhor=vadana-pañchakam). They are Īśāna, Tatpuruṣa, Aghora, Vāmadeva, Sadyojāta.[1] They face the four directions; the first face, the highest, is not carved, as a rule, on those images which are known as pañca-mukha-liṅga, the five-faced sign or symbol. Pañca-mukha-liṅgas have four faces, in the four directions, they are carved against the central liṅga pillar whose rounded top surmounts them.[2] Although only four faces are generally carved, they too need not all be visible; three, two, or one face only is required to be shown if the innermost sanctuary in which stands the liṅga has four, three, two, or one door, respectively.[3]

The names of the five faces are those of the five mantras, Sadyojāta, and so forth.[4] Mantras are rhythmical formulae; they evoke a supernatural presence, each mantra conjures up a corresponding vision of that supernatural presence. The rhythmic spell compels and constitutes its "body." Thus it is said of Śiva, the Supreme Spirit (Paramātman), that his body is mantra (vidyā).[5] It is made visible in the shape of a sign (liṅga). The liṅga is composed of mantras and is to be regarded as the body of Śiva, the place where he is present. Four of these mantras occupy the four regions of the manifested world and the fifth, Īśāna, lies beyond them, in the central direction. From there, it is at the same time everywhere, a subtle luminous presence. It condenses into a celestial light (divya-liṅga) equivalent to the vibrations released by the recitation of the respective mantras. The divya-liṅga, which is indivisible, forms the central "root pillar" (mūla-stambha) of celestial light called Īśāna; it is the liṅga, installed and consecrated on its base.[6] In the "root pillar" everything has its origin and finally ends in it. Thus, it is said, it was called the liṅga.[7] By the evocative power of the mantras, Śiva is realized throughout the universe; the universe is his body (śarīra)[8]; this body is of pure energy (śāktika śarīra), containing all the elements, itself the primordial substance (pradhāna) of the moving universe.

The "body" of Śiva, the sign (liṅga) of he who pervades the universe, faces all directions, is given a face in every direction; the faces are summed up and represented at the cardinal points and in the fifth direction. Each face conveys a particular aspect of Śiva, and its physiognomy indicates its nature. Certain signs also of identification are laid down in the texts; Sadyojāta holds the mātuluṅga or bījapūraka, a citron, in one hand, and a rosary (akṣamālā) in the other.[9] The bījapūraka is full of the atoms of the seeds of this universe[10]; the rosary is a symbol of the reintegration of this world.[11] In his crown of matted locks Tatpuruṣa wears the crescent of the moon; it is its sixteenth digit (amā-kalā), symbol of perfectedness and the power of the Lord (aiśvarya).[12] Aghora is fierce, terrific, like Time (kāla) itself; serpent and skull belong to him.[13] Vāmadeva is handsome; he is "woman's delight."[14]

The *Viṣṇudharmottara*, moreover, knows the five faces of Śiva under a double set of names. The first series, Īśāna, Tatpuruṣa, Aghora, Vāmadeva, and Sadyojāta, belongs to the Supreme Śiva in his mental "body of mantras"; they are the faces of the five-faced liṅga.

The second set of names is: Sadāśiva, Mahādeva, Bhairava, Umā, and

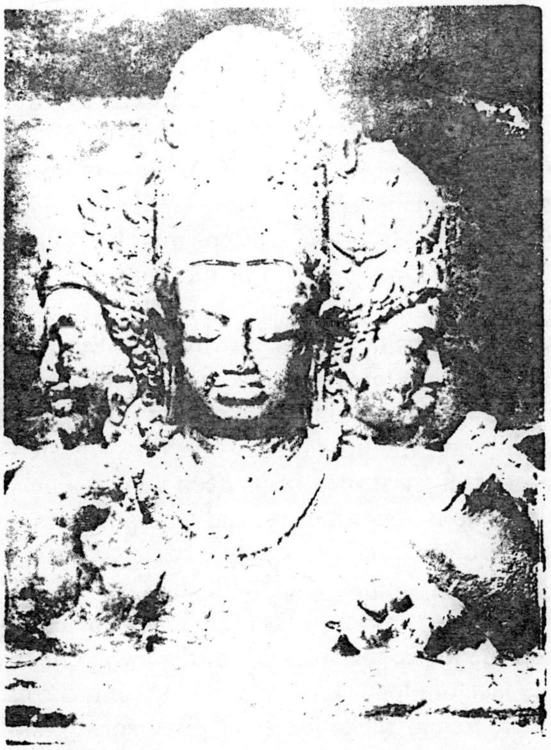

7-3. Mahādeva with scale of feet

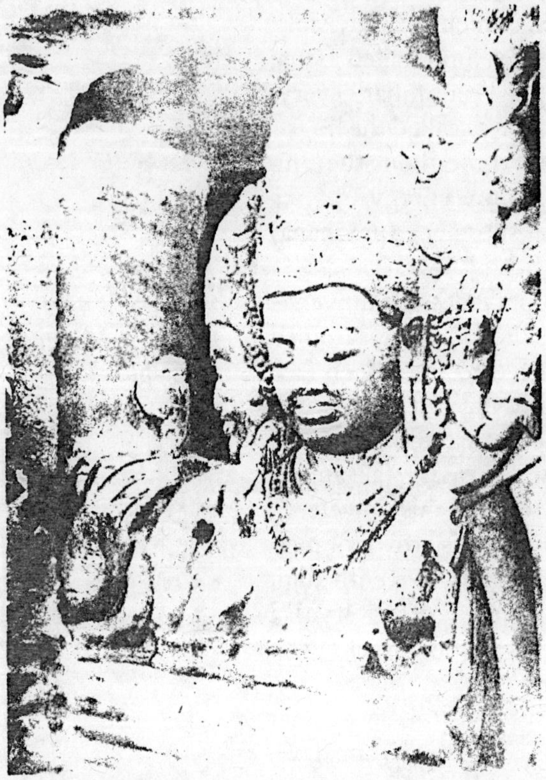

7-4. *Mahādeva*

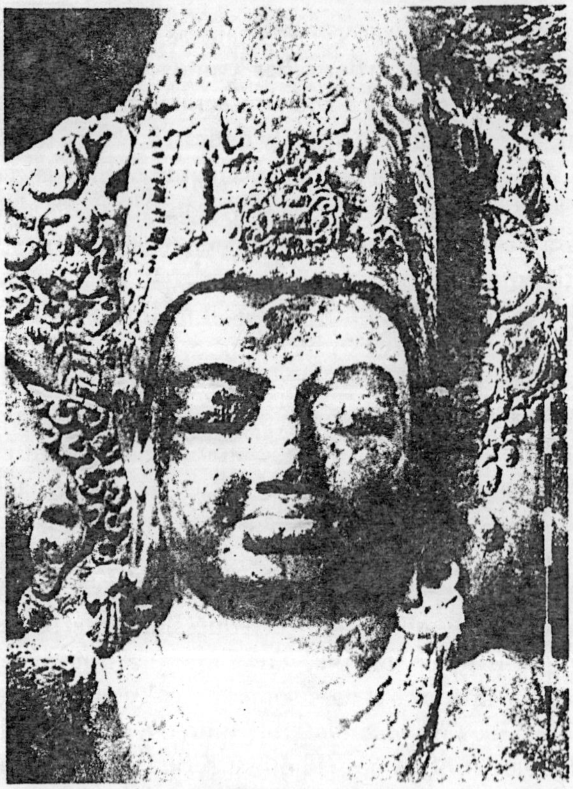

7-5. *Mahādeva Sadyojāta*

Nandī.[15] Thus the face in the middle is that of Sadyojāta-Mahādeva; Aghora-Bhairava is on the one side and Vāmadeva or Umā on the other. The latter face, which is that of the Beauteous God (Vāmadeva), is also that of the Goddess Umā, who is Śiva's Śakti, inseparably part of his nature.

The second set of names denotes the faces of the Supreme Śiva, fully manifest; he is the "Great Lord," Maheśa.[16]

Thus was carved the image of Mahādeva at Elephanta. It is symbol and image, liṅga and mūrti in one; the concrete form of the Supreme Śiva, fully manifest. Around this image, in separate panels, are carved his līlā-mūrtis, the various forms and actions in which is displayed his divinity. But the image of Mahādeva dominates the whole assemblage. It is the concrete form of Śiva whose liṅga is worshiped in the adjacent shrine. The plan of the rock-cut temple—and not only the disposition of the līlā-mūrtis—was thus adjusted to the image, the entire hall is laid out in front of it in its deep recess. The stage is set for that form (rūpa) of his who is beyond form, and who pervades the universe, which thus is his visible body.

The central pillar, the mūlastambha, rises with the face of Sadyojāta. His matted hair forms his cylindrical crown. It is clasped by a diadem of wide curves, clear cut. The serpentine locks, the splendor of the jewel crests which has its symbol in the leonine face of glory (kīrttimukha) in front, the crescent moon on its right, the tender, folded aśoka leaves of early spring, and their

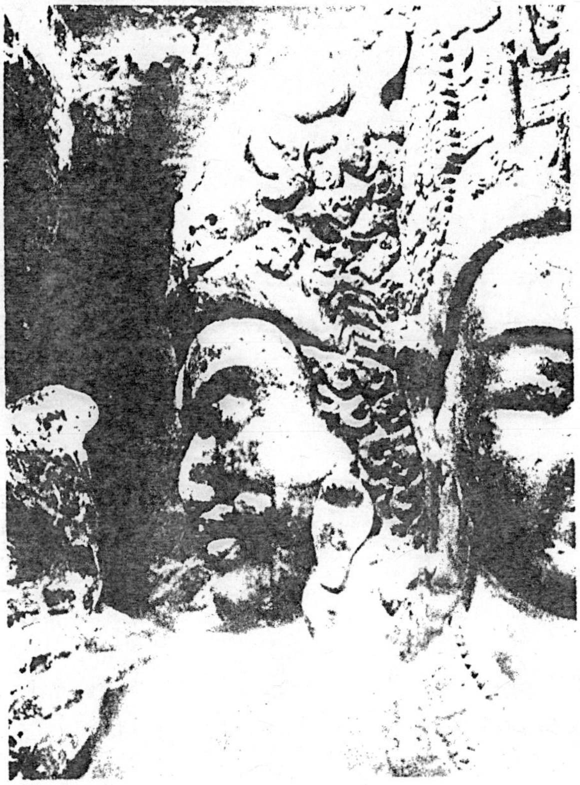

7-6. *Mahadeva Aghora, the Wrathful*

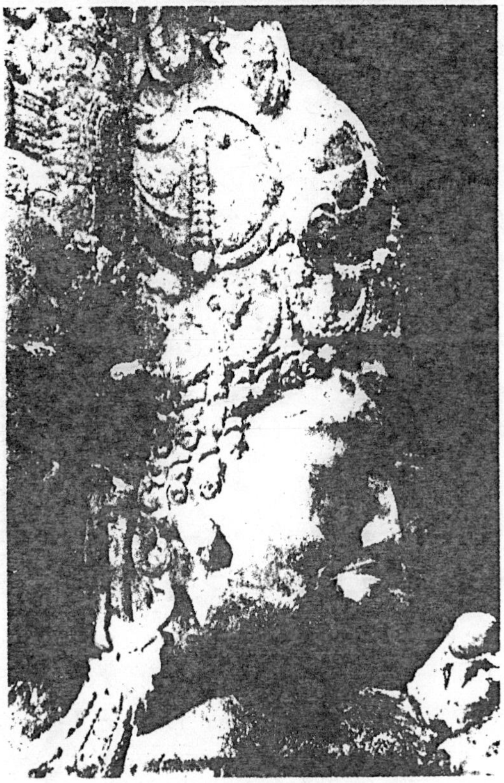

7-7. *Mahādeva Vāmadeva, the Blissful*

full flower-cups—all this precious, delicately carved, intimately agitated coiffure, full of meaning, closely adheres to the shape of the central pillar and none of its subtle detail is allowed to caress the august serenity of the face. The rim of the diadem with its wide curves tightly fits its planes; no curl transgresses, nothing disturbs its silence. The long curves of the ears are set against locks, a closely woven crop that frames each of the lateral faces; capricious, viciously encircled, tumescent, serpentine on Aghora-Bhairava's face, with drooping elegance they touch the cheek of the face on the right. Within their symmetry, each of these two crowns is truly a part of the nature of that god whose face bears his name and whose hands hold his insignia. Obstinate and coagulate, skull-adorned, the crown of Aghora-Bhairava ascends, then slopes back in a steep angle; whereas, above its diadem, the crown of Umā, on the right, is joined in one ripe roundness to the firm pillar of Sadyojāta's crown.

The wrathful aspect of Aghora or Bhairava, his face bulging with the curves of frenzied life, his moustache like lightning, flashing across the full lips; small and young, rapt in its bliss, the face of Umā, yet related by a structure of interlaced curving planes; deeply silent, the triune head holds its mystery, vital and deathly on the left, knowing and blissful on the right, and free of any attribute in the face of the middle. Ponderous yet weightless lips, relaxed in meditation, are the bar, the closed door, whereby the initiate and perfected alone may pass, and enter the state of Śiva.

8 An Image of Aditi-Uttānapad

An image of great significance is preserved in the museum at Alampur in the southern Deccan.[1] The image is carved in a dark stone. The surface of the recumbent figure was worked to a high degree of polish.

The mighty female shape lies facing upward on a nearly square plane. The rim of this surface frames the figure and allows the water that was poured over the image during worship to flow off through the spout at the proper left of the figure. The whole carved image with its squarish support (36" × 40") fulfilled the function of an altar (pīṭha).[2] It is replete with the high relief representing a majestic maternal body. It lies in the birth position. The broadly spread out legs are drawn up laterally and bent at the knees. The soles of the feet are turned upward. Their modeling and the contraction of the toes show the tension and struggle that attend the process of giving birth. The feet accentuate the corners of the squarish altar and the width of the figure, which is splayed out up to the knees. The elbows rest on them. The arms are bent upwards and the hands, each holding a lotus bud, are laid on the shoulders while the forefingers, in a sensitive and relaxed movement, touch upon the petals of the large and open lotus blossom that crowns the image, as its neck and head. A small and delicate bead necklace links chest and flower by the curve of its outline. It reposes on the surging modeling of the body which gains powerful volume in the large, flattened globes of the breasts with their lotus-nipples.[3]

Serpent armlets are coiled around the pillar shapes of the upper arms. Widely spaced bracelets join their broadening accents to the monumental form of the upper half of the image, whereas thin anklets, quickened with serpentine energy, cling to the feet. But for these serpent ornaments, the figure is naked. The lower half of her body is modeled in the throes of muscular convulsion,

This essay first appeared in *Artibus Asiae* 19(1956):259–70, and is reprinted here by permission.

from the palpitating flesh of hips and abdomen to their budlike opening in the middle. The upper half of the body, however, lies calm in monumental gravity and fulfillment, sealed by the lotus flower on top, whose limp petals, pointing upward, pointing downward, recline in low relief against the swelling buds upheld by the serpentlike fingers of the image.

None of the innumerable known shapes in which the goddess revealed herself to the Indian sculptors surpasses the power and consistency of the image in Alampur. It would seem to have belonged originally to one of the sanctuaries of this town of temples. The style of the modeling would assign

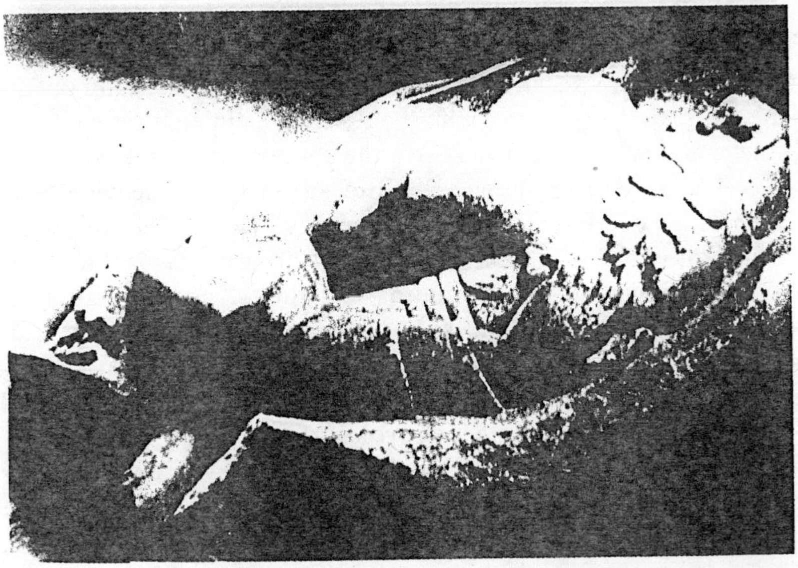

8-1. Image of Aditi-uttānapad; Alampur

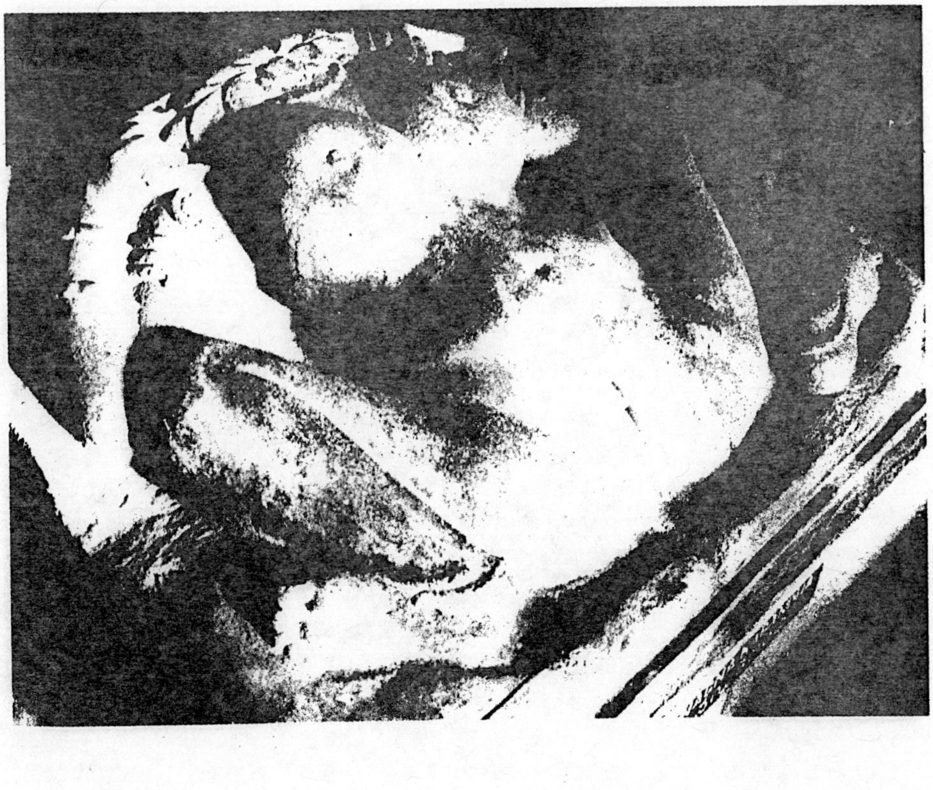

8-2. Image of Aditi-uttānapad; Alampur

the image to approximately the eighth century, although none of the images on the several temples or in the museum of Alampur are equal in quality.[4] None of them, moreover, portray a conception equal to that of the recumbent image. Nearer to it as a bodily type, though more schematically composed, would be certain images from Ellora, such as the Durgā in the Rāmesvara cave or the Indrānī in the Indra Sabhā.[5] The iconography of the image, though it has no known parallel, is nonetheless adumbrated, in one or several of its aspects, by more than one earlier work of art. Nearest in space and time is a fragment of an image in Mahakuteswar, in the southwestern Deccan (pl. 8-3). The temples there date from the later part of the sixth century A.D. or about the year A.D. 600.[6] This would also be the date of the fragment of the image of the goddess with arms raised from the elbows, each hand facing outward and holding in kaṭaka hasta the curved stalk of a lotus flower, just fully opening. They flank the main large flower whose outer circle of petals rests on the chest of the image and whose filaments form the center high up—level with the top of the stele—of the large flower that exceeds in width the shoulders of the slim, long-armed goddess and is her crowning glory. Like her mightier sister image, this figure, too—wearing a double pair of wristlets—although it seems to have been shown sitting or standing upright, is carved in front of a plain back slab. It was partly cut out so as to throw into higher relief and outline more sharply the contour of the image.

With the exception of two terracotta plaques from northern India,[7] of Kuṣāna or early Gupta date, no other representations of the goddess are known whose body carries a lotus in place of neck and head. There are cognate conceptions, however, in the more remote past of Indian art, the one from Sanchi of the second century B.C., the other from the Indus Valley of the third millennium B.C.

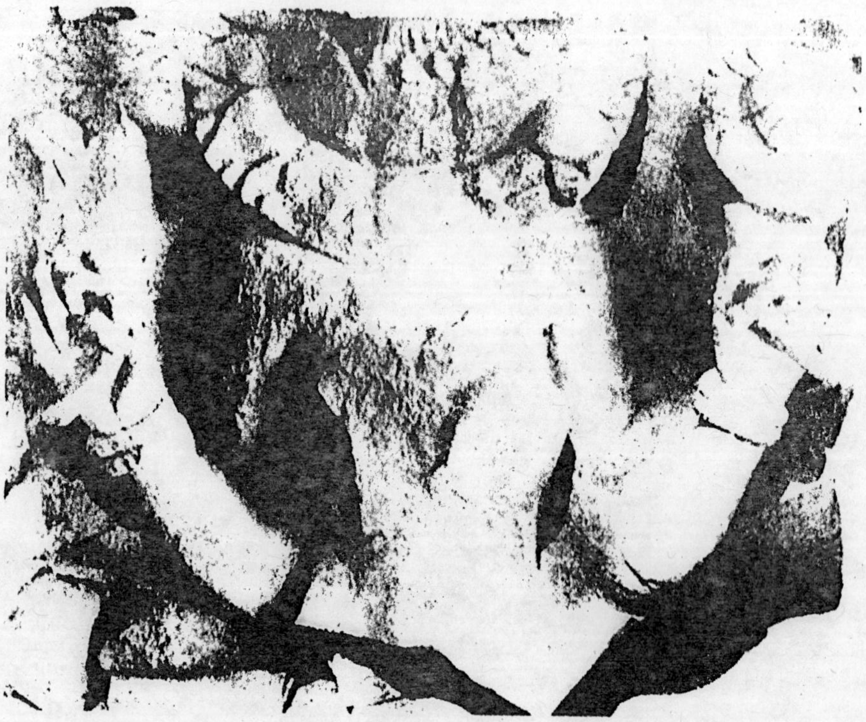

8-3. Image in Mahakuteswar

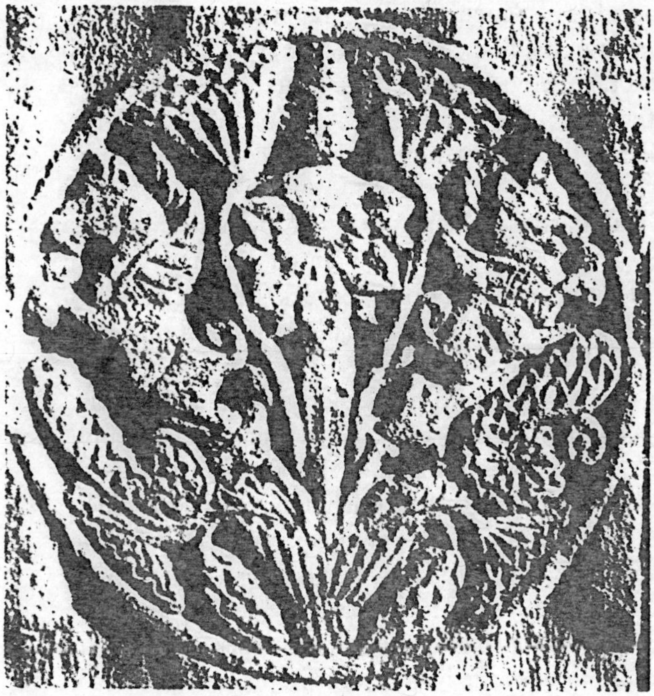

8-4. Roundel on railing post; stūpa 2, Sanchi

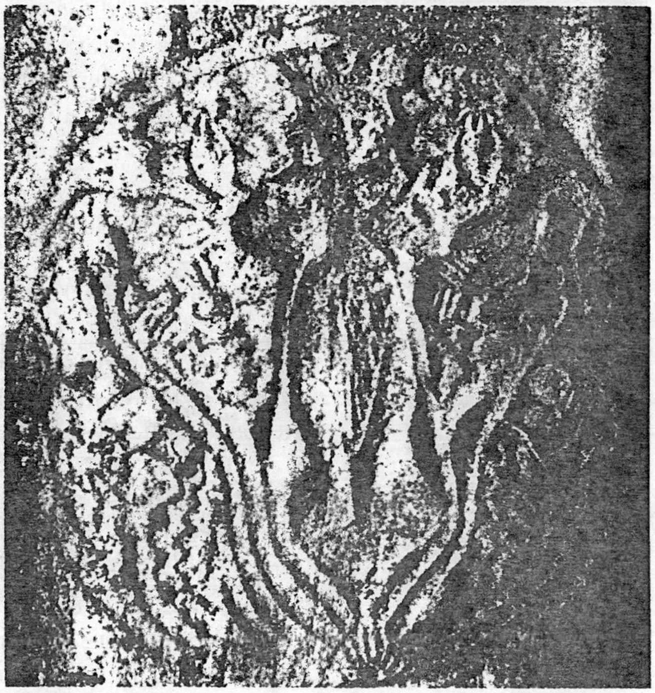

8-5. Roundel on railing post; stūpa 2, Sanchi

One of the roundels carved in low relief on the railing posts of stūpa 2 in Sanchi shows a typical configuration (pl. 8-4). In free but calculated symmetry, two winged lions prance forth from pod shaped bases carried on stalks that issue from a central device resembling an inverted flower shape. Indented leaf and bud motifs spring from the same center and fill the lower, lateral segments of the roundel. Above the lions two folded lotus leaves touch, with their chalice-like design, the apex of the circle. They are sent up on long stalks that likewise stem from the inverted floral fantasy at the bottom. Between their amphora-like lines, and at their widest divergence, a fully opened lotus flower tosses its petals and filaments around and below the emergent seed pod with its unusually broad top. The support of this central lotus bloom can hardly be described as a stalk. At either side of a thin, central ridge its shape, too broad for any stalk, is curved with the symmetry suggesting somehow lithe female limbs—topped by the lotus bloom. Above it, completing the vertical axis of the composition, garlands are suspended from one central point.

This roundel has a counterpart in another, similar design (pl. 8-5). Although this lacks the terse vivaciousness, the central figure emerges in complete anthropomorphic shape. Flanked by two birds instead of the lions and standing on a central "floral" support, the figure draws to itself the long lotus stalks and the large flowers are upheld by its hands to either side of the diademed head. It is crowned by two large lotus buds and a small rosette between them.[8] The figure here is male. A knee-length dhoti, draped around the thighs, shows its long end gathered and tucked in front.

Related to these two roundels in Sanchi is one more circular panel, from the railing of the stūpa of Bharhut of the first century B.C. (pl. 8-6). The winged quadrupeds here have well-toothed monster's heads, a lotus flower occupies the root position in the center. From the cuplike pericarp a small leafy tree emerges in front of a leaflike flame, the central, noniconic device of this composition.

Before entering into the underlying theme of these different sculptures in which the lotus occupies a central place, two painted potsherds from Mohenjo-daro with a circle of lotus petals around the neck[9] should be mentioned, for they seem to suggest in their own terms the plenitude and meaning of the image at Alampur with the lotus at its neck.

In Bharhut of the first century B.C., and particularly in Sanchi, on the gateways of the first century A.D., certain representations frequently occupy the same places. They would appear to be sculptural synonyms. In some of them, the center is occupied by a round pot, the "pūrṇa ghaṭa," from which lotus flowers emerge; in others, the anthropomorphic equivalent is a female figure, standing or seated on an expanded lotus flower, holding a lotus flower in her raised hand, and surrounded by flowering stems and growing leaves.[10] These latter compositions are well-established iconographic types of the Goddess Śrī or Lakṣmī. In none of them does she have a lotus in place of her head, and she is never in the birth position.

The lotus flower crowns the body of the images of Mahakuteswar and Alampur. In Alampur, the lotus is comprised within the outline of the body; it connects the curves of the shoulders (pls. 8-1, 8-2). It is edged and supported by the large lotus buds that converge on it from the hands of the image, whereas in the image in Mahakuteswar (pl. 8-3) the lotus faces upward and exceeds the shoulders in height. In the image at Alampur, the filaments of the flower are not shown, but only the double row of petals, and possibly the center and tip of the pericarp of the large, delicate and somewhat tired flower. The curves of the petals communicate the essence of their fragrance, just when the flower begins to fade. The vigor that had been in the petals is drawn inward, into the pericarp where the cycle of the lotus life begins anew. That is where the forefingers point to and where the large lotus buds are laid on with their soft, sheltering, fleshy shapes.

Embedded and floating on the surging modeled mass, the lotus crowns the woman who is all body, gravid mass, akin to that of the paleolithic Venus from Willendorf who, though she has a head of hair, is without a face. And there are Cycladic images whose rarified, extensive body has no head at all. For the mother goddess is altogether body, incarnate, purposive potentiality whose fulfillment, the womb, is between the symmetry, right and left, of the two breasts, hands, and legs. In one line from the center, over the roundnesses of the hill of the abdomen, lies the sheltered bank above, where the lotus rests and guards its secret, behind a double wreath of petals, locked by the bead chain, the only ornament laid on the body itself. Close by, laterally, on the armlet, the head of a serpent is raised.[11]

The image in Mahakuteswar, which has a lotus for its head, may be compared to images that have either human or animal heads. The human head, though it may be carved without a face, is the seat of consciousness and has its support in the body. The animal head in sculpture makes its carrier, the human body, into a support of its inhuman, more than human, power, that of the animal creation—which preceded men. Earlier still, in the hierarchy of creation, is the plant world. The innocence in the power of vegetation and the innocence of the animal shine forth from their shapes as formed in Indian art.[12] They are worthy to be carried by the body of man and with it conjointly convey a realization of divinity felt and known through the body, seen and felt in animal and plant, and thence placed at the seat of consciousness.

India's foremost sacred plant is the lotus.[13] It flowers on and above the surface of the water, rising from the mud under the water. The flower opens to the sun and closes in the evening. Other varieties of the lotus, however, respond to the moon: they open at night and are closed in the day. With its root in the mud, its stalk traversing the entire depth of the waters on which it rests its leaves, its flower open to the light of heaven, the lotus belongs to this world and those below and above, to light, earth and water. Its open flower emits a fragrance of the subtlest vibrations;[14] the petals, whatever their color, gleam with crystal freshness, their opening and closing fans into ripeness the seeds in the pericarp. It is seed pod, womb, and ground of the new plants, and on its high level of perfected beauty it holds the mystery of the lotus. This wondrous plant, having its being in earth, water, and light, enacts their transmutation from earth to light, from mud to scent, through water to gleaming color in the regularity of its shape, not only ordered as it is in all the directions of space, but also in the regularity of its movement, opening and closing with the measure of time, of days and nights.

With this series of functions a synthesis is effected of elements and forms of the cosmos, whereas the processes contained in the pericarp on high refer to the mysteries of generation.

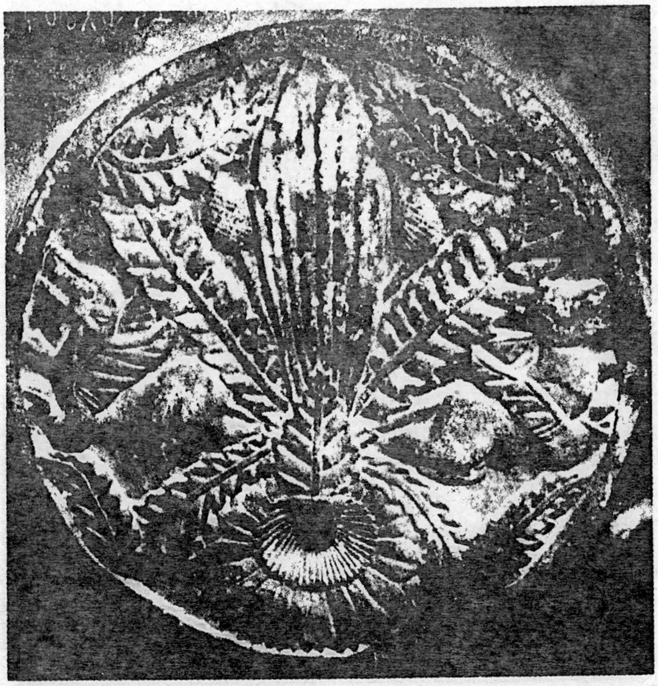

8-6. Roundel on railing post; Bharhut (courtesy Department of Archaeology, Indian Museum, Calcutta)

When the seeds of other sorts of plant are ripe, the bursting of the pod releases them, and they fall to the ground and germinate. It is otherwise with the lotus. The ripe seeds, instead of falling from the pod, remain in the cells where they have grown. Within these cells, whose openings are too small to let them out, the seeds send forth the young seedlings. The seed pod is their matrix until they are large enough to burst open their cells. The seedlings then sink to the bottom of the water where they take root in the mud.

Within the flower the reproductive power has its seat. There, high above the muddy ground, above the water, the whole cycle of vegetation is accomplished. Within the pericarp is held the continuity from bud to fruit and again to the new, young plant, the beginning and the end and the new beginning once more. The center of productivity and the cycle of generation reside above, in the flower. The earth below, the mud, is but the intermediate ground for the root. Productivity and generation above are one continuous process within the lotus flower. When the lotus flower is supported, not by its stalk in nature, but on the female body in art, the place of productivity and generation is also that of consciousness, which resides in the head, and which is concentrated in the several subtle centers (cakra) situated there. As the lotus extends over the region of the throat, it occupies the Viśuddhi cakra, the subtle center in the throat region, in the image at Alampur particularly (pls. 8-1, 8-2). Each of these centers or cakras is visualized in the shape of a lotus. Its name conveys its meaning. The lotus situated in the throat, Viśuddhi cakra or center of Great Purity, is realized as the door to liberation, for there the four Vedas are known, together with their secret meaning.[15] The throat, whence the vibration that causes speech is exteriorized in man, the microcosm, as articulate voice, the Viśuddhi cakra, is the place for the manifestation of the word, in its universal macrocosmic reference. The word is Veda, sum total of all knowledge. From the word was brought forth the universe.[16]

Supported by the entire figure, on top of her body is the place of the lotus, the place of the birth of the universe. Below, the figure is shown in the physical position of giving birth, above she is herself once more the giver of life, as lotus, the word that was in the beginning, genetrix of all that exists in the cosmos, genetrix once more of what is manifest as embodied cosmic consciousness.

For the image is that of the birthgiving mother in her shape as woman and in her shape as lotus, one in function and artistic vision, but dual in shape and in the hierarchy of meaning, offering her being to be beheld and worshiped as Goddess. The image at Alampur lies flat on her back, on a raised plinth, on an altar she completely fills. She herself is this altar.

She is the birthgiving mother. If head and face establish the identity of a person, she who has neither head nor face but a lotus instead is the lotus, padmā, foremost of all plants in India. "Plants, O ye Mothers, I hail you as Goddesses" (*Yajurveda* 4.2.6). The nourishing, lifegiving, lifesaving plants are mothers; in their miraculous power they are goddesses. In a physical sense, the earth (Pṛthivī) is the mother of plants and herbs, the all-producer (*AV* 12.1.17). She is this earth "on whose surface they enclose the altar" (*AV* 12.1.13). As large as is this earth, so large is the altar (*RV* 1.164.35; 10.110.4, *ŚB* 3.7.2.1; 9.4.2.3.; 12.8.2.36; etc.). This whole earth is one place of sacrifice, of transmutation of the lower earthly man into the higher spiritual man, and of attaining by sacrifice to the realm of the spirit, to heaven, while yet remaining firmly on this earth. So Mother Earth (*AV* 12.1.12) is invoked, as she who bears plants, that she, Pṛthivī (the wide one), may spread wide and favor us (*AV* 12.1.2).

The image as altar (pls. 8-1, 8-2) is the place of new birth—of which the mother is the figure and the lotus the symbol. Images vested in architecture and nature overlap, in the total configuration, colorful transparencies of the meaning that encompasses and surpasses them. It is said that herbs and plants—of which the lotus is the foremost—were "born first." The meaning here is not that of an event in time but of a prefiguration in those cycles of creation of causal images which do not lie within any time; they are known as timeless prefiguration of those essences which were to convey their meaning through the fragrance and shape of flowers and plants long before the conception of gods. "The plants which were born first, three ages before the gods" (*RV* 10.97.1), are prefigurative thought-forms. In the order of conceptual seeing or image-making, the essence to which the plants are to give substance is a mind-conceived reality that precedes that of the gods.

At the stage of the making of concrete images (mūrti), the "preceding" conceptual strata, in their causal and archetypal existence, though they are layered, are transparent. They imply and evoke each other.

The architectural form, the altar, as in Alampur, bases its symbolic suggestiveness on its horizontal extent which is spread out like the surface of the earth, Pṛthivī, the "broad one." As Mother Earth, Pṛthivī is the archetypal "altar."[17] In the sculpture at Alampur, the female shape carries the lotus in one line with her sex. Her generative power is along her middle line. On either side of it her width is spread. But when, for reasons of ritual requirement, the object used is of vertical extent, like the offering stands of the Harappa civilization, the head-lotus is expanded toward the sky, as it also appears on the upright image at Mahakuteswar (pl. 8-3), with the difference that the petals of the Mohenjo-daro lotus, painted on the underside of the pan or bowl of offering, formed a complete circle. And where the lotus is part of a capital of a pillar, the symbolism of this shape belongs to the same order, in all the varieties of its form and their particular applications. In this instance the petals of the upward-facing lotus are turned downward, as are those of the lower set, above the necklace, of the image at Alampur. Other adjustments of the head-lotus to its presentation with the image are the halo (Śiraścakra) in which the lotus is shown at the back of the head, generally as part of a stele, and also the lotus disc at the back of the head of South Indian metal images of divinities—where the anthropomorphic, divine head is the "face" of the image.[18]

A lotus, in the two images (pls. 8-1–8-3), is also held in either of the two hands. The images are "padmahastā," in addition to being "padmānanā" or "lotus-faced," as the goddess Śrī is described in the Śrīsūkta.[19] A lotus, "the nectarine essence of the Waters," is generally held by Lakṣmī, the mother of this entire earth, in her right hand where it also signifies one of the two oceans, that is the ocean of the upper region in contrast to the ocean that girds the earth and is symbolized by the conch shell.[20] Throughout the history of Indian sculpture, the goddess Lakṣmī, the auspicious, whose name is also Śrī, the beautiful, is represented as holding a lotus, occupying a lotus, as her seat or stand, and surrounded by lotuses. This goddess, in Indian iconography, is frequently the center of the lotus configuration, and her perimeter is a kind of lotus scene.

The image at Alampur (pls. 8-1, 8-2) does not hold full, open lotuses. The buds, which are closed, seem just then only to have acquired their pointed shape, petals and sepals have not as yet separated. They are nascent buds in which the embryonic seed pod is hidden. The lotus buds are not held aloft on either side of the body. Their curve extends the arc of the bent arms of the image upward from the knees. With this movement they reach to the apex of the central lotus flower as if in a rite of insemination. With great tenderness they are laid down by the large hands of the image and their serpentine fingers; they meet, support, and are part of one central, crowning lotus configuration, closing the cycle of the flower, sealing the sculpture of the genetrix as one self-contained form of the widest symbolic connotation.

Viewed as form, the mass of the sculpture appears replete with the vastness of its conception. This mass, carved in stone, is modeled throughout. The quality of the modeling is an intrinsic one, bringing to the surface of the relief the movement which sustains and pervades the curved planes of the image. They are fastened to and bounded by the square level of the altar. This seems to have risen up in the likeness of a gigantic female body, incorporating its shape and binding it by its square limit. The two conceptions, the "anthropomorphic" and the architectural are fused. They are not adjusted to one another, but constitute a formal unity.

Spread within, and coerced by the square limit of the base, the mass rises with curves which are as tense as they are elastic. Their arcs hold the tidal waves of the lifegiving body. Its boundless abundance is stemmed by the square field of the relief. The overall conception of altar and lifegiving body imparts monumental calm to the modeling. It is accentuated by a greater frequency of vibration in the modeling of the upturned soles, suggestive of muscular contractions in the agony of giving birth.

Whose is the life-giving image? Although related to that of Lakṣmī[21] it is not this goddess whom the great master of Alampur bodied forth. Here is a deeper message and a more primal vision. Like Lakṣmī, she is the All-Mother, born of the waters—by which she appears surrounded—floating on them on her altar, during worship. Like Lakṣmī, her shape is that of "our Lady of abundance," who is hymned in the Śrīsūkta, as of the lotus-face and lotus-thigh (padma-ūrū); the juxtaposition of these two of her lotus parts stresses their correspondence in the sculpture at Alampur.[22] Like Śrī of the hymn, her sculptured form is "ārdrā" (*Śrīsūkta* 4; 14) which means "billowing" as form and also "wet," in her element the water, the water on which her lotuses float. And she is earth, Pṛthivī, the broad one, spread on the water,[23] the support of all living beings (*Śrīsūkta* 9). For she "who at first was Water in the Ocean" Pṛthivī, the broad one, is invoked in the Atharva Veda, in her center and navel, with all the forces that have issued from her body, to set us amid those forces. "I am the son of Earth, Earth is my mother."[24] But this earth is the ground, the support of all existence, the all-sustaining. Abiding thus in the substantial and concrete aspect of the all-sustaining mother, the universe is ever borne along and supported by her. "Thou art the Earth, the ground, thou art the all-sustaining Aditi, she who supports all the World."[25] She, the wide one, the capacious, widely spread,[26] bounteous earth, is most truly, actively herself when "spreading wide," she is shown giving birth to all that is.

"In the first age of the gods the existent was born from the nonexistent. After this the regions were born. This [existent] was born of her with the legs spread open (uttānapad). The World was born of her with the legs spread open. From Aditi Dakṣa was born and from Dakṣa Aditi" (*RV* 10.72.3–4). And it is Aditi whom the singer of the hymn of the Atharva Veda invokes as the Vessel that contained all beings, "she who is granter of the wish, the far spreading, Earth, my mother."[27]

As Mother Earth, who never lets down,[28] whose lap holds all succor[29] and life immortal,[30] her navel is the center of the earth.[31] This earth, to the ancients was but one large altar—for "as large as is this altar, so large is the earth,"[32] one sacrificial place where man is restored to primordial unity. The sacrifice is the navel of the universe, the navel of the mother where in the beginning we were together, the place also where Aditi is invoked to restore this our relation.[33] Aditi, Mother Earth, is ritually the altar, who bears in her womb the sacrificial fire.[34] "May Aditi in her womb bear Agni as a mother in her lap, her son" (*Yajurveda* 11.57).

As altar and womb, the image of Aditi (pls. 8-1, 8-2) faces upward. The image is laved ritually by the water for which the sculpture provides rim and outlet. Symbolically it is the same water in which the gods danced in the beginning. The gods, born after Aditi was born, daughter of Dakṣa, stood closely embraced, in the flood, while thick mist rose from them like dust raised by dancers (*RV* 10.72.5–6).

As earth, womb, and altar, the image of Aditi is surrounded by the waters. The lotus flowers on them.

The lotus, symbol of creativeness, blooms above the waters. They nourish and sustain the plant as the body of the goddess, whose lap holds the elixir of life, the water of life, and the spark of life, the fire, supports the lotus flower as her head. In these two centers of creativity dwell the meaning and the power of the goddess and her image as altar. The navel of the earth is borne by the womb of this boundless goddess[35] who is receptacle and carrier of all "that is born and of all that is to be born" (*RV* 1.89.10), including those who are reborn through the sacrifice. This is how Aditi's head is spoken of as earth's place of sacrifice (*Yajurveda* 4.22). The head of Aditi thus is a lotus, for the lotus flower is also above, in the sky, where the sun is at the head of the universe (*MaUp* 6.1.2).

The navel of the earth is the center, where the earthly heat is consumed on the sacrificial altar. This is the place of the animal sacrifice, of the creative commutation of animal heat in the flame of the sacrificial fire. There burns the terrestial fire, Agni, in the flame of the sacrifice. But Agni has sprung from a lotus, "from the head of the Universe" (mūrdhno viśvasya, *RV* 6.6.13). In these two centers, the impartite, guiltless[36] Aditi is at one with herself, the Great Mother. For "Aditi is heaven, Aditi is the Air, Aditi the Mother, the same also Father and Son" (*RV* 1.89.10).

"From Aditi was born Dakṣa" (*RV* 10.72.4).[37] From the genetrix, in the act of generation, is generated the activity of the act, the creator spiritus, Dakṣa, the spiritual potency in the universe. "The Non-Existent and the Existent are in the highest heaven at the birth of Dakṣa, in the lap of Aditi. Agni indeed is the First-born of the Law in the Primal Age" (*RV* 10.5.7). The father and the son, creator spiritus, and the creative intellectual fire are born in the highest heaven, at the head of the universe, in the lotus, in self-sufficient, self-effected, creative generation, simultaneous with the perennial generation that takes place in the womb of the great impartite goddess, at the first age of the gods. It is thus that her lotus head rests on her shoulders in that sinless state of prefigured life in which the plants are born, three ages before the gods.[38] It is thus, too, that in a separate representation the birth of Agni is shown in the lotus flower (pl. 8-6), Agni who is the son of the Great Mother, the son of Aditi, and her gift (*RV* 1.185.3), the light of life and consciousness. For it is sung of Aditi "Thought art thou, mind, intellect—Aditi, with a double head" (*Yajurveda* 4.9).

The lotus head of Aditi, placed on her shoulders, overlays her throat with its petals. There the subtle center (cakra) of the articulate voice is situated, of speech, and of the word. As Vāc, speech and word, as microcosmic, articulate existence, and as macrocosm, Aditi raises her sinless lotus-head.[39] She is altar of the world, place of the sacrifice, genetrix who is mother, father, and son,[40] potent, parturient body vessel of fire within the water of life, and she is laved by primeval waters, lotus of self-renewal in the impartite. Who "will give us back to the Great Aditi? May I see Mother and Father again" (*RV* 1.24.1). Through the divine fire of creation and by the flame of the sacrifice we return to the lotus flower of guiltless, impartite, self-sufficient unity. "God Agni is the first of the immortals whose dear name we have in mind. He shall give us back to the Great Aditi. May I see Father and Mother again" (*RV* 1.24.2).

9 Pūṣan

Pūṣan in the Ṛg Veda is the Lord of the Way (pathas pate 6.53.1). He is invoked as the "Glowing One" (āghṛṇi).[1] His own name, Pūṣan, is connected in the Ṛg Veda with puṣṭi (nourishment; 4.3.7; 10.26.7) and can be taken to signify "the Nourisher."[2] His own sacrificial offering is gruel (karambha, 3.52.7; 6.57.3), a very special sacrificial food not given to any other god. Soma, the elixir of life, is their offering. Pūṣan is not offered any soma, but he drives one and the same chariot (2.40.3; 1.23.15) with Soma, that great divinity. Pūṣan's draft animal is the goat (6.55.3, 4). It climbs the steep and steady path of Pūṣan's perennial cycle. There he finds hidden treasure (nidhi, 8.29.6) and gives wealth in abundance (6.55.1, 3; 9.88.3; 8.31.11; 1.89.6). There he also puts his foot on the two-faced evil one (1.42.4), and he lacerates the heart of every man (6.53.8), yet he is the herdsman of creation (10.17.3). He guides all, the quick and the dead, and leads the bride on earth (10.85.37) as he leads the bride, the Great Goddess in heaven, whose name is that of the sun (Sūryā). Who is this god, who is invoked "O Liberator (vimocana), help us find the treasure (rai) by our inner vision (dhī)" (8.4.15)?[3] He has been called solar[4] and also pastoral, good shepherd and psychopompos[5] the guide of the departed, and he has been interpreted on the basis of natural phenomena and liturgically.[6] But, while he answers to these qualifications, they neither exhaust, nor do they constitute, his nature, which is one and whole, beheld in inner vision and hymned through the Ṛg Veda wherever his name occurs. One consistent image of this god, glowing in his ardor throughout his path, turns around with him so that he is beheld in all his aspects in time and eternity. The sun, the goat, the gruel, and the chariot, the right hand of Pūṣan and his golden beard, his wealth, his golden weapon, his cattle, all these are part of the symbolic picture drawn in verbal images, of the god-reality Pūṣan, who is present at all times when he

This essay first appeared in *JAOS* 81(1961), and is reprinted here by permission.

is invoked for he is always on the move, surrounds the cosmos, and is in every creature (6.58.2).

"Alles Vergängliche ist nur ein Gleichnis." Whatever is transitory is but a symbol, be it as firm as this earth and high as is the firmament. The shape of the animal, the body of man in all its parts, and man-made objects, all these are drawn into the picture. There they form part of one composition which paints in detail, in as many configurations as inner vision dictates, the nature and myth of the god. The myths are his actions, their stage is the heart and mind (manas) of the singer and he draws its lineaments in the frame and order of the cosmos which he sees and knows, in which he lives and is conscious.

He sees the sun's radiant face and glowing orb move on the vault of the sky, and understands its radiance, glow and movement as manifestations of a power to which he gives three names: Sūrya, the sun in manifestation; Pūṣan, the glowing innermost essence of this manifestation; and Savitṛ, "the impeller," the cause of its being and movement. Savitṛ, the impeller, the causa efficiens "becomes Pūṣan" (5.81.5; yāmabhiḥ), the primordial stress that was ante principium is beheld in Pūṣan, concreted in his ardor, the glowing essence of the sun, its "substance ante principium." Savitṛ is the efficient cause and Pūṣan the material cause of the sun that glows and shining moves. Savitṛ, Pūṣan, and Sūrya refer to the same symbol in the cosmos, the sun. It is validated as cause and effect. The cause is beheld in the effect and is named differently in the salient stages of its transition.

The sun mounts up on the vault of the sky as a surefooted goat climbs a mountain. This movement of the sun has its symbol in the goat, which is Pūṣan's animal; it refers to Pūṣan's nature in the image of a goat. The goat precedes the horse at the horse sacrifice, on their way to heaven (1.162.2–3). The horse is a symbol of the sun in manifestation,[7] it is preceded by its movement, which has its image in the goat, for ontologically the movement precedes the thing that moves in accordance with it, in accordance with its preestablished plan and order.

The various images have their substratum in the objects of the senses. These images, however, function in conformity with an order which operates not only in the outer world, the world of the senses, but is realized at the same time within the entire living being of the poet. By his word he gives effect to this twofold stage of his experience. The actors are the gods who move his mind while they move the cosmos. The herdsman of creation, of the entire universe (10.17.3; 6.58.2), is "inserted in every creature." Pūṣan takes the course of the sun in the cycle of the year and he takes the path of redemption in the heart of man. The first is charged with the emotions and realizations of mind and soul (manas), and the second takes on the images of the external world.

The polyvalence of each symbol is supported in two constant directions. The one refers to the cosmos and to the immanent and transcendent presence and activity of divinity, the other refers to the creative, inner world of man, with its two organs of manas, the "mind-soul" and dhī, inner vision or intuition and to Brahman, the creative power.[8] When, for example, the chariot is spoken of which Pūṣan, "the most perfect of charioteers," (6.55.2; 6.56.2–3) is driving, the image of the chariot is that of the "vehicle of the mind-soul" (manas) and at the same time it is an image of the cosmos as it exists and moves in time while the structure of the chariot comprises the timeless uncreated worlds and the point of their becoming manifest. The symbols operate in both these regions, the one with reference to the inner world of man, the other with reference to the cosmos. These symbols unite and interchange the contents of the two regions by subsuming them to a structure in which both have their home and each has its place.

The main image in which the presence and activity of Pūṣan is invoked is that of his path. The path is circular, that is cyclical, and has two focal points of the god's activity. The circular path with the two decisive points of its course refers to the annual cycle of the sun with the turning points of its course in the depth and darkness of the night of the year the one, and the other at the high noon of the year, in midsummer. Pūṣan glows in his majesty and wrath at the turning point from darkness to light, which is in the depth and he glows with love at the height of the year, the midday of creation. Pūṣan, the glowing one, the nourisher, leads all the way up from the depth to the height, and thence he conducts on the downward path to the point where he has arisen and overcome the darkness. The path (pathi) is eternally recurrent time which "like an ever rolling stream (sruti; 1.42.3) bears all its sons away"[9] from the peak of life, the peak of the world down to the halting place in the darkness, at the parting of the ways whence the direction changes from that of descent to ascent. All the while Pūṣan glows in the ardor of his nature, a steady guide who, on his way, never loses any of his herd, finds hidden treasure and nourishes and ripens all. The path of Pūṣan will first be traced together with the visions of the pit and of the peak which the path traverses. The chariot of Pūṣan and his draft animal, the goat, form part of the image of the path of the glowing god, Pūṣan, the nourisher, whose food is karambha, the food of life.

1. *Pūṣan's Path and Birthplaces:* "On the forward [leading] path of paths was Pūṣan born, on the forward [leading] path of heaven, on the forward [leading] path of earth. To both dearly beloved abodes he goes, to and fro, knowing the way" (10.17.6).

Pūṣan was born on the path of paths, on the very movement of that path, a child of the road, a wanderer. Pūṣan has two birth stations or halting places whence he moves on, ever anew. Thus he is said to be born twice on his forward path, up "in heaven" and down "on earth." Each time his birthplace is on the forward leading path of paths, in the superlative movement of the path, which is his hour of birth. High in heaven his ardor[10] glows most fervently in the midsummer of the year. Down, on the forward leading path of earth, he is born of old (10.26.8), in his innermost nature. He thence proceeds on the upward path.

The path of paths, at the beginning and end of his orbit, where he, the wonder-working (1.42.5; 6.56.4), has his fundament of treasure (10.139.3),[11] will here be viewed first. It starts at the midnight hour of the birth of Pūṣan, when the sun at midwinter is in darkness.

The birth of god is first at the heights, in heaven, from the source of light. This light source which is beyond manifestation, has "ante principium" broken out of the all engulfing darkness (10.129.3; tamas). Tamas, the darkness ante principium is an ontological symbol of the ultimate origin of the gods and of the cosmos.

The darkness of the midnight hour, on the other hand, is the symbolical night of the year in the cyclical movement of the sun. It refers to the cosmos in operation and, by analogy, to man, the microcosm where the midnight hour is that of the darkness and trials of the spirit.

The darkness ante principium which is prior to the light is without any definition (10.129.3) whereas the darkness of the sun's cycle belongs to the sat. Sat, the existent, comprises not only the manifest cosmos but also those stages of manifestation "in principio" which are beyond the visible universe, that is, the phenomenal and the noumenal worlds.

Part of the engulfing darkness (tamas) subsists "apud principium" and outside the sat (cf. note 15).

Pūṣan is born at the height where he choses his parents, the aśvins; Pūṣan is born again at the depth, in the pit. It is there that he is reborn in his innermost nature, as the liberator. His second birth in the depth on his ever renewed, unending path is therefore taken up here first.

The two stations, in the extreme south and the extreme north, of his path are Pūṣan's beloved places of birth. He journeys to and fro.[12] He knows, for he himself traces, the way, when he, the most perfect of charioteers (6.55.2; 6.56.2–3) travels on both sides (viṣu) in his car (2.40.3).

The one side of the journey is the path of light and day, the six months' journey of the sun to the north, from the midnight point of the winter solstice, in the darkness. The other side of the journey begins from the point on high of the sun in midheaven, and thence proceeds on its downward path.

2. *Pūṣan in the Pit:* The birth of Pūṣan, the glowing, is in the night (cf. 6.58.1) of the year at the midnight hour, in the darkness. As soon as born, he journeys forth with his bundle of luminous treasure (vaso rāśir; 6.55.3) on the way of the gods, to his other beloved abode and "birthplace." Symbolically, his one birth is at the midnight of the year, which is assigned to the south; and his other birth, at the high noon of the year, is assigned to the north. Between these two poles he leads his forward path upward and downward from birth to birth in perpetual, cyclical recurrence. Upward is the path of the gods, the devas, who travel with the light in which they have their origin. Deva means "shining." Heaven (div) is their station toward which they journey northwards from the point of his midnight birth. Here Pūṣan is born as the son of liberation (vimuco napāt; 1.42.1; 6.55.1). He is the liberator (vimocana; 8.4.15–16). He has removed the obstacles (1.42.1), on the downward path, on the evil way (cf. 10.135.2) where he drives away the evil wolf (1.42.2), the rapacious, devouring animal of darkness, he drives away the waylayer, the thief, and with his foot he tramples the burning hot weapon of the double-faced, evil-minded fiend (1.42.4). Pūṣan, the liberator, is an irresistible (6.48.15), watchful (6.54.8) lord (asura; 5.51.11), he removes the obstacle of greed which has its image in the wolf, the obstacle of self-deception, the waylayer, and of distraction, the thief on the single-minded path.[13] He removes the obstacles and his glowing power extinguishes the dark heat of treachery and insincerity,

when he puts down his foot on the double-faced fiend in the pit "whoever he may be" (1.42.4).

No allusion to the body of Pūṣan is made by this reference and no likeness of his should be conjured up by those few body parts which the hymns employ in order to illustrate his nature. They are used as symbols to the same degree as are the animals, the wolf or his goat-steeds (ajāśva; 1.138.4; 6.55.3; 6.58.2; 9.67.10) that draw his chariot. Aglow throughout, Pūṣan, in the ardor of his wrath, extinguishes the troubled heat of the two-faced enemy. His burning wrath is in the imprint of his foot, down in the abyss, on a fire now extinguished. His glow remains unperturbed, free from heat, when he arises, born as Liberator, and then proceeds to the green pastures of illumination. "Let there be no new heat [jvara (fever)] on the way to this pasture" (1.42.8) is the prayer at the end of this hymn (1.42) to Pūṣan, the son of liberation.

The fever and the burning belong to the hour of birth in the darkness in the pit, at the southernmost extremity of the sun's course in the year. This cosmical topography is symbolical to the same degree as is the burning and cutting and laceration of this hour. Here Pūṣan wields his weapons. He pricks and pierces the heart of the hoarder and miser, the paṇi (6.53.5), with his awl. He attacks and tears open not only the heart of those who withhold their wealth of knowledge and hoard their wisdom (6.53.7). He is the divine torturer who probes the heart and opens it (6.53.8), tears and rends the heart of everyone. In this hour of the midnight sun and its arising, in the pit, Pūṣan, the liberator, sharpens us like a razor (8.4.16), he grinds us, and makes us acute like the razor's edge so that our minds are freed from all obstacles, the dross that clogs the heart and intuition. With his weapon, the ārā, he incites toward Brahman, the creative operation (6.53.8).[14] He wields his golden adze (1.42.6) at the crossroads in the pit where he arises in his majesty as liberator from the two-faced evil, the pair of opposites, right and left, the downward and the upward path. He annuls and unites them by his onward movement.

In the dark and critical hour of his course Pūṣan as liberator operates on both the emotional and on the intellectual levels of the depth of the pit. The topography of the pit is given by its contents. They are the perils of darkness, the dangers of the road in the brutality of their animal nature, in their aggressive aspects, and on the defensive they are the oppressive, tightening fear of the miser and hoarder which reinforces the evil and makes it two faced, in its destructive obsessions of lie and deceit. Intellectually however, and fun damentally, the two-faced evil minded "whoever he may be" (1.42.1), is an embodiment of dichotomy and of the pairs of opposites. He is the great obstruction on the forward path on the way of wholeness or integrity. The emotional, moral, and intellectual stumbling blocks in the darkness of the pit, however, are not its only contents. Treasures are hidden, glowing in their own inner light.[15] It is then and there that Pūṣan's wealth shines forth, and the treasure of illumination is brought along the eternal path to the light of day.

The wealth of Pūṣan, the glowing one, is great and varied, rich in goods and rich in nourishment (2.40.40), in kine and horses (6.53.10). If some of it had been lost and some stolen, if an animal had fallen into the pit and broken a leg (6.54.7), they are retrieved by Pūṣan, whose herd is never lost (10.17.3).

He is the herdsman of creation (10.17.3), who beholds all (2.40.5). Pūṣan, the "good shepherd," is the liberator who glows in the midnight pit, where by his light he found Ṣoma, the hidden king (1.23.14), and where he himself, in his own hidden aspect, was found by Agni, the god fire.

3. *The Hidden God (Pūṣan and Agni):* The midnight hour of realization is the birthplace of Pūṣan, the liberator. He glows in the darkness at the crossroads, whose image is the "two-faced evil one whoever he may be" (1.42.4), dichotomy and doubt. His dark heat is extinguished by the one foot[16] of proceeding Pūṣan, the liberator, swinging his golden adze, while ascending on his endless path. It is then and there, at the critical birth hour that Pūṣan, glowing in the darkness, hidden in the pit, is found by Agni, the fire.

"Seven red sisters the Knower has eagerly brought out of the 'Sweet' (madhu) for beholding. He, born in ages past, halted in mid-air. Seeking a hiding place, he found that of Pūṣan" (10.5.5). The seven red sisters are the flaming rays or streams of the light of creation whom the transcendental Agni, manifesting, leads out of the madhu, out of the sweet secret of the source (9.86.10, 15; 10.32.5) in a fulgurating sunburst of manifestation of light and life. Agni, born in the beginning of things enters with his fiery light all the worlds. He halts in midspace. He seeks a hiding place, for he is overcome by the tremendous mystery of manifestation, by his breaking out of the source into the light of day which he surveys. He finds the hiding place (vavri) of Pūṣan, where the sun dwells in the dark (1.117.5).[17]

Agni, the knower (vidvān) knows all beings. When he finds Pūṣan, he finds his own hiding place, and there he finds himself sharing in the activity of Pūṣan. He makes over to the gods those who have died (10.17.3). This is his task, on the way of the gods, the upward path, the way of redemption, for he is cognizant of the other way, where Pūṣan makes over the dead to the fathers (10.2.7).

Agni, the fire, transmits in his burning flame the bodies of the dead, divests them of their mortality, and helps to lead them back toward celestial light, where Yama dwells, the first of mortals who found the way to the highest heaven (10.14.2) where he drinks with the gods under the well-leafed tree (10.135.1).

In relation to Pūṣan, the glowing, core of the sun's light, who is steadfast (10.26.8), from whom nothing is hidden (10.64.3), though hidden in the cover of darkness (vavri; 10.5.5), Agni, the fire, is the essence of that core as it is beyond even and in heaven, which is Pūṣan's other birthplace. One with Pūṣan, ante principium, Agni, it is told, returns to their source in his "flight" from this earth when he had become tired of his work of ministering, as sacrificial flame, to the sacrificial needs of men. When he bursts forth into manifestation and brings out of their source the seven fiery mares of light, he pauses in mid-air, seeks cover, and finds the hiding place of Pūṣan. By an infallible affinity of their natures, he is drawn to that selfsame secret depth. There, in the hiding place of Pūṣan, he finds himself—for Agni is Pūṣan (2.1.6).[18] In the identity of their natures and conjoint in their operations, Pūṣan leads the way, and Agni brings back to the gods those whom, while on earth, he helped to leave their dead bodies.

The division of functions of these great gods is as intangible as it is transparent. They manifest in light and flame. It is a division in degrees, of one proceeding power. Each progression, each intensity of the proceeding power from Savitṛ to Pūṣan to Sūrya—or in its diversification as Agni and Pūṣan—has its own name and place in the perpetual creation around which Pūṣan leads the way.

The hiding place of Pūṣan is in the pit, at the parting of the ways, where the pillar of life (āyu) stands, on its foundations (10.5.6). The pillar of life is a figure of that same axis which Pūṣan sets up when he puts his foot on the two-faced evil one, whose firebrand is extinguished on the "path of paths" where the downward journey of Pūṣan, who there has led the fathers (10.17.3) from this earth, on the pitṛyāna, the way of the fathers, swings over into the ascent of the gods, on the devayāna.

The origin of Agni's and Pūṣan's natures is in the heights, where Savitṛ is (1.35.6) and the dwelling of Yama. Their union is in the depth, where Pūṣan arises in his majesty and where he leads from the dark night, on the way to the gods, to the peak of manifestation. Agni is fire, and Pūṣan, illumination. Glowing in inner light, Pūṣan, the psychopompos, on his downward path, "whose herd is never lost" (10.17.3), becomes the liberator in the pit where he finds the treasure—and one flaming pillar of light and life (āyu) extends from the depth to the height.

4. *The Hidden King (Pūṣan and Soma):* In the depth "glowing Pūṣan found the king who was concealed, who was put into a hiding place on his shining sacrificial grass" (1.23.14).[19] Pūṣan, the herdsman of creation (10.17.3) found him, the king, on his shining sacrificial grass, as he finds a lost animal (1.23.13).[20]

King Soma, the elixir of life, the drink of immortality (1.91.18), is the "first milk of Heaven" (9.110.8) in his celestial home of flowing light, above the firmament, in the highest heavens of light (9.86.15).[21] In his celestial home he is placed in the lap of the stars (nakṣatra; 10.85.2).[22] The flowing light of the spheres (rocanā) of heaven, or also the stars are the carpet of Soma, the king, in the height and in the depth.[23] There, in the night of the year, glowing Pūṣan found the hidden king, on his shining carpet as he finds a lost animal or hidden treasure (8.29.6). Pūṣan knows the hidden treasures, finds all hidden, shining wealth (6.48.15), has all the treasures, is a stream of riches (6.55.3), an abundance of wealth. In him all wealth is founded (rāyo budhnaḥ; 10.139.3), all riches collected. He brings the hidden goods to light (6.48.15), comes as shining wealth itself (8.31.11), and gives wealth of all kinds and substance (9.88.3; 6.53.2; 6.56.6) to man. Those who seek riches address him (6.55.2): "Help us by our inner vision (dhī) to procure shining riches, O Liberator" (8.4.15).

The wealth of Pūṣan, which he, the master of all possessions (1.89.6) owns in abundance (8.4.15), he gives to him first who sees and invokes him (6.54.4). Glowing Pūṣan is the incandescence of light that is in the sun. He is and gives its very substance. He is the sun that never sets for all the time he proceeds on his way, from light to darkness and back to light. In the darkness, in the pit, he glows and by his light he finds the treasure that is hidden in the night, treasure of all kinds that has been lost and awaits being furthered into light. He finds all these riches by finding the king.

The substance of Pūṣan, the liberator, is illumination. It is this wealth which he procures for the sacrificer, the singer and the sage, vibrant (vipra) with the movement of his light.[24] In the darkness of the night, where he extinguishes the futile firebrand of the two-faced enemy, he finds the treasure. It is King Soma, the elixir of life.

Born in the depth of midnight, Pūṣan is found by Agni, and Soma is found by Pūṣan. Agni, the sacrificial fire, the spark of life, and soma the sacrificial "offering," the elixir of life, are essence and substance of the flowing light of heaven, whose path Savitṛ, the impeller, traverses on the "great drive" (mahat ajma, 4.53.4), when, by his movements he becomes Pūṣan, the glowing one (5.81.5). Pūṣan, born in the pit, is the liberator and illuminer, the guide who leads to light. He is creative fire kindled, when, having been found by Agni, they are one (2.1.6). Agni-Pūṣan, the creative fire, finds soma, the "offering," the luminous, formative principle, the treasure.

In his awesome majesty, Pūṣan, the glowing one, the liberator, gives this treasure to the inspired sage, the vipra, vibrant in the repercussions of the revelation. He does not give it to the unprepared. He tests whom he chooses, probes his heart, and sharpens his mind. With his pointed weapon he tears and rends the heart, opens it, and stimulates the spirit so that it arises in an upsurge of creative fervor (brahman; 6.53.8). He quickens inner vision (dhī; 1.89.5; 2.40.6; 6.58.2; 6.49.8), promotes sacred thought, and inspires the vipras, the vibrant seers (10.26.4). When Soma's inspiration is invoked, he is appealed to "like intuition inspiring Pūṣan art thou, O Soma" (9.88.3).[25] The treasure shines forth in the light of illumination, in the dark and decisive midnight hour of creation. It is then that Pūṣan is born and invoked by the ṛṣi "O Son of Liberation, glowing one, let us two unite" (6.55.1).

5. *Pūṣan Ascending:* Pūṣan, having found the hidden king, drives him hither (1.23.14) in their chariot (2.40.3), and while they ascend on the way of the gods, the vipra prays: "And may he with the Soma drops, driving forward for me the six-yoked together, plough as it were a grainfield with oxen" (1.23.15). In the chariot are Pūṣan and Soma, the treasure found, the elixir of life, sparkling with its drops, ready for work, arising to fertilize the field of the vipra. The chariot is drawn by the "six-yoked together," by the pairs of draft animals, which are the months of the year when viewed as positions of the sun. Each position of the sun occurs twice in the year, in the ascending and in the descending half.[26] Upward in the course of the new year that follows his birth in the pit, the chariot carries Pūṣan with the Soma drops. He sprinkles them on the yielding ground. Pūṣan sows, as it were, the seed of Soma on the field while his draft animals, which are the months, are plowing like oxen. Pūṣan ascending in his sun-chariot directs his energy downwards; he makes fruitful the field of which he is, as it were, the plowman. The herdsman of creation is the plowman of the field of the mind which he illumines and inseminates with the scintillating drops of Soma, the treasure and elixir of life.

In the elation of the arising of these two creator-gods, the ṛṣi chants: "O Soma and Pūṣan, creators of Treasure, creators of Heaven, and creators of Earth, you two born herdsmen of the whole world, the gods made you the navel of the immortal" (2.40.1).

"The gods rejoiced in the birth of these two divinities. May these two spread over the joyless dark. With them, with Soma and Pūṣan, Indra generated ripeness in the raw [dawn of days]" (2).

"O Soma and Pūṣan, mighty Bulls, urge on the chariot that measures the space [between heaven and earth], that has seven wheels, that does not carry everyone, that rolls to both sides, that is yoked by the Mind, that has five reins" (3).

"The one [Pūṣan] has made his dwelling in heaven on high, the other [Soma] on earth, up in midspace. May both open up and unfold the wealth full of treasures, rich in substance, the innermost center within us" (4).

"The one [Soma] has generated all creatures, the other [Pūṣan] travels, beholding all. O Soma and Pūṣan, further my inner vision. With you two may we win all battles" (5).[27]

Soma and Pūṣan as cosmogonic powers have arisen from the depth, on the cycle of Pūṣan's path, in the spring of life, with which they cover the joyless dark. Now the glowing one is a bringer of joy (1.138.1–2) and nourishment (4.3.7). He works wonders (dasra; 1.42.5; 6.56.4). Together with Soma, he joins powers with Indra, the creator of manifestation, and performs the miracle of generating "cooked" (pakva) milk in the raw cows.[28]

The miracle of putting the "cooked" white milk in the raw cows is the miracle of endowing the creature with creative power. The "raw" ones, the cows, are symbols of the dawn where the red cows of the coming day emerge from the black cows of night. This dawn is the dawn of creation, in the beginning, when light was discovered by Indra (2.17.4; 3.39.5), and he filled both the worlds with light. Into these cows of heaven, the dawn of manifestation, that are young and raw, Indra, the Creator of this universe, puts the "milk" which is cooked and ripe in their young raw bodies of a chilly morning at the dawn of the world. Such is the triune miracle of Indra, Pūṣan, and Soma. For this cooked "milk" is a great light (3.30.14)[29] alike to that of Soma himself, the "first milk of heaven" (9.51.2). It is the glory (yaśas) in the cows (4.1.16; 10.106.11), the glory in the creature, it is its creative power like that of the madhu, the "sweet" Soma (10.49.10). The creativeness in the creature is the white milk that flows in the verses of the hymn (mantra; 10.106.11).[30] The shining glory of creativeness radiates from the "creature" when it has ripened in wisdom. The miracle of the creative power of inspiration and sacred knowledge is a fire miracle by which the raw data of existence are "cooked" and ripened.

The cooked milk is of the nature of Soma, the milk of heaven. Soma is and generates the drink of life, of which the cooked milk is a symbol. The cause is in the effect. They are expressed in one symbol. Those who generate and create have entered into and are the things which they have generated and created. Soma is the drink of life, its elixir, its "wine." Pūṣan, the nourisher, sprinkles the Soma drops and tills the soil wherein he makes and becomes the food of life, its "bread." Soma and Pūṣan as cosmogonic powers contribute to the miracle performed by Indra the microcosmic image of the miracle of the hymn which is ripe and sweet in the secret act of its becoming, in the innermost center of the singer (2.40.4). While it is carried there, rich in substance, it is the wealth full of treasures. Soma and Pūṣan will open up this secret hoard and its contents will roll out, a mighty chariot, "which measures the space between Heaven and Earth" (2.40.3).[31]

6. *The Chariot of Pūṣan and Soma and Pūṣan's Goat:* In this chariot Pūṣan drives forward the "six-yoked together" (1.23.15), the syzygies of the sun's stations in the year, the course of the year, time in its cyclical unit. This chariot

has seven wheels. Like the seven red sisters whom Agni brings out of the "sweet" for beholding, the number seven here too indicates a coming forth into manifestation from the transcendental source as a totality in which all the degrees of manifestation are linked with their source.[32] This total cosmos, the "sat," includes this world and the two higher light worlds that are not visible to the physical eye.[33] They all are drawn by the "six-yoked together," at any moment, throughout all time. The seven wheels are a symbol of the total intelligible cosmos, of which this visible world here is but a part. This total cosmic structure is present at any moment of the chariot's course throughout time. It is the locus of the "hic et nunc," the "here and now" of the total, immediate intuition beholding the intelligible universe, this world and the light worlds beyond, together with their common source. It is a vision that carries Pūṣan and Soma in their timeless natures. This chariot does not carry everyone;[34] it is the vehicle of intuition, the vehicle of poesy.[35]

The reins or rays of the chariot are five in number.[36] Five in the *Ṛg Veda* is particularly the number of the five kins (pañcajanāḥ). The five kins occupy the levels from the earth to the sun (10.55.2) and represent mind in its various levels of attachment and activity.[37] Mind in its contingent aspects are the reins by which Pūṣan, the "most excellent of charioteers," (6.55.2; 6.56.2–3) and Soma check and urge on the movement of the chariot. It rolls to both sides, in the cycle of its course, upward from the parting of the ways in the depth, toward the height. It also travels the opposite way, down from the heights of manifestation on the other half of its course, the "evil way" (10.135.2), the path of the fathers.

Pūṣan and Soma ride in their chariot. Pūṣan is higher in station (2.40.4)[38] and wisdom (2.40.5).[39]

In the pit, Pūṣan had found Soma, the hidden king. He was hidden, not lost, in the darkest hour of the aeviternal round. Now Pūṣan, the glowing, moves on with his companion, steadfast (10.26.8) and watchful (6.54.8). He sprinkles sparkling drops of the treasure over the fields and pastures of man (10.26.3) and moistens the paths (8.29.6)[40] to earth. As they travel heavenwards, the mighty friend of nurture (10.26.7) beholds all. He is the bringer of good fortune (1.42.6), the augmenter of goods (10.26.9), the friend (6.55.2, 5; 10.26.8) of the sacrificers, the desired (10.26.7), beloved of all the gods (10.92.13). He is an all-bounteous (8.31.11) master of all possessions (1.89.6) who brings plentiful nourishment (6.48.14), for he is the lord of nurture (6.58.4), Pūṣan, the nourisher. He brings himself and he brings Soma. The bread and wine of life are in his chariot, as Pūṣan and Soma travel to the peak of the world. There, in the celestial heights, Pūṣan will lead the bride from the father's house, toward Soma.

The blessings on earth which Pūṣan brings are but a reflex of the joy that he brings to the wise and vibrant, the sacrificers, seers, and singers (1.138.1, 2; 6.55.3) when they behold Pūṣan, the glowing, their friend and illumination.

Pūṣan's animal symbol is the goat (aja). The word is derived from aj, and denotes agility. Pūṣan is called ajira or fleet (1.138.2), like a racer in his course. His course is that of the sun in its yearly cycle (cf. 6.58.1). The goat is in its element when, surefooted and swift, it climbs up the way of the gods, in the cycle of the year. It embodies the movement of Pūṣan on his path and represents that movement when goats draw Pūṣan's chariot. They are his goatsteeds (ajāśva; 1.138.4; 6.55.3, 4; 6.58.2; 9.67.10), his own fleetness in the shape of the goat.[41] It is in this function that the sacrificial goat, in the rite of the horse sacrifice (1.162.2–4) conducts the sacrificial horse, the symbol of the year or the sun in its annual cycle on its prefiguring circuit around the place of sacrifice, on the "way of the gods." It precedes the horse in this rite and will itself be sacrificed first, preceding the horse symbol of the sun on its way to heaven. The goat represents the power of solar movement which symbolically precedes the sun in the same way as ontologically Pūṣan "precedes" Sūrya, in the hierarchy of manifestation. In the ascension of the sun-horse to heaven, Pūṣan's goat goes straight ahead to heaven, their station. The goat is Viśvarūpa (1.162.2).[42]

Pūṣan and his path, his goat, and chariot belong together by logical affinity expressing the movement of the glowing god which the sun's disc shields from view. He is the glowing core of inner light in motion. The chariot is the realm of the god's power. Pūṣan's chariot, as the seven wheels show, drives right out of the source into the lightspace above and the worlds below the sun. The course of the chariot is controlled by the mind, which tightens the reins according to the five-fold needs of those who live under the sun. The light spaces above the firmament, the rocanā are invisible to the eye of man. They are part of the sat; they exist in the mind and correspond to degrees of illumination prior to, or in spatial symbolism, above their sensible expression. The light realms above the firmament, above the world of form, are effective cosmogonically. Flowing with suprasensible luminosity, they forecast this world under the sun. They are equally effective in the ontology of intuition or inspired thought (dhī, manas) before it is laid down in word and image.

The chariot carries the power of creative, inspired thought (dhī, manas) and the knowledge of the supramundane, luminous source of that power. Glowing Pūṣan, the best of charioteers, drives his chariot to the summit, and thence he will "drive down the sun's golden wheel" (6.56.3).

7. *Pūṣan at the Heights:* "Bright is thy one aspect, the other is awesome. Thou art like day and night with their different shapes" (6.58.1).

At the height, at the peak of manifestation, at the apex of the sun's annual cycle, at the noon hour of the year, Pūṣan glows like bright gold. His station is now at the other end of the axis, above the point where he extinguishes the firebrand in the pit and was "born" as son of liberation (vimuco napāt; 6.55.1). Glowing in wrath and majesty in the dark night of the cycle now, at the high noon, he is aglow with love (kāmena kṛta, made by love, 6.49.8; 6.58.3–4). Pūṣan in his glory makes his golden ships travel in the celestial ocean [of liquid light] and in midspace (6.58.3) and he shakes his golden beard from side to side (10.26.7).[43] Raying forth from his station above, his power, he is the lord of great munificence (6.55.2), greater still than on his ascent when he sprinkled in sparkling drops, the treasure of King Soma, on the fields and pastures of men.

With his golden ships[44] Pūṣan, activated by love and desiring praise goes on embassy for Sūrya, the sun god (6.58.3). To whom does his embassy take Pūṣan in his glory, at the heyday of the world? It is the time of the wedding of Sūryā. She is the daughter of Sūrya, the sun god (1.116.17), but it is

Savitṛ, the impeller, who acts as her father (10.85.9, 13).[45] He gives her in marriage to Soma. She is radiance to this world, and the flowing light oceans above the firmament reflect her shining presence.

Sūryā, the sun maiden, is the daughter of the impeller and of the impelled. She is fulfillment itself—as "daughter"—of the moving cause as well as of its effect. From the house of the father, she goes to her wedding in her chariot, "mind and soul" (manas, 10.85.10).[46] The chariot is drawn by the luminaries that shine from heaven and they are harnessed with the music and the words (ṛk sāma; 10.85.11) of the hymns. "Hearing" are the wheels of the chariot (10.85.11–12) which travels in heaven, to Soma, the bridegroom of Sūryā.

Meanwhile Pūṣan—"who knows the way"—has gone on Sūrya's embassy, impelled by love. Whither does he go, by what path, and what are the contacts which he establishes?

"With eloquence [we praise] the Guardian of every pathway. Activated by love, he won [our] laud" (6.49.8). The radiant song of praise (arka) ascends. Pūṣan "take[s] pleasure in this laud—as the bridegroom takes pleasure in his bride" (3.62.8). Activated by love, Pūṣan carries out for Sūrya his ambassadorial task, acting as the guardian of the pathway of illumination, the straight road from singer to God. Pūṣan, the glowing, is nearer to their common source than Sūrya, the sun. He brings about the direct connection between this source beyond and in the heart (manas; hṛd) of the ṛṣi. He goes on this embassy at the special occasion of the nuptials of Sūryā, the daughter of Sūrya. His embassy travels the straight and swift path from the source above to the vipra, from heaven to earth.[47] His golden ships run a straight course.[48] "Pūṣan is a good friend of Heaven and Earth, Lord of nurture, bounteous, wondrous in his glory, whom, activated by love, strong and swift, the gods gave to Sūryā" (6.58.4). As what do the gods give Pūṣan to Sūryā on her wedding day with Soma?—The wheels of her chariot "mind" hear his lauds (cf. 10.85.8–11).

While Sūrya dispatches his embassy and Pūṣan makes the golden fleet of illumination sail straightaway to their destination, father Savitṛ, the impeller, has taken leave of the sun maiden and her bridal procession (10.85.13). Sūryā has mounted her chariot. She has left the impulsion of Savitṛ. As bride, she proceeds in her own chariot of spirit-mind and soul (manas) at the heyday of the cosmos.

Sūryā, as daughter, is the fulfillment of Savitṛ, the "father." By his movements (yāmabhiḥ) Savitṛ becomes Pūṣan.[49] Pūṣan is Savitṛ by kinetic extension and condensation of the impelling luminous power of light.

In the hierarchy of manifestation of celestial light through the sun's orb, Savitṛ, the impeller of light, ontologically precedes Pūṣan, the glowing light, in movement. Savitṛ impels by his movements the insubstantial, transcendental essence, light in itself, to become glowing, heated by its movement into the golden splendor of the sun. In this movement and form of manifestation, the glowing substance, impelled by Savitṛ is Pūṣan. The ontological hierarchy of celestials is expressed here in terms of "becoming." It is also conveyed by the analogy of filiation, in the relation of father and son or father and daughter. Sūryā is the daughter of Sūrya. She is the active power of Savitṛ, at the height of manifestation. Twiceover related to Pūṣan, she is his sister.

Pūṣan is activated by love, he is all love (kāmena kṛta, made by love) when he goes on the sun god's embassy (6.58.3) and brings about the sudden flash of intuition that hits straight like a ray of the sun. He is activated by love when he gets the radiant song (arka). "Arka" is anything that radiates. It is ray, splendor, and lightning. It is the song. He takes pleasure in it as the bridegroom does in the bride (3.62.8).

To Sūryā, the daughter of Savitṛ-Sūrya, the gods had given Pūṣan, activated by love. Their relation is secret and subtle. Pūṣan is the lover (jāra) of [his] sister (6.55.4–5) and the suitor (didhiṣu) of his mother (6.55.5). He is, moreover, the son of the two Aśvins, whom he had chosen as fathers[50] when these heavenly twins, the lords of beauty, had come as her wooers (pṛchamānāu) to Sūryā's wedding (10.85.14–15).

In the marriage ritual of the human bride, Pūṣan is invoked to lead the bride by her hand from the house of her parents (10.85.26).[51] Pūṣan is to bring to the husband the bride "in whom men sow their seed" (10.85.37). Pūṣan is her guide on this path.

Sūryā is the archetypal bride, the bride in heaven in the chariot of the Spirit (manas). She is the light in the spirit, the light of heaven. "She spread to the gods her immortal and ageless glory" (śravas; 3.53.15). As a bridegroom takes pleasure in his bride so does Pūṣan, aglow with love, rejoice in the glory and radiance of the song (arka) that comes to him like a bride. It was the target of his love embassy. Sūryā, the archetypal bride is also the archetypal song in the "chariot" of mind-soul. As bride she is the inner readiness and radiance of the light in the spirit, at the high noon of creation. This is how Pūṣan loves the bride and leads her toward her husband.

The time when Sūryā, having taken leave of father Savitṛ, sets out from his house in the marriage procession is marked by the stars (nakṣatra) Aghā and Arjunī (10.85.13). These stars are also known by their names Maghā and Uttara Phalgūnī.[52] They are lunar mansions and are situated at the peak of manifestation, the high noon of the year.

The wooers are the Aśvins, the heavenly twins, the transcendental knights of movement in the cosmos. Sūryā now mounts their three-wheeled chariot and Pūṣan, as son, chooses them as parents. The bride, having left the father's house, was driven forward in her own spirit-mind-soul chariot. She now ascends the three-wheeled chariot of the three-fold creation and is raised to the throne which the Aśvins offer to her as Great Goddess (cf. 10.85.15) and mistress of the universe.

At this supreme moment in Sūryā's procession to Soma, her husband, Pūṣan chooses the Aśvins as his parents, in a flash of awareness of their all-encompassing sway and circuit. The Aśvins aeviternally drive their chariot prior to any sun that ever has arisen. They prefigure movement prior to its first vibration in the earliest dawn.[53] In the wake and within the orbit of their movement Pūṣan knows his way. He chooses, for he comes to know them as his parents at the high noon of the year, when he is born at the peak of manifestation on the foremost path of paths, in the heights of heaven (cf. 10.17.6). This is his other birth in the foremost path of paths in heaven, a birth by choice, the entry through the dual nature of the twins, as their son, into the ceaseless round of the path, the entry into manifestation at its peak, on its high pole right opposite to his birthplace in the deep, as son of liberation. Down there, the two-faced evil one "whoever he may be" lies trodden down. Here, at the upper pole of the axis of his circuit, Pūṣan is born of the Aśvins in their dual nature. He enters his course by the nature of duality, by the archetypal and inseparable pair of contraries which keeps the world in perpetual tension.

Pūṣan, having lovingly conducted Sūryā in her procession from the father's house, takes leave of her as sister. His love now belongs to her as the Great Goddess, in a transport of cosmic movement in which she is carried by the chariot of the Aśvins (10.85.26). She had chosen this chariot for the beauty of the Aśvins and the beauty of the chariot, which equals theirs, and she enjoyed its beauty (1.117.13; 1.118.5; 1.119.5; 4.43.2). This beauty is that of creative movement in its harmony.

Pūṣan is now the suitor of Sūryā, the Great Goddess enthroned. As the Great Goddess she is the great mother. She is Pūṣan's mother in the same way as the husband in his wife becomes her son (cf. 10.85.45). Proceeding from the source, from Savitṛ, the impeller, Sūryā, the sun maiden, becomes the Great Goddess. Pūṣan, who has the same origin, glows with the essence and substance of light. He glows with love which is the nature of light in creation. His love goes to Sūryā, his sister, nearest to him in cosmogonic procession, and who, as the manifesting power of light, becomes the Great Goddess of the manifest cosmos. Pūṣan, the inner glow of light in movement, leads her celestial incandescence to full glory for to her he is seed and kernel, the innermost core within the sun. In this way too, Pūṣan leads the bride toward her son.[54] Then Pūṣan proceeds on his path, laying his right hand around his descending way, in the cycle of the year.

At the heights, in heaven, Pūṣan is the Lord (asura) in his love. Pūṣan is the lover of his sister and mother, who are one, and son of the same, the Great Goddess, at the moment of her glory when she is enthroned by the Aśvins, the archangels of cosmic movement, his fathers. Lover and son, mother and father represent the integral and intimate, proceeding relation to and from the source, onward *into* manifestation, and referring *beyond* time and manifestation. The relation is that of a web of a perennial state and perennial process in which the identity of a god on his path emerges. In this web of congenital images there is neither contradiction nor incest. A visual logic of prefigured form traces the pattern of life in the cosmos and for man.

8. *Pūṣan Leads the Bride:* Similar to his role in leading the human bride (10.85.26), it is Pūṣan who gives the direction to the furrow in the field, but it is Indra who gives effect to it and presses down the furrow (4.57.7).[55] Pūṣan is and shows the way. He leads the bride the way of love and he leads the singer's mind the way of intuition where he beholds the bride in the chariot of spirit and mind-soul.

At the heights Pūṣan is the "Lord of her, the longing and thinking, the shining one and of him, the shining one" (10.26.6).[56] The "longing, thinking" one is the hymn as the expression of intuitive thought (dhī) and its direction. She, too, dhī, is the shining one in the coincidence with the aim of her direction, the light on high, the shining goddess, Sūryā, the bride. He, the shining one, is Soma, to whom Pūṣan leads the bride.

On the straight and swift road Pūṣan guides and incites the inner vision as forcibly as he knows how to probe, rend, and open the heart. With his goad he instigates the spirit to create and give form (brahman; 6.53.8), for in himself as Pūṣan is that swelling might (vātāpya; 10.26.2), the leaven, by which he stimulates (9.88.3) and quickens (2.40.6) this sacred wisdom (dhī). In this, his power, he is equal to Soma. "Like Soma, Pūṣan knows the hymning lauds" (10.26.3).

9. *The Eater of Gruel:* The herdsman of creation goes on his ever-proceeding path. Nothing arrests him, the perennial light, that glows in love in the day of life and in majesty at the depth, in the dark. Made of love (kāmena kṛta), at the height, he is the liberator, at the opposite end of the pole. Between them the way is as straight as a line or as endless as his eternal cycle. He always gives boundlessly of himself to his herd, which is never lost (10.17.13), of his property, which is never lost (6.54.8). He is the lord of wealth (6.54.8), abounding in riches (6.55.3), which he increases and makes grow (10.26.9). The wealth of Pūṣan, on which man lives, is food. Pūṣan, whose name is "the nourisher," is the "mighty friend of nurture" (puṣṭi; 10.26.7) and he is the lord of the food offering (iḍas pati; 6.58.4).

The sacrificial food, which is offered to Pūṣan exclusively and to no other god, is [barley] gruel (karambha; 6.56.7; 6.57.2). The other gods are offered soma; Indra is the greatest soma drinker. Karambha is sometimes added to his drink (3.52.1; 3.52.7; 8.91.2). Another god, too, seems to have been offered food, though not only karambha and not exclusive of the soma oblation. In the hymn to food (1.187), nourishment is extolled, the mighty strengthener of divine ordinance. It was Trita who, strengthened by food, dismembered Vṛtra in all his joints (1.187.1). In this feat Trita is a kind of double of Indra, the creator of the cosmos, who killed the dragon Vṛtra. In his fight with the dragon, Indra was invigorated again and again by draughts of soma, the elixir of life. Trita prefigures, and in part coalesces (10.8.8–9) with Indra in killing Viśvarūpa. But Trita derived part of his strength from food (pitu; 1.187.1). Pitu is nourishment, easily assimilated, liquid food, milk, butter, and gruel. This is why the plants are invoked to become gruel (karambha) first and then to be transmuted into fat (1.187.10). Karambha, the life-sustaining food, is the food of life. It is mixed with the elixir of life, the Soma, in the morning offerings to Indra (3.52.1) when it has been prepared for Indra, in the company of Pūṣan (3.52.7). Then a new day begins with yet another victory of Indra.

But as a rule Indra drinks Soma and Pūṣan wants karambha (6.57.2). Pūṣan shares equally with Soma in the sacrifice (10.26.5).[57] He receives a special sacrifice (6.50.5), the importance of his sacrificial food is stressed. His share is the food of life, "our daily bread." He himself is the nourisher (Pūṣan), dwelling in the sun. He is its glowing nucleus and the concreted substance of Savitṛ's vibrant impulsion. As such he is the stuff itself of the food of life. The relation of the food of life with the solar power underlies also a rite described in later scripture in which a piece of gold is placed on a disc made of flour. This is called "worship of the solar disc."[58]

Karambha, "gruel," the sacrificial food of Pūṣan, is equal in value (10.26.5) to Soma, the sacrificial drink of Indra and the other gods. Soma is the elixir of life, karambha is the food of life. Food sustains the body and, together with the body, it sustains existence on any of its levels. Existence lives by its desires. All objects of desire are its food. Pūṣan is karambhāt, the eater of the food of life (6.56.1). He is activated by desire (kāmena kṛta 6.49.8; 6.58.3, 4). Food satisfies desire. Where unceasing love and desire have their unending food, life is immortal. "Where love and desires [are met], where the highest place of the shining red sun is, where food is and satiety, there make me immortal" (9.113.10).[59] These are the inexhaustible and imperishable worlds where the sun dwells and eternal light (9.113.7). Pūṣan, whose sacrificial food is gruel,[60] the food of life, the food (svadhā) by which he as the sun, the red shining one (bradhna), glows (āghṛṇi), activated by desire and fulfilled in it, is self-offered (svadhāvan), complete and at rest within himself throughout the perpetual movement of his path. He is steadfast (10.26.8), this lord of nurture (6.58.4), an infallible guardian (1.89.5), of constant ordinance (10.139.3), the guardian of every pathway (6.49.8; pathas-pathaḥ paripatiṁ) all around, on the descending path of the fathers, at the crossroad in the depth, on the ascending way of the gods and at the heights where he leads Sūryā, the bride.

Pūṣan, glowing substance of solar power in its course, the giver of food, is sacrificially sustained by food. He is an "eater of food" (karambhāt; 6.56.1).[61] Karambha was added also at one special occasion to Indra's soma offering. Apālā, a young woman, was the daughter of Atri, a principal sacrificer, who had freed the sun from the magic of Svarbhānu, the demon of obscuration (5.40.8). Deserted by her husband because her skin was diseased and she had lost her hair, Apālā, "she without a protector," goes to the water of the river, where she finds soma (plants) on her way. She takes them home in order to press them for Indra and makes an offering to him so as to draw him toward her, so that he will let her hair grow again. She presses out the Soma juice with her teeth (8.91.2), Indra hears the grinding sound and comes to accept her offering of soma, pressed by her teeth, and mixed with karambha and other cereals.

Loss of hair indicates loss of creative power, loss of the inner light. To remedy this sickness, Apālā makes an offering to Indra by the strength of her teeth. The strength of the teeth shows will at work for the sake of survival.[62] This is one of the reasons for the use in India, to this day, of the tusks of the boar as an amulet.

Apālā's desire for union with the creator, with Indra, makes her creative will work through her teeth on the soma plant so that the elixir of life may bring to her Indra, in whom she will find her protector and in whom she will lose her identity, be rid of her isolation as one defiled by a failing of her inner light. Her connection had been cut off from the light on high and she had become hairless and unproductive. By the effort of her teeth, by her creative intent, she draws the creator toward her. The part which the teeth play in the story of Apālā's soma offering to Indra may account for an attribute of Pūṣan, which is given to him in later Vedic texts, in the epics and purāṇas, where he is spoken of as being toothless, although once the toothless god (karūḍatī) is invoked also in the Ṛg Veda (4.30.24).[63]

The Vedic myths[64] say that Pūṣan lost his teeth when he ate a certain part of the sacrifice. The sacrifice is Prajāpati, the god who sacrificed himself into creation. This is his perennial and ritual aspect. According to a widespread myth, through his self-sacrifice the cosmos came into existence in the manifoldness of its parts. When performing the sacrificial rites and building up the symbolic body of Prajāpati, which is the altar, man, the sacrificer who identifies himself with the altar, regains the original wholeness of Prajāpati. But the myth of Prajāpati, the Lord, tells of him as cohabiting with his daughter, the Sky or Dawn. This is his aspect as Prajāpati proper, which means "Lord of progeny." At that moment God Rudra aimed at him and pierced him. Half of Prajāpati's seed fell to earth. The gods applied remedies to Prajāpati and cut out of him the flesh pierced by the arrow. Rudra offered that morsel of Prajāpati—who is the sacrifice—to Pūṣan. Pūṣan ate the morsel and it knocked out his teeth.

Rudra's arrow pierces Prajāpati at the moment when first he spends himself into creation. The entry of God into his creation and his becoming manifest in it—where he is but a part of himself—is a fragmentation. Rudra himself was generated when part of Prajāpati's seed had fallen on earth.[65] All this happened when time was not as yet, at the dawn of creation. Rudra, born when Prajāpati's seed was shed and fell on earth, discharges his arrow. His arrow hits with the creative-destructive furor of Rudra just as, in later Indian myths, the arrows of the god of love and desire (kāma) infect with desire whom they pierce. This arrow, stuck in the wound of the progenitor's flesh, is the morsel of sacrificial food that knocks out the teeth of Pūṣan. Rudra's parricidal wrath is directed against the father spending himself into creation. The wound he inflicts and the dart in the wound, the furor of the existent on account of its existence—away from the wholeness which was prior to the beginning of things—is the sacrificial fare offered to Pūṣan to eat. It breaks his teeth—or, as the Bhāgavata Purāṇa says, "Pūṣan became childless, an eater of ground food, toothless" (*BhP* 6.6.41).

Pūṣan, the lord of nurture, is and eats his own food. Prajāpati sacrifices himself into creation. Pūṣan's offering returns to its source. He is self-offered (svadhāvan), whole. The glowing one moves undiminished on his paths. He illumines and liberates. He guides, finds, and gives.

10. *Pūṣan Descending:* "May Pūṣan beyond, protectingly put around the right hand, let him drive back to us what was lost" (6.54.10). The prayer goes to Pūṣan at his height in heaven. From the highest point of his orbit, he who beholds all (2.40.5), who is the weaver of the raiment of sheep (10.26.6), the golden fleece, may he hold out his right hand,[66] show the way and protect those whom he leads from this world where the sun shines, to the darkening realms of the fathers. "May he deliver them to the fathers" (10.17.3).

As soon as the heights of his path are reached, on the forward leading path, where he chooses to become the son of the Aśvins, Pūṣan carries forward the movement of the cosmos, the round of existence.

From the crossroad in the depth, Pūṣan, the son of liberation, had led up on the way of the gods,[67] to the highest heaven, the worlds of light, in the lap of Savitṛ (1.35.6)[68] whence those who have followed his path are set free from the round, in the third and highest heaven of the flowing light of the godhead. Having passed the high noon of his cycle, Pūṣan gathers his flock on the descending path and drives down the sun's golden wheel (6.56.3). On the downward path, and while still at the height of his orbit, Pūṣan is the friend of "everyone who desires" (10.26.8). The way he leads them depends on the nature of their desires. His herd, who desire well-being and the goods of this earth, riches and prosperity, he guides in his bounty down that way where those who are now the fathers have trod before them. Those who long for the light he contacts in his golden ships on the straight and quick road at the high noon of inspiration. He leads them straight to the treasure—and they know "here it is." Pūṣan leads the seer, the ṛṣi, and the herd, he measures out time to each on his way to the goal. The path to the treasure is an instant long or it leads round where Pūṣan holds out his right helping hand. Pūṣan leads *all* men to the place where their treasure is, their goal and destiny (6.54.2, 4, 7). It is a going together, and it is a union with Pūṣan.[69] "O Pūṣan, bring us together with the knower [of the way] who shall direct us straight ahead (añjasa) and who shall say: This here it is" (6.54.1). "May we be united with Pūṣan who shall point out the dwellings and say: These here they are" (6.54.2).[70] "May none be injured, may none be destroyed in the pit, rather arrive with them unharmed" (6.54.7). "May Pūṣan beyond give his right hand [leading us] around (6.54.10).[71] May he drive back to us what was lost" (6.54.10).

"This here it is," instantaneous illumination, the immediate recognition of those whom Pūṣan leads the straight, swift way. "These here they are," the dwellings of the fathers, where men of good action abide, whither they have gone (10.17.3–4). They have gone there on the downward road in the declining path of the sun, the round of the way where the dangers of darkness lie in wait for them, the evil wolf who watches with malicious intent, the waylayer, the thief, the two-faced evil one with burning dart (1.42.2–4). This is the darkness of the pit when the sun has gone down and the wolf takes charge of the perils of the night on the approach to the pit. On this perilous journey Pūṣan guards his flock. As he had helped "our fathers" so he should lead us fearlessly and undiminished in men and strength (10.17.5) beyond the pursuers, to a pasture rich in grass (1.42–45).

The perils of the way reach their depth in the pit (kevaṭa) where the two-faced evil threatens fall and destruction. But Pūṣan leads his flock, he leads to the houses[72] of the fathers those who will now join them. Through the flames of fire Agni leads the others to the gods (10.17.3), when Pūṣan as son of liberation (1.42.1) puts down his foot on the two-faced evil (1.42.4). Hence, from the parting of the ways Pūṣan, the liberator goes right before us (1.42.1) upward to the gods.

Pūṣan leads those who have died to their stations, and guides them to their homes in the cycle of his path. He leads the living, too, in the same direction, the sinners and seers as well, right down into the pit, where he probes, rends, and opens the hearts of the misers, the ungenerous, who have nothing to give, the unproductive, who hoard what they grasp (6.53.5–6). Here, in the pit, his goad (ārā) probes and pricks the conscience, tears, rends, and opens the heart of everyone. And those who tremble in their heart until they vibrate with the rhythm of his golden wand are the "vipras," the "vibrant" singers. Stung by the "brahma-stimulating goad" (6.53.8), they soar with form-giving power, the creative power of the poet.

To the parting of the ways Pūṣan leads the dead who are to join the fathers; thence he gives his hand to those who have died on earth and go the way of the gods. The herdsman of creation guides the living the same path. They come to their hour of trial, each one of the herd. He goads them to the two-faced evil one, and there he swings his golden weapon, the best wielder of the golden fire, and leads beyond their pursuers to pastures rich in grass (1.42.8) where the sun shines and there will be no "new heat," no burning firebrands which rage down in the animal nature of the herd.

Down there, whither the path of the fathers goes and whence the path of the gods ascends, a commutation takes place of the values of this earth with its material aims and death, and the immortal treasures of the spirit. At this parting of the way the son of liberation is born in whom Pūṣan has his other, his second birth. It is here, at the crossroad, that Agni the fire and spark of life finds and is Pūṣan. In the glowing union of their natures the flaming pillar of life shoots up to the heights. It is there, in the pit, that Pūṣan finds Soma, the hidden king of splendor, not of this earth, sparkling with the elixir of life, of immortality.

Pūṣan ascends and sprinkles with the soma drops the pastures of man. Their fields grow rich with the nourishment that Pūṣan dispenses, their mind-souls are saturated as giving of himself, he leads them upward.

Pūṣan is the guide of the quick and the dead, throughout the cycle of his course, eternally and in the hour of need. But on the straight, swift path of ecstatic absorption he leads the seers and the sages, right to the treasure, the shining wealth of illumination,[73] by his swelling, soaring might (vātāpyam) in their inner vision (dhīti; 10.26.2).[74] There they see as one and the same in his cycle the nourisher in his sacred aspect and majesty, glowing in the darkness of their night where he arises[75] as liberator (vimocana), swinging his golden weapon at the crossroad, at the depth of his cyclical path, where he finds the hidden king Soma, like a lost animal. And they see him, having found what had been lost (6.54.10), now at the other pole of his circuit, aglow with love, at the zenith of creation, at the wedding of Sūryā. Pūṣan leads the bride toward Soma, across heaven, in their home, the Sun.

IV

IMAGE AND TEMPLE

10 Figural Sculpture of the Gupta Period

The sculpture of the Gupta period represents one of the high points of Indian art. This art, patronized by rulers, monks, and laity, developed in a fertile historical context. It was a time in which there was a united kingdom that included almost all of northern India, a culture that was both rooted in indigenous tradition and enriched by foreign heritage and a religiosity that recognized the unity of all spiritual experience.[1]

Our knowledge has expanded since Vincent A. Smith attempted a survey of Gupta sculptures in 1914.[2] With the aid of works dated by inscriptions found in the same place as the sculptures, it is now possible to trace the diversity of Gupta sculpture, as well as to follow the origin of a particular style of Gupta art and its transformation at various centers of art. Though inscriptions of the Gupta era exist from the fifth century on, there are none in the fourth century. The generally accepted dating of two works hitherto ascribed to the Gupta era is contradicted by their artistic treatment. These are the Buddha from Bodhgaya[3] (pl. 10-1) with the inscription of Mahārāja Trikamāla of the year 64, and a relief of Śiva and Pārvatī from Kauśāmbī[4] (pl. 10-3) of the year 139. While in the latter case the date is unanimously accepted as referring to the Gupta period, different opinions prevail concerning the Buddha figure from Bodhgaya. Its inscriptions refer either to the Śaka period[5] or to the Gupta period,[6] which corresponds to the year A.D. 142 or A.D. 384.

The datings advanced up to now are not tenable on stylistic grounds. The doubts cast from this point of view are strengthened by the evidence of the inscriptions. The Buddha of Bodhgaya is carved from yellowish sandstone. The entire figure appears to have been originally overlaid with an eggshell-thin layer of plaster and painted. There are traces of the distinctive ocher color of

This essay first appeared as "Die figurale Plastik der Guptazeit," *Wiener Beiträge zur Kunst- und Kulturgeschicht Asiens* 5(1931):15–39. It was revised by the author in translation.

the robe and the dark red of the lips. The Buddha of Bodhgaya belongs to the Mathura tradition. It represents the highest realization of this school, examples of which are numerous from the second century A.D. It is not necessary here to elaborate on obvious features. The taut quality of the vajraparyanka posture the robe—tight and flat on the body and gathered only over the left shoulder and the left arm in stylized creases—the short neck, and the weighty corporeality, are generally well known. Despite these common traits, the differences are great. This is striking in the treatment of the torso and, above all, in that of the face. In works of the second century, the fleshy portions, despite their massiveness, appear soft and even flabby. The stomach muscles are defined in such careful detail that the body seems capable of breathing. In the Buddha of Bodhgaya the modeling is more summary, contours are sweeping and hardened. This is also true of the chest. In earlier Kuṣāna sculp-

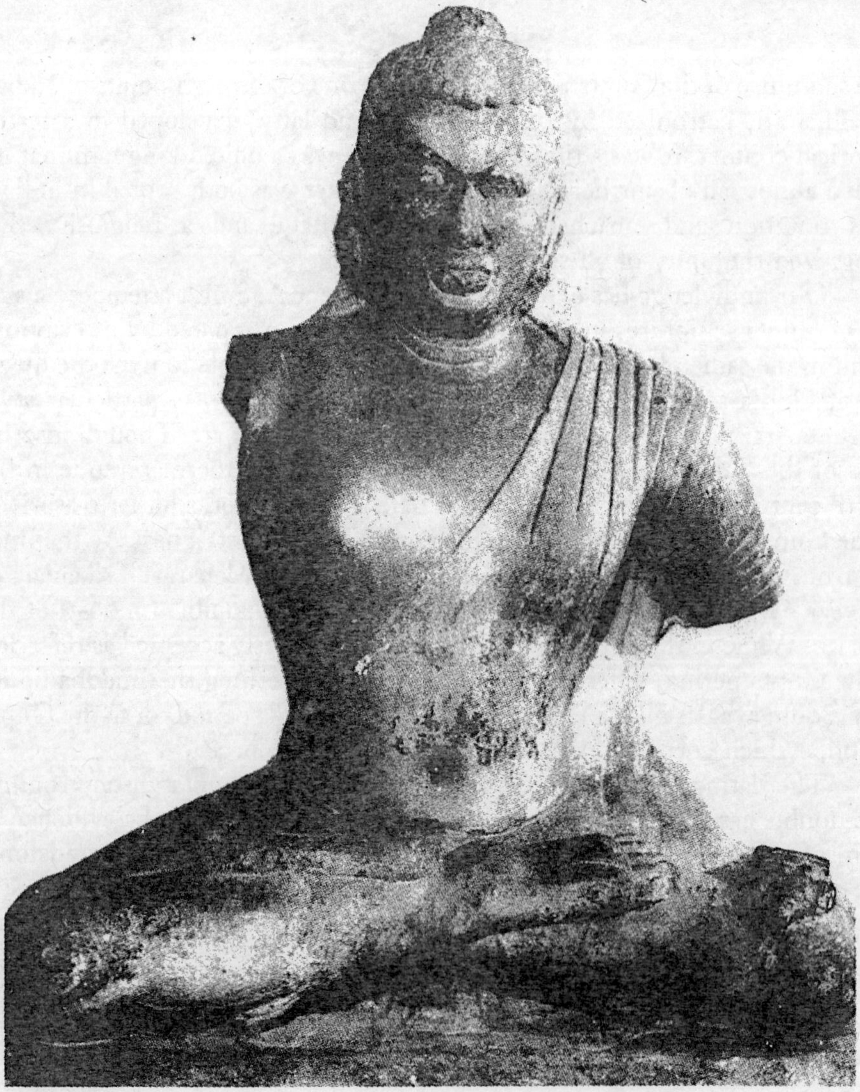

10-1. Buddha; Bodhgaya (Indian Museum, Calcutta)

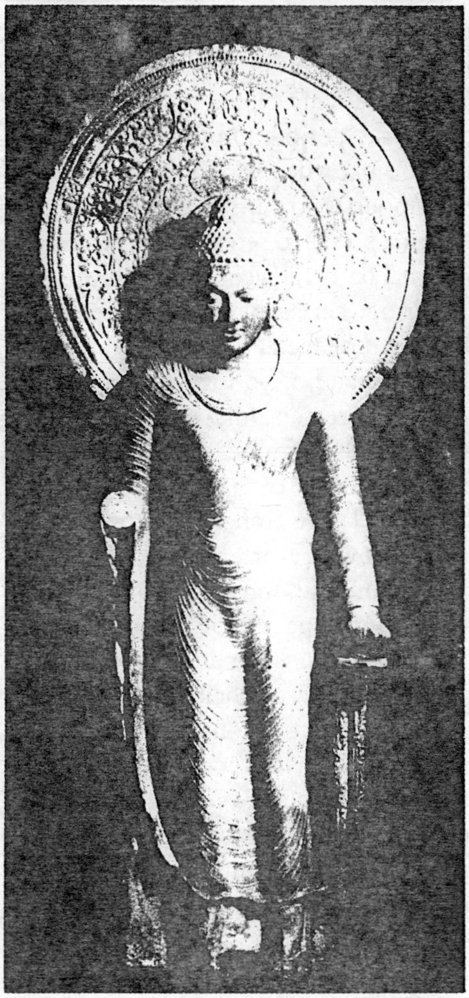

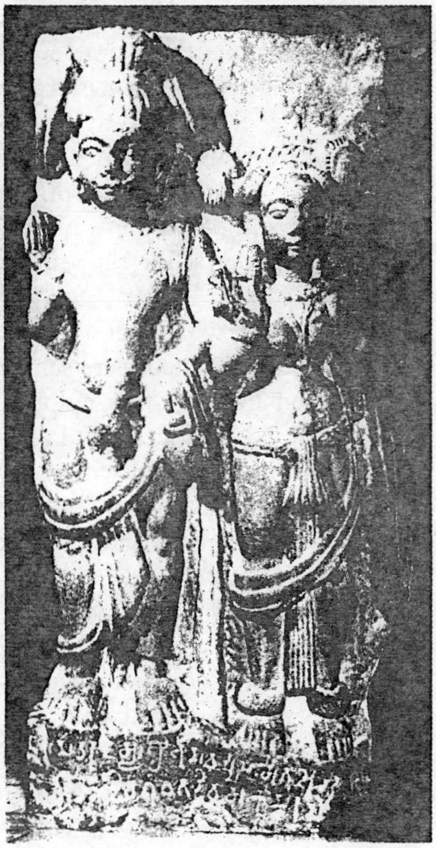

FAR LEFT:
10-2. Buddha; Mathura (National Museum, New Delhi)

LEFT: 10-3. *Śiva and Pārvatī; Kauśāmbī (Indian Museum, Calcutta)*

tures, there is an elaboration of the musculature, and the breasts project, gently swelling from the chest. In the image from Bodhgaya, they merge with its plane in one vaulted sweep. The "naturalism" of the first and second centuries has vanished. Volumetric and linear abstractions now confine the massive corporeality that the Kuṣāna period had preserved from more remote antiquity.

The face is without counterpart in works of the second century. Its features and expression, as they are rendered here, are unknown in the earlier monuments. The generous, full lips are sharply set off from the slant of the short, broad chin, as well as from the summarily rounded, heavy, hard cheeks. Second-century Mathura is ignorant of the ascetically closed lips that never smile. Though the mouth may smile in an archaic manner, Mathura generally favors features that are nearer to nature. The treatment of the eyes and forehead is the most original feature of the Bodhgaya image. Its grandeur lies in the elongated, boat-shaped slits of the eyes and in the wide planes of the lowered upper eyelids. These are extended at the corners, while the lower lid is barely indicated. The eyebrows are cut in steep sideward curves that extend into the broad, high plane of the forehead to give the whole face unity. The earlier period does not know such bold abstractions. They first appear in the fourth century and are further developed in the fifth century. The faces of the images of the Mathura school of the second century A.D. are too well known to need describing here, and the differences are clear. The year 64 of the inscription, therefore, cannot refer to the Śaka period. On the other hand, the connections with the school of Mathura in its earlier period are apparent. This means that the Gupta era as it is now understood cannot be considered relevant for dating this masterpiece. The year 64 seems to refer to another era.[7]

The second sculpture whose inscriptional date, the year 139, has hitherto been unanimously ascribed to the Gupta period, certainly cannot be placed in the year 458–59 if this chronology is followed. The facial type, the treatment of the clothing, and the way in which the right hand of both figures is raised to the shoulder while the left is held at the hip, are certainly features of the Kuṣāna period. Pārvatī's body, however, also calls to mind the style of the Śuṅga period, while that of Śiva presumes a knowledge of the Kuṣāna period, but the separate shapes are schematically joined. These archaic features allow one to conclude that this sculpture is a work of provincial art, rustically following in an old practice, only lightly brushed by contemporary movements, yet spontaneously imbued with a rhythm of its own. Its peculiarities include the hairstyles, particularly that of Pārvatī, who appears to wear a bamboo frame with tassels on her head, but also Śiva's crown of matted hair (jaṭāmukuṭa) with its pendant strands, as well as an awkwardness in the construction of the bodies, coupled with rhythmical assurance in the overall composition—the curving diagonals of the draperies and the vertical accents provided by the hands. There is no relationship to works of the mid-fifth century. These stylistic observations accord with the character of the inscription. The letters are considered to be of the early Gupta period, though in many cases they exhibit earlier forms as well. The posthumous inscription of Samudragupta on a pillar in Allahabad, which was brought there from Kauśāmbī and belongs to the mid-fourth century, supports this dating of the Kauśāmbī stele.[8]

Both works mentioned must fall in the early part of the Gupta period or even earlier. Their dates must relate to a chronology that corresponds to the inception of another era. The Cedi or Kālacuri[9] period fulfills that condition. It begins in the year A.D. 248. The year A.D. 312 would be the date of the Buddha of Bodhgaya, and A.D. 387 would be the year of the Śiva-Pārvatī stele from Kauśāmbī. Thus, the Buddha of Bodhgaya would have been carved immediately before the Gupta period, while the Śiva-Pārvatī stele would be the earliest dated work assignable to the Gupta period. However, it remains a work of provincial archaism, outside the mainstream of Gupta art. The Buddha of Bodhgaya, on the contrary, shows the Mathura tradition alive and creative at the beginning of the fourth century. Although it falls eight years before the Gupta period, the Buddha from Bodhgaya may be seen as the point of departure for Gupta art as it evolved out of the Mathura school.

Apart from these fourth-century works, it is the art of the fifth, sixth, and seventh centuries that constitutes the subject of this investigation. The following list gives a summary of the dated works of the Gupta period, or such works as were found near dated inscriptions. The latter are marked with an asterisk.

Buddha	Bodhgaya	312–13
Śiva-Pārvatī stele	Kauśāmbī (Kosam)	387–88
Vaishnavite rock-cut reliefs, Dvārapāla, etc.	Udayagiri (Bhopal)[10]	401–2
Relief pillar	Bilsad[11]	415–16*
Pillar and architrav reliefs	Gadhwa[12]	417–18*
Jain rock-cut relief	Udayagiri (Bhopal)[13]	425–26
Buddha (cf. coins)	Tanor (Rajshahi)[14]	432–33*
Buddha	Mankuwar[15]	448–49
Buddha	Mathura[16]	454–55
Jaina pillar reliefs	Kahaum[17]	460–61
Buddha	Sarnath[18]	473–74
Buddha	Sarnath[19]	476–77
Diverse inscriptions	Khoh[20]	476–515*
Ḍvaja-Stambha	Eran (Airikina)[21]	484–85
Buddha	Deoriga[22]	Undated inscriptions
Parinirvāṇa rock-cut reliefs	Kasia (Kucinagara)[23]	in characters of the
Stele and Buddhas	Sarnath[24]	fifth century
Śiva Temple	Bhumara[25]	508–9*
Pillar reliefs	Eran[26]	510–11
Colossal Boar (Varāha Avatāra)	Eran[27]	510–11
Śiva stele	Mandasor[28]	533–34
Buddha	Mathura[29]	549–50
Buddha pedestal	Bodhgaya[30]	588–89[31]

MATHURA

The currents in the sculpture of the Gupta period are manifold. Mathura, which was in the forefront during the Kuṣāna period, exported artisans and works; Mathura sculptures found their way as far as Sarnath, and are also known from Sanchi, Kasia, and Bodhgaya. The peculiarities of the Mathura style extend to Sind and are apparent in the fifth-century terracottas of Mirpur Khas.

From Mathura itself come several Buddha figures[32] of the beginning and middle of the fifth century (pl. 10-2). There is little that recalls the style of the Kuṣāna school. The new bodily ideal of the god-man Buddha shows no trace of the powerful corporeality of the previous centuries. The body parts cohere in planar contiguity, forming a rhythmic whole even more intimate and uniform than in the Buddha of Bodhgaya. The figure now becomes lighter and more ethereal. Steeped in an aura of grace, the features of the face portray perfect inner absorption. This attitude contradicts the earthbound serenity that characterized the Mathura school earlier. The new ideal, with its refined mode of expression, was molded in Sarnath. From there it found its way to Mathura, where the Buddha's likeness had first been created by local means in the Kuṣāna period. Sarnath, departing from the commanding image of the Kuṣāna period, proceeded to create a more lyrical, devotional image. It was this new type that returned to Mathura in the Gupta period.

The centers of the artistic development of the cult image in the northern part of India moved farther east from the fifth century onward. In the fifth century the center moved from Mathura to Sarnath, which remained the creative center during the Gupta period. Later Nālandā became the place where new Buddhist types originated, and finally, during the medieval period, Bihar and Bengal played a decisive role in the creative output of all sects and religions.

In the Gupta period the Mathura school maintained or transformed certain motifs of the Kuṣāna period. For example, the folds of the drapery of the monk's outer garment, originally taken over from Gandhāra, were changed into a flowing pattern of regular, fine ridges, which play over the gently rising and falling modeling of the body. Where the cloth hangs free without touching the body, it becomes a deep, concave foil for the subtle gradations of the body's modeling. The edge of the garment becomes an accompanying motif of the body's silhouette (pl. 10-2). Its curve transposes the boundaries of the body's reposing mass into linear motion. This function of the garment's hem remains

10-4. Head of Buddha; Kaukali Hill, Mathura (State Museum, Lucknow)

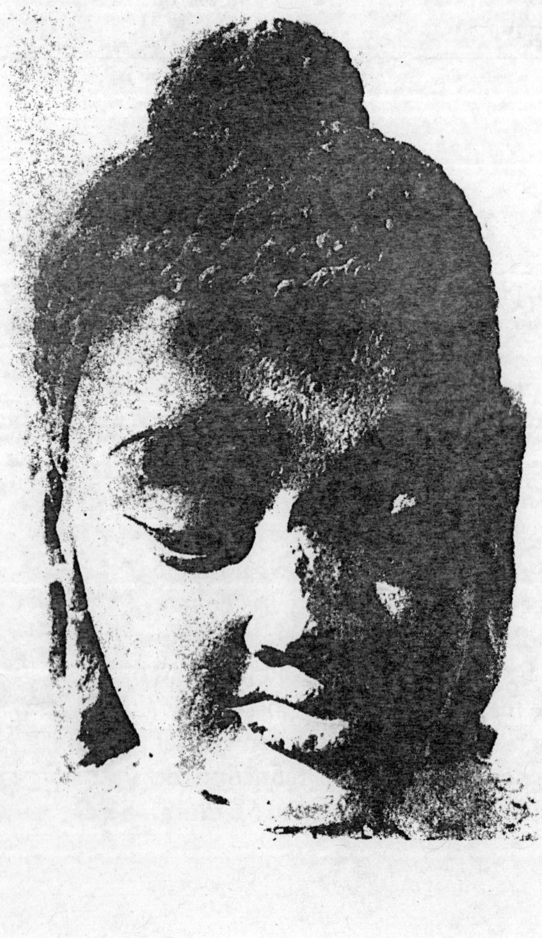

10-5. Vishnu; Mathura (National Museum, New Delhi)

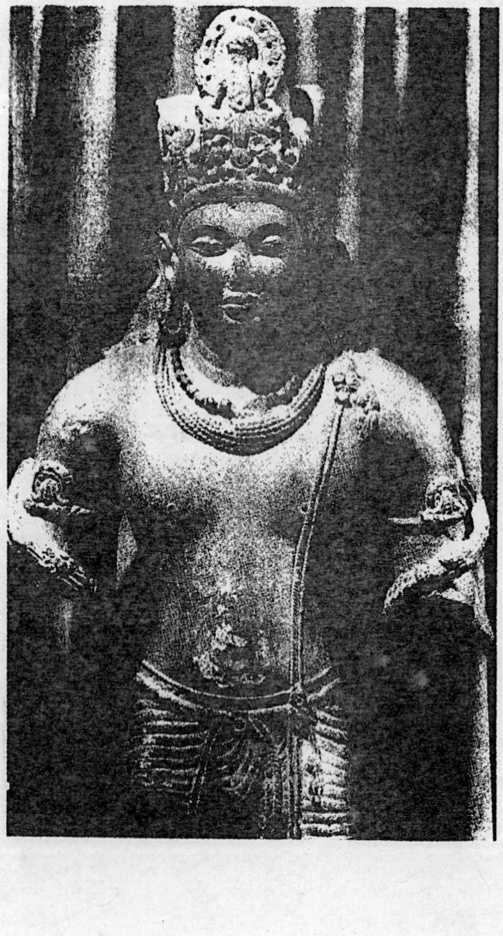

a characteristic of the Mathura school. In Sarnath, and farther eastward (Buddha of Sultanganj [pl. 10-16],[33] of a later date), the garment falls straight down, and rounded corners provide the transition to the horizontal hem.

The garment's ends, gathered in the lowered left hand, have a life of their own. It obeys an ornamental discipline. At this point, Indian tradition has absorbed volumetric motifs of Hellenistic art. For the rest—and in contrast to the barely visible undergarment in Sarnath—the skirt-like undergarment (antaravāsaka) of Mathura, though as thin as a membrane, is evident considerably below the slightly billowing lateral edges of the outer garment (sanghātī), while the cincturing cord (kayabandha) of the undergarment, with its hanging ends, is entirely visible and crossed by the parallel ridges of the sanghātī's folds, as is the modeling of the body. A further sculptural accent, which is less evident in Sarnath, is the draping of the upper garment, which leaves the neck free and accentuates its three creases (trivāli). The neck is longer than in the Kuṣāna school, and the head is carried with noble ease.

Characteristic of the Gupta sculptures of Mathura are the eyebrows rendered as antenna-like ridges, with eyelids and lips bounded by the same device. At times such a ridge is placed between the intersecting planes of the upper eyelids. The role of the ridges in the face, as on the body, is to bind the form of the figure, and to encompass and arrest the flow of the plastic modeling. This effect is also achieved by means of deep, round holes placed at the corners of the mouth.

As already mentioned, the lowered eyelids are carved as intersecting convex and concave planes, and shadows linger in the space thus created. They give to the sculpted faces of images from the latter half of the fifth century onward an expression of dream-like enchantment (pl. 10-4). This treatment of the eyelids is known from an earlier period on the stucco and slate heads of Gandhāra. Hellenism had no share in this particular feature, nor did Scythian art. Technically the intersecting planes of the eyelids are characteristic of the earliest monuments of the Indian tradition. But it is the downcast eyes that allow this technical potential to be developed as an element of creative form, particularly in the cult images of Buddhism.

The elaborately ornamented nimbus (śiraścakra) (pl. 10-2), richest in motifs in the Mathura cult images, had its origin in the Kuṣāna period toward the end of the first century. Then the nimbus was a plain disk with scalloped edges;[34] in rarer cases it was filled with an open lotus flower or some similar device. The nimbus in the Gupta period, with its rich, decorative detail, was not only derived from the Kuṣāna nimbus, but also from the ornamentation of the inner surface of the flat umbrella, a horizontal stone disk that originally shaded the head of the Bodhisattva (Bodhisattva statue of the monk Bala, A.D. 81). It is from here that the concentric circular zones and the variety of motifs they contain are borrowed. The nimbus is filled with radiating lotus petals, scrolls, garlands, twisting tendrils, rosettes, strings of pearls, and the traditional scalloped edges (also pl. 10-6). The flat disc of the umbrella was raised above the image after the Kuṣāna period. In Sarnath, the nimbus is rendered as a smooth plane, framed by the broad band of scrolls, the foliage cut in concave planes at an angle to the ground of the relief. The scrollwork of entwined shapes, enclosed by slanting, concave planes, became the central motif of deco-

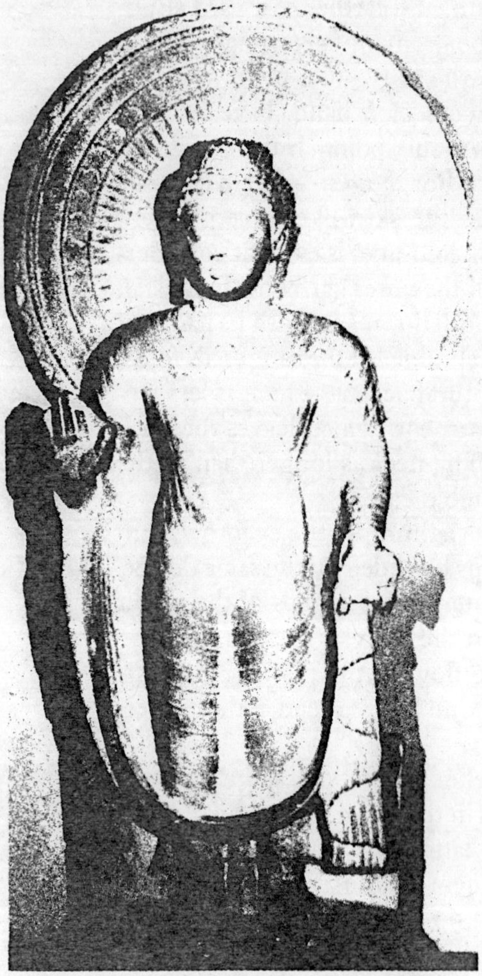

10-6. Buddha; Katra Hill, Mathura (State Museum, Lucknow)

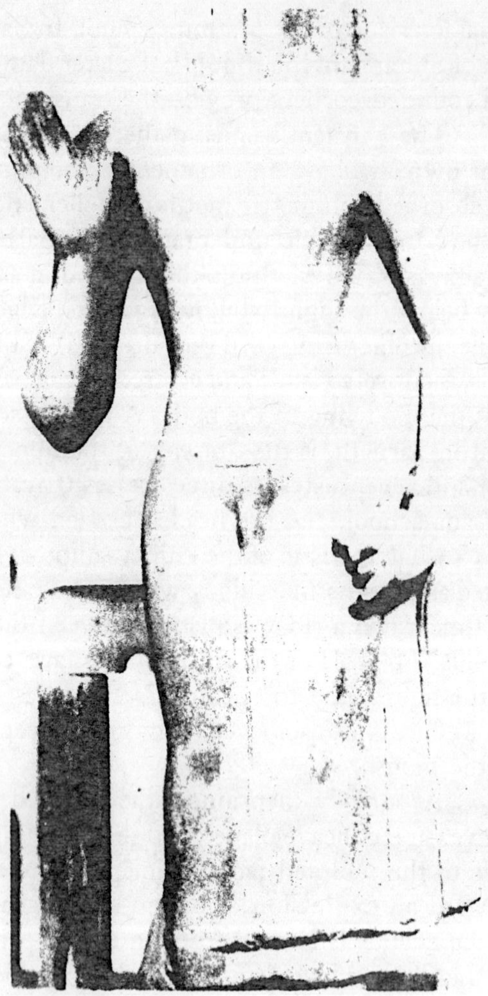

10-7. Buddha; Sarnath (Sarnath Museum)

rative sculpture in northern India in the following period. It had its ultimate triumph in Konarak, in Orissa, in the thirteenth century, and even earlier it found its way to the remote corners of "Greater India."

Although the non-Buddhist Gupta sculptures of Mathura (pl. 10-5) conform stylistically with Buddhist works, the absence of a monastic overgarment allows the modeling of the naked torso its full effect; no ridges indicative of drapery folds overlie the modeled planes. The flesh, swelling above the upper edge of the tight loincloth (dhoti) is depicted naturalistically, while the folds of the dhoti are only scratched in; they are not raised as stylized ridges, as are those of the Buddhist saṅghāṭī. Together with the opulent motifs of its jewelry, the Hindu images appear more sensually animated, more vigorous in contour and also in facial expression. Compared to the severe discipline of the modeling of the Buddha statues, the creative power of the Gupta period more freely unfolds here and is richer because of this freedom. The fragment of a Vishnu statue (pl. 10-5) belongs, like the Mathura Buddha (pl. 10-2), to the second quarter of the fifth century.

The later development within the Mathura school runs parallel to that in the Sarnath school, yet its peculiar characteristics remain. For example, the face of the Buddha image in the Lucknow Museum is rendered with unsurpassed expressiveness (pl. 10-4). The tension of the upper portion of the face with its steep forehead, highly arched brows, and eyes fixed in deep concentration, is balanced by a gently pouting mouth, the smooth roundness of cheeks and chin. The profound calm of the earlier faces has begun to vibrate.

In comparison, the standing Buddha from Mathura (Katra), likewise in the Lucknow Museum, with an inscription from the year 549–50 (pl. 10-6), can only be seen as an archaism, even if one considers the inferiority of the work. The lion between the feet of the image and the massiveness of the composition are in the Kuṣāna style; in contrast, the halo and the schematic quality of the clothing are in the style of the early fifth century. Noteworthy are the rays of the nimbus. The Śakya nun Jayabhattā, the statue's donor, possibly gave the relevant instructions to the sculpture. That this image may be a work of the sixth century is indicated, not only by the inscription, but also by the position of the right hand, which does not appear raised to the shoulder, as is characteristic of early Gupta work; here the forearm is outstretched, almost horizontally. The face makes use, however crudely, of the sculptural abstractions typical of the fifth century. This archaic sculpture is an exceptional case.

During the fifth century, the Mathura school undergoes the transition from a ponderous to a visually lighter form, though Mathura remains austere in its preference for static massiveness instead of the rhythmic flux of form in which Sarnath excelled.

SARNATH

Sarnath overshadows Mathura as an art center with respect to the age and quality of its work. The interaction with Mathura has already been alluded to. From the end of the first century A.D. on, works of the Kuṣāna school from Mathura were exported to Sarnath where they could be studied by its artists. How Mathura models were taken over in Sarnath is shown, for example, in a standing Buddha-Bodhisattva figure (pl. 10-7). It gives a new cast to the Mathura model. The Kuṣāna style, diluted by Hellenism and intensified in its naturalism, is here given a nervous suppleness alien to the more earthbound manner of Mathura. Invested with sensitive agility, the gestures, such as the right hand raised to the shoulder in abhayamudra, become full of expression and life. The same refers to the torso, though here the Kuṣāna style still prevails, and the modeling, though soft, is not yet imbued with fluent vibrancy. Especially characteristic of Sarnath is the undulating lower edge of this overgarment, which is otherwise exceptional for baring the one shoulder and for being depicted without folds. The lower part of the statue details much of the Kuṣāna style, with clear influence of Hellenism. This torso could belong to a transitional period, that is, to the fourth century.

In the beginning of the Sarnath school, its fully developed style is seen in statues like the Buddha of Tanor (pl. 10-8) from North Bengal, now in the Rajshahi Museum. It is a typical work, the product of a Sarnath artist; judging from the coins found in the same place, it was made in the year 432–33. The garment covers both the shoulders, but it is treated so that it is not visible on the body except for the modeling around the décolletage and a pair of barely noticeable incised lines on the shoulders. The upper garment forms a trough-like foil, a kind of stele for the body of the image. The relationship of the body and its garment is finalized by the hem of the rolls above the wrists, which are broken off here, and by the lower edge of the garment over the legs. The legs appear to be jutting through the concave plane of the garment. The body is flat and loosely follows the kind of "anatomy" that developed in the Kuṣāna period and was still tinged with realism during the transitional phase (cf. pl. 10-7). However, the new style of modeling regulates its convex and concave sequences and is unconcerned with realistic description; it follows a rhythm of its own. At the same time, this style of modeling presses the convex and concave shapes sidewards, so that the planar body is surrounded by a contoured curve. The proportions of the torso, according to convention, appear to be stocky and short. No attempt at representing the cincturing cord of the undergarment can be seen here. Instead, a deeply incised curve, dipping somewhat in the middle, defines the upper part of the body. We can assume that it was straighter at the beginning of the century,[35] as in the case of the Tanor Buddha.[36] In the next period, this originally horizontal curve sinks more and more toward the middle of the body, until it almost forms a sharp angle (pl. 10-10). Otherwise, linear definition is avoided within the modeling.[37]

In the transitional works leading up to the Gupta type of Sarnath (pl. 10-7), the flexibility of the joints has already been noticed. This involved only the finger, hand, and elbow joints, while the legs in rigid samapādasthānaka pose are as stiff as "inverted banana stems," a stance that becomes typical of the later medieval icons. Not until ca. 425 did a Sarnath craftsman succeed in making the knee joints supple and in distributing the body's weight over both legs (pl. 10-8). This achievement was taken over by Mathura as well.[38] In between these supple legs with their long, elegant curves, whether the legs are shown as if stepping forward or are standing still, the outer garment clinging to the body indicates or dissimulates the area of sex (e.g., pl. 10-8). But this vestige of a realistic style portraying the body disappears around the mid-fifth century, when the plane between the legs is assimilated to that indicating the garment (pl. 10-9). The feet of all the Sarnath icons appear swollen, padded from their ankles to the base of their long toes. This "deformity" is one of the signs of the Buddha as Mahāpuruṣa.[39]

The facial features of the Sarnath Buddha statues are generally rounder and animated with a lighter grace than is found in Mathura. This is due not only to the round physiognomy that is preferred at Sarnath, but to the way the face is sculpted. In contrast to the more detailed modeling of the facial features in Mathura, those of the Sarnath images imply a modeling of the entire face that ascends in a smooth curve from the lower jaw upwards. In this way the eyes appear embedded in their sockets, and the heaviness of the upper lids is mitigated, whereas in Mathura this same heaviness weighs on the cast of the other features. The sculptural treatment at Sarnath is altogether more delicate. Absent is the heavy accentuation of features we find at Mathura, such as the ridge lines around the mouth and eyes, or the deep, dark holes at the corner of the mouth; in Sarnath, the facial features flow into one another. All this gives the Sarnath heads their supernatural, serene calm. At Mathura the facial expression of the Buddha heads tends to become rigid; the danger for Sarnath lies in stereotyped sweetness. Apart from local differences, the Gupta Buddha heads have an unmistakable character of their own. No other phase of Indian art approaches their perfection in creating the superhuman features of a state of perfect knowledge.

The mid-fifth century marks the zenith of the Sarnath school. At this moment, the total effect is powerful, harmonious. Resilient curves define each profile of the modeling. The formerly ponderous limbs appear to be lightened; there is movement in all their joints, so that the body appears to hover weightlessly above flexed knees without encumbrance, and the broad shoulders are carried with ease. The perfection of Gupta sculpture lies in the fusion of the body's several parts into a vibrant total image in which the single physiognomical features are integral to the rise and fall of an uninterrupted rhythm, where

10-8. Buddha; Tanor (Rajshahi Museum)

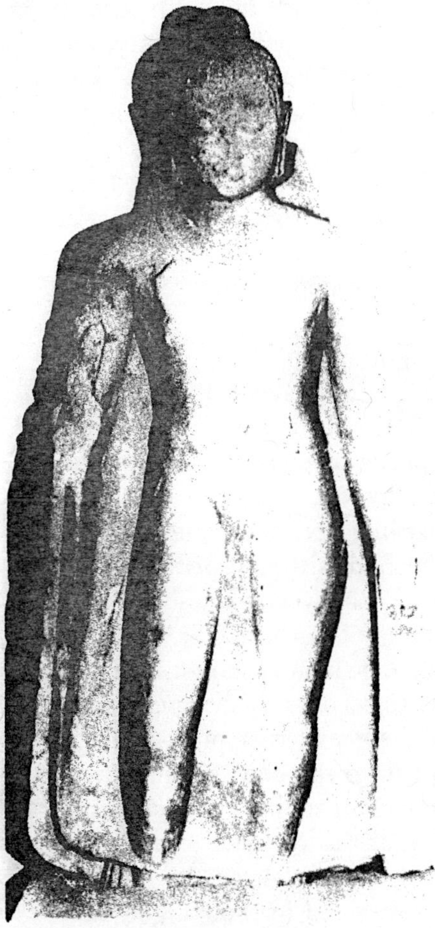

10-9. Buddha; Sarnath (Sarnath Museum)

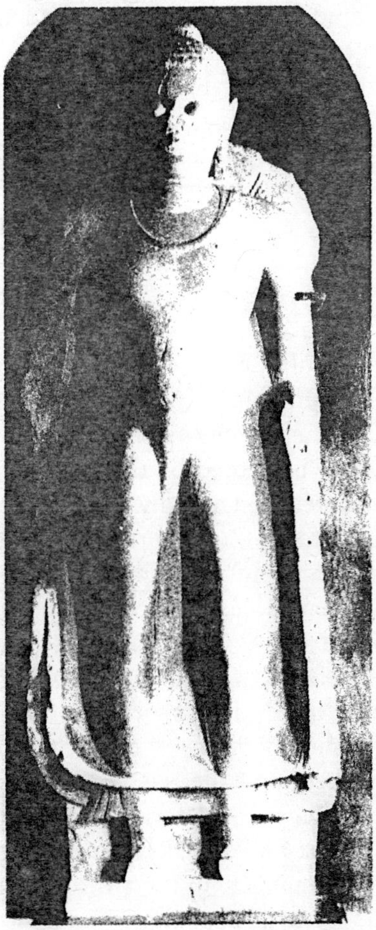

10-10. Buddha; Sarnath (Sarnath Museum)

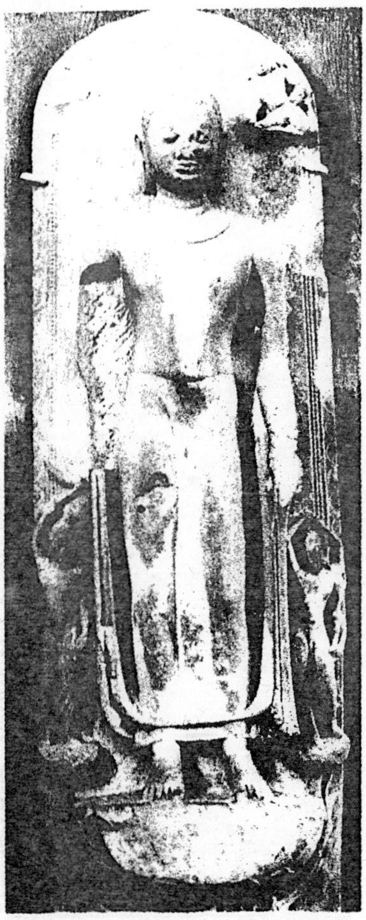

details of the garment are eliminated unless they intensify the impression of a body at rest in its vibrancy. It is evident that the incised line across the abdomen dips deeper in the course of time and that all other lines, such as those within the crook of the elbow, on the neck, ears, coiffure, eyebrows, and eyelids, follow its course. A comparison of the figures illustrated (pls. 10-8 and 10-9) points out this change, which came about within approximately a quarter of a century.

After the seventh decade of the fifth century, the shapes became even more delicate, even more subtly modeled, and the graceful features convey a spirituality that allows the corners of the mouth to point upwards as if a smile were passing over the lips (pl. 10-10). One of the standing Sarnath Buddha images has a dedicatory inscription of the year 473–74. This sculpture is a continuation in the evolution of the Buddha image (pl. 10-9). The edge of the robe is partially broken off;[40] on the broken surface are small, square holes, indicative of an ancient repair. However, even in the fifth century, single parts, such as the upraised hand, were often made from a separate piece of stone.[41] This technical procedure corresponds to a changed perception. The Buddha figures of the thirties had the right hand in the gesture of fearlessness (abhayamudrā), raised and stretched horizontally from the elbow. At the beginning of the fifth century[42] the palm of the hand came to be situated between the shoulder and the elbow. In transitional works of the fourth century (pl. 10-7), the hand is still rendered in Kuṣāna style, raised to the shoulder, with the palm turned toward the Buddha's body, whereas from the thirties of the fifth century, the palm is turned toward the worshiper. Similarly, the position of the left hand changes. In Mathura it was placed on either the hip[43] (as it was during the Sarnath transition period; pl. 10-7) or else it was brought back in some other way to the body.[44] In the fifth century, it sinks down and faces outward, away from the body and in front of the pendant hemline of the robe so that it marks the outermost limit of the Buddha statue's corporeal existence. Behind this gesture the body rests within a space of its own and its depth is limited by the plane of the back of the stele.

The sculptural treatment of the Buddha figure in fifth-century Sarnath, which then influenced Mathura, not only places the image within its own space, but concentrates its divine presence by the close layering of the anterior plane, which is formed by the hands, and the posterior plane, formed by the back of the stele. Enclosed within a space created by its own surface, the Buddha image of the Gupta age represents a departure from the compact mass of its Kuṣāna prototype. Layered in planes, the Buddhist icon of the Gupta period is given its classical proportions in the relation between planes and modeled corporeality.

Two Sarnath statues, dated 476–77,[45] one of which is shown here (pl. 10-10), make the Buddha's form a supple, delicate vessel of rarified, superhuman bliss. The shoulders have become narrower and somewhat sloping, the legs have stretched, and the modeling gives life-breath to the body's "anatomy." The noble elegance of form is evident in the accompanying figures, which stand on lotus flowers. For the first time, Vidyādharas (celestial "bearers of knowledge") appear, flying from the right and from the left on the nimbus. They are squat in appearance and somewhat restrained in their flight. Not until the sixth century are they pictured as masters of all the arts of rapid flight, which is convincingly rendered without external trappings, but simply by the way their limbs and bodies are placed. In the medieval period, flying Vidyādharas are the inevitable companions of practically all icons.

A further change took place in the rendering of the end of the robe gathered by the left hand. The zigzag folds that had been so popular earlier (cf. pl. 10-8) are now deemphasized; they form but a narrow pattern at the bottom of the robe. The honing of form to create a unified plastic effect tends to eliminate even linear decorative details inherited from earlier Indian traditions such as Bharhut.[46] Also noteworthy are the small figures of the donors, placed on either side of the scrollwork at the bottom of the stele, and the straight stalk bearing the lotus flower on which the figure of the Buddha stands.

Gandhāra and Mathura had introduced a scene of worship as a subject on the base of the image. Here the figures of the donors, the lotus flower, and the standing attendants have been integrated with the Buddha image into a unified composition. In the following period the lotus, the scrollwork, and the donors are all again relegated to the base. This is particularly true of the Eastern school of the Pāla period.

The scrollwork of the lotus must be noted. It consists of single concave planes cut at an angle to the plane of the relief and is a descendant of the early fifth-century scroll motifs that adorned the nimbus of the Buddha. Now the treatment of the scrolls has become fleshy. One might be tempted to call it a "roccoco motif," but the terms used for artistic epochs of European art are meaningless with regard to Indian art.

The famous seated teaching Buddha of Sarnath exhibits a feeling for form similar to that of the two standing Buddha images, but it is more extreme in the economy of its modeling.[47] The slight stiffness is partly traceable to the abstract, triangular scheme on which the composition is based (compare the modeling from shoulders to breast, and from there to the abdominal area). This stiffness marks the beginning of reduced plasticity and sensitivity to subtle tactile transitions. There is also a change in how the bodies and the impetuous flight of the Vidyādharas are conceived. According to a new ideal, horizontal sequences of plastic volume are accentuated. The seated Sarnath Buddha typifies the Sarnath school at the end of the fifth century.

The phases of shaping the icon at the Sarnath school within the fifth century are now clear. After the transitional forms of the fourth century, the early fifth century created the Buddha-type of the Gupta period in its normative form. Its still heavy limbs and expressive facial features each became a unique amalgamation of observation and abstraction. In the seventies a rarified subtlety of modeling and expression was achieved, but it lasted in this perfected form for only one generation. The turn of the century again shows a tendency toward a new formalization. This persisted during the entire sixth century, allowing nuances of introspective knowledge and compassion to form the images in subtle variations.

In the mid-fifth century each sculptural profile consisted of generous, flowing curves. The profile of the trunk, from the breastbone to the abdomen, showed a gradual rising, like an elastically stretched curve. In the seventies this profile was retained; yet, as a result of the narrower and more elongated shape of the figure, it now lacked the space that would allow a gradual lateral transition to the flanks. In the seventies this profile was more pronounced, and its curve recalls the female figures of Gothic art.[48]

A swaying stance characterizes an image of the Bodhisattva Avalokiteśvara, probably belonging to the sixth century (pl. 10-12). The figure is poised in a harmonious balance of form and movement, one might say, of matter and spirit. It is the spirit that sways the body and bends the limbs in a manner conducive to that motion. It is precisely in the sixth century that the motif of the flying figures occurs so frequently and is presented with such spontaneity.

The image of Avalokiteśvara (pl. 10-12) is endowed with all the characteristics of this new phase. Although the body's sway is accentuated by the countermovement of the garments, the curves of the scarf, and the edge of the dhoti, the main emphasis remains on the arching contour of the body. It is complemented by the bow-shaped lotus stalk, from which the flower is broken off. The richness of costume, coiffure, jewelry, and drapery shows motifs that the artists refrained from using in images of the Buddha. These several motifs add an aura of worldliness to the image of the Bodhisattva.

The lack of dated sculptures within the sixth century at Sarnath poses a problem in attempting to trace stylistic changes. Works from the seventh century show a tendency to stiffness and minimally articulated massiveness (pl. 10-11). Each part of the image appears stilted and is only connected to the next by placement, not organically or plastically, as was the case earlier. The

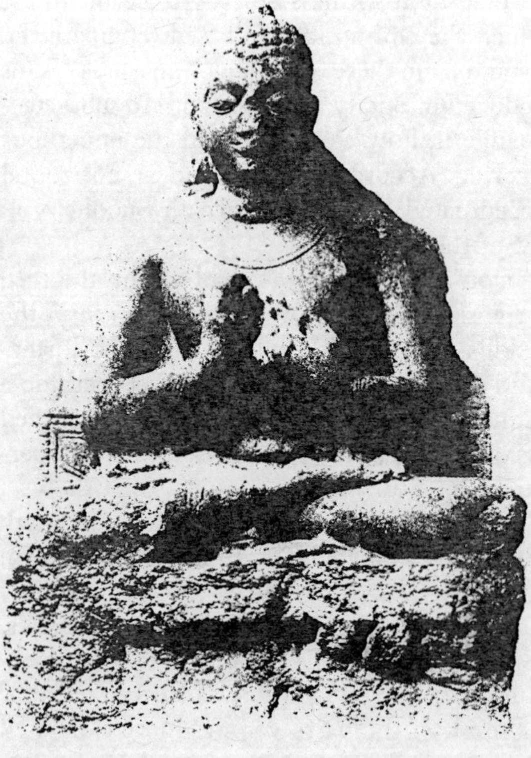

RIGHT:
10-11. Teaching Buddha; Sarnath (Sarnath Museum)

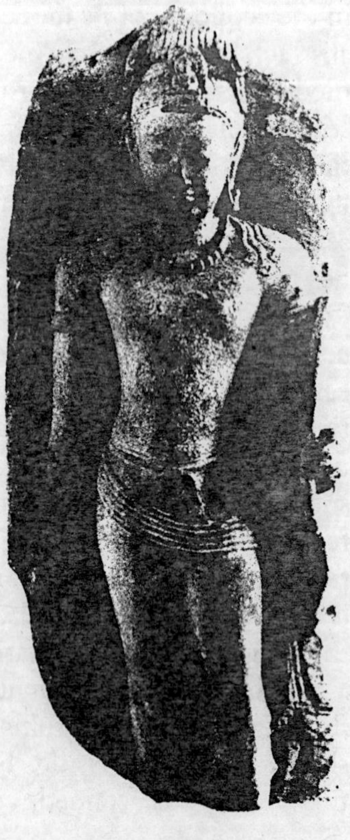

FAR RIGHT:
10-12. Avalokiteśvara; Sarnath (Indian Museum, Calcutta)

eyes are now opened somewhat more widely. Often a cushion is placed behind the Buddha's back, in order to make him comfortable.[49] This object seems to be without a symbolic meaning. A rigid contour, a schematic elaboration of detail, a general coarsening of form, and a pedantic respect for rules mark the end of the Gupta sculpture at Sarnath.

After the icons, the relief panels with representations of scenes from the Buddha's life are the most frequent works of sacred sculpture from Sarnath. They belong to the fifth and the sixth centuries and onward. Their early, aniconic predecessors are reliefs filled with symbols, such as a bodhi tree, a wheel, or a stūpa, on the railings and gates of the Śuṅga and Andhra periods. From then on, in Mathura as well as in Gandhāra, human figures lent pathos to the narrative scenes in a panel.[50] Sarnath follows the Kuṣāna prototypes from Mathura. The scenes now appear in separate panels framed by flat fillets, or in separate sections compositionally connected in one relief. With regard to style, these steles follow the changes that were observed in the representation of the Buddha image.

The question of whether the images were painted is answered at Sarnath. Some of the sculptures show remnants of color, which is also evident in the Bodhgaya Buddha. However, it is generally only the ocher color of the robe that is preserved.[51]

LOCAL SCHOOLS CONNECTED WITH MATHURA AND SARNATH

Gadhwa

From the fourth to the sixth century, Sarnath and Mathura were the major art centers. It has already been pointed out that Mathura artisans worked at various locales and that art works were exported to such places as Mankuwar, with its peculiar seated Buddha image,[52] and Kasia, where the sculptor Dinna of Mathura carved in the rock, and also to Kauśāmbī and Bodhgaya. In addition there are significant terracotta reliefs from Bhitargaon, in some of which the exaggerated musculature of the figurines does not conceal Hellenistic influence. However, the figures' manifold and powerful movement can be accounted for in the Indian tradition, for the manner of rendering them is freer in terracotta reliefs than in the contemporary stone reliefs.

The same currents are evident in works from other sites, among which Bilsad and Gadhwa are noteworthy; also the sculptures of Kasia (apart from the Parinirvāṇa Buddha, a work of a Mathura master) and Mirpur Khas in Sind. The Kuṣāna school of Mathura, as well as the Kuṣāna style influenced by Gandhāra, set the standard for the sites just mentioned. The works of the various centers are clearly distinguishable from one another; a lively artistic life in each locale contributed in its own way to the whole cultural context.

Vincent A. Smith has already drawn attention to the relationship between the pillar reliefs of Bilsad and Gadhwa.[53] Close in time and space,[54] these

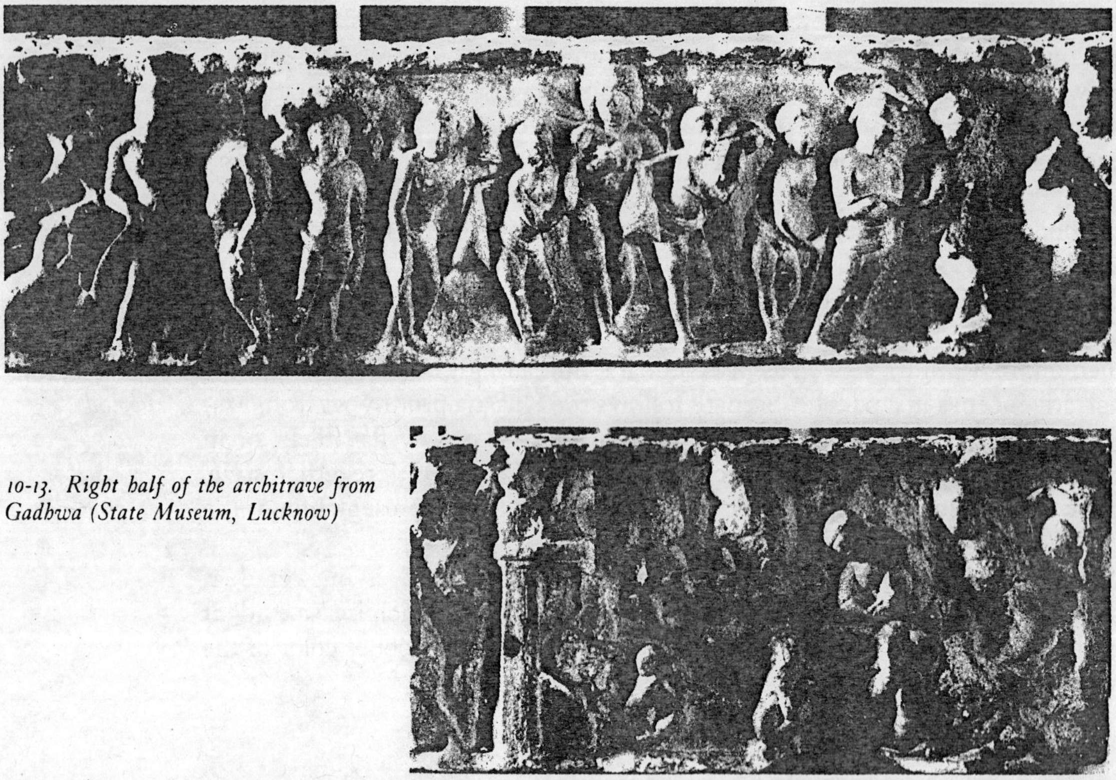

10-13. Right half of the architrave from Gadhwa (State Museum, Lucknow)

sites in Uttar Pradesh at the beginning of the fifth century share elements of style. But differences in quality and character exist despite the similar mode of composition and common decorative motifs. Aside from their ornamentation, the Bilsad reliefs are heirs to the early Indian tradition. The Gadhwa reliefs are unimaginable without the Hellenism that shaped the Kuṣāna school of Mathura. The distinct way in which various influences were transformed makes these reliefs masterpieces of early Gupta art.

No other work of Gupta sculpture surpasses the Gadhwa panels (pl. 10-13) for rhythmic harmony and delicacy of carving. Probably made to serve as the lintel of a temple doorway, these panels show scenes of celebration and worship, with Vishnu as the focal image (pl. 10-13b). The sun god Sūrya is on the right end of one panel (pl. 10-13a); Siva and Pārvatī are seated on the extreme left of the other. The celebration includes various offerings of food and acts of veneration. Free of the limiting norms that were applied to icons, the figures appear in groups of classical purity. As in the earlier reliefs of Amarāvatī, some figural motifs are reminiscent of the Kuṣāna school. The composition is characterized by its diverse elements: an understanding of the human form based on lively observation; gestures that speak in the nimble language of dance; natural grace of movement and balanced rhythm; varied physiognomies and costumes.[55]

The perfected classicism of the Gadhwa reliefs is confined almost exclusively to the human form; the juxtaposition of nature's shapes, so characteristic of early Indian art, has no place in this world of emotionally mature humanism. Hardly any use is made of the abstract spatial formulas of earlier times; the

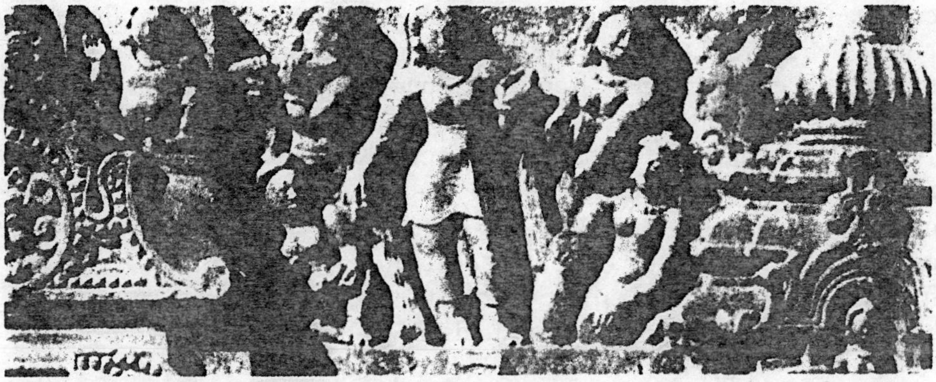

10-14. Music and dancing scene (Kṣāntivādin Jātaka); *Sarnath (Sarnath Museum)*

optical perspective accommodates itself effortlessly to the frieze and its figures. In this composition, the human figure, which can be godly as well as human, is the sole standard.

In the province of Gandhāra, the constituent artistic traditions (whether Indian, Hellenistic, or "Scythian") coexisted and commingled, while in the rest of India high artistic achievement was based on ancient indigenous traditions, and Hellenism was so transformed that its foreign origin was forgotten. This happened at Amarāvatī in the south, and at Gadhwa in the north.

Only a spontaneous and increasingly sensitive understanding of the human body, innate in the early period of the indigenous tradition, could fully respond to and integrate values that were ultimately Greek in origin. By the fifth century, the Graeco-Roman heritage had become "classical antiquity" in the West. Its impact in the India of the same time was vital, though it had come to Indian art centuries earlier. It had entered the fabric of Indian art like a foreign body and lay dormant until the new spirituality of the Gupta period made it effective in the northern part of India. Here, the Indian genius produced a rebirth of the classic Western forms, not inferior in quality and originality to the European Renaissance a thousand years later.

In the Bilsad pillar reliefs, the old Indian school is seen meeting the demands of the Gupta period. This is equally true of the narrative "architectural" reliefs in Sarnath[56] (pl. 10-14). This can be understood in two ways: on the one hand, the Kuṣāna style and Hellenism were incorporated into the complex form of the Gupta period; on the other hand, the old Indian tradition, continuing on its own path, was brought to efflorescence by the genius of the Gupta period. The influence of Sarnath spread to the eastern and western parts of the country, where it stimulated various local resources.

THE EVOLUTION OF THE EASTERN SCHOOL

The eastern sites of Gupta sculpture include Sultanganj, Bodhgaya, Rajgir, and Nalāndā, as well as Candimau.[57] They exhibit the eastern transformation of the Sarnath model from the fifth to the seventh centuries. Many reliefs, especially those from Candimau, possess an appeal coming from their locally determined character. One of the most outstanding works of the eastern style is the colossal copper Buddha from Bhagalpur-Sultanganj in the Birmingham Museum (pl. 10-16).[58]

The Sultanganj Buddha exhibits some distinctive traits: the summarily rounded stiff legs; the accentuated kneecaps; the almost horizontal, incised midline; the right hand raised to a level below the shoulder; the sensitively modeled flesh of the torso. The style of relating garment to body is derived from the Sarnath-Mathura tradition, but an innovative compromise operates here. In Sarnath any suggestion of folds, apart from those at the neck, was smoothed away, whereas in Mathura, a linear pattern of parallel curving ridges suggested folds. But in the Sultanganj Buddha these "folds" are indicated by faintly incised lines on the body, swinging downward in ever wider arcs. These lines are incised where the garment adheres to the body but not where it hangs free; they emphasize the body rather than the garment. While the Sarnath icons guide the eye downward from the face along the calmly relaxed curves of the limbs, the Sultanganj Buddha leads the eye upward from the firmly yet lightly resting feet to the head, which is carried with great dignity. The body is proportionately slimmer, but the shoulders are broader and the neck is longer than in the other schools, so that the overall impression of the figure is one of nobility and power rather than of the bliss of samādhi. The sensitive rendering of each individual finger and of the edges of the garment animates the silhouette of the image. Another characteristic of this sculpture is the facial type, which is longish and heavy, with more sharply defined features than in the Western schools. This eastern Buddha-type evolved in Nālandā[59] and Bodhgaya[60] (pl. 10-15, seventh century).

Among the sixth-century reliefs, the stucco reliefs at Maniyar Matha,[61] Rajgir, as well as some of the rock-cut reliefs at Sultanganj have no distinct "eastern" character, but pillar reliefs of the late fifth century from Candimau (pl. 10-17) are noteworthy. They demonstrate an eastern variant of the Gupta style, more nervous and more forceful in the gestures of its figures and rhythms of sculptural detail (such as the curve of the cloth hanging from the umbrella and the way that the snake curves around Śiva's neck). Such traits continue in the east into the ninth century and become commonplace in the Pāla period.

10.15 Stucco figures of the Buddha with the gesture of the renunciation of the world from the temple at Bodhgaya

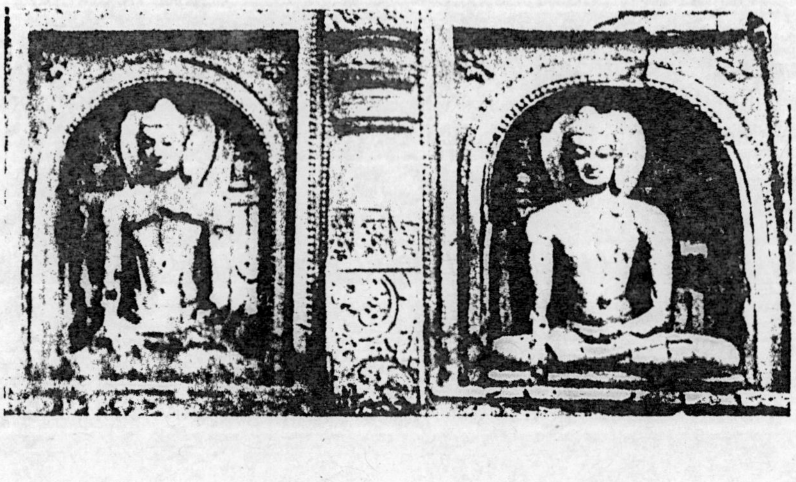

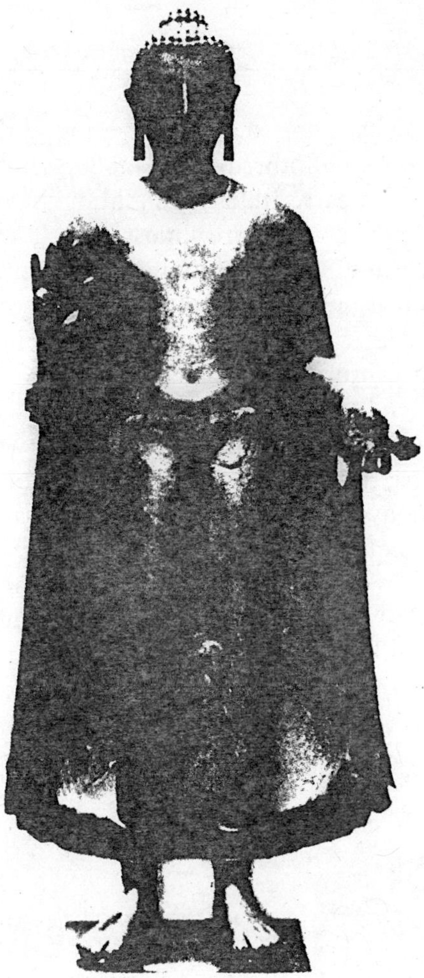

10-16. Buddha; Sultanganj
(Birmingham Museum)

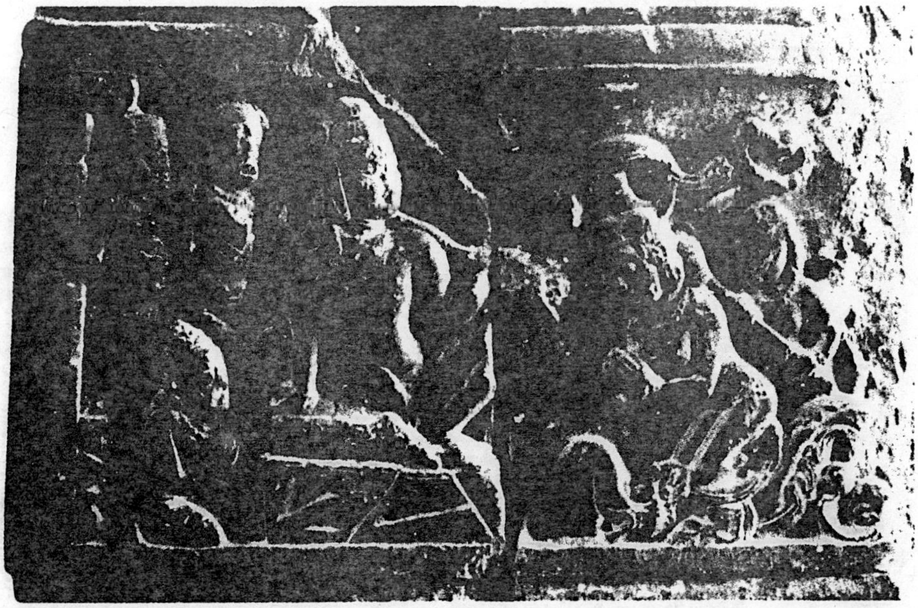

10-17. Intercession of Gaṅgā,
pillar relief; Candimau

CENTRAL INDIA

All that had made early Indian art so vital came to a full flowering in the fifth and sixth centuries in the areas where the sculpture of the Gupta period represents a direct transformation of trends of early Indian art. Although connecting works from the second to the fourth centuries are almost entirely missing, in the fifth century one can see how the strands interconnect. The central Indian monuments of the Gupta period are numerous; to do justice to them requires a more exhaustive statement than what can be given here.[62] However, the greatest monument of the fifth century is the Udayagiri rock relief of Varāha.

The rock reliefs at Udayagiri, Bhopal, are among the earliest works of the fifth century. The relief of Varāha, the Boar incarnation, is so famous that a description of it would be superfluous (pl. 10-19, detail). The colossal power and slow flowing plasticity of this unique relief blend harmoniously with the delicacy of detail carved in the flowers of the garland, the folds of the dhoti, and the jewelry of Bhūdevī. The entire rock wall and its adjoining sides were transformed into a scene of cosmic upheaval. A cosmic vision also underlies the Pārvatī temple at Nachna-Kuthara, built somewhat later in the fifth century. The walls here are reshaped into rocky boulders, the temple becomes an allegorical mountain, the cosmic mountain. Such gigantic visions assumed

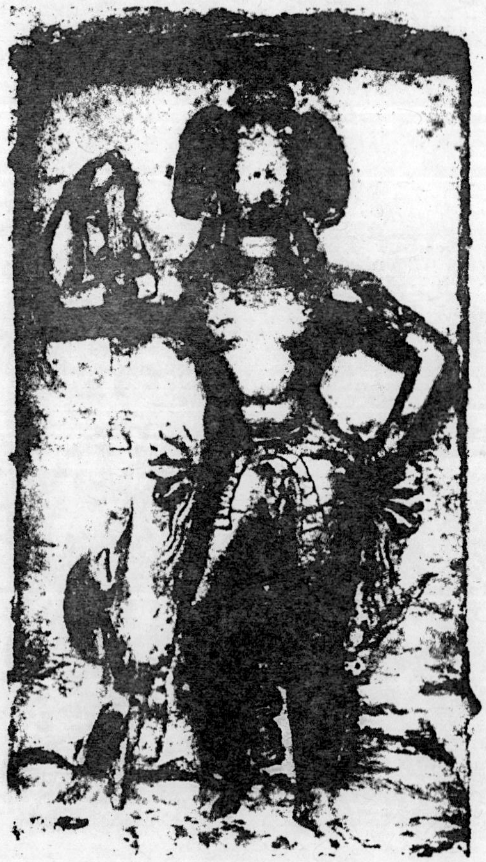

10-18. Dvārapāla; Udayagiri, Gwalior

OPPOSITE PAGE, RIGHT:
10-19. Bhūdevi; Udayagiri, Gwalior

OPPOSITE PAGE FAR RIGHT:
10-20. Śiva-gaṇa; Bhumara (Indian Museum, Calcutta)

concrete form for the first time in central India in the fifth century. The "Descent of the Ganges" at Mamallapuram and the related rock relief at Isuruminiya, Sri Lanka, have their northern forerunners here.

The Dvārapāla figure near the entrance to the Candragupta cave in Udayagiri (pl. 10-18), in its powerfully realized corporeality, forms the "first movement" in the symphony of central Indian sculpture of the fifth century. The refinement that pervaded Buddhist imagery at Sarnath and Mathura can be seen in central India in the treatment of such figures as that of Bhūdevī in the rock-cut relief of the Boar incarnation (pl. 10-19), the reliefs of the river goddesses at the Candragupta cave, and those from Besnagar[63] and the Tigowa.[64] Though they are the descendants of the female figures at Sanchi, a "classical" freedom and calmness of motion, as well as of the flowing contour, are characteristics of the new period.

This can also be seen in the overall sensitivity of modeling of the Śaiva figures at Bhumara (pl. 10-20).[65] These figures, like the flying Vidyādharas of the fifth and sixth centuries at Sarnath, are among the most charming realization of Gupta sculpture. Flying Vidyādharas, Gaṇas of every imaginable kind, full of verve, humor, and lightness are frequently found in central India, yet nowhere else do the Ganas have the childlike wisdom infused into classical form that they have at Bhumara.

The temple reliefs of Deogarh, which have been granted high praise, can be placed in the early sixth century.[66] It is not possible here to go into

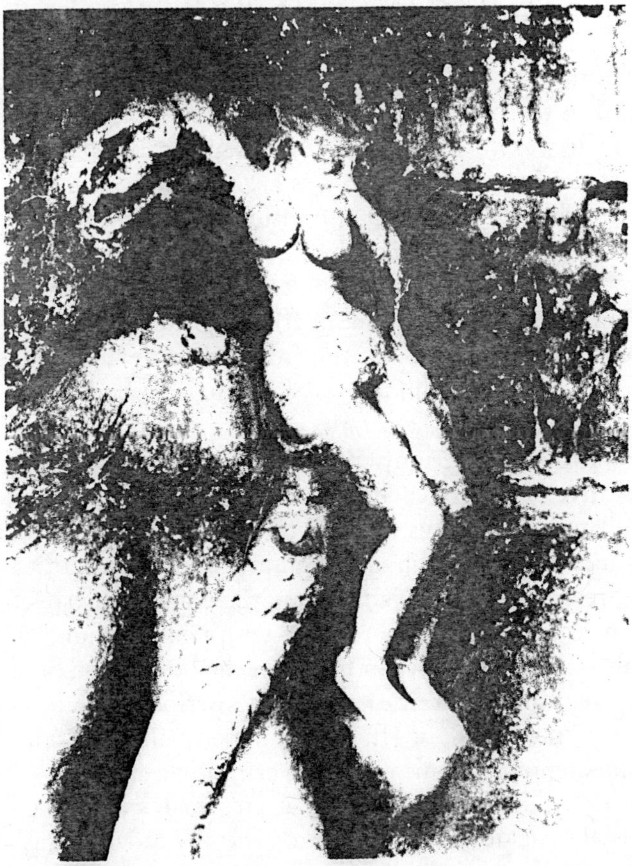

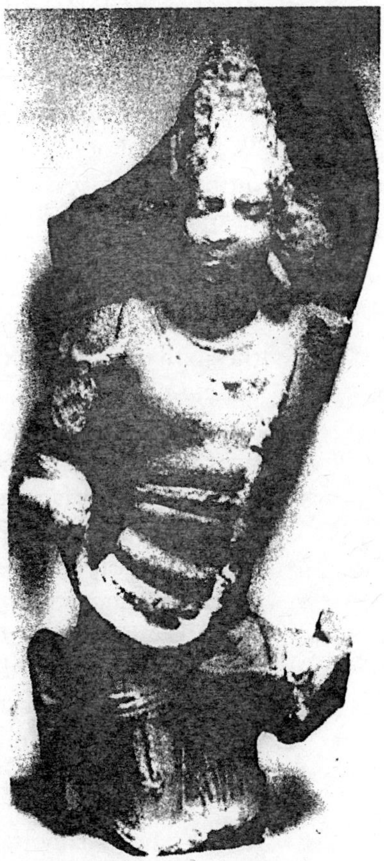

the details of the types of coiffures, drapery, and so on. The rendering of dhoti-folds (pl. 10-22) as small, tight undulations is not a local peculiarity, but is also found at eastern sites, such as the doorpost reliefs from Bihar in the Indian Museum, Calcutta. However, certain peculiarities of costume may be noted. For example, the Yaśoda of the Deogarh relief (pl. 10-22) is wearing a long-sleeved, kurta-like upper garment that is slit at the left breast. The dancer of the Kṣāntivādin frieze at Sarnath wears a similar kurta-like overgarment, although here the slit at the breast is missing (pl. 10-14). Whereas the dancer wears a long dhoti, the Deogarh Yaśoda is dressed in a richly pleated skirt. The long, flowing scarf does not rest on her hair, but is raised up by a conical frame, similar to certain medieval European headdresses. The heavily pleated skirt, the kurta-like overgarment, the high, conical bamboo frame over which the scarf is draped, are still worn in India today by women of the nomadic Banjara tribe, in Uttar Pradesh and Rajasthan. Another notable article of costume is found in the relief of the Gadhwa architrave. Here some of the women, for example those who are feeding the monks (pl. 10-13), wear a cap whose elongated sidepieces reach below the chin; similar headdresses are still worn by Kirghiz women. These features of costume point to the northern nomadic element in India during the Gupta reign. Though it left no trace in the form of figural sculpture, it did shape the ornamentation.

THE FORMATION OF THE WESTERN SCHOOL

The special character of the Eastern school emerged during Gupta times. The Western school was defined in the medieval period. In both the Eastern and Western schools, the new style was not yet pervasive in all work. The old tradition, which was concentrated in central India, was also widespread in the east and the west; it provided the matrix in which transformation and further development took place. The first symptoms of the new style, in the "west," appeared at the same time in Gwalior, Madhya Pradesh,[67] and Rajasthan.

The Śiva stele at Mandasor, Gwalior[68] (pl. 10-21), from the first half of the sixth century, can be compared with the Vishnu from Eran,[69] of approximately the same age, on the basis of the rigidity of Śiva's massive body. But other features, such as the draping of the loincloth, which forcefully emphasizes the naked lingam, point to a connection with the Northern school. The Northern style is most creatively integrated in the delicate modeling of the body and face of the Āyudhapuruṣas of Śiva (anthropomorphic embodiments of Siva's weapons). Another feature, which may remind one of an earlier northern conception, is represented by the Gaṇas along the edge of the stele, a motif reminiscent of the well-known Gandhara relief with its figures of soldiers and grimacing demons. The Gaṇas form a frieze on the base of the Śiva stele, and, by contrast, are genuine children of the Gupta period; their grotesque trivialities make up the base of the serene sensuality of the Āyudhapuruṣas and the threatening gloom of the towering Śiva figure.

Among all these currents, one trait in particular anticipates idioms of the Western schools. It is the sickle-shaped curve of the Āyudhapuruṣas'

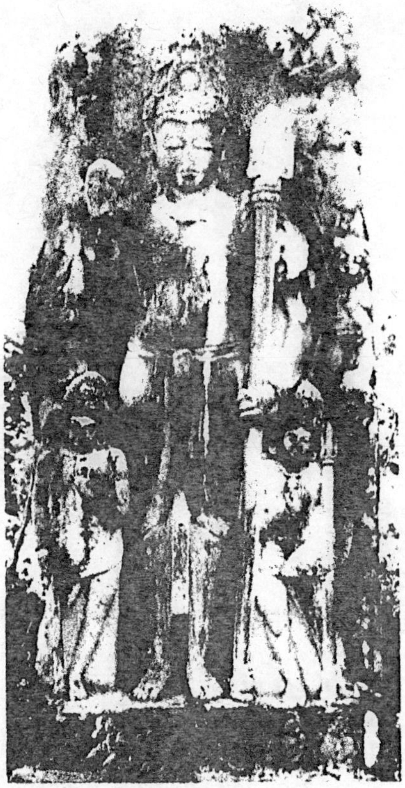

10-21. Śiva; Mandasor

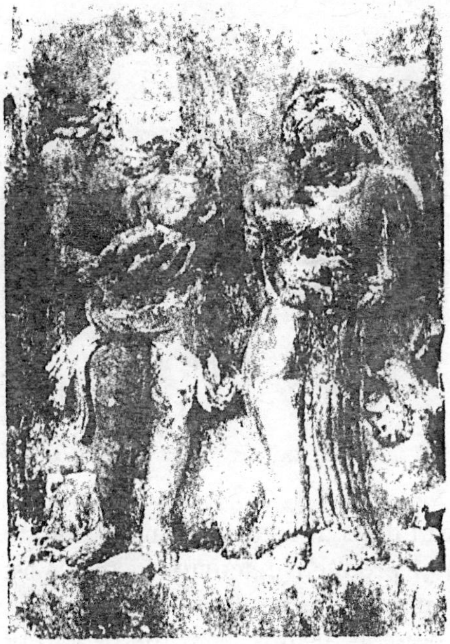

10-22. Scene from the Krishna legend; Deogarh

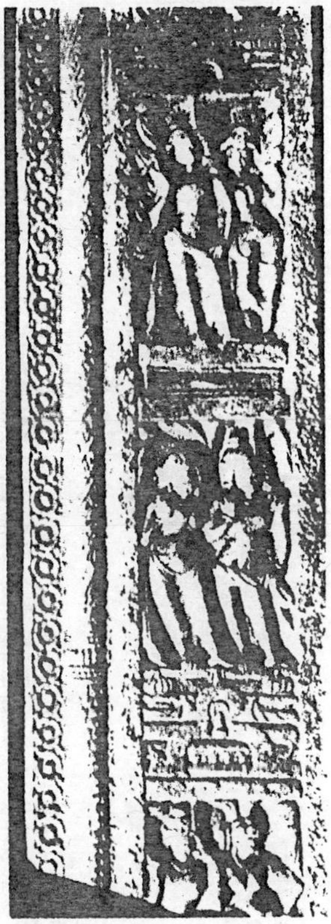

10-23. Door-post relief; Nagari, Rajasthan

stance, resting on one leg, stretched at the knee. This pose is unknown farther north or east. On the other hand, in its extreme form it marks the end of the Western school exemplified by many marble statues from Mount Abu. In the fifth-century Śaivite doorpost reliefs from Nagari (pl. 10-23), this particular motif appears clearly recognizable, not only as a particular posture, but as the symptom of a style. This may be due to its more western site, while in Gwalior this motif is only one among other features. Above all, the central relief panel (pl. 10-23) shows how sculptural values here form the base for a triumphant linear movement, to which the plastic quality of the relief has become subordinate, whereas in the other schools of Gupta sculpture, the plastic quality is paramount.

This chapter has attempted to show how a wave of genius, carried by uniquely favorable circumstances, raised the sculpture of the Gupta period to one of the peaks of Indian art. It has also attempted to trace how this took shape in relation to the Kuṣāna sculpture at Mathura in the north. Attention has been drawn to the regional varieties and changes of style during a three-hundred-year period—how the high crest in central India was supported by the old Indian local tradition and how, within the Gupta tradition, the Eastern and Western schools each began styles of their own.

11 Pāla and Sena Sculpture

Indian art differs in its development from the course of art in Europe. Every moment of productive activity in the West is usually the consequence of a previous moment. The effect of this is continuity. Indian art, on the other hand, repeatedly begins from the beginning. This, to a certain degree, was also the case in Europe when Christianity took over the traditions of classical antiquity. There, a syncretism, mainly Eastern in origin, found its way into the decaying mass of aged conventions and carried with it the germs of a new life. But the course of European art did not lose continuity because of these Eastern sources.

The reasons why Indian art "starts anew" are explained both by repeated foreign invasions and by indigenous political developments and religious ideas. Dynasties rapidly rise to power, retain it for a limited number of years, a few centuries at the most, and are rapidly overthrown. Then, after a short interlude, events once more take a parallel course. A vaster spectacle than this, however, is contained within the Indian notion of time, in which the process of art is ultimately rooted. Man in his reincarnations, the gods in their avatars, kalpa and pratikalpa, Brahmā-day and Brahmā-night of the world, cosmos and chaos, creation and dissolution, all of them are varied appearances of a notion of time that does not take its straight course from the past to the future, but seems to oscillate between two points. This notion of time almost could be considered a spatial one. Its movement proceeds on a stage, so to speak, built up by imagination and reality. There it goes on without ever coming to a dead stop, exchanging and connecting one extreme with the other, a sort of pendulum, whose mechanism swings according to the ever varying impetus of life.

This peculiarity is rooted in the texture of the peoples of the country

This essay first appeared in *Rūpam*, no. 40 (Oct. 1929), pp. 107–26, and is reprinted by permission.

and in their manifold racial origins. Not only had the Aryan invaders found pre-Aryan races who themselves had been immigrants to the country, but even the mixture that centuries brought about between those Aryans and pre-Aryans was not fed from the same sources throughout the first millennium of the Christian era. On the contrary, repeated immigrations from the north had infused new blood during the earlier part of that epoch and had brought about those combinations that distinguish the medieval phase of Indian culture. The influx of new blood suggested new trends in art; these in turn blended with the main tradition, itself already complex and changing. An ever-renewed fusion of trends and capacities on different levels again produced various levels. A progressive development from the primitive to the classical and from there to the baroque is unknown to Indian art as a whole and only certain phases, like that of the Pāla and Sena period, conform with this general rule. In spite of the uninterrupted chronological sequence and geographical limitation, the complexities of racial mixture and their expression in the artistic sphere follow general laws of organic growth that lead art forms from simplicity to perfection and from there through exaggeration to decay.

Indian art repeatedly seems to start from a fresh beginning; its monuments are conspicuous by their plastic quality, by a flowing connectedness of surface and depth. In the second century B.C. volume appears to lose its earthbound and static weightiness. At this time, the tradition of the Maurya period

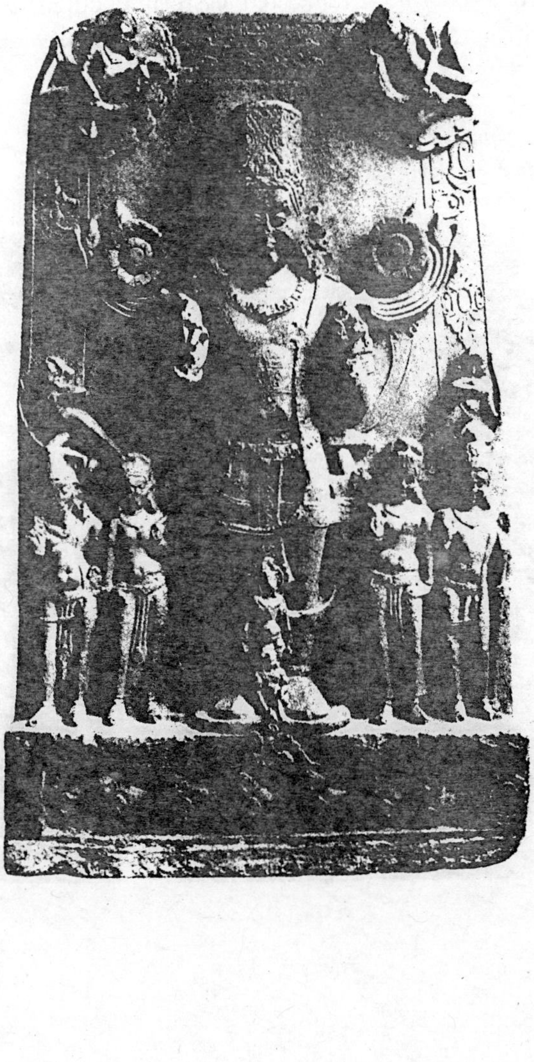

11-frontispiece. Sūrya of unknown provenance; beginning 9th century (South Kensington Museum, London)

(322–185 B.C.) loses its vitality. Its place is taken by the scrupulous narratives of the Śunga and Āndhra reliefs (185 B.C.–A.D. 225 approximately) with their demure figures, which in the course of four centuries become more agitated and more passionately modeled, but this style comes to an end after the second century A.D. But simultaneously, from the Kuṣāna period onward (20 B.C.–A.D. 226), the trend of the plastic development rises once more, its center now being situated in the northwest, in Gandhāra and in Mathura, whereas its radiations are noticeable in south India and in western Indian cave sculptures. This trend reaches its climax in the Gupta period (ca. A.D. 320–600). It is characterized by its blossoming fleshliness and by a dignity in which metaphysical knowledge and spiritual charm equally contribute to the mature freedom and disciplined mastery of form. Inertia, however, sets in by the seventh century, and drowsiness lies heavily in every limb. New energies seek expression, and new schools arise, united by the impress of the same age, differentiated, however, by the varieties of races and their mixtures in the different art centers.

At this moment the Eastern school becomes tangible. Few of its productions dating back to this early period are known. The Buddha image from Beharail, Rajshahi, ranks with the finest specimens of the Sarnath school of the first half of the fifth century. The black stone pillar from Candimau is another East Indian contribution to the Gupta style. The colossal copper image of Buddha from Sultanganj has the individuality of a masterwork, whereas the rock-cut images of the same locality are carved in the current idiom of Gupta sculpture. No work of marked eastern peculiarity, of the fifth century, is known hitherto, but sculptures of a high quality of the Sarnath tradition of Gupta art were worked then in eastern India.

11-1. Durgā killing a demon, seventh century; Bihar (Indian Museum, Calcutta)

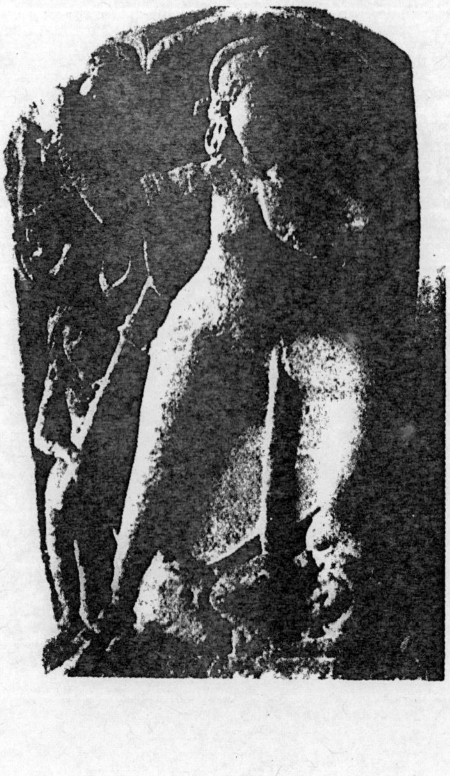

11-2. Vishnu, seventh–eighth century; North Bengal (Rajshahi Museum)

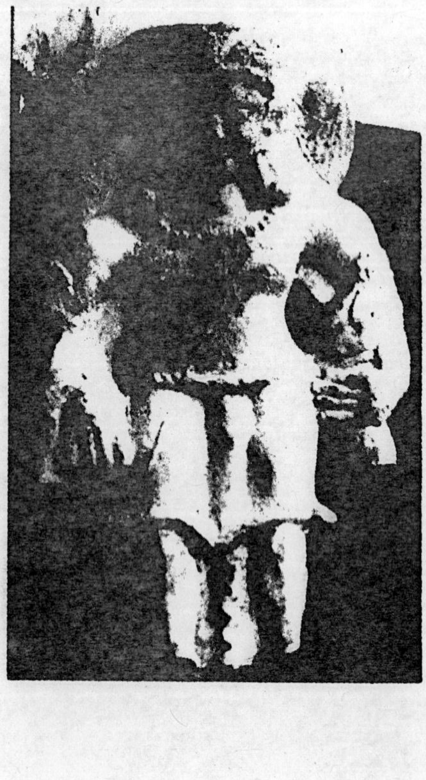

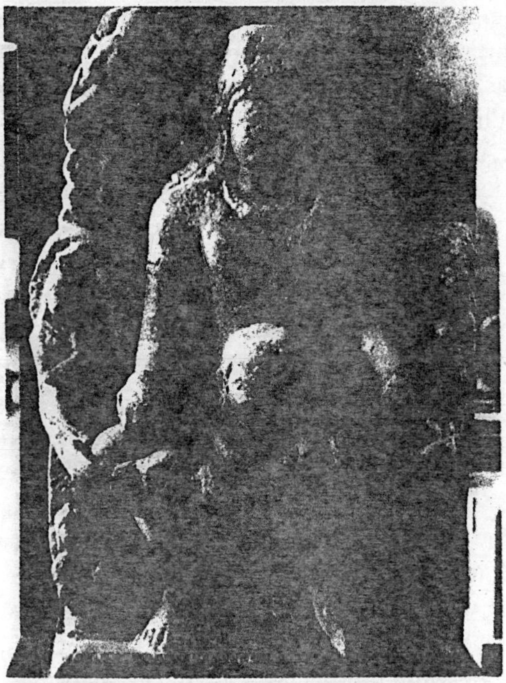

11-3. Vishnu riding on Garuḍa, eighth century; Bihar (Indian Museum, Calcutta)

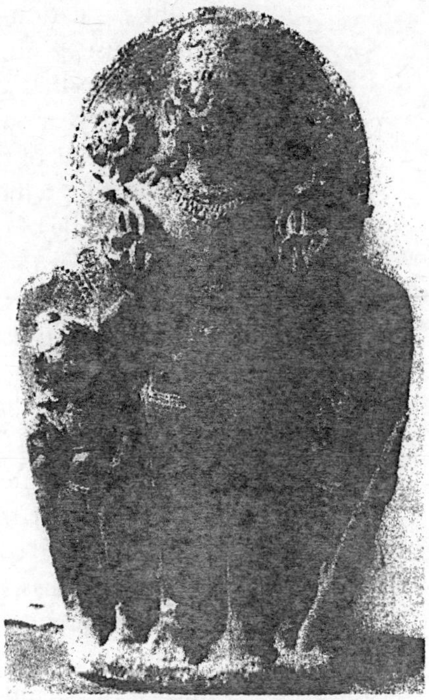

11-4. Sūrya, eighth century; Bihar (Indian Museum, Calcutta)

The Paharpur finds, northern Bengal, have shown that in the sixth century the Gupta tradition then current was followed, although the quality of these reliefs is inferior. One of them represents the divine couple of Rādhā and Krishna.

However, there are other panels in Paharpur, of crude execution, but full of decorative beauty and lively action, the work of local men, scarcely earlier than the eighth century, illustrating the Krishna legend. No other reliefs comparable to these are known but that their unsophisticated expressiveness and bold decorative quality are local features is corroborated by paintings of the *Rāmāyaṇa*[1]—although these are of later date.

The seventh and eighth centuries are represented by a relatively small number of known images. A third group of Paharpur reliefs also belongs to the eighth century.

A vigorous gesture asserts itself in spite of a drowsy heaviness of form in the seventh century (pl. 11-1).[2] By the eighth century, however, in eastern India as elsewhere, the high tide of the Gupta tradition had subsided, little remained of its refined sensuousness and of its sensitive abstractions, and yet the peculiar quality of early ninth century work is still indebted to it.

A large number of sculptures date from the ninth century, when under the Pāla dynasty many devotees dedicated images. At that time its fame spread far, so that Tāranātha, a Tibetan historian of the sixteenth century, mentions it with praise. This school grew up in an age agitated by political disturbances and reached its height while Indian and Mongolian troops continued their invasions. During a relatively consolidated and more successful period, it enjoyed the possession of the art form it had built up—it was now seized by a slight stagnation—but coming generations finally stirred it up with a baroque luxuriousness. Invading Islam suffocated it forever.

The Pāla dynasty came to the throne with Gopāla, a soldier-emperor, about the year 750.[3] The preceding century, after the death of Harṣa, had seen the invasions of the Gurjaras from the west as well as of the Rāṣtrakūtas from the Deccan, which, despite successful repressions by the Pālas, continued up to the middle of the next century. During this period the extension of the Pāla country kept changing; at the beginning of the ninth century it reached as far as Rajasthan; later on, however, it kept itself within the limits of the modern provinces of Bihar and Bengal. The rule of the Gurjara-Pratihāra dynasty was dissolved toward the end of the tenth century; the Rāṣtrakūtas also were weakened, but now the South Indian Cholas invaded Bengal, the home of the Pālas (A.D. 1025), who were no longer rulers over the whole of Bengal; in eastern Bengal three different dynasties rapidly succeeded to the throne. This invasion left permanent traces. The Sena dynasty, partly contemporary with that of the Pāḷas, ruled over the country of the latter and occupied the twelfth century; whereas in eastern Bengal they held sway for a quarter of a century more; the emperors were the descendants, most probably, of a Kannada chief of the Chola army who had remained in Bengal. In the year 1199, Bakhtiār Khilji conquered Bihar and Bengal. The followers of Islam smashed many of the extant images and left little room for creative power that would have been required for producing new ones.

The four centuries of continuous East Indian artistic productiveness cover a period of political unrest and belong to a country whose extension frequently changed. But neither of these circumstances touched the artistic vitality of Bihar and Bengal, for battles were an internal affair of the Kshatriyas of the warrior caste, which did not essentially act upon the occupations of the other spiritually, economically, or commercially productive castes. Even in the case of an ethnically foreign element settling down in the country, as for instance in the case of the Sena dynasty, this only modified the trend of art within the limits of its hieratically fixed forms and of its own inherent impulse.

The home of the art of the Pāla and Sena dynasties is the modern provinces of Bihar and Bengal; its most prolific schools are situated between the forty-eighth and the ninety-second degree longitude, between the twenty-sixth and twenty-second degree latitude, the present Chota Nagpur excluded. A few images were occasionally exported outside these limits as royal gifts, for example an image of Buddha that was sent on elephant back to Lalitāditya, the ruler of Kasmir.[4] Apart however from such an accidental token of the appreciation of eastern Indian sculpture, the art of Bihar and Bengal exercised a lasting influence on that of Nepal, Burma, Sri Lanka, and Java. But this extension no longer can be called eastern Indian art, which acted as a seed only, placed into the fertile and ready soil of new countries, where it germinated in a familiar yet indigenous fashion.

Many images were dedicated under the rule of the Pālas and Senas. Dedicatory inscriptions from the time of the various rulers are known up to now on almost two dozen reliefs and fragments of reliefs.[5] Yet no image has been found with an inscription of any of the Pāla rulers themselves, for the Pālas had an itinerant residence, always close to the battlefield for the time being.

This already suggests that no personal patronage of art is to be expected from their side. Also the donors of the different images had no personal relation to the work of art that was finally dedicated on their behalf. They were solely interested in the dedication itself, through which they expected to acquire religious merit. Nominally, this attitude remained the same under the Senas. They helped to revive Sanskrit literature, but at this epoch religious life was saturated with a luxurious worldliness, so that poetry as well as sculpture occasionally seemed to have satisfied the aesthetic taste of the royal patron, as for instance that of Vijayasena.

In spite of the religious subject matter, the art of the Sena dynasty belongs to the world and to the court and is replete with sensuousness. No artist of this period, that is, the twelfth century, is known to us by name, whereas the names of Dhīmān and Bitpāla, father and son, who flourished in the ninth century and had founded a school of sculpture, bronze casting, and painting, are remembered by the Tibetan historians. The name of the artist, however, by no means stands for individuality of artistic conception; that work only in India is extolled by fame, which rises above the rest by the accomplished quality of its craftsmanship. For the religious experience that underlies the work of art is anterior to its conception, and is moreover the common property of the initiated. The individual is just the channel, narrow or broad, through which it passes. Similarly, the artistic form meant to help it toward objective appearance is preexisting with regard to the single work of art. It is chiseled or molded by the master or his pupils under the guidance of a living tradition. This, with the most creative type of artist, amounts to a true inner vision and an identification of the self with that vision; in less favored cases, however, the well-fixed tradition itself about the appearance of the image yields a solid and reliable framework with the help of which the religious experience is evoked in the worshiping devotee according to the rules that are familiar to the craftsman. But the image, even when fully visualized and finished, is not yet fit to fulfill its purpose of being worshiped and of leading to the desired salvation. It has to be consecrated first; then only it is considered an arcāvatāra, descent of the highest for the purpose of worship.[6] Then at the proper season, with appropriate mantras, songs, and ceremonies, the breath of God is breathed into it (prāṇapratiṣthita). Then only the work of art becomes the visible body, suggestively animated by the divine presence.

The images of the ninth century are mainly Buddhistic, but there are also Brahmanic images; in the tenth century Brahmanic sculptures begin to increase in number; in the twelfth century Vishnu images are so abundant that they scarcely can be counted, but images of the various goddesses are equally widespread, whereas Śaivite and Jaina images are less frequently met with.

The figure of Buddha rendered in the ninth century generally exhibits a satisfied and enigmatic smile, and a plump smoothness of stiff limbs, but a novel and manifold grace is infused into the Bodhisattva figures (pl. II-13). Strangely enough, it reflects back upon the rendering of the Buddha image. A jewel crown and heavy, yet finely wrought, jewelry now become added to the sanghātī, the upper monkish garment, and they cover the symbolism of the uṣṇīṣa and the short locks (pl. II-17). Compared with the feminine and emotional grace of the Bodhisattva image, and to some extent with the image of the Buddha too, the goddesses appear either as their equal as graceful and emotional Śaktis, whereas others appear as mighty women; they are the mothers.

The main figures of Buddhism when it had become imbued with Tantric views are those of the goddesses in their two-fold aspect, as Śakti, that is, as working energy, and as mother and those of the Bodhisattvas, with their girlish charm. But not only Buddhism, but all the religious systems at that moment were tinctured by the Tantric view of life. A Vishnu image thus does not differ from the figure of a Bodhisattva in features or in composition; it can be distinguished by its position, only its attributes, and its accompanying figures. The goddesses, similarly, are differentiated from one another mainly by their names, which can be "read" with the help of the attributes they carry (pl. II-19). Śaivism, however, just at this moment invented two very pronounced types, that of the dancing Śiva in its peculiar East Indian version, and the united group of Śiva and Pārvatī, in the aspect of Śiva known as Umā-Maheśvara or Umāliṅganamūrti (pl. II-53) familiar to the whole of northern India, but especially widespread in the eastern districts. Jainism, again, has its iconographically established types. They are neither animated nor transformed by any peculiar artistic experiences. They are just some more images executed in the form idioms current at the different periods.

The artistic conception, in spite of iconographic and sectarian differences which then had reached a climax of pedantic observation, remains the same, exactly as the religious experience in its Tantric trend tinctures all the different sects. There are stelae, for example, with a relief on one side, representing Vishnu, and with another relief on the reverse representing Umā-Maheśvara. This may be looked upon as a widening of the conception of Hari-Hara, which unites Vishnu and Śiva, in one superhuman figure carrying both their attributes. Such a coordination may be attributed to religious eclecticism, but it will be better understood as the outcome of a knowledge, that considers all differences as names and forms of appearance of one and the same reality.

Facilitated by this attitude, one religious diapason, that of Tantrism, became established under different names and with varying rites. The goal of the much-discussed Tantric cults is the intuition of the cosmic spirit, its throwing forth female energy and their final union, the understanding of which brings about salvation and bliss. The ways that lead to the goal are adapted to the temperamental and spiritual aptitude of the various types of men. Even actual union in the flesh may be resorted to, when its aim and condition are the absence of all passion. This sexual yoga as a permanent form of the world and its life is symbolized by the image of Umā-Maheśvara. While the god holds Pārvatī seated in shy happiness, his aloofness and imperturbability are to be seen by the vertical position of the "ūrdhvaliṅgam." Nevertheless, it is quite likely that to some outsiders such a group did not convey much deeper a meaning beyond that of conjugal happiness. Not only the Tantric ceremony, but also the Tantric images have lent themselves to much misunderstanding.

This typical group of Śiva and Pārvatī, however, is the more significant, because it is not meant as a representation of the god and the goddess, but merely as a manifestation of the god in his form as Umā-Maheśvara. Umā, in this conception, has no existence of her own; she is part of the god in his unfolded appearance. Compared with this explicit form, the other images of gods and of Bodhisattvas (pl. 11-44) appear as hypostasis of the male permeated by the female principle, and the images of goddesses (pls. 11-18, 19, 22) as hypostasis of the female principle itself. It is so manifold that the emaciated, grinning skeleton of Cāmuṇḍā, the pot-bellied dancing Parṇaśabarī, the graceful nobility of Tārā, and the brooding motherliness of Pārvatī stand side by side.

The female principle as creative energy, as potential all-mother, seems to be preponderant in these sculptures. But every image also (pl. 11-39) contains a complex mixture of contents, consisting of abstraction, obedient to fixed rules regulating the proportion of the image, of a sensuously soft modeling of the flesh and of an overconscientious precision in the rendering of the rich goldsmith's productions that clasp and play over the smooth fullness of limbs. The same qualities are shown by the images of goddesses and gods; as the god carries within him the female part of himself, so the image makes it visible.

The female element that rules over the sculptures under discussion left its impress already long ago upon the religious experience. The cult of the mother is known to the remotest antiquity of India. A sculptured group of the Mātṛkās, of the seven mothers, for instance, exists from the later Kuṣāna period (Besnagar, now in the Gwalior Museum). The conception of Śakti, or female energy, becomes tangible during the early centuries A.D. and is enlarged and deepened later on through Chinese and High Asiatic influences. The image of Tārā (fig. 6), so frequently met with in the northern countries of Buddhism, in the art of the Pāla and Sena period, is utterly unknown in the south of India. Śaktism is not only one of the three main aspects of Brahmanism (i.e.,

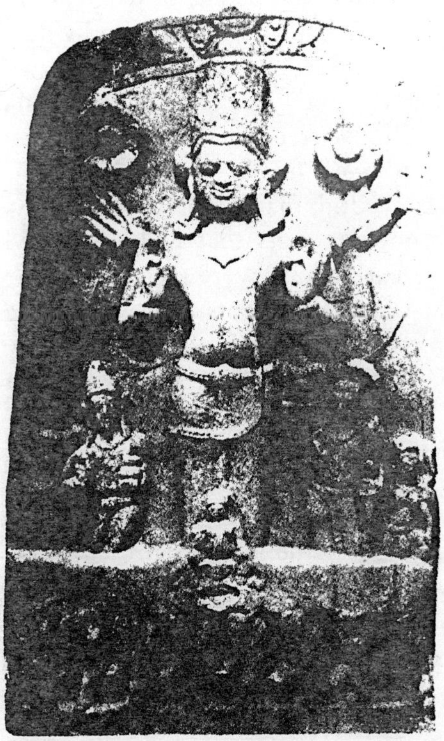

FAR LEFT: *11-5. Sūrya, middle ninth century; Bihar (Indian Museum, Calcutta)*

LEFT: *11-6. Khadiravanī Tārā, before* A.D. *820 (inscription: in the thirty-fifth year of Devapāladeva); Hilsa, Patna, South Bihar (Patna Museum)*

Śaivism, Vaishnavism, and Śaktism), but having its roots in the most remote antiquity, in the course of centuries it filtered into Śaivism and Vaishnavism; and it is responsible also for the last phase of Buddhism. The first century A.D. in the life history of Buddhism was a turning point on the way to salvation—a turning away from the Buddha to the Bodhisattva. A religion of faith and devotion toward divine mediators who had voluntarily renounced their own salvation, replaced a philosophy of the ideal of personal nihilism. This deviation, that had begun about 600 years after the parinirvāṇa of the Lord, once more, after six centuries, was reinforced and more and more directed toward Tārā and Śakti.[7] These, however, are the most conspicuous milestones only on a way, that, at the time of the beginning of the development, already contained the germs of some of the later stages. Such a phenomenon, however, is typically Indian. A section across the culture of any period simultaneously shows the most variegated trends of thought and possibilities of imagination; one or the other eventually surges into the foreground and leads the spiritual life for a certain period. Sexuality as a simile of the bliss of knowledge is emphasized already in the *Bṛhadāraṇyaka Upaniṣad.*[8]

An attitude of this kind later on became the keynote of religious experience. The five steps of devotion, as prescribed to the Vaishnavites, illustrate it well. The first step is permeated by śānti, by the peace that embraces the devotée, who, from the fearsomeness of existence, turns toward God. In the peace of his soul he now enters the next stage, where his attitude toward God is that of the servant (dāsya), while on the next higher step he approaches God already with intimacy (sakhya). In the fourth stage, he yields in tenderness and affection (vātsalya), and in complete dedication of his body he reaches the final stage (mādhurya). This attitude of religious experience, so strongly emotional, is kept in strict obedience; the details of daily life in their regular sequence are meticulously prescribed by ācāra—individual thoughts and personal emotions are thereby excluded. In the twelfth century this orthodoxy reaches the heights of pedantry under Vallāla Sena's Kulina system of rigorous caste observance. Emotional freedom had given many new contents, to the last phase of Buddhism, but it finally shattered its foundations. As compensation the opposite was needful, that is, a new orthodoxy. Bāuls, Nerā-Neris, Sahajiyās, and other popular sects that had originated within the garb of late Buddhism after its "extinction" were received by the Vaishnavites. The reaction set in against such movements under the Sena kings, of whom some were followers of Vishnu and others of Śiva, while the majority of the population, just as during the rule of the Buddhistic Pāla dynasty, remained within Brahmanism.

The Buddhist images, of which large numbers were installed in the monasteries (vihāra)—Bihar, the country derives the name from this—are of the same type as the Brahmanic sculptures that were worshiped in many large temples and small sanctuaries. The mood of the image represented always remains impersonal, whatever guṇa may be embodied, whether sattva, rajas, or tamas, however tenderly and roundly the features may be shaped, however rich the jewels, however full the limbs; grace or fury have the typical bearing laid down by the śāstras.

We may consider the character of these sculptures complex. It is con-

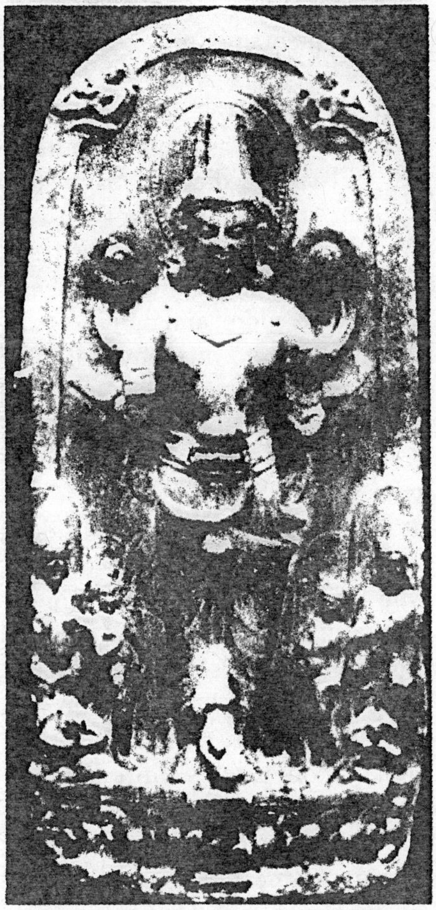

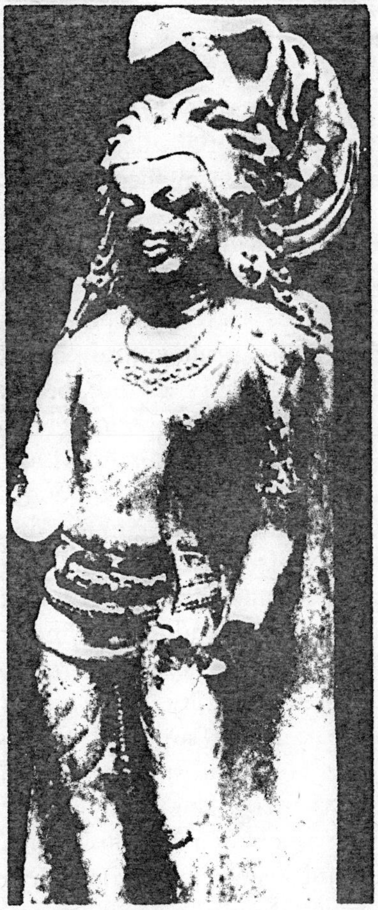

FAR LEFT: *11-7. Sūrya, beginning ninth century; Rajshahi, North Bengal (Rajshahi Museum)*

LEFT: *11-8. Cakrapuruṣa, beginning ninth century; Kasiabari, Bogra, North Bengal (Rajshahi [?])*

sistent, however, for an exuberant impersonal experience is passed through by the experiencing individual in perfect tranquility. But this art never has been the art of the people, of which the majority remained within Brahmanism, whereas the number of Buddhist images is very large compared with the Brahmanic images.

Thus within these four centuries art seems to be produced organically, within a well-surrounded district, of which the limits and chief factors are the court, the cult, the prosperous lay communities, and the workshops. Its quality, as well as its limitations, result from this high breed. Every sculpture of this period shows at the same time a more or less petrified bodily form and over-sensitive gestures, a baroque upheaval of the plastic organism and a well-calculated accuracy in every detail of the linear composition. Similarly, the bodily appearance of the images, though sensuous, is not the outcome of an equivalent experience; it is not spontaneous but is derived from the knowledge of the corresponding formula (sādhana).[9] With all that, the temptation to look for the gods of the common people and for their images is great. They were absorbed, however, partly into the pantheon of the educated classes, and like Caṇḍī and Manasā were worshiped with due rites and were represented in the current art language. Partly, however, they forever remained excluded from this higher and officially recognized community. To represent them, nothing more was needed than a conical shape made of clay. It was worshiped by the women of lower pre-Aryan descent who had married into the higher castes, and in spite of frequent mixtures considered themselves Aryans.[10]

A cross section through contemporary literature is as intricate in its texture as one through the images. Ballads, for instance, as those of eastern Bengal, cinema-like in their dramatic appeal and simple diction, originated with anonymous authors belonging to the lower strata. They are far away from the style of writing, called Gaudī, which Daṇḍin mentions in his treatise on poetry, *Kāvyādarśa*, as a peculiarity of Bengali literature.[11] These popular ballads are conspicuous by a gypsy-like freedom and intense passions. They take place entirely on this earth and have no metaphysical outlook. Although dates cannot be fixed, some seem to have become well known during the Sena period. There are, on the other hand, popular songs of the tenth century in praise of agriculture that celebrate Śiva as the tiller of the soil and Pārvatī as the good housewife. These homely and naïve tokens of the piety and the comfort of peasant life express an outlook considerably different from that of such later novels as Behulā or Caṇḍī. Although free from true metaphysical conceptions, the latter make goddesses human in their nature but endowed with some supernatural attributes—the punishing or helping powers that destroy or save human life—described with considerable sentimentality. Side by side with this popular literature, mystic songs were, and are, sung to the present day by the Bāuls, for example, that with a few words and similes suggest a spiritual mood. Of this entire popular literature, the language—Bengali—strangely differs from the art literature of the Senas, which, in a high-flown Sanskrit style, surrounds a few imaginative and graceful inspirations with cumbersome pompousness. The worldliness, almost frivolous, of the court atmosphere of the eleventh and twelfth centuries, breaks through the classical figures of speech, and both of them are surrounded by meticulous and stereotyped phrases. This mosaic of literary activity of the Pāla and Sena period is reflected in the entire artistic life and is compressed, so to speak, in every single work of sculpture. Frequently the most variegated trends are interwoven in one and the same image. This is due to the artist following the strict rules of iconographic tradition while working for a donor, frequently a man of the world, whose sphere of life, though inaccessible to the artist by caste, nevertheless lay before his eyes, while he himself belonged to the lower strata of the people, whose customs and notions were alive within him. The artist or workman, on account of his caste and profession, gathers within his person the upper and the lower layer of the contemporary civilization. The work of art thus becomes a repository of religiousness, tinctured by worldliness with its rich ornaments. It unites refined taste with homely sturdiness, and combines pedantic and uninspired formulas with the grace of a humanized vision of God.

When transplanted into a new soil this art, so comprehensive in its features, proved a great stimulus and provoked provincial and colonial art schools that variegated the language of the motherland by a vernacular of their own. Kashmir and Nepal were reached by land, Burma and Java by sea. Bengal, which today is mainly an agricultural country, at the time of the Pālas was the home of enterprising seafarers. Considerable wealth seems to have come into the country that way, in spite of the harassing and almost continuous wars that were going on. An expression of this well-being can be seen in the names of men and women. The captain of a ship, for instance is called Dulāldhan, that is, "highly prized wealth," an architect Hirāmānik, "diamonds and precious stones," a girl Kāncanamālā, "string of pearls."[12] The number of images dedicated by the prosperous community in order to secure religious merit for themselves, for their near relatives and for all sentient beings, may be imagined, when the large number of sculptures is considered that escaped destruction—although rarely only mutilation—by the invasion of Islam.

In the ninth century, as mentioned already, the art of the Pālas already had fully developed features. Only a few monuments are known at present in Bihar and Bengal that date back to the period after the decay of the Gupta tradition. The seventh and the eighth centuries especially, as far as can be judged from a scanty number of images (cf. p. 207) one of which only, the Chauddagrām Sarvvānī bears a dated inscription, may be looked upon historically as the critical moment from which eastern Indian art, as an art school of its own, takes its start. Nevertheless, the connection with Indian art as a whole is not cut off, for, from now onward as in the past, the country is the common basis, while every province and within it every local school contributes its own features.

The common denominator of Indian sculpture is obvious in the tenth, eleventh, and twelfth centuries. The most conspicuous data are, to indicate just a few—the sculptures from Tajore, in South India, about the year 1000, on one level with contemporary eastern form; the western and central Indian carvings of the eleventh century, corresponding to those of eastern India at the same moment, and similarly, the images of the twelfth century in the Deccan, which partake of the same exuberance that weighed heavily on the sculpture of the Senas.

Indian sculpture, however, in the various provinces during the eighth and ninth centuries, does not admit a common denominator of the stages in its development. The south, at that time, had proceeded on a straight line from the early classic Pallava style to the high classicism of the Chola temples. In the Deccan, too, the artistic movement went on without any significant incision. This was limited to the northern half of the country. For just then northern, and especially northeastern India, shaped a form-idiom of its own. The awakening out of a rigid state, the growth and exuberance of this novel spirit will be traced in the following pages with the help of dated images, and illustrated by those of artistic significance. One generation takes over the tradition from the other and adds its own vitality, scareely perceptible to the casual spectator, yet essentially differentiated on closer scrutiny. Tradition thus goes on through four hundred years in a steady course without stop, but also without making any of the moments especially significant or graced by supreme artistic achievement.

Most of the sculptures are carved out of a black stone, frequently highly polished. It has been quarried in the Rajmahal hills in the Santal Parganas of Bengal. It is known under the name kaṣti pāthar and is found in two varieties—one coarse grained, the other of a fine and even structure. The first variety is a basic phyllite, mainly consisting of chlorite and talc, the latter a cericitized slate.[13]

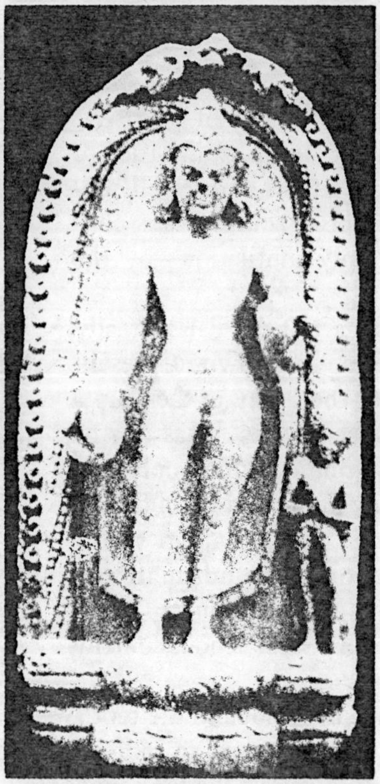

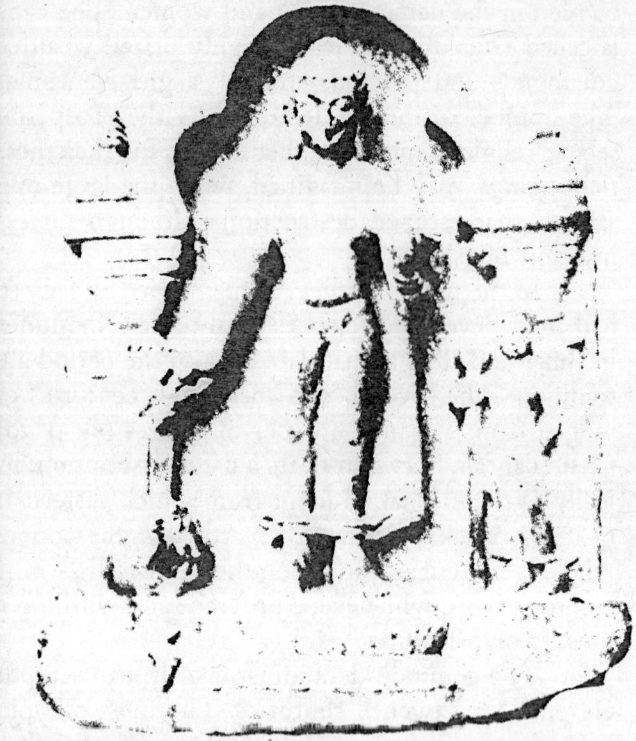

RIGHT: *11-9. Crowned Buddha on the way to Benares, beginning ninth century; Nālandā, South Bihar*

FAR RIGHT: *11-10. Buddha taming the wild elephant,* A.D. *820–830 (inscription: in the third year of the reign of Vigrahapala [or Surapāla I]); Bihar (Indian Museum, Calcutta)*

Both, when newly quarried, are said to be relatively soft and easily workable. Exposed to the air they harden quickly and scarcely weather. During the earlier centuries, bulkiness and dignity were features of the images, and for this the coarser stone sufficed[14] as well as the finer one; later on, however, with an ever increasing accumulation of ornaments, and with features growing sharper and sharper, the finer stone was more in demand. In the twelfth century it was used almost exclusively, and its surface became wrought with metallic precision. It is, however, difficult to say whether these images were painted, or tinted with color, as were those of the Gupta period. No trace of paint has been left on any of the images. That of the goddess Vāgīśvarī (pl. 11-18), in Nalanda, it is true, had been streaked with gold according to the inscription, but this has to be understood as an act of Buddhist worship, for to cover stūpas or images with gold leaf is held to be meritorious.[15] This devotional action, however, was free of any aesthetic or iconographic intention.

The metal images of the period are cast in brass or in aṣṭa-dhātu, an alloy of eight metals, that is, copper, tin, lead, antimony, zinc, iron, gold, and silver in varying proportions; at times these bronzes were enameled with a thin layer of kaolin or clay, green or brown, patina-like in its effects.[16] One small image cast in silver has been preserved, too, a solitary example of the gold, silver, and jeweled figures that in the course of time have disappeared, a prey of avidity. A special preparation of unburned clay may be mentioned, last, of which the magnificent head from Deopara, Rajshahi, is formed.[17] The material is extraordinarily light and elastic. It is covered and made watertight with the

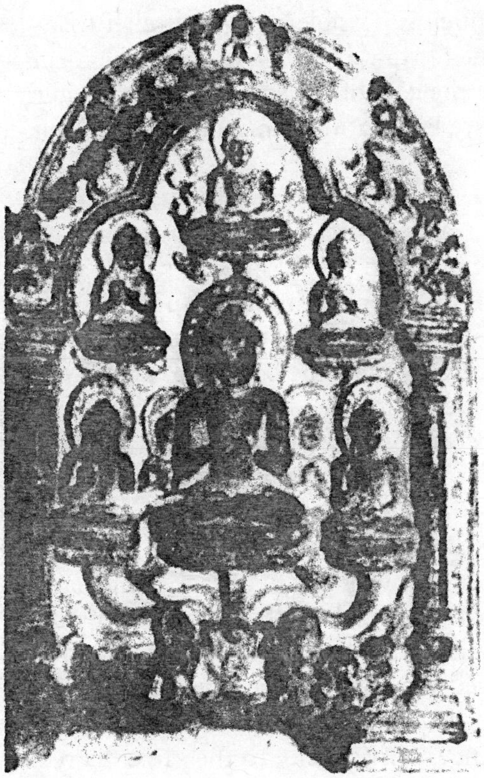

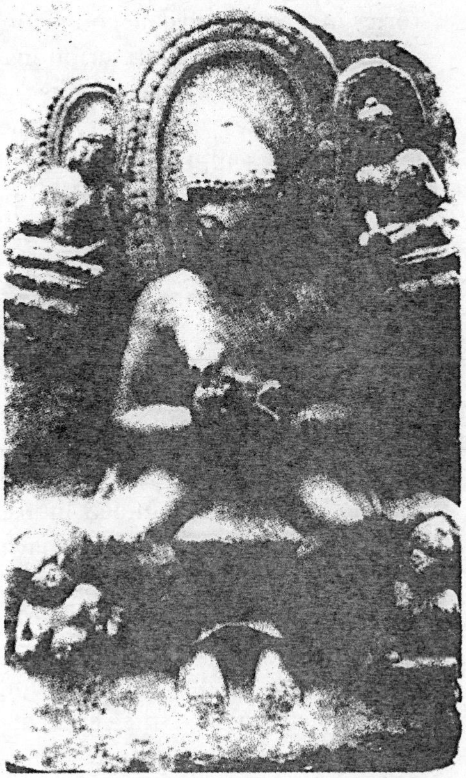

FAR RIGHT: *11-11. The miracle at Śrāvastī, middle ninth century; Nālandā*

RIGHT: *11-12. Buddha, middle ninth century; Bihar (Indian Museum, Calcutta)*

help of vajralepa, a decoction of buffalo hides.[18] A figurine carved in ivory (pls. 11-34–35) and some wooden carvings[19] also have come to our days. The formal treatment is essentially the same in every material; it is modified with that minimum of variety which the texture of the different materials demands.

The large majority of the stone images are stelae, carved in relief. The small bronzes too are treated as stelae, the figures there, however, being worked in the round as a rule. This setting results from a struggle between liturgical convention and artistic intention. The image made to be worshiped is turned toward the worshiper, and its back view is immaterial. Relief, therefore, is the proper style which the cult demands. It is peculiar, however, that pradakṣiṇa, the ceremony of circumambulation, did not favor images carved in the round. But orientation was the main goal, and the image has to face the appropriate direction, that is, the east generally. Circumambulation does not lend itself to aesthetic contemplation; it is a devotional procession around the divine presence which it has for its center. The image in the dim obscurity of the shrine lost much of the effect that appeals to the eye. The devotée thus did not see the image in its reality; the vision he beheld of it originated from his knowledge of the divine presence. The artist, on the other hand, far from calculating the artistic effect of his work, was guided by the elementary principles of artistic form, whereas the more specialized features were dictated to him by the śāstras. One trend, however, he added quite of his own—the tendency to model in the round. This urge is inherent in almost every Indian sculpture but perpetually it is repressed, either by another aim, that is, to tell stories in a clearly visible connection, which is possible only by a relief treatment, or by canonical prescriptions of the śāstras. The urge to shape the form in the round fully comes into its own in the case of the stūpa and in the later medieval temples; in either type the entire body of the monument is nothing but a colossal sculpture in the round.

During the Pāla and Sena period, the relief becomes more and more independent from its background. The single figures modeled in the round, when seen in front and side view, are connected finally by struts only with the back slab. The figure of the main deity, even during the Gupta period, had almost been made in the round; during the following centuries this mode became the favorite. It was effected by cutting away the back slab around the outline of the figure, so that it ends parallel to it. The distance between back slab and figure is filled by air, which, according to the inclination of the rays of light, appears as a dark or light border that accompanies the figure of the main deity with its rounded limbs. The back view of the figure is modeled in a sketchy manner only, but garments and jewelry in full reality, multicolored, golden, and silky, were attached and slung through, where limbs and body and the back of the slab have an opening, in order to heighten the joyousness of worship. But in spite of its isolation from the background, the effect of the figure remains flat and compressed into the surface. It is only in the twelfth century—at the end of the development—that a fully three-dimensional sculpture comes into existence, self-assuring to the same degree, as that of the Mauryan period. Not only figures of Garuḍa (pl. II-47) meant to adorn the top of columns but also actual images, as that of Ardhanārīśvara, are freed from two-dimensional restrictions.

The tendency of modeling in the round comes into its own at the end only of this period. The plastic imagination, on the other hand, as far as the relief is concerned, is untiring in increasing inventions of creeper-like scrolls, flame and feather arabesques, cloud-motifs, and those graceful creatures that go by the name of kinnara and kinnarī, haṁsa, śārdūla and gandharva (i.e., bird-men and women, swanlike geese, leogryphs, and flying aerial spirits). They bustle about on the back of the slab in all degrees from flat to high relief. Most of the images thus consist of two plastic layers, some even of three strata. Complex contents necessitate a complex rendering even in the matter of mere technical treatment. That it succeeded in remaining organic speaks for the vitality of this art.

The chief medium of this sculpture is the human figure. Its typical feature is the union of abstraction and realism with its religious and sensuous suggestiveness. The male figure seems endowed with the graceful roundness of the female body, yet both the masculinity of the male as well as the femininity of the female figure are overemphasized. A new type of man seems to be featured on androgyne base. His shoulders are broad as those of the elephant, and his waist slender as that of the lion; contrasting with these peculiarities are the exaggerations of the female figure that enhance her almost paleolithic beauty of motherhood by over-large, round breasts and bulging hips. These features, derived as they are from actual appearance, abstract however, that is, unnatural in their exaggeration, were not newly invented at the time of the Pālas. They were, on the contrary, taken over fully developed from preceding artistic tradition, and though placed in novel surroundings, remained unchanged, being a constant expression of an attitude essentially Indian. A twofold process led to these abstractions. An inner experience of an erotic nature lies at the bottom. It is stronger than the impression of the actual appearance, through which it is excited. In order to express itself satisfactorily, this actual appearance had to be exaggerated when reshaped as art, in order to be on one level with the inner experience. This exaggerated form loses its reality of appearance; it becomes a formula and as such it is lifted even outside the range of the inner experience that caused it. The same process, however, that led from exaggeration to abstraction, can be traced also in the opposite direction. For not only with the help of exaggeration, but also by suppression, an abstract form is gained, and this, too, was used as a current formula. The skeleton, sinews, and veins of most of the figures are invisible, most of the gods appear as if eternally sixteen years old[20] and free from all worry; some figures, however, are conspicuous by the portliness of a more mature age (Agni or Brahma), some again, representing destructive powers appear as emaciated, mere skeletons covered by a net of veins (Cāmuṇḍā).

In any case, a typical imagination is visualized by a suggestive selection, whether it overemphasizes or whether it suppresses certain portions or constituents of the body. This tendency toward abstraction is based upon actual appearance and is strengthened by the norms of the cult. Canons of proportion regulate the relative size of the single figures of the image as well as that of each single limb, with mathematical objectiveness. Symmetry, repetition, and balance equally do justice to the prescriptions of the cult and to the artistic composition. But the dignity and suggestiveness of these images are attained not only by a typical or idealizing treatment. Together, and this is no contradiction, with this abstract treatment, soft fleshliness is also suggested sensitively. Almost within every century, one generation of artists at least, is endeavored to model the supple roundness of the flesh. Although realistic anatomy is suppressed, as has been said above, the limbs show such fullness, and their outlines are of such caressing roundness that, it may be said, the artist by yielding to the emphasis of blossoming and perishable flesh has grasped the eternity of imperishable bliss. The scanty garments, in order to show more of the body with its firm skin, were made transparent, clinging to every modulation as if they were wet and the jewelry in its hard, metallic heaviness was chiseled with utmost intricacy, so that the sharp play of light and shade, set against the broader and soft modulations of the limbs, enhanced their smoothness. The different types of jewelry are most accurately described by the sculptor, but this realism is not based on a joyous optical perception. It is the result of a sense of orderliness, of a conscious appreciation of wealth and of a castelike self-assertion of the householder and of his property.

The appearance of the figures in this way belongs to a world, rooted in the spiritual sphere, yet supported by the smooth surface of sensuous satisfaction and proud possession. Their attitudes and movements also, though in a different manner, are the outcome of perception and imagination. The single figures are thoroughly static. If standing stiffly on both legs, the weight of the body is carried by legs without much articulation and resembling trunks of trees. This is especially conspicuous in the standing figures of Sūrya, Vishnu, and Buddha. There, the weighty massiveness of the lower part of the figure is emphasized to such a degree that in its solidity it appears to assert its existence beyond life with its changes, consolidated within itself, as a guarantee for the unshakable existence of God (II-frontispiece and pls. II-7, II-39, etc). The same effect (pls. II-17, etc.) is attained by the vajraparyanka motif, a seated posture on both legs, with soles turned upwards and resting on the thighs. Both these motifs are peculiar to representatives of the highest hierarchy of spiritual existence. Bodhisattvas, on the other hand, and their female counterparts, gods and goddesses, accompanying the figure of the main deity balance the weight of their bodies playfully and in gentle curves of a well-contented existence. This satisfied oscillation from right to left and back again, in diagonal correspondence (pls. II-23, and the accompanying figures in II-39, II-50, etc.) at times becomes exuberant, expressive of an ever-growing sensuousness that, especially during the last stage of this period, in the twelfth century, overwhelmed the single figures. The sitting figures, too, of the deities just mentioned are more easy in their attitudes, squatting in mahārājalīlā or with gracefully pendant leg in lalitāsana (pls. II-6, II-19, II-42, etc.), they rest in self-conscious gracefulness. But either attitude, whether rigid or animated, is the

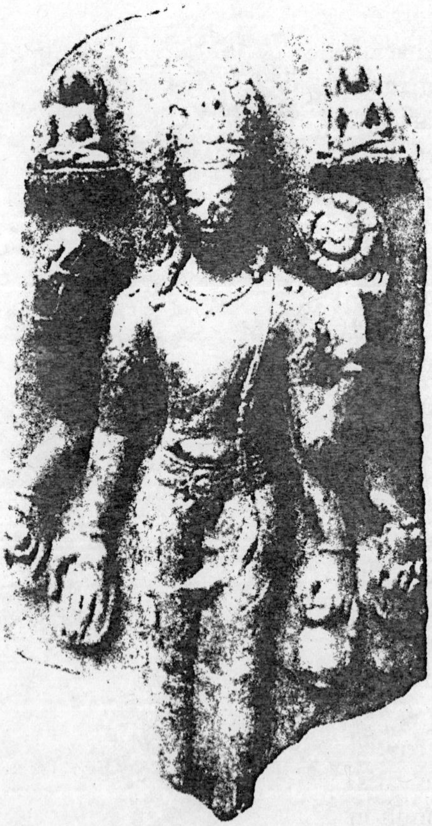

II-13. Lokeśvara Pretasantarpita, end of ninth century; Kurkihar, Gaya (Indian Museum, Calcutta)

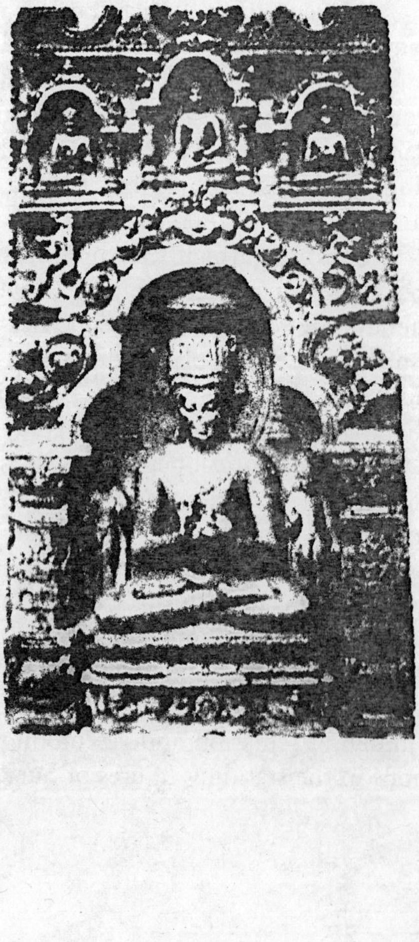

II-14. Dhyānibuddha Vairocana, middle ninth century; Kurkihar, Gaya (Indian Museum, Calcutta)

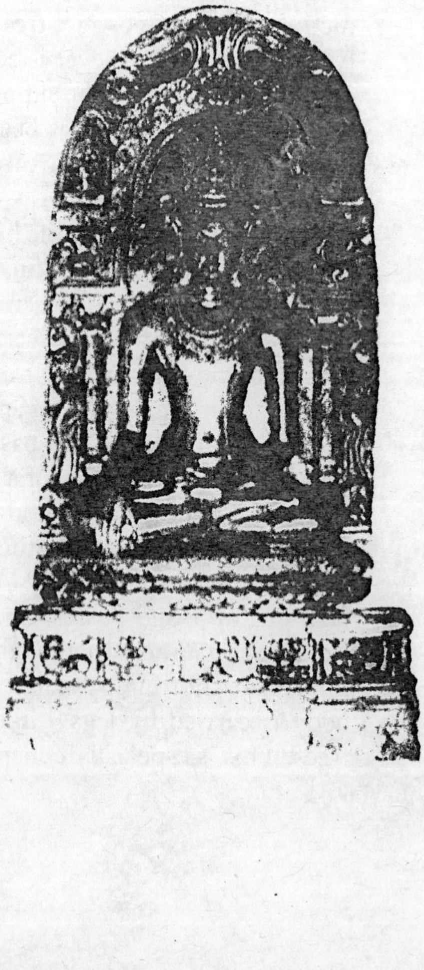

II-15. Crowned Buddha, middle ninth century; Muzaffarpur, North Bihar

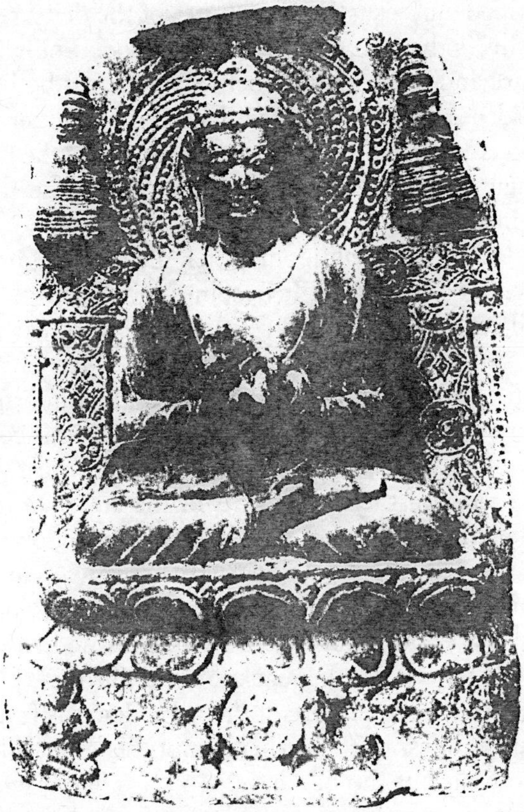

II-16. First sermon at Benares, end of ninth century; Bihar (Indian Museum, Calcutta)

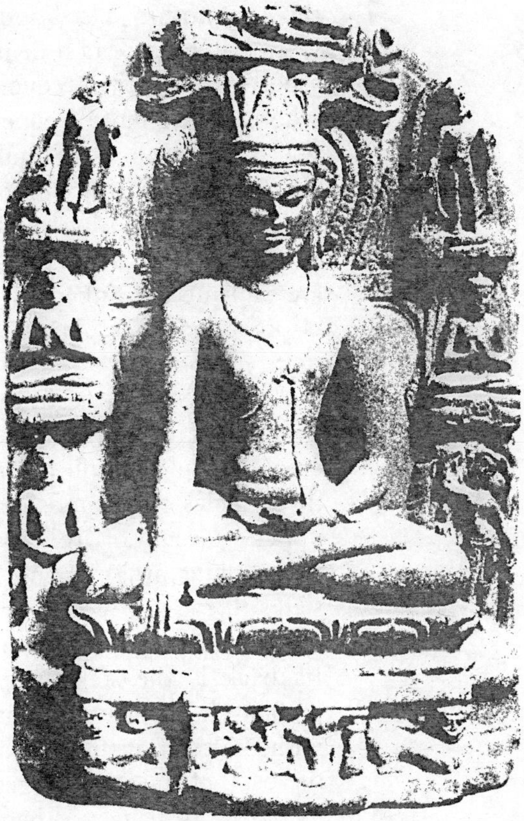

II-17. Crowned Buddha, end of ninth century; Bihar (Indian Museum, Calcutta)

outcome of an experience of restfulness. Even such vigorous and seemingly active movements (pls. II-1, II-25, etc.), as suggested by the forceful ālīḍha and pratyālīḍha postures or by the three steps of Vishnu (pl. II-27) or by the flying gandharvas, correspond to a state experienced in imagination and attributed as permanent character to that particular conception of the deity. An inner attitude is rendered as a state of movement with the help of a display of limbs. The representation of transitory motion by no means is attempted.[21]

The translation of an inner state of mind into posture is not the exclusive property of the Pāla and Sena period. The preceding tradition of the Gupta period in this respect, too, had evolved the essential norms, but it was left to the four centuries of eastern Indian tradition to exhaust all their latent possibilities. The same refers to the mudrā, that is, to the attitude of the hands. The extraordinarily varied touches of fingertips, the directions of palms and flexions in every joint convey a special, yet permanent, attitude of the mind of the respective deity. A deity may bless at the same time and threaten, with his hands; his multiple faces may express bliss and at the same time wrath. But the objectivation of the various qualities of the deity does not stop short with the differentiated attitudes (mudrā) of the hands. It is achieved also by permanent attributes, carried by the deity, of which the lotus of Avalokiteśvara, or the wheel, club, conch, and lotus of Vishnu may be especially mentioned (pls. II-42, II-49). The hands with their attitudes and the faces with their expressions, thus, are nothing else but objectified and visualized attributes of the deity represented. To a certain degree, this is the function of the body too. The wild aspects of the deity frequently are endowed with potbellied and squat bodies, whereas their more frequent and peaceful appearance is graced with eternal youth and loveliness. Simultaneously with this spiritual suggestiveness the features somehow, although remotely, are conditioned ethnically, while the attitudes are dictated by tradition inspired by artistic grace.

The great abstractions and charming realities of which the single figures are built up are linked by a severe composition. It becomes more and more elaborate and is replete with all its details in the twelfth century (pls. II-36, II-37, etc.).

The stele is meant to be the throne-carriage of the deity. It is supported by a plinth, which, as a rule, shows several projections, and frequently is covered by a lotus scroll (pl. II-44, etc.). In it are placed figures of devotees, of the vehicles of the gods (vāhana), and of the implements of the cult. On the upper surface of this pedestal lie the open or double lotus flowers (mahāmbujapīṭha), upon which the deity rests. Frequently they grow on long stalks that are shown in relief on the pedestal. The depth of the lotus throne measures the space occupied by the standing or seated figures of the deities. Its back is the stele proper, suggestive of the back of the throne. The prabhāvalī, the halo that surrounds the entire figure of the main deity, is fused with the back of the throne and at times, in the earlier sculptures especially, the back of the stele suggests nothing but the prabhāvalī (pl. II-9, etc.), with its border of flames. When, however, representing the back of the throne as such, the stele is richly decorated, and the decoration is the richer the later it is. Its full ornaments are the leogryph-motifs (śārdūla) on either side of the posts of the throne, the kinnara or haṁsa motifs above the throne-lintel, which frequently is terminated by makara devices. On it, generally, rests the prabhāmaṇḍala, the halo that surrounds the head of the deity. Above, to right and left, flying gandharvas display their alertness on cloud-motifs; the top of the stele, in the later examples (pl. II-50, etc.) is made into a point decorated by kīrttimukha, the face of glory. The middle of the entire composition is occupied by the figure of the main deity in high relief. On either side, and correspondingly smaller in size, figures of the accompanying deities are placed on separate lotus pedestals. Frontality, symmetry and triangular composition are the inevitable rule (cf., however, a slight divergence in pl. II-29). Within this linear scheme, the movement of the outline has only a relative freedom. Strongest curves are allowed when it accompanies the double and three-fold flexion (atibhaṅga and tribhaṅga) of bodies; but bows and fluttering garments, too, yield capricious possibilities. Yet the roundness and flexibility of the outline is never a factor by itself, but goes hand in hand with a corresponding plastic value, so that the entire slab appears in a rich variety of lively form, and the stele, as a whole, achieves its solemn and luxurious effect by the large, smooth, and economically modeled surfaces of the bodies of the deities set against the curly exuberance of the back and plinth of the stele and enlivened by the lighter sound of jewelry tightly clinging to head, neck, body, and limbs.

The plastic group as a whole is set against the back slab. It hereby gains connectedness. Along the figure of the main deity, fully modeled in the round, the back of the slab is cut away sharply, and parallel to its outline. The open space between figure and background (pl. 11-31, 11-39, and 11-49) appears according to the fall of light or according to the color of the wall behind, as a light or dark zone; it accompanies the outline and heightens its sharpness, while at the same time, by way of contrast, it accentuates the intermingling play of light and shade on the richly carved surface of the slab. But these effects scarcely can be considered as calculated, for the images, standing in the dim light of the shrine, could not become visible with all their intricacies. The effect, however, is there, not as a purpose, but as an outcome of the surety with which contents, whether experienced or merely traditional, were visualized. In rare instances inspiration graced the craftsman; norm and inner experience then became one and produced the masterwork, greater than all rules, but greater also than the single artist. In spite of the absence of a purely aesthetic appreciation of artistic quality, it may have nevertheless helped some impressionable souls toward an easier approach of the deity.

The single works of sculpture, by no means individual, fall into groups, mainly dependent upon time, and but slightly influenced by local tradition.

The few sculptures of the seventh and eighth centuries, that are known hitherto, in their formal treatment lead from the preceding Gupta tradition toward the form in vogue under the rule of the Pālas (cf. pp. 207, 215). The latter is conspicuous (pl. 11-1), especially in the relief of Durgā. A tender modeling of heavy bodily forms is inherited from the last phase of Gupta sculpture. Derived from the same source are the equal compositional accents placed on the main as well as on the accompanying figures and also the increased amplitude and flexion of limbs so as to suggest mighty movement. But these factors in the course of time have become over-emphasized. The moonfaces with their full and short features, the curly wigs, and the clumsy and simple jewelry also are of the same origin. The stone images from Barakar, Burdwan, Bengal are shown, though later (eighth century), in restful attitudes, yet replete with that selfsame boldness of composition.[22] They also are great in conception. The peculiar plastic scroll on either side of the images at Barakar further corroborates the early date of these stelae (cf. the treatment of the scroll in the earlier temples of Bhubaneswar).

A plastic and physiognomical type like that of Vishnu, however, has all the charm of the unexpected (pl. 11-2). The soft modeling has become compressed into a thin surface. The outline is sharpened and the relief in clearly indicated planes is graduated into depth, whereas in the former example, modeled as one unit in the round, it was set against its background. The accents are placed on the linear effect. The single narrow and rounded fillets of the jewelry and the upavīta are sensitively emphasized. The flat and broad face with its pointed chin has the form of a betel leaf, the long makara-like eyes rise from the root of the nose to the temples. The modeling of the eye is based on the oblique cut, which makes the upper eyelid appear lowered in a sharp angle. It partly covers the large and bulging eye-apple. The mouth is pointed into triangular shape, with corners raised high into the cheeks. Both these facial types, that of the Vishnu as well as that of the Durgā sculpture, are favored during the following centuries.

Other sculptures that may be assigned to the early Pāla period (the

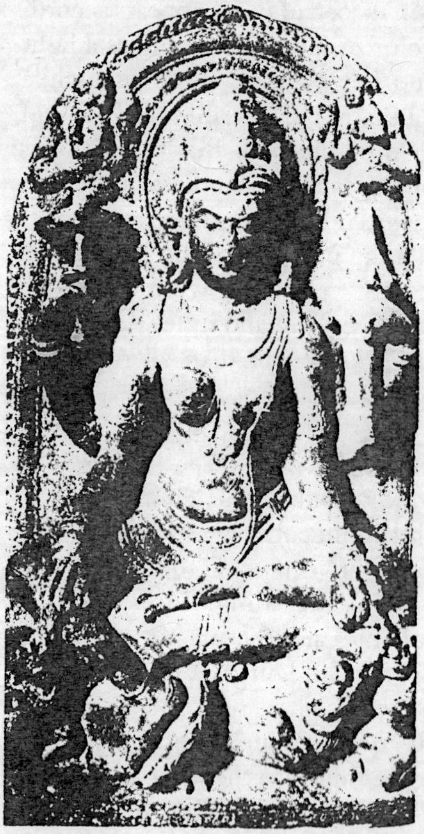

RIGHT: 11-18. Vāgīśvarī, A.D. 910 (inscription: in the first year of the rule of Gopāladeva); Nālandā, South Bihar (Indian Museum, Calcutta)

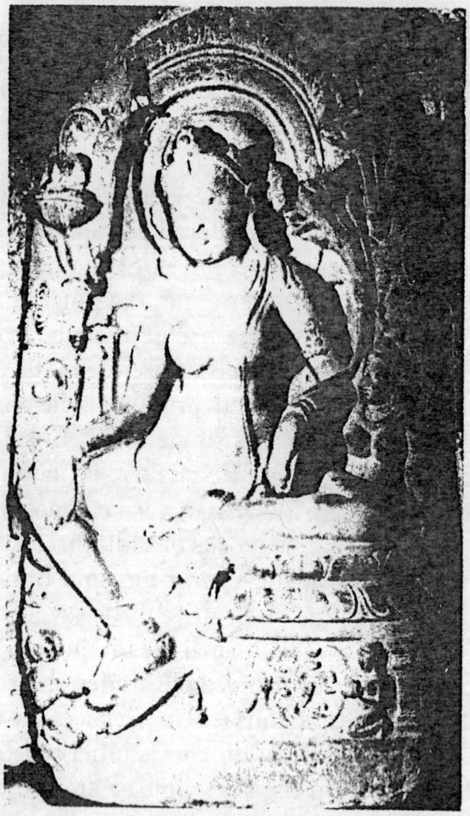

FAR RIGHT: 11-19. Śyāmā Tārā, beginning tenth century; East Bengal (Dacca Museum)

eighth century) maintain the thinned appearance of the relief, just described, while at the same time the single limbs appear more rounded, although stiffened (pls. 11-3 and 11-4).

From about A.D. 800 onward some dated images are the milestones of an uninterrupted evolution. It proceeds between two extremes (which entirely depend upon the modeling), whether endeavoring to do justice more to the matter of stone, "the abstract," or to the matter of flesh, "the realistic." In the beginning, for example, of the ninth century, fleshliness is more accentuated (pls. 11-7 & 11-8) and even within the more abstract type (pls. 11-9, 11-10), on the whole a relative softness is attained.

The beginning of the ninth century has bequeathed to us a number of images, especially some metal images found at Nālandā, some dated, others assignable to the reign of Devapāla. Compositions as that of Vishnu or the Avalokiteśvara group put into shade the work of the following generations.[23] An equal standard of artistic quality is reached again at the end of the development only under the Sena dynasty. The figures are modeled so as to suggest the soft texture of flesh and skin, an inheritance of the Gupta period. Yet they have become fuller and more earthly, their movements and expressions are supported, so to speak, by their well-being; sensuousness vibrates in their glances and in their limbs. Whether the figure is Brahmanic or Buddhist, Vishnu or Avalokiteśvara, the treatment is identical; it has Tantrism for its inspiration.[24]

Toward the middle of the century, the petrifying tendency increases however, and at the end of the century it ebbs down into mere extensiveness without zest and vigor. The stone images of the beginning of the ninth century, though they do not attain the high quality of the metal images, yet belong to the same form-complex (pls. 11-6, 11-7, 11-8, 11-9, 11-10, 11-28). In the stele of Sūryà (11-frontispiece), the plastic form appears as if embossed out of the surface, doing justice not to a cubical abstraction, but to an overemphasized fleshliness. This conception envelops the stele as a whole. For the latter is not articulated in an architectonic sense (pl. 11-6), but it is conceived altogether as if embossed (pl. 11-10) into rounded forms. The profiles of the three-lobed niche are of the same nature as the modeling of the Buddha figure, that is, widespread and of a sturdy heaviness. Minor devices joined with those swelling plastic masses at times have a capricious movement of their own. Thus stalks of lotuses and fluttering ends of bows are bent with pedantry (pl. 11-6 and frontispiece).

A stiffening of the fullness of the modeling and its becoming coagulated (pl. 11-11) denotes the work of a later generation, in the middle of the century. At this time also the stele becomes divided into three main portions, and this division for all the future becomes traditional. The pedestal is separated from the main group, the background, moreover, is made to consist of a lower portion suggesting the back of the throne proper, and an upper portion, with maṇḍala, kinnaras, and kinnarīs and manifold other motifs (pl. 11-15). At the same time the modeling becomes more flat, and a more slender ideal of bodily appearance is chosen (pls. 11-5, 11-11, 11-12, 11-14, 11-15, 11-48). Modeling finally, as well as composition, becomes rigid, governed by an architectonic discipline (pls. 11-16, 11-17). With this stage, the end of the century is reached. The plastic, whether it favors a more rounded or more flat modeling, a more weighty or a more slender bodily type, invariably connects elevation with elevation in an additive manner, without leading to synthetic unity, for the depressions are without plastic force or value (pls. 11-13, 11-16, 11-17, 11-20, 11-34–35).

This, within the fleshy type, makes the swelling masses appear of less articulate modeling (pl. 11-20), while in the more petrified type it resembles rounded pads, laid across the middle of the body, singly or doubly (pl. 11-17).

The evolution of the formal treatment is accompanied by a change and evolution of single devices. Certain motifs are leading at a certain period. This, however, does not exclude their full-fledged existence at an earlier or later period. From the surroundings in which they are found, the age may be assumed of the single sculptures.

The stele of the ninth century are rounded on the top. The outline varies from the rectangle with rounded corners (pl. 11-5) to the half round (pl. 11-9) and the slightly pointed half-round form (pls. 11-7, 11-10, 11-11, etc.). The border is either flat or slightly raised (pls. 11-5, 11-7, 11-9).

The garments, which in the main consist of shawl (uttarīya) and loincloth (paridhāna), have their folds indicated by schematic and parallel scratches or ridges with a diaper pattern of rosettes or of lozenge shapes[25] (pls. 11-8, 11-9, 11-16). The ornaments are heavy; the single motifs, lotus scrolls as a rule, are linked together in the shape of buckles or of triangles (purīta) (pls. 11-8, 11-14). Hairdress and headgear undergo considerable changes. Goddesses and gandharvas in the ninth century carry a flat-round chignon on the crown of the head, figures of Sūrya and Vishnu a kirītamukuṭa, of prismatic shape at times (pl. 11-5), higher already than in the eighth century, when it was more like a fez (pl. 11-4), and covered with lotus scrolls. Its height is still more emphasized when it approaches pyramidal shape (pl. 11-7). The jaṭāmukuṭa again, the high crown of matted hair distinguishes Śiva and other deities; it either looks like a high chignon or else it is heaped up into a pointed shape (pls. 11-28, 11-48). Toward the middle of the century, the single plaits are intertwined in loops and fastened together. Toward the end they cover the head like a cap (pl. 11-13). The Buddha figures of this century that do not wear crowns have their curly locks of hair frame the forehead in a double curve, and they show a pointed uṣṇīṣa (pl. 11-10) on the top of the head, whereas at times the locks covering skull and uṣṇīṣa are contracted into a kind of pointed cap that terminates into a flame. At the end of the century the uṣṇīṣa is more rounded (pl. 11-20).

The facial expression after the earlier part of the century maintains a comfortably mild peacefulness in keeping with the general artistic conception, that does not betray any exalted state of mind. A spiritual state of being is transferred into the stone with equanimity. Tradition guarantees calmness. But as nothing is being added and nothing enhanced, this tradition, heavy and inevitable, seems to weigh upon as well as to carry along every single work.

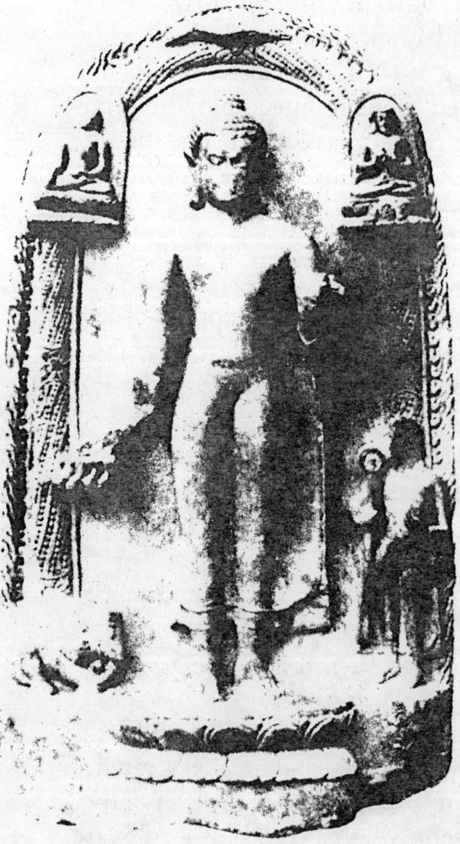

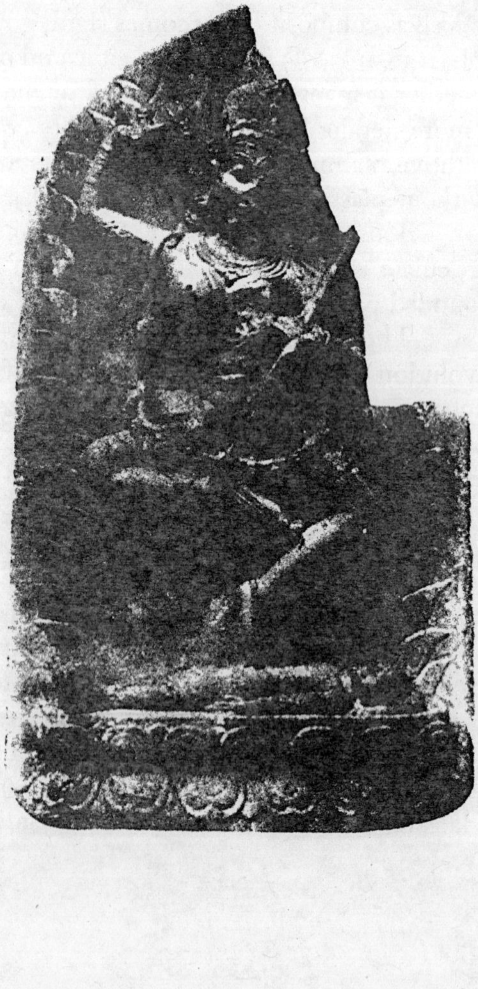

RIGHT: *11-20. Buddha taming the wild elephant, end of ninth century; Bihar (formerly: Collection Nahar, Calcutta)*

FAR RIGHT: *11-21. Nairātmā, beginning tenth century; Bihar (Indian Museum, Calcutta)*

Out of this calmness in the following period a new and mighty form arises. The tenth century starts with a powerful conception of the body, that in its wholeness is shaped with vigor (pl. 11-18). The additive manner of the preceding century is replaced by synthesis. A novel greatness lifts into significance the relief as a whole and every single part of it. The facial types in their features resemble those of the ninth century, but as a whole they are longer, although equally full as before. By this, the impression of massiveness is enhanced. The face is full of an earnestness that seems to have been condensed into pure and heavy matter.

This new conception on a grand scale subjects the slender bodily type too (pl. 11-23). At the beginning of the century a firm discipline of form prevails, with a slight tendency, however, toward petrifaction of the flesh (pls. 11-18, 11-21, 11-23, 11-24, 11-25). But this firmness is softened again, and the vigor is spread out into the surface in a sensuous and somewhat relaxed manner (pls. 11-19, 11-26, 11-29, 11-42). These significant preludes, however, are followed by a new impulse of great power, in the middle of the century, that seems to distend the figures from within (pls. 11-22, 11-27) and to mold them into high relief, so that the limbs are pregnant with a threatening movement. This high tide now

11-22. Aṣṭabhujapīta Mārīcī, middle tenth century; Nālandā, South Bihar

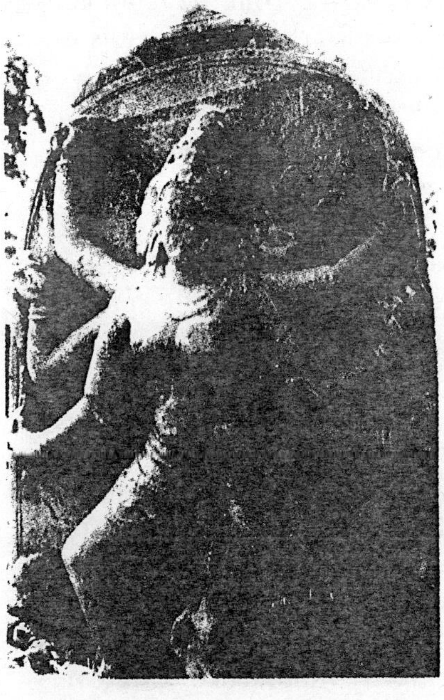

11-23. Sugatisandarsana Lokeśvara, beginning tenth century; Bihar (Indian Museum, Calcutta)

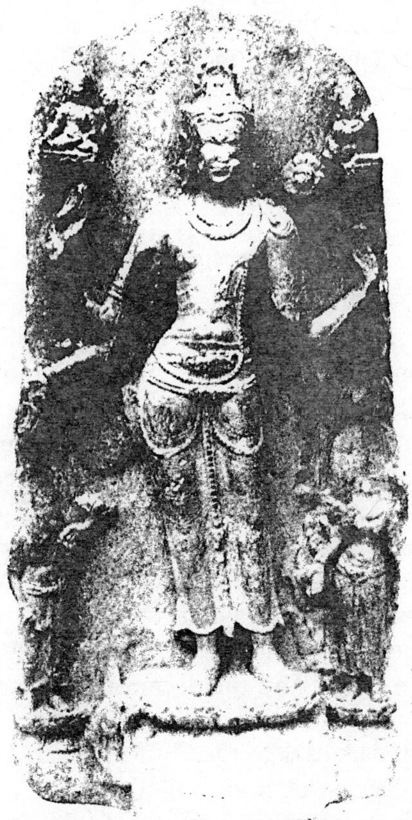

11-24. Vishnu Trivikrama, metal, beginning tenth century; Rangpur, North Bengal (Indian Museum, Calcutta)

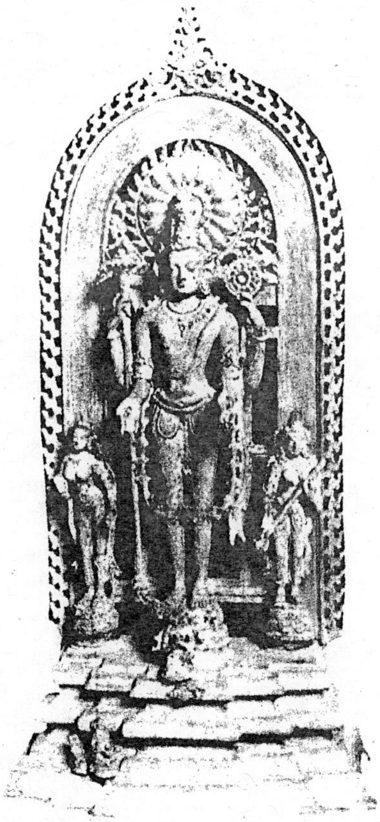

has reached its climax. The ending tenth and the beginning eleventh century see once more a stiffened outline (pl. II-30).

During the ninth century the petrifying tendency had seized the soft fleshliness more and more. This process of artistic hardening prepared the consolidated vigor of form in the tenth century. The latter equally does justice to the matter of stone and to that of flesh. At the beginning of the century it is unfolded in grandeur and dignity, while in the hands of the next generation it becomes weakened through the enjoyment of its own existence, whereas toward the middle of the century an added emphasis vitalizes it and enhances its own inherent strength beyond its limits. Stone and flesh are heaving into majestic roundness (pl. II-27) until finally the urging power relaxes, and the reaction sets in by forcing the stone into a stiffness of appearance, more rigid than ever.

The single motifs, up to the middle of the tenth century, did not undergo much change, except that the details of jewelry were more delicately chiseled. Toward the middle of the century, the kīrttimukha device occupies the top of the stele (pl. II-27) which formerly used to be decorated by a lotus flower if at all, or by different devices. Hairdress and crown have changed too; the chignon of the goddesses is placed further down the head; the pyramid of the kirītamukuṭa has grown more elaborate (pl. II-27); and the gandharvas now wear a pointed karaṇḍamukuṭa. The plaits of hair of the jaṭāmukuṭa now sometimes are horizontal, sometimes matted vertically and horizontally, while in some other instances they consist of single loops.

The beginning of the eleventh century takes over from the tenth century the broad vision, yet it makes it somewhat shallow and thin, and is not far from elegance and mannerisms. In pl. II-30 a stiffening of the legs may be traced. They seem to have abdicated all elasticity, even though placed in a posture suggestive of movement and in this way from below they seem to communicate the stiffness of stone to the body of the deity. In this manner, every image contains the rigidity of the stone in the columns of the legs, while the upper portion of the body is invested with blossoming flesh whereas the round and fleshy face is made the receptacle of an expression suggestively spiritual.

The solemn grandeur which characterized the tenth century gives way to a conscious gracefulness by the middle of the eleventh. The bodily type has become slender and its significance too has narrowed down (pls. II-31, II-32, II-33, II-51). At the same time, however, accessories are made more and more independent. The ornaments of the human figures and the motifs on the slab compared with the image itself, have an equal share in the effect of the stele, but frequently they surpass it by their spontaneous liveliness (pls. II-31, II-49). Soon they are on the way to become sumptuous and overladen; soon also the selfsame energy breaks through the postures and the limbs of the accompanying figures, while leaving that of the main deity untouched. An overexaggerated and bent posture scarcely seems able to contain all the exuberance (pls. II-49, II-50), and the decorative devices in the second half of the century reach a voluptuousness hitherto unknown. The motifs as well as their technical treatment date back to the Gupta period. The motif of the scroll is cut obliquely, with deep shade in its hollows, into one surface, which in its turn rises perpendicularly from another surface (pl. II-31), that of the ground, and is set into

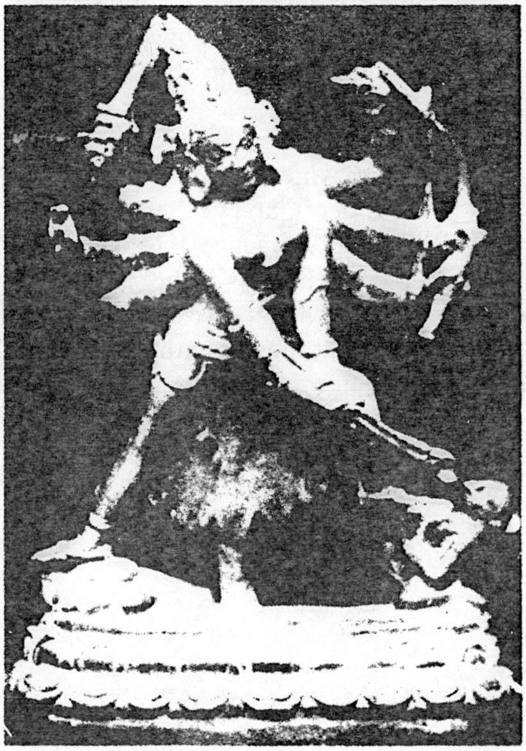

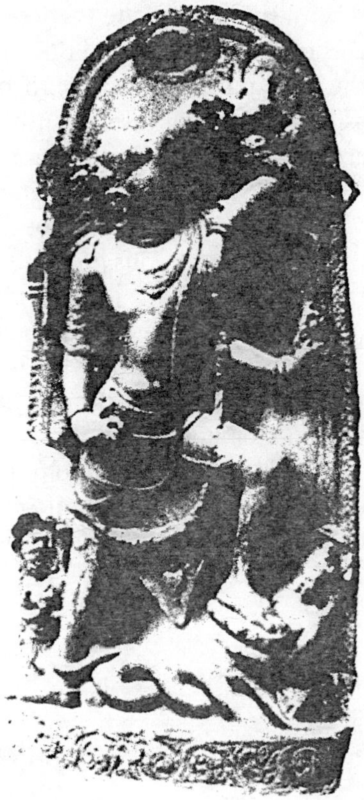

FAR LEFT: *11-25. Vāgīśvarī, metal, beginning tenth century; Vikrampur, Dacca, East Bengal (Rajshahi Museum)*

LEFT: *11-26. Varāha Avatāra, beginning tenth century; Bihar (Indian Museum, Calcutta)*

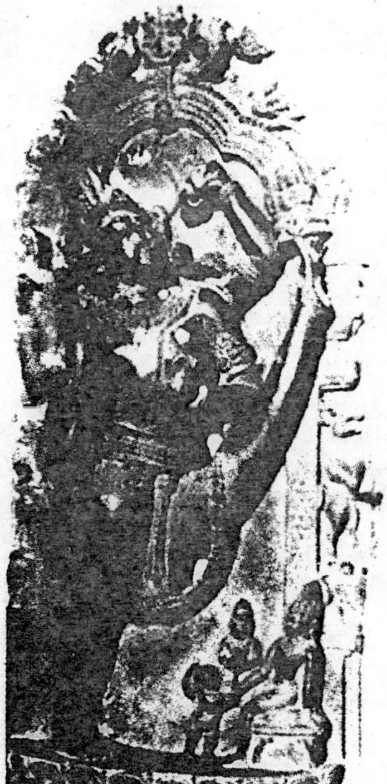

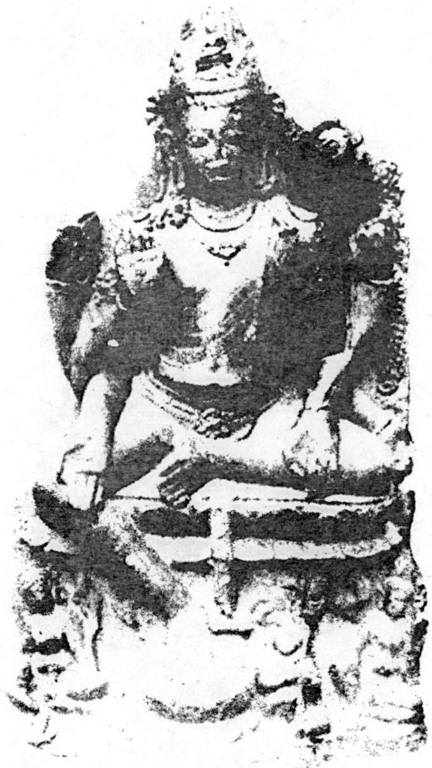

RIGHT: *11-27. Vishnu Trivikrama, middle tenth century; Bihar (Indian Museum, Calcutta)*

FAR RIGHT: *11-28. Lokeśvara (Pretasantarpita or Sugatisandarśana), beginning ninth century; Bargaon, Nālandā, South Bihar (Indian Museum, Calcutta)* contrast with the dark shade that covers the latter (cf. later pl. 11-36). Feathers of the tails of the kinnaras, and the curly breadth of the kīrttimukha mask consist of the same motif and fill the throne-slab. The stele of Sarasvatī shows the juxtaposition, typical of the eleventh century, of bodies modeled elegantly, yet in a stereotyped manner, and of a richly decorated slab.

The relative slightness and gracefulness of the sculptures of the eleventh century toward the end seem to become burdened by heaviness (pls. 11-43, 11-55). Once more a ponderous bodily type replaces the slender figure, yet despite the stereotyped rendering, it retains a vague loveliness. Independence of ornaments, the flexibility of the accompanying figures, and the richness of the slab keep on increasing. But this wealth is that of matter; it is not the visualized equivalent of a great force. It must be stated, therefore, that the eleventh century most spontaneously expresses itself in the rendering of the decoration, which plays about, round iconographic conventions. The facial type, too, is enriched by a novel note, full of sensitiveness and pliability. The cut of the eyes of all the faces, whether egg-shaped, moon-shaped, or in the shape of a

11-29. Gaṅgā, beginning tenth century; Iśvaripur, South Bengal

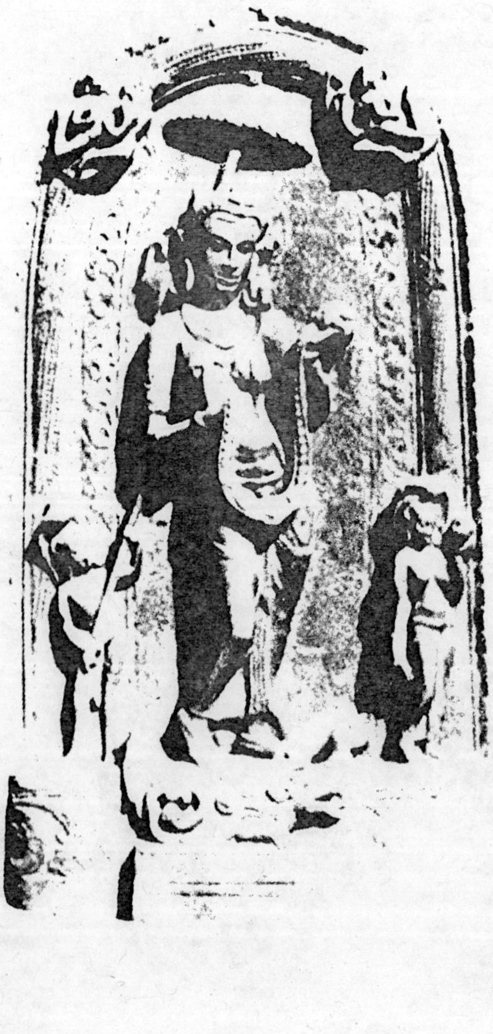

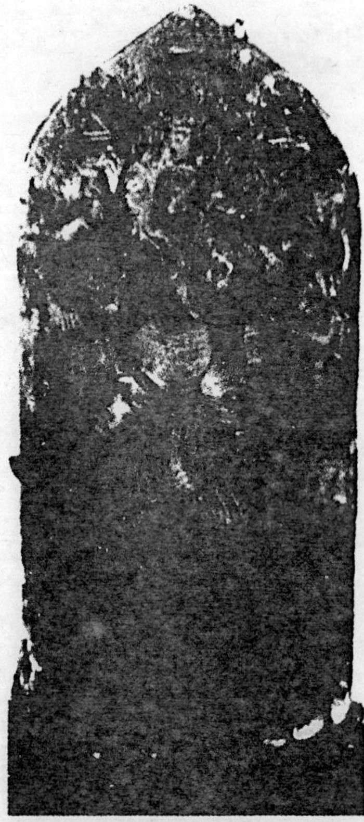

11-30. Aṣṭabhujapīta Mārīcī, beginning eleventh century; Bihar (Indian Museum, Calcutta)

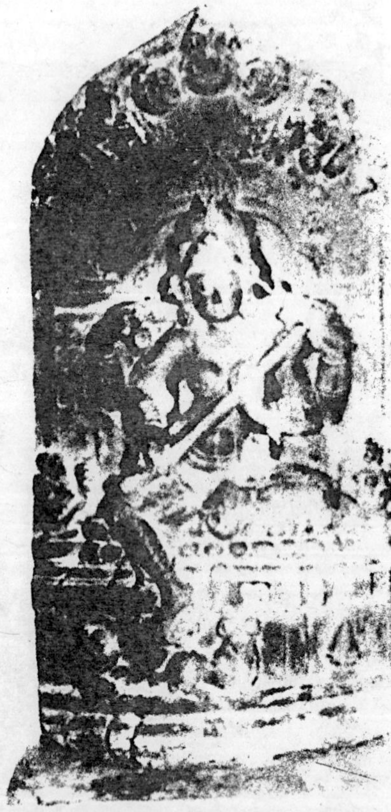

11-31. Sarasvatī, middle eleventh century; Chhatingram, Bogra, North Bengal (Rajshahi Museum)

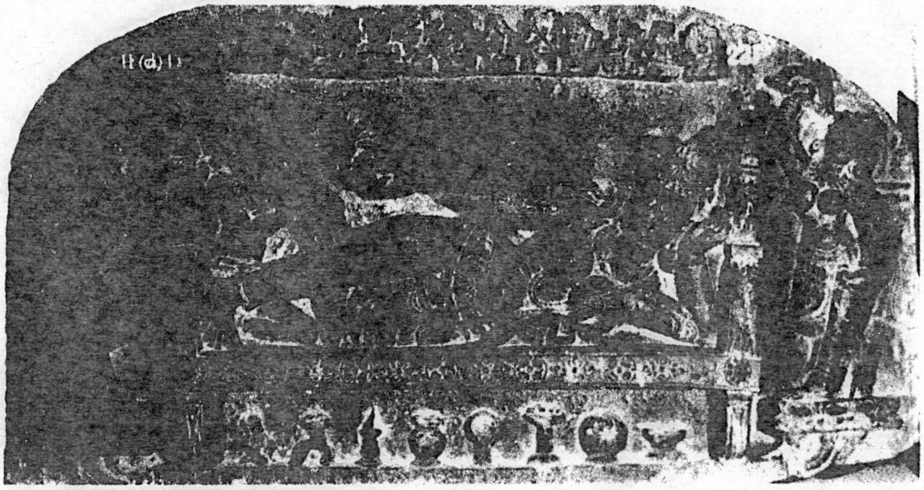

ABOVE: *11-32. Sadyojāta (?), middle eleventh century; Manda, Rajshahi, North Bengal (Rajshahi Museum)*

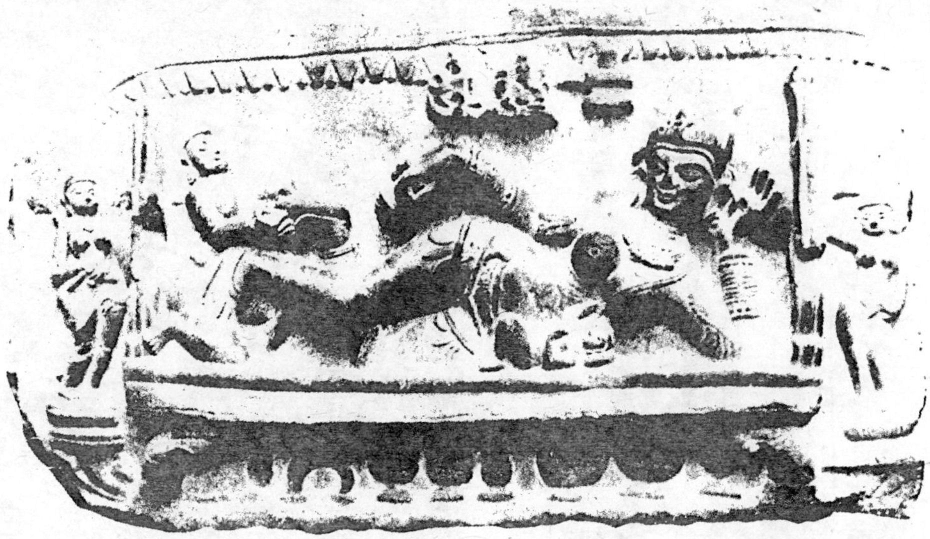

LEFT: *11-33. Sadyojāta (?), middle eleventh century; Tanor, Rajshahi, North Bengal (Rajshahi Museum)*

betel leaf, up to then had remained the same, varied only by iconographic prescriptions. Thus the images of Sūrya (11-frontispiece and pl. 11-4) have open and round eyes, whereas some other images are beautified by eyes long and with eyelids lowered, slightly modeled in oblique cut, and sharply set against the narrow slit of the bulging eye-apple (pls. 11-17, 11-23, 11-29, etc.). The eyebrows hitherto had been rounded bow-like (pls. 11-13, 11-16, 11-19, etc.); or else they sharply rose from the root of the nose to the temples (pls. 11-2, 11-17, etc.). But from now onwards these feeler-like brows become doubly curved, bending once more toward their outer ends (pl. 11-31). The upper eyelid, too, now is accentuated by an S-like curve drooping over the iris (pls. 11-30, 11-32) more emphatically than before (pls. 11-8, 11-16, etc.), a mannerism of the Eastern school suggestive of moist glances. The lips always full, whether lying horizontally (pls. 11-13, 11-20), or raised in a triangle (pls. 11-7, 11-2), are now once more bordered by a narrow ridgeline, a peculiar convention, in vogue already in the ninth century (pls. 11-30, 11-8), and to be traced back to the Kuṣāna period. Corresponding with these ridges, the folds of the garments are treated (pl.

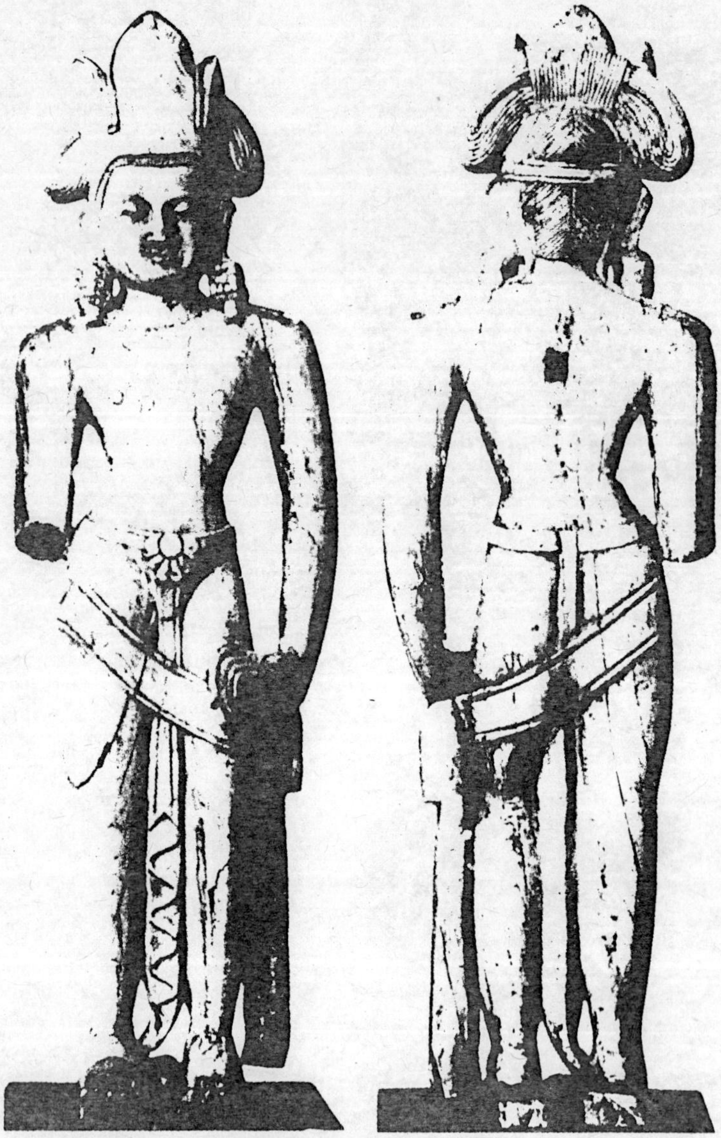

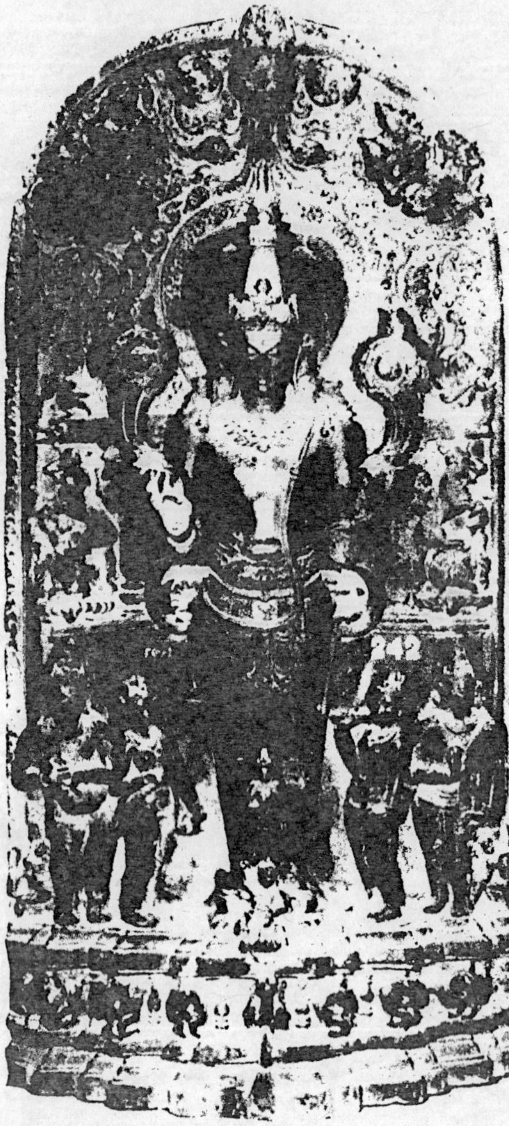

II-34–35. Ivory statuette, end ninth century (South Kensington Museum, London)

II-36. Sūrya, beginning twelfth century; Chopra, Rajshahi (Rajshahi Museum)

II-32). They are no longer incised as single or parallel lines, but are set as thin ridges against the modeling of the body.[26] This sensitive independence of the ridge-like line achieves its noblest results toward the end of the century, in the tenderness of the hem of the robe and the double curve of the feeler-brows of the Buddha image. Similarly, also the ornaments are further differentiated (pl. II-55). A necklace, for example, is dissolved into single pendants or flowers.

Toward the middle of the century the goddesses wear a flat and high chignon, either on the crown of the head or at the side and more backwards. At times the chignon on the crown of the head is quite flat or else in the shape of a gable (pl. II-32). But the latest fashion is a chignon of the shape of a mango or of a Phrygian cap, that either rests on the shoulder or projects from the back of the head (pls. II-31, II-49, the accompanying figures). The kirītamukuṭa now becomes cone shaped (pl. 11-51), while the very high jaṭāmukuṭa has plaits of hair undulating or intersecting in circles and crowned by a lotus flower. The gandharvas wear pointed karaṇḍamukuṭas with purītas, or "Phrygian" caps.

The trend of the sculptures at the end of the eleventh century is retained at the beginning of the twelfth century. The relief now generally occupies three planes (pls. 11-36, 11-41, 11-44, 11-53). The composition keeps on growing denser and denser on account of the multitude and heaviness of the accompanying details (pl. 11-36). By the middle of the century, however, a wave of creativeness, conspicuous by a spontaneous power of modeling, seems to be carried along by its own fullness (pls. 11-37, 11-46, 11-47). The high-relief of Gangā,[27] sculptured almost in the round, achieves a maximum of sumptuousness. The modeling, plump and tough and rippling, nevertheless yields a sharp and precise outline. But after this last climax there follows a final stagnation.

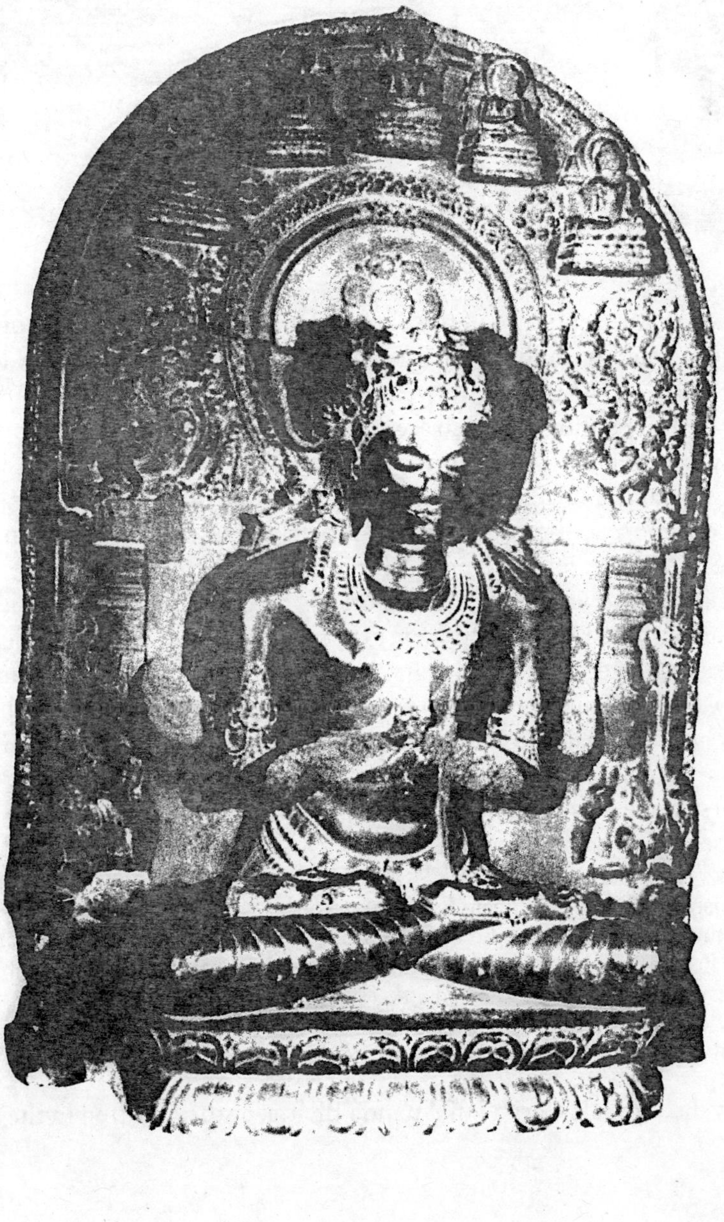

11-37. Ṣaḍakṣarī Lokeśvara, middle twelfth century; Colgong, Bhagalpur, South Bihar

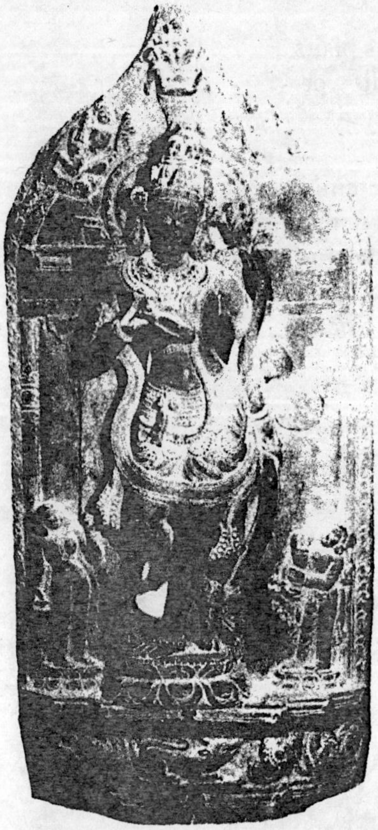 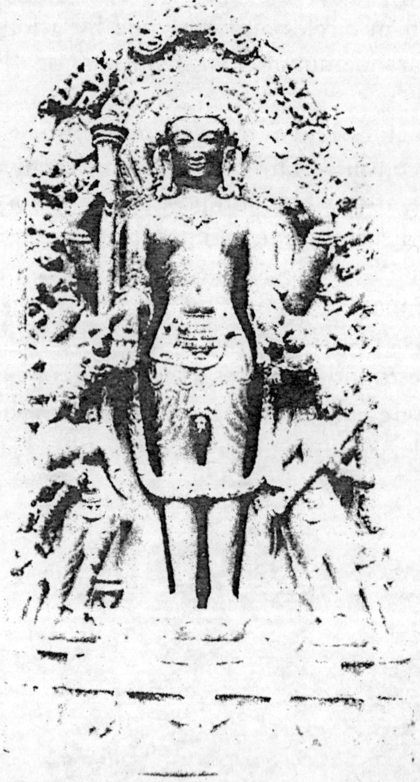 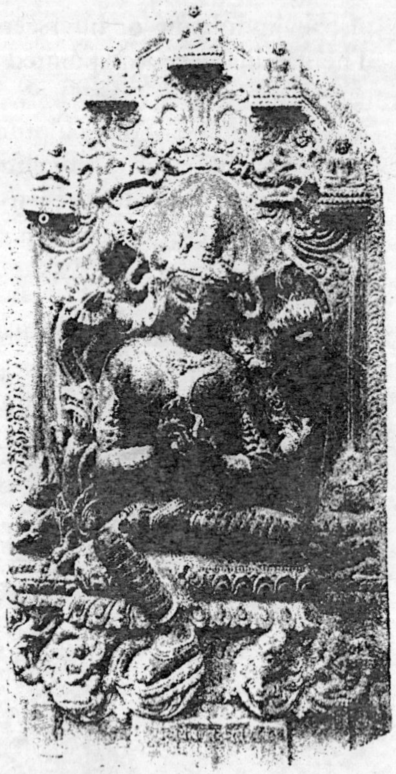

ABOVE LEFT: *11-38. Śaivite deity, end twelfth century; Padumshahar Tank, Deopara (Rajshahi Museum)*

ABOVE MIDDLE: *11-39. Vishnu Trivikrama, end twelfth century; Rajshahi, North Bengal (Rajshahi Museum)*

ABOVE RIGHT: *11-40. Khadiravanī Tārā, end twelfth century; Bihar (Indian Museum, Calcutta)*

Torpor seizes the sculpture of the Senas. Ornaments and folds, no longer artistically connected with the modeled body, rush over the image (pls. 11-38, 11-39, 11-40, 11-45, 11-52, 11-54). The movements of the accompanying figures, while exaggerated, are stiffened and so are the facial features. They are pointed, rigid, and drawn into length somehow. The architectonic threefold division of the back slab becomes effaced by a crowded disorder of clumsy scrolls. The volume grows more and more insipid and petrified. After the invasion of Islam, the little there was left of creative form died out, too.

Yet in spite of its lateness, the art of the Senas, which occupies the end of the eleventh and the twelfth century, represents the most significant phase of late eastern Indian sculpture. Its worldly exuberance lends an unexpected actuality to the religious theme. A stone inscription dating from the time of Vijayasena, found along with remarkable sculptures in the tank of Deopara in North Bengal, well evokes the attitude embodied in the sculptures. In the thirty-first verse of this memorial inscription, the poet Umāpatidhara describes the consecration of an image of Śiva:

> Instead of the elephant hide he gave (to the god) manifold garment of silk; instead of the enormous snake, he twisted round his breast a big chain of pearls; instead of ashes, he smeared his skin with sandalpaste; into his hands he placed a chain of sapphires instead of one made of seeds; the snakes he replaced by emeralds, the human bones by lovely ornaments of pearls. He decorated him so as to be agreeable to the wishes of him, who carries the skull at the time of the destruction of the world.

In the "Vallāla Carita" of Ānanda Bhatta, a story written in the sixteenth century but dealing with the Sena period, a sentence occurs: "When waving the caurīs while fanning, they discovered their armpits and looked as if their hands were in a dance." Similar in their mood are many Sena reliefs. The movement of the figures carries the entire charm. Strong bends are employed up to the last possibilities, until they seem to break in angles. But even in these figures, apparently so replete with movement, it is not of a transitory nature, but expresses a permanent attitude, exuberant in its tension.

It is possible that the lavishness of Sena sculpture was promoted by that of the Kannada country from where the dynasty came. A direct connection between southern and eastern Indian art may be seen in those colossal images that were found in the Sunderbands recently (cf. one head in possession of Mr. P. Tagore, Calcutta). But the animation of the Sena images boldly contrasts with the inert and overladen heaviness of Hoyśala sculpture. Its grace and sensuousness belong to eastern India.

The pliability of the body increases in the course of the artistic development. The standing posture, in the ninth century, was upright, or the weight was placed on one side only (11-frontispiece and pl. 11-5) and in exceptional

11-41. Betrothal of Śiva and Parvatī, beginning twelfth century; Chhatingram, Bogra, North Bengal (Rajshahi Museum)

11-42. Avalokiteśvara in the mountain cave, beginning tenth century; Kurkihar, Gaya, South Bihar

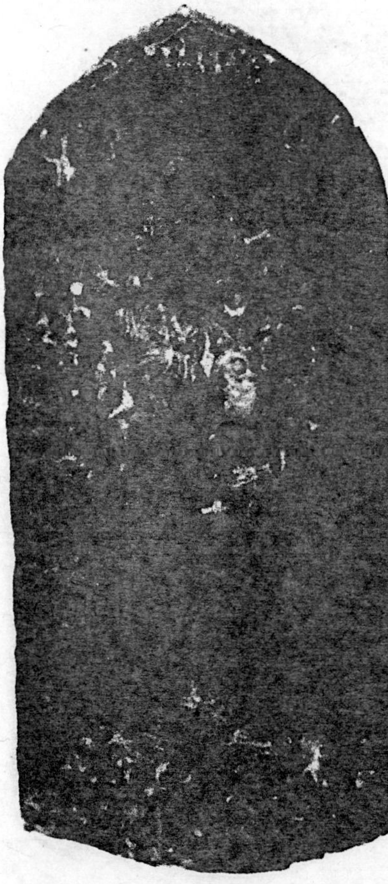

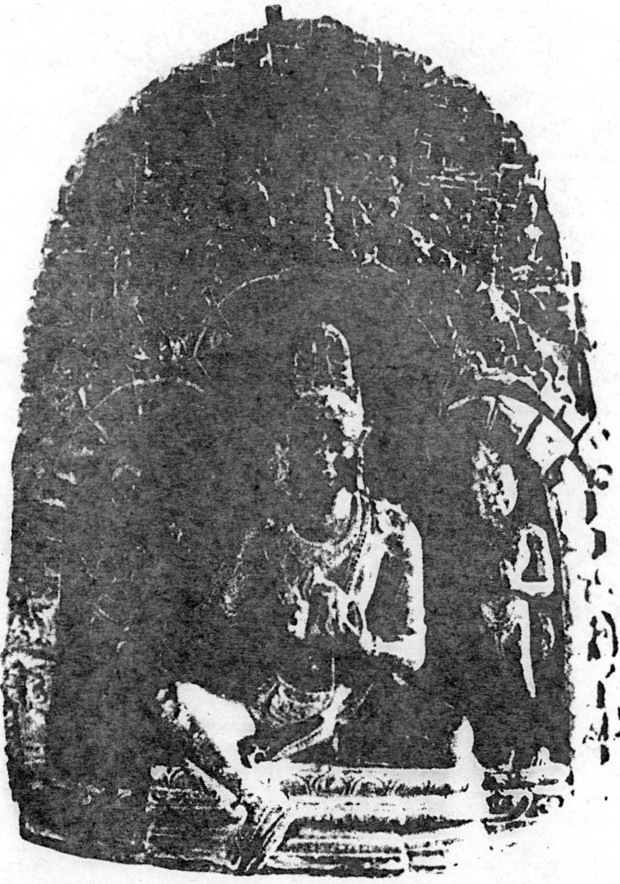

masterpieces (Avalokiteśvara, Nālandā) it was of the slightest tribhanga. This subtle threefold flexion and balance was taken up in the tenth century. The eleventh century gave greater amplitude to it until in the twelfth century the sway became extended to its utmost limits. In this manner the evolution from the slight to the overemphasized flexion keeps equal pace with the ever-increasing richness and liveliness of the ornamentation. It indicates the changing outlook of generations. The positions, on the other hand, of arms and legs, untouched by this evolution, throughout the centuries, by the sameness of their flexions and angles remain exponents of hierarchy, meditation, and grace. A singular exception to this is the attitude of sitting "ardhaparyanka," a pose of ease, which, in the tenth century becomes spread out into the surface, wider than usual (pl. 11-19). The treatment of the limbs themselves, of feet, arms, and hands, remains the same almost throughout the centuries. The degree of sensitiveness given to the fingers, slenderness or plumpness of limbs, depends upon the individual achievement of the workman. The legs, it is true, in the beginning of the ninth century, with carefully modeled knees (pls. 11-8, 11-9), give an impression of greater elasticity than those carved toward the end of the century and, later on, when they grow more and more into the likeness of columns, decorated by an incised round line, where the stiffly stretched knee has

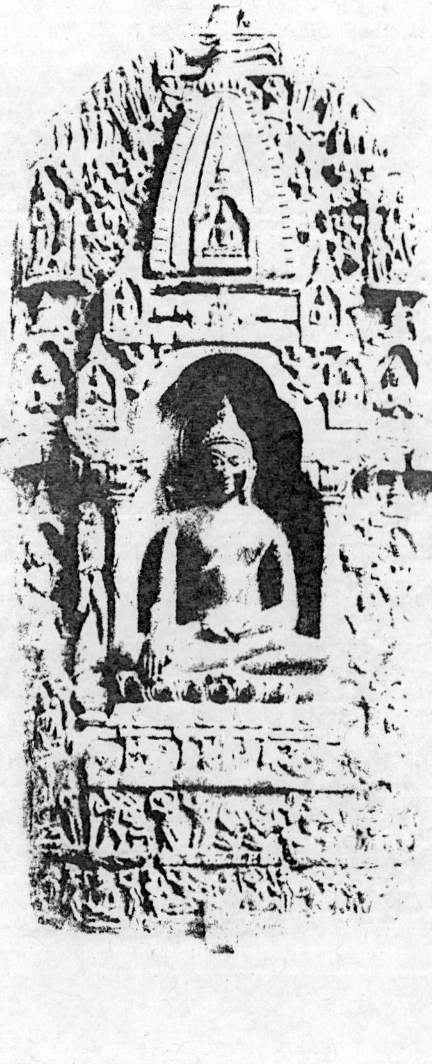

RIGHT: *11-43. Buddha calling the earth to witness, end eleventh century; Tetrawan, Patna, South Bihar (Indian Museum, Calcutta)*

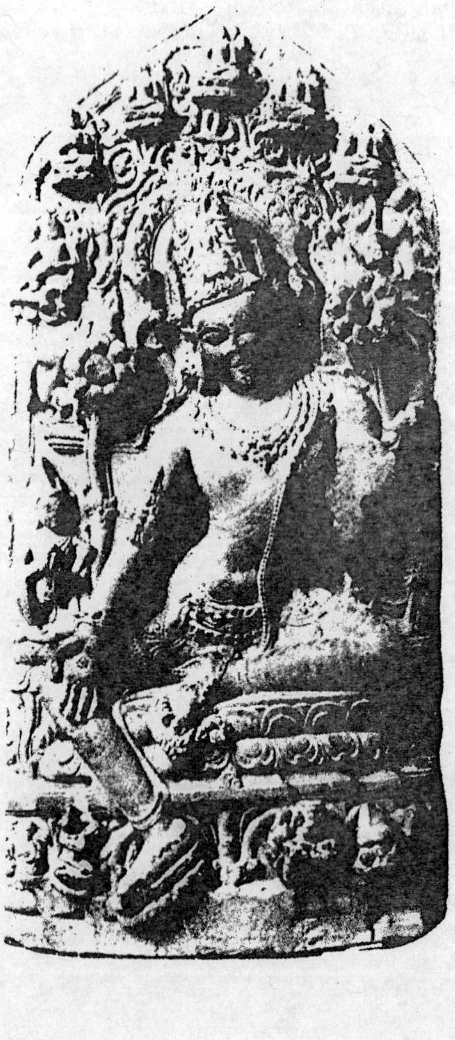

FAR RIGHT: *11-44. Lokanātha, beginning twelfth century, Bihar (Indian Museum, Calcutta)*

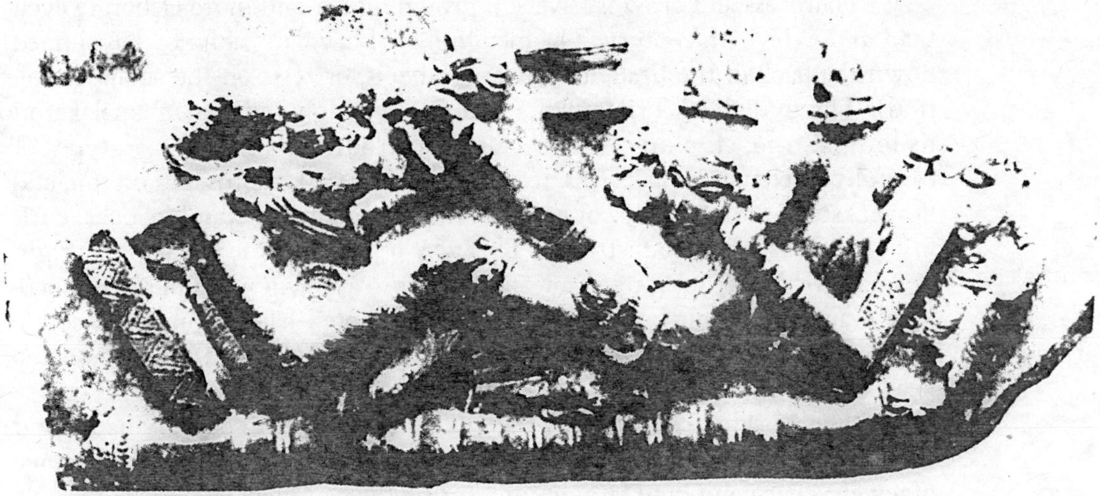

II-45. *Sadyojāta (?), end twelfth century (inscribed); Khetlal, Bogra, North Bengal (Rajshahi Museum)*

to be imagined (pl. II-20). Exceptions (pl. II-23) must be ascribed to a slow adoption or to an anticipation of the leading tradition.

Just as it is true generally that the treatment of arms and legs depends upon the quality of the work and not upon its age, the treatment of hems and ends of garments, too, remains unchanged up to the end of the eleventh century. It is left to the single craftsman, to make the hem of the garment straight, to place it in large undulations, to show it frizzled or to make it plain or folded. From the end of the eleventh century, however, a frizzly hem is favored. This is especially noticeable in the treatment of the uttarīya. Up to the end of the eleventh century, this shawl swayed in one great curve across the chest, or else it formed one undulation there (pls. II-27, II-28). But afterwards it becomes bordered by small waves, and the ends of the "drapery" are arranged in single plastic and parallel folds, of which the ends form a rounded zigzag. But by the middle of the twelfth century the uttarīya not only is frizzly, but its hem is frequently bordered with a narrow flounce. Even the loincloth at times shows such flounces (pl. II-45). Fluttering scarves in small undulations now accompany the figure on either side (pls. II-38, II-45, II-52, II-54).

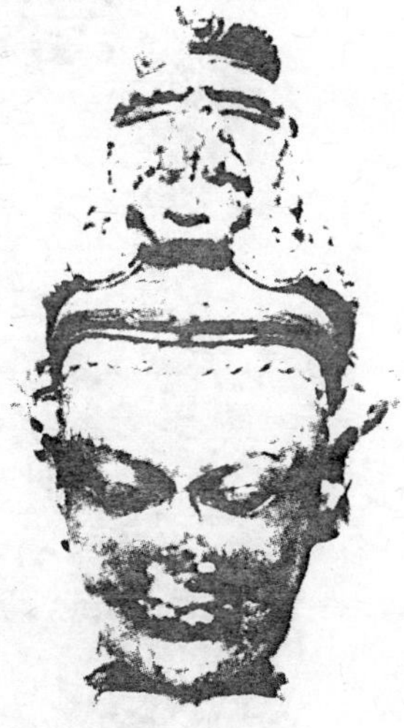

II-46. *Head of a colossal statue, middle twelfth century; Padumshahar Tank, Deopara, Rajshahi, North Bengal (Rajshahi Museum)*

The increased linear movement of the drapery and the profusion of ornaments no longer are connected organically with the figures. In a petty way they bustle over the body (pls. II-39, II-40, II-52). But whereas ornaments and accessories exaggerated to the utmost, and having become almost independent, degenerate into an effete scribble, the postures of some of the minor figures become replete with spontaneous movement (pls. II-40, II-45, Gandharvas and attendants respectively). An elementary experience, against all iconographic prescriptions, full of vigor and freshness, sets in at last, just before the final stagnation and only to be suffocated soon by the invasion of Islam. The facial type, too, of some female figures becomes individualized; not, however, by a portrait-like treatment, but by a closer approach to the actual type of women of the country, to which the artist belonged, than to an abstract scheme (pls. II-38, II-45, the companion figures). Even to the present day the round face with high cheekbones, a childlike chubby type, with some Mongolian admixture, frequently can be met with among the women of Bengal.

Hairdress and crowns have still grown higher and more elaborate even than in the eleventh century. The mango-like "Phrygian" chignon has slipped down the back of the head and towers above it, or rests on the shoulder (pl. 11-41). The pyramidal kirītamukuṭa is now very high and has an āmalaka on its top (pl. 11-36, cf. pl. 11-51). The jaṭāmukuṭa shows the accustomed types of carefully intertwined plaits (pls. 11-41, 11-44, 11-52, 11-53), a lotus bud on top, and flowers stuck into the loops of hair, but it is also embellished loose locks, curling capriciously and coquettishly. This way of dressing the hair has its origin in an ascetic habit, but is by no means inferior to any wig worn in the Rococo. The Gandharvas (pl. 11-38), as before, wear pointed karaṇḍamukuṭas, sometimes also a "Phrygian" chignon covered by a veil (pl. 11-41) as that on the head of Pārvatī.

The worldly trend, that by the middle of the twelfth century had found its expression in an enhancement of movement, in the frivolous exuberance of jewelry, garments, and fashions of wearing the hair, may be noticed to some extent in the facial expression, too. Although under the doubly curved feeler-like brows the lotus-eyes remain unchanged, the voluptuous and curly lips, triangular generally in outline and smiling, transform the general expression;

11-47. Garuḍa, middle twelfth century; Malda, North Bengal (Rajshahi Museum)

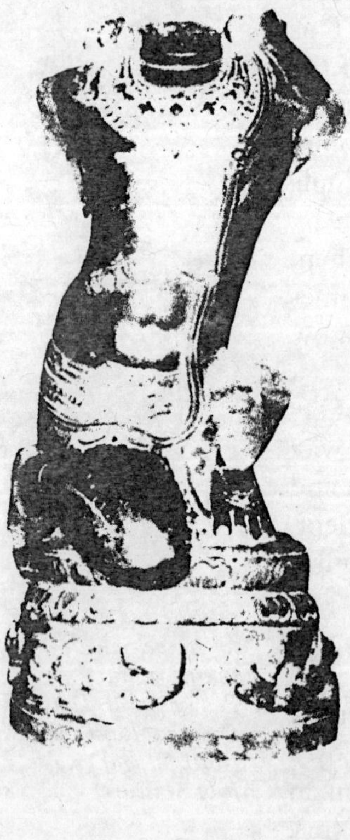

11-48. Avalokiteśvara, middle ninth century; Bihar (Indian Museum, Calcutta)

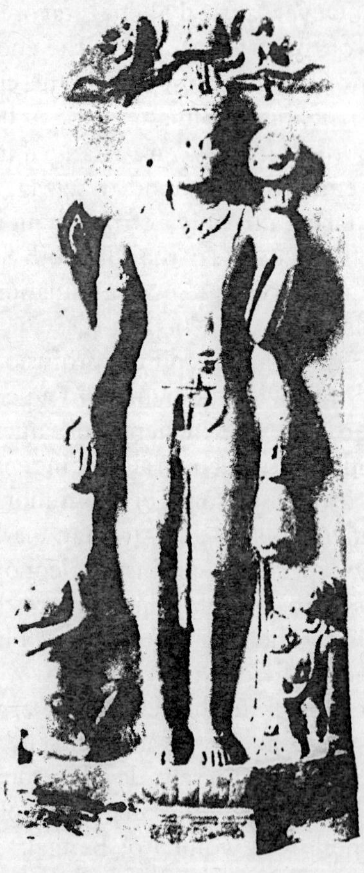

11-49. Vishnu Śrīdhara, middle eleventh century; Murshidabad, South Bengal (formerly: Collection Nahar, Calcutta)

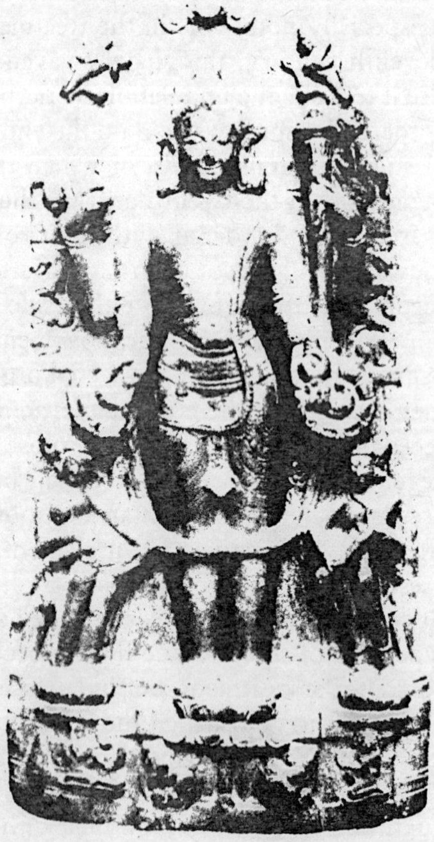

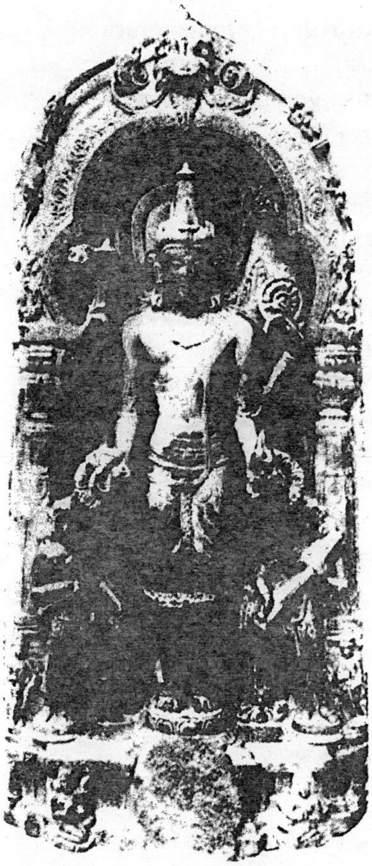

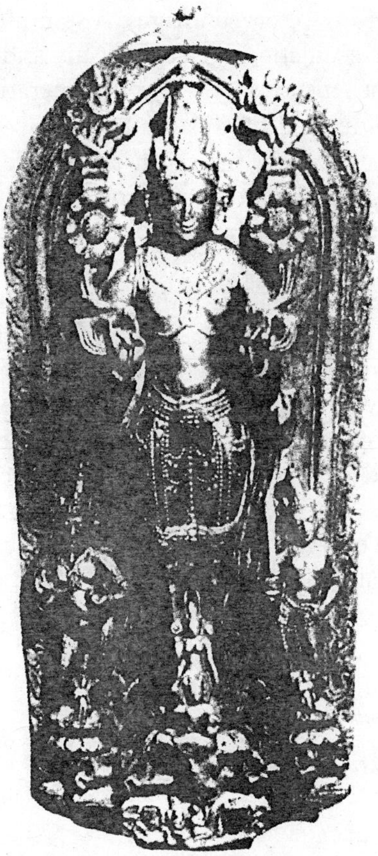

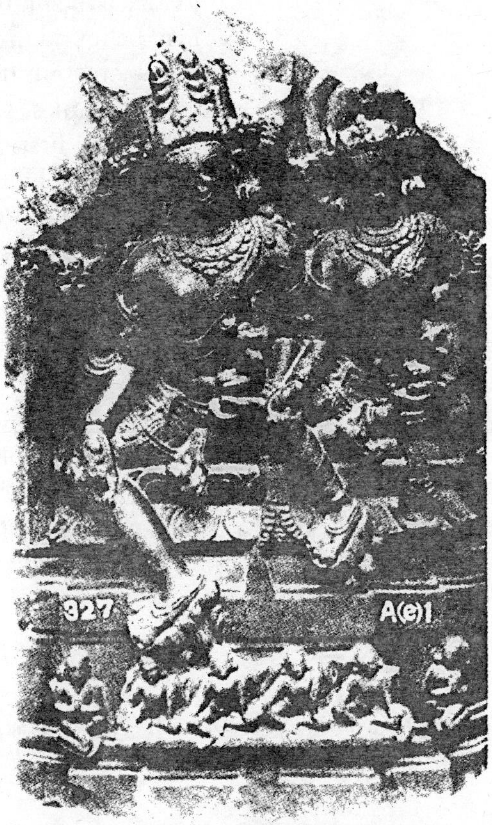

ABOVE LEFT: *11-50. Vishnu Trivikrama of unknown provenance, middle eleventh century (Indian Museum, Calcutta)*

ABOVE MIDDLE: *11-51. Sūrya, middle eleventh century; Katalipara, Faridpur, South Bengal (Bangiya Sahitya Parishad Museum, Calcutta)*

ABOVE RIGHT: *11-52. Hāritī and Vaiśravana, second half twelfth century; Deopara, Rajshahi, North Bengal (Rajshahi Museum)*

in the first half of the century it had been that of meditation, of listening to the depth of one's own being, whereas afterwards the smile becomes covered with the dew of contemplative enjoyment.

The art of the Senas culminates in the sculptures that were found in the tank of Deopara in North Bengal. It has to be assumed that an especially gifted artist who justifies the fame of the school of Varendra, to which Tāranātha refers, was at work there with his pupils. But at present it is impossible to point to certain centers of art with an outspoken tradition of their own. The reason is that to the vast material already known, many novel finds are constantly adding new information—the recent excavations at Paharpur for instance, or the find of sixty-five metal images at Jhewari, Chittagong, of which the bulk belongs to the tenth century and is peculiar through its "Burmese" features, whereas other earlier "bronzes" recall the style of Sarnath and of Nālandā; the individual craftsmen moreover just as the individual sculptures migrated from their centers to different destinations.

Some images, as the stelae of Vishnu and of Sūrya (pl. 11-51) have exceptional features, such as the angularity of the linear composition; but it is impossible at present to decide whether this is a local variety or a peculiarity belonging to a tradition of which examples may be found later on in other districts.

The sculpture of the Pāla and Sena period does not belong to the greatest moments of Indian art. Its merit lies in the local and chronological continuity of a large number of preserved images. A summing up of its entire evolution may be found in the oscillation between fleshly and abstract form, so that even the abstraction has a sensuous basis. From generation to generation, this process continues, safeguarded by a carefully followed tradition.

The first generation of the ninth century lends softly sensuous bodies to its deities. During the second generation, these stiffen, and during the third become still more severe and abstract, until at the beginning of the tenth century a new reality is given to the stiffened mass, the abstract treatment of which is replaced by a livelier form. With this transformation, the next two generations are engaged. The evolution in the ninth century leads from the reality of the flesh to that of abstraction. The tenth century achieves a ponderous, sensuous grandeur. The eleventh century in its turn works in a downward direction; it values cool regularity over the sensuous wealth of form, but in its second and third generation the sensuous perception grows strong once more, and celebrates its final triumph in the twelfth century. But for a short time only, for at the end of the century there are clear signs of the approaching end, with its inevitable rigidity.

11-53. Umā-Maheśvara, twelfth century (inscribed); South Bengal (Dacca Museum)

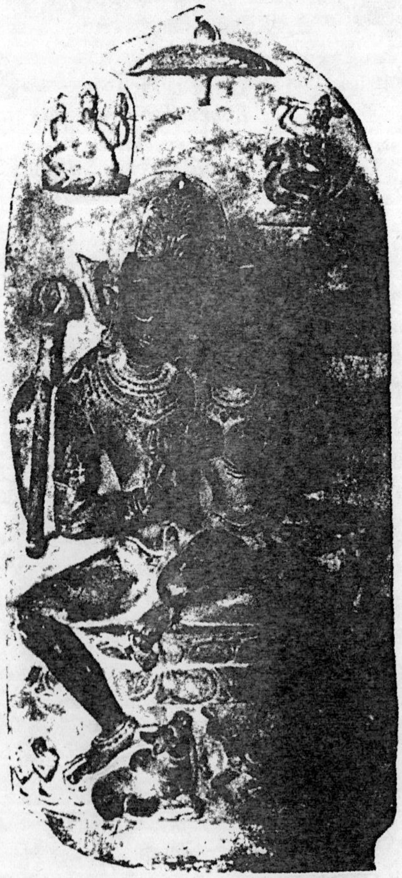

11-54. Jambhala, end twelfth century (inscribed on pedestal); Ghasikundi (Indian Museum, Calcutta)

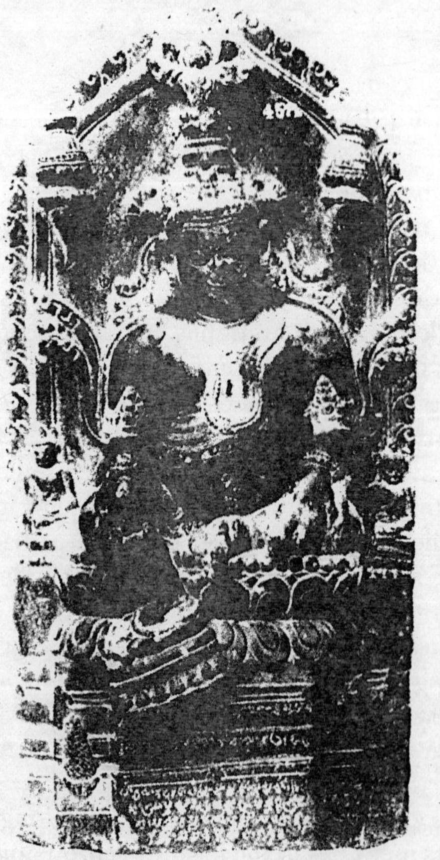

11-55. Jambhala, end eleventh century; Vikrampur, Dacca, East Bengal

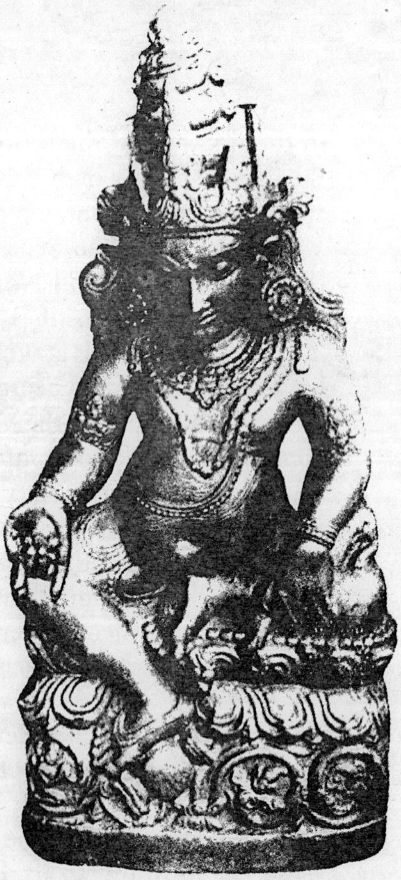

12 Candella Sculpture: Khajuraho

The stone, from which the temples of Khajuraho are made is a very finely grained sandstone ranging from a creamy buff to a deep golden hue. It comes from quarries in the area of Panna, not far from Chhatarpur, the site in Madhya Pradesh where the temples are located. Texture and color of the stone give warmth and fullness to the modeled surface. It is smooth where the stone is not weathered. Evenness of surface texture is one of the qualities on which the Indian craftsman insists throughout. The high polish so conspicuous in Mauryan sculpture is one of its extreme applications. Elsewhere, and especially in the caves, where the stone is porous by nature and cannot yield an even surface, this was coated with plaster and was painted.[1] The Khajuraho sculptures, too, are not free from traces of plastering. This appears to be modern. But even as a misuse it confirms a practice.

To make the surface smooth means that it was altogether mastered and that nothing was left to the accidents of the material. At times in Khajuraho, it was worked almost to a polished condition (pl. 12-9), but as a rule it was left in a condition where it absorbs, instead of reflects, the light. It appears luminous and warm.

On temple walls in the light of day or in the twilight of the interior, irradiated by such sun rays as pierce it, more or less clearly discernible or lost in an overwhelming number or dim and even invisible in some recess or nook are the single sculptures. The most negative aspect of their appearance, that they may be invisible, reveals that they are not so much meant to be seen as known to be there. A preconceived order, and an inexhaustible supply of form and figure are taken for granted by the devotee. Nothing is left to chance, and there is no room for surprise.

But with all this subordination under a given scheme, the single sculp-

This essay first appeared in *JISOA* 1 (Dec. 1933):129–47, and is reprinted by permission.

tures are of varied trends, and their coexistence and intermingling result in a highly strung form. Each sculpture, though part of the whole, is but a soliloquy that none need hear. It does not address itself to anyone and acts its part, because it is there.

The validity of set rules and the contributions of partly heterogeneous ethnical components[2] may be considered as given conditions. The stability upheld by the former and the tension brought about by the latter are the basis on which the peculiarly Candella-type of sculpture is formed: More complex than any other school, it is more subtle than most of them.

In it the animal is of importance (pl. 12-2). Modeled with taut economy, within curves that dilate upon a comprehensive sweep, the grandeur is acknowledged of lion, bull, or rat. These colossal animals—the rat is more than a yard long—are vāhanas, but they carry neither Durgā, Śiva, nor Gaṇeśa; unencumbered by any rider as in ancient Indian sculpture, their presence suggests that of divinity. But no longer does it "convey," that is, contain it, but refers to it. The reference is one of intent. Intent with lurking curves on something outside itself, submissive with placid bulk to the object of its intent, it postulates and creates a distance around itself oriented in the direction of its head, the meeting point of its curves, a distance which is not space or of any definite extension, but it is bound up centrifugally with the power in view of which the animal exists, while centripetally it is laid round the animal, an intangible taboo. Actually, however, its statue was placed either in a pavilion by itself (Nandī), or in a porch (lion), either supported by widely set pillars or else it stood right in the open (other lions).[3]

The figure of the animal and colossal statuary in the round belong together in these instances. So they did in Mauryan art, either the outcome of a readiness to become form, more ancient than the other and widespread version where vegetative connectedness binds form to surface. Yet the vegetative

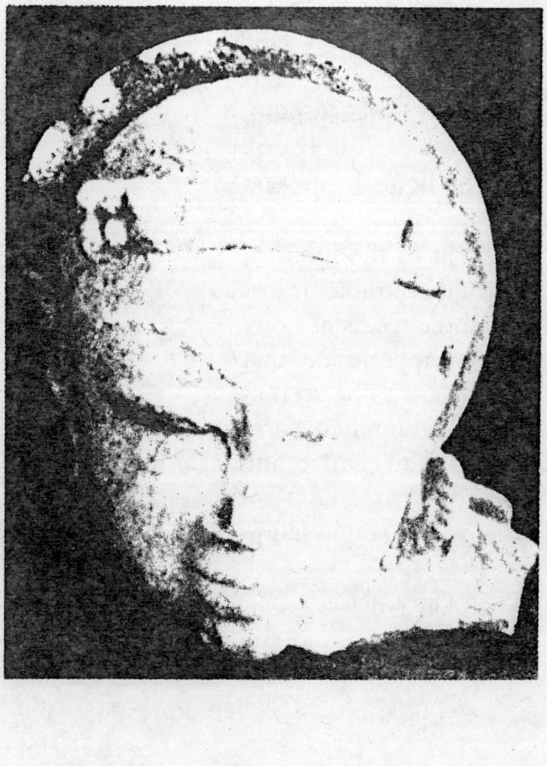

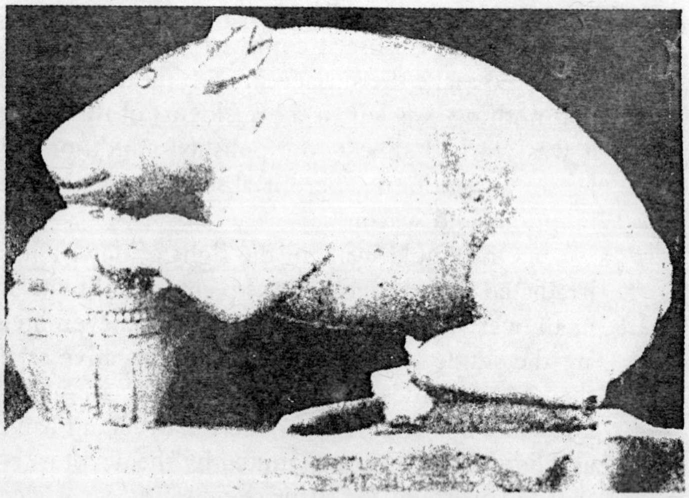

LEFT: 12-1. *Head of Nirṛiti (?). Private collection. The tightly fitting hair and the halo-like rim occur on figures of Nirṛiti, in situ.*

ABOVE: 12-2. *Muṣaka-vāhana; Khajuraho (Khajuraho Museum)*

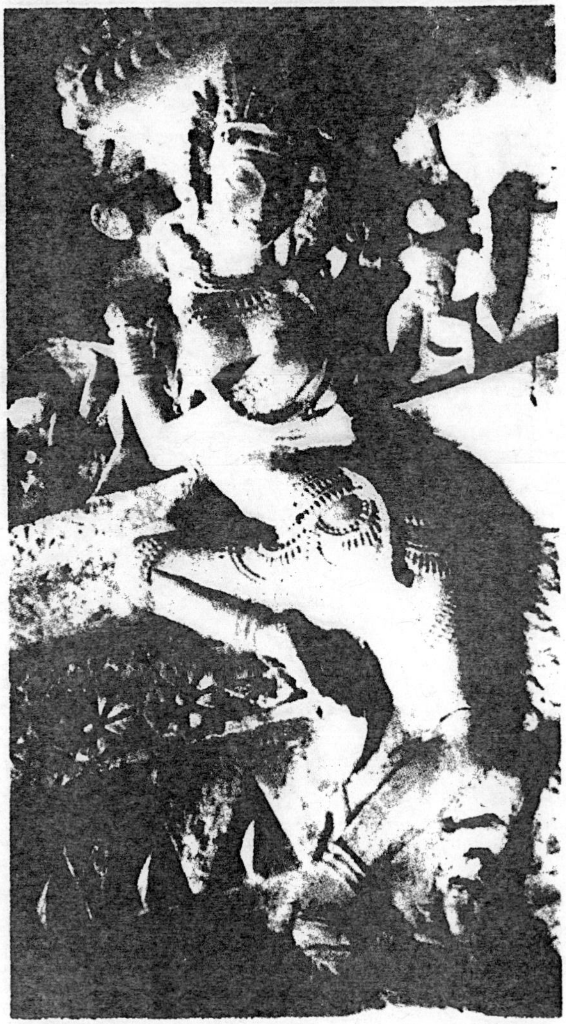

12-3. Bracket figure, in maṇḍapam of Dūladeo Temple. Although this temple has no dated inscription, its sculptures appear considerably posterior to those of the Lakṣmaṇa Temple but also to those from the Viśvanātha Temple dated A.D. *1002.*

aspect too is there in the animals of Candella sculpture. It is in the gliding modeling that knows of flux and transformation and smooths the particulars of the specific shape. It is carried and confined by curves of which the unbroken roundness is the linear equivalent to the modeled summary of the animal body, but at times these curves are as if caught by an invisible grip (for instance, the hindlegs). The latter is not rooted in the vegetative but belongs to the medieval factor. That moreover a lotus-petaled bowl is added, heaped with balls of sweetmeat, on which a trustworthy guardian, the rat, rests paws and jaw, is not only a device to make the mass of the sculpture more compact and to lead the curve of the profile down to the rectangular pedestal, but it makes more living the reference to Gaṇeśa in the expectation of which the rat dwells.

A lasting state of expectant submissiveness is embodied in animal shape, and this is formed in keeping with a doubly rooted tradition of modeling into which has entered, in this case, an arresting element. But never are the animals humanized.

Intent, a line that is slowly bent with force pent up and to such a degree that it seems to stagnate at times in angles, a darting weightiness of the mass which comes down with the heavy thump of a pestle (pl. 12-3) are peculiar to one aspect or component of Candella form. Though the line has no speed,

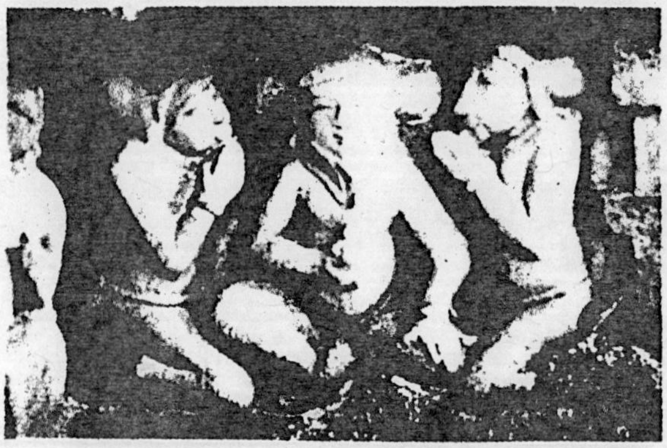

12-4. Ṛṣi with chelas, on back wall of Citragupta Temple. Frequently with ṛṣi figure in Khajuraho are the two lateral chignons at the back of the head. Such and similar architectonic reliefs—invariably on a relatively small scale and frequently belonging to a series of similar panels—are flanked by pilasters (see pl. 12-11).

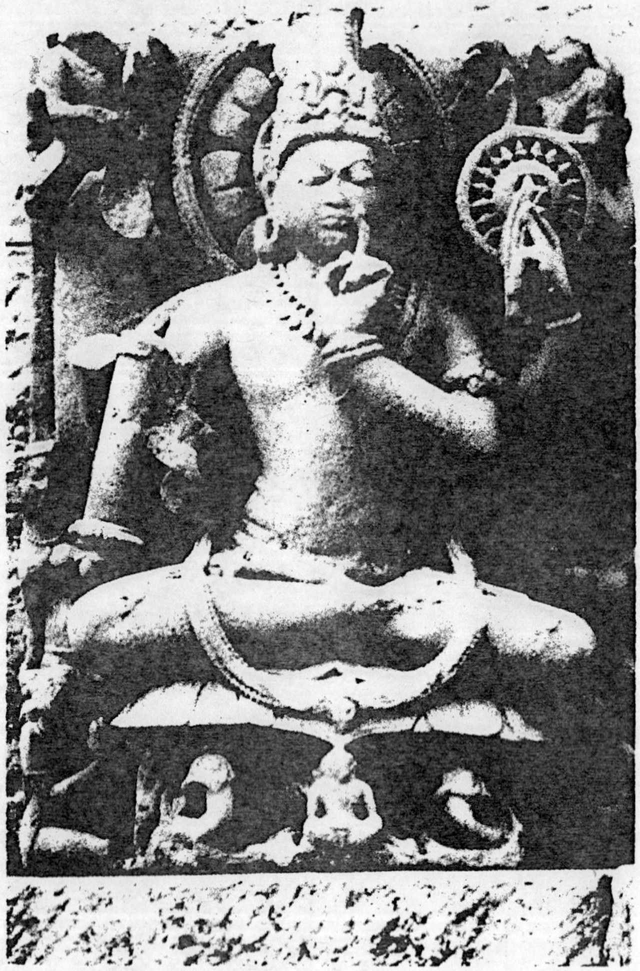

12-5. Vishnu; Khajuraho (Khajuraho Museum). The stele has been cut away on three sides. Vishnu is shown with the forefinger of his main left hand raised to the height of the lips, a gesture not recorded in any of the varieties of the Vishnu image, nor am I aware of any literary references to the hand raised as if indicating silence, as if Vishnu were shown as mauna-vratin. The usual accompanying figures, relatively large figures of donors, with añjali mūdrā to either side of the pedestal, Garuḍa in its center. The lotus scroll consists in Candella ornamentation mainly of stalks in full relief (contrast the version in Pāla-Sena sculpture), smooth or either knotty in more detailed examples.

it has determination and is decisive. The movement solely inheres in the mass. It depends upon the prevalence of the determined directedness or else of the heaving and living quality of the mass, whether angular intentness or reticence and a stagnating modeling (pls. 12–3, 12–4) or a thoroughly melting modeling result (pl. 12-5). The poles lie wide apart and solutions as those of pls. 12-4 and 12-12 seem incompatible.

Nowhere else in medieval Indian sculpture is the discrepancy so considerable between a twofold plastic treatment. The one is purposive, it has a direction toward something outside itself. This must not be misunderstood. The movements, that is, the actions of limbs and bodies, may be identical in both the types, and so they need not be taken into account in this connection. The purposive and directed mass movement squeezes out of the mass all that is surging and welling up from within. The heaving and as if breathing modeling is silenced in its vibrations, and its subtleties are ousted. The plastic mass tightens, and darts, heavy with its smoothed bulk. The other treatment makes the mass appear at rest while it is brought about by the process that builds it up from within. The latter is the manner traditional with "classical Indian" sculpture and is alive in Candella sculpture, too. There its particular version is one of spreading softness (pls. 12-1, 12-5, 12-12). Intent angularity against the swelling curve, stagnant hardness against vibrating softness, and along with these, outward directedness against repose within, will against being; such is the dual position.

Not always is the treatment as extreme in one sense as, for instance, in pl. 12-4. But even there the hard and directed version cannot wholly be without the other, that is, without the "classical Indian." The two celas have their arms, legs, and faces fitted into a zigzag pattern held symmetrically by the scales of attention situated between their eyes and uplifted hands, the latter directed toward the index, that is, the steadiness of the guru's absorption. The intent angularity of tubular limbs, the pointedness not only of the linear composition but of the facial features too are the more forceful because they seem as if held back by, while yet they break forth, from a widely curved cheek and bodies heavy with a roundness as if of strangely shaped bags of cement. This holding back corresponds to an expression of reserved beseeching and to a meditative surrender full of expectation. Spiritual absorption and plastic poise are in the central figure of the ṛṣi only. Either is negligible in this compo-

12-6. Tīrthaṁkara Dharmanātha, image in outside shrine on wall of Parśvanātha Temple. Siṁhāsana; the sthitāsanā marked with vajra and festoons on cloth. Peculiar are the elephants on console-like pilasters and the edge of the stele, altogether dissolved into figure.

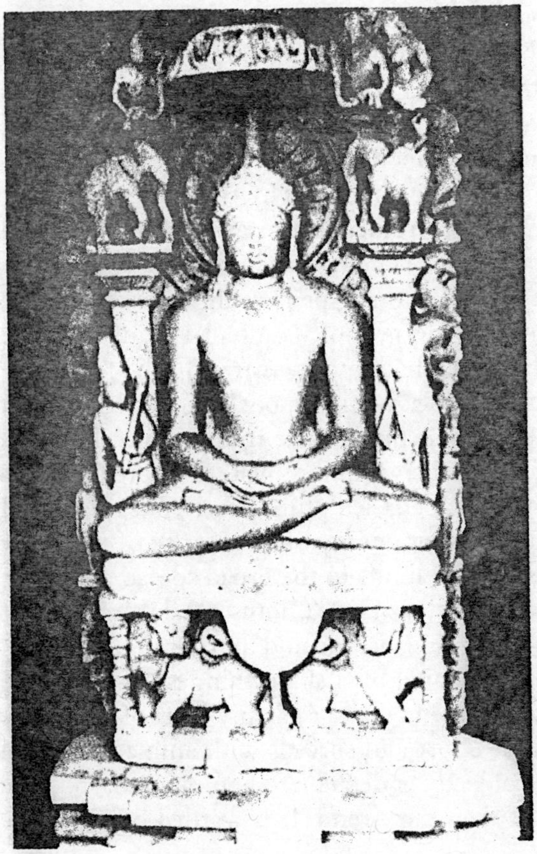

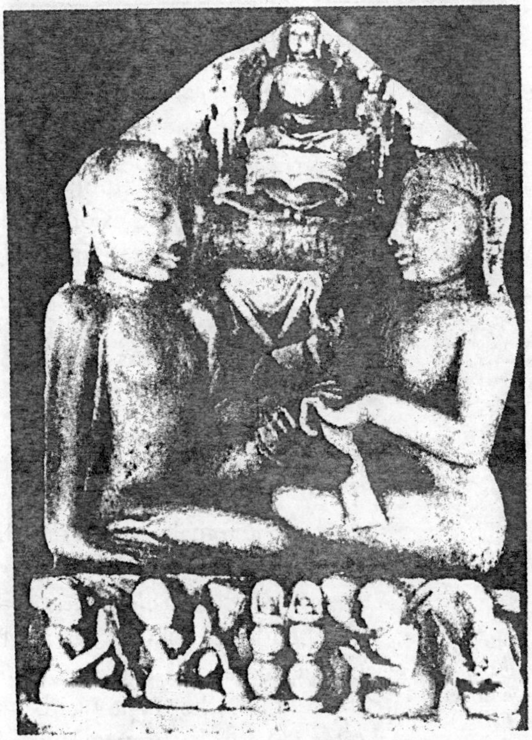

12-7. Conversation between two ācāryas. Set into a modern wall, Śantinātha Temple; plaster partly covers the upper part of the slab.

The discoursing ācārya on the right holds a palm leaf manuscript in his left hand. Between the two a tripod, on top a Tīrthaṁkara and two attendants. The pedestal shows four women disciples.

The two trends are embodied in this relief. Without the "medieval," the rigor of the right arm of the figure on the left would be impossible; this also applies to the simplified shapes into which plastic mass is packed and to the sharp angles of the facial profiles, the lips, etc. Without the "classical," the surging of the graded relief into globular elevations would also not be possible.

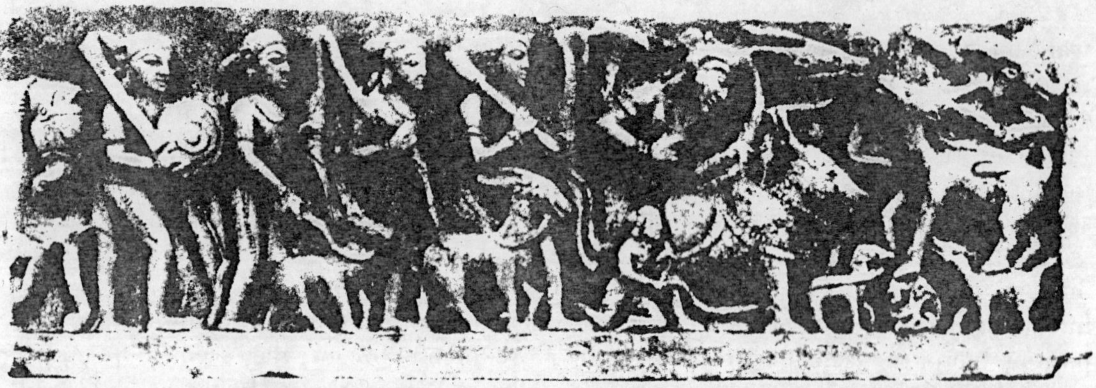

12-8. Fragment of an architrave, with hunting scene; Khajuraho (Khajuraho Museum). A scene of "antelope sticking" with two of the animals impaled, while an antelope, a bull, a ram (?), and two other animals are taken on leads toward the impaled victims. A small animal sniffs at one of the transfixed antelopes; next to it a scroll device fills the surface. The bearded hunter and the younger ones following him carry bows, dart, and sword. A smallish and kneeling figure in front allows the long lead of one of the two smaller animals (dog?) to pass between the legs of the caparisoned bull. A peculiar device behind the main hunter and behind the bull and antelope's head. A horse follows the hunters. What is the story? This narrative relief in its composition does not essentially differ from early Indian versions. But the modeling, etc., of men and animals is peculiarly Candella; plastically inert in this example, the volumes are stuck within their own weight. The marching rhythm, however, carried by these onerous shapes still has flux.

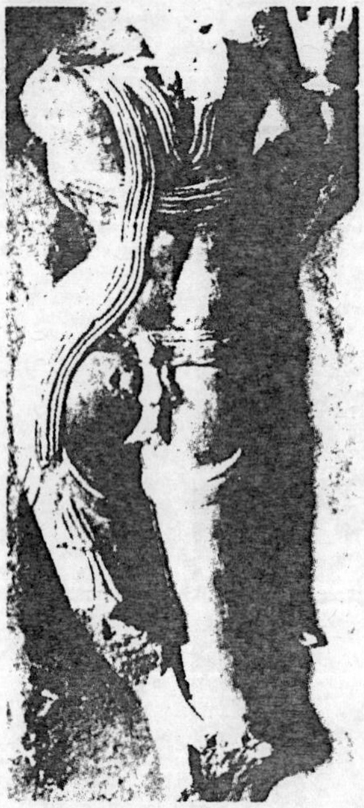

12-9. Fragment of back view of female figure (a flute player?) on interior wall of maṇḍapam, Citragupta Temple. This body clings to the surface as if tacked on. The heavy tightness of the modeling, the sharp outline of ample and manifold curves, the sleekly furrowed scarves, etc., which adhere, clasp, and partition its fullness, have as much more of the central Indian or "classical" in their composition as pl. 12-7 owes to the other factor. The hand is a failure on the basis of the same quality, by which the body succeeds.

sition, although it supplies the foundation toward which the celas turn.

If the two poles of Candella sculpture are integrated in varying degrees in one composition or in its single figures (pls. 12-6, 12-7, 12-11, 12-12), they are at times also placed next to each other (pl. 12-3). The large bracket figure, with all its turns around its axis, seems to come down upon the minute male at her feet with the pitiless weight of her superiority. Her raised left leg seems to dart far more than the actual dart which a figure in the frieze above carries in parallel direction, though with the swagger of a dandy. In these figures of the frieze—warriors by implement only—modeling and line are soft and fluid. They move in swaying rhythm, only to be cut across by the peaked harmfulness of the female "dancer's" diadem and profile, the one as rigid and indented as the other.

The linear element, on the whole, in this type of sculpture has no more independence than it has in the following group. Its intent is sunk into the plastic mass, and this accordingly, by embodying it, is transformed.

The other type yields its surface to a melting modeling, it spreads with relaxed ease. If the urge toward form is mainly active from within the stone in an outward direction[4]—the facets of the ground of plate 12-5 actually serve as stepping stones—it pours forth in Candella sculpture slowly. It spreads and accumulates in breadth, altogether without energy. The absence of the latter is made up by an added strictness. It puts limits to the broad spread and these are of a fatal hardness (see, for instance, vanamālā, lotus petals, and rim of śiraścakra, etc.). That hardness of heavy line, behind and in front of the spreading mass, may furthermore be accompanied by a sharp thinness of edge (the single lotus seat, pl. 12-5; pilasters, cloth, etc., pl. 12-6) at any level of the relief. While the mass pours forth without effort and spreads with animated leisure in the modeled bodies, accessory objects or details are hard and sharp. This incongruity shows the presence of the other trend. It is warded off from the main plastic conception but hardens in accessories.

Subtly differentiated and relaxed, the plastic mass spreads within this group of sculptures. Of preceding schools it bears the closest affinity to the work of Sanchi; it is genuinely of Central India. The quality passed on to it from Sanchi is the subtle warmth of modeling. The outbursting quality of the latter is nowhere manifest in Candella sculpture. This was bequeathed to the Haihaya school. With this minus and that specialization Candella mass appears vibrant in its outer layer. Its throbbing warmth does not go deep, it rests on an inert middle and bottom. Evanescent and as if breathing throughout, wrapped around a somnolent core, modeling tolerates as much of the precision of jewelry as it can carry, for the sake of its own definition and just before it becomes dead weight.

This evanescent quality of the modeling and its broad spread give also to the facial physiognomy its peculiar cast and expression (pl. 12-1). It is dilated sideways so that the cheeks cannot be broad enough to suffice for the spreading mass. Forehead and cheeks are laid around eyes and mouth. No attempt is made to set the eyes into their sockets; they float with the narrow slit between lowered eyelids across a broad expanse and carry their heavy freight of eyeballs bulging with a knowledge which their fixed glance takes care not to spill. Differentiated according to the more or less upward slanting shape of the slit and the width of its aperture, invariably rivetted on the tip of the nose, these superhuman eyes look out and are not meant to see. They do not give away anything, and their secret, which is their power, remains within the flat and broad expanse of the face. In keeping with their shape, the tendril eyebrows are drawn to the highest arch; where exactly it reaches its apex, whether nearer to temples or root of nose, is determined in each case by the eye itself of which its ridge line serves as an aggrandizement and echo. The high, obliquely cut and summarily modeled upper lid is all width and tension and veil; there is no lower lid but a dark line of shadow, at times even a deeply engraved furrow. Nothing from below trespasses this moat. So it must be, for the vibrant mouth betrays the fixed glance.

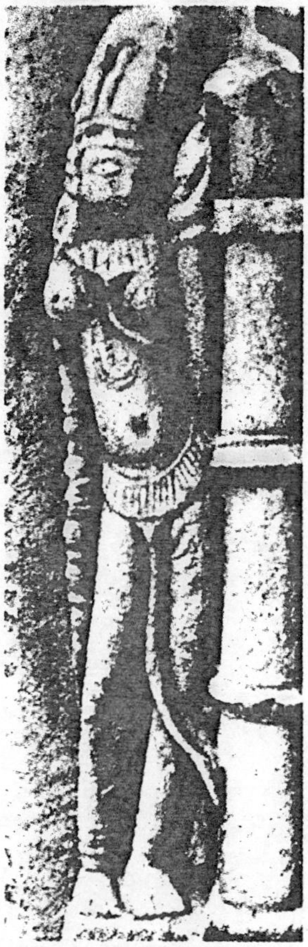

12-10. Architectonic fragment; Khajuraho (Khajuraho Museum). Rough surface due to weathering. The timid grace of the female figure, an animate companion of the round pilaster, if not exuberant in hardened plastic form as pl. 12-9, is rhythmical with a subdued plasticity. As if swept into this sheltered corner, this figure, too, does not come out of the stone, but just adheres to it. It is in such lesser and inconspicuous figures that lesser, if more intimate visualizations take form (also pl. 12-12). An indistinct object in the raised left; the right arm is unaccountably invisible, though the right hand clasps a knobbed and bow-like object.

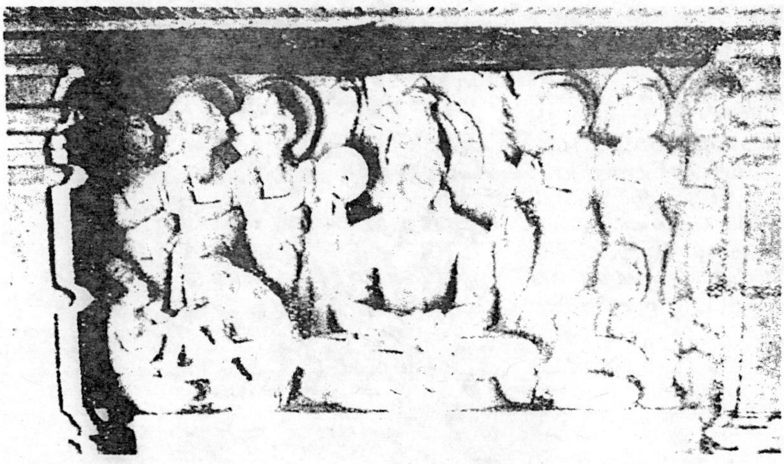

12-11. Vishnu in Vaikuṇṭha. Panel in interior back wall of garbhagṛha, Lakṣmaṇa Temple. This panel of standardized Candella quality has special iconographic features such as the two main arms of Vishnu in dhyāni mudrā, two figures bent over the homa fire, an emaciated ascetic squatting, and a cela facing him; behind a row of devatās, with añjali mudrā and the profile of each set against the disc of a halo.

Modeling is lifted, so to speak, from its innermost source, it spends itself at a distance from it and on the surface, in a broad flood of subtlety. This living quality of the plastic medium, so near to and on the surface, has its physiognomical equivalent in the rendering of the lips, blossoming forth or sealed. A last degree of sophistication plays on the surface; it does not belong to the intellect, but to the senses. Below the moat of darkness which underlines the eye they pass their criticism of what they cannot bridge over. Surely such an attitude is unknown to the contemporary drama, *Prabodhacandrodaya,* written under Candella rule. There, directness and vehemence of the acting of personified aspects of the mind are more akin to the purposeful and simplified trend of the other group of sculptures.

The two are distinct in some sculptures by the prevalence of the one or the other trend while they are inseparable in the majority (pls. 12-2, 12-8–11). If already the one component, the classical, with its sophisticated surface and numbed pith, in itself is complex, the absorption of the other makes it the more so. Candella sculpture embodies paradoxical qualities, relaxed sophistication on the surface, questioned by an emotionally conscious, that is, critical savoring of the situation, either of them referred to the permanent state of inwardness from which originates and by which is withheld the living and plastic essence, and on the other hand and less deeply rooted, but sunk into the plastic mass, an intent and purposeful movement. Such widely separate conditions are brought together within the peculiar plastic quality of Candella sculpture. Its twofold definition according to the prevalence of the one or the other—mass mollified, spreading, and vibrating on the surface, or else taut and simplified volumes charged with directedness—has, however, to be understood in its actuality as being borne by the innate tradition of central India and supported by the formulations throughout Indian sculpture in its later phases.

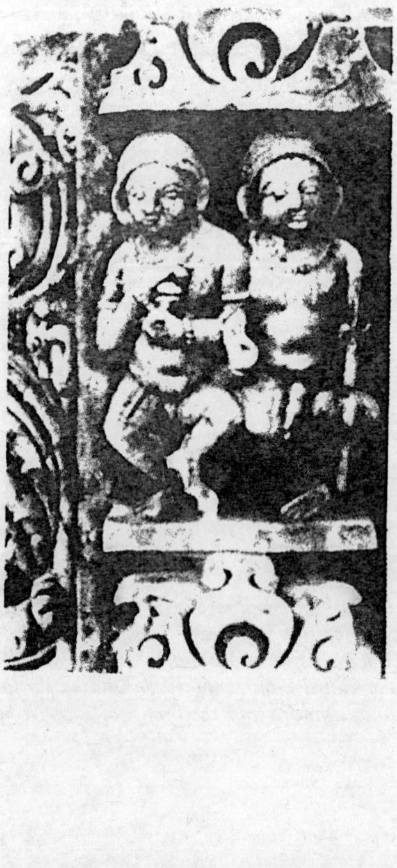

12-12. Dancing Gaṇas with cymbals and staff; Khajuraho (Khajuraho Museum). Architectonic relief, the highest stepping forth of a facet which has a plain ground. Next to it, a facet on a lower level makes a heaving surface, by virtue of the many rolled up and knobby, thickly flowing scrolls. Counterpoint to this surging roundness, the sun window triangle devices with their split halves on either side and the neat light and dark effect of their flat pattern set off the spreading and full modeling of the lugubrious. Gaṇa infants, with their stampeding dance and animal expression in blubber eyes and ill-content mouths, shifted outward in either face.

13 The Four-Cornered Citadel of the Gods

āyātayati . . . etāṁ caturaśrāṁ devapuram
BŚS 15.19.

The innermost sanctuary (garbhagṛha) of a Hindu temple is four cornered (caturaśra). Its walls are thick in proportion to the area of the innermost sanctuary.[1] The thick walls, moreover, project as a rule with buttresses (ratha), which increase the solidity and girth of the sanctuary and give to it the appearance of a bulwark or citadel (pura). The name of this temple proper is generally Prāsāda or Vimāna.[2] It is the house of god (devagṛha),[3] and it is also considered as the "body" of god.[4]

No four-cornered structural temple in stone or brick and built prior to the fifth century A.D. is known to have been preserved to this day. The antecedents, however, of the temple described above are found in the *Ṛgveda,* as far as the verbal image is concerned, and in certain śrautasūtras of the black *Yajurveda,* as far as the actual shape is concerned.

"Eine feste Burg ist unser God," it is said in the *Ṛgveda* repeatedly, of Agni and Indra, also of Sarasvatī.[5] This figure of speech was to be given effect in the Hindu temple, one of the prerequisites of the structure being that it should be "firm" (dṛḍha),[6] that it should be a dṛḍhaṁ puram, a firm citadel as which Agni is spoken of in *Ṛgveda* 5.19.2. The verbal image is the precursor of the architectural symbol. It would not have been necessary to stress the firmness of the structure, for the small building with its relatively thick walls could not but be firm, rising as it did above carefully laid foundations and, what is more relevant in the present context, on a well-packed plinth (pīṭha). The plinth or socle of the temple is one of its constituent parts. While there are relatively few temples without plinth or socle (pīṭha), a socle plus a subsocle (pīṭha and upapīṭha) are not infrequent. Moreover, the temple on its socle and subsocle may rise from a broad supporting platform which is ascended by

This essay first appeared in *JAOS* 75 (July–Sept. 1955):184–87, and is reprinted here by permission.

steps. While this type of architecture is finally developed about the year A.D. 1000, for example, in Khajuraho,[7] a number of earlier sanctuaries, all situated in northern India (Paharpur, in Bengal,[8] Lauriya Nandangarh in Bihar and Ahicchatra in Uttar Pradesh),[9] consist of piled terraces only. These terrace temples were crowned by a small sanctuary or by a symbol. The terrace temples are monuments, architectural solids, and are described in vāstuśāstra. The *Viṣṇudharmottara* of about the sixth century A.D. gives a detailed description of such a temple type. The type is called aiḍūka,[10] which means a wall, or the like, that is, a piled mass of whatever material. This type of temple is the utmost application as a structural form of the method of piling. The word for piling is cayana, piling being the technique proper of the Vedic altar, which was a pile made of bricks; on it rose the pile of firewood which fed the flame of the sacred fire.

The *Baudhāyana Śrautasūtra* 15.13–15.22, describes the preparations for the horse sacrifice (aśvamedha) and enumerates the artisans who establish themselves near the king, the sacrificer, that is, the carpenters, wheelwrights, and others, the brickmakers and potters, metal workers, and so forth, before the Adhvaryu, the priest who conducts the sacrifice and who acts on behalf of the sacrificer (the king) orders them to bring the firewood, one hundred and one cart loads[11] of bilva wood *(Aegle marmelos)* of which the bark must be removed before the logs are piled (or arranged like the spokes of a wheel; *BŚS* 15.14).[12] Besides, twenty-one trees must be felled for the twenty-one sacrificial posts to be set up in one line, parallel with and close to the eastern boundary of the sacrificial area (mahāvedi), in whose easternmost part the altar occupies the middle.[13] The altar for the Aśvamedha is thrice the size of the altar generally built for the sacrifice (agnicayana).[14] It measures twenty-one instead of the usual seven puruṣas (one puruṣa being the height of a man with arms raised and standing on his toes). While the brickmakers make the number of bricks that are required for an altar of twenty-one puruṣas or man's lengths, the chariotmakers make ready four or eight cars of Indra (indrāṇa) with four wheels so that they are as high as the upper end of the sacrificial posts. The next step is described in *Baudhāyana Śrautasūtra* 15.19. After having assembled in one pile, in the middle of the fire altar, twenty or twenty-four cartloads of bilva wood, the remainder of the wood is thrown on to it. This remaining wood has been cut in smaller and smaller pieces. This would indicate that a pile of a more or less pyramidal shape had to be heaped.

When this was accomplished, "one laid out that four-cornered citadel of the gods" (āyātayati . . . etāṁ caturaśrāṁ devapuram) on the body itself of the fire altar or one extended it outward on to the wings and the tail of the altar. *(BŚS* 15.19) The height of the four-cornered fort of the gods extended to the top end of the sacrificial posts.[15]

When this fort of the gods has been erected, one encloses it by a cloister. Therein one makes an opening on the north side. Then one brings the cars of Indra (inside the enclosure). One places the four cars in the four cardinal points, or, if there are eight cars one places the others in the four intermediate directions. Each car is mounted by four priests.

After these preparations for the night service (following the first day of the soma pressing) are completed, the oblations are offered all the night long.

They are called by some "oblations of the enclosure" (*BŚS* 15.22). After the morning litany, when dawn has come and the sun has risen, the enclosure is dismantled and the cars are taken away. Then the rites of the sacrificial posts begin. It is not said how and of what material the four-cornered citadel of the gods was built. Its height is given as extending up the upper end of the wooden sacrificial posts. These were planted outside the brick-built Agni and the Vedi. They measured each twenty-one cubits (*KŚS* 20.4.16 and 6.1.34) or forty-two feet (see note 14). The "citadel" was open to the sky, erected as it was on the four sides of the pile of wood in the center of the altar. This fort-like enclosure was finally surrounded by an enclosure. As high as was the Devapura, the citadel, so high were the cars each of which was mounted by four priests. Keeping in mind the height of wooden temple cars in use to this day in southern and eastern India, the impressive height of the "cars of Indra" is not surprising.

The fifth, that is, the topmost layer of the brick altar thus supported: a hypaethral sanctuary, the fort of the gods, with the pile of firewood in the center and surrounded by an enclosure around the citadel. Between the walls of the citadel and the enclosure were stationed four or eight cars; each as high as the walls of the citadel and in the middle of each or also at the corners.

The name Devapura, citadel of the gods, does not occur among the many names of the temple, whereas the term Devagṛha, house of god, and other synonyms are frequent. The temple as house of god had a roof supported by walls. The Vedic citadel was, it appears, without a roof. In that respect it can be considered a precursor of "hypaethral" types of the temple such as that of the sixty-four yoginīs.[16] The Devapura, the fort of the gods, as set up in the Aśvamedha, though it did not bequeath its name to the Hindu temple, passed on to it the underlying idea that was to shape its form. The firm walls of the Hindu temple project with mighty buttresses in the four directions of space. These buttresses are technically known as ratha, which means "car." In name and allocation they would correspond to the "cars of Indra," whose height, like that of the structural rathas was equal to the height of the wall of the garbhagṛha.[17] The lesser buttresses in the intermediate directions are also of the same height. A surrounding wall or cloister of the temple precincts belongs to most of the larger temples.

It was Agni who brought the gods to the sacrifice. They dwelled at the sacrificial fire. In the horse sacrifice the fire was fed by the high pile of wood of 101 cartloads. It rose from the center of the great altar, where it was piled above the high altar, the uttaravedi, embedded in the lowermost of the five layers of the brick altar. The flame rose right above the effigy of the golden man and in line with the sequence of svayamātṛṇṇā bricks.[18] In short, position and shape—as far as the tapering character of the pile of firewood is concerned—anticipate the high superstructures of Hindu temples. These latter, however, could consolidate as shapes of monumental architecture only after the "house of god" had come to be accepted for sheltering in its walls and below its flat roof the permanent presence of a god installed in his symbol or image.

The roof in Hindu temples covers the garbhagṛha; it is the lid of the garbha, and above this flat ceiling towers the high superstructure. It rests on thick walls with their buttresses. Between them and the enclosure of the temple precincts is the outer ambulatory—which makes the complete temple with its enclosing wall or cloister a hypaethral monument. Or, if the ambulatory is in the interior of the temple, the idea of the sheltering house with its roof is given wider extension and a ceiling closes the garbhagṛha with its one or more ambulatories. Henceforward the flat-roofed house of dolmen type has its walls coalesced with those of the fort of the gods. They carry the superstructure with its finial whose—one—ideational prototype may be seen in the pile of the firewood with its flame.

The Hindu temple is a symbolic monument in space that serves the requirements of the cult. In it is compacted as much of an accretion of visual concepts and their ritual execution, for it is built with the help of architectural shapes subservient to this purpose. The "four-cornered citadel of the gods" of the Aśvamedha is a precursor of the square house of god, the Hindu temple.

14 Wall and Image in Indian Art

The point of this chapter is that the divine power enshrined in the inner cell of the Hindu temple is viewed by Hindu architects and architectural treatises as though projecting itself through the walls of the temple and expressing itself on and beyond the walls as buttresses and images.

The foremost monument of Indian art is the temple, and it is the center of all the arts. It is, moreover, practically the only monument that has survived the ravages of climate, time, and wars. The temples that will be considered here are of stone. Their types belong to the millennium from about the fifth to the fifteenth century A.D. The relation of wall and image will be considered in three respects: architecturally, sculpturally, and with regard to the paintings on the walls.

The Indian temple, the house of God, is enclosed in walls of great thickness, one-fourth part, as a rule, of the inner width of the sanctuary, and these walls enshrine the symbol or image of the deity to whom the building is consecrated. The symbol or image occupies the center of the sanctuary and is known as the jīva, the "life" of the temple in which it dwells; it is to the temple what the principle of life, the vital breath, the soul, is to the body of man. The *Agni Purāṇa* (61.23–25), a text compiled in the ninth century but based on older sources, speaks of the jīva of the temple. The walls are its body. Permeated at the time of consecration by the Supreme Principle, the temple is at once both the house and the body of God. As his house, the temple is a work of architecture; as his bodily symbol, the walls of the building are imbued by the Supreme Principle. The conception of sacred architecture as house and at the same time as symbolic presentation is Vedic; the *Śatapatha Brāhmaṇa* (13.8.1.1) speaks of an altar as being both house and symbol (gṛhaṃ vā prajñānaṁ vā).

This essay first appeared in the *Proceedings of the American Philosophical Society* 102 (Feb. 1958):7–13, and is reprinted by permission.

The temple is the house of the divine presence and is its very body. The temple itself, therefore, should be worshiped as puruṣa, the essential and unchanging and unaffected Principle of all things, says the *Śilparatna* (16.114), a text on architecture compiled in the sixteenth century.

Stone, the building material, is converted by the rites of architecture into a potent substance, charged with the divine presence. Throughout their massive, three-dimensional extent, the building stones become representations of prakṛti, the unevolved material of the universe, which is capable of change and evolution and is different from puruṣa, the unalterable essence, which has the jīva of the temple for its center.

The material of the walls of the temple, of the work of art to be, is transmuted to a state when it too becomes potent and causal and its activity is felt by the architect who gives it expression on the temple walls.

In order to evoke the power of the temple stones, they are invoked as goddesses when the foundations of the walls are being laid, and they are addressed in rhythmical, magic formulae called mantras. These mantras invoke the stones by many names, such as pūrnā, "Fulfilled One," caturaśra, "Square," and handsome in all parts, "Perfect One," perfectly proportioned. This rite also goes back to Vedic practice (*VS* 20.9; 11.44, Kāṇva recension), and the mantra is repeated in many of the textbooks on architecture from the sixth century downward through the period when the great temples were built (*VDhP* 2.29. 84–89; *BṛS* 52.112).

To recapitulate, the substance of the temple walls is stated to be prakṛti, or undifferentiated matter, which is given form by the jīva and then as receptacle of the jīva becomes potent with the potency of the jīva or puruṣa, the Supreme Principle.

In some of the figurative expressions of the texts the temple as puruṣa, as the Supreme Principle in manifestation, is endowed with eyes and mouth, neck, chest, legs, and the other parts of the body of man. But unlike sculpture

BELOW LEFT: *Figure 2. Schematic sketch plan of temple "Sthaṇḍila," drawn according to Vaikhānasāgama, ch. 10.*[1]

BELOW RIGHT: *Figure 3. Schematic ground plan of temple "Kṣitibhūṣana," drawn according to SRSu 57, 760–80. This type of temple, as also fig. 4, has two sets of walls. The inner wall here is square, on both sides, and is surrounded by an ambulatory in the interior of the temple. The outer wall of this ambulatory is square on the inside, whereas the outside shows a buttress projected from the middle of each side.*

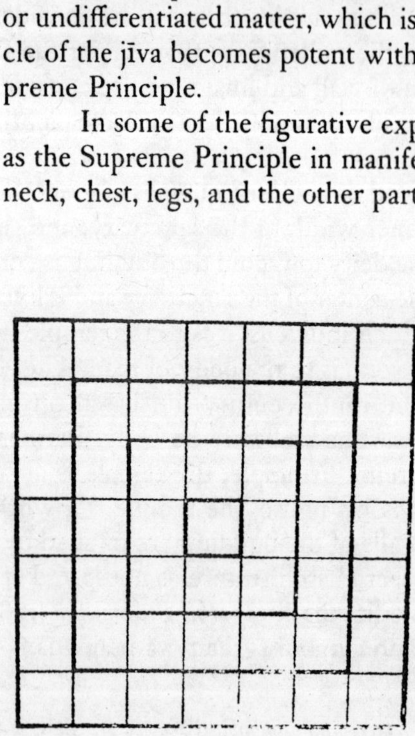

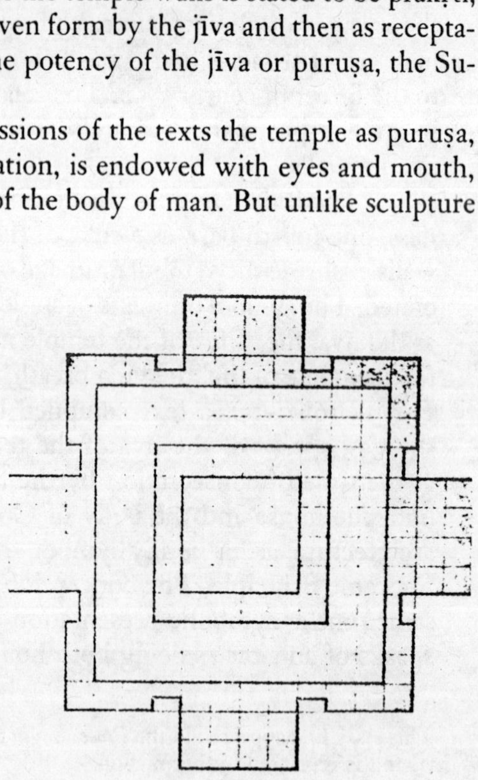

and painting, which produced images of the gods in the shape of man, architecture abstains from such physical representations. Though the architectural terms for parts of the temple include the words for leg (jaṅghā), chest (uras), or neck (grīvā), and the consecration of a temple begins with the ritual of the "opening of the eyes," the building itself has no anthropomorphic parts. Form is given to the in-dwelling spiritual essence and to the evolving power of the material substance by the ordering of the architectural shape so that it conveys by its masses their distribution and proportions.

The meaning of the temple is given full exposition at the height of the evolution of its architecture in the tenth and eleventh centuries. Before that time, the walls were less explicit or articulate, and, in the earliest forms of temples, the wall surfaces were altogether plain. In this summary and schematic sketch (fig. 1) of the division of a groundplan, based upon a description in a sacred text, the *Vaikhānasāgama* (chap. 10), compiled some time between the fifth and the seventh centuries, the temple is square, but it is not for long to remain bounded in its simple geometry. As another sketch plan shows (fig. 2), this one drawn from an early eleventh-century compendium on architecture (the *Samarāṅgaṇasūtradhāra*) describing a temple-type well established at that age, the walls are projected from the center of each face in aliquot parts of the area of the building to a multiple of the wall's own thickness, so as to form a buttress in elevation. In the next stage of evolution (fig. 3), which can be illustrated by a sketch plan from the same architectural text, the projection of the central buttress is extended and made more complex. The main buttress is flanked by lesser projections or offsets. There are many other possibilities of extending the buttress outward. However, the inside wall always retains its original straightness (fig. 4). In the most elaborate examples of multiple or complex buttresses, the walls become like many angled bulwarks, as in the temple of Ambarnāth, near Bombay, built in the year 1060. An additional hall may be built before the shrine and it, too, then develops its own system of buttress-

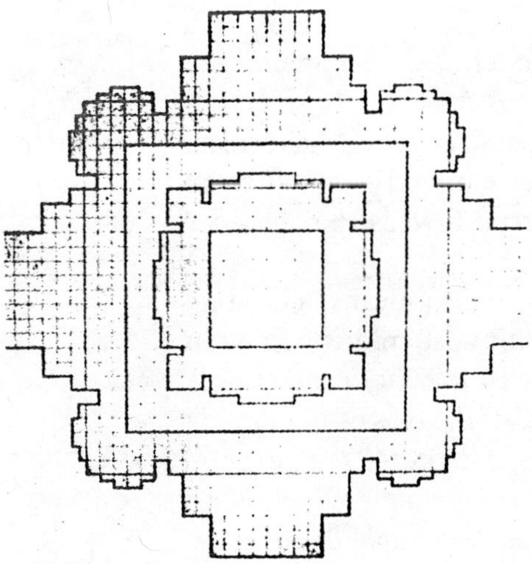

BELOW LEFT: *Figure 4. Schematic ground plan of temple "Hemakūṭa," drawn according to SRSu 57, 50–86. The innermost space of the sanctuary is square (cf. fig. 3), whereas the walls project into the inner ambulatory with their buttresses. The outer walls of the shrine are square on their inner side, whereas the outside shows its major buttresses widely projected into space in the center of each face.*

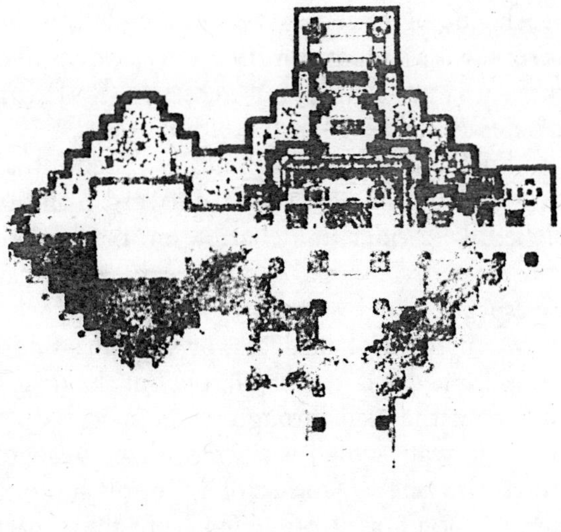

BELOW RIGHT: *Figure 5. Plan of Ambarnāth Temple, near Bombay, A.D. 1060. Lower half ground plan, upper half plan looking up. The smaller unit, on the left, is the sanctuary (prāsāda); that on the right is the hall (maṇḍapam) in front of the temple proper.*

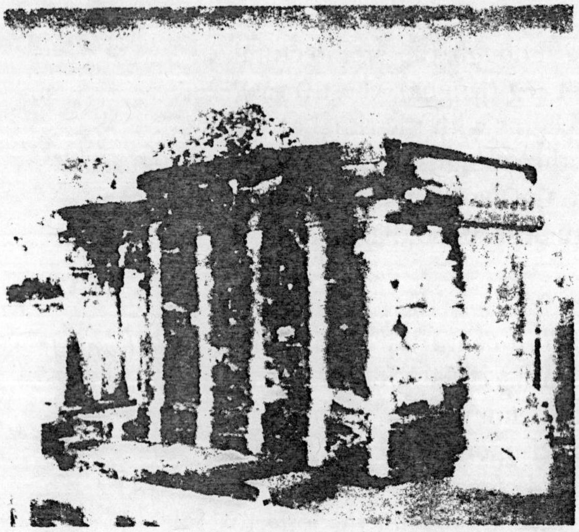

14-1. Temple 17 in Sanchi, Madhya Pradesh, fifth century. As seen in this side view, the walls of the flat-roofed shrine are plain but for the moldings at the base and top. These are extended to the small porch in front of the temple.

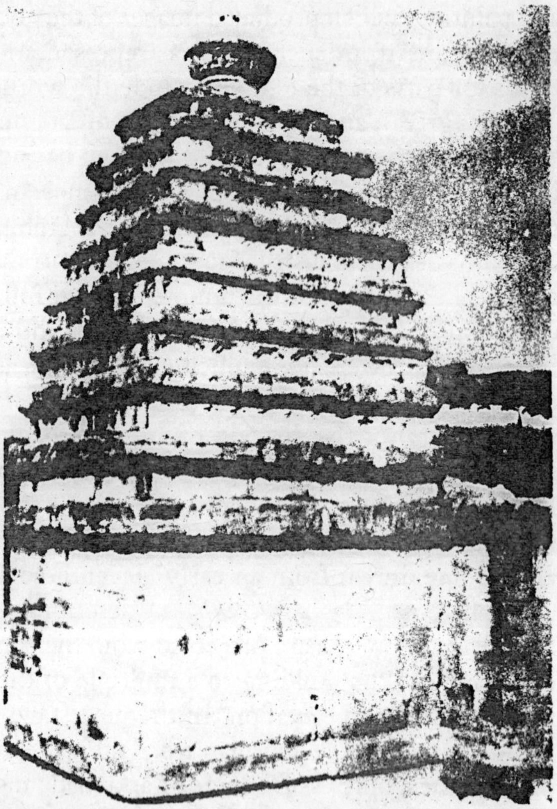

14-2. Temple 10 in Aihole. Sixth to seventh century. The large stones of the plain walls are joined without mortar. The high superstructure repeats the theme of the horizontal moldings.

es, of course observing the architectural proportions and style of the temple.

If we now retrace our steps to the earliest extant (pl. 14-1) examples of stone temples, we find in the fifth century a cubical building with plain walls. This construction is illustrated by a shrine at Sanchi, in central India, and by another temple (pl. 14-2) with plain walls, of about the sixth or seventh century in Aihole, southwest of Bombay. The walls in the latter example support a high superstructure. About the same time (pl. 14-3), a temple—the one on the right in pl. 14-3—in Mahakuteswar, close to Aihole, has the central projection on each side of its vertical walls extended to the superstructure. This central pier serves as a support for *itself* only; it does not receive or carry any outward thrust—it is not a structural necessity. Rather, it carries toward the beholder the potency held within the temple mass.

Such a buttress is technically called ratha, which also means "chariot." Like a chariot, the wall comes outward from its own midst, and it carries in a niche, like a rider in a chariot, an image of the deity to whom the temple is consecrated. The image in the niche is regularly of some one of the deity's main aspects, or of his consort, or of his son, or of one of his avatars. The name of such a niche is ghanadvāra, or solid-mass door; that is, a door which is no door. No one can enter through it, but the deity inside the temple has become manifest on the wall through it.

The wall, which is filled with power from the deity within it, makes manifest the deity by means of a progression of buttresses and of images. The walls are shown as if propelled from the center toward the four directions;

as such, they constitute a dynamic and symbolic architectural form. The walls also carry forward, in the images they bear, aspects of the deity. Thus the devotee looks at the temple first when he approaches the building, and then, particularly during the rite of walking around it, when he not only recognizes the images, but feels their impact. The wall now comes alive with images. Collateral niches on either side of the central ratha are barely indicated on this temple. But about a century later, on the Paraśurāmeśvar Temple in Bhubaneswar (pl. 14-4), on the northeast coast of India, the side niches have evolved into minor offsets of the wall. They occupy the entire height of the vertical surface only but do not fully accompany the ascent of the main buttress. All the rathas of this temple were originally full of images of the celestial host disporting themselves.

The host of images in this phase of temple architecture (pl. 14-5) appear as a rich texture of the wall. Single figures or groups are inscribed between flat pilasters whatever may be the bodily contortions and moods conveyed by the design, as of this acrobatic celestial dancer whose shape is fitted in the shallow rectangle which it fills.

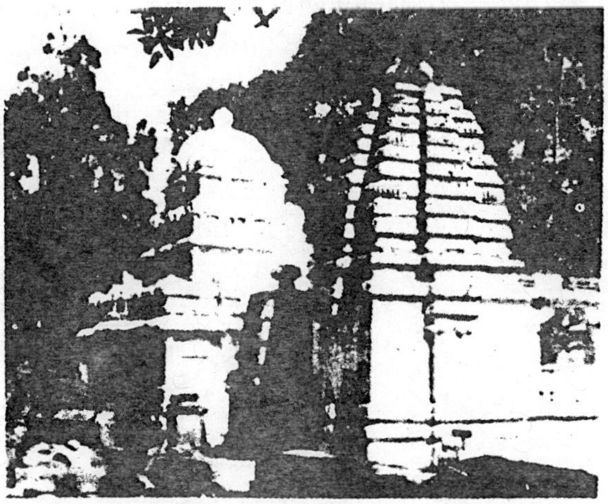

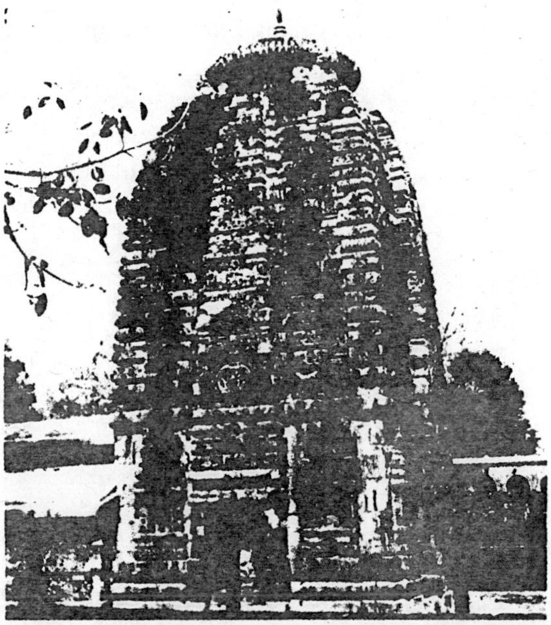

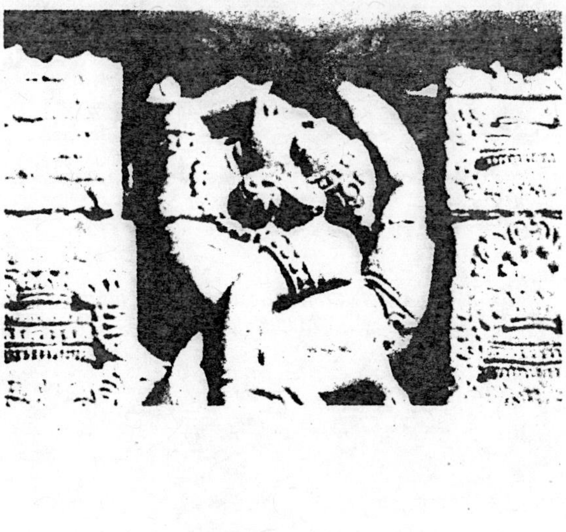

ABOVE: *14-3. Saṅgameśvara and Makuṭeśvaranātha Temples, Mahakuteswar, ca.* A.D. *600. The offset in the middle of the wall is flanked by pilasters. They accentuate the vertical theme of this building (the temple in the foreground, on the right). It is carried on by the buttress of the superstructure, in the middle of each of its sides.*

ABOVE RIGHT: *14-4. Paraśurāmeśvar Temple, Bhubaneswar, Orissa, ca.* A.D. *700. The importance of the central buttress of the wall is increased by its greater width and the introduction of horizontal moldings similar to those of the superstructure. The perpendicular walls and the curvilinear superstructure are coalesced into one theme.*

RIGHT: *14-5. Celestial dancer. Detail of carvings on wall of Paraśurāmeśvar Temple, Bhubaneswar (cf. pl. 14-6).*

The next stage in the development is shown in the ca. tenth-century Siddheśvar Temple (pl. 14-6), and also at Bhubaneswar, Orissa. In the mighty projections of its central buttress and the lesser rathas, the wall seems to have taken several steps forward. Its entire body appears furrowed by chases and recesses, which set the single piers into boldest relief. This edifice is singularly free from anthropomorphic and theriomorphic images, except for those in its main niches and on the four main projections from the spire. But the architectural image is systematically organized so as to progress into space at every one of the spire's many levels. Further progressions are embodied in the miniature replicas of the whole tower. These replicas are purely architectural symbolical forms, without structural function. They make manifest (vyakta) the potential which exists unmanifest (avyakta) inherent in their material substratum, called prakṛti. In them it has now become informed by the puruṣa, the Spirit, whose vital essence they hold.

The leonine shapes jutting into space midway of the ascending curve of the tower proper are theriomorphic symbols of power. At all times, Śakti, or power, conceived as the female energy of divinity or goddess, is symbolized in the shape of a lion. This power was present in the building stones which were invoked as goddesses at the laying of the foundation. (In front of the temple is a hall structure which has piers that are proportionately adjusted to its purpose.)

In this temple, the buttresses facing the four directions are akin to the form of a four-faced Śiva-Liṅga (pl. 14-7). The symbol of Śiva, the Liṅga, is a cylinder, rounded at the top. It is replete with the presence of Śiva; and this is visualized by a form where four faces or aspects of the god are seen to have

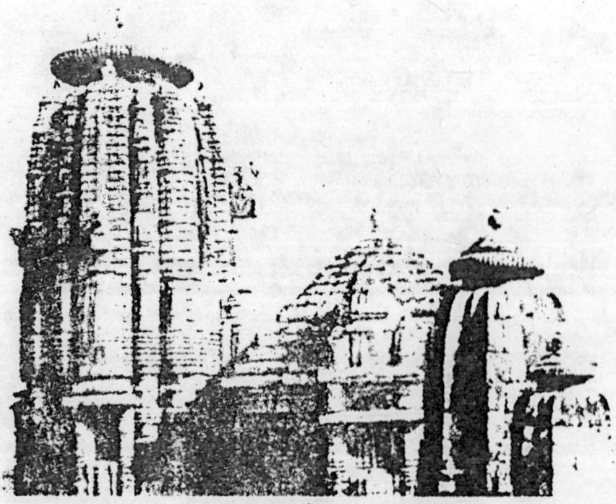

14-6. Siddheśvar Temple, Bhubaneswar, Orissa, ca. tenth century.

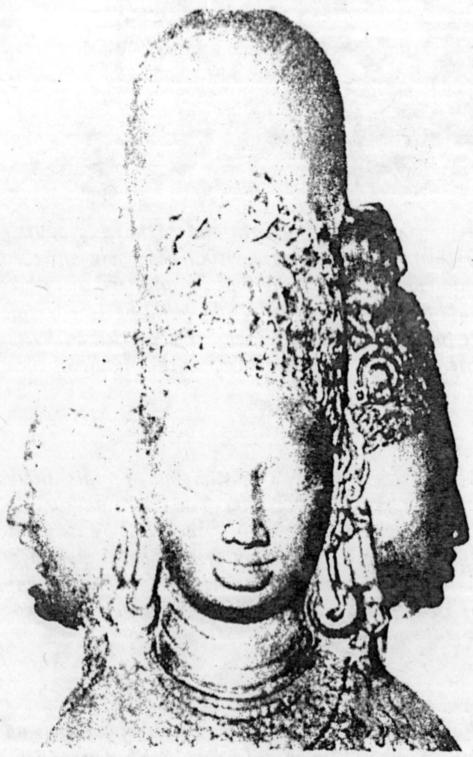

14-7. Four-faced Śiva Liṅga, Nachna-Kuthara, Madhya Pradesh, ca. eighth century.

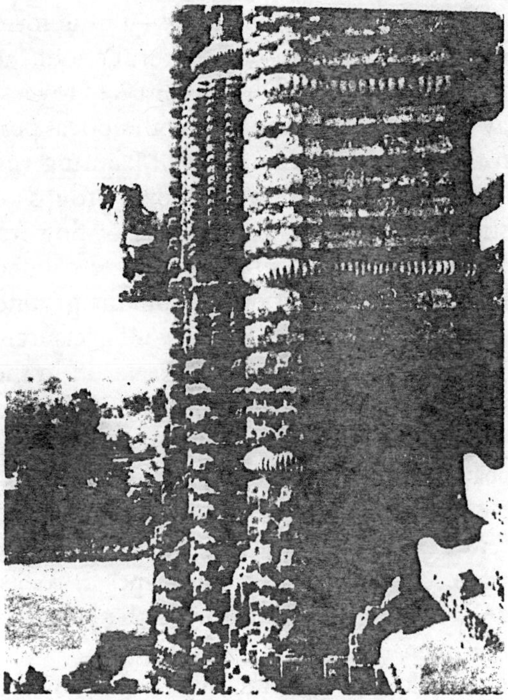

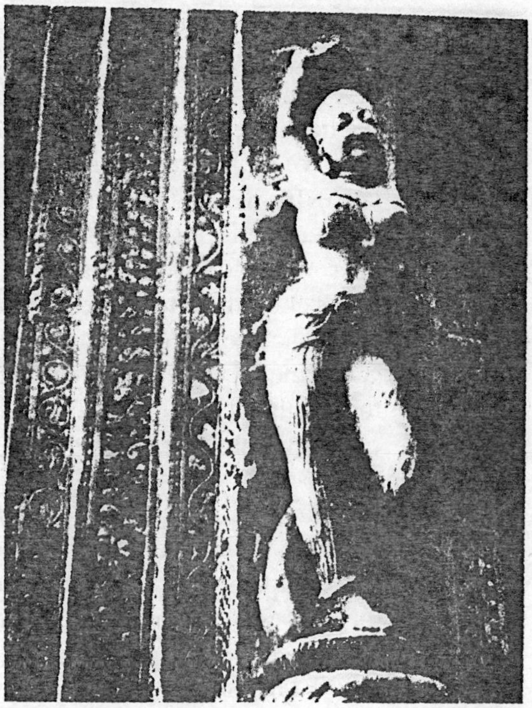

ABOVE LEFT: *14-8. Detail of Sikhara (superstructure) of Liṅgarāja Temple, Bhubaneswar, Orissa, eleventh century.*

ABOVE RIGHT: *14-9. Detail of buttress with figure of a tree-goddess from temple in precincts of Liṅgarāja Temple, Bhubaneswar, Orissa, twelfth century.*

emerged from its central pillar. This four-faced Liṅga of the eighth century in Kuthara, in Central India, is, in anthropomorphic imagery, analogous to the architectural symbolism of the temple buttresses facing the four directions.

The climax of this development of the buttress appears in the Liṅgarāja Temple, Orissa, of the eleventh century (pl. 14-8). This projects its multiple buttresses so far into space that some of the moldings seem to be clutching the pier and drawing it back toward its wall. This is especially marked in the ring shaped and ribbed Āmalaka devices here extended into moldings and seeming like ties to consolidate the monument. This virtuosity of organization of symbolic structure in all its intricacies gives final exposition of the power held to be inherent in the temple walls. Looking backward from this temple to the early shrines, we see that in it the walls express logically the meaning which was only latent and unexpressed in the early buildings.

Where sculptures appear on the fully evolved wall, as on a twelfth-century shrine in the Liṅgarāja Temple precints, the images appear to be propelled into position from the wall to which they still cling (pl. 14-9). Such images are the highest accents on the outward progression of the wall. A tree goddess, in the ease of her posture and radiance of her shape, leans on her ratha. Behind her, projecting not so far from the wall, are the steps of the subjacent rathas, textured with carved scrollwork, which constitute degrees in the forward manifestation of the indwelling Principle.

When the sculptural image on the wall is carved in high relief and sometimes almost completely in the round, the power active in and through the massive walls is communicated *to* the sculptural form. The images of the divinities have come forward toward the beholder, discharged from the core of the bulwark of the walls. For all their amplitude they appear weightless.

A corresponding vision prevails in Indian wall paintings—in the form in which they are known to us from the beginning of our era throughout the first millennium. They are organized in a perspective which is directed toward the beholder instead of leading away from him, as is the case with optical perspective in Western painting from the Renaissance on. A wall painting (pl. 14-10) from Ajanta of the middle of the first millennium shows groups of women, children, and flying celestials on a sloping ground, full of flowers, in front of and close to a grotto. The grotto is built up by means of painted cubes and other stereometric shapes. Like a trumpet it opens from the ground of the picture with its dense tapestry-like vegetation and sets forth the leisurely gathering of women and children. The scene of the painting breaks off in the foreground at the bottom, with beam-like protruding shapes, a convention for rocks such as those of the grotto. Together they create the illusion of the pictorial space in which the figures appear to move. All the figures in the Ajanta paintings are fully modeled by means of color, shade, and outline. They stand out from their opaque background. The lithe roundedness of their appearance is accompanied by a phantasmagoria of cubes and crags, the shapes of rocks, the shapes of nature and imagination, coming forward toward the beholder from their ground together with the main images.

The ancient texts on painting speak of the painter as drawing toward himself the required form of his inner vision. The image, they say, is led forward (ānīyate) by him from the wall, which the texts call the "white wall of attention."[2] There, the image should be rounded into relief, burgeoning forth in color. Thus the painting emerges on the "white wall of attention" from that innermost level of reference, which is at one, in the monumental structure of the temple, with the jīva, the innermost life.

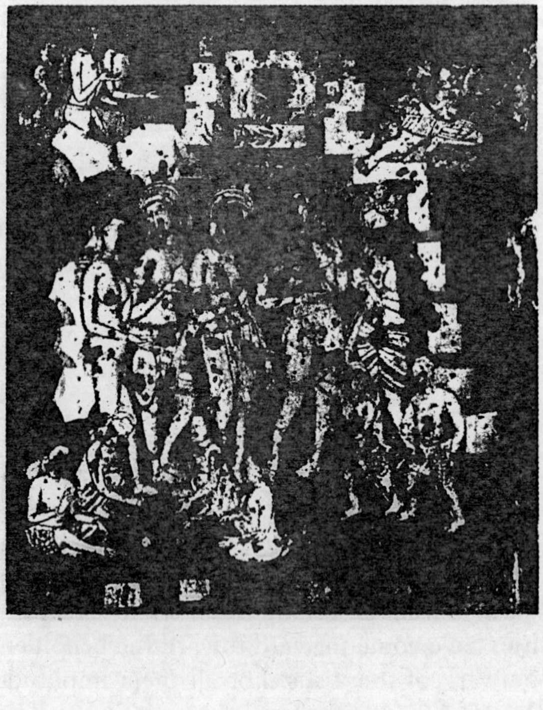

14-10. Women and children on their way to worship. Wall painting in sanctuary, cave 2, Ajanta, middle of first millennium A.D.

V

THEORY AND PRACTICE OF PAINTING

15 Introduction to the Viṣṇudharmottara

He who paints waves, flames, smoke, and streamers fluttering in the air, according to the movement of the wind, should be considered a great painter. VDhP 43.5.28.

Painting is the best of all arts, conducive to dharma, pleasure, wealth, and emancipation. It gives the greatest pleasure, when placed in a house. VDhP 43.5.38.

The *Viṣṇudharmottara* is a supplement or appendix to the *Viṣṇupurāṇa*. Part 3 of the *Viṣṇudharmottara* gives the fullest account known of the various branches, methods, and ideals of Indian painting. It deals not only with its religious aspect but also, and to a far greater extent, with its secular employment. It proclaims the joy that colors and forms and the representation of things seen and imagined produce. Speaking of artistic representation in relation to religion, it points out their mutual limitations:

> Vajra said—The Supreme Deity has been described as devoid of form, smell and emotion and destitute of sound and touch—so how this form can be (made) of Him?
>
> Mārkaṇḍeya replied—Prakṛti and Vikṛti (come into existence) through the (variation in) the form of the Supreme Soul. That form of Him (which is) scarcely to be perceived is called Prakṛti. The whole universe should be known as the Vikṛti (*i.e.*, modification) of Him, when endowed with form. Worship and meditation (of the Supreme Being) are possible (only when He is) endowed with form. . . . The best position of the (Supreme) Soul (however) is to be imagined without form. For seeing the worlds (He) possesses eyes closed in meditation. . . .[1]

This essay first appeared as the Introduction to the *Viṣṇudharmottara (Pt. III): A Treatise on Indian Painting and Image Making* (Calcutta: University of Calcutta, 1928) and is reprinted by permission.

This concession made, life in its entirety becomes fit for artistic representation, and the realm of imagination is as close within the reach of the artists as nature that surrounds him, for tradition guides him in the one case and observation checks and inspires him in the other.

The *Viṣṇudharmottara* admits in several places that it is but repeating and compiling from older sources. These being lost to us, our text represents the earliest exhaustive account of the theory of painting. Its date can be ascertained partly from chapters copied from earlier sources, and partly from a custom of setting up statues to renowned personages with which the text deals.

Vyāsa, the reputed author of the *Mahābhārata,* was worshiped as a deity. Directions for making the image of Vyāsa are given in the chapters dealing with image making, following the chapters on painting.[2] Directions are also given for making images of Yudhiṣṭhira, Bhīma, Arjuna, Nakula, Sahadeva, Krishna; of Sumanta, Jaimini, Paila, Vaiśampāyana (the four disciples of Vyāsa); and of Devakī, Jaśodā, Balarāma, Rukmiṇī, Satyabhāmā, Śāmba, and Aniruddha.

At the time of the compilation of the *Viṣṇudharmottara* the *Mahābhārata* must have been held sacred to such an extent that not only its heroes, but also its so-called author and his disciples were worshiped as deities. Vālmīki, too, was worshiped as a deity and the *Viṣṇudharmottara* also tells how to make his image.[3]

The complete book of the *Rāmāyaṇa* is not anterior to the *Mahābhārata,*[4] and since the *Mahābhārata* in its present shape is assigned to a period between A.D. 200 and 400, the *Viṣṇudharmottara* cannot date earlier than the fifth century A.D. This date is also evident from that of the *Viṣṇupurāṇa,* of which the *Viṣṇudharmottara* is an appendix. The *Viṣṇupurāṇa* bases its genealogical accounts on those of the *Bhaviṣya, Matsya,* and *Vāyu.* "The *Vāyu* borrowed the *Bhaviṣya's* augmented account about or soon after the year A.D. 330 or 335."[5] The *Viṣṇupurāṇa* cannot, therefore, be earlier than the second half of the fourth century A.D.

The lower age limit of the *Viṣṇudharmottara* must, however, be pushed still further. For Part 3, chapter 27, dealing with colors, is borrowed verbatim from Bharata's *Nāṭyaśāstra,* and the number of rasa's in the *Viṣṇudharmottara* is nine, while only eight are dealt with by Bharata.

The upper age limit of the text may be conceived from an iconographic peculiarity of its pantheon. In it every god, hero, philosopher, or sage finds his place somewhere round the central figure of Vishnu, the God Supreme. Yet no mention is made of Śaṅkara, who up to the present day is worshiped in the form of an image. Had Śaṅkara existed at the time of the compilation of the chapters on painting, the author would have incorporated him into the Vaiṣṇava pantheon in spite of his being an incarnation of Śiva.

The chapters of the *Viṣṇudharmottara* dealing with painting must have been compiled in the seventh century, contemporary with the latest paintings of Ajanta; and so we get acquainted with the theories prevalent at the time of the full maturity of their practice. But it must not be forgotten that our text is but a compilation and that its recipes and prescriptions go back to a remoter past. Valuable as these various kinds of information are, we have to be aware that, like all theories, they are derived from, and subservient to, the practice.

They left every freedom to the artist, to work, as the text says, "according to his own intellect." What Śrī Kumāra modestly states in his *Śilparatna* (verse 14) also holds good for our text: "I describe the methods of *Chitra* for the benefit of the ignorant."

Painting in ancient India, especially in the Gupta age, was of great importance in the life of the citizen. The interest taken in pictures varied with the education of the spectator. "The masters praise the rekhā's . . . (delineation and articulation of form), the connoisseurs praise the display of light and shade . . . , women like the display of ornaments, to the rest of the public richness of colours appeals." The artists, therefore, should take great care that the painting may be appreciated by every one. There was ample opportunity for contemplating and appreciating paintings.

From the great hall built by the Bodhisat—according to the *Mahā-Ummagga-Jātaka*[6]—painted with beautiful pictures, and the subterranean palace of the same Jātaka, with its stucco-coated walls, bearing paintings of the splendor of Sakka, the zones of Mount Sumeru, the sea and the ocean, the four continents, the Himavat, the lake Anotatta, the vermilion mountain, the sun and the moon, the heaven of the great kings with the six heavens of sense and their divisions—to the picture gallery (cittāgāra) in the royal pleasure grove of Prasenajit, king of Kosala, where many people used to go, among them the Bhikkhuṇis, who were forbidden to do so[7]—to those many portraits and landscapes painted by artists of the royal and the servant class alike, as mentioned in the *Ratnāvalī*, *Raghuvaṁśa*, *Śākuntala*, and *Uttararāmacarita*—we see an unfading delight taken in the magic and the sensuousness of painting. Wherever there was a festival, painting enhanced its mood—"from the city-gate to the palace, and from the palace to his own house, on both sides of the road, he erected lattice-work, and covered all over with mats, covered all with pictures, scattered flowers upon the ground, hung flags and banners."[8]

As permanent or temporary decoration, on the floors, on the walls and ceilings of private houses, palaces, and temples, and in the streets, paintings instructed and enlivened the mind of the public. Even religious teachers used painting as the most popular means of communication that could be understood by the illiterate and the child. "There is a class of Brahmanical teachers, known by the name of Nakha. They make a (portable) framework upon which they cause to be drawn a variety of pictures, depicting scenes of good and evil destinies, of fortunes and misfortunes, and causing the labels to be inscribed: 'By doing this deed one attains this,' 'By doing that, one attains that,'—thus showing different destinies, they wander about with these pictures."[9]

That every cultured man had in his house a drawing board and a vessel for holding brushes and other requisites of painting is evident from Vātsyāyana's *Kāmasūtra.*[10] But one should not have a painting by one's own hand in one's house, says the *Viṣṇudharmottara.* Certain objects are only to be painted in private residences, suggesting love, gaiety, and peace, while the supernatural and the terrible aspects of life were reserved for the walls of temples and royal audience halls.

The paintings were executed in various types; wall paintings, pictures on board, and on canvas were equally frequent (cf. *Kāmasūtra* and

Viṣṇudharmottara). The latter were sometimes in the shape of rolls, exhibiting continuous representation. Such a roll was spread out by a spy of Cāṇakya before the people in Candanadāsa's house and was exhibited by him with songs.[11] The figures were of oblong, squat, and rounded shape and the *Viṣṇudharmottara* accordingly enumerates four types of depictions: (1) satya—true, realistic, as we may say, of an oblong shape; (2) vaiṇika, which may mean lyrical, of squat shape; and (3) nāgara, of the citizen, gentry pictures of rounded limbs; while the fourth type simply is (4) miśra, mixed. In connection with wall paintings the *Viṣṇudharmottara* also alludes to floors inlaid with precious jewels. From the *Śilparatna,* on the other hand, we know that Dhūlicitra, powder painting, familiar to Bengali ladies as alpona, was applied as temporary coating of powdered colors on a beautiful piece of ground.[12]

Since painting took such a wide part in secular and religious life, it was only natural that legends were invented to explain the origin of the art. The *Viṣṇudharmottara*[13] gives a long account of how the sage Nārāyaṇa, in order to put the apsarases to shame, created the most beautiful nymph, Urvaśī, by drawing her outline with mango juice. The *Citralakṣaṇa*[14] again tells us how King Nam-grags a Jigs t' ul, ordered by Brahma, painted the likeness of a deceased son of a brahman; whereupon Brahma made it come to life, and having thus defeated Yama, restored the son to his father. In either legend the origin of the art of painting is seen in the outlining of a human figure[15] for the purpose of creating a living human form. This reconstructed origin is magic and nonaesthetic. A similar notion is to be found in Bhāsa's *Svapnavāsavadattā,*[16] where King Udayana and Princess Vāsavadattā, with whom he had eloped, are though absent, married by their parents in effigies, by drawing the portraits of the two on a board. These instances prove that the artist draws from his memory when visualizing a portrait. With this tradition another has to be compared. A Tibetan text of the eighteenth century, the *D'pag bsam ljon bzair*[17] tells us how King Udrayana of Raura caused a picture of the Buddha to be made by taking a reflex of the figure of the Daśabala as his model. This picture has become known under the name of l'u lon-ma (derived from the water). The *Śilparatna* accordingly defines painting as what bears a resemblance and looks like a reflex in a mirror.[18] The imitative and the imaginative origins of pictorial representation, therefore, were felt as equally true. The *Viṣṇudharmottara* quotes the Urvaśī legend, yet the text never grows tired to point to things seen as ever fresh sources of artistic inspiration, when dealing with the dṛṣṭa (i.e., with things seen). But not only the twofold origin of painting in observation and imagination was theoretically known to the authors of the various treatises; the *Viṣṇudharmottara,* moreover, introduces its chapters on painting with a discourse, where Mārkaṇḍeya instructs King Vajra that without a knowledge of the science of dancing, the rules of painting can scarcely be understood. In another passage, the observation of nature and of the rules of dancing are indicated as the ultimate resources of the painter. This does not mean that the positions of dancers have to be painted. None of the nine positions of the treatise on painting in the *Viṣṇudharmottara* coincides with any of the 101 positions explicitly described in Bharata's *Nāṭyaśāstra*. What is meant by the derivation of painting from dancing is the movement in common to both these expressive forms; it asserts itself in purity through dancing; it guides the hand of the artist, who knows how to paint figures, as if breathing, the wind as blowing, the fire as blazing, and the streamers as fluttering. The moving force, the vital breath, the life movement (cetanā), that is what is expected to be seen in the work of a painter, to make it alive with rhythm and expression. Imagination, observation, and the expressive force of rhythm are meant by the legends of the origin of painting to be its essential features.

The *Viṣṇudharmottara* clearly distinguishes between dṛṣṭa and adṛṣṭa, the latter comprising things invisible or rarely to be seen. The dṛṣṭa, things that are seen easily by ordinary mortals, excel in what we call landscape painting. The hours of day and night and the seasons are described (chap. 42). There we find a close connection of mood and time, which reached its height in the Rāgmālā pictures, where season, hour, emotion, and music became fused as painting. At the same time details are observed with the same sincerity as we find in the pictures of Dutch masters, for instance, in the description of the drinking place. The light effects sought to be produced show a very sensitive reaction to optic effects, as the faded light of the candle in the morning dawn. Yet we are told that moonshine should be shown by a Kumuda flower in full bloom, and sunshine by drawing creatures suffering from heat. In one instance, atmospheric effects are observed, while in the other, the behavior of one object or the other, reacting to the atmospheric change, is represented suggestively. This interest in the living individuality of the single forms of nature gives to Indian landscape the charm of storytelling.

Side by side with the naïve joy in the variegated forms of nature, we learn that rivers are to be represented in human shape, as was the case with them in Greece, but they should stand on their vāhanas, their knees should be bent, and their hands should hold full pitchers. What an amazing association of ideas! The personification of the river put again into action as an ordinary human being, bending down under the load of the full pitcher of water drawn from the river. This versatility in visualizing abstraction and actual action replaces the mere observation of nature. That seas should have water depicted instead of a halo, or that an artist should show a pitcher to suggest a tank, a conch shell in representing a conch shell, and a lotus flower in representing a lotus flower, once more points to a matter of absorbing interest, namely, the single form of nature exercised on the mind of the artist. He rendered it faithfully. Yet where large appearances like whole rivers and seas, or landscapes with rising suns had to be painted, he took his refuge and delight in introducing personifications or such actions of some members of the scene appropriate to, and indicative of, their surroundings. The Indian artist never took the world at a sweeping glance.

Observing the details of appearance, the author of the *Viṣṇudharmottara* describes the different types of men. Country people, the nobility, widows, courtesans, artisans, wrestlers, soldiers, and so forth, are vividly described in movements, habits, and features peculiar to their class, while, at the same time, most of them belong to one of the five standardized types of men, called (1) Haṁsa, (2) Bhadra, (3) Mālavya, (4) Ruchaka, and (5) Śaśaka. Their respective measures should be 108, 106, 104, 100, and 90 aṅgulas in contradistinction to the measurement given in the *Bṛhatsaṁhitā,* where the relation of sizes is inverse, 96, 99, 102, 105, and 108 aṅgulas, respectively. A detailed description of the five types is given there.[19]

The figures may appear in various positions, of which nine are the leading attitudes:

(1) Ṛjvāgata—the front view;
(2) Anṛju—the back view;
(3) Sācīkṛtaśarīra—a bent position in profile view;
(4) Ardhavilocana—the face in profile, the body in three-quarter profile view;
(5) Pārśvāgata—the side view proper;
(6) Parāvṛtta—with head and shoulder belt turned backwards;
(7) Pṛṣṭhāgata—back view with upper part of the body partly visible in forlorn profile;
(8) Parivṛtta—with the body sharply turned back from the waist upwards, and lastly
(9) Samānata[20]—the back view, in squatting position with body bent.

In a further passage thirteen positions are enumerated—which, however, is clearly an interpolation.

These positions are obtained in painting with the help of kṣaya and vṛddhi, decrease and increase, that is to say, the science of foreshortening.

Foreshortening (kṣaya and vṛiddhi) and proportion (pramāṇa) constitute with regard to single figures the working of observation and tradition. The law of kṣaya and vṛddhi was as intensely studied by the ancient Indian painter as was perspective by the early Italian masters. Pramāṇa, on the other hand, was the standardized canon, valid for the upright standing figure and to be modified by every bent and turn. The Haṁsa measure is detailed in full; it is of the uttama navatāla type.[21]

Though not distinctly mentioned, it is evident that the body of a deity should be of the size of a Haṁsa. Ṛṣis, gandharvas, vidyādharas, daityas, dānavas, ministers, Brahmans, Saṁvatsara (i.e., Śiva), and the family priest (purohita) should be of the size of a Bhadra. Yakṣas; prostitutes, and Vaisyas should have the size of a Ruchaka. Kinnaras, rākṣasas, Nāgas, and domestic women should have the size of a Mālavya, while the chief among men and the Shudras should be of the size of a Śaśaka (chap. 42).

Together with pramāṇa and kṣaya and vṛddhi, the knowledge of modeling or shading (varttanā) was fully known to the Indian masters of old. It is stated to be threefold:[22] (1) patraja—cross lines; (2) airika—stumping; and (3) vinduja—dots (chap. 41). How much observation and technical experience is needed to state their results in such clear terms will be understood. Yet "whatever the artist represents he should avoid placing one figure in front of another" (chap. 43). Once more, one notices the same counteraction of abstraction and observation as in the case of landscape painting. A logical employment of kṣaya and vṛddhi would have implied oversecting. But the Indian artist cherishes every single form as a whole, as containing all he has to express and as containing the whole of nature. So he cannot bring himself to cover and hide one of its parts.

As for the employment of color, we have the following information from the *Viṣṇudharmottara* and other sources. Five primary colors consist of white, yellow, black, blue, and the color of the myrobalan, according to our text (chap. 40), or white, red, yellow, black, green, according to our text (chap. 27) and the *Nāṭyaśāstra;* white, red, yellow, soot, and dark blue or black (śyāma) according to the *Śilparatna.* The *Abhilaṣitārtha Cintāmaṇi* knows as pure colors white made of conch shell, red (prepared from red lead or from alaktaka juice, i.e., lac, or from red chalk—gairika), green-brown (haritāla), i.e., sulphureted arsenic, and black from kajjvala (soot, used as eyeblack).[23]

The mixing of these colors is left to the ingenuity of the artist. He may coat them with lac and resin. Coloring substances are gold, silver, copper, mica, deep colored brass, red lead, vermilion, tin, yellow orpiment, yellow myrobalan, lac, indigo, and some kind of iron oxide. Prescriptions for the preparation of these vegetable and mineral colors are given in the *Śilparatna.*[24] Red chalk, for instance, ought to be ground on stone and left covered with water for a day; red lead also ought to be ground and covered with water for half a day; red arsenic, however, should be made into powder, but it should not be covered with water. Then the colors should be ground once more and again put into water for five days. Afterwards they should be mixed with the exudation of the Nimba tree, then at last they are ready to be applied on walls and in pictures.

Gold leaf should be divided into finest leaflets, and then ground with a well-smoothed stone; afterwards it has to be mixed with water and with a small amount of sand. When this paste is well ground, it should again be put into water so that all dirt may rise to the surface. The gold paste should then be pressed, mixed with vajralepa and applied with suitable brushes. There should be nine brushes for every color.[25] When dry, the artist should rub it slowly with a boar tusk until it becomes bright. Then again he may place over this very fine gold leaves and rub them with hard cotton. The same prescription is to be found in the Abhilaśitārtha Cintāmani.

As to the preparation of the ground, buffalo skin has to be boiled in water until it becomes soft as butter. The water then has to evaporate and sticks have to be made of the paste and dried in the sunshine. This hard plaster is called vajralepa.[26] If then boiled in a mud vessel with water, it will make fast any color with which it is mixed. If mixed with white mud, it has to be used as coating for the wall, in three layers, each layer being allowed to dry before the application of the next. On this the painting may be applied.[27] Previous to the process of vajralepa coatings, the wall has to receive a thick coating, consisting of bricks, burnt conches, and the like, powdered according to the *Śilparatna,* and mixed with sand, the watery preparation of molasses, and drops of the decoction of mudga (*phaseolus munga,* mung pulse) amounting to a fourth part of the mortar powder. Into this, smashed ripe banana fruits have to be put, also a fourth part of the amount of the mortar. After three months, when this mixture has dried up, it shall be ground again. Then it must be mixed once more with molasses water until it gets the touch of fresh butter. In this stage it should be applied to the wall with a spoon, the wall having been cleansed with cocoanut fibers and having been sprinkled for some time with molasses water. This is the twofold process by which the wall is made ready for the drawing and the application of colors.[28]

The outlines ought to be drawn in yellow and red color, as a rule

> The painter should think of the proportionate size of the thing to be painted, and think of it as having been put on the wall. Then calculating its size in his mind, he should draw the outline marking all the limbs. It should be bright in prominent places and dark in depressed places. It may be drawn in a single color where comparative distinction is required. If depressed places are required to be bright, jet black should be used.[29]

The modeling capacity of the outline is also described in the *Vṛddhaśālabhañjikā*. This outline has to be filled with the first color wash which, as a rule, is white, but according to the *Viṣṇudharmottara* also may be green.

The coloring of things seen, says the *Viṣṇudharmottara*, is true to nature. Great emphasis is laid on the thousandfold mixtures of colors left to the imagination of the artist, and on the light and dark shade of every tone. The range of colors must have been wide enough to render with subtlety the local color of objects. The different tribes and castes of India are thus distinguished as dark, when belonging to the Pulindas and people of the South, to Pañchālas, Śūrasenas, and Magadhas, to Aṅgas, Vaṅgas, and Kaliṅgas, to Shudras—to sick men and to family men engaged in toilsome work. Śakas, Yavanas, Pallavas, and the Vālhikas should be predominantly white, and so are the twice-born and the Kshatriyas, kings, and prosperous people. Those who are oppressed by evil stars are of dark color. And it is also clear that evildoers ought to be of a dark complexion. The color thus has partly descriptive and partly suggestive significance. The dṛṣṭa and adṛṣṭa hold their sway; symbol and illustration are amalgamated into an expressive language, keenly alive to all those visual impressions that are on a small scale, obtrusively finite, and seem to carry their meaning expanded within their outlines, as local color. But this ambiguity of the color in its suggestive and descriptive faculty was clearly kept apart. Taken in a naturalistic and descriptive sense, the sky or the atmosphere has to be painted as almost without any special color.[30] The sky, on the other hand, is of the color of the blue lotus and wears a garment of that color, if represented as a statue, when it should carry the sun and the moon in its hands.[31] Color symbolism underlies not only the painting of statutes which, according to their Sāttvika, rājasika, and tāmasika aspects, had to be painted white, red, or dark, but was respectively selected for rasa-citras, the pictures of emotions, which, according to the *Śilparatna*, formed a group by themselves, distinct from the realistic paintings that were resembling what is actually seen in nature and looked like a reflex in a mirror.[32] Each rasa (emotion) had to be painted in its expressive color, the śṛṅgāra (erotic) was of śyāma hue, the laugh-exciting (hāsa) of white color, the pathetic (karuṇa) of grey color, the furious (rudra) of red color, the heroic (vīra) of yellowish-white color, the fearful (bhayānaka) of black color, the supernatural and amazing of yellow color, and the repulsive (loathsome, bībhatsa) of blue color.[33]

The expressionism of colors visualizes a temperamental attitude and is concerned with the wide range of emotions. Yet side by side with it, color in its descriptive quality was made use of to a large extent. It was not only known as local color, distinctive of, and unchanging with, the various objects, but also its modifications due to light and surroundings were considered: "Vajra said: my curiosity (runs) high, and I wish to hear (more) about the true and untrue colours of water, mentioned by you. Mārkaṇḍeya replied: The untrue colour of water resembles that of lapis lazuli. It is the effect of the reflexion of the sky in water. But the natural colour of water is seen in the falling down of water-falls; it resembles moonlight."[34]

The abstract and the realistic vision, which, as a rule, we hold apart as poles in the evolution of art, isolated from one another by gradual steps of development or by the sudden gap of reaction, are but the two sides of Indian art, contemporary and organic, for the obverse is turned toward that which lies outside, changeable, alluring in its variety and provoking observation, while the reverse faces the within, essentially unchangeable, because continually stirred up by emotions, of which *cetanā,* the life movement, is the common source. To do justice to them, a language of symbols comprises colors and measurements in solemn hierarchy.[35]

After having dealt with the theory of painting, the *Viṣṇudharmottara,* 44–85 proceeds, giving directions how to make images of various deities, more than eighty in number. The purpose of these images is to have the deity nearby (cf. p. 31 and p. 65) to be in actual contact with it; the images thus actually have become "mingled with men," as it had been declared by the Rupnāth and other rock inscriptions of Aśoka, about a millennium before our text was compiled.[36] Out of the pantheon, leaving aside the avatars of Vishnu and his aspects as Brahma and Śiva in their respective varieties including the corresponding goddesses, prescriptions for the making of images of deities scarcely known at present as actual sculptures demand attention. The Nāsatyas, for instance (p. 72), physicians of the gods, the Manus (p. 92), the Maruts (p. 95), the images of Artha (p. 96), of the *Sāmaveda*, and of the *Ṛgveda* (p. 98), are personifications of a most variegated nature. Beside these, however, another group of "visualizations" is of no small importance. Directions are given with regard to the making of liṅgam, vyoman, and aiḍuka. Whereas the first symbol is widely used, the more complex forms of vyoman and aiḍuka (pp. 100, 108) are hitherto unknown as actual objects of worship. Both of them seem to be the remnants of an aniconic cult, the plastic equivalent to some degree of the graphic yantras. Their geometry strongly contrasts with the florid features of the anthropomorphic forms. Yet a connection is established between them, the yantra and the anthropomorphic image, by the minute description of the lotus (p. 66) on which the worship of the gods should be performed. This lotus should be of metal or some other material. Metal is mentioned in the first place because of the possibility of minute execution, allowing for a precise description with regard to the number of petals, the distance between pericarp and petals, and so forth.

It is said that by worshiping aiḍuka, the worship of this world should be regarded as accomplished. The form of aiḍuka consists of a combination of various stereometric figures, the liṅgam and the figures of the four lokapalas. It is a complex rendering of the liṅgam "by worshiping which" the adoration of the world should be (regarded as) accomplished and of the vyoman "by the worship of which the worship of the world should be (regarded as) accomplished" too (pp. 99, 100). Vyoman (the upper regions) consists of cubical and spheroid parts on which is established an eight-petaled lotus with the sun god in the center, and the Dikpālas in their proper places.

The yantra-like nature of the lotus pedestal is suggested by the lotus shape which yantra and maṇḍala as linear representations take. Its yantric character moreover, is pronounced by the *Viṣṇudharmottara* (p. 67), stating that "that god only and no other should be worshiped on the lotus, by contemplating whom in mind, it was set up." The lotus therefore is no mere pedestal. It is magically linked up with the image it carries. A similar magic can be assumed as connecting not only the various stereometric parts of vyoman and aiḍuka, but of all the bhadrapithas that serve as pedestals to the images along with the lotus, and serve as plinths with or without lotus profiles to medieval Indian temples. The temple builder and the imagemaker were working on the same foundation of a magical suggestiveness of form-connections. But the rules, valid for both, apply to painting too, as far as they can be applied there. The prescriptions translated in the following pages are valid for images as well as for book illustrations.

This common basis of architecture, sculpture, and painting—it was shown that it primarily underlies dancing—at times is responsible for a fusion of the various disciplines of sculpture and painting, for a desperate attempt of visualizing what perhaps is beyond visualization. Says the *Viṣṇudharmottara* with regard to the image of Hari-viśvarūpa (p. 107), "according to the capacity of the artist that god should be made. . . . By the way of painting one should show according to the rules of the Śāstras the whole aggregate of the three worlds attached to his body." This prescription, in its endeavor to render abstractions in a concrete, tangible, and visible form, stands in glaring contrast to a prescription like the one about the making of the image of vyoman. Two utterly different trends of mind, two utterly different traditions, are placed side by side and intermingle in this treatise on image making. It stores up old heritage and the practice of the day and at times proves that both are older than its words; it cannot avoid at times interpreting scholastically what imagination and representation had achieved spontaneously. It speaks, for instance, about the mottled skin of the black antelope, explaining its contrasting colors because all sacrifice is propagated by work white and not white (pious and impious). Nevertheless such doctrinal scholasticism does not detract much from the value of this treatise. It is common to all ecclesiastical literature on art.

For most of the images definite colors are prescribed (cf. also p. 33). Nevertheless no trace of color is to be found on stone images after the Gupta period. Probably the coloring referred only to representations of gods as book illustrations and in pictures.

About the form of worship, only one allusion is made (p. 102) with regard to the image of Dharma. "Only if anyone is accompanied by his wife and then is initiated (into the mysteries of Dharma) then Dharma should be (regarded as) established." This reference to the Dharma cult, exclusively made, corroborates the dating of the treatise as belonging approximately to the seventh century, when the cult of dharma, being new, deserved special mention. No allusion is made to any form of the other well-established cults.

16 Ajanta

A. PRINCIPLES

1. Space

Indian painting of the Ajanta type, known to us from the second to the sixth century A.D. (pls. 16-1–4), is not conceived in terms of depth. It comes forward. It is not visualized as starting from a plane near the spectator and leading away from him, but departs from a level at the bottom of its visible expanse and from there it opens up and shows its contents simultaneously from within many compartments.

It does not lead away., but it comes forth. All other types of painting obey two possibilities. They treat the ground as surface and exist within its two dimensions, or they create, in one way or another, an illusion of leading into depth.

Painting in terms of surface, however, is the rule in the Deccan from the sixteenth century onwards. This vision, as in Ellora, is forecast from the eighth century and earlier. Painting conceived in terms of depth does not exist in the Deccan, although from the sixteenth century onwards, contacts with Western painting introduce some of its spatial conventions.

The two modes of painting, the one in terms of surface, the other, as in the Deccan during its most relevant phase, in the direction of forthcoming, do not aim at giving a picture of the world as it is beheld by the eye. Both show it as it exists in the mind. Painting in the direction of forthcoming will first be investigated as this direction is the essential one of classical Indian painting, preserved as it is mainly in the Deccan.[1] It is, moreover, relatively the least exploited in painting outside India.

This essay first appeared in *A Survey of Painting in the Deccan* (Calcutta, 1937).

Viewed historically the two modes of painting, the one in the direction of forthcoming and the other in terms of surface, overlap after the sixth century. When the latter gains supremacy in the last phase of Deccani painting, strengthened by Turko-Persian confluences, it is upheld by an Indian past of long duration. The latter mode has to be referred to and defined with reference to the former.

The naïve outlook on life depends on where one stands. From that standpoint things are seen. The prospect may include the near and the far, heaven and earth.

INTERNAL SPACE

With the Ajanta painter we look, however, into the opposite direction. Aware of ourselves as experiencing the world, we turn back upon ourselves as the place that holds the world, and there we behold it in a direction that does not lead away from us, but points back toward ourselves. We are stage and spectator of the world as we see and live it. There is nothing to lead us away into a distance outside ourselves, and there is no room for nostalgia or perspective. There are no places to be gone to for they are all within us, seen, visualized and remembered. No time is lost, for it does not exist, to take us from the one to the next. Past and present events are there all together and nothing has happened which does not hold good and nothing holds good that will not endure. Memory transmutes time with a rhythm of simultaneous sequences on the stage which we ourselves make up and behold.

The world with its objects and events and their sequence in time is localized within ourselves. Memory assigns them their position and the world picture is on view to our mind all at a time, as far as it matters. The stage on which the panorama is laid out does not exist apart from ourselves, and its space is not external. We hold it—without pictures—in the hollow of our hand or in the cavity of the chest, a space within us. There it is not lit up by imagination nor is it charged with meaning. It fills the internal cavities and is part of our body. There is no such space if the hand is stretched out and the chest rent open.

Such a bodily experience of space actually or potentially within ourselves underlies the vision of space in paintings in the Deccan of the type of Ajanta. Primarily this space is not seen as is external space, the undefined. The latter yields the boundless symbol of the infinite and refers to it on a higher plane where bodies do not exist. The wide and open spaces beheld by the eye or felt to connote the infinite, have not entered painting as in Ajanta. Space there appears as a condition of the world of bodies, and what is situated in space makes up space itself. It has reciprocal reality and acts as a receptacle. The world is such a receptacle. It holds men, animals, gods, and other "walks of life."[2] They are all interlaced in a network. While they move in it, they knit its meshes. This receptacle is closely filled, each being has its definite residence and what separates them is the space, the condition itself which shows them as separate. This internal space of the world-receptacle has a substantiality of its own in function of its reciprocity with extended bodies. "Space is form and . . . as space penetrates into form, form is space."[3] The sensation of the internal space within our own living body is the analogy according to which the world is known to us, experienced and beheld within ourselves.

Space, a primary experience within our body, simultaneously makes us aware of its limits and of external space, its wider correspondence. This vacuity, outside our body, is filled with air, and with breath inside. While we think, we breathe. During the movement of breath, thoughts take shape. The painter thinks in pictures, and when he paints them, he shifts their stage from within his consciousness onto the other side of the limits of his body. He turns the figures around and also their whole setting so that they confront him. They have come out from his mind to be seen by his eye. The process of turning them round, turning the contents of his vision inside out is, however, a later stage of his work. It presupposes the "return" of his mind, at the moment of beholding the objective world as a manifestation of mind itself.[4] His consciousness returns toward itself with articulate vision and settles at the fringe of the vastness of mind where forms and names are not, the names and forms that now dwell there. These ultimately the painter projects onto the wall as in Ajanta; steeped in color, the world as he knows it comes forward to meet his glance.

The wall paintings at Ajanta show the internal space[5] of consciousness and its contents. They are a picture of the world-receptacle[6] teeming with people, spirits, and gods, their mansions, hermitages, and pleasances, with their arising and then being dismissed from the vast store of the mind. This is their ground. Once arisen they take their proper place. This taking place of form, its progression from the storehouse of the mind into visibility, is painted in Ajanta in a direction which leads from within the picture outward.

THE DIRECTION OF FORTHCOMING

There is no background in the accepted sense, and it is just from there that all the visualized world proceeds, full of itself, with its bodies and their spaces, compact in its density. Its progression is uninterrupted in the simultaneousness of closely set scenes. They are shown as coming forth from within the storehouse of the mind, and their movement in an outward direction proceeds in each case up to the point where the one instant or scene of a story is strung together with the next in a sequence in which time has no share. Although many stories are painted, their course is not visualized. Such moments and scenes which endure in their importance throughout the story are laid out and are linked rhythmically. Rhythm sways the surfaces of the walls while it meanders across all the scenes, pregnant at any phase with the movement that started it. The scenes are threaded on it, poised. This movement is the web on the surface, and keeps it intact. Across this transparent web, we see the scenes. It cannot be removed without disturbing the process itself of scenes and figures coming forward from their starting point. While the painting as a whole appears to come forward with all its scenes in uninterrupted progression, the latter is closely bound together by the rhythms which play over the surface. The entire compact mass of the painting results from movement.

Its space is charged with directions. The major direction is the forward movement, and its origin is metaphysical. From beyond the world of bodies, it sets them forth, each with its name, and most of them have their shape while their form is produced as they come forward, along with and in between the pillared palaces and pavilions and embracing as much space as each has body. The forward direction itself concreted into prismatic shapes is the principle according to which rocks are painted (pl. 16-1) when they show three surfaces, front, side, and the bottom simultaneously of the single boulders, in contrasting colors and with a shading which gives volume toward the edges. Such rocks are grouped around caves and also serve as platforms for the figures. The blocks and the rafter-like boulders come forward, each with the energy of a train shown in a cinema with the ever-growing engine coming, larger and larger, toward the spectator. Each has a special direction and this makes it detach itself from the neighboring block with a maximum volume. Rocks appear cleft with their insides out; they push forward and slide along like rafters or they settle in a stepped order. Wherever recesses open, human figures dwell, animals and trees. The constituents of this rock architecture in the process of be-

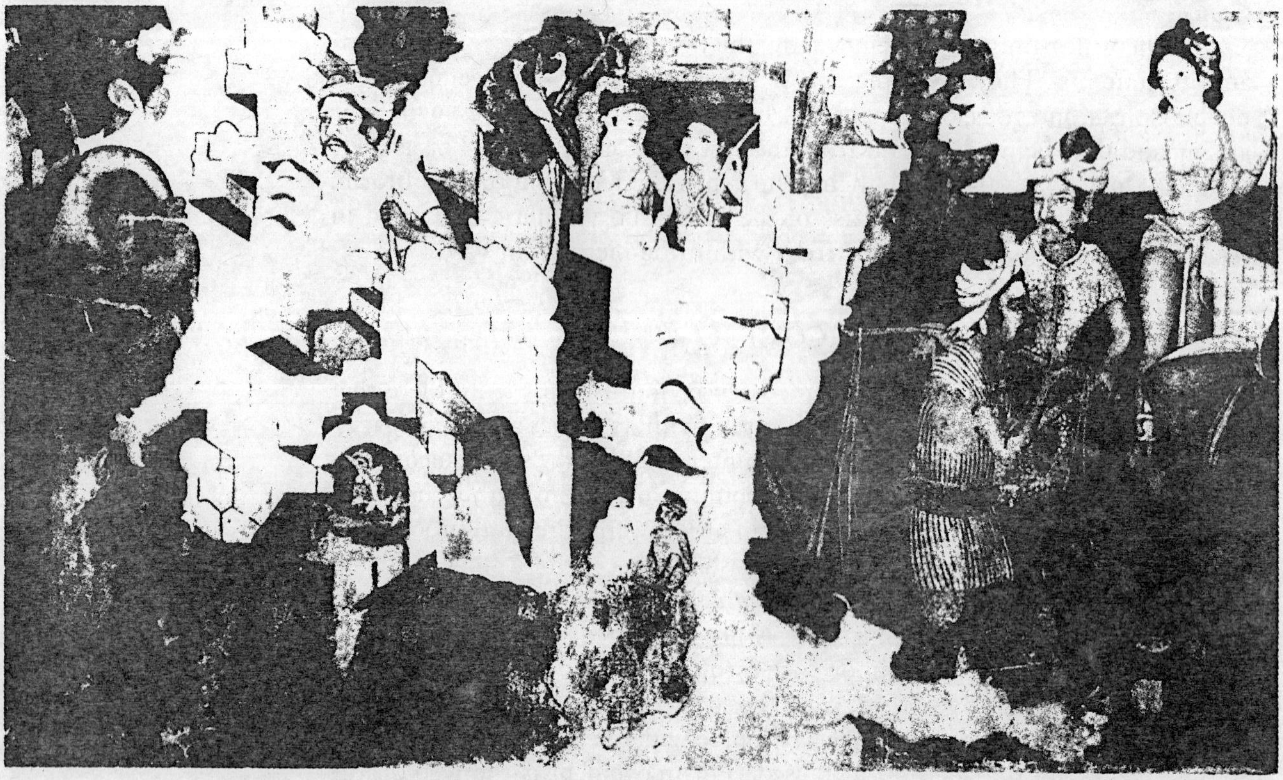

16-1. Copy of part of frieze, Ṣaddanta Jātaka, cave 10, Ajanta.[7] *The colors as they appear at present: Rocks of the Suvarṇa ridge: front surface grey with yellow lines, or else whitish. The other surfaces are reddish brown. Other rock cubes are yellow or white with yellow, the cave in which the two figures are set is dark brown-red in its interior. The colors of Sonuttara, the hunter: reddish brown complexion, red turban, white coat with black stripes; that of the other figures, including the second appearance of the hunter, is light yellow or grey with a black pattern.*[8]

The foliage is bluish green, shaded in color, with young leaves, reddish. Modeling in color is applied throughout. The light surface on either side of the rocks appears as a neutral ground. The upper edge of the dark portion below does not indicate the horizon. In the subsequent scene, curtains are suspended[9] *and above them flowers appear scattered on the ground of the painting.*

coming are the single prisms or rafters and their reciprocal space volumes. They have gained pictorial visibility by the mind of the painter placing itself behind the rocks and before they have come into existence. It produces the solid mass of the rocks by traveling inside and along each of their prisms, layer by layer, and in as many directions as will lead forward. The crystalline structure of the volume of rocks is built out of the directions forward which its shape has to traverse so as to acquire form on the stage on which play the scenes of the Ajanta paintings. These rocks are not described in any of the known texts on painting. They are, however, essential requisites. Their stereometry proceeds from points that have to be imagined behind the painting itself, where they lie hidden like the germs of things to come. Their stereometry is charged with the spell which shows their form in the making.

Adapted to the metaphysical movement and resulting in cubic shape is also the "multiple perspective." Not only the rocks, but also houses and objects, are painted as if seen simultaneously level with the eye and from above, or simultaneously level with the eye and from below (pls. 16-2 and 16-3).[10] Things are actually not seen as they appear, but imagined as they are. Not only Indian art shows three dimensional objects in this way. Functionally interdependent in the multiple view that they proffer, they are as closely knit in their meaning as they are in their connected forthcoming from within the unseen which discharges them compact in their balance across the levels of the painting so that they fill the entire stage. As a restrained mode of sculpture, their colorful display within the outermost surface, that is, that of the rhythmic web and the but fractionally visible innermost color surface, comprises in its density the space held in between them. The entire borderland of the mind with its contents is shown situated between the vertical plane of the inmost color surface and the transparent rhythmical web of which the outer surface consists; it is shown in the process itself by which it comes forth. Houses open like magical boxes. Without walls they hold their figures within the space marked by their pillars. None of them slips down or out of the picture. The rhythmic web, which they themselves make up, keeps them in place.

Within the forward direction of movement and the space which it constructs there is room also for backward movements. These, however, extend only as far as the forward movement allows, now here, now there, a shiver across its impact, a tendency to sink back into its origin. It remains in that stage and does not go further back, carried as it is by the metaphysical movement of forthcoming. Elastically it is replete with its antagonistic tendency. The forward direction builds up the borderland space of these paintings. Within it figures may turn and move backwards or laterally. Every possibility of extension is held within this borderland. It is not to be seen as having dimensions. These paintings do not give an illusion on a flat surface of the three dimensional conditions of concrete appearance or reality. They are precipitated from a reality teeming with possibilities of manifestation of which some are shown as they proceed from within it. This reality cannot itself be pictured. Formless, it lies at the bottom, behind the entire display which it emits; a fringe of its robe is held forth for the eye to view. It is beset in its entire width with receptacles of rock and house shape. Like magical boxes they show their contents which will not slip nor drop out of them if tilted.

THE DIRECTION OF FORTHCOMING AND ITS OBJECTS

With this forward movement the borderland is replete; while filling it with its objects such as palaces, pavilions, rocks, and the many figures that these hold, it makes itself the fabric of the fringe on which the many dwelling places are set as its building material. The space of this borderland is the visible outcome of the movement of forthcoming. Such visualization of movement constructing existence has its mythical counterparts. Dancing, Śiva creates and also destroys the world. Vishnu with three strides takes possession of the universe. Their movement holds its space. The world is built out of movement. The *Abhidharmakośa*,[11] for instance, describes how the winds increase until finally they constitute the circle of wind. Then is born the whole receptacle, circle of water, the golden earth, the Mount Meru with its terraces, the palace of Brahmā, and then all the castles up to those of the Yamas, in all twenty-two kinds of devatās, dwelling in the world receptacle with definite residences. The entire world is brought about by movement, its structure with all the various levels of existence, and the beings in them all in their definite residences.

A. Receptacles

The definite residence of every figure, group, and scene is the visible unit within the borderland which fills the paintings. The borderland, like a thick fringe, slips forth in between the slits of doors and curtains and any colored surface, which leads from nameless plenitude at the back to the fullness of figures in front. They are contained within definite residences and these are stable receptacles for the manifestation of their activities and the part they act within the stories. Viewed, however, within the whole, their stability is relative and each scene and the place where it is enacted itself is part of, and goes to make up, the forward movement. This movement persists even when it appears upheld in definite places on the slopes of Mount Meru. Such is the cosmographical aspect of the setting of the scenes at Ajanta. With palaces and rocks, the slopes of the world-mountain are covered.

Palaces and rocky scenery in their own small way act like magical boxes. They hold the manifestation of the activities of scenes and moments of many stories. Held and comprised within their receptacles, the movements of the actors are at liberty. Not only is the moment illustrated by telling gestures of figures which can be identified. By their movements and gestures the scene coheres and its constellation, its moment, is caught within their movements and within the further direction of their movements beyond their bodies. With its direction every movement transcends its carrier; when men sit down to play a game (pl. 16-2), their position round the dice board is assigned to them by their interest in each other and in the game, and they show it by their movements and the way they are turned toward one another. The charged moment of their play is replete with such communication. Its threads are intangible but nevertheless conspicuous as directions from the one to the other and within the group, which sets up its own space body, a reciprocal condition of their forming a group, and replete with directions, charged with them as the moment itself is fraught with meaning. Such are the contents of one magical box, and those of the next may vary in theme but not in the manner of its presenta-

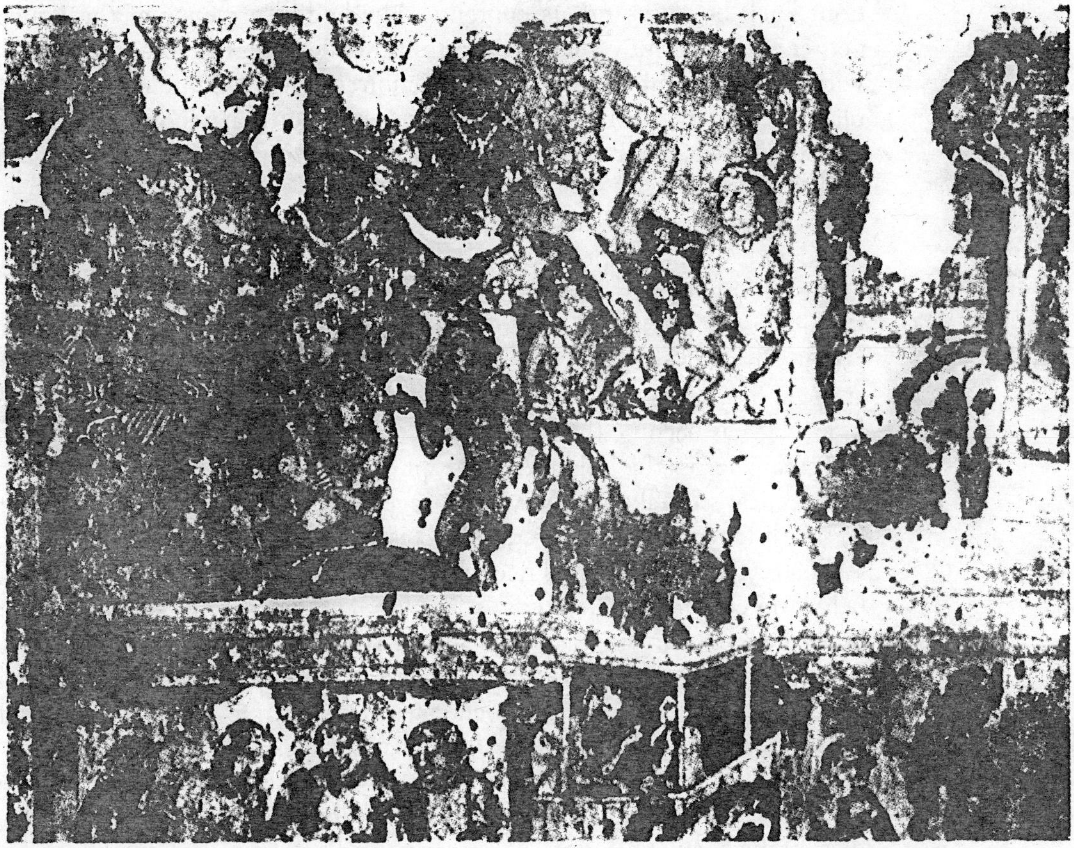

16-2. Vidhurapaṇḍita Jātaka (left part), cave 2, Ajanta. In this part of the painting, the figure of the magic horse is shown carrying the action from scene to scene. It is turned hither and thither, a link between the several compartments, shuffled the one into the next, along the direction of forthcoming. It is shown flying through the air and over the vaulted roof of a high building; the rocking horse stillness of two more of its appearances in this part of the painting functions as part of the rhythm of the simultaneous layout of the story.

The main group to the left makes a kind of ellipsoid; it fills the compartment diagonally, from the corner of the parapet "above" on the right, with the figure of Vidhurapaṇḍita squatting in front, to the corner of the balustrade "below" on the left. Similarly also the "gaming hall," intersected by a corner of the first apartment, is full of an elliptical grouping of all its figures and in a corresponding direction.

The standing figure of Pūrṇaka, in the first scene, is apart from the main group and connects this scene vertically, and with the help of the pillar with the compartment beneath it below. Its forward bending movement is reiterated by Pūrṇaka squatting in the second scene, near the pillar on the right, where the vertical direction also is upheld. It rests in either case on the broad horizontal of the wall, and is further strengthened by many more verticals.

At the same time, coordinates and ellipsoids are traversed by large rhythms; the two main compartments by a rising arch from the corner on the left to the highest figure of a king in the compartment on the right; another arch parallel with it carries the two appearances of Pūrṇaka, and a third, once more parallel, runs across the figure of the queen in her own compartment with her attendant, and across that of the magic horse turned to the right, into a subsequent scene which plays in the pillared hall of the residence of the Nāga king (only part of one figure is shown in the reproduction, to the utmost right).

Simultaneously these widely flung arches are crossed by others in the opposite direction; one comprises the horse turned to the left, and the figures of Pūrṇaka, the squatting minister, and King Dhanaṁjaya, in the first compartment; another passes the horse turned to the right and the "gaming hall" in a parallel sense. These movements are not confined within the several compartments and are shown in this part reproduction in one or several phases only of their course. The smaller and the wider rhythms are interknit, and where a point is fixed by their crossing, it is also carried in more than one direction. Paradoxically complex, the coherence of form defies a reduction to one or the other scheme of composition. The scenes below again are similarly connected among themselves and with those above.

tion. Each box presents its contents. The bodily presence of the figures together with their movements, conditions, while it fills the actuality of the space within the magical box. No lids are required, for the contents exactly fill the place of their performance, and terrace or balcony, pavilion or hermitage fit the charged space as the glass walls of an aquarium hold the water within it with the fish, gravel, and plants.

The receptacle and its contents cohere. Together they arrive on the scene and remain suspended by their impact at the spot where the meaning of the story will have it. In an extreme case in one painting of no great quality, massive rock cubes are the requisite setting and are laid out in crystalline compounds to one side of a scene of cattle at rest; two of the animals have got up at the appearance of rākṣasas. The neck of the one in back view is inordinately long.[12] It has become the receptacle of the space which the animal is bent on traversing across the hills and to this purpose its neck is stretched in the direction it means to take not only with eagerness, but also in spatial anticipation of the distance "to be covered." It takes that distance into the disproportionately stretched length of its neck so that the crystalline arrays of rocks extend below on either side of the cow's shoulder and head. The error of making the body itself, or part of it, a receptacle of space other than that which belongs to it is one of the most revealing blunders of an Ajanta craftsman. His mistake is set off by the tradition in which it has its place. He wrongly constructs on valid tracks when he exchanges the relative roles of space and volume.

While there are no massive front or side walls to the rooms in the Ajanta paintings, they are upheld by pillars. Their long verticals are carried like candles by the heavy horizontals of parapets and balustrades. Together they form systems of coordinates, and a separate one for each scene. Tightly, and definite in its frailty, each is raised above or by the side of another constellation. Balanced on multiple planes, at various phases of forthcoming, the several constellations are set, each with reference to its coordinates. Like trays with tall candles their systems are balanced, and viewed on the entire expanse of the painted wall, they seem as if handed on from here to there.

The forward direction of the Ajanta paintings leads charged space within open receptacles visualized in multiple perspective across a borderland of which the outer limit is a transparent web of rhythms. Wholly continuous throughout its planes and levels, it is replete with dwelling places, almost every one a palace. This world truly is like a stage, like the city of the Gandharvas. It is neither existent nor nonexistent.[13]

Kant, viewing the Western position of art, opposed the world as reality and the world as beauty. The latter he took to be the world of art inasmuch as it made concrete reality unreal. Such an unclothing of reality and its translation into beauty belong to a sphere altogether different from that of Buddhist or Brahmanical art in India. There, concrete reality itself is known as unreal and in this knowledge it is painted as it is known. It abides in the mind and is beheld by it.

The world itself is divested of its concrete reality. Such as is beheld is not separated from us, it is within ourselves, a reflection in a mirror, and in this indissoluble phantasmagoria of ourselves and the world there is no scope for shadows.[14] Similar is the vision in Hiuan Tsang's *Vijñāptimātratasiddhi.*[15]

It describes how the Bodhisattva introduces all "rūpa," the visible world, the villages, mountains, and so forth, into his own substance in the presence of a large gathering which recognizes itself entered into his substance.

Such a mirage is made manifest, proceeding continuously and closely bound together within the borderland that extends from the color surface of doors, screens, walls, and carpet-like floors, forward to the interwoven web in which it is caught up, transparent, in the texture of flowing rhythms. Correlated to its plenitude, the narrow space in which its figures dwell is charged with their gestures and glances and with the intangible movements of their breathing and thoughts.

The visualized stage of these paintings extends from opaque planes denoting walls, doors, or at times a screen of verdure, to the web of rhythms in front. Fully rounded, the figures hold their place by an instantaneous correspondence of their varied movements, within buildings or surrounded by rocks, on a ground strewn over with flowers in the borderland into which they have been dismissed from the invisible and undefined. Each is set forth by the impact of the whole.

Still life, "nature morte," is a branch of painting altogether unknown and alien to Indian art. Projected from within the mind and along with the other contents, inanimate objects share its movement and are part of its life. In living reality, movement always goes on. In the paintings it makes its carriers appear divested of part of their weight, just as a dancer's movement gives to his body the sensation and appearance of lightness. No object figured in these paintings can be considered isolated and each is carried by its origin.

B. Group and Figure

Groups are threefold in their connections. In relation to the unformed, they are its exponents; each group one whole within its setting of house or rocks. Within the borderland they are strung together by the rhythm of existence; each group moreover coheres by a participation of the figures which form it. Each figure, however, once more and straightaway is bodied forth by the impact of the unformed.

The group by itself has not come out from the unformed. It does so within and along with its receptacle. It may at times largely fill its extent as one cohesive massive (pl. 16-2, bottom on left); as a rule, however, the figures are more loosely set in loops and parabolic curves. In any case, the impact from the ground is not guided along their limbs. The groups taken as a whole are freed from the forward direction, for they dwell in and are supported by it. In its movement they are staid and yield themselves to the connections that bind them as inmates of the borderland. Still, in the way in which the figures are modeled the impact is felt; they are "bodied forth," embodied from within the colored surface in three-quarter profile view, in front or back view and very rarely in pure profile. Their movements, however, are effortless. They well up from the deep, from the innermost foundation of life. Physiologically from the region around the hips, psychologically from the flowing wealth of the unconscious.

The inner world which dwells in the figures, to the extent that they may entirely dwell within it, is their depth. From there their movements come forth. The way in which the human figures appear shaped in these paintings is analogous to the form itself of the entire painting.

The figures are brought forth and modeled by the impact from the deep. This is their sturdiness. But their agility, the bending and resilient curves are the oscillations of the rhythm of life in the guise of human shape. To allow them a smooth functioning, the joints are of importance, most of all the hip joint, where all these figures, seated or standing, have their center of gravity. The knowledge these figures have—for they embody it—is that of their depth. This is their secret.

The metaphysical movement has no share in the arrangement of the group—in respect to it the latter is a unit—while all the time it sustains every single figure in the wellbeing of its smooth shape. Every one of them holds its place in a twofold mission, as an exponent bodied forth into the borderland from the region that lies behind it, and as a part and passage of the movement itself within the borderland. By these two movements, one an impact, the other a rhythm, every figure is upheld. The architectonic receptacle or the one made of rock boulders (pls. 16-2 and 16-3) hold the presence of the group, and the volume of body and limbs encompasses the single figure.

MUDRĀS AND PHYSIOGNOMIES Their movements are mudrās, that is, seals of contents that they convey. Over and above this, they are charged with the non-communicable secret of being alive. Every body in those paintings has the face that belongs to it, and the physiognomy of the different types extends from top to toe on all sides. As the faculties and the mental disposition of a figure are, so also are its proportions and movements. The noble frame and face and the poised gesture belong to the figures who are members of the "family of Nirvāṇa." To this the figures belong with the mental disposition, inborn and acquired as well, of attaining Nirvāṇa.[16] According to other and lesser inborn and acquired dispositions, membership of other and lesser families results, and in conformity the figures look, move, and act. A hierarchy of types assigns their appearance to the single figures of men and gods alike. Those are the most accomplished types where physiognomy is altogether built up by measure. It is the proportion of the gods, and the lower the type, the less proportionate are body and face. The faces of demons and their bodies are altogether disproportionate and distorted. This is their standard. Further specifications are the attributes due to country of origin and occupation. These, however, are secondary marks. With reference to every sphere, none can be mistaken for something he is not.

Truly at home in the borderland, the bodies with ample curves and volume, and the faces which are as much part of them as are the hands, consist of what a person sees, hears, feels, tastes, and smells of the outer world and within the body itself. Scholastic texts from the *Mahāvibhāṣa* to Vasubandhu consider the objective world in the way it affects a human being, along with the sense organs in their connection with the objects and as supports of consciousness as making up the body of a human being.[17] All this is painted and the figures participate in the constellation under which they have come together, and each preserves its integrity.

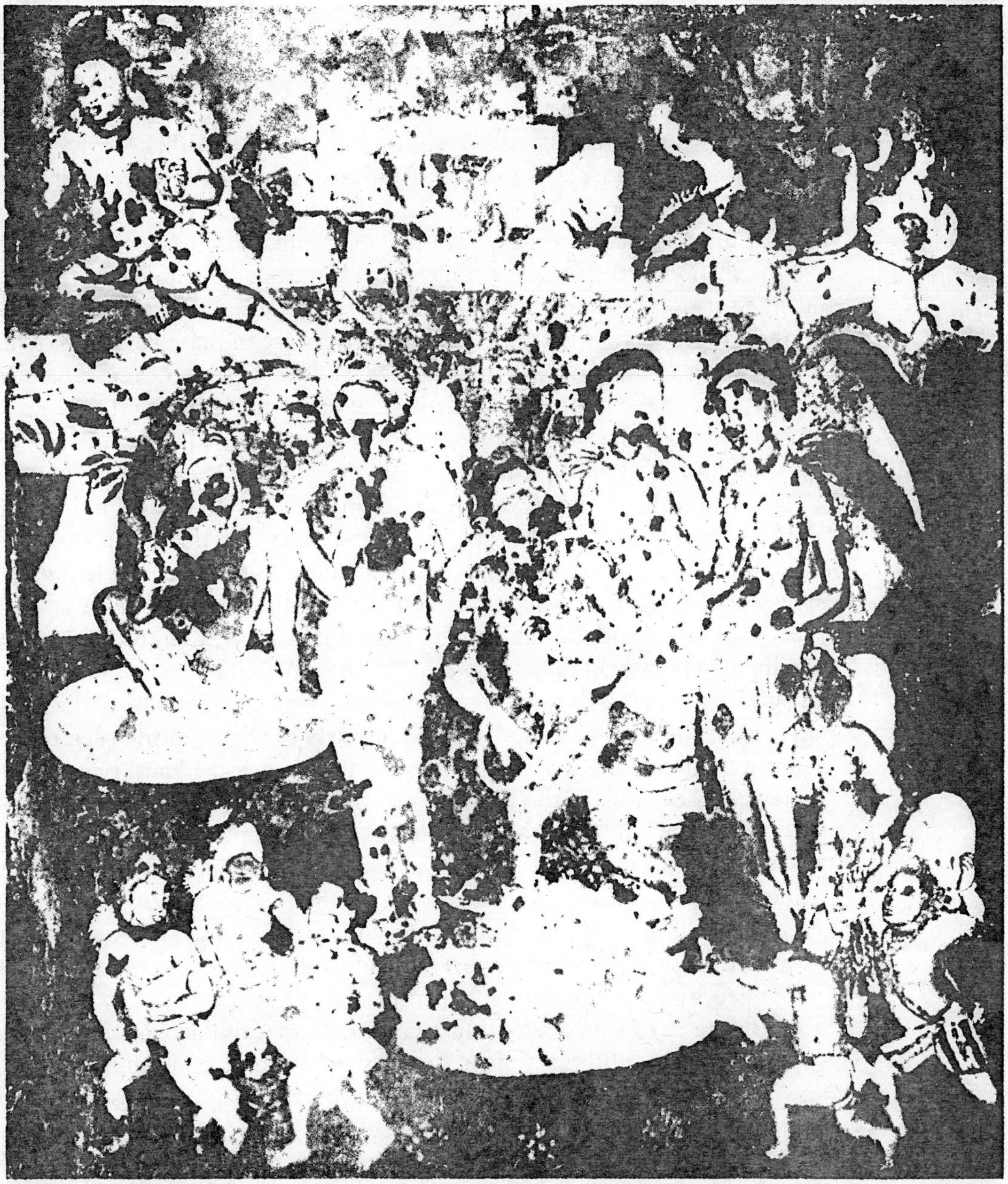

16-3. Votaries with offerings for Hāritī and Pañcika cave 2, Ajanta. The children are well accounted for in a scene devoted to Hāritī. Short and crisp curves bind their groups, the one horizontal, the other vertical, and each near the outer end of the forthcoming of the scene. It diverges from the middle and maintains a dynamic symmetry with weighted diagonals, with only the one figure of a flying vidyādhara intact on the left. The tall woman with the fly whisk is part of either diagonal movement. Her swaying vertical is reiterated by that of the other figure near the banana plant. Between their arms, the one raised with a fly whisk and the other lowered above the corresponding gesture of a small figure, turned and poised in the opposite direction, they rock the painting into balance. Round tray heaped with offerings, round seat of a Bodhisattva-like youth are rotating islands spinning into steadiness with the load they carry. Cave and banana plant, leaf and rock, on left and right, they clasp with their arches, quick with young sap and an adapted structure, the staid advance of this scene. It has its counterpart on the other side of the bay and its goal in the main direction of its figures, and at a right angle, on the back of the bay where the large images of Hāritī and Pañcika are carved.

MODELING AND ABSENCE OF SHADOWS The integrity of the single figure with regard to the group or in whatever connection it may be shown is the index of its balance. It measures the distance the body maintains from the inner person and from the outer objects that in any particular connection also belong to it. No shadows intervene.

The borderland is a land of no shadows. It is bathed in the full light of the mind; no corner is dark, and fully rounded, each object shines forth, as illuminated as it is informed. Nowhere else in the world of painting are bodies fully shaded in their plastic modeling and yet they cast no shadows.

Shadows are accidents. They are, moreover, destructive of form while its integrity is as essential to the figures in the painting as their name is to them in the story. There is no source of light anywhere in these paintings. The figures carry it in the modeled color of their bodies. A painter raises a painting,[18] he gives life to the figures by modeling them, by rounding them off with shading in color,[19] tone, and highlights. These are also raised and actually at times laid on with thick white color.

The highlight is the final mark of their mode of progression. It is neither derived from an outer source of light nor does it render the figures transparent. It makes their solid volume complete. The luminosity of the single figure does not extend further than its limits and belongs to its substance.

It corresponds to the opaque color intensity of the ground beset with the light stars of uncounted flowers (pls. 16-2, 16-3). They shine forth also like the gleam of the jewels worn by the figures. Whereas in sculpture the intricate carving of the jewelry sets off the smoothness of limbs, in the type of Indian painting which corresponds to it the highlight of beaded and twisted strings of jewelry accentuates the modeling of the smooth-skinned bodies.

Their attitudes are built upon the most complex relations with regard to their axis. Sitting or standing, their volumes sway around it. This swaying around the own axis is the mode in which the flux of life appears as personal grace in the single figures. Comprised within their ambient lines is the space between the axis and their limbs. It weighs on the hips of standing women, is hugged by seated figures left behind, and driven forward by flying ones. Each figure in this way sets forth a volume of space which corresponds to its own. It is the counterpart of its rounded appearance and mobility.

The modeled volume, however, of the single figures is still more intimately bound up with the space that belongs to it. Modeled as if breathing, the air inhaled can be followed into the neck, heart, nombril, hips, thighs, and down to the feet.[20] At the same time, and within the space enclosed by or clinging to their modeled bodies, they follow the exhaled air to the distance of the length of forearm and hand.[21] The living breath within the figure is shown in the modeling of the latter and still belongs to it outside the body in its corresponding space-volume. The figures appear upheld in it and their massive bodies are relatively weightless. They breathe their life into the moment of their presence.

This is carried by the linear rhythm on the varied levels to which the single receptacles appear pushed forth, having reached their destination by the impact which sets them forth. Their presence is kinetic. Shuffled in layers, the receptacles intersect in the direction of forthcoming (pl. 16-2).

2. *Limits*

OUTER LIMIT AND RHYTHM

The veil of rhythms, the plane most exteriorized, is not torn anywhere. It is kept in position by the impact of houses and scenes. They are set forth from a region behind the colored ground. The spectacle takes place on a well-defined stage. There are, in fact, as many stages as there are scenes, and that each scene has its place makes the consistency of this edifice all on different levels. The scenes being open, abandoned as they are to be looked at, not only from the front, but also laterally, are permeated by a connecting rhythm. Its movement, more than any balustrade, maintains the integrity of the scenes and prevents them from appearing as if spilled or shed from within the painting. The whole painting is beheld as one spectacle and it always remains at the same distance. These paintings cannot be entered by the eye from the front and traversed in the third dimension for the fact that their impact is too great; all of them while they open in front are activated by an even and imperceptible but unrelenting pressure. Where the painting stops, this pressure that shuffles forward its rooms ceases. It is here that the height of the painting, its imaginary foremost surface, is reached.

Having come forth from the storehouse of consciousness, the pictures are fully laid out and their sequence is not in the direction of time. The "multiple perspective" does not refer to space alone, but equally applies to time. The scenes are not shown in the sequence in which they happened and from whatever episode narration proceeds, past and future are equally present. They are present in the mind and there they are stored, and when they step out into appearance they are remembered. "Manas is the consciousness of the preceding moment,"[22] and it supports the consciousness of the coming moment. In this way the three are linked in their simultaneous coming forth into the field of visualized projection. Through the functioning of "manas" they cohere rhythmically, the end is in the beginning, and the stream of consciousness flows steadily and unbroken. Wherever the eye rests on the surface of these paintings it is compulsorily carried along, for beginning and end are in every one of their instants or points. Rhythm is not confined within any group, scene, or sequence of scenes. In its main cascades it floods the walls from left to right in oblique and wide open arches, while others, cast in the opposite direction cross them, and both have loops in common, eddies and rests. Those are brought about by an interaction of the metaphysical direction. Single figures are the points of crossing between the linear rhythm, the movement of existence confined to the borderland itself, and the forward movement, the metaphysical direction which leads from beyond, that is, behind the borderland, across it and up to its foremost limit.

Nor are the linear rhythms ever exposed, embodied as they are from figure to figure, in their plastic shapes. The space bodies are equally traversed by them. For the borderland is held in position by the rhythmic flux of existence. The widely flung curves across the vertical plane of the paintings make them cohere in the surface. They are drawn with such largess that they quietly guide the eye across the tension of the single scenes that they connect without being affected by them. These curves are invariably slow in their ascent and in their ebbing away. They have to be considered, far more than figures, groups and scenes as the ultimate performers on the painted stage of the Ajanta walls. They sum up figures, groups, and scenes. They allay their many directions while they pass across every one of the phantasmagoric rooms and connect them. As far as these leisured curves are concerned, the folding screen scaffolds that divide the scenes are traversed and carried by them to the same degree as the single constellations within the space volumes in which the scenes are enacted; partitions do not stay this major movement. Surging and sinking, it is the incalculable discipline, and times the painting according to one standard. Any movement of figures or groups, be it pensive or agitated, takes place within its measure. No agitation accelerates, nor does lack of gesture frustrate, the rhythmical movement. Figures shown rushing (pl. 16-3) appear upheld in their movement; direct and purposive as it is, it appears as if this were not the real movement, but only a quiver quickly arising and quickly extinct.

The metaphysical direction may be taken to be the visual analogy of "cetanā," the active force that directs consciousness and the linear rhythm equivalent with "saṁtāna," the consistent movement of life. The latter fills the borderland with its current. Within waves of fluctuation the objects are set forth from a ground. Its opaque surface, the plane of forthcoming or of reflection, is the colored wall of the storehouse of consciousness. With innumerable and fluffy pinheads of flowers, this common ground of unfoldment is held in position, a magic carpet throughout the scenes. Lightly are the figures borne by it. None is there who would tread upon the flowers with his gross weight. This has been transmuted in every figure before its coming into appearance, into flowing outlines and a round modeling carried by the rhythm of life, and it is this that passes over the blossoming ground with a tread which leaves no impress.

UPPER LIMIT (CEILING)

The magic borderland of the paintings has its place on the walls of the caves. It does not extend to the ceilings. These are bedecked with paintings; flowers and fruits,[23] scrollwork, animals, and scenes squarely fit into small-sized panels and the large circles of dome-like centers. Here the limit is definite and the memory of structural ceilings determines the layout of those cut in the rock. Architectural memories are met with the resources at the disposal of the painter of the borderland. The mythical figures and the few scenes up there betray by modeling and color the country of their origin. They conform to a plan, whereas on the walls they bring it about themselves while they are part of it. Exposed from within the borderland, they rest on the surface and within neat limits of the ceiling. It is in a playful spirit that they appear high up there, samples of the painter's art in an architectonic fancy.

Neither forthcoming nor a metaphysical direction can be seen in these circumscribed and well-filled panels. The "city of the Gandharvas" does not extend over a horizontal expanse. The slopes of Mount Meru are peopled in a vertical sequence of terraces and the plane of reflection, as a mirror is set up vertically. The metaphysical direction has no downward impact. The beyond lies at the back of all form, not above it, and sets it forth. It does not emanate into form. In that case form would be altogether weightless and static.

INNER LIMIT AND COLOR

Where the ground of the paintings on the walls is not covered by figures, it shows itself as a surface, as that of houses, screens, or door openings, for example, while for the largest part and with the help of the multiple perspective it is the ground itself on which the figures stand and act. Slanting, for it lies also on the slopes of Mount Meru, its surface is moss green, or Indian red or deep purple and is beset with flowers. They grow in the open and are scattered across the floors of rooms and verandas. In every case their light stars, with a feathery grace, fix the deeply colored surface of the ground to the vertical wall of the cave. There it is kept in position; saturated with color it emits the ripe roundness of the figures and covers all that lies in the region behind them and from where they have originated.

While the outer limit, the veil of rhythms, is transparent and shows the borderland coherent in their order, the inner limit is opaque. Charged with color, as the space of the borderland is charged with directions, it is at the same time the ground from which the figures arise in their plastic forthcoming as form and the floor or ground on which they are seen standing as figures. Ground and support in a dual sense, it becomes one in appearance and meaning if the scenes are beheld playing on the slope of Mount Meru. Such a view is afforded by the mythical world picture, and actually the borderland holds a view of existence itself, that is to say, of mind itself with its contents. They are tangibly exposed from within a depth which cannot be seen. It can be surmised from the colors with which its surface is saturated. The visible world, the borderland, is painted as a manifestation of mind itself. With all its objects exposed the latter lies itself with eyes closed, behind the saturated color surface with flowers strewn all over it.

The saturated color of the ground is the smooth surface of the invisible reservoir of form. Color is that visible quality which is nearest to its nameless condition. Across the colored ground and from the unfathomed depth behind, its contents become tangible on being set forth. They are connected from the origin, supporting in every point, the rhythm of the whole. The scenes (pl. 16-2) with their figures are carried high or low, to the top or bottom, and they do not leave existence,[24] which is painted as a land between rhythms and colors. In this insoluble connection, rhythm or line is the exposed or outward quality of form, and color is the inward quality of form.

The storehouse of consciousness[25] admits nothing outside itself while it is never spent in the wealth of its manifestations. It is of one kind, always uninterrupted, firm as the sesame seed that takes the scent of flowers, or as the fabric that takes color. The visualized equivalent of the fabric that takes color is the colored ground of the painting.

The visible, according to the *Abhidharmakośa*, is color and shape,[26] and the Sautrāntikas held that colors alone are realities and the shape constructions of the mind, superimposed upon color as an interpretation.

Color occupies the first place along the metaphysical direction of the forthcoming of form. It is the ground, opaque and saturated. Shape is bodied forth from it. It is secondary in the ontology of the paintings. Technically however, the outlines are drawn first and then only is the color applied. This process of demarcation is necessary in order to allot to color its position, in plots. These, in the next step taken technically, are modeled in color and tone,[27] by dots, cross lines (patra), and wash (?),[28] and it is then that shape comes forth where figures necessitate it, whereas elsewhere the colored ground remains flat, charged with its own density and beset with the light dots of flowers. Behind it, in the storehouse of consciousness, the whole universe of objects lies, indiscriminate and with its eyes closed. The charged density of the color lies still, while it flickers namelessly with uncounted flowers, where it is the ground on which the figures stand and which also extends behind them, in scenery and dwelling place. Behind and below are frequently coterminous, and actually these relations do not exist in the paintings. The ground preserves its nameless density irrespective of its situation. When finally the outlines are drawn once more on top of the first lines of demarcation, then only do they give definition and precise name to the figures. Before this is done, the process of modeling within the figure fulfills, in relation to the charged color surface, a function analogous to that of the flowers that flicker up as colored dots where no outlined and modeled shapes are.

"Some make of the empyrean which appears like a wall of lapis lazuli, a colour," says the *Abhidharmakośa.* Its undefined expanse is viewed as compact. Its substance is color. The *Abhidharmakośa* words describe adequately, and more comprehensively than the technical treatises, the function of color as it was felt, not only in Buddhist India.[29] Indefinite extensiveness is compressed into an intensity, for instance, into the deep and saturated color of lapis lazuli. Space accordingly is a certain category of substantial color.[30] Color in painting holds space.[31]

No vague distance, no haziness, is compatible with this space. It is transmuted into the opaqueness of color. The cavity or void is called the element space. This, one says, is light and darkness. The cavity or void of the door, of the window, and so on, is the external element space and this is contrasted with the internal space in the cavities of the human body. The extensiveness of space is compressed into color. It has "body" or substance. The space in between the modeled volumes of figures acquires compactness of color, and they are set off against its foil.

Space thus appears in a dual mode in the paintings. Contingent inasmuch as it is built up by, and contains, the figures as they are bodied forth; and in its own pictorial form, that is, compressed into the charged density of the color surface. The latter, of necessity, has no exact position "in space" being itself a mode of visualizing space as if within the void of a door, and free of figure. The color surface is the surplus of "space." As much of space is condensed in it as is not the counterpart of volume. In the borderland that has come forth from the storehouse of consciousness, it fills, for instance, the void of the door, as part of the plane of reflection. From there, on the hither side, form is made manifest. The anonymous and protean quality of the ground of the paintings makes possible the forthcoming of contingent form. Substantial with color, the texture of the ground is akin to that of modeled form to be laid out on it.

Innumerable are the tones of colors. Pure colors occur and are enumerated in the texts. These dwell at length on the secondary colors and their untold and tempered varieties. In the paintings they glow with an intensity which has substance, topaz dark or monkey dark, lotus-flower blue or blue-neck bird blue.[32] Modeling, moreover, is also done in color. It makes the rock crystal-cold, the human figure blood-warm, the plants turgidly cool. The temperature, the solid or liquid state yield color, which is the intensity of the body. These colors are not symbolic. They are not of the appearance, but of the nature of the objects. Mind born they are and, when visualized, substantial. This peculiar quality is at one with the modeling itself in the shapes. As the adept is said by an intense application of the mind (adhimukti) to be able to change the great elements, earth, water, and so on, the one into the other, and color and figure into sound, resolving the gross into the more subtle,[33] so does the painter absorb color the sensible qualities and substance of things.

Substantial color shining forth with its impact, in classical Indian painting corresponds to the text of the sixth prapāṭha of the *Chāndogya Upaniṣad* of which the fourth khaṇḍa starts with saying:

> What is the red quality (rūpa) of fire, that is the (intrinsic) form of light (tejas), what is the white quality of fire, that is the (intrinsic) form of water, what is the dark quality of fire, that is the (intrinsic) form of earth. (Thus) has vanished the fire-universality of fire. . . . What is real is the three intrinsic forms.[34]

Red, white, and dark neither designate nor describe brilliance, wateriness, and solidity. They are one with these qualities. They are spoken of as "rūpa," intrinsic form. This intrinsic quality invests with substance the colors in the paintings.

Color as intrinsic form is analogously worded in the *Kathāvatthu*, where it is said that the visible material, visible object and element as such is either blue-green, yellow, red, or white, is cognizable by the eye, impinges on the eye.[35]

The *Viṣṇudharmottara* distinguishes between the twofold possibility of every color, the dark and the light.[36] The quality of darkness is that of compactness or substantiality and the quality of lightness (aloka) is of the light of the moon, stars, fire, herbs, and gems.[37] These twofold possibilities are present in the opaque and yet luminous color of painting as in Ajanta, Bagh, Badami, and so on. They refer to color itself and to shape which is raised into appearance.[38]

Color is the place of transformation from the invisible to the formed. Its quality is an intensity, and by itself it has no defined extension. As nonexistence is considered by Indian thinkers to be grasped by the senses through a special contact,[39] the invisible storehouse of consciousness makes its presence felt to the painter by a substantial sheet of colors that rises into his field of vision. It is firm and charged with its contents and exposes them tangibly, that is, plastically. The variegatedly colored ground is the first specification of the totality from which the multiform world of the paintings arises.

But ground and figures cannot be imagined separately. The role of the ground is twofold; it is a phase prior to and itself containing the figures in their passage from the formless to form. According, on the other hand, to the multiple perspective, it appears as meadow, or as the floor of rooms and terraces and also as their wall, screen, and door.[40] It is manifoldly one with the figures, in their progression and as condition of their appearance. The figures inhere in it in the process of forthcoming, and they are projected at the same time and dismissed into the borderland, into the space of the painting itself. The ground is but a visualized phase of the painting acquiring form. From the outset it has no reference to any visible reality. The process itself of the painting acquiring form makes the setting of the painting. The colored ground, besides, acts as a sheet of refraction. Up to it from the fathomless beyond forward, there was no possibility as yet for the painting to come into existence. While the painter is himself aware of the picture arising in him, his experience of himself, simultaneous with and at one with the vision, makes the ground which cannot be severed from the picture in the making. This awareness of himself cannot be given a name. It is immediate and becomes the color ground from which the figures arise. In itself it has no definite shape. It is an intensity, and across it the figures condense in substantiality and appear fully rounded in front of it.

Neither is it a barrier nor does its color taint that of the figures. The movement of forthcoming passes across it as water runs through a sieve. The color ground is the plane of intervention in the process and form of the picture. The storehouse of consciousness, nameless and formless and teeming with all the possibilities of form, lies on one side and is invisible; its contents appear in front of the color ground. For consciousness as it is painted here is not split into two parts; process and content conform.

The forward movement within the visualized borderland of consciousness, that is, within the painting, is metaphysical. Rhythmical movement, as well as the movement of the figures, has to be distinguished though connected with it. The painter puts down in visual terms that reality which he carries within himself. When painting it, he transfers it to the wall, or whatever surface. This is made congruous with the ground of reflection which his awareness of himself provides. In this way the painting remains within its natural place. The figures in it belong to some extent to the external world, although none of them is brought from there into the painting by a separate observation.

THE OBJECTS BROUGHT INTO THESE LIMITS

That sight goes out to the object, seizes it, and brings it back, refers to Indian sculpture as far as it is modeled. Sculpture and plastic form in India do not always result from the same visualization as painting. History confirms it. Where sculpture in India in its plastic quality no longer is productive, especially in western India after the twelfth century, painting almost totally devoid of any plastic factor is strong with its own means, line, and color. The plastic quality to some extent preserves in its form the impress of contact. By it the external world is transmuted. The quality of Indian sculpture, and also of painting such as in Ajanta which gives a large share to the modeled body in color and shading, is due to some extent to tactile memory residues at work within the part seen of the storehouse of consciousness. This aspect, too, comes forward and is swelled from within into smooth shapeliness. Only living sap distends form so evenly and rounds off limbs and bodies, columns, and the stems of plants in the paintings. The condition of the waters underlies their fluid shape and grace.

Exposed from within consciousness, the space of the paintings has no externality. It has the dimension of the mind and is reflected with its contents from the color ground of the wall. To that space the many figures are adjusted inasmuch as they themselves have brought it about. Their origin, too, they do not leave behind the saturated ground whence they have come forward; they keep on showing this in their demeanor and appearance, in the way they seem pushed forward and held, each in its proper place, by the movement itself that has set them forth. This gives them a likeness and coherence. They are kept in suspense, in a charged atmosphere, which they themselves create by the movement which in them comes to act. It distends their surface into plastic roundness. The saturated quality of the ground, its color, discharges its potentialities into the manifold movement which fill the space of the paintings. Still, flowers strewn between the figures, on the ground, into the crevices of the rocks and across them, restore the peace of the surface to this dense crop of volumes which fills the space of the paintings. Over this flowery ground a web of rhythms is cast. This too levels the figures that have been bodied forth.

Figure next to figure, as they detach themselves from the ground, they carry their impact one step further, an indefinitely graded step, when all their movements of forthcoming are interlaced in a web of rhythms. It keeps them from falling out of this enchanted borderland.

There they exist, each of them doubly connected with the other one, caught within the web of rhythms which they uphold while they are sent forth, albeit to a varying height, yet from one and the same ground and with an equal impact. The movement that sets them forth and sustains them in the forward direction does not belong to any one of them. It is their metaphysical direction, and within the web of rhythms their movements severally are in consonance. Pattern and gestures are cognate and must not be severed.

The charged precision of the movements of the hands has given them the name of "mudrā," that is, seal. It means to communicate its intention. So also is the whole of the painting a "mudrā," charged with impact and gravid with the meaning it communicates. On this seal the rhythms are drawn. They show the pattern according to which the borderland is displayed.

Its closed world is situated in the internal space of the mind in which participation, observation, and tactile memories play their important and yet subordinate parts.

It is the test of a good, that is, "auspicious" painting if the figures appear as if breathing.[41] The ups and downs, the hills and dales of the modeling of living figures are the visible outcome of, and are held in shape by breathing. The dead are without movement and corpses lack resilience. Breathing, the craftsman participates in the form which he paints.

The living world where rocks too are felt as "jīva," endowed with life, is only quasi-external.[42] It exists inwardly and is grasped with a simultaneous awareness of its whole substance. An all around modeling verifies in every instance that life has shaped the whole of the tree or of any other figure. Magically the eye is fastened on its surface and notices that as the figure is shaped, so also does it move: the turgid banana leaves when others ramble, crisp and curly lancets (pl. 16-3). Shape and movement are beheld as different phases; shape belongs to the past and yet the living breath sustains it and casts its mold afresh incessantly.

Plastic volume and life movement are the conditions under which the quasi-external world is beheld. Such participating seeing is not a creative act on the side of the craftsman. It is the mode in which the world is felt and known in ancient India prior to and apart from his work. Within it, however, it assumes its proper place. Metaphysical movement, the impact from within his consciousness, propels while further inflating the plastic volumes into the dense web of the painting. This web has the fleeting rhythm of life. It takes as its own and into its wide curves the movement of every figure. Such is the situation of the borderland, the part seen and painted of the storehouse of consciousness. Every part is the visible outcome of its own origin and carries in its own manner the whole.

LATERAL LIMITS

The major part of the wall paintings at Ajanta are without a frame (pl. 16-2).[43] They extend all over the walls and as far as these go. That the wall has to come to an end and actually is of limited extent, the paintings do not convey. It has not entered their structure. They cover the walls entirely, and one and the same subject may begin on one wall and be continued on the adjacent one, at an angle of ninety degrees, and there is no break in the continuity of the picture. Far from being architectonically conceived, they harbor their own consistency and leave no room for anything outside themselves on walls, ceiling, and pillars. The only outside they admit is the void of the cave, which is held by their figured presence on all sides. So is also the mind of the devotee who has entered the cave and beholds them.

Few scenes or figures appear in panels, forming to some extent, limited compositional units.[44] They are painted on pilasters. The painted wall sometimes is ended by carved and painted figures. These compositions, however, are seemingly only concluded within themselves. Actually they are arranged in pairs facing one another. Their setting of rocks or pavilions with the multiple perspective shows them forthcoming within magically widening receptacles without front and side walls. By referring to one another and by bordering on sculpture on which the modeling of the figures verges anyhow, they are brought into a context in which is comprised the space receptacle itself of the cave. It ends where the web of rhythms screens off the paintings.[45]

The setting of the scenes and the groups in which they are displayed carries with it the frame of each constellation. Its shape is a system of coordinates brought about partly by the bordering outlines of the scenes next to it, laterally as well as above or below. Parapets intersect at right angles (pl. 16-2). Such intersections of vertical and horizontal fleetingly fix points. The crux is laid now here, now there, instrumental in building the architecture of the city of the Gandharvas.[46] It must be imagined as consisting only of frameworks, and their positions appear as if incessantly reshuffled while the figures within their compartments remain unperturbed.

Not only on one level, but throughout the thickness of the borderland, the coordinates are interlaced. The city of the Gandharvas is ordered throughout. Around each single cross a new constellation of figures is wreathed and in its turn links up with those nearby. The coordinates are not always "architectonic" in shape. The vertical of a thin pillar, for instance, is continued by the massive legs of a watchful horse (pl. 16-2). Horizontals and verticals have an equal share in this weightless system of coordinates. It maintains as much balance as it imparts stability to the changing scenes steadily laid out. It is relevant mainly in the forward direction. In the linear composition, connecting rhythms take it for granted and wreathe their patterns around. The rectilinear order belongs to the metaphysical movement of the paintings. It does not enter, while yet it sustains, flowing rhythms. This rectilinear order is condensed in the formula of the rocks. With them its framework is given substance. There is no room for jungles. Nature in these paintings embodies order. Rich in sap and with a delicate movement, vegetation is assigned its place (pl. 16 3). Clouds, too, have their allocation. Cusped and voluminous, their vaporous bodies tower above rocks, above the tilted bottom of magical receptacles on the slope of Mount Meru.[47]

B. PHASES

Caves 9 and 10

Almost a millennium of pictorial tradition, albeit preserved incompletely in the paintings of Ajanta, Bagh, Badami, and other cave temples and monasteries, appears recumbent on one tradition. Consistently and across the centuries the elements are maintained and enlarged upon. The earliest paintings which are preserved may be assigned to approximately 100 B.C, and they follow principles analogous to those of the reliefs of Sanchi and Amarāvatī, for example.[48] The scant number of wall paintings preserved and known hitherto precludes the attribution of this type of painting to the Deccan exclusively.[49] At present the term Deccani can be applied to this tradition only in a certain geographical sense, as wall paintings of a subsequent phase from South India (Śittaṇṇāvasal[50] and Tirumalapuram,[51] seventh century; Kailāsanātha Temple, Kanchipuram; Bṛhadīśvara Temple, Tanjore, twelfth century[52]) are based on a similar vision.[53] When, by favorable accident, fragments are preserved[54] and we can discern them, their maturity is on a level with contemporary sculpture. They do not mark a beginning. They are friezes contained by panels. The mode of setting forth a jātaka story is one of compartments within an oblong frieze (pl. 16-1). The "walls" of these compartments come forward at various angles from the ground of the painting. The *Ṣaḍdanta Jātaka*[55] in cave 10 contains an elephant frieze akin in density and relief to similar scenes in Sanchi. It is a version in painting of such carved and modeled groups. The animals are modeled in color in a dense variety of positions. The thin and hanging roots of the Nyagrodha tree interfere, more intimately perhaps than a sculptor would have had it, with the bulk of elephantine bodies (pl. 16-1). The leaves are shaded in color, in various greens and the young leaves reddish, a mode of painting foliage which in the sixteenth century has an equally fresh pattern.[56]

It is, however, only to the right of this tree that the painting, with means of its own, amplifies the range of relief treatment. A phantasmagoria of rocks wells forth in diagonal direction. Sculpture does not know such voluminous and varied conglomerations.[57] Some of the single boulders of trabeated cast have their front surfaces grey with yellow streaks, the other surfaces variously reddish brown. There are whitish rocks too, and the whole in its own way builds up the stratification of bare rocks. A compact of stone logs slants across the painted frieze, its driving power cut off at diverse vertical planes and exposed with a color of its own and a modeling. The latter does not round off a shape. It exposes a texture, in the sense of a repleteness of form with the principle which, while building up the form within definite outlines, makes it full of itself. Crevices and caves are filled with a void similarly banked. Appropriately a tree sallies forth, sleek and undulating with sap, verdure and birds perched, smug. In its swaying movement the driving power of the rock phantasmagoria is transmuted and deflected upwards, from the forward thrust. To some extent such formations, bare boulders of stone, are peculiar to the country in several places in the Deccan, around Hyderabad for instance, where stray rocks, barren and massive, are cleft all of a sudden by the growth of one or the other tree with glossy leaves. In Ajanta itself the hills are mild and wooded. They were not exposed, except by the craftsmen who excavated the caves.

The story of the *Ṣaḍdanta Jātaka* is shown from right to left and then again from left to right,[58] and the hunter on the right who is deputed to kill the six-tusker has gone out on his errand on the left (pl. 16-1) amidst the rocks and has returned, in a scene painted between the two scenes mentioned and on the other side of the rocks, with the signal weight of the tusks as if on scales, to the queen who had asked for them and seeing them, faints. Beyond these scenes, on the extreme left, are painted the elephant scenes.

The hunter, his companion, and a maid-in-waiting are arrayed in a diagonal, parallel to the forthcoming of the rocks (pl. 16-1). Once more and parallel to this appearance, they stand before the royal couple enthroned. A group of trees set equally slanting across the breadth of the scene marks the third "wall" against which the current of the story is stemmed. Between these compartmental walls[59] which themselves are partly made up of the figures of the story, of the hunter and others, or the royal couple enthroned, groups cohere, rows of figures one behind the other and parallel, or else parabolically and diagonally connected so that each compartment or receptacle aslant between its two lateral and figured walls is replete itself with figures in the direction of forthcoming.

The ground in part is colored in horizontal stripes not meant to indicate the horizon. The division of the ground by two or three horizontal bands of color is peculiar also to paintings of cave 17 for example, where the ground in the *Ṣaḍdanta Jātaka* is streaked reddish, brown, and greyish between palace and elephants. The painted frieze in cave 10 with its scenes is part of the borderland of the mind. It is unrolled ribbon-like with all the scenes present in one layout while its setting implies the depth from which it is forthcoming, precipitated into cubical compartments meted out across the width of the band; its charge in front of a colored and nameless ground fills the compartments in parabolic curves or straight rows parallel with the edge of the frieze, or else in parabolic curves or loops laid in the forward direction; all of these are held within the partitioning walls built of rocks, groups, and clusters of trees.

To bring forward into the field of mental vision, and to people the slopes of Mount Meru, two methods of grouping are resorted to. The elephant group of the *Ṣaḍdanta Jātaka* in cave 10, for instance, or the figures of men (devatas ?) in cave 9,[60] who are shown approaching a stūpa within a walled quadrangle, entirely fill the part of the frieze allotted to them. In superimposed rows and in a manner corresponding to relief tradition they are given form. They are visualized in a final stage of forthcoming. Their full mass issues up to the outermost plane. There they are arrested, painted in relief, and mostly in three-quarter profile on the ground from which they have come forth. The other mode visualizes the scenes in an earlier moment of forthcoming and in the process itself, arrayed within cubical compartments with walls aslant across the width of the painted frieze. They are emptied out into visibility while they are held in the strictly defined realm of the painted band. This mode of visualization is also familiar to sculpture, especially at Amarāvatī.[61] The two modes alternate in the painted friezes of caves 9 and 10.[62] Their juxtaposition, however, is elastically consistent. Viewed as a whole, and it is meant thus to be seen, the story now bounces forward and then again the impact is relaxed and room is made for other scenes. The mass of shapes, herd of elephants, or procession of human figures is entirely dismissed into the plane of visibility and completely cover the ground. The interplay of action, on the other hand, in contrast to this form of corporate activity, has its own stage. On it the impact is made to halt. Such cubical compartments each contain a significant moment within the story. The latter is laid out breadthwise across the ups and downs, the hills and dales of its course. In cave 9, the part of the frieze still left has two rows of human figures, superimposed. From the stūpa quadrangle which they approach a gate leads into another enclosure with trees and buildings,[63] by the side of which once more are human figures superimposed. The quadrangle, with the two lateral walls slanting in either direction, seems to empty its contents forward on its sloping ground, from back to front. A figure with a tray of offerings is shown in the gate on the way to the stūpa. The figure in the gate is one of the generally employed requisites to show connection or separation of the scenes. It acts in the sense of direction and, as a rule, laterally in between the single scenes. It appears arrested in the momentariness of its movement, on its way from one compartment to the next. It closes a scene or story when it stands at the gate, a guardian. Similarly, also, other figures turned this or that way at a corner or near the edge of a scene act as a full stop, or else they lead from one scene to the next. Themselves of little consequence in the story, they usher in its current in the way it wants to go.

Two sides of a building are drawn into view, besides the top, while the stereometry of rocks adds the bottom surface to the two sides. This elasticity in beholding the extensiveness of volumes is not tantamount to a change of viewpoints, and this perspective has no reference to things unfolded before the physical eye. While the mind dwells on the volume of a house, the roof is an integral part. Rocks, however, are understood as part of the earth and potential holders of caves. According to its function, each is shown in due manner. All the other figures are also fully "bodied forth." Much experience in color modeling goes to their making. The modeling capacity of the line is equally known.

With eyes wide open, and mildly expressive of emotional states, the figures are not in touch with one another. Distinct in their appearance with a high- or low-class physiognomy,[64] and the appropriate complexion and costume, they are made to act at some higher order, aloof the one from the other even where they are placed closely together. Their reference is to the context and not to one another.

Smoothly, the sturdy figures carry out their movements. With their large heads and turbans, they are near in appearance to figures as carved in Sanchi. A reticent sleekness levels the manifold types and their movements.

Two modes of visualization appear side by side, the one of the type of reliefs as in Bharhut, and to a considerable extent also in Sanchi, the other of cubical conception.[65] They visualize degrees of forthcoming. The former mode belongs to the past and does not appear in subsequent paintings of the Ajanta type. The latter, of which the rocks are emblematic and the function they fulfill, along with the cubical compartments which empty their contents in forward, are among the leading exponents of painting as in Ajanta. The metaphysical direction, that is, that of forthcoming, is seen at work in them. The rhythm according to which the several compartments are linked is that of the wavy line of unbroken flux. Its emblem in the shape of a "lotus stalk" can be seen rambling across jātaka scenes carved on the coping stone of the Bharhut railing. The "composition" is based on the two comprehensive factors, of forthcoming and of rhythm. The modeling of the figures, in that it bodies forth the figures with a rounded and voluminous appearance, is an aspect of the working of the metaphysical direction. The smooth contour of rounded limbs and the flux of movements are aspects of the living rhythm which percolates the whole painting in every part.

These main trends of form, however, carry figurines, and they respond with restraint and shyness to the principles laid down for their appearance. Without their being aware of it, they follow an order and act their parts; viewed from paintings of later phases, below its level. The human figures throughout, as painted in caves 9 and 10, are an outcome of the vision that had precipitated their dense rows into the surface in the manner of earlier reliefs from central India.[66] This discrepancy in the conception of the paintings on the one hand and the relative immaturity of the figures on the other, would justify these paintings being called comparatively early, in view also of the later correspondence of identical means of "composition" and the type of figures through which it then finds its more specified utterance.

Caves 16 and 17

It takes time for a vision to mature and to manifest all its possibilities. Centuries lie between the work in caves 9 and 10 and the paintings of caves 16 and 17. As aspects of one unanimous tradition, they show the essential formulations in different stages. The bands in which formerly the stories were laid out have broadened on the whole to the full width and length of the entire wall; as long as the wall continues, the paintings go on and one scene or story may extend not only on one wall, but also at a right angle to the painted field on the adjacent wall, or else it is carried over on the face of a pilaster (cave 17).[67] Such painting on adjacent walls corresponds to some extent to cave sculpture where, as for instance in Bhaja (Sūrya relief, second century B.C.),[68] the whole extends from one wall to the next in continuity, irrespective of the changed direction of the wall and with a technical adaptation only of the design to the edge. In Ellora, however (Nāga and Nāginī, on the outer wall of the Kailāsanātha Temple; Tripurāntakamurti,[69] eighth century A.D.), the carving is carried on over the edge and comprises the space between the walls as part of its form. This is not so in the paintings. The web of rhythms screens them from the space of the cave.

Not altogether, however, do the paintings extend without frames over the entire available wallspace. Frames occur, albeit negatively with regard to the paintings, inasmuch as broad borders replete with scrolls surround, not the paintings, but the doors of the cells that are cut into the walls in regular intervals. This refers to cave 16, whereas elsewhere there are no such painted frames laid around the doors.

The wide surfaces now overlaid with paintings are not usually divided into horizontal bands, although vestiges of such an array occur in cave 17 and take the shape of plain separating lines or of rocks, houses, and roofs linked in horizontal continuity. The *Matiposaka Jātaka*,[70] for instance, is divided from the *Śarabha Jātaka* by a straight horizontal line while it is painted itself in two rows separated by horizontal roof lines.[71] Two panels again on a pilaster[72] are bounded by plain or shaded bands of color. Horizontal demarcations are brought about by an alignment of architectonic shape in the *Mṛga Jātaka* with the kitchen scene, where the coping of a wall draws the line. Not a division, but an articulation along horizontal lines is effected in the large painting of the *Viśvāntara Jātaka* by rocks set in horizontal sequence. In vestiges, which are transformed into parts of a more comprehensive mode of painting, the frieze with its horizontal limits survives. The stories now are laid out on the whole of the wall. Yet the painting does not end with the presentation of one story. Imperceptibly, and this is the main trend, one glides into the next, and they are joined in the whole painting as the single scenes in their turn are comprised within the painting of one story. The whole wallspace, the front, sides, and back of the cave, unheeding demarcation and brimming with paintings, shows the scenes next to one another, laterally, above and below, spread out in simultaneous validity. Collateral scenes are connected so that they can be read in the direction of the main rhythmic flux while the scenes appended below or added on above are linked with the main current by a tree, for instance; it grows from the one scene into the other which is superimposed (*Mahākapi Jātaka*, cave 17). Or the scenes are shuffled in several compartments to convey their connectedness (scenes from the life of Buddha, cave 16).

CAVE 16

In the large painting of the conversion of Nanda (cave 16), a building with a pent roof comes out of the depth from left to right, and the rocky formations behind also sally forth across the width of the painting, but at a different angle. In the opposite direction a high rock looms large with platforms. Elements embodying the metaphysical direction, that is, that of forthcoming, are combined in staging the scenes of Nanda's and the Buddha's flight through the air. Charged with their forthcoming at multifarious angles, the painting is solid with the impact of forward movement. In the earlier caves similar devices are employed.[73] In this painting large volumes emerge against a dark sky.[74] It is beset with flowers. Although remains are scanty to witness the ground, strewn over with flowers, they can still be discerned, as in the earlier paintings also (p. 276). In the present scene,[75] a tree with its leaves shaded in yellow-green tones stands out against the dark ground.[76]

A very round modeling, carefully outlined, gives a bodily warmth and stable wellbeing to the figures. Whatever their size, their inner measure is not conceived on a large scale. Possibly the paintings most balanced in Ajanta in the relation of modeling and outline belong to the right and left walls, respectively, of cave 16 with the scenes of the conversion of Nanda and those from the life of Buddha. The inner measure of these paintings, however, does not attain to the implicit possibilities of the means of visualization which are here perfectly poised. Reserve holds every form from within and keeps it trim with a glowing presence. Movements are decorously ample, and fiercely collected at times (the flight of Nanda and Buddha). The angles are rounded off and nowhere can the mobility of the line be witnessed to greater advantage than in the shallow curves of the now long and liquid eyes and the multiform arches of brows. Of the same type, though of lesser achievement, are the elephant scenes[77] and with a further recrudescence, a slack modeling, and loose line, the scene of Mahosadha's judgment from the *Mahā-ummagga Jātaka* is painted.[78]

The paintings in cave 16, fragmentarily preserved in parts, are not all the work of one phase. The remnants of scenes with Buddha preaching, on the left wall, as well as those on the back wall, modeled profusely in color, brown modeled with red, and light yellowish-red with deep Indian red and with highlights, have none of the suavity of the paintings just mentioned. In the scene of the sermon on the right half of the back wall, the modeling shadows condense into thick rims along the outlines. They are deeper at the edge and lighter inside. Such summarizing deftness means quick work and presupposes a knowledge of a more intimate modeling taken for granted. This applies to the three fragments of scenes preserved on the back wall, that is, Buddha preaching on a lotus supported by Nāgas, an elephant scene, and a fragment of warrior figures, as well as to the sermon scene on the left wall. They are on one level of technical maturity with paintings in caves 1 and 2.[79] The yakṣa on the right wall, to the left of the first door, has the highlights of his jewels laid on in a thick relief of dots of white color. Such technical facility comes late and is worthy of note as it shows the "forthcoming" ever more obvious of the modeled form in painting.

CAVE 17

Bands of jātakas are unrolled in disguised alignment or with a dividing line casually interpolated in cave 17. They are lavish with small figures endowed with ease amounting to elegance where efficient craftsmen work in the tradition which had been consolidated by such paintings as that of the Buddha and Nanda scenes in cave 16. These small-figured jātaka scenes on the back wall and the adjacent parts of the right and left walls[80] are painted in the idiom of the day.[81] It has several dialects and these are gathered in the vast and complex composition of the *Viśvāntara Jātaka* on the left wall. Wind passing over a ripe field of corn bends it in waves as dense in their sequence as are the widely flung arches of rhythm across the entire height of the wall, above and below the door lintels, and extending right to the door openings which have no painted borders that would stem the tide of this multiple procession.[82] It is astir with rhythmical sequences and where one movement glides downwards, another has started already within its arch and rises in its turn.

Into this great cortege of ambient rhythms, the royal chariot drives forward, diagonally outward into the painting; the gate next to it similarly set against a row of shops in the bazaar marks one compartment while once more the same forthcoming from the depth marks another phase in the jātaka. Metaphysical and rhythmical movement here are joined in a comprehensive conception on the largest scale. It is filled with middle-sized figures, varying accomplishment, and with different formal treatments. Such paintings of vast conception are the integration of the possibilities of composition in Ajanta. The penetration of metaphysical direction and rhythmical movement absorbs all the possibilities and requisites hitherto devised. The *Viśvāntara Jātaka* and the *Siṁhala Avadāna*, the one occupying the middle of the left, the other of the right wall, of cave 17, and the *Mahājanaka* (?) *Jātaka* in cave 1 are integrations on one level. Beyond such compositions painting in Ajanta does not go. They are complete and altogether exhaustive. None of the possibilities present in previous paintings have been left aside and all of them are carried out to the last. This compositional fulfillment, however, is not always accompanied by an equivalent maturity of the figures which it carries. All have not fully grown up as yet and have not reached the measure they have internally as well as externally, in "the offering of the handful of dust," another painting in cave 17.[83] Actually the mode of visualization in this tradition is often ahead of the things visualized. The setting, for instance, of the *Ṣaddanta Jātaka* in cave 10 (pl. 16-1) held the direction of forthcoming in the rocks as well as in a cognate massing of other devices, and strung together the whole by an undulating movement in the surface, and forward and backward as well. The figures entrusted to this forthcoming and sway were not its equals. They were unaware of it and unawakened. They looked with open eyes into a festive life. They glow, with a bodily warmth of modeling and the foreboding of its transience, in cave 16. This makes them supple, with a wistful elegance, in cave 17. Slender and silent, they avert the glance and behold themselves. Their eyes are long and devoted to their own wondrous presence. Carried now by integral waves, they lean with grace on their plantlike surrender to being alive and passing away, as if by enchantment.

The fullness and warmth in which the bodies were glowing in cave 16 had been based on the stolid roundness of limbs of the earlier versions (caves 9, 10). Now the figures are attenuated. Elegant and versatile in all the arts of movement and emotion, their glance sways in their boat-shaped eyes and does not detach itself from the sea of living experience on which they sail. The narrow and long slits of their eyes are as yet not burdened by an ultimate realization which is to make them droop their lids over a knowledge akin to that which the painters now formulate in compositional terms. This gradual awakening with lowered lids to a final absorption is not conveyed only by the eyes. It is equally manifest in the gradual transformation of the body, its proportion, mode of modeling, and outline.[84]

Such comprehensive painting may be executed with pervading mastery, as of the *Siṁhala Avadāna*, but this need not be so and the lesser attainment in parts of the *Viśvāntara Jātaka* is yet carried by a subordination to the integral scheme. In the *Viśvāntara* painting modes of form occur which are to occupy a wider range in caves 1 and 2.[85] Although some are of a relatively lesser achievement, they appear by the side of a type of painting which gives to cave 17 an equal distinction, albeit of a different type, as the work of the Nanda and Buddha scenes to cave 16. It is especially in the figure of Mādrī—as she appears twice, encased by rocks, where she had gone to pluck fruits for her family and where she is retained by Indra, transformed into a lion—swayed by the wide silence of her eyes and the pliancy of her being, that a more tenuous modeling relegates its fullness to the line. Swaying, it is rocked into ambient roundness. Such swaying and modeling linearism tends toward an association with floating, transparent veils, and of similar curves (cf. *Siṁhala Avadāna* painting). This type of figure is interspersed in the *Viśvāntara Jātaka* with a more clotted type while it is sheer in the entire *Siṁhala Avadāna* painting, in the *Śibi Jātaka* painting, which follows it, as well as in the scene of the *Haṁsa Jātaka* that precedes the *Viśvāntara* painting, and in the single figure on a large scale that follows upon it, painted on the second pilaster of the left wall. It is perceptible to a lesser degree in an unidentified scene on the facade of the veranda of cave 17.[86]

The painting of the *Siṁhala Avadāna* is born of this vision. Figure and composition, ground, line, and volume are cognate. The ground, with the deep red, saturated surface is bestrewn with flowers. It is the condensed and transmuted, the "original" body of any setting merged in it, and for which it stands (see p. 290). Few rocks flame up, burning copper red and the house of the Rakṣasas is thrown up acutely. But the bodies of the many figures in intrinsic concatenation, desubstantialized like a beating of wings and scimitars, are its angelic pattern. Such elation and acuteness are the lightning flashes of mastery. The ineluctable urge to become form is not ahead of its means any more; an ardent and responsible guide, the means now keep pace with it.

Other paintings in cave 17 are akin in their figures to those of the

Śaṅkhapāla Jātaka of cave 1,[87] in proportion and movement, looseness of knees, and energy of gestures. The paintings in cave 1 carry on, in many respects and strightway, the idioms of cave 17. It may be mentioned that large figures of Bodhisattvas in the shrine of cave 17, carved, plastered, and painted, in their expansive generalizations and clear-cut physiognomies, are equivalent with the magnificent Bodhisattva, carved, plastered, and painted to the right of the image of Buddha in the shrine of cave 2.[88]

Caves 1 and 2

Aggrandized in outer and inner form, the large Bodhisattva paintings of cave 1 have completely come forth. Entirely laid out with all its possibilities attained, the impact which shapes the figures full in substance, sustains them. As if weightless in their amplitude, they are held forth on the ground of which they are the ultimate exponents. Upheld, they lean on it. All that tends forward teeming with life and form, in them it falls back upon itself and halts. Lowered eyelids screen the return of life gone out in its plenitude and come home. The silence of this return resounds in the music and elation of child and animal form; monkeys and kinnaras gambol and strum their instruments. Ribbons flutter from Bodhisattva Padmapāṇi's crown tossed by a gale of stillness and the crystalline rock cubes flame and consume their own shapes. A fierce combustion of crystalline definition still urges ahead while it has already reached its limits.[89]

Of equally wide lineaments is the large Avalokiteśvara painted on another part of the wall.[90] Yet his figure is grave, a bar to the inward step of return. This need not necessarily be shown in painting in the expression of the figures. Their cast and also their setting conveys it. In this painting, garlands and crown are stellar webs of scintillation and leafy flowers are winged on evergreen rocks. Their icy cubes are sparks crystallized. Within this transcendental filigree the large figures are staid. Their movements and their gestures lack the amplitude of their frames.[91] The achievement of this painting has not the omnivalence of the former. But its setting belongs to the same sphere. In the one, the vortex of matter in the momentariness of its consummation makes the rocks themselves into flames; in the other their ice green crystals sparkle with the white heat which has gone to their making. Such painting of rocks draws the ultimate consequences of an attitude that from the earliest paintings on followed the rocks on the way of their acquiring visualized shape (pl. 16-1).

It resolves them now into their primeval precedence and living essence. This stepping backward, in visualizing the concretion of rock form, is concomitant with the transformation of traits of the human figures and the way they are limned. As the cube of construed stone is now suggestive of a less dense, more ardent and fluid state, so also does modeling now not show off a rounded body. Modeling in its own nature is bodied forth in terms of substance, color, and line.

Not always is this ultimate level of vision and attainment within the reach of the craftsman. While some of them are great masters of painting, they yet remain "pṛthagjanas" who have devotion, though not the understanding of the transforming power; others with adept hands may be in the current of things, unawares, and their work also fits into the whole while it may not in itself be convincing. Carried by one unanimous tradition which sustains his work, any experienced craftsman is fit to fill in any part if this does not hinder the flux and consistency of the whole.

Immediately to the left of the large Padmapāṇi painting, and oversected by the tail of one of the monkeys sporting on its rocks, are the red pillars of a palace, with lustration and renunciation scenes. These belong to a jātaka,[92] and below this trim and slender building there is another of flaccid shape and pallid color.[93] Each tells its own story in subject matter, form, and meaning. The various modes of painting are in the closest proximity, and with the same ease as the tales they tell. Each in its way, they all have the same reference. There is only one final goal of all the jātakas and one ultimate source from where the many trends and waves of painting issue. The figures in the red building are relatively small, sparse, and dedicated. They do not occupy much room, and the ceiling is high above them. Flexed in every joint they sway and amble, arrayed within the building, in impetuous diagonals. Their short and animated faces are rich in modeling with highlights on forehead, nose, lips, chin, and a flash in the eyes. The outlines are potent, by the side of and not one with the modeling. The large eyes are not drawn toward the temples in an aggrandized and simplified shape, nor do their brows show the calligraphic and unbroken sweep of two widely flung arches and a steep vale toward the root of the nose.[94] They differ in every face,[95] and the main figure has triangular brows, those of another are smoothly arched, while in a third face they are straight lines. Their thickness also varies and the quality of the hair as it is painted agrees in each line with the total physiognomy of the figure. But all have a thrilled swaying, so that even the low-caste type, for instance, of the second man who leans on a staff in the prince's palace, is purged of the dull grossness of his features. A dedicated participation reverberates in the figures and the vibrancy of the moment makes fly up with alike zest the end of a "cāmara." With sparse and brittle shapes accomplished in their slightness within a spacious setting, this scene is the work of a master craftsman of a humbly dedicated mind.

The large figures, however, in the pale green pavilion of the next scene below, reach to its ceiling, obtuse and drowsy. They are modeled with large surfaces of different tones of color, and there is no highlight. Flaccidly spread, their three-quarter view is given only one distended, sweeping curve, with an outline vaguely descriptive in rambling torpor. Their languor and opulence, however, do not occur only sporadically, that is, in this special scene. The paintings of other scenes are of similarly ample curves, around blubber features, obfuscated, and bedematous with large surfaces. Their sodden spread has a thick modeling color to strengthen the contour, and the line has a breadth that is blunt.[96]

By the side of one another, one merging into the next, the differing modes of painting of the three scenes. The Padmapāṇi scene and the two others, one in the red building, the other in the green building, exemplify different possibilities within one tradition. The type of painting of the large Bodhisattva scenes has attained to its climax, while that of the lustration and abdication scenes within the red building, ripe in pictorial means and on a lower level of realization, is painted in a manner forestalled in the earlier caves. The transformation of the pictorial means, however, is taken for granted while it is not itself gone through by the painter of the "salver scene" in the green building, and of the other scenes referred to. Of the two latter types of craftsmen, the painter of the red building has the frame of mind of an earnest and humble lay-follower, and his understanding he paints with the highest efficiency. This is not the case with the painter of the green building with the salver scene. His mind is that of a worldling, and as a craftsman he has no special attainment either. But he also paints within the tradition, and while he dilutes it, he can neither do without nor break it. Leaving aside the quality of these paintings, their sequence from the point of enlightenment and of its transforming power—also of the pictorial form—would give a place before the climax to the red house scene, and another albeit inferior one after the climax to the scene in the green pavilion. This implies a potential chronology, although not in terms of date. The red house scene could have been painted without the mastery of the large Bodhisattva paintings having been there. Not so the salver scene and a good number of other paintings.[97] The inflated mannerisms of the latter rest on the largeness of their fulfillment. They encumber and dilute it.

Stages in the process of integration of pictorial form are: the layout of stories (cave 10, pl. 16-1); the vast and comprehensive composition on the entire wallspace as of the *Viśvāntara Jātaka* of cave 17 and of the *Mahājanaka Jātaka*, cave 1; the ultimate stage of the forthcoming of modeled form is held by the large Bodhisattva paintings of cave 1. The principles of form seize the whole from the outset and accommodate to it the appearance of the single figures. The larger, that is, the compositional vision, is there from the beginning, if only "in nuce";[98] it expands intrinsically within every shape comprised in its organism and finally invests it with a physiognomy fit to embody its metaphysical and rhythmical components, in traits of awareness. This growing up of the figures is not only an inward process. Visibly, too, they expand. Size, not only in Indian art is an index of importance. The colossal size of Kuṣāṇa Bodhisattva images shows it in a naïve sense. The large and phantom-like Buddha figure painted in cave 17 in the scene of the offering of the handful of dust[99] forestalls the large Bodhisattva figures painted with a full awareness of their state of consciousness.

A painting as vast and comprehensive as the *Mahājanaka Jātaka* employs modes of presentation partly based on this ultimate aspect of forthcoming. It does however not by far rise to the level of the large Bodhisattva scenes. Parallel to the *Viśvāntara* painting in cave 17, various modes of painting fall each into their proper place, with analogous cadences of arched rhythms and following upon another as breath follows breath. On the whole the painting is not distinguished. A stolid mannerism of arched lines holds an unfeeling modeling.[100] The painter of the sermon scene around the hermit applies the idiom he has learned with a sober earnestness[101] and the palace scene is painted with a liquid brush and a florid flutter.[102] Its cast is in the current of things and sweeps also across the next scene, the exit of the prince. This facile idiom is readily employed in cave 1. Exuberant or torpid in the mannered sinuosity of modeling and line, it occupies a lower level of pictorial means which have been brought up to date.[103]

Imperceptibly merging as far as the rhythmical continuity of "composition" is concerned, into the *Mahājanaka Jātaka* but painted differently, is the *Śaṅkhapāla Jātaka.*[104] The figures that people either jātaka are turned into their respective context as far as the stories are concerned. The mode of painting, on a level with that of scenes in cave 17,[105] makes modeling of relatively little consequence, and the outline has much to say. The male figures like those of children, with big heads and slight limbs, do not attain to the sophisticated alertness of curve, around the back view of the female figures, for example; it is sprightly tame as of young domesticated animals, the bullocks nearby. To this type of painting belongs also the first group of the *Campeya Jātaka,*[106] spontaneous with relatively angular movements and diagonally planned. The other scenes of this jātaka,[107] which are separated from the first by rocky boulders strewn among the flowers on the ground, show within a pavilion a pictorial fluidity of higher achievement than that of the *Mahājanaka Jātaka* painting, while the keen briskness of the preceding scene is not absent from the voluble scarves of the central portion of this episode. The third scene, within a pavilion, has the simple earnestness of the sermon scene of the *Mahājanaka Jātaka*. Although some of the figures are standardized types, none is merely applied. Each is painted afresh in exactly the way to which it owes its existence.

This is less so in the Māradharṣaṇa panel,[108] which has a dull lethargy of form. This painting is symmetrically laid out and does justice vertically and horizontally to the rectangle it fills. According to the available wallspace, some of the paintings conform in extent and composition with its limits, in cave 17, the offering of the handful of dust as also the magnificent figure on a pilaster,[109] and so on. All in one panel and to be seen as one composition are also the "preaching in the Trayastrimsa heaven," the descent from this heaven, and Sariputra's question,[110] in cave 17.

Coarsened, with summary outlines and modeling, with an extensive spread of highlights and the "rounding off" shadows shrinking toward the outline, which now, with a mannered sickle-sweep may comprise an entire figure,[111] the Māradharṣaṇa painting and others dwindle in one direction, whereas another group, more flaccid and less obtuse, more mannered even in line than in modeling, is similarly inured to a sunken level and scattered quality.[112] Into such degeneration only paintings that employ types of the ultimate attainment fall, and the group of smaller range,[113] the easier and more popular idiom, maintains an eager style and does not slur over it. On the contrary, sterner accents of will or emotion enter into its fabric. They thin it out to a lesser dimension, purposive and linear.

In the *Śibi Jātaka*[114] angular and animated movements spurt into the lineaments of the figures. They supersede the fluent curves and the plasticity of the modeling and relegate them to a subservient role. The architecture is shown in this painting to a lesser extent with molded profiles than with patterned bands, and the formerly rounded shafts of the columns are streaked with lines of an even heaviness. Aridly ornate, they are shuffled in slight layers, thinly following established formulae of forthcoming. Within their shuffled frames, flat and erect like posts, the figures conform with their setting. One of the major figures turns its sharp profile, coarse, intense, and angular into a context that as yet is indebted to a suaver idiom. Still, palm trees and flowering shrubs rattle spiky or tin-sheet-like leaves into the cries and the pang of a group of women, all elbows and jutting facial angles.[115] Their fierce context cuts across the flux of things. This type of painting, possibly posterior to any other in this cave, is not due only to a lessening of quality. The obvious deformations (the right arm and hand of the prince enthroned) result from a clash of the linear elements belonging to the domain of will and emotion, on the one side, and the metaphysical direction of forthcoming along with the uninterrupted rhythm of existence, on the other.

The harsh fabric of the reception scene[116] is akin to that of the *Śibi Jātaka.* With a vertical and horizontal structure into which the figures fit rigidly upright and the bundled folds of their costumes, the painting is stark. And yet the mode of modeling and grouping the figures, dismissed as they appear from door and intercolumniae, absorbed some of them in a state beyond purposive intention, places them, more than the painting of the *Śibi Jātaka* within the tradition of Ajanta.[117]

CAVE 2

Embossed to the highest degree of forthcoming, some of the paintings in cave 2 appear burdened with their impact. Ingrained, the color itself throws up the form, bubbling. Its substance is tone and shape in one. This color is neither symbolic nor descriptive and has more than two dimensions. It is substantial. It is the pictorial analogy of such substances, as for instance of the pearl. Color, shape, and irradiation are not to be separated. The color and its quality are ingrained in its texture. The incarnate appearance of the paintings in cave 2 is a last mode of the forthcoming of form. Color there is consubstantial with form.[118] In this it agrees somehow with the quality of color of the ground. Through it, however, form passes on its way into the "borderland." The color ground holds it prior to its getting into shape, that is, potentially. Color in cave 2, ingrained in form, incarnate, has attained to its ultimate possibilities of forthcoming. So did modeled form in cave 1. A looming power is laid out in it. It burdens while it dilates the figures.[119] Analogously it weighs at this moment in sculptured form. Of the ultimate fulfillment of the function of color, there is no painting preserved equally great in conception as of the ultimate phase of "volume" in the Bodhisattva scenes in cave 1.

Lesser painters now adhere to the manner of the *Mahājanaka Jātaka* of cave 1. They endow a further coarsening with a new ponderosity. Jewelry with them is a cumbersome adjunct in the way it is painted unfeeling of the body it is meant to adorn.[120] In other paintings of this type, the figures are torpid with large and contrasting stretches of color.[121] Thick and dark color modeling condenses near the edges and frames the lighter parts of the body, as lead rims a stained-glass window.[122] A slackening at this stage cannot always be dismissed as merely the contribution of mediocre craftsmen. It is symptomatic of a devolution in another direction. The offering scenes (pl. 16-3)[123] have figures summarily modeled in large surfaces. The darker tones, productive of the roundness of modeling, have receded from the center and condensed toward the outlines. Such reductions tend toward a final elimination of the modeling function of color.[124]

Another type of painting, corresponding to those of smaller range in cave I, is represented extensively by the contiguous scenes of the *Vidhurapaṇḍita Jātaka* (pl. 16-2) and of the *Pūrṇa Avadāna.*[125] Related to the type of painting of the *Saṅkhapāla* and *Campeya Jātakas* in cave I, they share some of its peculiarities such as the slight bodies of men appended to relatively large heads and this childlike appearance, especially in some Purṇavadana episodes, adds an eager humbleness to the shuffled scenes, room upon room, one forthcoming telescopically in front of the other. Meting out its setting to every scene, in this kind of painting, runs parallel and synchronous with the great conceptions of the Bodhisattva configurations in cave I and the great color

16-4. The betrothal of Śiva and Pārvatī, cave 3; Badami, A.D. *578.*

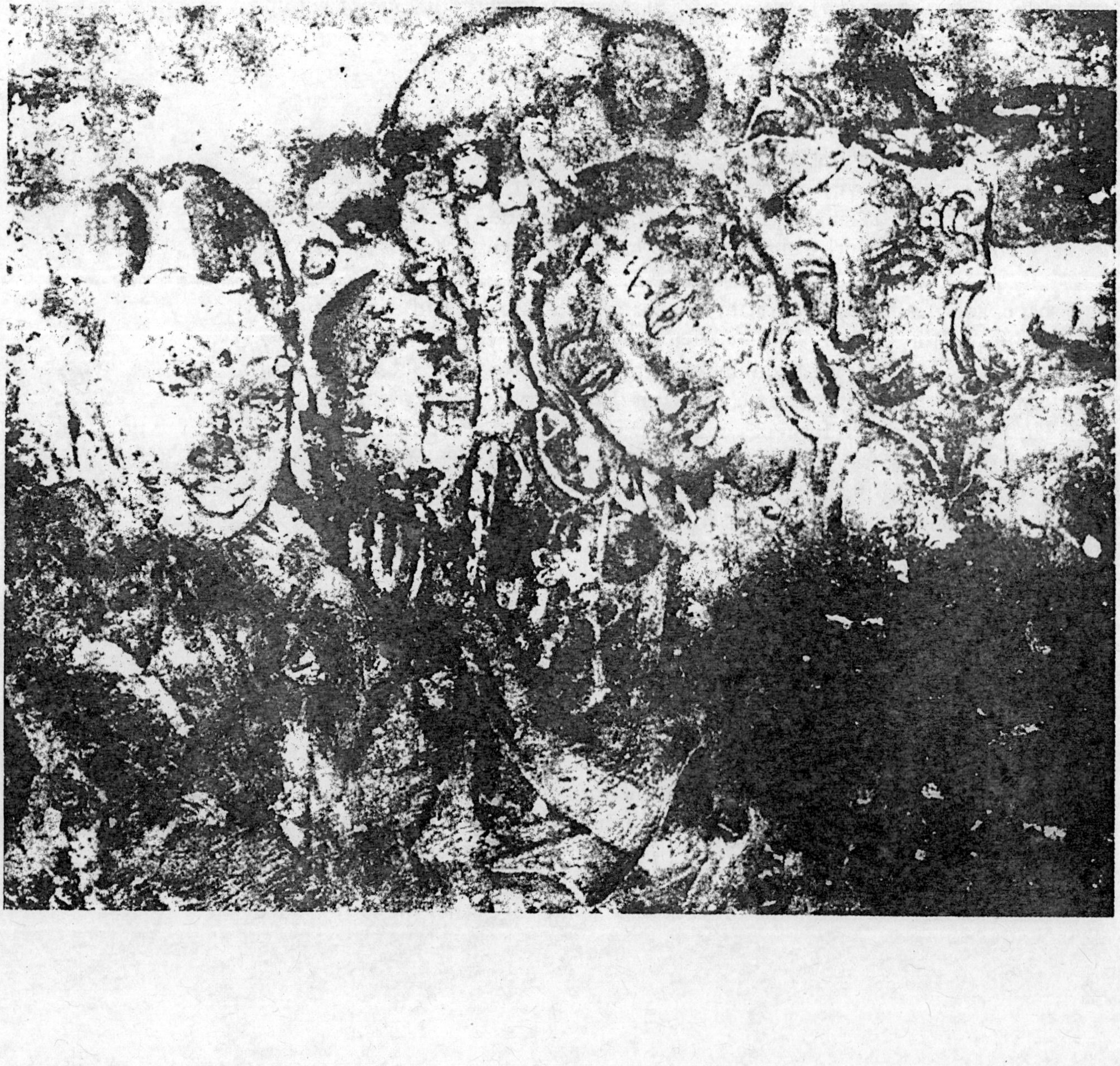

form of painting (Indra, etc.) in cave 2.[126] This reliable mode of painting neither touches upon the climax nor is it subject to dissolution. From the paintings in caves 9 and 10 (pl. 16-1) to the last mentioned in cave 2 (pl. 16-2), including related paintings in the other caves, sanctioned types remain spontaneous in the security of their tradition. It outlives the great moments and supports them. Its mutability rests on a permanently available stock. Its total repertory is drawn upon within the phase of approximately half a millennium outlined hitherto. Subsequently full use is not made of the entire heritage, and in a context less resilient, the line hardens.

The *Śibi Jātaka* type of painting in cave 1 is partly of a different lineage. It allows modeling to become insipid and to peter out in line as well as in color. The vitality of the painting belongs to a new and lower level to which the achievements of Ajanta could sink, with a setting still reminiscent of its meaning and yet part of another life. But in the tall figures of the offering scenes in cave 2 the plastic conception of forthcoming is still incandescent in pale limbs (pl. 16-3). Elbows there are dreamily hooked into sparse movements. Frail glances from wondrous eyes are held in smooth ovals of faces ensconced by simple bands and elegant coiffures. A thin sap flows in limbs turned round to perfection. Some of the Buddha and Bodhisattva figures in this cave are akin in type.[127]

In other paintings a mannerism of careless drawing brushes over residues of the whole range of conventions; overelongated figures are packed into pavilions, which they entirely fill, a slatternly congeries.[128] In these paintings, large with disintegration, although no renewed forces stir, yet a clear trend is at work, if only by elimination of a redundancy by which some of the paintings in cave 1 and those like it were benumbed.[129]

Neither are the paintings of caves 9 and 10 a beginning, nor those of caves 1 and 2 the end of a tradition. When all the possibilities of ultimate realization have matured and been given form, in Ajanta and in Bagh,[130] undercurrents of smaller range yet persist for centuries. Some of the paintings in Ellora, others in South India,[131] and some book illustrations of the same date as the last, of the "eastern school,"[132] are products of the same tradition.

In the eight centuries (second century B.C. approximately to sixth century A.D. and shortly after), the possibilities of this tradition have altogether been bodied forth; "space receptacles" and the prisms of the rocks are among the formulations preceding that of the color incarnate, which is substance itself modeled. Along with the intensification of pictorial means, the physiognomy of the figures becomes concentrated in psychological awareness. The latter is carried by the sensibility of the line which in its turn shares in the burden of modeling. Decreasing and increasing in thickness in that function, it is at times invested with a calligraphic definition in caves 1 and 2. With a thinned modeling and slackened contour, the paintings in cave 3, Badami, dated A.D. 578 (pl. 16-4)[133] follow this style of Ajanta[134]

List of Abbreviations

Serial Publications and Periodicals

AKM	*Abhandlungen für die Kunde des Morgenlandes*
AO	*Acta Orientalia*
ASB	*Asiatic Society of Bengal*
ASI	*Archaeological Survey of India*
ASIAR	*Archaeological Survey of India Annual Reports*
ĀSS	*Ānandāśrama Sanskrit Series*
BEFEO	*Bulletin de l'Ecole Française de'Extrême Orient*
BI	*Bibliotheca Indica*
CII	*Corpus Inscriptionum Indicarum*
GOS	*Gaekwad's Oriental Series*
HOS	*Harvard Oriental Series*
IA	*Indian Antiquary*
IHQ	*Indian Historical Quarterly*
IPEK	*Jahrbuch für prähistorische und ethnographische Kunst* (Leipzig)
JAOS	*Journal of the American Oriental Society*
JASB	*Journal of the Asiatic Society of Bengal*
JBHS	*Journal of the Bombay Historical Society*
JBORS	*Journal of the Bihar and Orissa Research Society*
JISOA	*Journal of the Indian Society of Oriental Art*
JRAS	*Journal of the Royal Asiatic Society*
JRASB	*Journal of the Royal Asiatic Society of Bengal*
KSS	*Kāśī Sanskrit Series*
MASI	Archaeological Survey of India *Memoirs*
PTS	*Pali Text Society*

SBB *Sacred Books of the Buddhists*
SBE *Sacred Books of the East*
SBH *Sacred Books of the Hindus*
TSS *Trivandrum Sanskrit Series*
ZDMG *Zeitschrift der Deutschen Morgenländischen Gesellеschaft*

Texts and Translations

List of Abbreviations

NOTE: Because articles often do not contain citations to specific editions, abbreviations given in the left-hand column indicate the edition cited in *The Presence of Śiva*, Stella Kramrisch's most recent book; otherwise the standard edition; translations are cited by author and title.

AB — *Aitareya Brāhmaṇa.* Edited and translated by Martin Haug. 2 vols. Bombay, 1863.
———. *Rigveda Brāhmaṇas: The Aitareya and Kauṣītaki Brāhmaṇas of the Rigveda.* Translated by Arthur Berriedale Keith. *HOS* 25. Cambridge, Mass., 1920.

AbhK — *Abhidharmakośa.* Translated by Louis de la Vallee Poussin. 6 vols. Paris, 1923–31.

AitUp — *Aitareya Upaniṣad.* Edited by pandits of Ānandāśrama. *ĀSS*. Poona, 1889.

AP — *Agni Purāṇa.* Edited by Āchārya Baladeva Upādhyāya. *KSS* 174. Benares, 1966.

ĀpGṛS — *Āpastambha Gṛhasūtra.* Edited by Morris Winternitz. Vienna, 1887.

ĀpŚS — *Āpastamba Śrautasūtra.* With the commentaries of Dhūrtaswāmi and Rāmāgnicit. Edited by Vidwan T. T. Srinivasagopalacharya. Vol. 2. Oriental Research Institute Publications, Sanskrit Series, 93. Mysore, 1953.

AV — *Atharva Veda Saṁhitā.* Edited by R. Roth and W. D. Whitney. Berlin, 1856.
———. With the commentary of Sāyaṇa. Edited by Shankar Pāndurang Pandit. 4 vols. Bombay, 1895–1898.
———. Translated by Ralph T. H. Griffith. 2 vols. Benares, 1895–1896.
———. Translated by William Dwight Whitney. 2 vols. *HOS* 7–8. Reprint of 1st ed. Delhi, 1962.
———. Translated by Maurice Bloomfield. *SBE* 42. Reprint of 1st ed. Delhi, 1964.

BDP — *Bṛhaddharma Purāṇa.* Edited by Haraprasād Shāstri. *BI* 120. Calcutta, 1889.

BG — *Bhagavadgītā.* Translated by J. A. B. van Buitenen. Chicago, 1981. With the text of Poona critical edition; see *Mbh.*

BhP — *Bhāgavata Purāṇa.* With the commentary of Śrīdhara. Edited by Pāṇḍeya Rāmateja Śāstrī. 1962.
———. Translated by N. Raghunathan. 2 vols. Madras, 1976.

BhvP — *Bhaviṣya Purāṇa.* Bombay, 1910.

BrP — *Brahma Purāṇa.* Edited by Nārāyaṇa Āpṭe. *ĀSS* 28. Poona, 1895.

BṛS — *Bṛhatsaṁhitā of Varāhamihira.* Edited by H. Kern. *BI*. Calcutta, 1865.
———. Translated by H. Kern. *JRAS*, 1870, 1871, 1873, 1875.

BṛUp — *Bṛhadāraṇyaka Upaniṣad.* With the commentary of Madhva. Edited and translated by Śriśa Chandra Vasu, with the assistance of Rāmākṣya Bhattāchārya. *SBH* 14. Reprint of 1st ed. New York, 1974.
———. Translated by Robert Ernest Hume in *The Thirteen Principal Upanishads. See AitUp.*

BŚS — *Baudhāyana Śrautasūtra.* Edited by W. Caland. 3 vols. *BI* 163. Calcutta, 1904–1924.

BVP — *Brahmavaivarta Purāṇa.* Edited by Jīvānanda Vidyāsāgara. 2 vols. Calcutta, 1888.
———. Translated by Rajendra Nath Sen. 2 parts. *SBH* 24. Allahabad, 1920–1922.

ChUp — *Chāndogya Upaniṣad.* With the commentary of Madhva. Edited and translated by Śriśa Chandra Vasu. *SBH* 3, *The Upaniṣads* Part 2, Reprint of 1st ed. New York, 1974.
———. Translated by R. E. Hume in *The Thirteen Principal Upanishads. See AitUp.*

HIIA — *History of Indian and Indonesian Art.* By Ananda K. Coomaraswamy. 2d ed. London, 1950.

ĪPad — *Īśānaśivagurudevapaddhati* of Īśānaśivagurudevamiśra. Edited by T. Gaṇapati Śāstrī. 4 vols. *TSS* 69, 72, 77, 83. Trivandrum, 1920–1925.

Jātaka — *Jātaka.* With commentary. Edited by V. Fausboll. Reprint of 1st ed. London, 1963.
———. *The Jātakas or Stories of the Buddha's Birth.* Translated by E. B. Cowell. Reprint of 1895–1907 ed. 6 vols. in 3. London, 1973.

JB — *Jaiminīya Brāhmaṇa.* Edited by Raghu Vira and Lokesh Chandra. Sarasvatī-Vihāra Series 31. Nagpur, 1954.

KaṭhUp — *Kaṭhopaniṣad.* Edited by S. C. Vasu. Allahabad, 1905.

KB — *Kauṣītaki Brāhmaṇa.* Edited by B. Lindner. Vol. 1, Text. Jena, 1887.
———. Translated by A. B. Keith. *See Aitareya Brāhmaṇ (AB).*

KŚS — *Kātyāyana Śrautasūtra.* With extracts from the commentaries of Karka and Yājñikadeva. Part 3 of the White Yajurveda. Edited by Albrecht Weber. London, 1859.

Manu — *Manusmṛti.* Edited by M. G. Jha. Calcutta, 1932.
———. *The Laws of Manu.* Translated by G. Bühler. *SBE* 25. Oxford, 1886.

MaUp — *Maitrī (Maitrāyaṇīya) Upaniṣad.* With the commentary of Rāmatīrtha. Edited and translated by E. B. Cowell. *BI* 42. London, 1870.
———. Translated by R. E. Hume in *The Thirteen Principal Upanishads. See AitUp.*

MBh — *Mahābhārata.* Edited by Vishnu S. Sukthankar, et al. 19 vols. Poona, 1933–1959.
———. *Mahābhārata with Nīlakaṇṭha's Commentary.* Edited by Kṛṣṇa Śāstrī Gurjar. 7 vols. Bombay, 1888–1890.
———. Translated by J. A. B. van Buitenen. 3 vols (Books 1–5). Chicago, 1973–1978.
———. Translated by P. C. Roy. 13 vols. Calcutta, 1883–1896.

MP — *Matsya Purāṇa.* Edited by Nārāyaṇa Āpṭe. *ĀSS* 54. Poona, 1907.
———. Translated by "A Taluqdar of Oudh." *SBH* 17. Allahabad, 1916.

MUp — *Muṇḍaka Upaniṣad.* Edited by Johannes Hertel. Indo-Iranische Quellen und Forschungen 3. Leipzig, 1924.
———. Translated by R. E. Hume in *The Thirteen Principal Upanishads. See AitUp.*

PGS — *Pāraskara Gṛhyasūtra.* Edited by Adolf Friedrich Stenzler. *AKM* 6.2. 1876.
———. Translated into German by Adolf Friedrich Stenzler. *AKM* 6.4. 1878.

PrUp — *Praśnopaniṣad.* Edited by the pandits of Ānandāśrama. *ĀSS*. Poona, 1889.
———. Translated by Robert Ernest Hume in *The Thirteen Principal Upanishads. See AitUp.*

Ṛ͏V	*Ṛg Veda Saṃhitā.* With the commentary of Sāyaṇa. Edited by F. Max Müller. 6 vols. London, 1849–1874. ———. Edited by Theodor Aufrecht. 2 vols. 3d ed. Berlin, 1955. ———. Translated by Manmatha Nath Dutt. Calcutta, 1906. ———. *Der Rig Veda.* Translated by Karl Friedrich Geldner. 3 vols. *HOS* 33–35. Cambridge, Mass., 1951. ———. Translated into German by Hermann Grassmann. 2 vols. Leipzig, 1876–1877. ———. Translated by Ralph T. H. Griffith. Reprint of 2d ed. Delhi, 1973. ———. Translated by H. H. Wilson. 7 vols. Reprint of 1st ed. Delhi, 1977.
ŚB	*Śatapatha Brāhmaṇa.* In the *Mādhyandina Śākhā.* With extracts from the commentaries of Sāyaṇa, Harisvāmin, and Dvivedagaṅgā (Part 2 of the White Yajurveda). Edited by Albrecht Weber. London, 1855. ———. Translated by Julius Eggeling. 5 vols. *SBE* 12, 26, 41, 43, 44. Reprint of 1st ed. Delhi, 1963.
ŚGS	*Śāṅkhāyana Gṛhyasūtra.* Edited by Hermann Oldenberg. Indische Studien 15. 1878, pp. 1–166.
ŚRa	*Śilparatna* of Śrī Kumāra. Edited by T. Ganapati Śāstrī (vol. 1) and K. Sāmbaśiva Śāstrī (vol. 2). *TSS* 75, 98. Trivandrum, 1922–1929.
SRSu	*Samarāṅgaṇa Sūtradhāra* of Mahārājādhirāja Bhoja. Edited by T. Ganapati Śāstrī and Vasudevan Saran Agrawala. *GOS* 25. Baroda, 1966.
ŚS	*Śivasaṃhitā.* Edited and translated by Śriśa Chandra Vasu. 2d ed. New Delhi, 1975.
ŚŚS	*Śāṅkhāyana Śrautasūtra.* With the commentaries of Varadattasuta Ānartīya and Govinda. Edited by Alfred Hillebrandt. 4 vols. *BI* 99. Calcutta, 1888–1899.
ŚUp	*Śvetāśvatara Upaniṣad.* Edited and translated by Siddheshvar Varma Shastri. *SBH* 18.2 Reprint of 1st ed. New York, 1974. ———. Translated by R. E. Hume in *The Thirteen Principal Upanishads.* See *AitUp.*
TĀ	*Taittirīya Āraṇyaka.* With the commentary of Sāyaṇa. Edited by Bābā Śāstrī Phaḍke. 2 parts. *ĀSS* 36. Poona, 1897–1898.
TB	*Taittirīya Brāhmaṇa.* With the commentary of Sāyaṇa. Edited by Nārāyaṇa Śāstrī Goḍabole. 3 parts. *ĀSS* 37. Poona, 1898.
TUp	*Taittirīya Upaniṣad.* With the commentaries of Ānandagiri and Śaṅkarānanda. Edited by Vāmanaśāstrī Islāmpurkar. *ĀSS* 12. 2d ed. Poona, 1897. ———. Translated by R. E. Hume in *The Thirteen Principal Upanishads.* See *AitUp.*
VDhP	*Viṣṇudharmottara Purāṇa.* Third Khaṇḍa. Edited by Priyabola Shah. *GOS* 130. Baroda, 1958. ———. Part 3. Translated by Stella Kramrisch. 2d ed. Calcutta, 1928, based on the Venkatesvara Press edition (Bombay; 1923).
VP	*Viṣṇu Purāṇa.* Edited by Śrīmunilāla Gupta. Gorakhpur, 1967. ———. Translated by H. H. Wilson. Reprint of 1st ed. Calcutta, 1961.
VS	*Vājasaneyi Saṃhitā* in the *Mādhyandina* and the *Kāṇva Śākhā.* With the commentary of Mahīdhara (Part 1 of the White Yajurveda). Edited by Albrecht Weber. London, 1852.
Yāj	*Yājñavalkya Dharmaśāstra.* Edited and translated into German by Adolf Friedrich Stenzler. London, 1849.

Notes

1 Artist, Patron, and Public in India

1. *Śukranītisāra;* see Durgādatta Tripāthī, "The 32 Sciences and the 64 Arts," *JISOA* 11(1943):40–64.
2. *Īśānaśivagurudevapaddhati,* Part 4 *TSS* 83 (Trivandrum, 1925), chap. 34, 3.
3. *Epigraphia Indica* 24(1937–38):56.
4. For a full account of the guilds, see Aranda K. Coomaraswamy, *The Indian Craftsman* (London, 1909), passim.
5. *IA* 9(1880):74.
6. *Epigraphia Indica* 1(*ASI,* n.s. 13[1892]):159.
7. Stella Kramrisch, *The Art of India* (London: Phaidon, 1954), pl. 137, p. 211.
8. D. R. Bhandarkar, "The Kīrtistambha of Rānā Kumbha," *JISOA* 1(1933):52–56.
9. "*-sthūla-sūkṣma-parā.*"*-Viṣṇusaṃhitā* (ca. twelfth century). *TSS* 85(Trivandrum, 1925), chap. xiii.
10. *Suttavibhaṅga; Vinaya Piṭaka,* III, 36. For further sources see B. M. Barua, "The Antiquity of Image Worship in India," *JISOA* 11(1943):67–68.

    The *Ṣaḍviṃśa Brāhmaṇa,* X, 5, speaks of laughing, weeping, . . . opening and closing images of gods.

2 Traditions of the Indian Craftsman

1. The sixty-four arts (kalā) are listed in Vātsyāyana, *Kāmasūtra* 1.3. Cf. Yaśodhara's commentary, *Jayamaṅgala.*
2. Stella Kramrisch, *The Hindu Temple* (Calcutta: University of Calcutta, 1946), p. 11.
3. *Arthaśāstra,* 1.3.7.
4. *Viṣṇusmṛti,* 2.10–14.
5. *Baudhāyana,* 15.13–22.
6. D. R. Bhandarkar, "Foreign Elements in Hindu Population," *IA* (1901): 16f.
7. *Manu* 5.129; cf. *Vishnu Purāṇa* 23, 48.
8. *Gautama* 17.17; cf. *Manu* 4.214–221.
9. *Mānasāra,* ii. 1–20.
10. *JISOA,* vol. 13 (1945): pl. 15.
11. *Brahmavaivarta Purāṇa,* 1.10.20–23f.
12. *VDhP* 3.90.29; *SRSa,* 32.28.
13. Kramrisch, pp. 18–85.
14. "South Indian Inscriptions," *Epigraphia Indica,* 3, p. 82.

15. Bāṇa, *Harṣacarita*, ch. IV, ed., P. V. Kane (Bombay, 1918) p. 14 (trans. Cowell-Thomas [London, 1897], p. 123).

16. *Epigraphia Indica*, 1, p. 159.

17. *Epigraphia Indica*, 24, p. 56.

18. *Īśānaśivagurudevapaddhati*, *TSS*, Trivandrum, 1920–24, Introduction to vol. 2. See also *Epigraphia Indica* 1, pp. 251, 354; 3, p. 297; 21, p. 149; 22, p. 127; 24, p. 241, and *MASI*, no. 23, pp. 110–15.

3 Indian Terracottas

1. Cf. C. C. Das Gupta, "Bibliography of Ancient Indian Terra-cotta Figurines," *JRASB* 4(1938):67–120.

2. The error of assigning an early date to certain supposedly archaic types is based on finds in excavations in India (Mohenjo-daro, Harappa, etc.) and outside India, in Kish, Susa, and Assur, Tall Asmar, Jemdet Nasr in Mesopotamia; in Anau, Turkestan; Alishar (Anatolia), Troy, Adalia, and other sites in Asia Minor, on early Cycladic and Cretan works, etc., to name only a few early occurrences. The nearest likenesses of the "primitive types" are within Cycladic work in marble and in terracotta, also in Crete, under Mycenean rule where geometrical volumes and rounded lines are charged with similar rhythms. This refers to human figures and to some female shapes from Buxar especially (see below), but also to twentieth-century terracottas from Bengal, etc., whereas the figures of animals, i.e., horses in the main, have more than one trait in common with those from Cyprus (third through sixth centuries B.C.).

3. I.e., rūpa-bheda, the first of the six limbs of art (citra, i.e., sculpture and painting) as enumerated in Yaśodhara's commentary to the *Kāmasūtra*. "Proportionate measurement" is the second limb.

4. On the sixth day of the birth of a child, the Goddess Ṣaṣṭhī (the "sixth" part of Prakṛti) is invoked and set up as an image, to remove calamities and grant health and long life to child and parents. On the sixth night the Vidhātā Puruṣa writes the future of the child on its forehead.

5. *TB* 1.7.6.7, *SB* 2.2.1.19.

6. *AB* 8.5.

7. *Yāj* 11.56.

8. C. W. Crooke, *Religion and Folklore in Northern India* (London: Oxford University Press, 1926), p. 28.

9. S. C. Mitra, "On a Curious Cult of Orissa," *JASB*, n.s., 30(1934):20.

10. P. N. Bhattacharjee, "Folk-custom and Folklore of the Sylhet District," *Man in India* (1930), p. 118.

11. This ontology of form may be compared with the description of Agni, when "first born in his ground" and referred to as "footless and headless, hiding both his ends" (*RV* 4.1.11–12); Ananda K. Coomaraswamy, "Angel and Titan," *JAOS* 55(1935):411.

12. Star-shaped figurines like the one from Buxar (pl. 3-1.1) are always roughly modeled by hand, flattened on back and front with four points marking the ends of "arms" and "legs," and the whole topped by a rounded outline which terminates the head. The face is pinched so that the nose ridge results. The Buxar figurine is purest in type, the one from Patna (pl. 3-1.2) has lost (or was made without) the arms, which, to judge from the legs, must have been more differentiated, as is also the face with holes for the eyes.

Baskets full of such "star-shaped" figurines have been collected in Kauśāmbī and Bhita and are now in the Municipal Museum, Allahabad.

This type may still be further articulated (pl. 3-1.3; from Taxila) and the arm stumps bent forward, the eyes modeled, etc. Related to this type are also the bodies of a whole group of male figurines from Mathura, for instance Ananda K. Coomaraswamy, "Archaic Indian Terra-cottas," *IPEK* (1928), fig. 33; Takacs, *JISOA* 5(1937), pl. 19, fig. 6.

13. There are more varieties of traditional types among the female figurines. Of the standing figurines found in the Ganges Valley, none is shown with a child, while the seated figurines clasp a child's figure, separately modeled against the breast. Among the standing figurines, types range from that of plate 3-1.8 (from Bulandibagh) to that of plate 3-1.10 (from Patna). The former is of dark grey terracotta and has a rectangular torso, and separate pellets are affixed for the dog collar and the broad girdle that covers the hips with its double row of ornaments. The pointed breasts, too, are separately modeled and affixed. In shape, this figurine is akin to many from Mohenjo-daro; these differ also with their diminutive and band-like skirts from such types as plate 3-1.10. There are few exaggeratedly female figurines in Mohenjo-daro (E. J. H. Mackay, *Further Excavations at Mohenjo-daro*, New Delhi: Government of India, 1938, pl. 75, 5). The Pāṭaliputra fragment (pl. 3-1.10) has the shape of a tuning fork with the excessive narrowness

of waist, bulging hips, and leg cones held apart, the abdomen flattened and with a double ringlet for the navel.

Figurines of the seated variety are preserved in especially large numbers in Buxar and Pāṭaliputra. There are two varieties, one a timeless type; the other with time-bound traits (cf. Banerji-Sastri, "Remains of a Pre-Historic Civilisation in the Gengetic Valley," *JBHS* 3[1930], fig. 6, Buxar Terra-cottas, "Series B.") The "ageless type" is seated on a two-legged stool, i.e., a flat shape making an arch. Her own legs and arms are bent cylindrical shapes; the body, an upright cylinder with a neck of equal width, supports the head. Cylindrical breasts are modeled along with it, and the child's figure, where present, is another volume added to the balanced coordination of geometrical shapes. The face here is broad and flat, with a partly pinched and partly modeled nose; a small line indicates the mouth and large lozenge shapes the eyes. The hair may or may not be indicated above the high brows; large ears stand up high and have a cup-shaped ear plug (?) impressed with a "lotus" design. The head in this, and in all the other examples of both the varieties of this type, has, as a rule, three double holes, and in a few specimens a different number of holes. They must be present, it seems, to allow a high headdress to be inserted. No single part of this headdress has been preserved, and it is possible that it was made of materials other than terracotta. The shape of the head varies; it is dome shaped or straight and has also in some examples two horn-like hillocks. The Pāṭaliputra examples of this type have only occasionally lozenge-shaped eyes. Elliptical shapes are the rule there, frequently suggestive in their curves, of the lozenge shape.

Often a greater amount of modeling is introduced (the lips, especially the lower, the nose with nostrils, the hair, which is affixed and incised), and there is a long, conical neck. Gone furthest in the dissolution of the surface through modeling is a face found in Patna (cf. K. P. Jayaswal, "Terra-cottas Dug Out of Patna," *JISOA* 3[1935], pl. 30, fig. 4, where the head has been wrongly identified by Jayaswal). The broad and spatulate head with four double holes sends forth laterally the flat ear surfaces. They frame a face in which the smile of contentment, an "archaic" smile—that hovers on the modeled variety of Buxar faces—has deepened and grooved the face. The high cheek bones are an upper limit to the enormous mold-like depression (cf. stone reliefs from Bharhut) around the mouth with its very heavy lower lip.

14. They are holed across the pointed top so that they can be hung up. Relief plaques of the time-bound varieties are similarly holed.

15. Ananda K. Coomaraswamy, *The Darker Side of Dawn,* Smithsonian Miscellaneous Collections 94 (Washington, D.C., 1935), p. 7.

16. Crooke, *Religion and Folklore,* p. 50.

17. *SB* 4.6.9.16; Vāc turns away from the gods, creeps away along this earth.

18. Coomaraswamy, *Darker Side,* p. 18. Because its verses are "recited mentally" (manasā stuyante), hence the name of the well-known Bengali snake goddess, Manasā Devī, who is the Earth.

19. According to Sāṁkhya; the other ten senses are external, five of sensation (buddhīndriya) and five of action (karmendriya).

20. In the Manasā Mangal by Vijaya Gupta (quoted by D. C. Ṣen, *Bengali Language and Literature,* p. 282), the merchant king Cānd Sadāgar, a devotee of Śiva, possesses mahājñāna, the "Great Knowledge," intellectual intuition. He foils the plots of Manasā. But when he falls in love with her, he dispenses with mahājñāna, and he bestows it on her. Beheld from the level of intellectual illumination, Manasā is seen in her malign aspect.

21. Coomaraswamy, *Darker Side,* p. 2.

22. The Buxar figurines are reproduced by Banerji-Sastri, "Remains of a Pre-Historic Civilisation," p. 187ff., and also in the K. B. Pathak commemoration volume, 1934, p. 248ff.

23. Cf. *Annual Bibliography of Indian Archaeology,* vol. 12, pl. 5.

24. V. S. Agrawala, "Mathura Terra-Cottas," *Journal of the U.P. Historical Society* 9, pt. 2(1936):6–38 (reprint), pl. 7, fig. 23, etc.

25. Stella Kramrisch, "Emblems of the Universal Being," *JISOA* 3, no. 2(1935):149 reprinted here.

26. Sarat Chandra Mitra, "The Cult of the Tree Goddess in Eastern Bengal," *Man in India* 2(1922):228.

27. Kramrisch, "Emblems," p. 153; the sun is "maṇiśṛṅga" (jewel-horned), *Harivaṁśa*, 12, 367.

28. C. W. Crooke, "The Headdress of Banjara Women," *JBORS* 4:247–56.

29. Cf. Ṛṣya Sṛṅga (*JISOA,* vol. 4, pl. 11). The horn in these instances implies procreative power.

30. Re other varieities of conical or triangular headdress of women, cf. figurines from Buxar.

31. S. Beal, *Si-yu-ki, Buddhist Records of the Western World,* 2 vols. (London, 1906), Introd.; cf. also corresponding medieval European headwear of women.

32. Sāyaṇa explains opaśa as ā-upa-śī, to rest against, and interprets *RV* 1.173.6 Indra's opaśa as horn. Cf. Vedic Index 2, p. 313, visāṇin, i.e., having horns, a tribe mentioned in the *Ṛg Veda.*

33. References given by Crooke, "The Headdress," p. 251.

34. Coomaraswamy, "Archaic Indian Terra-Cottas," fig. 14; Banerji-Sastri, "Remains of a Prehistoric Civilisation," plate facing p. 251.

35. *Annual Bibliography of Indian Archaeology* 12, pl. 5; a similar although coarser plaque (head portion only preserved) has been excavated recently in Kauśāmbī and is now in the Indian Museum, Calcutta. Professor Johnston in the report for the years 1938–39 (Curators of the Indian Institute) assigns the former to about 200 B.C.

36. Durga Prashad, "Classification and Significance of the Symbols on the Silver Punch Marked Coins of Ancient India," *JASB* 30(1934). The following correspondences of the five devices (from below upwards) are:

(1)	Aṅkuśa; cf. Durga Prashad, "Classification," pl. 24, fig. 236; pl. 31, coin 21, symbol 7.
(2) and (4)	The main symbol is identical; it is a kind of triśūla; it is topped by a different device in each case, i.e., (2) by a comb-like device pañca vāṇa (?), cf. Durga Prashad, "Classification," pl. 27, fig. 97; from Mohenjo-daro; (also pl. 28, symbol 4, etc.); pl. 24, 179, pl. 4, nos. 44, 46; pl. 23, 108.
(4)	by a triangular (arrowhead) device, cf. Durga Prashad, "Classification," pl. 28, symbol 30 (from Mohenjo-daro), pl. 24, fig. 183.
(3)	Arrowhead-like device; it issues horizontally from an upright staff; cf. Durga Prashad, "Classification," pl. 26, fig. 22; pls. 13, etc., symbol 2; arrowheads may be an analogy of the rays of the sun. On the lesser Kauśāmbī terracotta plaque, symbol (1) = 1 of the Oxford plaque, the aṅkuśa being rectilinear instead of curvilinear; (2) = 3; symbols 3-5 are indistinct and appear to belong to the type of symbols 2 and 4 on the Oxford plaque.

37. They frame the forehead of the female faces at Buxar, Mathura, etc.

38. Durga Prashad, "Classification," p. 18, from Kālīvilāsa Tantra, chap. 25, śl. 27–29.

39. Re the bindu, cf. "Ein Punkt der in den Zirkel geht
Der im Quadrat und Dreyangel steht,
Kennst Du den Punkt, so ist es gut,
Kennst Du ihn nicht, so ist's umbsonst."

This German medieval quatrain applies to the bindu in every Yantra.

40. *Ramāyaṇa* 5.11.

41. The moon is beheld as a white bull radiant with a pointed, full horn; *Ramāyaṇa* 5.20, cf. "cornucopia." The various symbols lie close together in meaning, shape, and position.

42. Ananda K. Coomaraswamy, "The Buddha's Cūḍa, Hair, Uṣṇīṣa, and Crown," *JRAS* (1928), pl. 4, figs. 2, 3, and "Uṣṇīṣa and Chatra," *The Poona Orientalist* 3:2.

43. *MBh* 13.3.11 = 191; 13.38.2 = 2203; Adolf Holtzmann, "Die Apsaras nach dem Mahābhārata," *ZDMG* 33:637 renders pañcacuḍa as "with five tresses."

44. *MBh* 13.38.2 calls her Puṁścalī (meretrix).

45. Kālīvilāsa Tantra, 33.13.

46. Mitra, "Cult of the Tree Goddess," p. 228, re Midnapur, Bengal.

47. Crooke, *Religion and Folklore,* pp. 99, 199.

48. Re Uttarāyaṇa and Dakṣiṇāyana, see B. G. Tilak, *The Arctic Home in the Vedas* (Poona, 1903), p. 67 passim.

49. Cf. Durga Prashad, pl. 22, 16–25 (Paramābīja mudrā), p. 20, the emblem of "astravidyā," the science of arms and warfare.

50. Pl. 23, fig. 140; pl. 25, fig. 109; pl. 26, fig. 53, considered to be an insect (?), p. 46.

51. Cf. Sūcīmukha, in medieval stone carvings from Bihar, for instance, Stella Kramrisch, "Pāla and Sena Sculpture," *Rupam,* no. 40 (October 1929), fig. 46.

52. The symbolism of the wheel, hub, axle (*RV* 10.89.4) and body of the chariot is the subject of many texts.

The chariots from Kauśāmbī have a front wall on which are two or four bullocks or bulls in relief; the carts are open in front and have raised sides, against which the members of a so-called "pleasure-party" recline. Cf. Stella Kramrisch, "Madhupāna Scenes," *JISOA* 6(1938):

197. The subjects of the large stone carvings dealt with there and the occupants of the terracotta carts have the same aim. They are shown in various stages of "pilgrimage" and engaged in "rites" that are also continued while on pilgrimage. These carts and their passengers are "timed" and follow in their appearance and execution the style of their period.

53. In Kauśāmbī the body and head of the ram are shaped into a massive and fleecy lump; the Vaiśālī (Basarh) type is articulate and elegant with a smooth surface of head and body impressed with flowers and leaves.

54. The insertion of time-bound traits into ageless types has various results. Pl. 3-1.14 (from Patna), a light grey, very hard terracotta with traces of black slip, has a flat topknot on the left, similar to that of the vase-bodied male figurine found at the same spot (cf. Jayaswal, "Terra-cottas Dug Out of Patna," pl. 32 $_{2-5}$). It appears despite the "primitive appearance" also to belong to the same age. Moreover it is to be compared with terracottas found in the Nilgiris (J. W. Breeks, "An Account of the Primitive Tribes and Monuments of the Nilagiris," pl. 36). Pl. 3-1.13 (from Bulandibagh) has a larger amount of time-bound traits. The double earrings (spirals), the topknot, etc., assign it as well as pl. 3-1.14 to the first century A.D. approximately, to which date also belongs the vase-shaped figurine referred to. Pl. 3-1.15 is another variety and has a light ocher slip.

55. Mackay, *Further Excavations,* p. 260.

56. A combination of terracotta shapes with other materials is peculiar to bird figurines that have small holes into which legs made only of metal could have been inserted. This technique, however, is also represented in Mohenjo-daro (Mackay, pl. 75, 5).

57. Jayaswal, "Terra-cottas Dug Out of Patna," pl. 30.3.

58. *JBORS* 10:190–92, 194–201; 17:410–11.

59. The "Dampatī" couples from the Bhir mound, Taxila, of which a considerable number of replicas in the Taxila Museum and elsewhere are among the few exceptions.

60. Cf. Ananda K. Coomaraswamy, *Early Indian Terra-cottas* (Boston: Museum of Fine Arts of Boston, 1927), pp. 90–96, and "Archaic Indian Terra-cottas," pp. 64–76; K. deB. Codrington, "A Note on the Pottery of Bhitab," *Man* (1929), p. 136ff., "Some Indian Terra-cotta Figurines," *Indian Antiquary* (1931), p. 141ff.; D. H. Gordon, "The Problem of Early Indian Terra-cottas," *Man* (1935), p. 117; Agrawala, *Mathura Terra-cottas,* pp. 6–38, pls. 1–19; D. H. Gordon, "Age of Frontier Terra-cottas," *Iraq* 5:85–88, pls. 6–9; for Buxar, see Banerji-Sastri, note 70 below.

61. Cf. *ASIAR* 1915–16, pt. 1, p. 14ff.; 1917–18, pt. 1, p. 27ff.; 1926–27, pl. 31; A.S. Eastern Circle, *Annual Report, 1914–15,* p. 45ff., *Annual Report, 1915–16,* p. 27ff.; Jayaswal, "Terra-cottas Dug Out of Patna," p. 125ff.

62. Stella Kramrisch, "Die indische Kunst," in Anton Springer, ed., *Die aussereuropäische Kunst, Handbuch der Kunstgeschichte,* vol. 6 (Leipzig: Alfred Kroner Verlag, 1929), p. 241, fig. 246; Coomaraswamy, "Archaic Indian Terra-cottas," fig. 51.

63. Coomaraswamy, "Archaic Indian Terra-cottas," pl. 2, fig. 14.

64. Ludwig Bachhofer, *Early Indian Sculpture,* vol. 1 (New York, 1929), pl. 12. They are possibly of late Maurya date.

65. *ASIAR* 1926–27, fig. k. The figurines of this type have heavier cheeks, and their faces conform with types from Sanchi.

66. For instance, J. Charbonneaux, "A Nike from Kyme," *Les Terres-Cuites Grècques,* no. 62.

67. W. W. Tarn, *The Greeks in Bactria and India* (Cambridge: Cambridge University Press, 1938), p. 132.

68. Jayaswal, "Terra-cottas Dug Out of Patna," pl. 31.

69. Cf. male figure, upper story, Rānī Gumphā, Udayagiri, Orissa, carved out of the living rock.

70. *Journal of the Bombay Historical Society* 3:187–91, and in the K. B. Pathak commemoration volume, 1934, pp. 248–61.

71. For instance Coomaraswamy, *Early Indian Terra-cottas,* 5, 18; K. deB. Codrington, "Some Indian Terra-cotta Figurines," *IM* 163, 166 (1929), "Some Indian Terra-cotta Figurines," *IA,* pl. facing p. 141; Agrawala, *Mathura Terra-cottas,* pl. 3, fig. 9; pl. 4, fig. 12.

72. Stella Kramrisch, *Indian Sculpture* (Calcutta: YMCA Publishing House, 1933), fig. 32. There is more affinity of "school" between certain stone sculptures from Patna and the carvings in Sanchi than with Bharhut.

73. Coomaraswamy, *Early Indian Terra-cottas,* figs. 18, 19.

74. Codrington's dating of these female types from Mathura in the late second–first century B.C. rests on comparisons of fashions (*IA,* p. 144) and on the fact that the "molded features have nothing primitive about them"; Lieutenant Colonel Gordon, following Codrington, goes

even further in "The Problem of Indian Terra-cottas," p. 111, when he sees no essential difference between early Mathụra terracottas and the Yakṣī on the Bhuteśvar railing.

75. *AṢIAR* 1913–14, pl. 44b. Plate 3-2.2 is a cast from a mold found in Basarh, *ASIAR* 1913–14, no. 336; of Suṅga date, a specimen of the local work, untouched by Hellenism.

76. The terracottas illustrated on plates 3-1–3-3 are in the Patna Museum, Patna.

4 Unknown India

1. Surajit Sinha, "Tribal Cultures of Peninsular India," in *Traditional India,* ed. M. Singer (Philadelphia: American Folklore Society, 1959), pp. 298–311. The figures in the preceding paragraph refer to India proper, not to the entire subcontinent.

2. G. N. Das, "The Funerary Monuments of the Nilgiris," *Bulletin of the Deccan College Research Institute* 18 (Poona, 1957): 140–52; James W. Breeks, *An Account of the Primitive Tribes and Monuments of the Nilgiris* (London, 1873), pls. 36–39.

3. Verrier Elwin, *The Tribal Art of Middle India* (Oxford, 1951), p. 2. The statement by Pāṇini (6.2.62) classifies without evaluation. A distinction, however, recorded in later days, though not aimed at the visual arts but at music, is relevant. The *Saṁgītā Darpaṇa* (1.4–6) contrasts mārga with deśi: mārga implies the path of sacred tradition, deśi a local or "country" style, the one safeguarding the purity of the tradition on the side of the performer and the knowledge of its subtleties on the side of the audience, the other being unconcerned with its rules. Applied to visual art, deviations from the established iconometry would make a work of art deśi, i.e., belonging to "folk art." This term does apply to the work of the rural citrakaras of the later nineteenth and early twentieth century in Bengal, whose scroll paintings illustrate Hindu themes. It does not apply to works of art outside the Hindu tradition, and in which content and form correspond the one to the other.

4. *Indian Archaeology 1959–60—A Review* (New Delhi, 1960), p. 18, pl. 16; M. G. Dikshit, "Excavations at Rangpur, 1947," *Bulletin of the Deccan College Research Institute* 11 (Poona, 1950): 51, pl. 17.

5. W. Koppers, "Die Bhil in Zentral Indien," *Wiener Beiträge zur Kulturgeschichte und Linguistik* 7 (Vienna, 1948):17.

6. Ibid., p. 20. C. von Fürer-Haimendorf, in T. B. Naik, *The Bhils* (Delhi, 1956), p. x.

7. Mathias Hermanns, *Die Religiös-Magische Weltanschauung der Primitivstämme Indiens,* vol. 1 (Wiesbaden, 1964), p. 13.

8. Koppers, "Die Bhil," p. 14.

9. W. Koppers, "Monuments to the Dead Erected by the Bhils and Their Neighbours," *Annali Lateranensi* 6 (1942): 119–206, passim.

10. *RV* 1.163.2.

11. *AP,* 51, 3. Images of Sūrya, the sun-god, on horseback are in the great sun temples of Martand, Kashmir, of the eighth century and in Konarak, Orissa, of the thirteenth century. Cf. H. Goetz, "The Mediaeval Sculpture of Kashmir," *Marg* 8, 65f, fig. 3; H. Zimmer, *The Art of Indian Asia* (New York, 1955), pl. 371; M. Th. de Mallmann, *Les Enseignments Iconographiques de l'Agni Purana* (Paris, 1963), p. 76.

12. Cf. *RV* 4.40.5; 7.77.3.

13. Hermanns, "Die Religiös-Magische Weltanschauung," pp. 403–26, treating of the Bhagoria Bhil, and Koppers, "Die Bhil," p. 207ff. The accounts differ in some respects according to variations of the Nukto rites in different localities within the Bhil region.

14. Koppers, "Die Bhil," pp. 147, 260.

15. J. Abbot, *The Keys of Power* (London, 1932), p. 10.

16. For example, see *1000 Years of Iranian Art,* Smithsonian Institution, exhibition catalogue, 1964–65, fig. 104.

17. Leonhard Adam, *Primitive Art* (London, 1954), pl. 11b.

18. The surface patterns of the wire-technique in metal recall those produced by the coiled withes of Siki grass of which figurines and baskets are made to this day in North Bihar. See Ruth Reeves, *Cire Perdue Casting in India* (New Delhi, 1962), p. 17, passim. In the equestrian figurines from western India, the body of the horse is sometimes cast hollow.

19. *AB* 3. 33.

20. J. Dowson, *A Classical Dictionary of Hindu Mythology and Religion* (London, 1914), p. 311.

21. Brahmanic texts know not only the skin but also the horn of the black antelope to be full of secret powers. Cf. H. Oldenburg, *Vorwissenschaftliche Wissenschaft: Die Weltanschauung der Brahmana Texte* (Göttingen, 1919), p. 42. During the soma sacrifice, the priest wrapped a

horn of the black antelope into his robe, saying "Thou art the maternal lap of Indra." The skin of a black antelope is the initiation garment of a Brahman (*Institutes of Vishnu* [*SBE*] 7, p. 115).

A black antelope skin is also the seat of a Brahman during meditation. An early Chola relief shows the antelope as Vāhana of Durgā, the Great Goddess (S. R. Balasubrahmanyam, *Early Chola Art* [Bombay, 1966], pt. 1, pl. 1b.). Horse and deer are also known as the vehicles of the luminaries (Abbot, *The Keys*, p. 142), the solar symbolism of the horse being pervasive. In the small metal images the shapes of deer and antelope are assimilated the one to the other.

22. The "wire" technique is being practiced by itinerant or settled metal workers in West Bengal, South Bihar, Mayurbhanj, Orissa, and in Madhya Pradesh as far south as Bastar. It is not always possible to assign on grounds of style alone each figurine to its place of origin. However, the Kaser of Bastar evolved a distinct style of the wire technique. The figurines made for the Kutiya Kond tribe of Orissa are another style group by themselves. Other figurines from Orissa do not resemble them. The work of Ruth Reeves (note 18) devoted to the hereditary metal craftsmen working for tribal and nontribal peoples in certain parts of central and eastern India needs to be carried on wherever vestiges of traditional crafts survive.

23. Hermanns, "Die Religiös-Magische Weltanschauung," p. 499, pl. 13, fig. 24. The wheel is a symbol of the sun (*RV* 4.30.4). Sun wheels are imprinted on the palms and soles of the Buddha.

24. A. J. Patel, "Folk Terra-cottas of Gujarat," *Journal of M. S. University of Baroda* 12 (1963): 63–67 discusses such "substitute" offerings donated in lieu of the actual animal. P. Jayakar, "Some Terra-cotta Figurines from Tribal Gujarat," *Marg* 7 (1953): 27–32, states that the terracotta figurines of the Rani Paraj areas of Surat are made by the potter women solely for the tribal people. The Rani Paraj terracottas have a fantastic, flamboyant style.

25. Their number is not accidental, 72 being 9 times 8, the sacred number of the "city of Ayodhyā," the "perfect dwelling," that is, the body of man. Cf. Stella Kramrisch, *The Hindu Temple*, vol. 1 (Calcutta: University of Calcutta, 1946), p. 49.

26. A. Chandras, "Gujarat Fairs and Festivals," *Census of India* (New Delhi, 1961), vol. 5, pt. 7, B, p. 228.

27. Ananda K. Coomaraswamy, *The Indian Craftsman* (London, 1909), p. 21.

28. Louis Dumont, "Definition structurale d'un dieu populaire Tamoul: Aiyanar, Le Maître," *Journal Asiatique* 246 (1953): 256–70.

29. Pyyappan, *Lord Ayyappan* (Bombay: Bharatiya Vidya Bhavan, 1962), p. 55.

30. Dumont, "Definition Structurale," p. 263.

31. H. Whitehead, *The Village Gods of South India* (London, 1921), p. 26.

32. *Folk Arts of India*, catalogue section by Ruth Reeves (Syracuse, 1967), pp. 33–34.

33. Stirrups on horses are shown in Indian stone sculptures of ca. the first century B.C. to the first century A.D. in Sanchi, Bhaja, Pitalkhora, and Mathura. S. D. Singh, *Ancient Indian Warfare with Special Reference to the Vedic Period* (Leiden, 1965), p. 63, asserts that this is the first occurrence in any representation not only in India, of stirrups, however primitive they are.

34. W. G. Archer, *The Vertical Man, A Study in Primitive Sculpture* (London, 1947), p. 44.

35. B. K. Sarkar, *The Folk Element in Hindu Culture* (London, 1917), p. 111.

36. A. Bhattacharya, "The Cult of the Village Gods of West Bengal," *Man in India* 35(1955):19–33.

37. Reeves, *Folk Arts*, p. 33.

38. Kramrisch, *The Hindu Temple*, p. 32.

39. Cf. note 37.

40. The votive images of bullocks and horses in some of the South Indian village sanctuaries form large herds of animal statuary whose impact by sheer number of their repetitive shapes is as powerful as that of the human votive figures, offered for warding off epidemics. They form a dam of cumulative units against apprehensions and fears. Similarly, in Malabar, local ghosts, the servants of the goddess who could bring misfortune, must be offered bullocks and horses. E. Kathleen Gough, "Cults of the Dead Among the Nayars," in *Traditional India*, ed. M. Singer (Philadelphia: American Folklore Society, 1959), p. 260.

41. While Bhagavan, Supreme Deity, is without an image, the gods of Hinduism accepted into the tribal pantheon, as well as the lesser, originally tribal gods and also the tribalized versions of Hindu gods, have their images set up for worship, for instance by the Bhil (Ramesh Chand, "The Painted Terra-cotta Wall Plaques of Molela Village," *Folk Arts of India* [Syracuse, 1967], pp. 63–68). It must not be overlooked that some of the Hindu gods were of pre-Hindu or tribal origin. But it was within Hinduism that their iconic shapes were conceived.

42. According to the information given by the Victoria and Albert Museum, London, the figurines are "playthings for the use of the bridegroom (generally about ten years old)."

43. Elwin, pp. 173, 175, fig. 196.

44. Outside the work of Verrier Elwin, Ruth Reeves, and W. G. Archer, no local studies have been made. Anthropological publications have given no further attention to tribal and rural art but that of bare reference to its existence and hardly any illustration.

The metal statuettes travel easily. When they finally reach a dealer, he mostly does not know their place of origin. They are summarily known as "Jungli bronzes."

45. Elwin, *Tribal Art,* p. 2. The name of these metal smiths is variously spelt: Kaser, Ghadwa, or Ghasia. W. Grigson, *The Maria Gonds of Bastar* (Oxford, 1938), p. 179, spoke of them as "one of the lowest of the untouchable castes." "Even in Bastar where many of them are skilled artisans, the wildest Maria hold them in profound contempt." The untouchables, or "scheduled castes" or "God's people" (Harijan) as Gandhi called them, are mainly of tribal or "aboriginal" stock. Outcast and despised, they remained creative and kept their craft traditions intact.

46. Elwin, *Tribal Art,* figs. 136, 138, 140, 141; the carvings by the Hill Saora of Ganjam, Orissa, representing Sahibosum.

47. James Tod, *Annals and Antiquities of Rajasthan,* ed. C. W. Crooke (London, 1908), vol. 1, p. 262.

48. A large group of figures from the temple at Darasuram, carved in stone and representing "The Wives of the Rishis" (now in the Tanjore Art Gallery) is an exception. *The Tanjore Art Gallery Guide Book* (Tanjore, 1957), p. xxvii.

49. S. C. Roy, *The Oraons of Chota Nagbur* (Ranchi, 1915), p. 185.

50. The masks, collected by V. Elwin and now in the collection of the National Museum, New Delhi, are all too few. They do not allow generalizations on behalf of their form with reference to the tribe that made them.

51. Sarkar, *Folk Element,* p. 110.

52. Cf. Balwant Gargi, *Folk Theater of India* (Washington, 1966), pp. 166–81.

53. Ananda K. Coomaraswamy, *History of Indian and Indonesian Art* (New York, 1966), p. 108, pl. 91, fig. 273. King Hemaprakasha was the donor of this mask from Nirmand.

54. From Buddhist monuments of the later part of the first millennium B.C. (with their golden plaques of the Earth-goddess) and possibly from the Vedic age with its effigy of the "golden man."

55. On the east gate of Sanchi (first century B.C. to first century A.D.). J. Marshall and A. Foucher, *The Monuments of Sanchi,* 3 vols. (London: Probsthain, 1940), vol. 2, pl. 49a. On the door jambs of the Daśavatāra Temple at Deogarh (early sixth century), Stella Kramrisch, *The Art of India* (London, 1965), pl. 48.

56. Grigson, *Maria Gonds,* p. 281; Elwin, *Tribal Art,* p. 71.

57. The horseman, however, as Spirit Rider, whose past extends from Hindu and Aryan to pre-Aryan times is not only the ancestral symbol of the Bhil, where it is cast in metal and carved in stone, but also of the Korku of Middle India (Elwin, *Tribal Art,* p. 90), whose wooden memorial posts show the figure of the ancestral Spirit Rider with the sun and moon, the ultimate ancestors, above.

58. Dakshinaranjan Shastri, "Cult and Images of Pitris," *JISOA* 7 (1939): 72–73.

Ancestral effigy and sacrifice post (to which in Vedic rites, the animal was fastened before being immolated) are amalgamated here. In Hindu thought, the bull is a symbol of righteousness and cosmic law, or dharma, (*VDhP* [Baroda, 1958] 3.48.18).

59. Cf. the hobbyhorse of the Durjat Shamans, in W. Koppers, "Pferdeopfer und Pferdekult der Indogermanen," *Wiener Beiträge zur Kulturgeschichte und Linguistik* 4(1936): 374. The hobbyhorse of the Muria and Maria Gond is the subject of an article by V. Elwin on "The Hobby Horse," *Illustrated Weekly of India* (Bombay, July 5, 1953). Cf. Sarkar, *Folk Element,* p. 111, and Stephen Fuchs, *The Gond and Bhumia of Eastern Mandla* (New York, 1959), p. 448.

60. Control of the senses is also enjoined for the Hindu craftsman. (*SRa*, 1. 2ff.)

61. C. von Fürer-Haimendorf, *Naked Nagas* (Calcutta, 1962), p. 52.

62. Verrier Elwin, *The Art of the North-East Frontier of India* (Shillong, 1959), p. 5.

63. Similar in shape to the mukh-dibba, the face-casket used in Bengal for serving pān.

64. When erecting a new building, the sacrifice of a human being strengthened the new building. This belief is widespread in India, too, and seems to underlie the myth of the Vāstupuruṣa.

65. This aristocrat (he was alive in 1962) was—or is—a blacksmith; his brothers are wood carvers. C. von Fürer-Haimendorf (*Naked Nagas,* p. 114) says that "the only things he was really serious about were his works of art."

66. A comparison with wooden Muria figures from Middle India of about the same degree of tribal form shows the "elegance" of this Naga style.

67. Elwin, *Tribal Art,* p. 173.

68. Cf. pictures painted on the walls of their houses by the Saora following the inspiration of a dream. Ibid, figs. 209–16, 222.

69. *SRa,* chap. 46. 143–45.

70. By Oraon, Munda, Kharia, and Birhor; cf. S. C. Roy, *Oraon Religion and Customs* (Ranchi, 1928), p. 285ff. The drawing on the ground of an enclosure (square or circular) and quartered is common to the Bhil, Baiga, etc., as it is with the Hindus; cf. Fuchs, *The Gond and Bhumia,* pp. 267, 452.

71. C. W. Crooke, *The Popular Religion and Folklore of Northern India,* vol. 2 (London, 1896), p. 191.

72. Tantric religion gives prominence to the female principle in divinity and to the union with it. Tantric ritual uses complex diagrams as symbolic and magical contrivances (yantra) in and by which deity is beheld in its cosmic manifestation and primordial unity.

73. Cf. G. Tucci, *The Theory and Practice of the Mandala* (London, 1961), pp. 49–84.

74. Abbot, *The Keys,* p. 14.

75. They are strictly geometrical in western and South India and are called maṇḍana in Rajasthan, rangoli in Maharashtra, sathiya in Gujarat, and kōlam (and muggu) in South India. They are richer in symbolic shapes in Bengal, Bihar, and elsewhere in northern India where they are known as alpona and aripana; apnā is their name in the western Himalaya, caukā pūrṇa and sonā rakhnā in Uttar Pradesh. The paglya of Rajasthan include footprints in their designs as do certain alpona.

Cf. W. T. Elmore, *Dravidian Gods in Modern Hinduism* (Lincoln: University of Nebraska Studies, 1915), p. 27, pl. 4; J. Layard, "Labyrinth Ritual in South India," *Folklore* 63–64 (1952–53):463–72.

76. T. M. Chatterji, *Alpona* (Calcutta, 1948), no. 32, p. 58. Also, S. K. Ray, *The Ritual Art of the Bratas of Bengal* (Calcutta, 1961), pp. 41–48.

77. C. G. Diehl, *Instrument and Purpose* (Lund, 1956), p. 252, re: the encircling of power; Abbot, *The Keys,* p. 83; re: the function of the ground.

78. *VDhP,* pt. 2, chap. 169. The text is of the sixth century but goes back to older sources. The "lotus flower" here is a symbol, a *rose des vents,* pointing into the eight directions. An actual lotus flower has petals in multiples of five.

79. Purāṇas are encyclopedias of traditional knowledge, dealing with everything from the creation of the cosmos onwards.

80. *BrP* 28.23–33; *BhvP* 48.52, 205. *Shamba P.* 29.2–6, saying that the sun was worshiped in a circle by his devotees "in early days," that is, prior to the anthropomorphic image of the sun-god. This is shown on coins dating from ca. 200 B.C. to the first century A.D. (J. N. Banerjea, *The Development of Hindu Iconography* [Calcutta, 1956], pp. 138–39, pls. 2, 8). Here the circular sun symbol is raised on an altar.

81. Haradatta commenting on Gautamasūtra 11.20 says that when the sun stands in Aries young girls paint the sun and his retinue on the soil with colored dust and worship this in the morning and in the evening. This is to illustrate the meaning of the Sūtra that enjoins that customs, though not expressly founded upon a passage of the Veda, are to be observed if they are not against the principles of the sacred writings. Max Müller, *History of Ancient Sanskrit Literature* (London, 1859), p. 53. That the sacred symbol was drawn on the ground was a non-Vedic practice.

All the same, the Vedic altars range in plan from circle and square to complex geometrical configurations such as the shape of a bird. The laying of the bricks in these patterns would presuppose their being drawn on the ground.

82. Stella Kramrisch, "Kanthā," *JISOA* 7 (Calcutta, 1939): 141–67; Kramrisch, "Kanthas of Bengal," *Marg* 3 (1949/50):18–29.

83. *RV* 6.9.3; 10.130.1, also *BṛUp* 3.8.3–8 and *MUp* 2.2.5.

84. M. Lalou, *Iconographie des étoffes peintes (pata) dans le Manjusrimulakalpa* (Paris, 1930), p. 27.

85. Crooke, *Popular Religion,* p. 161.

86. Sarkar, *Folk Element,* p. 33.

87. Cf. K. K. Ganguli, "Kantha, The Enchanted Wrap," *Indian Folklore* 1, no. 2:3–10.

88. Kanthās, however, made by women of the weaver caste, imitate the effect of weaving and are meant to be seen on one side only. G. S. Dutt, "The Art of Kantha," *Modern Review* (Calcutta, October 1939).

89. J. C. Mathur, "Domestic Arts of Mithila," *Marg* 20 (1966): 43–46.

90. W. G. Archer, "Maithil Painting," *Marg* 3 (1949): 24–33. Mildred Archer, "Notes on [Maithil] Paintings," *Marg* 20 (1966): 47.

91. Crooke, *Popular Religion*, p. 28.

92. Pran Nath Mago, "Murals and Mosaics from Villages Around Delhi," *Design* (New Delhi, August 1967), pp. 22–25. The peacock, bird of immortality, is painted on funerary urns of Harappa, cemetery II, of the second millennium B.C. In the rites of Sanjhi, the figures not only have their place on the wall, but also their specific time when they come to exist visually, in scale with the dimensions of the wall. If taken out of its ritual context, "the skilled work of those who practice folk art as a commercial craft" immediately degenerates into inane "decoration." Cf. *Design*, p. 30, showing a "village mural made by village women near Delhi for the Indian pavilion at Expo 67."

93. Ananda K. Coomaraswamy, "Picture Showmen," *IHQ* 5 (1929):182–84.

94. S. K. Ray, "The Artisan Castes of West Bengal and Their Craft," *Census of India* (West Bengal, 1951), pp. 293–349.

95. Stella Kramrisch, *The Hindu Temple*, p. 9, quoting *BVP* 1. 10.20–23f.

96. G. S. Dutt, "Tiger's God in Bengal Art," *Modern Review* 52 (1932):521–29; G. S. Dutt, "The Living Tradition of Folk Arts in Bengal," *Indian Art and Letters*, n.s. 10 (London, 1936): 34; G. S. Dutt, "The Indigenous Painters of Bengal," *JISOA* (1932), p. 21. Contrary to G. S. Dutt, "Tiger's God," W. G. Archer considers the "portraits" the work of chitrakaras and not of jadu-patuas (in a note to the writer).

97. S. K. Ray, "Artisan Castes of West Bengal," p. 311.

98. A. Ghose, "Old Bengal Paintings," *Rupam* (Calcutta, 1926), pp. 27–28, pls. 2 and 3, was unable at that time to assign these paintings to Hooghly or to Bankura. Cf. A. Mookerjee, *Folk Art of Bengal* (Calcutta, 1946), pl. 21.

99. D. P. Ghosh, "An Illustrated Ramayana Manuscript and Patas from Bengal," *JISOA*, 13 (Calcutta, 1945): 134ff.

100. Coomaraswamy, "Picture Showmen," note 92, referring to the Mudrārākṣasa of the seventh to eighth century.

101. Practically all the paintings come from West Bengal. However, the style of the Ghazi-pats in East Bengal is closely related to work of the jadu-patuas in the Santal Parganas of West Bengal and Bihar.

102. C. Dev, "An Outline of the Folk Art of Bengal," *Indian Folklore*, 2 (Calcutta, 1959): 203.

103. W. G. Archer, *Bazaar Paintings of Calcutta* (London, 1953). In W. G. Archer, *Kalighat Drawings* (Bombay, 1962), this term, however, is no longer used.

104. Binayak Mishra, "Folklore and Pauranic Tradition About the Origin of God Jagannātha," *IHQ* 13 (1937): 600–609. The shape of a log of wood—which is that of the image of Jagannatha worshiped in the temple at Puri, Orissa, on the east coast of India—serves also the tribal Muria and Maria Gond of central India as nucleus of their log symbol called peṇ (Grigson, *Maria Gonds*, p. 194), and it underlies the shape of the goddess Kālī as painted by the paṭuās of Kalighat, Bengal.

105. Tod, *Annals and Antiquities*, 1, 329; 2, 893.

106. Stella Kramrisch, *Drāviḍa and Kerala in the Art of Travancore* (Ascona: Artibus Asiae, 1963), pls. 33–37.

107. Most of the stone images of this phase, while fit for the purpose of worship, are outside the realm of art.

108. K. K. Ganguli, "Chamba Rumal," *JISOA* 11 (Calcutta, 1943): pl. facing p. 70.

109. Shown in the present exhibition are only a few varieties of textiles of rural character which are more closely connected with the celebration of rites.

110. Wooden puppets moved by strings were known at the time of the *Mahābhārata* (3.30. 21f) where the actions of men are compared to those of wooden puppets moved by strings, controlled by a power beyond them. Puppet plays, one of the oldest forms of the theater in India, have a large audience to this day in Rajasthan. Their themes, however, belong to a large extent to the life of the court. Cf. Ananda K. Coomaraswamy " 'Spiritual Paternity' and the 'Puppet Complex,' " *Psychiatry* 8, no. 3 (1945):287.

6 Emblems of the Universal Being

1. Enumerated in *Mahāpadāna Sutta, SBB* 3; *Lakkhaṇa Suttanta, SBB* 4; *Abhiniṣkramaṇa Sūtra, Romantic Legend of Sākya Buddha*, trans. by Samuel Beal (London: Trübner, 1875), p.

55; referred to in *Ambaṭṭha Suttanta, SBB* 2, p. 131; *Dhammapada, SBB* 7.352; *Milindapañha, SBB* 3.6.3; *Suttanipāta, SBB* 3.7; discussed by M. E. Burnouf, *Le Lotus de la bonne loi* (Paris: Imprimerie Nationale, 1852), App. 8, p. 357; Émile Sénart, *Essai sur la légende du Buddha* (Paris, 1875), pp. 106–91.

2. These "lesser marks" are of minor importance.

3. *BG, SBE* 8, p. 102 (chap. 13) "This body is called kṣetra."

Buddhistic and non-Buddhistic texts of all ages have been consulted. The Mahāpuruṣa Lakṣaṇas belong to brahmanical tradition, and later sources (and images) frequently make explicit a meaning implicit from the outset. This does not refer to later texts as, for instance, the *Bṛhat Saṁhitā* where the original meaning is but faintly present.

4. *RV* 5.44.6. The indissoluble nāma-rūpa relation of the image or "work of art" invalidates a purely formal treatment, as there is no rūpa without nāma, no substance without essence, and, conversely, a treatment of the meaning only may dispense with the form and be strong by the support derived from texts of which it may see sculpted and painted versions secondary in value to the written word. The tradition, however, is carried equally by the visible and by the audible, and none has priority within the realm of the other. In either of them, form is of the same age and always "the youngest" in view of the principle.

5. Images from Mankuwar, Amarāvatī, Romlok (Phnom Penh). Cf. Ananda K. Coomaraswamy, *HIIA*, figs. 162, 100; "Gold Image of Buddha from Hmawza (Burma)," *ASIAR*, pl. 41a, etc., p. 177; metal images of the tenth century from Jhewari, Chittagong, Bengal (Calcutta Museum, nos. 8148, 8150).

6. Coomaraswamy, *HIIA*, figs. 84, 158, etc.; Ananda K. Coomaraswamy, "The Buddha's Cūḍa, Hair, Uṣṇīṣa, and Crown," *JRAS* (1928), pp. 815–41.

7. Ibid. See infra, p. 157.

8. This occurs in India among the Kurkihar Bronzes, cf. K. P. Jayaswal, "Metal Images of Kurkihar Monastery," *JISOA* 2, no. 2 (1934), pl. 35, and those from Negapatam, *ASIAR* (1927–28), pl. 38, fig. 1, with flame only, fig. 3 with Uṣṇīṣa and flame; also on Pāla stone images, cf. Stella Kramrisch, "Pāla and Sena Sculpture," *Rupam*, no. 40 (1929), fig. 43.

9. "Uṣṇīṣa has been accepted by the Buddhists in a particular sense," Burnouf, *Le Lotus*, p. 560; see infra, p. 153.

10. *Histoire de la vie d'Hiouen-Thsang et ses voyages dans l'Inde*, vol. 2, trans. Stanislas Julien (Paris: Imprimeries Imperiale, 1853), p. 10.

11. Ibid., vol. 1, p. 108.

12. *Pratimālakṣaṇa*, ed. and trans. by J. N. Banerjea, *Journal of the Department of Letters, University of Calcutta* 23(1933):10.

13. *AV* 10.7.39.

14. Māyā being measured out is limited and so is the cosmos, the totality of manifestation.

15. *AitUp* 2.4.3.7.

16. *TUp* 1.6.1.

17. *KaṭhUp* 2.6:16; *MaUp* 6.21.

18. *Satcakra Nirūpaṇa*, 44.

19. *MaUp* 6.30.

20. Karli, cf. Coomaraswamy, *HIIA*, pl. 5, fig. 8.

21. Kramrisch, "Pāla and Sena," fig. 17.

22. Bardo Thödol (W. Y. Evans-Wentz, *The Tibetan Book of the Dead* [Oxford, 1927], p. 89).

23. *BṛUp* 1.3.9. "It" has been employed instead of "he" on account of the alternative use in this essay of prāṇa and breath.

24. *Anugītā, SBE* 8:258.

25. *BṛUp* 1.3.19.

26. *TUp* 2.2. "Different from this which consists of the essence of food is the other, the inner self which consists of breath. The former is filled by this. It also has the shape of man. Like the human shape of the former, is the human shape of the latter." The image is identical in the worded and in the sculpted or painted version.

27. Anuvyañjana, Burnouf, *Le Lotus*, p. 616.

28. Julien, *Hiouen-Thsang*, vol. 1, p. 359.

29. Thomas Watters, *On Yuan Chwang's Travels in India* (London: Royal Asiatic Society, 1904–5), p. 197.

30. Cf. Sénart, *Légende du Buddha*, p. 111.

31. *Saddharmapuṇḍarīka, SBE* 21, p. 427.

32. *Satcakra Nirūpaṇa*, 45; cf. *BG, SBE* 8:79.

33. It may be mentioned that Savitṛ is called Hiraṇyastūpa, *RV* 10.149.5.
34. *AitUp* 2.4.3.7; *TUp* 1.6.2.
35. Arthur Avalon (Sir John Woodroffe), *Principles of Tantra*, 2 vols. (Madras, 1914–16).
36. *AV* 11.4.15.
37. Cf. *BṛUp* 3.7.2; 9.9; 9.26.
38. *BṛS* 67.5.76; cf. J. N. Banerjea's lucid account of Uṣṇīṣa-śiraskatā, etc., *IHQ* 7:499.
39. Sumangalavilāśinī, *IHQ* (1918), p 77.
40. Burnouf, *Le Lotus*, p. 562, samavipulalāṭaḥ.
41. Amalā Ṭippaṇī, in Avalon, *Principles of Tantra*, p. 179.
42. Satcakra Nirūpaṇa, 42.

43. Mention has already been made (Stella Kramrisch, "Marks of the Great Being: Mahāpuruṣa Lakṣaṇa," *The Golden Book of Tagore* [Calcutta, 1931], p. 288) that the images of all the deities in India are high above the forehead. Crowns are commonly employed, also for the Sambhoghakāya image of Buḍdha (cf. Mus, "Le Buddha Paré," *BEFEO* 28:153), or the hair is piled up high (Jaṭāmukuṭa of Śiva and Avalokiteśvara), and Jaina images have the broad and high skull frequently tapering into a point. Ananda K. Coomaraswamy, "The Buddha's Cūḍa," p. 828, quotes from the Aupapātika Sūtra. There the appearance of Mahāvīra is described with a projection on the top of his head. The head as seat of the higher possibilities of being is enlarged as if to hold them. From the point of view of presentation by the craftsman the means employed, i.e., increased height, is the same that he gives in reliefs, etc., to figures of outstanding importance.
44. Kramrisch, "Marks," and Waddell, "Buddha's Diadem or Uṣṇīṣa," *Ostasiatische Zeitschrift* (1914), p. 155.
45. Julien, *Hiouen-Thsang*, vol. 1, p. 359.
46. Ghulam Yazdani, *Ajaṇṭā*, 4 vols. (London: Oxford University Press, 1930), vol. 1, pl. 28. The trellis pattern does not show clearly in the plate due to the great reduction from the original.
47. I.e., ūrṇā, see infra, p. 156.
48. Amitāyur Dhyāna-sūtra, *SBE* 49:166.
49. Bodhicaryāvatāra, p. 419.
50. The "upper" and "lower" Meru stand in the relation of dharmakāya and nirmāṇakāya. The returned ray of the Amitāyur Dhyāna-sūtra encompasses the universe on its way from the ūrṇā to the uṣṇīṣa. Beginning and end of this manifestation are synchronous in the dharma substance.
51. Cf. *Praśna Up.* 3.7; 3.9.
52. *AV* 10.7.
53. Cf. *BṛUp* 2.2.1.
54. *MaUp* 6.21.
55. *JB* (Oertel *JAOS*) 1.29.1. (The ray) consisting of breath stands firm aloft.
56. Cf. *BṛUp* 3.9.26.
57. Ibid., 3.7.2.
58. *MaUp* 6.30.
59. Ibid., 6.33.
60. Ibid., 2.6 "This heat is the Puruṣa and this Puruṣa is Agni Vaiśvānara."
61. Ananda K. Coomaraswamy, *A New Approach to the Vedas* (London, 1933), p. 11. Re Buddha, Agni Vaiśvānara, the fiery pillar, the tree of life, see Ananda K. Coomaraswamy, *Elements of Buddhist Iconography* (Cambridge, Mass.: Harvard University Press, 1935), p. 101.
62. Arthur Avalon (Sir John Woodroffe), *Serpent Power* (Madras, 1931), p. 251.
63. Cf. *BṛUp* 1.3.9; *Avataṁsaka Sūtra* (Samuel Beal, *Catena of Buddhist Scriptures* [London, 1872], p. 41). "On certain signs at the time of death: if from the summit of the head . . . the flame departs. . . . (a Buddha)."
64. Cf. *BṛUp* 4.4.2. "He has become one, they say. The point of his heart becomes lighted up and by that light the self departs . . . through the skull."
65. Uṣṇīṣa, "heat gleaning"; Vārttika on Panini, 6.1.94, has uṣṇam īṣate hinasti, obviously in order to explain the current sense of "anything wound round the head" to protect from heat. Another meaning of is is to glean.
66. The deep samādhi called uṣṇīṣa vidarśana (the highest stage of the vidarśana process of meditation), Waddell, "Dhāraṇī," *IA* (1914), p. 49; cf. also Mahāvyutpatti 244, 82 mentioned in ibid.
67. *ASIAR*, 1904–5, p. 79. The Uṣṇīṣa is missing. A cavity is cut in its place (into which an uṣṇīṣa of precious material must have been inserted).

68. Re maṇi (jewel) of the uṣṇīṣa, cf. Beal, *Romantic Legend of Śākya Buddha*, pp. 289, 413.
69. Julien, *Hiouen-Thsang,* vol. 2, p. 145.
70. Cf. *AitUp* 2.2.11, "for he who shines (the sun) is the breath."
71. References could be quoted in an indefinite number.
72. *BG* 8.10.
73. Cf. Sénart, *Légende du Buddha,* p. 155.
74. I.e., of the world of the senses and of the intellect.
75. Ananda K. Coomaraswamy, "Angel and Titan," *JAOS* 55(1935):396ff.
76. The Gandhāran disguise, the chignon that conforms with anthropomorphic standards, is of no consequence.
77. *The Ṛg Veda as Land-Nāma-Bók* (London: Luzac, 1935), p. 31.
78. Julien, *Hiouen-Thsang,* vol. 1, p. 53.
79. *Bodhisattvabhūmi;* cf. Louis de La Vallée Poussin, *Bouddhisme, Études et Matériaux* (Brussels, 1897), p. 279.
80. Krishna, for instance, is called Keśava in the *Bhagavadgītā;* the (terrestrial) Agni is hairy (keśī) with flames, the middle one with lightnings, while that (celestial) one is hairy with rays. *Bṛhad Devatā,* 94; also Keśara, Caesar, cf. Festus, p. 44, "qui scilicet cum caesarie natus est"; etc.
81. Cf. for instance *Lalitavistara,* 7, second lakṣaṇa.
82. Cf. *AitUp,* 1.4.11.
83. *Lalitavistara,* lakṣaṇa 20.
84. *AitUp* 2.1.4.10.
85. Cf. *CnUp* 3.12.3.
86. Anugītā, p. 258.
87. *SBB* 3:15; 4:138.
88. Ibid., vol. 4; cf. Mahāvyutpatti list no. 16 (citāntarāṁsa).
89. Ibid., vol. 3, p. 131.
90. *ŚUp* 3.8; cf. Ṛgveda passim.
91. *MaUp* 7.11; "(The ray) consisting of breath stands firm aloft." *JB* 1.29.1.

This has been repeatedly shown by Coomaraswamy, cf. *A New Approach to the Vedas,* p. 30; *The Ṛg Veda,* p. 8; *Elements,* pp. 7–10, etc.

Mus, *Barabuḍur, BEFEO* 32(1935):385, has well summed up the interchangeability of the images of the cosmic axis under the four main forms of mountain, pillar, tree, and giant (puruṣa) and their reference to the principle of air (=breath).

92. According to Gegan Lungtok Puntsok, trans. Van Manen, *JISOA* 1(1933):107.
93. Mus, *Barabuḍur,* based on the Dharma pradīpikā, f. 2b and 3a deals exhaustively with the first lakṣaṇa of the Pāli lists that figures last in the *Lalitavistara,* i.e., that of the well-placed feet with level tread (supratiṣṭhitasamapādaḥ).
94. Cf. *ChUp* 3.12.3. That earth again is the body in man, for in it the prāṇas rest.
95. The Pāli lists do not allude to the "swelled" feet as a Mahāpuruṣa-lakṣaṇa. Number 25 of the *Lalitavistara* may refer to this mark. Some of the lakṣaṇas, as for instance "forty teeth" (the inhabitants of Śvetadvīpa have sixty, *MBh*), are not within the scope of the craftsman. Those that are within this range he not only visualized, but in order to show them convincingly, the "image" that in their totality they imply, must have been the object of his contemplation. He does not show single marks, here and there, but the substance itself of the Buddha or Mahāpuruṣa that makes the body of the image. That it is a transfigured body, beyond the appearance of any figure, need not be repeated. Altogether it is emblematic, and the Uṣṇīṣa, its "supreme" mark, is nothing but an emblem. The Buddha's substance comprehends the cosmos. The lakṣaṇas, etc., are not physiognomic features but cosmognomic emblems.
96. *AitUp* 2.1.4.1.
97. Banerjea, *Pratimālakṣaṇam,* p. 19; *Citralakṣaṇa,* ed. and trans. Berthold Laufer (Leipzig: Otto Harrassowitz, 1913), pp. 161, 176.
98. 68.2.
99. The robe of the monk is the only allusion to his earthly career. No image of the Buddha shows him as a monk.
100. *TUp* 2.2.5. "Different from this which consists of the essence of food, is the other, the inner self which consists of breath. The former is filled by this. It also has the shape of the latter."

"Inverse" is meant in the sense of the valuing which in the case of the image does not proceed centripetally from the grosser to the subtler aspect.

101. J. N. Banerjea, "The 'Webbed Fingers' of Buddha," *IHQ* (1930), pp. 717–27; *IHQ* (1931): 654–56; Coomaraswamy (1931), 365–66; Stutterheim, "Le Jālalakṣaṇa," *AO* 7:232, have more recently expressed their views on this lakṣaṇa. Foucher's views, incorporated as they are in J. N. Banerjea's papers, need not be taken into account here. These partly anthropomorphic and partly technical, i.e., "simple craftsman's device," interpretations leave untouched the traditional meaning of the lakṣaṇa.

102. Cf. Beal, *Romantic Legend of Śākya Buddha*, p. 55. The fingers and toes severally connected with a fine, net-like membrane.

103. Cf. Chinese translation of Madhyamāgama text noted by Banerjea, "The 'Webbed Fingers,'" p. 655.

104. Agni is also called the thread, *RV* 10.5.3; 10.57.2 (Agni) the thread, drawn out for the gods.

105. *RV* 6.9.3.

106. *RV* 10.130.1.

107. *BṛUp* 3.8.4.

108. *AV* 10.2.13.

109. *BṛUp* 3.7.2.

110. *AV* 10.8.37.

111. *MaUp* 6.28, 38. The fabric symbolism is also valid in the three guṇas (strands) of Prakṛti.

112. *AV* 2.1.5.

113. Cf. *SBB* 3, p. 214.

114. Bachhofer, *Early Indian Sculpture*, pls. 25–27; Coomaraswamy, *HIIA*, fig. 47 and elsewhere. The coping stone of the railing is called Uṣṇīṣa.

115. Coomaraswamy, *HIIA*, fig. 31.

116. Beal, *Catena*, p. 57, note 2.

117. *Lalitavistara* (Bibl. Ind.) 4.

118. Cf. Mus, *Barabuḍur*, passim.

119. *Lalitavistara*, ed. and trans. R. Mitra (Calcutta: Asiatic Society of Bengal, Text 1877; trans. 1881–86), 5.

120. Ibid., 7.

121. Ibid. (trans. R. Mitra), p. 159.

122. The latter is not indicated in sculpture, nor are all the images of Buddha invested with this lakṣaṇa. The same can, however, be said about the ūrṇā.

123. *Saddharmapuṇḍarika*, *SBE* 21, p. 321.

124. *AV* 12.3.38; *RV* 4.40.5; Citralakṣaṇa, p. 161, says that the web of the feet of the Cakravartin resembles that of the mallard.

125. *AV* 10.2.29.

126. Cf. *Mahāpadāna S.*, 1. c. p. 15 and other lists.

127. This does not convey any special length of the arms. It is the average proportion of the human body. Another lakṣaṇa says: Standing and without bending he can touch and rub his knees with either hand. Not every lakṣaṇa can or need be rendered by word and also by figure. (These two lakṣaṇas, i.e., proportions, cannot possibly be employed in one and the same image.)

128. *AV* 10.35; *RV* 10.90.1.

129. *AV* 10.2.28.

130. *AV* 10.8.19.

131. Detailed measures are given, for instance, in *Pratimālakṣaṇam*, p. 13.

132. *AitUp* 2.4.1.6.

133. Ibid. 2.4.2.4. Cf. Anugitā, p. 350, "all the quarters residing in the ear."

134. Julien, *Hiouen Thsang*, vol. 2, p. 59.

135. This is symbolized, moreover, by the lakṣaṇa of the long tongue (Lakkhaṇa Suttanta No. 27). In the legend of Pūrṇa (Sela Sutta), Buddha shows the miracle of his tongue that touches his ear (cf. also Ambaṭṭha Sutta, *SBB* 2, p. 131). In the *Saddharmapuṇḍarīka*, 20 (Burnouf, *Le Lotus*, p. 234) the tongues of the Buddhas Sākyamuni and Prabhūtaratna reach to the world of Brahmā. All this means, as the small Sukhāvatīvyūha (*SBE* 49, 2, p. 49) says: "the Tathāgatas cover with their tongues the worlds where they teach." This makes it clear why it is said that the tongue reaches to the ear. The ear holds all the worlds where the Tathāgatas teach. The Buddha-word and his substance are one. Cf. *JB* 3.18. "In me the worlds, in me the four quarters." Sénart, *Légende du Buddha*, p. 125, has dealt with the long tongue of Agni.

136. *JB* 3.35.1.

7 *The Image of Mahādeva in the Cave-Temple on Elephanta Island*

1. Īśāna is the first "form" in the hierarchy of manifestation of the Supreme Śiva; Tatpuruṣa is next and is followed by Aghora, Vāmadeva, and Sadyojāta; they are thus also likened to the elements of which the universe consists, the first being ether, invisible and everywhere; the others are air, fire, water, and earth (*VDhP* 3.48.1–3).

2. The pañca-mukha-liṅga from the Śiva temple at Nachna-kuthara is the most perfect of its kind. It was carved in the later Gupta Age.

3. *Rūpamaṇḍana* 4.94. T. A. Gopinatha Rao, *Elements of Hindu Iconography*, vol. 2 (Madras, 1914), p. 97. A chaturmukha, etc., liṅga may, however, also be placed in a shrine with one door only.

4. The five mantras are given in the *TĀ* 10.43–47.

5. *ĪPad* 3.5.1.

6. Cf. G. Rao, *Elements*, p. 366.

7. *Suprabhedāgama;* G. Rao, *Elements.*

8. *VDhP* 3.48.20.

9. *ĪPad* 3.12.35; *Rūpamaṇḍana* 4.12–13. The dhyānaślokas in the various texts are not identical in detail. There are as many, if not necessarily the same, variations there as in the images. The vision held by signs and words is the same: different ages and different schools see it under particular modifications. The *VDhP* 3.48.9, assigns to the face in front (Mahādeva) the rosary and the water vessel (kamaṇḍalu) instead of the citron (mātuluṅga or bījapūraka).

10. *VDhP* 3.48.12.

11. *VDhP* 3.46. For its resorption by Time (Kāla), *Vāchaspatya*, s.v.

12. *VDhP* 3.48.17.

13. *ĪPad* 3.12.36–37; *Rūpamaṇḍana* 4.5–12.

14. *ĪPad* 3.12.38, strīvilāsa.

15. *VDhP* 3.48.4–6.

16. He is the immanent and primordial cause of the universe and its primordial substance (Prakṛti). The *VDhP* 3.48.19, says that Maheśvara is white, as white as Prakṛti. The image of Maheśvara (Mahādeva) must originally have been painted white.

8 *An Image of Aditi-Uttānapad*

1. I.e., in the former state of Hyderabad. The image is labeled as Nagna Kabandha, or "naked, headless body," which shows complete ignorance of the meaning of the sculpture.

2. The stone slab is at present installed on a cement base. The rim is damaged on the right proper of the image. There was, it seems, another outlet for the water.

3. Actual decoration of the breasts with flower or leaf pattern (patralekhā; see Amarakośa) was used as an erotic and symbolic device (cf. *Kādambarī*, ed. M. R. Kale [Bombay, 1928], p. 98).

4. See Stella Kramrisch, *The Art of India* (London: Phaidon, 1954), pls. 73–75, 77.

5. See Heinrich Zimmer, *The Art of Indian Asia* (New York, 1955), pls. 234, 243.

6. See Kramrisch, *Art of India*, pl. 37, and Rambach and de Golish, *The Golden Age of Indian Art: 5th–13th Centuries* (London, 1955), pls. 24–26. The image was lying uncared for, the left arm broken, on a corner of the enclosed grounds of the temples in Mahakuteswar.

7. One is from Bhita, the other from Kosam. A large lotus, which may be compared with the lotus flower of pl. 8-3, covers the shoulders and part of the chest of the figure on the Bhita plaque; the upper row of petals is above the shoulders, where the neck would be; the womb is lotus-girt. See *ASIAR*, 1927–28, pl. 23, fig. 40, p. 75. For the similar figure from Kosam, see ibid., p. 67.

8. The small shape between the large lotus buds of pls. 8-1–8-3 could neither be identified on the image nor in its photographs.

9. Sir John Marshall, *Mohenjo-daro and the Indus Civilisation*, vol. 3 (London: A. Probsthain, 1931), pls. 87, 3 and 90, 25. One side of a scaling from Harappa (I, pl. 12, 12, pp. 52, 70) shows an inverted female figure with knees wide apart, hands resting on knees, and a tree-like plant issuing upside down from the womb.

10. Ananda K. Coomaraswamy, "Early Indian Iconography, II," *Eastern Art*, 1, no. 3(1929):178, distinguishes accordingly three varieties of the image of Lakṣmī: (1) with lotus in

hand, padma-hastā; (2) padmāsana, or padmapīṭha, the lotus seat or lotus on which Śrī Lakṣmī rests; and (3) Lakṣmī as the dweller in the lotus, "padmavāsinī, kamalālayā."

11. Another instance of the connection of serpent and lotus, in the iconography of Śrī Lakṣmī in particular, are the Nāgas amid lotuses in the lower part of the rock-cut panel of Śrī Lakṣmī in the Rāvana-ka-khai cave, Ellora, Ananda K. Coomaraswamy, *Yakṣas,* pt. 2 (Washington, D.C.: Smithsonian Institution, 1931), pl. 24.

12. *BDP* 48. Siva cut off the head of Dakṣa, for the offense he had committed of excluding Śiva from the sacrifice. Siva then says, "Fix the head of an animal on Dakṣa. It will be sinless and replace his sinful face." Dakṣa was given the head of a ram or goat.

13. From the days of the Indus Valley civilization, in the third millennium B.C. where the lotus as a conventionalized, geometric pattern is painted on the underside of the bowl of an offering stand, the lotus flower is a perennial symbol of Indian art.

The circular lotus pattern painted at Mohenjo daro is similar in its mature stylization to the carved versions of the lotus petals on Mauryan pillars (Marshall, *Mohenjo-daro,* pl. 87, 3), whereas the abbreviated version (ibid., pl. 110, 25) is more closely connected with carvings of Stūpa 2, Sanchi, and in Bharhut, with paintings on the vault of Cave 9, Ajanta, and with carvings on fountain stones of Chamba.

Ibid., vol. 2, pp. 321, 329, considers the design on the underside of these two pans as quite unusual. "It may have been derived from a flower or from fluted metal work." But no fluted metal work has been found in Mohenjo daro; the designs, moreover, do not resemble the fluted metal work found in Kish, Cemetery A, to which Sir John Marshall refers (see E. J. H. Mackay, *Report on the Excavation of the "A" Cemetery at Kish* [Chicago: Field Museum of Natural History, 1925], pl. 57, 13).

14. Gandha, scent is known to be the subtle essence of the element earth, as rasa, flavor, is that of water.

15. *ŚS,* 5.117.

16. *Manu* 1.21.

17. Pṛthivī is derived from pṛthu, which means "broad."

18. Re the Lotus-halo, see Heinrich Zimmer, *The Art of Indian Asia: Its Mythology and Transformations,* ed. Joseph Campbell (New York, 1955), cf. p. 242, fn. 5, pls. 100, 101, 108b. The lotus above the images is carved also at the more-or-less pointed top of the back slab of the stele where, however, the "Kīrttimukha" or Face of Glory frequently takes its place. The same vicarious occupancy of a significant position on the monument by the lotus (of earlier occurrence) and the Kīrttimukha that takes its place gives special emphasis to the Śikhara of Hindu temples above the point where the roof of the porch terminates. The skyline of the subsidiary buildings must not exceed in height this particular point.

Analogously, too, lotus and Kīrttimukha are the main frontal or top ornaments of the crown of divinities. Their significance at these places is elaborated in the various schools of sculpture.

The lotus that stands for divinity and is that divinity as made by art belongs also to Egypt. There it represents the god Nefertem; or else the lotus is shown above the head of the god who arose from the primal water (Nun), who arose from Earth, cf. S. Morenz, *Der Gott auf der Blume* (Ascona, 1954), pp. 16–21, pl. 1.

19. Srīsūkta 25, in Pañcāmṛtādhyabhiṣeka Sūkta: Isidor Scheftelowitz, *Die Apokryphen des Ṛg Veda* (Khilani, 1906), p. 79.

20. *VDhP* 3.82.1–16.

21. The image of the Goddess Mother Śrī, Sirimā Devatā, in Bharhut comes nearest to the shape of a "Mother Goddess." See Ludwig Bachhofer, *Early Indian Sculpture,* 2 vols. (New York, 1929), pl. 21.

22. Śrīsūkta, 17a; Scheftelowitz, *Die Apokryphen,* p. 77.

23. *ŚB* 7.4.1.8.

24. *AV* 12.1.8–12.

25. *VS* 12.18.

26. *VS* 13.17.

27. *AV* 12.1.61, 63. Also *RV* 10.11.12; Dr. W. Norman Brown referred to Uttānapad, *RV* 10.72 as soon as he saw the photograph of the image at Alampur.

28. *RV* 6.51.5, "pṛthivi mātar adhrug," "deceitless Mother Earth."

29. *RV* 7.88.7.

30. *RV* 9.26.1; 9.71.5; 9.74.5; i.e., Soma, the elixir of life (as offered on the sacrificial altar).

31. *Yajurveda* 1.11.

32. Ibid., 1.8.

33. *RV* 10.64.13.

34. *Yajurveda* 14.5.

35. *RV* 2.40.6. "Aditi, the Boundless" (anarvā).

36. *RV* 1.94.15. Being at one within herself, the boundless, impartite is guiltless (anāgā) and makes guiltless (*RV* 4.39.3; 1.162.22). The fetters of guilt and sin fall in her boundlessness.

37. In a later text, at a phase when Brahmā had taken the place of the creator-god, it is from his intellect that Dakṣa is known to have sprung (*VP* 1.7.7). The birth from the seat of the intellect, from the head, like that of Pallas Athena from the head of Zeus, is equal in meaning to a tradition according to which Śrī Lakṣmī was born on a lotus that had sprung from the forehead of Vishnu (*MBh* 12.59.2253–54). Brahmā borne on a lotus, sprung from the navel of Vishnu.

38. The animal head of the gods similarly represents the state without guilt, of divinity, see note 12.

39. The "double head" is also interpreted as "facing both ways, as speech does, for good and evil, now going to the gods, now to the Gandharvas" (cf. *AB* 1.29).

This concept, however, is not "in Aditi" but belongs to a subsequent stage of articulate speech having left the body of Aditi, the impartite, the sinless. The double head as lotus flower faces both ways, upward toward the macrocosm, and down toward the embodied creation (microcosm).

40. And also daughter, reborn in the intellectual act, of Dakṣa, the creator spiritus.

9 Pūṣan

1. S. D. Atkins, *Pūsan in the Rig Veda* (Princeton, 1941), p. 98ff., Index of epithets applied to Pūṣan.

2. Or poṣa (2.40.4), although these words are not necessarily derived from the same root. See A. Bergaigne, *La Réligion Védique,* Bibliothèque de l'Ecole des Hautes Etudes, vol. 53 (1883), p. 425, note 2. Synonyms for nourishment (puṣṭi) are also associated with Pūṣan, such as vāja, which means refreshment or also well being (6.54.5; 6.57.1; 6.58.2; 8.4.18; 10.26.9), or bhoja, which again means nourishment (6.48.14), or iḍa, which is liquid, sustaining food offered to the gods and whose Lord is Pūṣan (iḍas pati; 6.58.4). Another root from which the word Pūṣan could be derived is pū, referring to flame and fire, and meaning "to purify," to make bright, to enlighten. Pū in the sense of flame and fire agrees with Pūṣan's exclusive attribute āghṛṇi, the glowing.

3. The translations given in the present context differ to some extent from those by Atkins, *Pūṣan,* K. F. Geldner, *Der Rig Veda* (Cambridge: Harvard University Press, 1951), and others, to whom they are indebted.

4. Bergaigne, *Réligion Védique,* p. 420. This is the traditional Indian view. A resumé of the various interpretations is given by Atkins, *Pūṣan,* pp. 2–8.

5. The obvious association of solar and pastoral traits of Pūṣan with his function as God of Paths has been seen by H. Oldenberg, *Die Religion des Veda* (Stuttgart: Cotta, 1917), p. 235.

6. Bergaigne, *Réligion Védique,* pp. 420–26; N. Flensburg, "Bidrag till Rigvedas Mytologi Om Goden Pūṣan i Rig Veda," *Lunds Universitats Arsskrift,* N. F. Afg. i V, no. 4 (1909):1–49 (translated in part by Atkins, *Pūṣan*).

7. Horses draw the chariot of Sūrya. Horses draw the chariot of Phoibos Apollo. The horse as symbol of the sun in manifestation figures in 7.77.3.

8. Manas has the meaning of "mind-soul" or noûs, or "intellectus vel spiritus." In later, Sāṁkhya terminology, however, manas is mind and is subordinated to buddhi, intellect (intuitive intellection). Brahman is the power of giving form to the inner vision (dhī) or intuition as shown by P. Thieme, *ZDMG* 15(1952):91–129. The usual translation of dhī as "prayer" does not convey the meaning of the word, although its mood is that of "Andacht." The level of this mood is that of wisdom. Dhī means "inner vision in its sacred wisdom."

9. From a hymn by Isaac Watts (1719). The words designating Pūṣan's path are: adhvan, 1.42.1; pathi, 1.42.2, 6.49.8, 6.53.1, 4, 8.29.6, 10.17.6, 10.59.7 (pathyā); sruti, 1.42.3 and yama, the latter is said of Savitṛ, who by his movements becomes Pūṣan (5.81.5).

10. Āghṛṇi, "glowing," is the most frequently employed attribute of Pūṣan and belongs to him exclusively (cf. E. Siecke, "Pūshan," *Mythologische Bibliothek,* vol. 7 [Leipzig, 1914–15], p. 10), whereas tejas (heat, ardor) takes its place in *BṛUp* 5.15.2.

11. This passage refers to Pūṣan, according to H. Oldenberg, *Ṛg Veda. Textkritische und exegetische Noten* (Berlin, 1909–12), 7–10, p. 352; and not to Sūrya or Savitṛ as held by other scholars.

12. "As soon as born" a god fulfills the mission for which he is born. Indra, as soon as born, drinks for the first time the Soma (3.48.2); as soon as born, he "masters the Seven who

found no master" (8.96.16). Lord Buddha, too, as soon as born, took the seven steps. The two symbolic journeys, the way of the gods (devayāna) and the way of the fathers (pitryāna), are described in *BṛUp* 6.2.15–16; *ChUp* 5.10.3–7; *BG* 8.23–26. The names devayāna and pitryāna are established in the *Ṛg Veda.* The concept of the way of the gods is well established (see Grassmann, *s.v.*). The way of the Fathers, the ancestral spirits, is mentioned once only (10.2.7) explicitly, whereas it is referred to as the other way, different from that of the gods, the path of Death (mṛtyu; 10.18.1). Agni is invoked on the path of the fathers (10.2.7), but the way of the gods is particularly that of agni, the sacrificial fire, 10.51.2; 1.72.7; 5.43.6; 10.51.5; 10.99.11. Agni, the fire, burns on earth in the flame, and it burns in heaven in the sun. Agni as sacrificial fire is the messenger between heaven and earth. Agni, the fire that burns in the sun, and Pūṣan, the glowing one, are continguous conceptions. It is Pūṣan's goat that climbs up and goes ahead on the way of the gods (1.162.4).

13. *RV* 10.26.5 invokes Pūṣan as Ṛṣi, friendly to men and a protecting friend of the inspired singer-priest (vipra, "vibrant"); Ṛṣi, generally translated as sage or seer, conveys the fleetness, the immediacy of a pouring and shining forth alike to the light of the luminaries. *BṛUp* 6.15.2 invokes Pūṣan as "sole Ṛṣi," the only light. *AV* 6.112.3 Pūṣan delivers from sin.

14. Brahman is here rendered as creative operation (see note 8) as against J. Charpentier, *Brahman I and II* (Upsala, 1932). L. Renou, "Sur la notion de brahman," *Journal Asiatique* (1949), p. 71; Jan Gonda, *Notes on Brahman* (Utrecht, 1950).

15. Below the pit of danger and treasure lies the lap of nirṛti (7.104.9), the lap of destruction with its endless pit (7.104.17) below all creation (7.104.6). This deep dark place is the asat, the nonexistent, "The Ṛg Vedic Equivalent for Hell," as shown by W. Norman Brown, *JAOS* 61(1941):76–80. This deep substratum of the ordered cosmos, of the existent (sat), the abyss that yawns at the bottom of the pit, in the lap of destruction (nirṛti) is the necessary opposite in the first pair of contraries. There they are from the beginning of things prior to which neither of them existed.

The asat, the nonexistent below the pit, is the remainder "apud principium" of the all-engulfing darkness, ante principium. The cosmic darkness ante principium is distinguished from the darkness of the "night of the cycle."

The hymns of the *Ṛg Veda* do not dwell to any length on the tedium of nonexistence. Its hells become staggered in later layers of Indian thought. In the *Ṛg Veda* it is those who are accursed because their actions had gone contrary to cosmic order (ṛta) who fall below all creation and never see the sun shine. They are outside Pūṣan's realm; they are neither fiends nor sinners but nonexistent nonentities.

And yet, this outcasting of hell provided a safety valve at the base for the protection of an ordered cosmos full of meaning. For the nonexistent is the place where dwell the root-gods (mūradevā) and/or their worshipers (7.104.14). They are roots without trunk or "neck" (7.104.24), their stem is cut, they are dead. It is to such roots that the fathers slip, the ancestral spirits (*SB* 13.8.1.20). In this domain of the outlaws from ṛta, cosmic order, is the place of the sorcerers. Their dubious remedies have their origin there. In a hymn of the *Atharvaveda* (6.44.3), medicinal poison, a plant (viṣāṇakā) having sprung from "the fathers' root," is invoked to effect a cure. Whether "in a likeness" or literally, the fathers' root produced a shoot from the world of the dead, the cosmic outlaws, for the benefit of the sick. The line that separates the chasm of nonexistence and the ordered cosmos is not sharply drawn. Eternal damnation—as a possibility—must underlie at its lowest point the path of Pūṣan, the liberator.

16. In this aspect, before he goes farther on his path, Pūṣan shines forth as aja ekapād, the uncreate one-foot. Aja ekapād is an image of the vertical axis of Pūṣan's cyclical path. Aja ekapād connects Pūṣan's two poles of being. Aja means uncreate but it also means goat. The goat is the animal symbol of Pūṣan. Aja ekapād is the axis of the cosmos, preestablished as the upholder of its movement. Aja ekapād is the central pole from the birth on high to the birth in the pit.

17. The myth tells of the flight of Agni, the sacrificial fire, and how he absconded from his office, the sacrifice. Having taken flight, he was found by Yama, the first mortal (10.51) and himself an aspect of Agni (1.66.8; 1.164.46). This hide-and-seek of the primal powers, in and out of manifestation, in their return to the source where they find themselves as one another, is staged in different places, at the height or at the depth. Pūṣan's hiding place lies on its path at its lowermost station.

18. Agni is Pūṣan, whereas Savitṛ becomes Pūṣan (p. 105).

19. Barhis is the sacrificial grass that is spread on the place of sacrifice, the Vedi. The "shining" sacrificial grass is that of the celestial soma, the effulgence on which he rests (or the stars) (cf. Johannes Hertel, *Arische Light- und Feuerlehre,* Indo-Iranische Quellen und Forschungen, Heft 6 [Leipzig, 1925], p. 15).

20. Soma (1.23.13) is evoked as "the support of heaven," that is, as coincident with the pillar of life and with Pūṣan, the liberator and aja ekapād. For Soma as the support of heaven, see 6.47.4–5; 9.74.2; 9.76.1; 9.86.35; 9.86.46, and for Soma, the king, 1.23.14; 1.91.43.

21. 6.44.23; 9.86.15; 9.110.8.

22. The nakṣatras are the stations of the moon in other Vedic texts.

23. In later Vedic texts, as also in the marriage hymn (10.85.2), Soma is evoked as moon. The light of this luminary, however, is in its origin, the one light of the heavenly luminous spheres, above the firmament.

24. Images of kine, horses, wealth, riches, and substance (vasu, rāi) are symbolic synonyms (cf. pecunia-pecus) of the treasure that Pūṣan finds and disperses. His "substance" is illumination. He gives to each one according to his light. Should it be dim, showing only the tangible shape of things, the treasures are taken for factual possessions of cattle and the like.

25. "Pūṣeva dhījavano 'si soma." Dhī has the meaning of light in the sense of "leuchten" and "Erleuchtung." Dhīvat and all other terms derived from or combined with dhī are generally translated as "pious, devout, prayer or worship." Dhī, however, means seeing and thinking in the sense of inner vision, intuition, and wisdom. All these are carried by "devotion" in the sense of "Andacht," which is an intellectual, rather than an emotional, mode.

26. The six yoked together have been taken by Sāyaṇa to refer to the six seasons of the year, each of two months' duration (cf. *MBh* 1.3.141–43).

27. In this hymn (2.40) Soma and Pūṣan are invoked as cosmogonic powers whose conjoint share in creation is specified. They are the "navel of the immortal." The navel is the center whence generation proceeds into manifestation. This is illustrated in later Indian iconography by the god Brahmā seated on a lotus flower whose stalk issues from the navel of Vishnu lying on the waters. In the second stanza "birth" means coming into being, which is here the light of consciousness arising from cosmic darkness, the darkness ante principium. The epithet "bull" in the third stanza means creative power.

28. This miracle of Indra is frequently evoked in similar terms, as in 8.89.7 and in 1.62.9. "In the raw ones you put the cooked milk, the white in the black, in the red ones" (also 2.40.2; 3.30.14; 6.17.6; 8.32.5). The white, luminous milk is contrasted with the black and red cows; cf. the later theory of the three guṇas, the white sattva-guṇa, the black tamo-guṇa, the qualitative potentials of existence, the one, luminous and pure, the other dull and dark, while the middle term of the aggregate is turbulent, red. Bergaigne, *Réligion Védique,* vol. 2, p. 83, identified "raw" with cold, with night, dawn, or cloud.

29. 3.30.14 sings of "a great light (mahi jyotir) hidden in the udders [of the cows]. The raw (cow) moves on carrying the cooked [milk]."

30. 10.106.11 calls the hymn (mantra) the cooked sweet (madhu), which is the glory in the cows. This "white, desired [milk] in the udders and bellies of the cows is sweeter than sweet" (10.49.10).

31. The hymn as a chariot is a recurrent image (2.31.4; 10.26.9). The driving power of inspiration is spoken of by the ṛṣis as their chariot. The whole cosmos is "comprehended" by it. The sacrifice with its rites is a symbol of the cosmos as "universal sacrifice" and has the same significant numbers as the chariot (Bergaigne, *Réligion Védique,* vol. 2, p. 430).

32. The several heptads of the *Ṛg Veda* refer to the source. The seven ṛṣis are, or act as, the "seven rays" of the sun. Ṛṣi or radiating is generally translated as "seer," but would mean "rushing" or outpouring from ṛṣ or arṣ; this meaning is taken as referring to the singer who pours out his songs. The seven ṛṣis, however, are celestials, and the meaning of "raying forth light," the word raying being taken as transitive, appears even more suitable than the intransitive meaning. This would make the ṛṣis themselves rays of light pouring forth or rushing out into manifestation from their source on high. Cf. note 13.

Another fundamental significance of the number seven is given by the three pairs of heaven-and-earth. They make the triple universe with its three heavens and three earths into which the one undivided principle became differentiated while holding or "carrying" all. Images of the "one carrying the six" are given in 3.56.2; and of the "one in the shape of aja who has separated these six worlds" in 1.164. 6, also 1.164.10. Aja cf. aja ekapād (note 16) with reference to Pūṣan.

33. The word translated here as worlds is rajāṅsi (1.164.6), the world spaces. Rajas connotes the space that came into being by the separation of the—ante principium—undivided heaven-and-earth. Rajas thus denotes not only the "atmosphere" between this earth and the sky, but is used also to signify the spaces (rocanā) of eternal light in the two higher, invisible worlds, when spoken of as three rajāṅsi. Rajas, in the singular, however, here denotes the atmosphere.

34. 2.40.3. The word aviśvaminvam has generally, though not unanimously, been translated as "not carrying everyone" (Ludwig, *Der Rig Veda,* vol. 5, p. 302; Geldner, *Der Rig Veda,*

vol. 1, p. 296). This meaning agrees with 1.164.10, which is the only other occurrence of this word in the *Ṛg Veda.*

Atkins, in *Pūṣan,* p. 45, translates aviśvaminvam as though it were equivalent to viśvaminvam, "who pervades all." Viśvaminvah is, by intended contrast, the attribute of Pūṣan in 2.40.6.

35. The chariot, in this respect, is also the hymn (note 31). The seven wheels, the five reins, allude as little to the appearance of an actual chariot as the foot of Pūṣan—or the three heads of other gods—are meant to suggest human shape. Nothing here is descriptive or anthropomorphic. The vocabulary of experience is used in combinations that defy experience and conjure up an immediate and coherent vision. They do it with a shock, not altogether unintentionally.

36. Raśmi signifies rein or also ray.

37. The names of the five kins are given (with some variations) in the *Aitareya Brāhmaṇa* (3.31.5) and *Bṛhadevata* (7.67–71). They are the serpents (nāga), fathers, or ancestral spirits, men, gods, and Gandharvas, in ascending hierarchy.

38. Soma in this context is evoked not as the celestial Soma, but as his correspondence on earth, the soma plant, which grows on the high mountain, in midspace (9.79.4; 9.110.8; 9.82.3).

39. A prayer says: "May Soma restore the body (tanu), Pūṣan the way which saves" (10.59. 7).

40. Soma is god and elixir of life just as "Dionysus, himself a god, is poured out in offering to the gods, so that through him mankind receives blessing." Euripides, *The Bacchae,* in *The Bacchae and Other Plays,* trans. L. P. Vellacott (Baltimore: Penguin Books, 1954), p. 190.

41. Equally surefooted, the goat climbs down the mountain slope from the height of the cycle of the year on the path of the Fathers. If this cyclical movement is viewed in one direction—which is the direction of time—the graphic sign is the chevron pattern of zigzag outline, which owes its name to the goat (chèvre).

42. In notes 16, 32, the approximation of Pūṣan and Aja Ekapād, the goat one-foot, or the "uncreate" (nonmanifesting) one-foot, was shown to rest on more than the name of the goat. In 3.56.2 the "one" carries the six burdens. In the following stanza, 3.56.3, the Bull Viśvarūpa is envisaged having three bellies and three udders. If the steeds of Pūṣan are goats, Pūṣan himself (2.40.3) can be spoken of in his potency as a (mighty) bull.

43. Hair is a symbol of vital power and of the inner light. The golden hair of the god is solar power, raying downwards, as his "beard," throughout the cosmos. Cf. the divine power in the hair of Samson (Judges 13.3–16.30). In later Indian art and thought, Gaṅgā, the celestial river, the water of heaven, comes to earth in Śiva's hair; cf. also the story of Apālā (above) and the story of the Viṣṇupurāṇa of the white and black hair that Vishnu pulled from his head and in which Lord Krishna and elder brother Balarāma were incarnated.

44. The gods readily, and for soteriological reasons, change their chariots for ships in their journeys in the ocean of flowing light and the vapors of the air.

45. Savitṛ is the great father (7.52.3). The daughter of the Sun (Sūrya) (1.34.5) is Sūryā. Sūryā is Sāvitrī. *AV* 6.82.2; 14.2.3. The Sāvitrī mantra follows immediately the evocation of Pūṣan (3.62.7–9) and the image of the bride.

46. The chariot of Sūryā is Manas itself (cf. the chariot of Pūṣan, pp. 166-68). Manas, in 10.84.1–12 and in 10.60.8–10 corresponds to Gk. noûs, the mind-soul that leaves the body at death.

47. This path leads in a straight line and coincides with the vertical axis that Pūṣan establishes when he puts his foot down in the pit. Its starting point here is in the heights. The heart of the ṛṣi lies on this line. The straight swift path, the central vertical axis viewed from above or below, has its image in the one who bears the sixfold burden in the name of Aja Ekapād.

48. The ship is the ship of sacred thought (nāva matīnām 1.46.7), which here starts from "the other shore." If the ship takes the return journey from man to God, it is the sacrifice that fulfills this function: Yajñiyām nāvam (10.44.6). In 1.140.12 ship, chariot (and house) are coordinated in their function of carrying man "to the other shore." The ship of the ritual (ṛta) is at the same time the ship of ṛta, the order in the cosmos. This ship takes "the straightest course" (9.89.2). The house is also synonymous with the body.

49. Re the relation of Tvaṣṭṛ-Savitṛ-Viśvarūpa on the one hand with Savitṛ-Pūṣan-Viśvarūpa on the other, and with the "One" or Aja-Ekapād, the Uncreate-One-legged, or the One-legged goat, see notes 16, 20, 32, 42, 47.

50. Pitarāu means fathers, but it also designates the Aśvins as parents in the same way as the dual janitrī (mothers) designates heaven and earth as parents (10.110.9; 1.185.6).

51. *Kauṣika-sūtra,* 76.10.

52. *AV* 19.7.2–3; *Āp. GṛS* 1.3.1–2. Although the Nakṣatras are not given in the *Ṛg Veda* in their full number of 27 or 28, they are enumerated in later Vedic texts. Nakṣatra, however, in the *Ṛg Veda* connotes a lunar mansion like those of Aghā and Arjunī. Arjunī (Uttara Phalgūnī) is a Nakṣatra favorable for marriages (*PGS* 1.4.6; *ĀpSS* 1.3.2.f.).

53. Pūṣan's sonship of the Cosmic Twins, one of whom is mortal, the other immortal (1.181.4), corresponds to his own cosmogonic station between Savitṛ and this "mortal" sun. The Aśvins also fathered Agni (10.24.4–5; cf. 10.184.3). They churned Agni into being, acting themselves as the firemaking drill.

54. Pūṣan's role has frequently been misunderstood. He is not the bridegroom of Sūryā, nor are the Aśvins the bridegrooms of Sūryā (and Pūṣan does not lead the Aśvins to the marriage of Sūryā, as R. Pischel and K. Geldner, *Vedische Studien* [Stuttgart, 1889–1901], pt. 1, p. 114, and Atkins, *Pūṣan,* p. 10, interpret, 1.184.3). The various attempts by Oldenberg and other scholars clarify some passages but fail to see the meaning of the "marriage of Sūryā" and of the roles of the members of the bridal party. Atkins rightly observes that "an adequate explanation of the details in naturalistic terms appears a hopeless task." The Aśvins (1.119.5) are friends and protectors of Sūryā. Cf. 8.26.19, where the Aśvins drive together with shiny white vision (śvetayā dhiyā) the "radiant song." The Aśvins as protectors (pati) are invoked in 2.31.4, 8.5.5.

55. Woman as the field in which man sows his seed is a frequent figure of speech. The agricultural rite is seen as performed in the human sphere.

56. Bergaigne, *Réligion Védique,* vol. 2, p. 425, translates ādhīṣamāṇāyāḥ patiḥ śucāyāś ca sucasya ca as "maitre de la brillante qui pense et du brilliant." "La brilliante qui pense" he interprets as "prayer" and "le brillant" as soma. Bergaigne comes nearest to the meaning of this verse to which the preceding verses of the hymn (10.26.1–5) lead up. None of the other translations render the meaning, nor did Sāyaṇa.

57. Pratyardhir yajñānām refers to Pūṣan and Soma (10.26.5) and not to Pūṣan and the other gods, as suggested by Geldner, *Der Rig Veda,* vol. 3, p. 163, and Atkins, *Pūṣan,* p. 89. The relation of Pūṣan to karambha on the one hand and of Indra to Soma on the other is the subject of 6.57.2, 6; 6.56.1, 2; 3.52.1, 7; 7.53.1, and in view of this relation, Pūṣan is called Indra's brother (6.55.5).

58. Atharvaveda Pariśiṣṭa 12, *The Pariśiṣṭas of the Atharva Veda,* ed. G. M. Bolling and J. V. Negelein (Leipzig, 1909–10).

59. Food: svadhā. Svadhā has two meanings, (a) self-determination, and (b) satisfaction of one's own desire (Grassmann, *s.v.*). In the latter sense it means sacrificial food, and particularly the food offered to the Fathers. It appears that self-determination or independence is a secondary meaning based on that of "self-procured, self-offered" (svadhā). In this sense the gods, including Pūṣan, are called "svadhāvan" (6.58.1), which is translated as independent and could be rendered as self-offered.

Food (svadhā) is given its place in the creation hymn 10.129.5. There the gods are spoken of as being this side of creation (10.129.6) where food (svadhā) is, here below, whereas above this line are the creative powers who give their seed.

This dichotomy of creation is "in principio," in the beginning of things. Ante principium no division exists; desire and satisfaction coalesce in the imperishable world of light, in heaven (cf. 9.113.9, 10).

60. Gruel (made of rice) and the gruel pot are symbols of the sun: Leopold Schroeder, *Die Wurzeln der Sage vom heiligen Graal,* Sitzungsberichte der Wiener Akademie der Wissenschaften, vol. 166, p. 8.

61. Thus he might have been called in blasphemy, by those to whom soma was the elixir of life. (Cf. Franklin Edgerton in *JAOS* 40[1920]:101–2). The assurance "Pūṣan, I do not slight thee" (1.138.4; cf. also 1.42.10) conveys a similar attitude. It would appear that Pūṣan is an ancient god and so is Trita, the alter ego of Indra. Food offerings were the share, it appears, of the ancient gods; grain, and the marrow and milk of animals. These receded in the worship of Indra, the creator-god of the *Ṛg Veda,* in the transports caused by soma drink and expressed in the symbol of the elixir of life.

62. Cf. on the other hand, the "creative" or "seed" quality of teeth, in the sowing with the serpent's teeth by Cadmus, at Thebes, and by Jason, in the field of Ares, by the order and gift, respectively, of Athene.

63. In 4.30.24 first Aryaman is invoked, then Pūṣan, Bhaga, and the toothless god (devaḥ karūḍatī). The toothless god is most probably Pūṣan (according to Yāska and Sāyaṇa's commentary). In connection with the "toothless god" as sun god, the sun as "Jungfer Mundlos" may be thought of. "Maiden Mouthless" would express silence. Cf. W. Schwartz, "Zur Indogermanischen Mythologie," *Zeitschrift für Ethnologie* 13:170.

64. They are told in the *SB* 1.7.4.1–9, and the *TS* 2.6.8.3–5, and less fully in the *KB* 6.13.

65. 10.61.6, where it is told that the gods fashioned Vāstoṣpati. Vāstoṣpati is Rudra (*TS* 3.4.10.4).

66. The hands and the feet are the "organs of action." Pūṣan's specific activity requires him to put down but one leg—the axis of the cosmos—and to hold out one hand, the right one, in the direction of his course. The right hand is the hand of action, in particular, and it remains unstained in its shining purity even where it points forward on the downward path "the evil [sinister] way" (10.135.2).

67. The belief in the two ways, the Dakṣiṇāyana, the way to the South, the way of the Fathers, and the Uttarāyana, the way to the "north," which is the way of the gods, the way of Liberation, is the belief in Pūṣan's path. The terms Dakṣiṇāyana and Uttarāyana, however, are not used in the *Ṛg Veda.* They are synonyms of the Pitṛyāna and Devayāna.

68. "Three are the heavens of Savitṛ, two are his lap, one in the world of Yama." The lap of Savitṛ, the Impeller, which is on high, is at the very end of the axis, opposite to the "lap of Nirṛti" (note 15) at the lower end of the axis. Below, in the lap of Nirṛti, yawns the chasm, into which have fallen beyond release those who have gone against the ṛta, the cosmic order. Above, in the lap of Savitṛ, at the height, is the opposite place of "no return" where the Liberated dwell.

69. Samnaya, bring us together (6.54.1), may we be united samgamemahi (6.54.2), and Samtira (1.42.1) traverse together [with us], are terms of union with God.

70. The word gṛha, house, dwelling, is used here. These dwellings are to be distinguished from the dwellings (sadhasthe) of Pūṣan; see note 72.

71. Pari hastam dadhātu, "give [put] his hand around," parastāt "beyond" is replaced by purastāt (in front) in *AV* 7.9.4, "ahead, leading."

72. The dwellings or houses (gṛha; 6.54.2) are where the pious have their seat (yatrāsata), whither they have gone (10.17.4). The two stations of Pūṣan, on the forward (leading) path of heaven, on the forward (leading) path of earth, are the supreme stations or dwellings (10.17.6).

73. "Vasu" is Light, splendor, the "treasure," wealth. The wealth and prosperity that Pūṣan leads is expressed in terms of cows and horses. They represent the substance and power, respectively, of light.

74. Pūṣan is viśvaminvaḥ (2.40.6) pervading all and bhuvane viśve arpitaḥ (6.58.2), which can be understood as "inserted in the whole universe" but also as "inserted in every creature." Pūṣan is here the inner guide.

75. At the moment when his foot holds down the firebrand of the two-faced evil one. In this moment Pūṣan is symbolically one with Aja Ekapād and with the pillar of life (10.5.6; note 16).

10 *Figural Sculpture of the Gupta Period*

1. Hemachandra Raychaudhuri, *Materials for the Study of the Early History of the Vaishnava Sect* (Calcutta: University of Calcutta, 1929; rev. ed., 1936), p. 104.

2. Vincent A. Smith, "Indian Sculpture of the Gupta Period, A.D. 300–650," *Ostasiastische Zeitschrift* 3 (1914–15): 1–27.

3. Alexander Cunningham, *Mahābodhi or The Great Buddhist Temple at Buddha Gayā* (London, 1892), pl. 25; Ludwig Bachhofer, *Early Indian Sculpture* (New York: Harcourt, Brace, 1929), pl. 89.

4. *ASIAR,* 1913–14, p. 262; Alexander Cunningham, *ASI* 10:3.

5. Cunningham, *Mahābodhi.*

6. R. P. Chandra in *ASIAR,* 1922–23.

7. Author's revision: Cf. J. C. Harle, *Gupta Sculpture* (Oxford: Clarendon Press, 1974), p. 43; the date of the image would be A.D. 384 and the strength of the Kuṣāṇa tradition would be remarkable at this date.

8. J. F. Fleet, *Inscriptions of the Early Gupta Kings and Their Successors, CII* 3 (Calcutta, 1888):2.

9. Alexander Cunningham, *Book of Indian Eras* (Calcutta: Thacker, Spink and Co., 1883); F. Kielhorn, *IA* 17:215 ff.

10. Fleet, *Inscriptions,* p. 21.

11. Ibid., p. 42; Smith, "Indian Sculpture," pl. 11, fig. 5.

12. Fleet, *Inscriptions,* p. 39; Smith, "Indian Sculpture," pls. 12–13, figs. 6–7.

13. Fleet, *Inscriptions,* p. 258.

14. Ibid., p. 146; J. C. French. *The Art of the Pāla Empire of Bengal* (London, 1928), p. 1.
15. Fleet, *Inscriptions,* p. 45.
16. Ibid., p. 262; Cunningham, *ASI* 3:36.
17. Fleet, *Inscriptions,* p. 65; Cunningham, *ASI* 1:91, pl. 29; 16:129, pl. 29.
18. *ASIAR* 1914–15, p. 99, p. 63, fig. b.
19. Ibid., figs. a and c.
20. Fleet, *Inscriptions,* pp. 93–100, 112, 121–35.
21. Ibid., p. 88; Cunningham, *ASI* 10:87, pls. 25, 26.
22. Fleet, *Inscriptions,* p. 271; Cunningham, *ASI* 3:48, pl. 18.
23. Fleet, *Inscriptions,* p. 272.
24. Ibid., p. 281; cf. *Catalogue of the Indian Museum, Calçutta,* pt. 2, nos. 11, 12, 14.
25. Fleet, *Inscriptions,* p. 110; R. D. Banerji, *The Temple of Siva at Bhumara, MASI* 16 (1924).
26. Fleet, *Inscriptions,* p. 89; Cunningham, *ASI* 10, pl. 23.
27. Fleet, *Inscriptions,* p. 158.
28. Ibid., p. 142; Cunningham, *ASI* 10, pl. 22.
29. Fleet, *Inscriptions,* p. 273.
30. Ibid., p. 278.
31. In each of these figures, there remains only the pedestal, with an inscription, and a fragment of sculpture.
32. Smith, "Indian Sculpture," fig. 15; Ananda K. Coomaraswamy, *History of Indian and Indonesian Art* (Leipzig, London, and New York, 1927), fig. 158.
33. Author's revision: This is of a later date, i.e., seventh century. See Frederick Asher, *The Art of Eastern India* (Minneapolis: University of Minnesota Press, 1980), pp. 56–58.
34. Cf. Bachhofer, *Early Indian Sculpture,* pls. 81, 86, 87 and pls. 84, 85.
35. Stella Kramrisch, "Die indische Kunst," in Anton Springer, *Die aussereuropäische Kunst, Handbuch der Kunstgeschichte,* vol. 6 (Leipzig: Alfred Kröner Verlag, 1929), fig. 285.
36. Kramrisch, "Die indische Kunst," fig. 278.
37. Author's revision: The reference to the Sultanganj image in the original text is not valid, since the image belongs to the seventh century.
38. Cf. Smith, "Indian Sculpture," fig. 16.
39. Cf. Stella Kramrisch, "Emblems of the Universal Being," *JISOA* 3, no. 1 (June, 1935): 148–65; and in this volume.
40. Cf. *ASIAR* 1914–15, p. 100, no. 6.
41. D. R. Sahni and J. Ph. Vogel, *Catalogue of the Museum of Archaeology at Sarnath* (Calcutta, 1914), p. 45, B (b) 19.
42. Kramrisch, "Die indische Kunst," fig. 285.
43. Bachhofer, *Early Indian Sculpture,* pls. 75, 80, 81–84, 87.
44. Ibid., pl. 86, on the left.
45. Cf. note 19.
46. In the third quarter of the fifth century, before the steles of the seventies, is the standing Buddha, *ASIAR* 1903–1904, pl. 62, 1; Smith, "Indian Sculpture," fig. 9.
47. Smith, "Indian Sculpture," fig. 14; Coomaraswamy, *HIIA,* sec. 161; Harle, *Gupta Sculpture,* fig. 70.
48. It is also possible that various stages of inhaling and exhaling are captured in separate works. The inhaling position is in accord with the powerfully accentuated figures of the first half of the century; the more relaxed position conforms to those of the following time.
49. Sahni and Vogel, *Catalogue.*
50. A. Foucher, *L'Art grécobouddhique du Gandhāra* (Paris, 1905), fig. 74; J. Ph. Vogel, *Catalogue of the Archeological Museum at Mathura* (Allahabad, 1910), pl. XII.
51. Sahni and Vogel, *Catalogue,* pp. 53–59.
52. Coomaraswamy, *HIIA,* sec. 162.
53. Smith, "Indian Sculpture," p. 10, fig. 5.
54. Cf. notes 11 and 12.
55. Only the left half of the lintel is shown here. Cf. Smith, "Indian Sculpture," fig. 7, where the whole lintel is reproduced, although in sections, and Kramrisch, "Die indische Kunst," fig. 280, where the right half is reproduced, along with the figure of Viṣṇu; also Harle, *Gupta Sculpture,* figs. 71–78 for both halves, with details.
56. Cf. Smith, "Indian Sculpture," figs. 13a and b.
57. *ASIAR* 1911–12, p. 161ff.
58. Kramrisch, *Calcutta Review,* 1923.
59. *ASIAR* 1920–21, pl. 18c.
60. Cunningham, *Mahābodhi,* pl. 15.

61. Coomaraswamy, *HIIA*, sec. 176.

62. Cf. Kramrisch, *Indian Sculpture* (first published Heritage of India Series, 1933; reprinted Delhi: Motilal Banarsidass, 1981, pp. 68–69).

63. Smith, "Indian Sculpture," fig. 3; Coomaraswamy, *HIIA*, sec. 177.

64. Smith, *History of Fine Art in India and Ceylon* 2d ed. (Oxford, 1930), pl. 46.

65. Banerji, *Bhumara;* Banerji places the temple "in all probability" in the middle of the fifth century; Sir John Marshall places it in the sixth.

66. Smith, *History*, pls. 48–49.

67. Cf. the fragment from Sondani in the Gwalior Museum; Coomaraswamy, *HIIA*, sec. 173.

68. Cf. note 28.

69. Cf. note 27.

11 *Pāla and Sena Sculpture*

1. *Rūpam* (1920), p. 100.

2. J. C. French, *The Art of the Pāla Empire of Bengal* (London, 1928) does justice in the early period of Pāla art, cf. fig. 1 with pl. 5, a work of the eighth century.

3. R. D. Banerji, *The Pālas of Bengal, Memoirs of the ASB* 5, no. 8(1915):47–112.

4. Cf. R. P. Chandra, *Gaudarājamālā* (in Bengali), and R. C. Kata, *Handbook, Sri Pratap Singh Museum* (Srinagar), p. 72.

5. The most significant sculptures that are inscribed are reproduced in pls. 11-6, 11-10, 11-18 and in R. D. Banerji, *Banglar Itihāsa*, 1st ed., passim. For other dated inscriptions see M. M. Chakravarti, "Pāla Inscriptions in the Indian Museum," *JASB* (1908); D. R. Sahni, *Catalogue of the Museum of Archaeology at Sārnāth* (Calcutta, 1914), p. 88, pl. 11; Banerji, *Pālas of Bengal*, pp. 61, 65, 77, 103, and 105; "Bangiya Sahitya Parisad Patrika," *Bengal District Gazetteer* 15(1916):13; and French, *Art*, pls. 2, 9, 10, 11, 20, 27, and pp. 11–15.

6. G. A. Grierson, "Gleanings from the Bhakta Mālā," *JRAS* (1908), p. 627.

7. Vajrayāna, the ruling form of Buddhism at the period under discussion, emphasizes in Sunya, Nirātmā, the female principle, united with whom the Bodhisattva rests in eternal bliss. Cf. B. Bhattacharyya, *Indian Buddhist Iconography* (London: Oxford University Press, 1924), p. 16.

8. Cf. also D. C. Sen, *Vaiṣṇava Literature of Mediaeval Bengal* (Calcutta, 1917), p. 221; and D. C. Sen, *History of Bengali Language and Literature* (Calcutta, 1911), p. 63.

9. For instance, Bhattacharyya, *Buddhist Iconography*, pp. 123, 82.

10. D. C. Sen, *Folk Literature of Bengal* (Calcutta, 1920), pp. 246, 267.

11. Chanda, *Gaudarajamāla*, p. 8; D. C. Sen, *Ballads of Eastern Bengal*, 4 vols. (Calcutta: University of Calcutta, 1923–32); and Sen, *Bengali Language and Literature*, p. 246.

12. Sen, *Folk Literature*, p. 67.

13. I am indebted to the Office of the Director, Geological Survey of India, for the analysis.

14. In several instances the earlier images were made of different varieties of stone, cf. pl. 11-2, and N. K. Bhattasali, *Iconography of Buddhist and Brahmanical Sculptures in the Dacca Museums* (Dacca, 1929), p. xix.

15. Aṣṭa-dhātu images sometimes were gilded, cf. "The Viṣnu Image from Gomilla," *Rūpam* (1928), pp. 33, 34, 26; and the Chauddagrām Sarvvānī.

16. The Rangpur Bronzes do not contain gold or silver. Cf. Annual Report, *ASI*, 1911–12. D. B. Spooner, "Viṣnu Images from Rangpur, Found near Dacca," now in the Calcutta Museum (R. D. Banerji, *Banglār Itihāsa*), and S. Kumar, "A Note on the Bengal School of Artists," *JASB*, n.s. 12(1916):23–28.

17. Cf. Stella Kramrisch, "Grundzüge der indischen Kunst" (Hellerau bei Dresden, 1924), pl. 47. Terracotta plaques and figures were found in Nalāndā and in eastern Bengal, but the large terracotta reliefs from Pāhārpur, with their lively and careless treatment, form a group by themselves.

18. Stella Kramrisch, "The Viṣṇudharmottaram," *The Calcutta Review*, 3d ser., 10(1924): 15.

19. In 1922 in the possession of Raj Pandit Radha Krishna Bahadur of Mathura; Bhattasali, *Iconography*, pp. xxi, 273–74.

20. Kramrisch, "Viṣṇudharmottaram," p. 41.

21. The difference becomes clear in the case of the kneeling figures of devotees with their more momentous movements. This difference, however, is especially marked when the ritualis-

tic stone sculptures are compared with decorative reliefs, made of terracotta and fixed into the walls of the vihāra at Paharpur, where the single figures with the full freedom of motion run and hover about, enjoy themselves, and cut grimaces.

22. See French, *Art*, pls. 6, 7. Cf. also Tārā prom Sukhavāspur, Bhattasali, *Iconography*, pl. 20.

23. See French, *Art*, pls. 10, 15. The Sūrya at Chandimuda, Bhattasali, *Iconography*, pl. 59, and the Lokanātha from Sylhet, pl. 4, belong to this period and maintain the same high standard. The Vishnu from Lakṣmaṇakāti, ibid., pl. 32, belongs to the end of this century.

24. French, *Art*, pl. 18, is of the tenth century; pl. 8 illustrates a sculpture that belongs neither to the art of the Pāla tradition nor to the eighth century.

25. The robe of the Buddha images (sanghāti) makes use of the same convention in order to indicate folds. In some later instances, cf. Bhattasali, *Iconography*, pl. 14, of the twelfth and eleventh centuries, respectively, some goddesses wear either a short bodice (colī) or a longer jacket-like and tightly fitting bodice. They are marked by their hemlines only and by the pattern, if any, of the cloth.

26. This treatment, too, is met with in the early ninth century. Cf. pl. 11-3.

27. Stella Kramrisch, "Notes on Bengal Sculpture," *The Modern Review* 33(January 1923): 62.

12 *Candella Sculpture: Khajuraho*

1. Traces of plaster in Ellora.
2. Stella Kramrisch, *Indian Sculpture* (Calcutta, 1933), pp. 103, 109.
3. The statue of the rat is now in the Khajuraho Museum, and there is no record of where it stood originally.
4. Kramrisch, *Indian Sculpture*, p. 31 passim.

13 *The Four-Cornered Citadel of the Gods*

1. According to general (sāmānya) norm, the thickness of the wall has half the width of the floor of the garbhagṛha. See *MP* 269, 1–6; *BṛS* 55.11–16. The recently revised dating of the Bṛhatsamhitā is in the early fifth century A.D.

2. See Stella Kramrisch, *The Hindu Temple*, vol. 1 (Calcutta, 1946), pp. 131–36.

3. Devagṛha and near equivalents of the term "house of god," i.e., Devatāgāra, Devālaya, Devakula, occur in *Manu* 9.280, *SGS* 2.12.6, etc.; Pañcatantra, Book 1, story 1; Bhāsa's *Pratimānāṭaka* 3; Mora well inscription, *Epigraphia Indica* 24:194; also (a Gupta inscription) *Epigraphia Indica* 21:81.

4. *AP* 61, 11; Viṣṇusaṃhitā 13, 61–69; Kramrisch, *Hindu Temple*, passim.

5. 1.189.2agne . . . pūś ca pṛthvī bahulā na urvī bhavā
"Agni . . . be thou a broad, large, wide
fort [for us]."
5.19.2 ā dṛḍham puraṁ viviṣuḥ
"they [the sacrificers] have entered the firm
fort [i.e., Agni]"; cf. also 7.15.14;
10.87.22.
7.95.1 sarasvatī dharuṇam āyasī pūḥ
"Sarasvatī is a bulwark, an iron fort"
8.80.7 indra dṛhyasva pūr asi
"Indra, stay firm, you are a fort (cf. also
8.69.8)."

6. Vaikhānasāgama, ch. 7. *IPad*, vol. 3. ch. 27.82.

7. B. L. Dhama, *A Guide to Khajuraho* (Bombay, 1927), pls. 4–10.

8. K. N. Dikshit, *The Temple of Paharpur* (Archaeological Survey of India, Memoir 55), passim.

9. Kramrisch, *Hindu Temple*, p. 176.

10. *VDhP* 3.84.1–15.

11. The significance of the number 101 = 100 + 1 is that it exceeds 100. One hundred is the ideal lifespan of man. Man has one hundred energies, and his ātman, he himself, is the one hundred and first (cf. *SB* 13.2.1.6).

12. It does not appear likely that the small pieces of wood were thrown between the spokes of the wheel-like arrangement of the larger logs, i.e., ācāyam (for ācayam) appears to

be the correct reading, and not aracāyaṁ (for aracāyāṁ); see P. E. Dumont, *L'Aśvamedha: description du sacrifice du cheval* (Paris, 1927), pp. 312 and 320.

13. The significance of the number twenty-one is given in the *ŚB* 13.4.4.11, with reference to the Aśvamedha by explaining that the sun is composed of twenty-one parts. "For there are twelve months, five seasons, these three worlds [i.e., the earth, the air, and the heaven-world] and the sun on high is the twenty-first. And it is the Aśvamedha, and the Aśvamedha is Prajāpati." The meaning is that the sun encompasses the entire manifest universe, and that this power, vested in the number twenty-one is known to be communicated to the sacrificial posts. The twenty-one sacrificial posts are not known to have been part of the Hindu temple. In number and shape, however, the twenty-one posts have their place in a specific type of the Buddhist stūpa. There they are called āyaka and also āyakakabho. They are distributed, five at a time, at the four cardinal points of the stūpa on projections of the drum of the stūpa facing the gates. The twenty-first pillar, identical in shape although differently proportioned, is set in the body of the stūpa and raised above it at the apex of the dome shape of the stūpa. The āyaka posts distinguish the stūpas of Andhra, in the southeastern Deccan, with Amarāvatī as the main site in the second century A.D. and Nāgārjunakoṇḍa in the third century.

The name Āyaka-post (-kabho) has remained unexplained hitherto; it signifies approach and also arrival (āya: from √i). In the four directions of space, the groups of five posts, facing the gates of entry to the stūpa, do justice to their name. In the fifth, the upward direction, arrival is symbolized by the square railing of the harmikā, which encloses the central post. This square railing has no entrance. It faces the cardinal directions and is closed to them. The "entry" or "exit" is in the fifth, the upward direction.

The groups of five pillars are, in certain cases, accentuated each by their middle pillar, the fifth. The four flanking pillars terminate uniformly, with rounded tops that are either plain or, if decorated, carry four "ray-windows" (gavākṣa). It is, however, the fifth or central pillar only that sometimes carries a stūpa and exceeds thereby its surrounding group of four just as the twenty-first pillar emerging from the center of the top of the dome exceeds the four groups of five pillars on the platforms of the drum of the stūpa. The number symbolism of twenty-one is here applied in a Buddhist context as $4 \times 5 + 1$, whose reference is to the "fifth" state of consciousness (ekaggatā) in the realm of Pure Form (rūpa dhātu) (for descriptions of āyaka posts, cf. C. Sivaramamurti, *Amarāvatī Sculptures in the Madras Government Museum*, pp. 25, 173, 264–72; and D. Barrett, *Sculptures from Amaravaṭi in the British Museum*, pp. 34–38).

14. The altar has the shape of a bird (the falcon). Its "body" is a square. Right and left, that is, on the north and south sides, a smaller, near-square rectangle is joined to the body. These are the wings. Similarly, a smaller, near-square rectangle is joined to the body in the middle of the west side. This is the tail. The standard measure of the altar is seven puruṣas (3 plus 4 puruṣas). A puruṣa is equal to 10 feet. The measure of seven puruṣas is the sum of the maximum east-west measure and of the maximum north-south measure. In this standard measure, the longer side of the rectangles of the wings measures 1.2 puruṣas, whereas the longer side of the tail rectangle measures only 1.1 puruṣas. So the "seven puruṣa" measure amounts actually to 7.5 puruṣas. The altar of the horse sacrifice is thrice as large as the standard altar. It has 21 puruṣas (actually 22.5 puruṣas) as the maximum measure of its east-west and north-south dimensions, i.e., 9 plus 12 puruṣas respectively, or 120 and 90 feet (cf. Dumont, *L'Aśvamedha*, p. 73). The standard size of "bricks is 6-2/5 aṅgulas or 4-4/5" in a seven puruṣa altar (cf. N. K. Majumder, "Sacrificial Vedis and Agnis," *JISOA* 7:82). In an altar thrice the size of the seven-puruṣa altar, the bricks are each said to be thrice the standard size. There are five layers of bricks, and the last svayamātṛṇṇā brick above the fifth layer (cf. *KSS* 16.8.26). Below the first layer of bricks, the height of the "High Altar," the uttaravedi, whose perimeter measures 40 feet in the seven-puruṣa altar, has to be taken into account.

15. Cf. Dumont, *L'Aśvamedha*, p. 320.

16. Kramrisch, *Hindu Temple*, p. 198.

17. The number of the priests stationed in the eight cars was thirty-two, in eight groups of four corresponding to the number—and position—of the thirty-two pada-devatās in the plan, the Vāstupuruṣamaṇḍala of the Hindu temple.

18. *VS* 17.72–73; 18.68–74.

14 *Wall and Image in Indian Art*

1. Figures 2–5 are reproduced from Stella Kramrisch, *The Hindu Temple*, vol. 1 (Calcutta: Calcutta University Press, 1946), pp. 60, 251, 247, and 230, respectively.

2. *Sādhanamālā*, 98.

1. Part 3, 46, 1–19; page references are to Venkatesvara Press edition (Bombay, 1923).
2. Part 3, 85.65–79.
3. Part 3, 85.63–64.
4. E. Washburn Hopkins, *Great Epic of India* (New York: C. Scribner's, 1901), pp. 58–84.
5. F. E. Pargiter, *Dynasties of the Kali Age* (Oxford, 1913), Intro., pp. xiii, xvi.
6. *Jātaka*, vol. 6, pp. 159, 223.
7. *Vinaya Piṭaka*, vol. 4, *Pāchittiya*, no. 41, p. 289.
8. *Mahā-Umagga-Jātaka*, p. 212.
9. *Sārattha-Pakāsinī*, Siamese edition, part 2, p. 398. Cf. B. M. Barua's *History of Pre-Buddhistic Indian Philosophy*, p. 110; "Maskari-Gósala's Early Life," *Calcutta Review* (June 1927): 364–66.
10. Benares ed., pp. 32, 44.
11. *Mūdrārākṣasa*, Act 1. Cf. *Harṣa-Carita*, Nirṇaya Sāgara Press Edition, V, p. 153, quoted and discussed by Barua in the *Calcutta Review* (June 1927), pp. 370–71.
12. *SRa* 46.143–45.
13. *VDhP* 1.129.1–19.
14. *Citralakṣaṇa*, trans., Berthold Laufer, *Dokumente der indischen Kunst* (Leipzig: Otto Harrassowitz, 1913), pp. 129–36.
15. Cf. A. K. Maitra, "Aims and Methods of Painting in Ancient India," *Rūpam* (1923).
16. Trans. S. Subbarao (Madras, 1917), p. 48.
17. Ed. by Sarat Chandra Das (Calcutta, 1901); cf. Laufer, *Dokumente*, p. 186.
18. *ŚRa* 4.46.145–46. Greek tradition, agreeable only to an appreciation of the naturalistic aspect of art, has it that painting began with the outlining of a man's shadow (Pliny the Elder, *Natural History* 35.15).
19. *JRAS*, vol. 7 (1875). The *BṛS* (trans. H. Kern), pp. 93–97:

(2) By Jupiter being in its power will be born (the personage denominated) Háṁsa; by Saturn, the man Śaśa; by Mars, the Ruchaka; by Mercury, the Bhadra; and by Venus, the Mālavya.

(7) The length and stretch of the Haṁsa is of 96 digits. The personages going by the names of Śaśa, Ruchaka, Bhadra and Mālavya, are each taller than the preceding one by three digits.

(10) The Mālavya will be marked by arms resembling an elephant's trunk, and by hands reaching to the knees. His members and joints are fleshy, he has a well-proportioned and neat frame, and a slender waist. His face, of oblong form, measures 13 digits, the transverse measure between the ears being three digits less. He has fiery eyes, comely cheeks, even and white teeth and not too thick lips.

(11) Having by his valour obtained wealth, he will, residing in the recesses of Mount Pāriyātra, reign as a wise king over Mālava, Broach, Surāṣṭra, Lāṭa, Sindh, and so forth.

(12) This Mālavya will at the age of seventy years piously depart from life at a place of pilgrimage. Having in due form indicated the characteristics of this man, I now proceed to mention those of the others.

(13) The man Bhadra is marked by having the arms thick, equal, round and long, his length is equal to the stretch of his arms from one side to the other; his cheeks are covered with soft, small and dense hairs.

In his constitution skin and sperm are predominant; his breast is broad and thick; his prevailing quality is goodness. He has a tiger-like face, is steadfast, forbearing, virtuous, grateful; he has the pace of an elephant, and knows many sciences.

(15) He is sagacious, handsome, clever in the arts, constant, an adept in ascetic philosophy; has the forehead and temples well-shaped; the loins likewise, the hands and feet lined like the lotus calix, the nose fine, the eyebrows even and well-knit.

(16) His person smells like earth when moist from fresh rain, or cassia-leaf, saffron, frontal juice of elephants, agallochum. The hair of his head is black, curled, and such that each single hair has its own pore.

(18) Should his length come to 84 digits and his weight to one bhāra, then he will be lord over the Middle country; but if he have the full measure implied in the words "taller by three digits" he will be emperor of the whole country.

(19) After dutifully ruling the country he acquired by his bravery, the Bhadra, at eighty years of age, will depart from life at a place of pilgrimage and go to heaven.

(20) The Śaśa will have somewhat projecting, otherwise fine teeth, fine nails, blubber

eyes; a swift pace; he takes delight in science, mining and trade; has full cheeks, is false, a good general; fond of love's sport and partial to other men's wives: restless, valorous, obedient to his mother, and attached to woods, hills, rivers and wildernesses.

(21) The same Śaśa is suspicious, and a keen observer of another's weak points. He is 92 digits in length, and, not being very heavy, has a soft step. The chief constituent of his body is marrow.

(22) His waist is slender.

(23) This Śaśa will be a border chieftain or provincial governor. . . . He will, seventy years old, reach Yama's home.

(24) The marks of the Haṁsa are: the mouth red, the face gold-coloured, and, showing thick cheeks and an elevated nose; the head round; the eyes honey-like, the nails wholly red;—etc.

(25) He delights in water. . . . His length according to the statement of the Sages will be 96 digits.

(26) The Haṁsa will possess the country of Khasa, Śūrasena, Gāndhāra, and the land between the Ganges and Yamunā; after exercising the royal power for 90 years, he will meet death within a wood.

(27) The worthy Ruchaka by name will have good eyebrows and hairs; a red tinged dusky colour, a neck marked with three folds like a shell; an oblong face. He is brave, cruel, an egregrious counsellor, a chief of robbers, and a practised soldier.

(28) The measure of Ruchaka's face, in length, being taken four times, gives the measure of his middle. His skin is thin.

(29) . . . His length is a hundred digits.

(30) He is an adept in charms and spells, and has thin knees and legs. When this Ruchaka has reigned as king over the Vindhya, Sahyagiri and Ujjain, he will on reaching seventy years, find his death by sword or fire.

(31) There are five other men, who will be the attendants of the fore-mentioned monarchs.

(105) The number of digits which make the measure of men's height is, for the tallest, 108; for those of middle height, 96; for the shortest, 84.

20. Cf. *ŚRa* 64.60–110.

21. *MASI* 5(3):22–25.

22. A photo taken before restoration of one of the female figures painted on the rock of Sigiriya shows the various manners of shading.

23. Ms. 12ct., Mysore library. B. M. Barua draws our attention to an important passage in the *Saṁyutta-Nikāya,* part 3, p. 152, where the Buddha has incidentally mentioned the following vegetable substance used by the dyers or painters for preparing dyes or colors: (1) resin (rajanā), lac (lākhā), turmeric (haliddā), indigo (nīlī), and madder (mañjeṭṭhī).

24. *ŚRa* 46.119–30.

25. Cf. K. P. Jayaswāl, "A Hindu Text on Painting," *Modern Review* 33:734.

26. For the preparation of vajralepa, see *BṛS* 57, Abhilaśitārtha Cintāmaṇi 86ff., and *ŚRa* 131–33.

27. For the preparation of the wall underneath the vajralepa cover. Cf. *VDhP* 3.40.1ff. and *ŚRa* 41–42.

28. Abhilaśitārtha Cintāmaṇi, p. 60.

29. *VDhP* 3.27. Cf. *Nāṭyaśāstra.*

30. *VDhP* 3.42.

31. *VDhP* 3.62.1–2.

32. *ŚRa* 145–47.

33. *Nāṭyaśāstra* 6.42–43.

34. *VDhP* 52.10–12.

35. The *Visṇudhārmottara* declares the rules for painting as valid also for sculpture, which either may be hollow or massive (ch. 43); worth noticing as an example of hollow sculpture is the use of skin, coated with clay and painted over. Hollow figures must have stood among other places also on the stage, where images of gods, demons, yakṣas, elephants, horses, deer, and birds were to be made of clay, wool, cloth, leather, or iron (27.3).

The commentary to the *Kāmasūtra* by Yaśodhara, when speaking about the Ṣaḍanga, the sixlimbs of painting, i.e., rūpa-bheda, pramānam, bhāva, lāvaṇya-yojanam, sādṛśya, and varṇika-bhaṅga, refers to the categories of types, proportion, rendering, of mood (rasa), embodiment of grace, point of view with reference to sthānam, and to the preparation of colors (cf.

Ananda K. Coomaraswamy, *HIIA,* p. 99); all these categories are dealt with by the *Viṣṇudharmottara.*

Since the publication of the first edition, a number of passages referring to painting have been added to our notice. The following deserves special mention: *Samyuttanikāya,* part 3, p. 152, verse 11, where paintings of male and female figures on wooden boards, walls, and on cloth are discussed. This is the earliest known reference to wall painting, painting on wooden board, and on cloth. Another interesting quotation from Buddhaghosha's commentary to *Vinaya Bikkhu Pachittya* 26 throws light on the reason why Buddha objected to the representation of figures: "The objection was raised because the Mera Lāludāyi, after having dyed a yellow garment, made various objectionable representations in it of male and female figures in the act of dalliance" (references made by Prof. Dr. B. M. Barua). This text also shows that not only were paintings made on cloth, but cloth itself was dyed so as to be decorated with figures, a technique for which Masulipatam in South India became famous much later.

36. "Those gods who during that time had been unmingled (with men) in Jambudvipa, have now been made (by me) mingled with them." Cf. R. P. Chandra, *The Beginnings of Art in Eastern India, MASI,* no. 30 (1921), p. 21.

16 Ajanta

1. Deccan, Sanskrit: Dakṣiṇāpatha designates the southern region of India, i.e., south of the river Narmada. The word has not always denoted the same extent of land. Today it is the name of the country between the Narmada on the north and a variable line along the course of the Krishna to the south, exclusive of the provinces lying to the extreme east (R. G. Bhandarkar, *Early History of the Deccan* [Calcutta, 1884], pp. 1–3). The modern designation covers the country between Bagh in the north and Badami in the south. The ancient and wider designation of Dākṣiṇatya or Dakṣiṇāpatha includes the monuments in the south also. These will be only referred to in connection with the paintings within the narrower zone.

2. gati, see *AbhK* 3.1*a.*

3. *Laṅkāvatārasūtra,* trans. D. T. Suzuki (London, 1932), 2.12.53. Space as visualized in the paintings corresponds to some extent to the element space, i.e., to ākāśadhātu, and not to ākāśa, which is unconditioned (asaṁskṛta). The latter is said to be infinite, boundless, immeasurable, *Milindapañha* 7.3.29. Besides, space as a part of painted form is always manodvāraviññāṇaṁ, discerned through the gate of the mind, and never cakkhuviññāṇaṁ, discerned by the eye; *Kathāvatthu,* PTS, p. 193.

4. *Laṅkāvatārasūtra* 2.6.40. Nivṛtti, return to unconditioned being, and pravṛtti, outturn toward embodiment, cf. Ananda K. Coomaraswamy, *Elements of Buddhist Iconography* (Cambridge, Mass., 1936), p. 83, note 108.

5. *AbhK* 1.28. Re internal space, see also *Majjhimanikāya* ("Further Dialogues of the Buddha," 5.137). "It is by and because of bones and sinews, flesh and skin, that a space is enclosed which is called a visible shape" and *Visuddhimagga,* PTS, part 3, p. 521: "Space element has the characteristic of delimiting material objects and of being their holes and openings"; the same in *Atthasālinī,* PTS, p. 425.

6. bhājanaloka, *AbhK* 3.1*b.*

7. Cf. G. Yazdani, "Note on Frescoes Discovered at Ajanta," *Annual Bibliography of Indian Archaeology* 7:32, pl. 5*b,* where the painting is photographed in its present condition. The reproduction there comprises the scenes from the rocks to the right inclusive of the fainting of the queen.

8. Here as well as in Bharhut (Ludwig Bachhofer, *Early Indian Sculpture,* 2 vols. [New York, 1929], pl. 22), the stitched garment is worn as a shirt or coat by warriors or hunters respectively. In Ajanta it is short sleeved, fastened in the middle, and held around the waist by a broad sash.

9. This device is resorted to throughout the classical tradition of Indian painting and is conspicuous with a strong red in Badami, Cave 3, A.D. 578. Cf. *JISOA* 4, pl. 7.

10 All these views, as in pl. 16–3, may be assembled in one painting or scene.

11. *AbhK* 3.90 and 3.68.

12. Cf. J. Griffith, *Paintings in the Buddhist Cave Temples of Ajaṇṭā,* part 1 (London, 1896–97), pl. 19. G. Yazdani, *Ajaṇṭā,* vol. 1 (Oxford: Oxford University Press, 1931), p. 45.

13. *Laṅkāvatārasūtra,* 2.35.90, etc.

14. As in all Asiatic painting, no shadows are cast in Indian painting either. Modeling

shades, however, are the rule, and the rounded plastic appearance of the figures throws the absence of shadows into stronger relief. The actual sense perception of shadows is frequently worded in literature, for instance, "the cool shadows thrown by dark clouds wandering round the mountain's zone" (Kālidāsa, *Kumārasambhava*, 1.5). This has nothing to do with the vision of the world with reference to the painter who holds this world within himself.

15. *Vijñaptimātratāsiddhi* 2.5 (a commentary of the *Triṁśikā* of Vasubandhu), trans. de la Vallée Poussin, 2 vols. (Paris, 1928–29), p. 792.

16. Ibid., p. 721 (gotra).

17. *Mahāvibhāṣā*, compiled at the council of Kaniṣka; Vasubandhu, fifth century A.D.

18. Cf. Ananda K. Coomaraswamy, "Ābhāsa," *JAOS* 52(1932):210.

19. Shading and adding highlights: Buddhaghosa, *Atthasālinī*, p. 64; cf. also Ananda K. Coomaraswamy, "An Early Passage on Indian Painting," *Eastern Art* 3:219, note 8.

20. *AbhK* 6.12*d*.

21. Ibid.

22. Ibid., 1.17*a;* and 2.34*a–b;* see also *Kathāvatthu* 1.6.4–5; PTS, pp. 86–87.

23. These are of the same value as the scrolls, animals, and other devices. They also intermingle. Apart from their implied symbolism, none of these paintings can be called a "still life."

24. *Vijñaptimātratāsiddhi*, p. 125.

25. ālayavijñāna, ibid., p. 184.

26. *AbhK* 1.10*a;* i.e., varṇa and saṁsthāna. The investigation of color, pp. 25–30, as also that of space, is based on its painted "form." Correspondences in texts not referring to painting corroborate the validity of the function of color in painting. The latter, however, does not differ in Brahmanical or Buddhist works, nor have the views held by the different Buddhist schools their precise correspondences in any special types of painting. The basis itself is painted from where the logical possibilities or discrepancies are given scope to arise, and not the dialectical differences. Varṇa and saṁsthāna are two aspects of rūpa and correspond to color and line of painted form.

27. See also C. J. Herringham, "The Frescoes at Ajanta," *Burlington Magazine* 17(1887): 136–38.

28. *VDhP* 3.41.5.

29. Color as in Ajanta is employed in this sense. There is no scope, for instance, "to show the sky without any special colour," as enjoined by the *Viṣṇudharmottara* 3.42. Where, however, the sky is painted in Ajanta, as in Cave 16, in the scene of Buddha's and Nanda's flight, its color is dark, suggestive of the element ākāśa; cf. also the use of black in Ellora.

30. *AbhK* 1.28, varṇa, rūpa, i.e., color as intrinsic form.

31. *Mahāyāna Sūtrālaṁkāra* 9.36, trans. S. Lévi, p. 79. One speaks of the profundity of the Buddha on the immaculate level as a sign . . . as one speaks of painting space with colors.

32. *VDhP* 3.27.

33. *Vijñaptimātratāsiddhi* 2.i.8, p. 792.

34. *ChUp* 6.4.1 and also 6 and 7. The translation (*SBE* 1:95–96) of "rūpa" as color is not correct. Rūpa denotes quality or intrinsic form; cf. the guṇas and their "colours," E. Sénart, "La theorie des guṇas," *Études Asiatiques*, pp. 285–92.

35. *Kathāvatthu*, PTS, p. 193. Consistently, the question "what is that form, which is the sphere of (visible) form" is answered: "The Form which, derived from the great principles, is visible under the appearance of colour and produces impact" *Dhamma Saṅgani*, trans. C. A. F. Rhys Davids, *Buddhist Psychological Ethics* (London: Royal Asiatic Society, 1900), p. 183.

The elements, the cosmical quarters (horizontally) and the strata, cosmologically and psychologically in vertical sequence, are shown by their respective colors, in Hindu and Buddhist tradition. In painted maṇḍalas altogether six colors, yellow, red, blue, green, white, and black, are used systematically. Cf. for instance, *Śrīcakrasambāra Tantra, Tantrik Texts* 7:15. B. Bhattacharyya, *Indian Buddhist Iconography* (London, 1924), fig. 7*a*. The reduction of painting to these principal colors, however, is outside the realm of the "borderland" as painted in Ajanta.

36. *VDhP* 3.27.

37. *AbhK* 1.10*a;* āloka in this connection corresponds to tejas in the *ChUp*.

38. Many of the paintings in Ajanta have been discolored by a coat of varnish applied more than half a century ago, i.e., between 1872–1885. The remarks refer to paintings that have escaped or else have been relatively least discolored.

39. According to Sāṁkhya and Tarkabhāṣā, cf. F. Th. Stcherbatsky, *Buddhist Logic*, 2 vols. (Leningrad: Academy of Sciences of the USSR, 1930), p. 22.

40. In the latter function the ground appears also in Persian painting in accordance with multiple perspective.

41. *VDhP* 3.43.

42. alīkam bāhyam; Stcherbatsky, *Buddhist Logic,* vol. 2, p. 413.

43. This does not refer to the panels painted on the ceilings or to the frames painted around some of the doors.

44. Ajanta, Cave 17, wall on right, first pilaster; wall on left, last pilaster.

45. Cave 2, cf. Yazdani, *Ajaṇṭā,* part 2, pl. 33.

46. The visible world (cf. *Laṅkāvatārasūtra,* Sagāthakam, 272, 62) is likened to the city of the Gandharvas.

47. Reproduced in color, Yazdani, *Ajaṇṭā,* part 2, pl. 35, the subject being described in ibid., pp. 36–38.

48. Caves 9 and 10, Ajanta, about A.D. 100. There is an inscription on the arch of Cave 10, of the second century, cf. Yazdani, *Ajaṇṭā,* part 1, p. 2, note 2; Caves 16, 17, 1, 2; approximately within the fifth and sixth centuries A.D. Some paintings in Cave 1 about A.D. 600 and possibly somewhat later; Bagh, paintings of Cave 4, correspond to Caves 1 and 2, Ajanta; Badami, Cave 3, A.D. 578; Kanheri, Cave 14; J. Burgess, *Report on the Buddhist Cave Temples, Archaeological Survey of Western India* 4:63–69; faint traces in Aurangabad, Caves 3 and 7; *Pithalkorā,* Hyderabad, in Caitya Cave 1, cf. *ASI* New Imperial Series, 1914, photographs nos. 3955*a* and *b.*

49. The traces of paintings at the Jogīmāra cave, Sirguja, show in some of the figures (for instance, in the third panel) the garment treated similarly to reliefs from Jaggayapeṭa (Bachhofer, *Early Indian Sculpture,* vol. 2, pl. 107) and Sanchi, ground balustrade of stūpa 2. The long and skirt-like dhoti makes dilated curves around the legs; the actual mode of wearing it that underlies this convention is shown on the Yakṣa statues from Patna (ibid., vol. 1, pl. 10). The uttarīya flutters away from the body as also in Jaggayapeṭa.

The ceiling of the Jogīmāra cave is an irregular vault, and the paintings in yellow and ocher earth colors are arranged in sections in accordance with its shape. In those nearest to the end of the vault, the figures on either side face opposite directions (see Uchayappa Maṭha paintings of the sixteenth century in Ānegundi, pls. 8 and 9). Their feet are nearest in each case to the end of the vault. In the four intervening sections the majority of the figures and groups face the respective broad sides of the vault.

These irregular compositional bands across the vault of the ceiling are framed on the one narrow side and near it by a band with large aquatic animals, makara, etc.

In the single sections, foreshortening and oversecting are employed with ease in the agile human figures, mostly in three-quarter profile. Vaulted buildings exhibit, as a rule and in conformity with their representations in sculpture, two sides with but little foreshortening. The groups of the figures are varied. They are arranged in parallel rows that are superimposed in the single sections. Freely and rhythmically, these are connected in the paintings. The third dimension forms part of the setting of the several groups; these are set loosely, always at some distance from one another, and connected in balanced alignments in the whole of each painted section (cf. *ASIAR* 1914–15, pt. 1, p. 12). These are clearly discernible despite the layer of paintings subsequently added.

50. Photographs 1301–1305 of the Office of the Superintendent of Epigraphy, Southern Circle; ASI, Southern Circle, photographs of outline sketch no. C. 143; cf. E. B. Havell, *Indian Sculpture and Painting,* 2d ed. (London, 1928), pl. 50.

51. *JISOA* 4, pl. 13, copies.

52. Photographs of paintings of the Kailāsanātha Temple at Kanchipuram, ASI, Southern Circle, D. 1780; re the paintings in the Bṛhadīśvara Temple, see *JISOA* 1, pls. 20–23.

53. Fragments of wall paintings in the manner of Ajanta are said to have been discovered by Jouveau-Dubreuil in the central provinces in the Chanda district [Chandrapur] (according to T. N. Ramachandran).

54. From the time when copies were made by Griffith in the third quarter of the last century, to the time when protection was given to the caves by H.E.H. the Nizam's Government, these paintings were badly disfigured by scratches, etc.; cf. the reproduction from the original paintings as they appear today, *Annual Bibliography of Indian Archaeology,* vol. 7, pl. 5, with the photo of a hitherto unpublished copy made by Griffith (pl. 1) corresponding to the left half of pl. 5*b, Annual Bibliography.*

55. Cf. the drawings by Griffith, *Paintings,* vol. 1, pl. 41.

56. In Deccan and Mughal paintings, cf. Ernst Kühnel, *Miniaturmalerei im Islamische Orient* (Berlin, 1923), pl. 104; Ivan Stchoukine, *La Peinture Indienne* (Paris, 1929), pls. 5, 6, etc.

57. Rocks are shown in relief as irregular chips, as indented cubes, etc., in Bharhut, Amaravati, etc.; cf. Bachhofer, *Early Indian Sculpture,* vol. 2, pl. 118. The peaked outline of hills is rarely to be met with. The mass of the rock in its crystalline structure is given form. The nearest approach in relief to the rendering of rocks as painted in Cave 10 is made on a pillar of the north gate, Sanchi, cf. Waldschmidt, *Grünwedels Buddhistische Kunst in Indien,* fig. 81.

58. The story does not proceed in continuous narration. The moments that matter are laid out on the unrolled band of the frieze in simultaneous presentation of the entire story. See also Waldschmidt, *Grünwedels Buddhistische Kunst,* pp. 54–55, fig. 91, reproduced from a copy of the first scene; fig. 93, part of the elephant group.

59. Compartmental walls aslant across the frieze also demarcate the scenes in the painting on the wall of Cave 9.

60. Waldschmidt, *Grünwedels Buddhistische Kunst,* fig. 90. See also Taki, "An Example of the Earliest Indian Painting," *Kokka,* no. 353 (December 1919).

61. Bachhofer, *Early Indian Sculpture,* pls. 116, 122 top.

62. The reliefs, as far as they are preserved, would suggest an earlier date for the first mode (Bharhut, Sanchi, etc.) and a latter for the second (Amaravati, second century A.D.).

63. Part of this is reproduced from Griffith's photographed copy, by Waldschmidt, *Grünwedels Buddhistische Kunst,* fig. 95.

64. The wide open eyes look frankly outward, in all the faces, whatever the type.

65. The former mode is subordinated to the latter and has its place in it.

66. Their positions and allocations are many. The movements of the heads, their turns, and the angles at which they are held against the axis of the body are numerous. While the three-quarter profile is the preferred position, the profile and back view are endowed with equal volume and movement. The animals, too, are given volume and freedom of movement in any position. (Cave 9, animal frieze with human figures, corresponding to Amarāvatī; Cave 10, *Syāma Jātaka,* gazelles jumping, in profile; a horse in three-quarter profile, and *Saddanta Jātaka,* elephants seen from any angle).

67. Cave 17; left wall where a pavilion scene is painted over edge on a pilaster; and corner of left wall and back wall.

68. Coomaraswamy, *HIIA,* pl. 7, fig. 24.

69. Stella Kramrisch, *Indian Sculpture* (Calcutta, 1933), pl. 30.

70. Re the identification of most of the jātakas and their position on the walls, see A. Foucher, "Lettre d'Ajaṇṭā," *Journal Asiatique,* 11th ser., part 17, pp. 237–42. The copies of the respective scenes, by Griffith, *Paintings,* and by Lady C. J. Herringham and others, *Ajanta Frescoes,* India Society (1915), may also be consulted in this connection.

71. Below the monkey scenes of the *Mahākapi Jātaka,* Cave 17, is a light colored and broad band.

72. Herringham, *Ajanta Frescoes,* pl. 5.

73. For instance in Cave 9, Griffith's copy (*Paintings,* pl. 37) shows a blank where actually rocks are painted with buff-colored front surfaces and the undersides orange.

74. In Rajput paintings of the late sixteenth and early seventeenth centuries the sky is also dark blue or black.

75. Re the tradition of shading the leaves of trees.

76. The notes on which the present study is based were taken on the spot during repeated visits. Photographs and reproductions are solely reserved for the Archaeological Department of Hyderabad and will be available when the monumental standard work on Ajanta will be published in all its parts. (Hitherto parts 1 and 2 with reproductions of the paintings in caves 1 and 2 have appeared.)

77. *Annual Bibliography of Indian Archaeology,* vol. 7, pl. 7*b*.

78. Ibid., pl. 7*a*, "An Unidentified Buddhist Legend"; re the identification of this scene, see E. B. Cowell, *The Jātaka,* vol. 6 (Cambridge, 1907), p. 163.

79. Re the meaning of the lotus throne, see Coomaraswamy, *Elements,* pp. 39–59; P. Mus, "Barabudur, VI," *BEFEO,* vol. 34, fasc. 1, p. 204 passim.

The meaning of the subjects painted is kindred to that of the painted form. The latter is investigated here in its own substance. In classical Indian painting, subject and form are cognate; medieval painting in India, with readaptations, conveys a traditional meaning.

The stylistic process is not to be dissolved from the meaning of the visible form. On the contrary, it exposes it at work with a consistently accumulative, condensing, or else reduced display of its possibilities.

The excavation of Cave 16 must have preceded that of Cave 17. This is not only shown by the paintings, but equally by the form of the pillars. Cf. note 134.

80. Excepting the scene on the terrace preceding the *Sutasoma Jātaka.*

81. This refers also to the jātakas to the right half of the front wall and others.

82. The middle door between the pilasters is painted with a zigzag border inside and on a lower surface than that of the painted scenes. It is outside the level of the paintings, belongs to the door, and does not refer to them.

83. Havell, *Indian Sculpture and Painting,* pl. 46. The long band unrolled and the scenes within their compartments shuffled together are stages now embodied in comprehensive presentation.

84. The transformation runs parallel with that of contemporary sculpture. Cf. Kramrisch, *Indian Sculpture,* p. 54, etc.

85. Cf. female figure next to the door, with the one on the left of the pavilion in the *Mahājanaka Jātaka,* Cave 1, Yazdani, *Ajaṇṭā,* vol. 1, pl. 12, or the male figure to the left of the horses of the chariot with types of the same painting, whereas the part of the *Viśvāntara Jātaka* painting above the third door, forestalls in type the painting of the *Vidhurapaṇḍita Jātaka,* Cave 2; pl. 16-2 of the present treatise.

86. Coomaraswamy, *HIIA,* pl. 47, fig. 179.

87. Yazdani, *Ajaṇṭā,* part 1, pl. 11.

88. They differ from the other images carved in Ajanta as broad and weighing masses, and are an equivalent in sculpture to the painted types. This does not result from the fact that the coat of plaster and paint is still preserved in their case and has disappeared in the other sculptures. The carving itself is of a different type and is also to be found elsewhere in the Deccan, for instance, at Nasik, cf. Kramrisch, *Indian Sculpture,* pl. 25, fig. 69.

89. Yazdani, *Ajaṇṭā;* part 1, pls. 24–27. V. Goloubew, "Documents pour servir a l'étude d'Ajanta. Les peintures de la première grotte," *Ars Asiatica,* vol. 10, pls. 15, 16.

90. Ibid., pls. 31–33 and p. 35.

91. This type on a lower level of achievement may be seen also in the Māradharṣaṇa scene, ibid., pls. 28, 29; also in pl. 30.

92. *Mahājanaka Jātaka* (?), ibid., pls. 20–22.

93. With the salver and severed heads (story of Amarā Devī?). Cf. ibid., pls. 20 and 23*a.*

94. The fluid doubly curved eyebrow line, modeling and calligraphic, is prepared in the paintings of caves 16 and 17. It attains perfection along with the other symptoms of transformation in the large Padmapāṇi painting, Cave 1.

95. Ibid., pl. 22.

96. Ibid., pls. 6–9.

97. For instance, parts of the *Mahājanaka Jātaka,* ibid., pls. 16–19.

98. In parts of the early paintings of caves 9 and 10 the relief-like occupation by the figures of the ground was still valid. This type of vision, however, has no actuality in the later paintings.

99. Havell, *Indian Sculpture and Painting,* pl. 46.

100. Yazdani, *Ajaṇṭā,* vol. 1, pls. 12–15*a.*

101. Ibid., pl. 15*b.*

102. Ibid., pls. 16–18.

103. Cf. also ibid., pls. 6–9 and 23*a* referred to above; also pl. 37.

104. Ibid., pl. 11.

105. See note 87.

106. Yazdani, *Ajaṇṭā,* vol. 1, pl. 34.

107. Ibid., pls. 34–36.

108. Ibid., pls. 28–29.

109. Cf. p. 53.

110. Foucher, "Lettre d'Ajanta," pp. 226, 227. An interpretation of the relation of the paintings and the available wall space, in terms of architectural application or tectonic principle, would be extraneous to these paintings.

111. Yazdani, *Ajaṇṭā,* vol. 1, pl. 29*b.*

112. Cf. note 103.

113. Yazdani, *Ajaṇṭā,* vol. 1, pls. 20–22; 11; 34*a.*

114. Ibid., pl. 5.

115. Ibid. The cloud motif, peeping forth above the scales, anticipates clouds painted in Ellora, cf. pl. 5. This form, in a nascent stage, appears in the Śaṅkhapāla Jātaka, cf. ibid., part 1, pl. 11.

116. Ibid., part 1, p. 46, suggests a later period, about A.D. 600, for this painting (pl. 38). Not only in this scene, but also in other paintings in Caves 10, 17, 1, and 2 (Griffith, *Paintings,* pls. 42*a,* 54, 94 no. 4, 95 no. 4, 29; V. Smith, *History of Fine Art in India and Ceylon* [Oxford,

1911], pl. 56, fig. B; Yazdani, *Ajaṇṭā,* vol. 2, pl. 30), the Sassanian motif of fluttering ribbons is noticeable. The most interesting occurrence of this motif is in Cave 10, where the flying figure of a vidyādhara has a lock of hair on his forehead not unlike that of the figures on a central Asian painted wooden box, cf. W. Norman Brown, "A Bronze Vessel from Central Asia," *JISOA,* vol. 2, pl. 38.

117. With the scanty documentation of painting of this phase, it is as yet not possible to show the process of the lowering and transference of levels and to trace it to its sources. It is feasible that repeated immigrations from the north, from that of the Śakas onward, and for considerably more than half a millennium, resulted in a fusion of heterogeneous traditions.

According to D. R. Bhandarkar, "Foreign Elements in the Hindu Population," *IA* (1901), pp. 16–24, the following northerners ruled over the Deccan or parts of it: The Kṣaharātas, a Śaka family; the Ābhīras—Ahīr Sonārs and Ahīr Sutārs, i.e., Ahīr goldsmiths and Ahīr carpenters working side by side in Khandesh with Sonārs and Sutārs of the previous population. The original tribal name soon sinks to a division or to a mere surname, and the whole tribe is thus absorbed into the general class. A separate dialect in Khandesh known as Ahirāṇi is mentioned by Daṇḍin in his *Kāvyādarśa*; the Kālacuri, a sept of the Haihayas, ruled over Khandesh, Nasik, etc. A portion of the present Hyderabad [Maharashtra] was governed by a Haihaya chieftain. In the first half of the seventh century, a century after their coming into India, the Gurjaras, intimately connected with the White Huns, had become Hindus and actually acquired the rank of Kshatriyas. In Khandesh the husbandmen belong to two main divisions, local and Gurjara Kuṁbis. In the last quarter of the sixth century, one horde of Cālukyas migrated from the Savālakh Mountains and spread as far south as the Madras Presidency; cf. also D. R. Bhandarkar, "Gurjars," *Journal of the Bombay Branch, Royal Asiatic Society* 21:413–33.

118. Yazdani, *Ajaṇṭā,* part 2, pls. 7–11; 15–16; 45, 46.

As in painting, so also in dhyāna. Re color and the rūpajhāna, see *Atthasālinī,* 12, PTS, p. 255, of which the following is a summary: "In doing the preamble of (1) blue-green, (2) yellow, (3) red, and white respectively as to one's own body, one does it (1) with reference to the hair, the bile, or the pupil of the eye; (2) with reference to the fat, the skin, or the yellow spot of the eye; (3) with reference to the flesh, the blood, the tongue, the palms of the hands and feet, and the red of the eyes. In doing the preamble of white it is done with reference to the bones, the teeth, the nails, or the white of the eye."

119. The outline retains its delimiting function. Colored, it is part of the entire color modeled substance. See Yazdani, *Ajaṇṭā,* part 2, pls. 9, 10*a*.

120. Ibid., part 2, pls. 18*b*–23; cf. also ibid., p. 19, note 1.

121. Ibid., pls. 12–14.

122. Such ponderous expanses, further thinned out, are frequent in Tun Huang.

123. Ibid., pl. 33, *a, b.* See also pl. 32.

124. Ibid. Figure on utmost left of pl. 33*a*.

125. Ibid., pls. 35–44.

126. Ibid., pls. 9, 10*a;* Indra and Yakṣas; vidyādharas.

127. Ibid., pls. 27, 29.

128. Ibid., pls. 24, 25.

129. See p. 57. Cf. also Cave 16, p. 50.

130. *The Bagh Caves,* India Society, 1927, pls. 16, 17, and A-i; the paintings are contemporary with the paintings, Caves 1 and 2, Ajanta.

131. See part 1, notes 50–52.

132. For instance, Stella Kramrisch, "Nepalese Painting," *JISOA* 1(1933), pl. 37. A. Foucher, *Etude sur l'iconographie Bouddhique de l'Inde,* 2 vols. (Paris: E. Leroux, 1900–1905), pl. 10, etc.

133. Stella Kramrisch, "Paintings at Bādāmi," *JISOA* 4(1936), pls. 7–10.

134. The pillars in these caves show a change of form of which the speed keeps pace with that of the paintings. The majority of those in Cave 16 are of an early type. On both the sides and at the back of the hall they consist of plain octagonal shafts only and are without capitals. Only in the front row do they have bracket capitals and the two middle pillars are more articulate; with a square part at the base, an octagonal and subsequently polygonal shaft, large cubical abacus, and a thinner, projecting one above, they show small and simple bracket capitals.

The pillars of Cave 17 are further differentiated. Square at the bottom, octagonal and subsequently polygonal as the shafts of Cave 16, they terminate with a round band across the polygonal endpiece and an octagonal jeweled band below the square scroll abacus. Above this is a roll bracket. In Cave 1 the pillars have the shaft round, above its third, polygonal part. This may or may not be fluted vertically or diagonally. On the shaft rests an āmalaka, and above this is a plain and narrow plinth. On it rests the bracket capital which has no rolls. On some pillars (in the middle of the right side) figures of gaṇas issue in the four directions from the round or fluted part of the shaft to the abacus; flat lotus plaques intervene between them. There is, however, no āmalaka. These two varieties are contracted into one yet more complex type. The pillar to the left of the sanctuary (in its florid decoration, it is akin to pillars in Cave 2) makes the gaṇas start from the āmalaka, whereas the pillar to the right is equally florid in its decoration, but there are no gaṇas.

The pillars of Cave 2 have a square, hexagonal, and then a polygonal part and above this a highly decorated octagonal part, then āmalaka with gaṇas, then low abacus and a plain bracket capital.

Index